The KPI Compendium

20,000+ Key Performance Indicators used in practice

Editorial coordination: **Aurel Brudan**

THE KPI INSTITUTE

This report is the result of primary research conducted by eab group. It is available in PDF format on the smartKPIs.com website. Terms of use available at: http://www.smartkpis.com/terms-of-use.html ('Premium content terms').

An appropriate citation for this report is:
The KPI Institute (2013), The KPI Compendium, Melbourne, Australia

Indemnity statement
The KPI Institute has taken due care in preparing the analysis contained in this report. However, noting that some of the data used for the analysis have been provided by third parties, The KPI Institute gives no warranty to the accuracy, reliability, fitness for purpose, or otherwise of the information. The KPI Institute shall have no liability for errors, omissions or inadequacies in the information contained herein or for interpretations thereof. The opinions expressed herein are subject to change without notice. For the latest version of the documentation, *smartKPIs Premium* should be consulted.

Published by:

THE KPI INSTITUTE

The KPI Institute
Life.lab Building
198 Harbour Esplanade, Suite 606
Melbourne Docklands, VIC 3008, Australia

Telephone (international): +61 3 9670 2979
E-mail: office@kpiinstitute.org

www.kpiinstitute.org | www.smartKPIs.com

Table of Contents

How to use the book

The Compendium is a concise, but comprehensive work that summarizes thousands of Key Performance Indicators (KPIs) available on the smartKPIs.com platform. The original word "compenso" comes from Latin and it means "to weight together or to put in a balance".

This is similar to what The KPI Institute has done in creating this book. By assembling the largest collection of KPIs in printed format, it has provided professionals and practitioners with a powerful tool to weight together or to compare practical examples of KPIs coming from hundreds of business areas. One of the most important benefits that this Compendium brings is the abundance of options that will assist you in identifying and selecting the most relevant KPIs.

The present work enlists the names of more than 20,000 KPIs. In front of each KPI name, a KPI number is listed so that those interested in a specific KPI can easily find further information by looking up the KPI number on the smartKPIs.com platform.

To make the search process as easy as possible for readers and smartKPIs.com users alike, the book's structure mirrors the taxonomy available online, which can be described as follows:
1. **The context level** - with three areas: organizational, global and personal;
2. **The group level** - each area is divided into two groups, as it follows: the *organizational* context includes the Functional Areas and the Industries; the *global* one includes Human Development Areas and Environmental Sustainability; and the *personal* one, Personal Productivity Areas and Well-Being Domains;
3. **The category level** - each group covers hundreds of business fields, from widely popular ones such as Accounting, Government and Healthcare, to more specialized one such as Biodiversity, Sport Management and Personal Development;
4. **The subcategory level** - further on, each category has subdivisions, where related KPIs are clustered together, in order to offer direct readers from their general area of interest to the exact information they are looking for.

The Compendium was designed to facilitate the identification and usage of KPIs in practice. Managers, consultants, researchers, academicians – now, they can all have a better access to the largest existing database of key performance indicators. The importance of these indicators in the decision making process turns this Compendium into an indispensable tool for both individuals and organizations.

For instance, imagine you are a Marketing Manager working in the Oil & Gas industry. Your company is looking at improving its performance management framework, and you are trying to find those KPIs which are the best in tracking your Corporate Social Responsibility (CSR) related objectives. Here is an example of the steps that you could take and that would help you identify the KPIs you are looking for in order to further customize them:
1. Depending on the industry and functional area in which you activate, identify key terms such as Marketing, CSR, Oil, Gas;
2. Take a look at our context level classification; since this is a work related project and not a personal one, the organizational context would be the most appropriate choice; given your CSR focus, globalization could be a secondary area to review;
3. At group level, you could look both in "Functional Areas" at "Industries"; let's assume you are first interested in identifying industry specific CSR KPIs;
4. Look up your industry at category level; here, you should search for "Resources", which includes the activities of extracting and refining natural resources such as gas, oil and coal. Also included here are the KPIs for energy production from sustainable sources, using, for instance, the solar, water, wind or geothermal power;
5. The next step is to find your suitable subcategory, which in this case would be "Oil and Gas". This offers you access to more than 60 KPIs you should take into account, such as "# Primary energy consumption" and "# Amount of oil spills".

The ways in which you could use this Compendium are extremely diverse so we invite you to discover them on your own. Remember that you are also welcomed to share some of the KPIs and relevant performance management tools you with the smartKPIs.com community. Additional resources including articles, specialized reports, customizable templates, best practice highlights, as well as specialized courses and services can also be found there.

Be a part of the KPIs' world!

About Key Performance Indicators (KPIs)

In many domains of human activity, the use of tools is essential for the achievement of results. Measurement and evaluation make no exception, being equipped with both conceptual and physical tools. Of the first category, at the core of any performance measurement and management system are the measures, metrics, indicators or KPIs used.

Both academic and practitioner literature use interchangeably these terms, oftentimes even within the same organization.

At smartKPIs.com, we have adopted the following definitions for these terms:

Measure - A number or a quantity that records a directly observable value. All measures are composed of a number and a unit of measure. The number provides magnitude (how much) for the measure, while the unit gives the number a meaning (what). Examples of unit measures are: dollars, hours, meters, inches, etc.

Indicator - Indicators are defined in many ways, but the common meaning for all of them is that they refer to specific information. Thus, the Organisation for Economic Co-operation and Development (OECD) defines an indicator as "a qualitative or quantitative factor or variable that provides a simple and reliable means to measure achievement, to reflect changes connected to an intervention, or to help assess the performance of a development actor".[1]

Metric, Performance Measure or Performance Indicator - A generic term encompassing the quantitative basis by which objectives are established and performance is assessed. It helps quantify the achievement of a result, the quantifiable component of an organization's performance. In the context of measuring and managing performance these terms are used interchangeably.

Key Performance Indicator (KPI) - A selected indicator considered key for monitoring the performance of a strategic objective, outcome, or key result area important to the success of an activity and growth of the organization overall. KPIs make objectives quantifiable, providing visibility into the performance of individuals, teams, departments and organizations and enabling decision makers to take action in achieving the desired outcomes. Typically, KPIs are monitored and communicated through dashboards, scorecards and other forms of performance reports.

While on paper the terms listed above can be differentiated, in practice, the difference between them is blurred and, at some extent, irrelevant. As long as their purpose and use is clear and understood by members of the organization, whether they are called performance measures or KPIs is a matter of preference.

At smartKPIs.com, we assess each example entered in the online database and label it as measure, performance indicator or KPI. It is an empirical and subjective approach to catalogue each entry based on relevance. Ultimately, all entries in the online database are considered KPI examples. In addition, to single out the entries that stand out in terms of relevance, we introduced a new label:

smartKPI - A Key Performance Indicator example available on smartKPIs.com, that is recommended as being the most relevant and truly "Key" for organizational performance. They are selected by the editorial team of the website based on criteria such as:

- Listing in academic and practitioner publications that analyse their usefulness;
- Frequency of use by Functional Area / Industry;
- Fulfillment of the criteria of how good KPIs should be defined and used.

1. Organisation for Economic Co-operation and Development, 2002, Glossary of Key Terms in Evaluation and Results Based Management, OECD Publications, Paris, France

KPIs ... Naturally

Measurement as a human activity is not new. It emerged in early history as means for discovery and sense making. Archaeologists consider the first measurement tool used in human history to be the Lebombo bone, a baboon fibula containing 29 cut notches. Dated 35,000 BC, this tally stick was discovered in the Lebombo mountains in Swaziland.

Evaluation, as a form of measurement was used as early as the 3rd century AD, when emperors of the Wei Dynasty rated the performance of the official family members. The biased nature of individual performance evaluation was noticed by Chinese philosopher Sin Yu, who reportedly criticized a rater employed by the Wei Dynasty with the following words: "The Imperial Rater of Nine Grade seldom rates men according to their merits, but always according to his likes and dislikes".

A major milestone in making the connection between measuring as a human activity and performance was in 1494, when Luca Pacioli published in Venice 'Summa de arithmetica, geometrica, proportioni et proportionalita' ('Everything on arithmetic, geometry, proportions and proportionality'). It detailed a practice the Venetian sailors had in place to evaluate the performance of their sailing expeditions, which became the basis of the double-entry accounting system.

In time, the subjective nature of individual performance evaluations and the dominance of financial indicators for evaluating enterprise performance became stepstones for performance management in human activities.

The industrial revolution added to this combination the "organization as a machine" metaphor that played a major role in driving improvements in efficiencies and effectiveness. The result was an organizational performance management model based on mechanistic, command-and-control thinking, driven by subjective individual performance assessments and financial indicators and crowned by pay-for-performance arrangements.

Did it work? To a certain extent, yes. Many organizations flourished and matured based on this model.

Does it have flaws? Many. And while historical circumstances attenuated them in time, today's environment amplifies and exposes them at an accelerated rate.

Is there a better way? Yes, but it is not simple. It requires a change at multiple levels, from the underlying philosophy of performance, to mentalities and processes. This is not easy.

Over time, the use of Key Performance Indicators (KPIs) became synonym to performance measurement and management. KPIs are the link between the old and the new in performance management. Their use, however, is much richer and rewarding in an environment based on organic performance architecture principles:

Organizations are echo-systems in their own right. They vary in terms of maturity and the environment in which they operate. As such, their use of performance management systems should reflect their own "personality". You can try to build an igloo in Sahara, but it won't be sustainable. The performance architecture of each organization needs to be unique and to reflect its internal and external environment.

Systems thinking provides a much richer context for understanding and improving performance. Command-and-control worked in time for the army, for increasing productivity of unskilled workers during the industrial revolution and for managing large organizations (such as the public service). Today, knowledge workers form the majority of the workforce in developed economies, operate in a much more interconnected environment and have to make decisions at an accelerated pace. Understanding the systems in which we operate, analyzing flow and learning based on data become ever more important today and complement the traditional simplistic managerial approach of executing orders from above.

KPIs should be used primarily for learning. The role of KPIs should be the one of providing the required information to assist in navigating towards the desired results. The same principle is used by ants, who leave pheromone trails to assist each other in navigating towards the food source. Similarly, the nerve impulses travel through the different points of the nervous system, transmitting information. KPIs results should travel through the organization, facilitating communication, providing a base for analysis / synthesis and ultimately decision making across all levels of the organization.

Data accuracy in human administration is an elusive desideratum. Neils Bohr once said: *"Accuracy and clarity of statement are mutually exclusive"*. Accuracy is a challenge in exact sciences and even more in human administration. Striving to obtain any KPI data is a challenge in itself for many organizations and data accuracy is an even bigger ask. The use of KPIs should acknowledge this aspect and be oriented towards making the most out of existent data, oftentimes by using variance intervals. This approach is used by the human body. If the temperature drops under a safe limit, we shiver. If the temperature increases, we sweat. Both are performance improvement initiatives of the body, aimed to regulate its temperature back to safe limits. The KPI here is the temperature. While it is not a constant, its trend is good when within certain safe limits.

The use of KPIs for rewards and punishment should be limited and driven by self-assessment. Purposeful oriented behavior is a characteristic of living organisms. For humans and many other species, this behavior is amplified by rewards and punishment. Along with this amplification, risks are amplified, too. Gaming of results, lack of cooperation, decreased morale and work accidents are some of the undesired consequences. On the other hand, the majority of nerve impulses in the human body transmit general information. Only in particular situations pleasure or pain signals. Similarly, the use of KPIs for rewards and punishment should be the exception to the rule, rather than the norm.

Embedding KPIs in organizations through visualization and communication of KPIs results is the key to maximizing their value added. Variations in the KPIs used by the human body are felt by our senses as their impact is sensory rich. Similarly, KPIs used in an organizational context should be embedded in everyday use and be a part of the working experience. The most important aspect of communicating KPI results is their visual representation. This is key, both in terms of optimizing the layout of the data representation and the presence of visual displays in the working environment. The range of media is diverse today: posters, whiteboards, banners, LED and LCD monitors should be combined to bring results to life across the organization. KPI results should not be restricted to paper reports and computer screens anymore.

New philosophy of performance, driven by self-assessment and purposeful achievement as a mean to happiness. While happiness means many things to many, a common expression of this feeling is the result of the purposeful achievement of a desideratum. Achieving something we want, while shared with others, is about us and reverberates strongly in our inner self. Transposing this powerful catalyst of performance in both our personal and organizational life is facilitated by a new paradigm: Happiness is driven by achievement. Achievement is an expression of performance. If we want to be in control of our happiness, we should be in control of our performance.

Self-assessment of performance results is not easy. However, if more emphasis is placed on building this capability in each employee, organizations can benefit by creating a rewarding environment conducive to happiness. In this environment, managers can focus on understanding and improving the working system, while employees can focus on self-assessment of the results' achievement, learning and communicating. Purposeful achievement of results in a well-structured working system would bring both individuals and organization much closer to happiness and fulfillment compared to the payment of bonuses in the current command-and-control driven dominant paradigm.

KPIs are here to stay. The question we have to answer is how do we want to use them: mechanistically or naturally?

Aurel Brudan,
Performance Architect
smartKPIs.com

Functional Areas

Accounting

Accounting includes activities related to the preparation of internal Financial Reports in order to support decision making by existing and potential capital providers. KPIs in Accounting refer to specific monetary measures of stocks and flows as well as to efficiency in operation management, systems and control.

Accounting Systems

Accounting Systems include all related procedures, controls and accounting methods employed to register, classify and interpret accurate financial data for enabling top management in decision making.

sKPI #	Key Performance Indicator name
sK65	# Interest cover
sK529	$ Cash flow after taxes (CFAT)
sK2959	% Customer invoices paid through electronic sourcing
sK3025	# Times interest earned
sK3189	% Accuracy of expense reimbursement requests
sK3340	% Electronic invoices
sK3341	% Employees managing the accounting processes
sK3344	% Employees allocated to accounts payable and expense reimbursement
sK3347	% Employees allocated to evaluate and manage financial performance
sK3349	% Employees allocated to fixed asset management
sK3350	% Employees allocated to general accounting and reporting
sK3351	% Employees allocated to internal controls
sK3353	% Employees allocated to manage and process adjustments/ deductions
sK3354	% Employees allocated to manage and process collections
sK3355	% Employees allocated to manage financial policies and procedures
sK3356	% Employees allocated to manage payments
sK3358	% Employees allocated to payroll
sK3362	% Employees allocated to perform financial reporting
sK3364	% Employees allocated to perform general accounting
sK3365	% Employees allocated to perform planning/ budgeting/ forecasting
sK3366	% Employees allocated to manage financial performance evaluation
sK3369	% Employees allocated to report on internal controls compliance
sK3370	% Employees allocated to report payroll taxes
sK3372	% Employees allocated to tax
sK3373	% Employees allocated to treasury operations
sK3385	% Manual payroll payments
sK3387	% Cost of outsourced finance function
sK3401	% Accounting system downtime
sK3460	# Bias ratio

sKPI #	Key Performance Indicator name
sK5903	% On-time trade settlement rate
sK5904	% Transaction items requiring reconciliation
sK5905	% Returned items from total transactions
sK5910	% Straight through processing
sK6157	# Time to process the secondary COB billing
sK6961	# Scheduled maintenance related downtime

Cash Management

Cash Management refers to short term operational activity. It is important in tracking and sustaining day-to-day activity. KPIs are indicated to track cash reserves relative to short term obligations.

sKPI #	Key Performance Indicator name
sK67	$ Net cash flow
sK514	# Acid test ratio
sK526	$ Working capital
sK528	$ Cash earnings per share
sK540	$ Operating cash flow (OCF)
sK3122	# Liquidity ratio
sK3260	$ Cash and cash equivalents
sK3262	$ Cash flow from investing activities
sK3268	$ Cash inflow
sK3270	$ Cash outflow
sK3271	$ Cash-at-hand
sK3290	$ Net change in cash
sK3367	% Cash flow return on sales
sK3419	% McDonough ratio
sK6147	% Collection of client payment balances
sK6149	% Collection of elective service deposits
sK6165	$ Cash revenue
sK6166	% Point of service cash to net revenue ratio
sK6170	# Time between credit balance report due date and submission date
sK6182	% Cash factor analysis
sK6206	% Client cash net revenue
sK6212	% Referrals and net fees of total collection agency recoveries
sK6216	# Time spent by collector per detailed review
sK14073	# Days cash on hand

Control

Control is necessary in order to meet legal and duty of care towards stakeholders, but also to ensure that the financial information provided possesses the fundamental characteristics of relevance and faithful representation. KPIs measuring this activity capture the effectiveness of control processes, methods and financial policies in place.

sKPI #	Key Performance Indicator name
sK3033	$ Bid and proposal costs
sK3383	% Financial reports submitted as correct and on time
sK3394	% Non-compliance statements solved
sK3397	% Time allocated to control financial data
sK3398	% Time allocated to decision support
sK3399	% Time allocated to financial management activities
sK3402	% Accurate financial reports
sK3448	$ Economic value added per employee
sK3457	$ Claims severity
sK6267	% Revenue leakage from total revenue

Cost Analysis

Cost Analysis represents a valuable activity providing feedback on internal performance and adequacy of resource allocation. Measures of costs relative to revenue or assets indicated by relevant KPIs support economic decisions.

sKPI #	Key Performance Indicator name
sK140	% Wages cost from sales
sK314	% Contribution margin ratio
sK316	% Gross profit margin
sK2267	$ Costs per FTE employee
sK3053	% Overhead cost ratio
sK3088	$ Total acquisition cost (TAC)
sK3094	# Marginal propensity to consume (MPC)
sK3132	% Interest expense to debt
sK3136	# Accounting rate of return (ARR)
sK3140	# Audit ratio
sK3145	# Burning cost ratio
sK3146	# Cash available for debt service (CADS)
sK3149	# Cash conversion cycle (CCC)
sK3153	$ Discretionary costs
sK3158	# Cost accrual ratio
sK3159	% Operating costs
sK3214	# Expenses claims processed per employee
sK3217	$ Fixed cost per employee
sK3218	# Fixed-charge coverage ratio
sK3254	$ Overdue invoices
sK3255	$ Back taxes
sK3257	% Repairs and maintenance expenses to fixed assets
sK3282	$ Fixed costs
sK3284	$ Indirect costs

sKPI #	Key Performance Indicator name
sK3286	# Sales to general and administrative expenses
sK3289	$ Marginal costs (MC)
sK3306	$ Phone costs per employee
sK3320	$ Variable costs
sK3321	$ Working capital per employee
sK3333	% Cost with employees from the operating revenue
sK3334	% Cost of the finance function from revenue
sK3337	% Department cost from revenue
sK3339	% Discretionary costs from sales
sK3409	% Indirect expenses per sales
sK3439	% Royalty rate
sK4732	$ Spent on equipment
sK5945	$ Payroll tax paid by the employer
sK6139	% Charity write-offs
sK6254	% Obsolescence costs from total inventory
sK6949	$ Cost to maintain vendor master data
sK7057	$ Savings achieved
sK7059	$ Life cycle cost (LCC)
sK13980	# Amortization period in months
sK14056	# Cost improvement plan

Planning and Reporting

Planning and Reporting is the activity of establishing financial targets in terms of costs and revenues as well as reporting on how those targets are met within the financial year. KPIs outline the extent to which the targets were adequately planned and achieved during a financial year.

sKPI #	Key Performance Indicator name
sK190	$ EBIT (Earnings Before Interest and Taxes)
sK192	$ Operating expenses
sK414	$ Cost of goods sold (COGS)
sK466	# Asset turnover
sK468	$ Earnings per share (EPS)
sK479	% Budget variance
sK513	# Price to sales ratio
sK517	# Berry ratio
sK520	# Current ratio
sK525	# Working capital turnover
sK535	$ Earnings before interest, taxes, depreciation, amortization, and restructuring or rent costs (EBITDAR)
sK538	$ Net debt
sK539	$ Net income after taxes (NIAT)
sK549	$ Shareholders' equity
sK550	$ Tangible book value per share (TBVPS)
sK551	$ Earnings before interest, taxes, depreciation and amortization (EBITDA)
sK652	# Breakeven point (BEP)
sK770	$ Fixed assets per FTE (Full Time Equivalent)

sKPI #	Key Performance Indicator name
sK3043	$ Extraordinary expenses
sK3044	$ Extraordinary profit (loss)
sK3045	$ Extraordinary revenue
sK3046	$ Financial profit (loss)
sK3049	$ Gross profit
sK3050	$ Gross sales
sK3067	$ Operating revenue per employee
sK3114	% Effective tax rate
sK3219	# Goodwill to assets ratio
sK3231	# Years debt
sK3251	# Amortization term
sK3258	$ Liabilities
sK3277	$ Current liabilities
sK3279	$ Discretionary accrual
sK3280	$ Financial expenses
sK3281	$ Fixed assets
sK3283	$ Goodwill
sK3285	$ Intangible assets
sK3292	$ Non current liabilities
sK3310	$ Selling, general and administrative expenses (SG&A expenses)
sK3312	$ Tangible assets
sK3313	$ Tax base
sK3314	$ Tax paid
sK3315	$ Taxable income
sK3316	$ Total assets
sK3322	$ Write-offs
sK3323	$ Accounts receivable turnover
sK3335	% Current liabilities to inventory ratio
sK3338	$ Depreciable amount
sK3374	$ Payroll tax for employees
sK3376	$ Excise tax
sK3378	% Financial reports issued on time
sK3379	% Gross-receipt tax
sK3392	% Reserve ratio
sK3396	% Tax deduction
sK3406	# Business development to administrative expenditure ratio
sK3969	$ Selling general and administrative (SG&A) costs per employee
sK4534	% Selling general and administrative (SG&A) costs per sales
sK4804	$ Expenses
sK6318	% Marginal tax rate
sK6848	$ Revenue from door fee charges
sK6876	$ Earnings (revenue)
sK6887	$ Sales revenue

sKPI #	Key Performance Indicator name
sK7046	% Operating budget spent
sK7047	% Stratex budget spent
sK14060	# Current asset turnover
sK20515	% EBITDAR margin

Planning and Reporting is the activity of establishing

Transactions/Accounts payable/Accounts receivable in Accounting represent the records on balances with entity's creditors and debtors. Control of such balances is a sign of good operational practice. Specific KPIs enable analysis and control on transactions processing and meeting payment/receipting terms.

sKPI #	Key Performance Indicator name
sK66	# Days in accounts receivable
sK279	# Days in accounts payable
sK280	# Days of purchases paid
sK2779	# Delayed receipts
sK3142	# Value per outstanding invoice
sK3150	# Closing days
sK3154	# Collection period to payment period
sK3162	# Time to process expense reimbursements
sK3169	# Time to dispatch a wire transfer
sK3170	# Time to reconcile a bank account
sK3173	# Time to resolve invoice errors
sK3223	# Outstanding invoices
sK3225	# Overdue invoices
sK3229	# Sales to accounts payable
sK3232	% Accounts payable invoices paid late
sK3236	# Days payable outstanding (DPO)
sK3243	$ Accounts payable
sK3244	# Accounts payable turnover ratio
sK3245	$ Accounts receivable
sK3287	$ Invoice processing costs
sK3291	% Net receivables
sK3299	$ Outstanding invoices
sK3326	# Accounts payable to sales
sK3328	% Bad debts against invoiced revenue
sK3336	% Customer receipts processed error free the first time
sK3375	% Entry line items processed error free the first time
sK3380	% Disputed invoices
sK3381	% Invoices requiring special payment
sK3382	% Invoices under query
sK3384	% Low value invoices
sK3389	# Payment errors
sK3400	% Time allocated to transaction processing
sK3404	% Bad debt to turnover
sK3405	% Billing accuracy

sKPI #	Key Performance Indicator name
sK3408	% Customers paying cash up front on commencement of project
sK3412	% Payments (non-payroll) right amount paid on time
sK3413	% Payments made by direct credit
sK3430	# Book-to-bill ratio
sK4704	# Time per processed invoice
sK4705	# Invoices processed per accounts payable FTE
sK4708	# Remittances processed per accounts receivable FTE
sK4711	$ Cost per invoice
sK4712	$ Cost per remittance
sK4715	$ Billable fees write-downs
sK4886	# Bad debt in days of billing equivalent
sK5289	% Invoices paid within established time frame
sK6135	% Accounts receivable value aged more than 90 days
sK6164	# Net account receivable days
sK6167	% Transactions posted in backlog
sK6169	% Gross credit balance A/R in days
sK6190	% Cash collection amount recovered
sK6191	% Bad debt netback
sK6197	$ Cost to produce and mail outsourced guarantor statement
sK6200	$ Backlog of final bills or claims not submitted
sK6205	% Cost to collect
sK6210	$ Cash collection amount recovered per vendor placement
sK6211	% Bad debt and charity expenses
sK6252	% Expedited fees
sK6255	% Billing error rate
sK6256	$ Unapplied cash
sK6258	% Value of billing disputes from revenue

sKPI #	Key Performance Indicator name
sK6259	% Billing disputes approved
sK6260	# Time to respond to a billing dispute
sK6261	# Time to resolve a billing dispute
sK6262	# Days past-due invoices
sK6263	% Value of billing in disputes as a percentage of value of past-due invoices
sK6264	% Cost of billing as a percentage of total value billed
sK6265	% Cost of collecting revenue as a percentage of value billed
sK6266	% Cost to handle errors as a percentage of value billed
sK6269	% Aging of uncollected bills
sK6737	# Vouchers processed per accounts payable FTE
sK7062	# Customer payback period
sK13966	# Accounts per collector
sK13967	# Accounts receivable balance
sK13995	# Attempts per collector
sK14000	# Days of debtors
sK14001	# Days of trade creditors
sK14002	# Payment period
sK14037	# Collections as a percent of total receivables
sK14075	# Days in A/R
sK14076	# Days outstanding
sK14077	# Days outstanding of bills
sK14078	# Days revenue in net accounts receivable
sK14095	# e-check collections per collector
sK14141	# Fees imposed
sK14142	# Fees waived
sK14187	# Hours non billable pre contract
sK19652	$ Operating revenue

Corporate Services

Corporate Services represents a support area that assures the management of basic and standard internal services within the organization.

Administration / Office Support

Administration/Office Support refers to all the processes related to sustaining the organization in its day-to-day administrative activities. KPIs focus on having well implemented procedures intended to reduce the time spent on administrative work, as well as general office/program equipment and customer service delivery needs.

sKPI #	Key Performance Indicator name
sK284	% Applications / pieces opened
sK287	% Correspondence service level
sK288	% Applications / mail in processing
sK289	# Application cycle time
sK290	% Applications completed

sKPI #	Key Performance Indicator name
sK291	% Answered calls within Automatic Call Distribution system
sK293	% Answer accuracy
sK3029	# Guest complaints on reception services
sK3030	# Frequency of checking inbound call messages
sK3031	% Inbound call answered and transferred to appropriate persons
sK3052	% Incoming call message taking accuracy
sK3068	% Administrative tasks completed accurately and efficiently
sK3070	% Office supplies adequacy
sK3081	% Minutes accurately recorded
sK3082	% Minutes distributed within agreed time-frames

sKPI #	Key Performance Indicator name
sK3087	% Documents filed according to standards
sK3093	# Projects and events supported by administrative staff
sK3113	# Meeting room booking errors
sK3115	# Time of handling visitor inquiries
sK3125	% Positive feedback from internal users on office support services
sK3127	% Positive feedback from guests and callers on office support services
sK6719	$ Losses due to administrative errors
sK6721	% Compliance with administrative standards
sK6729	% Documents in standardized style

Corporate Travel

Corporate Travel Management indicates the company's strategic approach to business travel. The KPIs focus on the travel policy implementation, vendors negotiation activities, day-to-day operation of the corporate travel program, traveler safety and security, credit-card management, travel and entertainment cost management.

sKPI #	Key Performance Indicator name
sK169	$ Ticket price
sK170	$ Lowest fare obtained
sK171	% Online booking adoption rate
sK3071	% Travel and accommodation requests fulfilled
sK5838	# Mechanisms used to manage travel policy compliance
sK5862	% Pre-booked travel tickets
sK5868	% ROI of business travel
sK6606	% Travel management services coverage
sK6607	% Virtual meetings
sK6608	# Travel policy compliance
sK6609	% Share of corporate credit volume
sK6610	# Travel expense productivity
sK6611	# Travel agency productivity index
sK6612	% Business travel share of carbon footprint
sK6613	# Per trip footprint intensity ratio
sK6631	# Age of supplier fleet
sK6651	# Trips per week
sK6652	# Trip duration
sK6653	$ Travel savings
sK6654	# Cost of videoconferencing versus travel costs
sK6662	# One-day business trips
sK6663	# Traveler satisfaction
sK6664	# Unused tickets
sK6704	$ Cost of trip
sK6705	% Out-of-policy bookings
sK6707	$ Cost per attendee
sK6709	$ Agency transaction fee

Facilities / Property Management

Facilities/Property Management coordinates and oversees the safe, secure, and environmentally sound operations and maintenance of these assets in a cost effective manner aimed at long-term preservation of the asset value. The KPIs refer to both the efficient management of day-to-day operations of the facility, as well as managing the liaison between the landlord and/or the management firm operating on the landlord's behalf and tenant. Duties of property management include renting, responding to and addressing maintenance issues, providing a buffer for those landlords desiring to distance themselves from their tenant constituency.

sKPI #	Key Performance Indicator name
sK141	$ Monthly depreciation
sK142	% Office capacity ratio
sK300	# Built area
sK301	# Facility age
sK302	$ Maintenance expenditure per square meter
sK303	# Building performance index (BPI)
sK304	# Maintenance efficiency indicator (MEI)
sK355	% Repairs completed within time limit
sK424	# Space usage efficiency
sK569	% Daylight factor (DF)
sK3054	# Security incident response time
sK3063	% Scheduled availability of security systems
sK3147	# Space per employee
sK3152	% Facilities management schedule compliance
sK3155	# Physical work environment index
sK3156	# Life safety or building code index
sK3157	% Fire sensors in good order with testing up-to-date
sK3160	% Fire extinguishers within effective service time
sK3163	% Mandatory evacuation exercises completed successfully
sK3164	% Emergency exits tested and unlocked
sK3166	% Fire warden positions filled
sK3180	% Asset space utilization rate
sK3181	# Facilities revitalization rate (FRR)
sK3182	# Hours of guarding delivered by security services staff
sK3183	% Security budget committed to improvement of security services
sK3184	# Safety condition index
sK3185	% Compliance with Cleaning Service Level Agreements
sK3186	# Frequency of cleaning services
sK3187	# Area leased
sK3188	# Area leased to owned
sK3190	$ Churn cost per staff workstation relocation
sK3191	$ Current replacement value (CRV)
sK3192	$ Deferred maintenance (DM) to facilities
sK3193	$ Capital renewal budget
sK3194	% Facility condition index (FCI)

sKPI #	Key Performance Indicator name
sK3195	# Indoor environmental quality (IEQ)
sK3196	% Building occupant satisfaction with facilities
sK3197	% Safety meetings participation
sK3198	# Actionable alarms
sK3199	$ Expenditure with preventive maintenance to facilities
sK3200	# Utility outages
sK3201	# Quality inspections completed to Facilities Management staff members
sK3202	# Customer Custodial Concerns (CCC)
sK3203	% Customer Custodial Concerns (CCC) compliance
sK3204	# Days to complete a work order
sK3205	# Urgent work orders
sK3206	$ Plant replacement value (PRT)
sK3211	% Reported security incidents dealt with in accordance with agreed procedures
sK3212	% Successful validation of security procedures
sK3213	% Security validation programs completed
sK3216	# Functions and events requiring security resources
sK3220	# Functions and events supported by Facilities Management
sK3302	% Staff workstation relocation churn rate
sK3317	% Landscape condition index
sK3318	$ Cost with ongoing maintenance of facilities
sK4044	$ Occupancy expense per person
sK4045	$ Occupancy expense per square foot
sK4049	$ Water costs per square meter in operational property
sK4052	$ Recurrent to capital expenditure ratio
sK4067	# Maintenance requests
sK4072	% Emergency repairs completed on time
sK4073	% Repairs completed on first visit
sK4078	% Unplanned repairs completed on time
sK4079	% Routine repairs completed on time
sK4086	% Properties compliant with security standards
sK4093	# Floor space per employee

sKPI #	Key Performance Indicator name
sK4100	# Repairs per managed property
sK4129	% Tenants satisfied with the overall repairs and maintenance services
sK4501	# Staff per parking space
sK6499	# Cleaning frequency for restroom facilities
sK13969	# Acquisition
sK13987	# Maintenance labor input
sK14058	# Critical maintenance backlog
sK14239	# Maintenance ratio
sK14240	# Management churned

Legal Services

Legal Services aim to support the preparation and execution of legal matters within the organization. KPIs in this area refer to both outsourced and internal legal services performed by lawyers and the workload involved, the legal cases handled, as well as the success rate of legal procedures initiated.

sKPI #	Key Performance Indicator name
sK341	$ Cost per lawyer hour
sK342	$ Cost to litigate a lawsuit
sK362	# Legal staff per billion revenue
sK363	% Legal spending from revenue
sK364	$ Total cost to resolve (TCR+)
sK365	# Legal dispute cycle time
sK366	% After action review usage (AAR)
sK367	# Caseload
sK15178	# Legal actions opened
sK15179	$ Revenue per lawyer
sK17404	# Billable hours per legal assistant FTE
sK17760	% Client growth rate
sK18657	% Lawyers per clients
sK20968	% Growth in top clients
sK20991	% Legal actions opened per client
sK21116	% Partner hours

CSR / Sustainability / Environmental Care

CSR/Sustainability/Environmental Care refers to the added value that the organization brings through responsible actions towards their community, stakeholders and the environment.

Corporate Social Responsibility

Corporate Social Responsibility represents the organization's policy related to its responsibility for voluntary practices towards the growth and development of the community, environment, consumers, employees and stakeholders. The KPIs refer to applied measures towards adherence to law, ethical standards and international norms.

sKPI #	Key Performance Indicator name
sK584	$ Funds raised per employee
sK586	$ Investment in the community

sKPI #	Key Performance Indicator name
sK588	# Hours volunteered by employees
sK589	# Partnerships with non-profit organizations / non-governmental organizations
sK1379	# Community satisfaction index
sK1381	% Local residents in total workforce
sK1387	# Sponsorship projects
sK1388	# Students recruited for holiday work

sKPI #	Key Performance Indicator name
sK1436	# Activities with a significant risk for the incidence of forced or compulsory labor
sK1437	# Activities with a significant risk involving the incidence of child labor
sK1438	# Cases of not following regulations in terms of consumer information
sK1439	# Community awards won
sK1440	# Consumer complaints regarding company's incursions into their private lives
sK1441	# Community complaints
sK1442	# Corporate community involvement initiatives
sK1443	# CSR awards
sK1444	# CSR events
sK1445	# CSR studies and research
sK1446	# Disabled employees
sK1448	# Employees dedicated to social investment projects
sK1449	# External NGO volunteers trained by company staff
sK1450	# Employees involved in up-skilling local community organizations
sK1451	# Grievances of an ethical nature
sK1452	# Infringements of publicity and marketing regulations
sK1453	# Legal cases relating to infringements of antitrust and monopoly regulations
sK1454	# Sponsored organizations dedicated to CSR
sK1455	# Media coverage of environmental and community activity
sK1456	% Media coverage of Corporate Social Responsibility (CSR) initiative
sK1457	# Programs for clients, customers and employees with information and training on healthy eating habits
sK1458	# Reported ethics-related incidents
sK1460	% Security personnel trained in aspects relating to human rights
sK1461	# Corporate sponsorship for community projects
sK1462	# Hours of human rights enlightenment training
sK1463	$ Donations
sK1464	$ Penalties and fines incurred for non-respect of consumer information regulations
sK1465	$ Social contributions per employee
sK1467	$ Sums paid to political parties or their candidates
sK1468	% Benefit utilization rate (BUR)
sK1469	% Donations from operating income
sK1470	% Employees who consider that their business acts responsibly
sK1472	% Hours utilization rate (HUR)
sK1473	% Profit (pretax) dedicated to philanthropy
sK1474	% Spending on local suppliers
sK1475	% Subsidiaries for which sustainability action plans are developed
sK1476	% Subsidiaries which have implemented a supplier code of conduct

sKPI #	Key Performance Indicator name
sK1477	% Suppliers and contractors that have undergone screening on human rights
sK1495	% Energy saved due to conservation and efficiency improvements
sK1589	# Upheld cases of prosecution for environmental offenses
sK1596	$ Environmental protection expenditure and investments
sK4734	% Unbleached paper use ratio
sK4735	$ Product purchases from minority and women-owned suppliers
sK6560	$ Donation of assets
sK6731	# Hours of Organizational Health and Safety (OH&S) training conducted
sK14185	# Hours donated to the community

Environmental Care

Environmental Care refers to the organization's practices towards the utilization of natural resources, particularly tight control of greenhouse gas emissions and energy efficiency. KPIs refer to natural environmental protection measures through the company's activities and efficiently use of required natural resources.

sKPI #	Key Performance Indicator name
sK59	# Energy consumption
sK61	% Energy produced from renewable sources
sK111	# Paper documents to electronic format ratio
sK182	# Energy used per unit of production
sK183	$ Penalties resulting from environmental non-compliance
sK184	# Water consumption per capita per day
sK186	# Carbon dioxide emissions per capita
sK436	% Energy used from renewable sources
sK574	# Recycled paper
sK576	# Paper pages used per employee
sK577	% Landfill volume in use
sK578	# Volume of recycled waste
sK587	% Consumption of recycled paper
sK590	# Initiatives to promote greater environmental responsibility
sK591	% Hazardous operational waste
sK592	# Aircraft emissions
sK593	% Recycled hazardous operational waste
sK594	# Wastewater
sK595	% Biodegradable carrier bags
sK756	% Paper reduction
sK757	% Reduced paper consumption due to duplexing
sK1382	# Entries to environment / community awards
sK1389	% Marketing projects that are environmentally friendly
sK1480	# Accidental releases of substances

sKPI #	Key Performance Indicator name
sK1485	# Petrol and diesel used
sK1486	# Biochemical oxygen demand (BOD)
sK1487	# Chemical oxygen demand (COD)
sK1488	# CO2 emissions from company car fleet
sK1490	# Non-contact water reuse
sK1493	# Discharges to water
sK1496	# Environmental complaints received
sK1498	# Habitat protected or restored
sK1499	% Halogenated volatile organic compounds
sK1511	% On-site energy
sK1513	# Packaging consumption
sK1514	# Packaging recycling rate
sK1518	# Pollution incident rate
sK1520	# Radioactive waste
sK1521	% Raw materials consumption
sK1523	# Oil spills
sK1528	# Total organic carbon (TOC)
sK1529	# Total suspended solids (TSS)
sK1531	% Volatile organic compounds (VOC)
sK1533	# Water recycled and reused
sK1536	% Non-hazardous operational waste
sK1537	# Baseflow salinity
sK1539	% Current projects that are environmentally friendly
sK1540	# Environmental performance index (EPI)
sK1542	% Intensity of salt affected areas
sK1543	% Products that incorporate sustainable materials
sK1544	% Recycled input materials
sK1545	% Input waste materials
sK1546	% Organic products purchased
sK1547	% Recycled paper packaging
sK1548	# Primary energy consumption
sK1551	% Recycled non-hazardous waste
sK1552	# Soil acidity
sK1557	% Staff that received environmental training
sK1558	% Subsidiaries achieving cost savings due to waste management initiatives
sK1559	% Subsidiaries that use recycled and secondary aggregates
sK1561	% Water from non-traditional sources
sK1562	# Water abstraction
sK1563	% Electrical and electronic equipment recycled from past sales
sK1565	# Heavy metal emissions
sK1568	# Electricity consumption per employee
sK1569	# Electricity consumption per manufactured product
sK1573	# Hazardous raw material per kilogram of product
sK1577	# Packaging weight per product

sKPI #	Key Performance Indicator name
sK1583	# Waste per product
sK1586	# Water footprint
sK1587	# Successful initiatives to reduce indirect energy consumption
sK1588	% Achieved initiatives to reduce the emissions of greenhouse gas
sK1590	$ Environmental penalties
sK1591	% Raw materials recycled from consumers
sK1594	% Suppliers with a ISO 14001 or equivalent certified Environmental Management System
sK1595	% Subsidiaries covered by Environmental Management ISO 14001 certification
sK1600	# Emissions from production
sK1730	# Air quality index (AQI)
sK1731	# Soil alkalinity
sK1757	# Net area to be reforested (NAR)
sK1758	# Annual allowable cut (AAC)
sK1760	% Cost savings due to waste management initiatives
sK2121	% Reused grey water
sK3488	# Carbon dioxide vessel efficiency
sK3495	# Aircraft emissions per payload capacity
sK3724	# Operational spills
sK4731	$ Energy consumption cost
sK4733	$ Water use value
sK4778	# Hotel waste per occupied bed night
sK4779	# Tonnes of hotel waste per year per employee
sK5101	# Fresh water withdrawn for business use
sK5111	% Recycled water used
sK5112	% Fresh water used
sK5934	# Sustainability reports
sK6400	# Water quality index
sK6414	# Greenhouse gas emissions per capita
sK6415	# Carbon dioxide emissions per kilowatt of electricity generated
sK6558	# Environmental legal contraventions
sK6559	# Materials containing dangerous substances disposed of
sK6782	% Use of raw materials from renewable sources
sK6928	# Environmental infringements
sK13983	# Energy use
sK13984	# Environmental reviews
sK13990	# Water use
sK14021	# Carbon intensity
sK14028	# CO efficiency
sK14029	# CO2 emissions
sK14030	# CO2 emissions from NCC sites in COT carbon trading pilot
sK14031	# CO2 emissions generated by fuel, gas and electricity consumption

sKPI #	Key Performance Indicator name
sK14032	# CO2 Emissions Intensity
sK14034	# CO2 emissions per shipping unit
sK14035	# COx,NOx, SOx, VOC emissions
sK14090	# Direct energy consumption by primary energy source
sK14091	# Direct greenhouse gas emissions by weight
sK14098	# Electricity consumption
sK14103	# Emissions of ozone-depleting substances by weight
sK14104	# Emitted mass of CO
sK14105	# Emitted mass of NOx
sK14106	# Emitted mass of SOx
sK14116	# Energy conservation
sK14117	# Energy consumption by country
sK14118	# Energy consumption by region and format
sK14119	# Energy intensity index
sK14120	# Energy intensity of selected products
sK14121	# Energy saved due to conservation and efficiency improvements
sK14122	# Energy Star labeled
sK14123	# Energy Star rating
sK14124	# Energy use
sK14125	# Energy use by type
sK14126	# Energy use intensity
sK14130	# Environmental approval
sK14131	# Environmental incidents
sK14132	# Environmental promotions
sK14133	# Environmental protection initiatives
sK14148	# Fluoride emissions to air
sK14151	# Fresh and recycled water use
sK14152	# Fresh water consumption
sK14153	# Fresh water intensity index
sK14166	# General waste disposed to landfill

sKPI #	Key Performance Indicator name
sK14167	# GHG emissions
sK14169	# Green leases
sK14170	# Greenhouse gas emissions
sK14171	# Greenhouse gas emissions by weight
sK14172	# Greenhouse gas emissions intensity from buildings
sK14173	# Greenhouse gas emissions intensity from new construction and redevelopment activity
sK14174	# Greenhouse gas intensity index
sK14175	# Greenhouse intensity of selected products
sK14176	# Groundwater consumption
sK14177	# Habitats protected or restored
sK14178	# Hazardous waste disposed to landfill
sK14179	# Hazardous waste in tonnes
sK14183	# High-quality water consumption
sK14190	# Hours of sustainability training
sK14202	# Indirect greenhouse gas emissions by weight
sK14205	# Initiatives to enhance efficiency and mitigate environmental impacts of products and services
sK14206	# Initiatives to provide energy-efficient based products and services
sK14207	# Initiatives to reduce greenhouse gas emissions and reductions achieved
sK14208	# Initiatives to reduce indirect energy consumption and reductions achieved
sK14221	# Land leased in, or adjacent to, areas of high biodiversity value outside protected areas
sK14222	# Land leased in, or adjacent to, protected areas
sK14223	# Land managed in, or adjacent to, areas of high biodiversity value outside protected areas
sK14224	# Land managed in, or adjacent to, protected areas
sK14225	# Land owned in, or adjacent to, areas of high biodiversity value outside protected areas
sK14226	# Land owned in, or adjacent to, protected areas
sK14237	# Low-quality water consumption

Finance

Finance deals with sourcing, budgeting, lending and spending money while managing their time value and risk attached with the aim of generating high returns. KPIs generally relate to asset and portfolio management, financial stability, forecast and valuation, liquidity and profitability matters.

Asset / Portfolio management

Asset/Portfolio management activities focus on determining the optimal allocation of capital among various categories of assets that are in line with a specific time horizon and risk tolerance. KPIs give investors the ability to monitor performance of such allocations and flag any adjustments that become apparent.

sKPI #	Key Performance Indicator name
sK464	% Earnings yield
sK465	% Dividend yield
sK490	% Net interest margin (NIM)
sK513	# Price to sales ratio

sKPI #	Key Performance Indicator name
sK516	% Annual equivalent rate (AER)
sK525	# Working capital turnover
sK2962	# Bid-to-cover ratio
sK2963	# Bond equity earnings yield ratio (BEER)
sK2965	# Bull to bear ratio
sK2967	$ Capital recovery factor (CRF)
sK2996	# Incremental capital output ratio (ICOR)
sK3008	# Preferred dividend coverage ratio
sK3009	# Price to cash flow ratio

sKPI #	Key Performance Indicator name
sK3010	# Price-to-innovation-adjusted earnings
sK3013	# Profitability index
sK3023	# Swap ratio
sK3024	# Tangible common equity ratio (TCE)
sK3026	# Treynor ratio
sK3027	# Upside/downside ratio
sK3086	# Shares outstanding
sK3090	$ Value of loans and investments
sK3091	% True interest cost (TIC)
sK3097	% Annual percentage yield (APY)
sK3106	% Corporate franchise tax
sK3119	# Hedge ratio
sK3133	# Up-down capture ratio
sK3134	% Yield gap investment
sK3178	# Tracking error (TE)
sK3288	% Management expense ratio (MER)
sK3319	% Total expense ratio (TER)
sK3329	% Before reimbursement expense ratio
sK3332	% Cash-on-cash return (CCR)
sK3403	% Administrative expense per gross premium
sK3415	# Information ratio (IR)
sK3416	# K-ratio
sK3420	# Nova/Ursa ratio
sK3422	% Placement ratio
sK3425	# Sortino ratio
sK3431	# Calmar ratio
sK3437	$ Redemption premium
sK3438	$ Redemption price
sK3450	% Sterling ratio
sK3453	% Cooke ratio
sK3455	% Exclusion ratio
sK5909	% Shares debited to Depository Trust and Clearing Corporation (DTCC)
sK14134	# Equity financing
sK14146	# Fixed asset financing

Financial stability

Financial stability dictates the right balance between capital and debt used to generate returns. KPIs in this area focus on measuring debt relative to assets and shareholders' equity.

sKPI #	Key Performance Indicator name
sK65	# Interest cover
sK470	% Weighted average cost of capital (WACC)
sK491	# Altman Z-Score (for public manufacturing companies)
sK494	# Altman Z-Score (for privately held manufacturing companies)
sK495	# Altman Z-Score (for privately held non-manufacturing companies)

sKPI #	Key Performance Indicator name
sK510	# Debt ratio
sK511	# Debt-to-equity ratio
sK530	$ Cash flow per share
sK534	% Debt-to-capital ratio
sK1532	# Expense coverage days
sK2980	# Current liabilities to sales
sK2987	# EBITDA coverage
sK2992	# Fixed assets to short term debt
sK2995	# Gearing ratio
sK2999	# Loan life coverage ratio
sK3000	# Long-term debt to capitalization ratio
sK3005	% Net debt
sK3020	# Short to long term debt
sK3025	# Times interest earned
sK3034	$ Capital employed
sK3038	# Cash flow to long term debt
sK3041	$ Debt-adjusted cash flow (DACF)
sK3101	% Capital acquisition ratio
sK3107	# Liabilities to net worth
sK3109	# Current liabilities to net worth
sK3118	% Operating assets ratio
sK3123	$ Interest expense
sK3124	% Long-term debt to total debt
sK3129	% Short-term debt to total debt
sK3130	% Solvency ratio
sK3269	# Cash maturity coverage
sK3327	# Common shares
sK3426	# Texas ratio
sK3433	# Defensive interval ratio (DIR)
sK5842	$ Firm exposure
sK5945	$ Payroll tax paid by the employer
sK6138	% Bad debt write-offs from gross revenue
sK6185	# Time to resolve credit balances
sK14019	# Capital gearing
sK14020	# Capital return for the current and prior three quarters
sK14082	# Debt to assets
sK14083	# Debt-Equity ratio

Forecasts & Valuation

Forecasts and Valuation are activities that stay at the core of company valuations and equity investments. Specific elements are combined to generate estimation of targeted firm value ranging from economic growth to future cash flows.

sKPI #	Key Performance Indicator name
sK468	$ Earnings per share (EPS)
sK469	# Price-to-earnings ratio
sK475	$ Economic value added (EVA)

sKPI #	Key Performance Indicator name
sK481	# Price per dividend ratio
sK501	% Sustainable growth rate (SGR)
sK512	# Price-to-earnings growth ratio
sK523	# Price-to-book ratio
sK533	$ Cost of equity (COE)
sK537	$ Book value per share (BVPS)
sK547	$ Revenue per share
sK548	$ Free cash flow (FCF)
sK2071	% Equity risk premium
sK2072	$ Discounted cash flow (DCF)
sK2964	# Book-to-market ratio
sK2968	% Capital reinvestment ratio
sK2969	# Capital to non-current assets
sK2972	% Cash flow return on investment (CFROI)
sK2974	% Cash reinvestment ratio
sK2976	% Consumer price index
sK2977	# Conversion ratio
sK2981	$ Current purchasing power (CPP)
sK2984	# Preferred shares
sK2986	# Discounted cash-flow (DCF)
sK2990	# Enterprise value to sales ratio
sK2991	# Equity multiplier
sK2993	# Franchise factor
sK3006	# Operating cycle
sK3021	# Shares unissued
sK3048	$ Future value
sK3056	$ Net asset backing (NTA)
sK3057	$ Net assets
sK3069	% Plowback ratio
sK3083	# Average propensity to save (APS)
sK3085	$ Shareholders funds per employee
sK3100	$ Breakeven yield
sK3102	% Capital appreciation
sK3103	% Capitalization rate
sK3105	% Combined loan to value ratio (CLTV ratio)
sK3131	% Tax rate
sK3161	# Restricted shares
sK3246	$ Enterprise value (EV)
sK3308	$ Savings
sK3309	# Treasury shares
sK3330	# Benefit cost ratio (BCR)
sK3343	$ Market capitalization
sK3348	% Outstanding shares that are considered public float
sK3418	% Margin of safety
sK3427	# Tobin's Q
sK3429	# Issued shares

sKPI #	Key Performance Indicator name
sK3434	# Envy ratio (ER)
sK3436	# Shares authorized
sK3445	# Marginal propensity to save (MPS)
sK4547	$ Net cash flow per customer
sK5231	# Turnaround time for audits
sK6249	% Planned cash break-even point to actual cash break-even point
sK6253	% Accurate forecasts of planned expenditure

Liquidity

Liquidity indicates the assets' ability to be converted into cash with minimum loss of value on the market or within an entity. Measuring and monitoring liquidity through KPIs provide an idea of the short term financial health of the organization.

sKPI #	Key Performance Indicator name
sK514	# Acid test ratio
sK1549	# Cash zero date
sK2063	# Debt-service coverage ratio (DSCR)
sK2970	# Cash flow adequacy ratio
sK2971	# Cash flow coverage
sK2973	# Cash flow to debt ratio
sK2982	# Days of liquidity
sK3014	# Put-call ratio
sK3028	% Working ratio
sK3036	# Cash flow from operations to net income
sK3037	# Cash flow from sales to sales
sK3040	# Cash turnover ratio
sK3075	$ Quick assets
sK3092	% Working capital per sales
sK3116	# Fixed assets to net worth
sK3122	# Liquidity ratio
sK14022	# Cash and cash equivalents to revenue ratio
sK14023	# Cash flow to total debt
sK15008	# Debt to equity

Profitability

Profitability indicates organization's ability to generate returns through effective allocation and use of available resources. Financial ratios are calculated to measure such ability and progress in time. KPIs in this area have often as main component profit or return.

sKPI #	Key Performance Indicator name
sK190	$ EBIT (Earnings Before Interest and Taxes)
sK316	% Gross profit margin
sK398	% Return on equity (ROE)
sK400	% Return on assets
sK431	% Return on security investment (ROSI)
sK463	% Return on total assets (ROTA)
sK466	# Asset turnover

sKPI #	Key Performance Indicator name
sK467	% Net profit margin
sK472	% Return on funds employed (ROFE)
sK474	% Return on net assets (RONA)
sK476	$ Net operating profit after tax (NOPAT)
sK502	% Dividend payout ratio (DPR)
sK517	# Berry ratio
sK524	# Fixed asset turnover
sK531	% Cash return on capital invested (CROCI)
sK541	$ Operating income before depreciation and amortization (OIBDA)
sK605	% Return on capital employed (ROCE)
sK1566	% Retained earnings
sK2062	% Risk-adjusted return on capital (RAROC)
sK2961	% Basic earning power ratio (BEP)
sK2966	# Capital expenditure to sales ratio
sK2975	% Cash return on assets
sK2988	# EBITDA to fixed charges
sK2997	% Internal rate of return
sK2998	% Like-for-like revenue growth
sK3016	# Sales to cash
sK3017	# Sales to cash flow ratio
sK3032	% Return on fixed assets
sK3039	% Cash return to shareholders
sK3047	$ Financial revenue

sKPI #	Key Performance Indicator name
sK3065	# Operating leverage
sK3066	$ Operating profit
sK3076	$ Retained earnings
sK3077	% Return on assets Du Pont (ROA Du Pont)
sK3080	% Return on investment (ROI)
sK3084	$ Profit per customer
sK3096	% Return on net asset value
sK3098	% Asset coverage ratio
sK3099	% Assets to sales
sK3111	% EBIT margin
sK3112	% EBITDA margin
sK3121	% Income growth
sK3126	% Return on assets managed (ROAM)
sK3128	# Sales to working capital ratio
sK3141	% Average accounting return (AAR)
sK3331	$ Burn rate
sK3407	$ Contribution margin
sK3421	# PEG payback period
sK4629	% Return on net investment
sK4672	# Labor multiplier
sK6876	$ Earnings (revenue)
sK19650	$ Operating margin
sK22607	$ Net present value

Governance, Compliance and Risk

Governance, Compliance and Risk indicate how the organization is meeting legal and business standards, implied either by the law, international standardization, shareholders or any other governance body. KPIs indicate how efficient management of corporations should support promoting corporate fairness, transparency and accountability, by using incentive mechanisms, such as contracts, organizational designs and legislation.

Compliance and Audit Management

Compliance and Audit refer to conducting business activities in accordance with established guidelines, specifications or legislation. KPIs focus on tracking if these guidelines and related legislation are followed and met.

sKPI #	Key Performance Indicator name
sK1459	# Reported regulatory incidents
sK1471	% Employees who signed the Code of Conduct and Ethics Policy
sK1589	# Upheld cases of prosecution for environmental offenses
sK1590	$ Environmental penalties
sK1996	% Security violations per audit
sK2000	% Audits conducted on schedule
sK2082	% Employees that received the Code of Conduct
sK2084	% Employees that are tested to confirm understanding of Code of Conduct
sK2085	$ Spent per employee for compliance / ethics training

sKPI #	Key Performance Indicator name
sK2086	% Employees trained on compliance and ethics responsibilities
sK2087	% Employees that have performance evaluation incentives aligned with compliance / ethics objectives
sK2088	% Employees that understand how to use the ethics helpline
sK2089	% Employees that believe there is an open environment to raise issues and questions
sK2090	# Ethics hotline calls
sK2091	# Cycle time to resolve ethics hotline report
sK2092	$ Costs due to business interruption (including debarment)
sK2094	% Employees aware of the Compliance Program
sK2096	# Frequency of compliance reviews
sK2097	$ Cost of non-compliance
sK2098	# Non-compliance critical issues identified
sK2099	# Non-compliance issues reported
sK2100	# Time between identification of a non-compliance issue and resolution

sKPI #	Key Performance Indicator name
sK2102	% Policies reported as non-conformal
sK2104	# Postponed internal audits at the request of the auditor
sK2105	# Postponed internal audits at the request of the auditee
sK2106	% Coverage of total audit universe
sK2108	# Time between internal control deficiency occurrence and reporting
sK2109	# Internal control improvement initiatives
sK2110	# Time between new regulation and initiation of compliance review
sK3165	# Time to investigate a procedural violation
sK3303	$ Penalties received due to non-compliance
sK3346	% Employees allocated to establish internal control policies and procedures
sK3357	% Employees allocated to operate controls and monitor compliance
sK3391	% Updated policy and procedures
sK5787	$ Penalties paid for poor performance
sK5894	% Procedure compliance
sK6221	% Functional areas that undertook annual business planning
sK6225	% Deals where current state due diligence is performed
sK6239	# Frequency of inventory audit
sK6241	% Transformation programs where baselining is performed
sK6268	% Regulatory fines due to billing noncompliance
sK6655	# Security incidents
sK6909	% Processes compliant with workplace safety and sanitation requirements
sK6928	# Environmental infringements
sK14050	# Composition of governance bodies on diversity
sK14205	# Initiatives to enhance efficiency and mitigate environmental impacts of products and services
sK14206	# Initiatives to provide energy-efficient based products and services
sK14207	# Initiatives to reduce greenhouse gas emissions and reductions achieved
sK14208	# Initiatives to reduce indirect energy consumption and reductions achieved
sK14573	# Audits across departments: planned vs actual
sK22663	$ Cost per regulatory activity processed
sK22664	# Regulatory actions processed

Governance

Corporate Governance defines the structure and the relationships with stakeholders, by which companies are directed and controlled. KPIs focus on both the adequate formulation of Corporate Governance principles and compliance with them.

sKPI #	Key Performance Indicator name
sK1717	% Outstanding shares considered as free float
sK1719	# Board meetings
sK2111	# Board director tenure
sK2112	% Executive directors

sKPI #	Key Performance Indicator name
sK2113	% Independent directors
sK2114	% New board members with industry expertise
sK2115	% Strategic objectives achieved
sK2116	# Corporate governance index (CGI)
sK2117	% Board nominees
sK2119	% Non-board members attendance
sK2122	# Channels of access to information
sK2123	% Board meetings attendance
sK2124	# Days in advance to send out notice of general shareholders' meetings
sK2125	# Cases of insider trading involving company management
sK2127	% Annual General Meetings (AGMs) attended by the managing director
sK2128	# Agreements arrived at during the meeting
sK2129	# Ownership rights, beyond voting
sK2130	# Boards the CEO serves
sK2131	# Codes of conduct
sK2132	# CEO mandate years
sK2134	% Board members who are financially literate
sK3151	% Concentrated stock
sK6081	# Board size
sK6082	% Board member attendance to board meetings
sK6083	% Outside directors serving on the board of directors
sK6084	% Outside director attendance of meetings
sK6085	% Outside blockholders presence
sK6086	% CEO's shares
sK6087	% Directors ownership (block ownership) other than CEO and Chairman
sK6217	# Time lapse between gathering of market intelligence and strategic response
sK6774	# Board meetings dedicated to organizational performance reviews
sK6775	# Briefing notes on performance
sK7050	% Compliance with performance architecture
sK13970	# Actions taken in response to incidents of corruption
sK14005	# Board members who are women or minorities
sK14008	# Business conduct and fraud hotline categories of calls
sK14009	# Business units analyzed for risks related to corruption
sK14040	# Community contributions through planning agreements with local authorities

Risk Management

Risk Management consists of identifying, assessing and prioritizing organizational risks related matters and the allocation and economical application of resources to minimize them. KPIs focus on the monitoring and control of the probability and/or impact of unfortunate events.

sKPI #	Key Performance Indicator name
sK277	# Detective risk controls
sK386	# Amendments made to controls

sKPI #	Key Performance Indicator name
sK429	$ Cost of insurance
sK430	$ Annual loss expectancy (ALE)
sK432	$ Risk assessment value (RAV)
sK519	# Field visits for risk assessment
sK543	# Regular risk reviews conducted
sK544	# Physical security system activations
sK545	# Contingency plans
sK711	# Reviews of risk management plans
sK714	# Risk likelihood level
sK1525	# Risk consequence level
sK2061	# Risk Grade-TM
sK2064	% Value-at-risk (VaR)
sK2067	# Employees allocated to risk management activities
sK2070	% Requirements changed during project execution
sK2073	% Unassessed risks
sK2074	$ Risk exposure
sK2075	# Risk events
sK2078	% Currency risk exposure
sK2083	$ Unexpected loss (UL)
sK2093	$ Costs due to reputation damage
sK2268	# Risk level
sK2296	# Risk Management Index
sK2989	% Business plans containing risk management considerations
sK3011	# Formal written strategies for risk management
sK3059	# Crisis management team members
sK3062	# Risk management reports
sK3108	# Regulatory changes
sK3253	% Risk responses that follow company emergency response procedures

sKPI #	Key Performance Indicator name
sK3410	# Corporate risk profiles
sK4556	# Detected instances of inadequate segregation of duties
sK4604	% Risk damage and loss assessments completed
sK4638	% Risk assessors who have completed primary risk assessment training
sK4805	# Debriefing sessions conducted with recovery teams
sK5853	# Recovery time objective (RTO)
sK5863	# Maximum acceptable outage (MAO)
sK5877	# Risk management clock-speed
sK5883	# Business Continuity Index
sK5889	# Preventive risk controls
sK5891	% Risk controls meeting intended objectives
sK14101	# Emergency response
sK14102	# Emergency simulations
sK14137	# Fatalities at controlled operations
sK14180	# Health and safety deficiencies
sK14181	# Health and safety topics covered in formal agreements with trade unions
sK14182	# High potential incidents
sK14194	# Incidents of non-compliance with regulations concerning health and safety impacts of products and services
sK14195	# Incidents of non-compliance with regulations and voluntary codes concerning marketing communications
sK14196	# Incidents of non-compliance with regulations concerning product and service information
sK14197	# Incidents of violations involving rights of indigenous people
sK14198	# Incidents per one thousand kilometers of pipeline per year
sK14200	# Incidents where senior management needed to instigate the remedial
sK22658	% Adoption of risk management approaches

Human Resources

The prime role of the Human Resources function is to support the achievement of organizational goals by ensuring that relevant and innovative people policies, practices and systems are in place so that the organization can attract, retain and develop valuable staff.

Compensation and Benefits

Compensation and Benefits includes the remuneration of compensation to employees in the form of money, fringe benefits and equity compensation and their level of satisfaction with these benefits. Cash compensation includes base salary, bonuses and other amounts paid to employees. Fringe benefits come in the form of health, well being, car allowance, housing, education funding and other non-financial benefits. Equity is represented by stock options granted to and exercised by employees.

sKPI #	Key Performance Indicator name
sK46	$ Compensation per employee
sK83	% Compensation revenue rate

sKPI #	Key Performance Indicator name
sK85	# Entry level wage to local minimum wage
sK86	$ Bonus payout
sK195	% Actual to potential bonus paid
sK715	% Compensation and benefits cost to annual sales turnover
sK726	$ Wage rate
sK728	$ Social insurance cost per employee
sK729	$ Medical insurance cost per employee
sK730	$ Hourly compensation per employee
sK731	$ Income per employee by position
sK737	% Workforce on individual employment contracts

Organizational » Functional Areas

sKPI #	Key Performance Indicator name
sK775	% Employees who have received recognition
sK776	# Recognition events and awards for staff
sK1854	$ Cost rate of contractors
sK1855	$ Hourly FTE compensation rate
sK1856	% Bonus eligibility rate
sK1857	% Bonus receipt rate
sK1858	# Compensation satisfaction index
sK1859	% Direct compensation operating expense rate
sK1860	% Direct compensation breakdown
sK1861	$ Direct compensation expense per full time equivalent (FTE)
sK1862	# Market compensation ratio
sK1863	$ Overtime expense per full time equivalent (FTE)
sK1864	% Overtime payment rate
sK1865	% Salary increase occurrence
sK1866	$ Benefit expense per full time equivalent (FTE)
sK1867	% Benefits expense type breakdown
sK1868	% Benefits operating expense rate
sK1869	# Benefits satisfaction index
sK1870	% Benefits total compensation rate
sK1871	# Stock options per employee
sK1872	$ Net proceeds of options per employee exercising stock options
sK1873	# Stock options exercised per employee
sK1874	% Contingent labor rate
sK1875	% Employee stock ownership
sK1876	# Performance based pay differential
sK1877	% Compensation packages with pay-for-performance arrangements
sK1878	% Employee ownership rate
sK1879	% Stock incentive eligibility rate
sK1880	# Vacation days per employee
sK1881	# Female to male salary ratio
sK1884	% Payroll losses
sK1885	# Fringe benefits to basic salary ratio
sK1887	$ Salary per full time equivalent (FTE) employee
sK1889	$ Value of sick leave per full time equivalent (FTE) employee
sK3174	# Time to resolve payroll errors
sK4761	% Labor costs from total sales
sK6440	% Expense of temporary staffing to labor cost
sK14003	# Basic salary and remuneration of women to men
sK14160	# FTEs who receive 90 % of total amount of bonuses, incentives and stock options
sK19457	$ Employee salary

Efficiency and Effectiveness

Organizational efficiency and effectiveness reflect the results achieved by the workforce as per the set objectives. KPIs focus on workforce productivity and achievement of individual performance plans.

sKPI #	Key Performance Indicator name
sK89	$ Human capital value added
sK90	% Human Capital Return on Investment (ROI)
sK444	$ Lost time accounting
sK681	% Low performing employees
sK682	% High performing employees
sK683	$ Profit per employee
sK684	$ Sales per employee
sK685	$ Office space cost per staff
sK718	% Employees with decreased performance rating
sK719	% Employees with increased performance rating
sK722	# Time lost by starting work late
sK724	# Labor costs to sales
sK725	$ Revenue per FTE (Full Time Equivalent)
sK769	% Performance appraisals completed on time
sK777	% Employees in self-managing teams
sK1917	# Perceived work ability
sK2004	$ New products and services revenue per full time equivalent (FTE)
sK2005	# Performance appraisal rating
sK2006	% Peer review rate
sK2007	% Performance appraisal participation rate
sK2008	% Performance rating distribution
sK2009	% Self review rate
sK2010	% Upward review rate
sK2011	% Staffing rate - high potential
sK2014	% Staff who received a verbal feedback
sK2016	% Employee cost over sales revenue
sK2017	% Employee cost over net income
sK2019	$ Telephone / communication cost per employee
sK2278	% On-time delivery of HR service requests
sK3172	# Time to process payroll
sK3274	$ Cost of payroll process
sK3390	% Labor cost from operational cost
sK5845	$ Revenue per home office staff
sK5943	# Internal reports to members
sK6238	% Work performed by staff over-skilled for the job complexity
sK6718	% Productivity lost due to infrastructure
sK6788	$ Payroll expenses per employee
sK7058	% Time spent on work generating real value
sK13963	# Absenteeism
sK14108	# Employee lost time frequency

sKPI #	Key Performance Indicator name
sK14184	# Hours absent per employee
sK14209	# Injuries in relation to FTEs
sK14210	# Injuries per one thousand kilometers
sK14227	# Lateness
sK14235	# Lost time sickness frequency
sK14236	# Lost workday cases
sK18851	# Staff with sick leave of equal or more than 50 days per 100 employees
sK22456	% Staff attendance rate

Recruitment

Recruitment is the process of filling job roles with internal or external candidates. KPIs generally focus on external recruitment, internal movement of candidates and the overall effectiveness of the recruitment process.

sKPI #	Key Performance Indicator name
sK2	# Employment brand strength
sK49	$ Cost per hire
sK50	# Time to start
sK51	% Internal promotion rate
sK53	% Job offer acceptance rate
sK241	# Open job requisitions
sK242	# Open requisitions to current staff
sK243	# Recruiter to open requisitions ratio
sK480	$ Signing bonus expense
sK672	# Open time of job positions
sK673	# Applications received per vacancy
sK674	% Interviews from submitted CVs
sK688	# Time to fill a vacant position
sK710	$ Recruitment costs
sK763	% Staffing rate
sK765	% Applicants referred by current employees
sK768	% Rehired employees
sK779	% New staff with post-employment interview completed
sK1777	% Succession plans for key positions
sK1779	% Junior and middle managers who were promoted internally
sK1781	% Employment offers made within the target timeframe
sK1782	% Signing bonus rate
sK1783	# Career path ratio
sK1784	% Cross functional mobility
sK1785	% Internal hire rate
sK1786	% Internal placement rate
sK1787	% Employees lateral mobility
sK1788	# Promotion speed ratio
sK1789	% Employee transfer rate

sKPI #	Key Performance Indicator name
sK1790	% Recruitment source breakdown
sK1791	# Recruitment source ratio
sK1792	# Interviews per hire
sK1793	# Recruitment referral
sK1795	% Applicant interview rate
sK1796	% Interview employment offer rate
sK1797	# Interviewee ratio
sK1798	% New hires terminated within 30 days
sK1799	# New hire performance satisfaction index
sK1800	# New hire satisfaction with recruiting index
sK1801	% External hire rate
sK1802	# Net hire ratio
sK1803	% New position recruitment rate
sK1804	# New position recruitment ratio
sK1805	# Applicant ratio
sK1806	# On time talent delivery
sK1808	% Employee probation reports assessed
sK1812	# Long term vacancies per total number of jobs
sK1813	# Applications received by recruiting source
sK1814	# Response time for recruitment inquiries
sK1816	% Newly recruited employees screened
sK1819	$ Interviewing cost
sK1823	% Internal appointments above level
sK1824	# Hired to needed personnel ratio
sK1825	# Applicants average age
sK1826	% Unsolicited applications rate
sK1828	% Employment requests filled on schedule
sK1829	% Promotions and management changes publicized
sK4723	# Requisitions handled per recruiter
sK4726	# Absenteeism per new hire
sK4727	# Inquiries per open job positions
sK5492	# Recruit to hire ratio for job placements
sK6251	% Resource requests overdue
sK6422	% Executive positions filled internally
sK6825	% Traineeship job openings
sK6826	# Recruitment partnerships
sK6919	# Administrative staff per recruiter
sK6922	# Candidates database size
sK6924	% Candidate files up to date in database
sK14107	# Employed persons
sK14213	# Internal promotions
sK14214	# Interviews conducted
sK14247	# Officers employed

Retention

Retention deals with the desire of staff to continue working for and contributing to the organization, as well as their eventual termination of employment. KPIs generally focus on employee satisfaction, engagement and turnover.

sKPI #	Key Performance Indicator name
sK1	% Employee turnover
sK8	# Employee tenure
sK52	% New hire failure
sK91	$ Turnover cost
sK244	# Time to promotion
sK588	# Hours volunteered by employees
sK1830	# Employee empowerment index
sK1831	$ Employee termination value
sK1832	$ Voluntary termination cost
sK1833	$ Termination value per full time equivalent (FTE)
sK1834	% New employees turnover cost rate
sK1835	# Employee commitment index
sK1836	# Employee engagement index
sK1837	% Employee retention rate
sK1838	# Employee retention index
sK1841	% Staffing rate less than 1 year tenure
sK1842	% Involuntary termination rate
sK1843	% Terminations by performance rating
sK1844	% Employment termination reason breakdown
sK1845	% Voluntary termination rate
sK1846	% New hire turnover
sK1847	# Employee perceptions of external job opportunities index
sK1849	% Early retirements
sK1850	% Employees taking ill health retirement
sK1852	# Length of service of senior level staff
sK2069	# Unplanned personnel losses
sK3442	$ Job abandonment cost
sK4403	% Unavoidable officer terminations
sK5912	% Employee satisfaction
sK14241	# Management lost
sK22960	# Workers retaining employment after relocation

Service Delivery

Service Delivery is the core responsibility of the HR function represented by transaction processing and other general HR processes. KPIs focus on general profile of the HR function, its structure, efficiency and effectiveness of processes (such as payroll), use of technology and other aspects related to the HR team in the organization.

sKPI #	Key Performance Indicator name
sK43	$ HR department cost per FTE
sK44	# FTEs per HR department FTE
sK45	% HR outsource rate

sKPI #	Key Performance Indicator name
sK752	# Absent days per employee during peak operational periods
sK1890	% Employees who interact with customers
sK2021	% HR outsourcing costs
sK2033	% Availability of Human Resources IT system
sK2037	# HR corporate staffing ratio
sK2038	# Satisfaction of employees with HR services
sK2039	% HR mobility rate
sK2040	# HR staffing mix ratio
sK2041	% Human resources staffing breakdown
sK2042	# HR staffing coverage ratio
sK2043	% HR staffing rate
sK2044	% HR expense distribution by function
sK2045	% HR expense distribution by type
sK2046	% HR operating expense rate
sK2047	% HR revenue expense rate
sK2048	$ HR revenue per HR Full Time Equivalent (FTE)
sK2049	% Human Resources Information Technology (HRIT) investment rate
sK2050	# Human Resources IT (HRIT) system average days to data entry
sK2051	% Human Resources IT (HRIT) system late transaction rate
sK2052	% Human Resources IT (HRIT) system transaction error rate
sK2053	$ Overpayment value
sK2054	% Direct deposit participation rate
sK2055	% Overpayment rate
sK2056	% Payroll error rate
sK2057	$ Payroll expense per employee
sK2059	% Time sheets incorrectly filled
sK2060	# Human Capital related suggestions resubmitted and approved
sK14193	# HR deficiencies

Talent Development

Talent Development deals with the administration of the talent pool of the human capital in the organization. This is achieved through assessment and development of personal and professional skills. KPIs focus on evaluation of the educational and development programs that employees took part in. They also focus on assessment of general staff skills as well as managerial and leadership skills. Training and other learning opportunities are also monitored through a separate set of KPIs.

sKPI #	Key Performance Indicator name
sK6	$ Training investment per full time equivalent (FTE)
sK7	# Training hours per full time equivalent (FTE)
sK217	# Industry specific training sessions for personnel
sK249	% Management successor pool growth rate
sK250	% Training return on investment

sKPI #	Key Performance Indicator name
sK251	% External training programs
sK689	% Training certificates
sK690	% Operational budget spent on training
sK691	# Time to competence
sK692	% Training penetration rate
sK693	% E-learning courses utilized
sK709	$ Cost of training per year
sK713	% Training cost / sales turnover
sK723	# Training duration per session
sK753	# Technological competence of staff
sK764	% Employees assessed in an assessment center
sK771	% Employees cross-trained
sK774	# Time employees spend in mentoring
sK780	% Employees with higher education
sK781	% Employees certified for skilled job functions or positions
sK1263	% Managers with satisfactory IT literacy
sK1891	% Rising stars with mentors
sK1892	% Successor pool coverage
sK1893	# Mentoring meetings by each high performer
sK1894	% Re-skilled employees
sK1895	% Training course content by type
sK1896	# Time in training
sK1897	% Managerial positions without ready candidates rate
sK1898	% Employees that have improved skills during last six months
sK1900	% New staff who attended an induction program
sK1901	% Competence development expense out of payroll cost
sK1902	% Educational attainment breakdown
sK1903	% Requests for tuition reimbursement
sK1904	% Cross-function job rotation of managers
sK1905	% Employee satisfaction with leadership
sK1906	% Leadership development plans (LDP) prevalence rate
sK1907	% Manager instability rate
sK1908	# Managers quality index
sK1909	# Training class size
sK1910	% E-learning abandonment rate
sK1911	% Employee satisfaction with training
sK1912	% Training channel delivery mix
sK1914	# Training quality
sK1915	# Training staff ratio
sK1916	% Training compensation expense rate
sK1918	% Skill attainment rate
sK1921	# Employees completing sponsored Master in Business Administration (MBA) programs
sK1922	% E-Learning pass rate
sK1923	% Cross training of employees

sKPI #	Key Performance Indicator name
sK1925	$ Training cost per hour
sK1928	$ In house learning and development cost per full time equivalent (FTE) employee
sK1929	$ External learning and development cost per full time equivalent (FTE) employee
sK4182	% Training rate
sK4648	% Certified accountants
sK4659	# Certifications per employee
sK4673	% Employees meeting continuing professional development requirements
sK4800	% Staff holding a degree
sK5217	% Training sessions evaluated as satisfactory or better
sK5811	% Training provided that uses e-learning
sK5812	% Trainees who receive constructive feedback on their learning
sK5813	% Participants in training programs from underrepresented groups
sK5837	% Trainees working on interdisciplinary tasks
sK5841	% Trainees in fieldwork
sK5843	# Short term trainees
sK5847	# Long term trainees
sK6353	$ Training investment per customer
sK6421	$ Expenses on further education per employee
sK6591	% Education and training workplace delivery
sK6701	% Employee IT literacy
sK6702	# Professional events attended by employees
sK6703	% Employees attending professional events
sK6760	% Professionally qualified employees
sK6761	# Skills gap index
sK6769	# Strategic skills coverage ratio
sK6771	# Hours of strategic skills training
sK6772	# Strategic skills development programs
sK6777	% Employees that received a minimum accepted level of training
sK6871	% Employees reaching competence after training
sK6872	# Post training evaluations
sK6873	% Training objectives met
sK7011	# New staff recruitment cost vs. current staff skill enhancement cost
sK7048	% Core skills coverage
sK13996	# Attendance
sK13997	# Attendance hours at formal training lessons per staff member
sK14054	# Continuing education activities offered by the Board for licensees
sK14080	# Days training support provided on a per student basis
sK14113	# Employees studying for a related vocational qualification
sK14114	# Employees used for development
sK14128	# Enrollment

Organizational » Functional Areas

sKPI #	Key Performance Indicator name
sK14145	# Firms employees involved in working or up-skilling a local
sK14186	# Hours in mentoring
sK14188	# Hours of employee training on policies and procedures concerning aspects of human rights
sK14189	# Hours of staff development related to job performance per employee
sK14191	# Hours of training per year per employee by gender
sK14192	# Hours training per employee
sK22472	# Hours of training per FTE
sK22598	# Staff key competencies
sK22648	% Training course by discipline
sK22654	# Participant in training courses
sK22655	% Respondents who undertook formal training by region
sK22657	% Primary producers that undertook formal training in the areas specified

Workforce

Workforce describes the demographic, structural and tenure characteristics of the workforce. Measures of status are more common for this sub-category.

sKPI #	Key Performance Indicator name
sK9	# Headcount
sK193	# Span of control
sK194	# Management-to-staff ratio
sK245	# Workforce age
sK246	# Gender ratio
sK247	# Ethnic diversity ratio
sK252	% Independent contractors
sK698	% Employees nearing retirement age
sK762	% Accession rate
sK1840	% Organization employment staffing breakdown
sK2023	# Employees with delegated spending authority
sK2024	% Part time employees
sK2025	% Managers who are women
sK2026	% Age staffing breakdown
sK2027	% Disability staffing rate
sK2028	% Customer-facing time rate
sK2029	% Employment level staffing distribution
sK2030	% Employees distribution by functional area
sK2032	# Rookie ratio
sK3368	% Employees per process
sK3377	% Employees per department
sK5890	% Operations staff to total staff ratio
sK6759	# Ratio of support to total staff
sK6770	% Strategic job coverage
sK6824	# Traineeship programs

sKPI #	Key Performance Indicator name
sK6884	% Core areas of expertise covered at desired level
sK6948	# Length of contractor assignment
sK13971	# Active management
sK13977	# Age of staff
sK13978	# Age staffing breakdown
sK14059	# Cumulative work experience in current management team
sK14096	# Education levels
sK14154	# Full Time Equivalent (FTE) employees
sK14155	# Full Time Equivalent (FTE) library staff
sK14156	# Full Time Equivalent (FTE) per 100 adjusted discharges
sK14157	# Full Time Equivalent (FTE) per adjusted day
sK14158	# Full Time Equivalent (FTE) per age group
sK14159	# Full Time Equivalent (FTE) per average daily census
sK14164	# Full-time positions
sK14219	# Labor hours
sK14220	# Labor productivity
sK14229	# Length of service
sK14231	# Level of diversity of skills
sK22455	# Workyears
sK22470	# Ratio of production staff to administrative and supervisory staff
sK22474	# Clerks
sK22523	# Employees by union code
sK22961	# New labor force

Working Environment

Working Environment is about creating and maintaining a highly motivational, safe, fair and productive environment for employees to perform their duties. KPIs focus on absenteeism issues, workforce relations (conflict resolution, industrial actions),organizational health and safety related aspects.

sKPI #	Key Performance Indicator name
sK47	# Overtime hours per employee
sK48	# Sickness absence days per full time equivalent (FTE) employee
sK87	# Lost time due to accidents per 100,000 hours worked
sK88	# Accidents per 100,000 hours worked
sK542	# Harassment and discrimination complaints received
sK686	# Paid time off
sK687	# Intimidation, hazing, bullying or retaliation complaints received
sK694	% Fatal accidents
sK695	$ Health and safety prevention costs
sK720	# Hours lost due to absenteeism
sK721	% Lost time due to strike action
sK732	% Employees with working home agreements
sK733	% Job sharing agreements

sKPI #	Key Performance Indicator name
sK734	% Employees with flexible work agreements
sK735	# Formal union grievances
sK736	% Employees covered by collective bargaining agreements
sK778	% Employees trained in first aid
sK914	# Incidents outside working hours
sK1277	# Feedback received from employees, partners and customers
sK1457	# Programs for clients, customers and employees with information and training on healthy eating habits
sK1930	% Employees satisfaction with work / life balance
sK1931	% Employees attendance for social club activities
sK1932	% Employees involved in community activities
sK1933	# Lost time injury frequency rate (LTIFR)
sK1934	% Staff attending stress management trainings
sK1935	# Working days lost by reason
sK1936	% Staff working flexible hours
sK1937	# Days working overseas on jobs
sK1938	# Employee complaints resolution timeliness
sK1939	# Staff with more than 30 days leave owing
sK1941	# Safety inspections per month
sK1942	% Staff with adequate occupational health and safety (H&S) training
sK1943	# Safety non-conformances cleared up
sK1944	% Health and safety representatives (HSR) positions filled
sK1945	# Non-compliance with legal standards in safety inspections
sK1946	% Corrective actions completed within time
sK1949	# Work week
sK1950	$ Compensation value of unscheduled absences per full time equivalent (FTE)
sK1951	% Paid time off (PTO) hours utilization rate
sK1953	% Unscheduled absence breakdown
sK1954	# Unscheduled absence days per employee
sK1955	% Unscheduled absence rate
sK1956	% Alternative dispute resolution (ADR) success rate
sK1957	% External complaint factor
sK1958	% Grievance rate
sK1959	# Time to resolve grievance
sK1960	# Industrial dispute absence days per full time equivalent (FTE)
sK1961	# Time lost per health and safety (H&S) incident
sK1962	% Health and safety expense breakdown
sK1963	$ Health and safety (H&S) expenses per full time equivalent (FTE)
sK1964	% Health and safety (H&S) incident type breakdown

sKPI #	Key Performance Indicator name
sK1965	# Health and safety incidents per 100 full time equivalents (FTEs)
sK1966	$ Workers compensation insurance per full time equivalent (FTE)
sK1967	# Work related injury return ratio
sK1968	# Occupational diseases per 1,000 employees
sK1971	% Adult education credential rate
sK1977	# Sexual harassment complaints received
sK1979	$ On site search average order value (AOV)
sK1980	% Employees lateness
sK1982	% Employees on sickness leave
sK1984	% Women returning to work after maternity leave
sK1990	% Lost time incident ratio (LTIR)
sK1991	$ Occupational health and safety cost factor
sK1993	# Safety suggestions from employees
sK1997	% Safety equipment checked per schedule
sK2001	% Safety problems identified by management
sK2002	# Safety violations by department
sK2058	% Schedule flexibility rate
sK3148	# Workers' compensation claims
sK5102	# Employees exposed to an 8 hours noise dose of more than 85 dB
sK5928	% Adherence to values and mission
sK6273	# Employee advocacy for products and services
sK6390	% Employees willing to recommend the organization as an employer
sK6434	# Employee advocacy for the organization as an employer
sK6731	# Hours of Organizational Health and Safety (OH&S) training conducted
sK6776	# Top leadership communication sessions
sK6903	% Complaints with workplace safety and sanitation
sK6910	# Reported work accidents
sK13964	# Accidents per employee
sK14025	# Classified injuries
sK14026	# Classified injury frequency rate
sK14097	# Education, training, counseling, prevention, and risk-control programs regarding serious diseases
sK14109	# Employee satisfaction survey conducted
sK14111	# Employees recognized as disabled workers
sK14112	# Employees rewarded
sK14140	# Fatalities in relation to FTEs
sK22471	# Work hours lost to accidents
sK19715	$ Radiation safety cost per authorized user and radiation worker

Information Technology

IT is the functional area in charge of making available, easy accessible and secured information within the organization, by studying, designing, developing, implementing the computer-based information systems, particularly software applications and computer hardware.

Application Development

IT - Application Development refers to using different technologies to design, develop, and implement software applications within own or client organizations. KPIs refer to both quantitative and qualitative aspects of the applications development process generally relating to design and functionality aspects.

sKPI #	Key Performance Indicator name
sK13	% Schedule adherence in software development
sK14	% Assignment content adherence
sK15	% Cost adherence in software development
sK16	% Fault slip through
sK130	# Time to repair (TTR)
sK230	# Design to development time ratio
sK231	% Software build failures
sK232	% Features requested by users
sK233	% Bugs found by application developers
sK234	% Time spent on fixing bugs
sK437	% Trouble report closure rate
sK670	% Software upgrades completed successfully
sK785	# Software versions released
sK787	# Untested software releases
sK788	% Data redundancy
sK789	% Applications constantly modernized
sK794	# Fixed bugs
sK802	% Availability errors
sK803	$ Cost of maintenance per 1,000 lines of code
sK804	# Lines of code requiring rework per person
sK805	# Persons needed for rework due to requirements capturing inefficiency
sK806	% On time completion of software applications
sK807	% Quality of software applications developed
sK808	% Additional requirements satisfied
sK809	# Additional requirements requested
sK810	# Defects found over a period of time
sK814	# Unique requirements
sK815	% Unique requirements completed
sK816	% Requirements to be reworked
sK818	% Requirements satisfied in the initial design
sK820	# Extra months spent for the implementation
sK822	# Applications data transfer time
sK823	% Unique requirements to be reworked
sK827	# Entry points for a module
sK828	# Discovered defects that are known as software vulnerabilities

sKPI #	Key Performance Indicator name
sK831	% Modules that contain vulnerabilities
sK832	% Defects that negatively impact the security posture of the system
sK833	% New systems that have completed certification and accreditation prior to their implementation
sK934	% Defects removal efficiency
sK987	# Different technology platforms
sK1089	% Failed software releases
sK1158	% Releases implemented without operational assurance
sK3600	# Build application failures
sK3607	# Unauthorized reversions to previous releases
sK3841	% Issues raised by latest test still to be addressed
sK4635	# Planned changes per application
sK6095	$ Coding cost per line of code (LOC)
sK6096	% Cost of testing and debugging
sK6097	# Bugs per 1,000 lines of code (KLOC)
sK6098	# Time to market (TTM)
sK6099	# Software process execution time in seconds
sK6100	% Lines of reused code
sK6102	# Software defects per testing minute
sK6103	% Single-user licenses sold
sK6104	% Multi-user licenses sold
sK6105	% Software sales from revenue
sK6106	$ Single-user license price
sK6107	$ Profit per software product sold
sK6111	# Software errors to application run time ratio
sK6112	# New features per software version
sK6115	% User inputs with improper error handling
sK6693	# Tests written per feature
sK6694	% Out of date test cases
sK6695	# Bugs uncovered in system test
sK6696	# Trouble reports density
sK6697	# Trouble reports to test cases
sK6698	% Code churn
sK6706	% Testing pass rate
sK6708	# Static analysis tools
sK6710	# Cyclomatic complexity
sK6712	# Velocity per programmer
sK6714	% New defects introduced by fixes
sK6717	# Team velocity estimate
sK6720	% Productivity loss due to code lost
sK6723	# Application breakdowns per day of usage

sKPI #	Key Performance Indicator name
sK6724	% Bugs reported by clients
sK6725	# Unit test failures per programmer
sK6726	# Testers to developers ratio
sK6727	# Bugs per developer
sK6728	# Bugs assigned not in pipeline
sK6945	# Firmware updates released or conducted

Data Center

Data Center is a facility that contains technology equipment able to perform functions such as: storage, management, processing and dissemination of digital data and information organized around a particular body of knowledge or pertaining to a particular business. A data center houses the software, hardware and network infrastructure and it ranges in complexity from a computer closet to a network operations center.

sKPI #	Key Performance Indicator name
sK575	% Corporate average data efficiency (CADE)
sK583	% IT asset efficiency
sK679	# Power usage effectiveness (PUE)
sK680	% Data center infrastructure efficiency (DCIE)
sK786	% Data center availability
sK836	# Data center temperature efficiency
sK837	% Servers located in data centers
sK7014	# Supply temperature
sK7015	% Relative Humidity Range at IT Inlet
sK7016	% Return temperature index
sK7017	# Data center cooling system efficiency
sK7018	# Cooling system sizing factor
sK7019	% Air economizer utilization factor
sK7020	% Water economizer utilization factor
sK7021	# Airflow efficiency
sK7022	# Uninterruptible power supply (UPS) load factor
sK7023	% Data center uninterruptible power supply (UPS) system efficiency
sK7024	# Data center lighting power density
sK7025	# Data center area (electrically active)
sK7026	# Return air temperature
sK7027	# Cooling system power consumption
sK7028	# Cooling load
sK7029	# Installed chiller capacity
sK7030	% Fan efficiency
sK7031	% IT power to data center power
sK7032	# HVAC effectiveness index
sK7033	% Rack cooling index (RCI)
sK7034	% Uninterrruptible power supply (UPS) loss
sK7035	# Carbon usage effectiveness (CUE)
sK7036	# Water usage effectiveness (WUE)
sK7037	# Carbon intensity per unit of data

sKPI #	Key Performance Indicator name
sK7038	# PAR4
sK7039	% Massive array of idle disks (MAID) level
sK7040	# Node input to output
sK7041	# Node paging hierarchy - scan rate
sK7042	# Disk service time

Enterprise Architecture

IT - Enterprise Architecture sustains the organization to establish a decision framework that enables its various parts to articulate how information and technology can be used in the context of business strategy. KPIs refer to the role Enterprise Architecture plays in business development and the business methods used for assuring the organization's structure and processes connected to the strategic objectives.

sKPI #	Key Performance Indicator name
sK375	$ Costs savings from service reuse
sK381	% Financial management processes supported electronically
sK1038	# Business disruptions caused by IT problems
sK1133	% Timely implementation of new technology
sK1156	% Web applications not compliant with enterprise architecture
sK1157	# Frequency of updates to the enterprise architecture
sK1164	# Services under development
sK1165	% Effective service development rate
sK1166	% Service oriented architecture (SOA) services reused
sK1168	# Current state applications that could be replaced by Service Oriented Architecture (SOA) services
sK1170	# Services managed by Service Oriented Architecture (SOA) registry
sK1171	% Assets encapsulated as services
sK1172	% Architecture with service interface specification
sK1173	% Architecture with service data taxonomy
sK1174	% Architecture with service security requirements
sK1177	# Web application outage due to Service Oriented Architecture (SOA) services down-time
sK1178	% Service Oriented Architecture (SOA) service validation errors
sK1179	# Response time of SOA services
sK1180	% Cost saved from Service Oriented Architecture (SOA) service reuse
sK1181	$ Cost of service change
sK1183	$ Added development cost of SOA service implementation
sK1184	$ Cost savings from faster application integration
sK1186	# System interfaces with public sector partners
sK1190	% Cycle time reduction
sK1191	% Reduction in redundant data sources
sK1192	% Data quality improvement
sK1195	% Visibility into the application portfolio
sK1198	# SOA applications at the end of their useful life

sKPI #	Key Performance Indicator name
sK1199	# Redundant technology products
sK1200	# System Development Life Cycle (SDLC) exceptions granted
sK1201	% SOA requirement fulfillment
sK1202	% Service Oriented Architecture (SOA) requirement accuracy
sK1255	# Frequency of independent reviews of IT compliance
sK1256	# Frequency of IT governance as an agenda item in the IT board meetings
sK1266	% Configuration changes approved and implemented
sK2688	# Variances from the business plans and capacity plans
sK2887	% Timely incorporation of business plans in capacity plans
sK2983	% Business disruptions caused by a lack of adequate IT capacity
sK3608	% Bought-in software compliant with legal restrictions
sK3609	% Non-standard hardware equipment
sK6140	% IT systems integrated
sK6218	% Cost of strategic investments in technology
sK6230	# Days to refresh one desktop
sK6423	# Enterprise applications used per employee
sK14024	# Changed posts on Oracle ERP
sK14088	# Deleted posts on Oracle ERP

IT - General

IT is the functional area in charge of making available, easy accessible and secured information within the organization, by studying, designing, developing, implementing the computer-based information systems, particularly software applications and computer hardware.

sKPI #	Key Performance Indicator name
sK99	$ Cost per PC
sK857	# Obsolete IT infrastructure
sK860	# IT network equipment replacement time
sK874	# Server connection time
sK1054	% IT operations staff with advanced ITIL certification
sK1064	% IT operations staff ITIL aware
sK1074	# Joint IT / business planning meetings held
sK1097	# IT steering committee meetings held
sK1152	# Timeline for regulatory compliance to new IT regulatory requirements
sK1169	% IT budget spend on service delivery
sK1182	$ Maintenance cost per application
sK1204	$ IT spending per employee
sK1206	% Time dedicated to creative IT activities
sK1207	% IT spending for IT maintenance
sK1209	$ IT spending per customer
sK1210	% IT budget from total company revenues
sK1211	% IT capital spending

sKPI #	Key Performance Indicator name
sK1214	% IT work outsourced
sK1215	% Strategic business initiatives driven by IT
sK1216	% IT budget growth
sK1227	% Critical business processes not covered by a defined service availability plan
sK1234	% IT budget spent on risk management
sK1245	% IT service bills paid by business management
sK1251	# Frequency of IT reporting to the board
sK1253	# Frequency of review of the IT risk management process
sK1261	% Spending of current technology capital budget
sK1271	$ Spam filtering cost per email mailbox
sK1274	$ Cost per available terabyte
sK1275	$ Cost per stored terabyte
sK3395	% Expenditure with financial system
sK4612	# Affected users by IT infrastructure incidents
sK4626	# System login time
sK4627	% Peak infrastructure utilization
sK4628	% Disk utilization
sK4633	# IT Infrastructure changes completed
sK4634	% IT infrastructure change success rate
sK6025	# Cases cleared using the new technology
sK6026	# Automated information exchanges in use
sK6028	% Case dispositions recorded in repository
sK6042	% Personnel who log on a Court Management System module each day
sK6718	% Productivity lost due to infrastructure
sK6942	# Age of PCs
sK6943	# Handheld devices in the enterprise
sK6944	% Laptop rebuilds to address stability issues
sK6947	# Laptop to desktop ratio
sK14089	# Desktop and role play exercises performed during the quarter

IT - Security

IT - Security is concerned with protecting the information and the IT systems, assuring the confidentiality, integrity and availability of data regardless of its form. KPIs track both the availability, efficiency and effectiveness of security systems in place.

sKPI #	Key Performance Indicator name
sK92	# Security control duration
sK93	% IT security policy compliance
sK94	# Detected network attacks
sK125	% Security awareness
sK127	% IT security related incidents
sK128	% Downtime due to security incidents
sK131	% Email spam messages stopped
sK223	% IT security budget

sKPI #	Key Performance Indicator name
sK224	# Incident efficiency
sK225	% Compliance to password policy
sK226	% IT security staff
sK562	# Unauthorized changes
sK563	% Intrusion success
sK564	# Password policy violations
sK565	# Viruses detected in user files
sK567	% IT systems monitored by anti-virus software
sK568	# Unapplied patch latency
sK570	% Critical patch coverage
sK571	% Incidents after patching
sK572	% Spam not detected
sK655	# Time to detect incident
sK656	% False detection rate
sK657	% Security intrusions detection rate
sK830	% Discovered vulnerabilities that have been mitigated
sK834	% Information systems that have a contingency plan
sK880	% Users with access to shared accounts
sK897	% IT systems with anti-virus protection
sK899	$ Cost of virus incidents
sK903	# Security defects per 1,000 lines of code
sK906	# Outgoing viruses discovered
sK907	$ Cost of patches
sK910	% Service calls addressing a security issue
sK911	# Time lag between detection, reporting and action upon security incidents
sK912	$ Cost of security incidents
sK915	% Successful backup operations
sK917	% Physical backup / archive media that are fully encrypted
sK919	# Age of file backup
sK924	% Users who do not comply with password standards
sK925	% Systems where security requirements are not met
sK926	# Frequency of testing of backup media
sK928	# Incidents of unauthorized access to computer facilities
sK929	# Incidents due to physical security breaches or failures
sK930	# Major internal control breaches
sK931	# Backup every night this month
sK936	% Impact of security threats and attacks compared to competitors and peers
sK937	% Accuracy of threat analysis
sK938	% Responsiveness to emerging threats
sK940	# Identified vulnerabilities
sK942	% Adoption of prescribed software security best practices in organization
sK943	# Security incidents before and after the introduction of policy, principles or procedures
sK944	# Security events related to improper technological security controls

sKPI #	Key Performance Indicator name
sK945	% Information security events that affect business operations
sK946	% Security compliance against the most common vulnerabilities
sK948	% Successful test backup restores
sK949	# Substantiated complaints regarding breaches of customer privacy
sK950	% Information security risks for which satisfactory controls have been fully implemented
sK952	# Information security related risks
sK954	# Employee malware incidents
sK955	# Employee custodianship of sensitive data
sK956	% Critical vulnerabilities mitigated after discovery
sK958	% System and service acquisition contracts that include security requirements
sK959	# Computers that perform cryptographic operations
sK960	% Viruses detected in e-mail messages
sK961	% Invalid logins (failed password)
sK962	# Intrusion attempts
sK963	% Unauthorized website access
sK964	% Invalid logins (failed username)
sK965	% Unauthorized internal access attempts
sK966	% Administration violation (unauthorized changes)
sK968	% Fully patched hosts
sK969	% Host scan frequency
sK970	% Host exempt from vulnerability scanning
sK971	% Hosts without high priority patches
sK972	% Hosts with unknown vulnerabilities
sK973	% Host classified as having severe vulnerabilities
sK975	% Patch success rate
sK976	% Patches applied within established protocols
sK977	% Vulnerability exposure time
sK978	# Vulnerability remediation time
sK979	# Missing patches
sK981	% Patch coverage for IP subnets
sK982	% Patch coverage for latest critical patch
sK983	# Devices having problems after patching
sK984	# Applications with problems after patching
sK1082	% Incidents caused by software releases
sK1083	% Invocation of incident response team to remediate the security incidents
sK1142	# Email incidents per user
sK1150	# Time required to resolve business debilitating information security events
sK1154	% Accuracy of data analysis compared to actual events and activities
sK1254	# Frequency of IT physical risk assessments and reviews
sK1257	# IT policy violations

sKPI #	Key Performance Indicator name
sK1264	% Awareness of information security programs and capabilities
sK1265	% Effectiveness of remediation plans and controls for identified IT vulnerabilities
sK1267	% Individuals screened before being granted access to organizational information system
sK1276	% Information security events related to improper technological controls
sK2219	# Information security incidents before to information security incidents after training solutions have been put in place
sK2510	# Incoming spam messages missed
sK2557	# Inbound connections to Internet facing servers
sK2627	# Unapproved open ports on business critical servers
sK2628	# Incoming spam messages detected and filtered
sK2631	# Malicious codes detected on websites accessed
sK2632	# Banned sites access attempts
sK2659	# Outgoing email viruses and spywares detected
sK2669	# Successful virus attacks
sK2687	# Malicious code incidents requiring manual cleanup
sK3211	% Reported security incidents dealt with in accordance with agreed procedures
sK4208	# Detected attacks targeting servers
sK4449	# Malicious codes detected in computers
sK4759	% Clients computers covered by antivirus software
sK4768	% Computers with latest anti-virus signature
sK4811	# Legal actions taken against an organization related to information security
sK4814	# Legal issues underlined through the analysis of legal and regulatory trends and activities
sK5918	# Transactions recorded from a single IP address
sK6116	% Encrypted servers
sK6270	% Information security-related incidents that impact the operational effectiveness of the business
sK6271	% Information security objectives aligned with business goals and initiatives
sK6272	% Positive compliance audit reports from internal and external auditors
sK6722	$ Loss due to identity theft

Network Management

IT - Network Management includes the operation, administration, maintenance and provisioning of state of the art network systems within the organization.

sKPI #	Key Performance Indicator name
sK17	$ Cost per trouble report
sK95	$ Cost per device
sK96	$ Cost per terabyte transmitted
sK97	% Data network utilization
sK122	# Devices per FTE
sK123	# Terabytes managed by one Full Time Equivalent (FTE)

sKPI #	Key Performance Indicator name
sK124	% Data network growth rate
sK219	$ Voice network - cost per minute
sK220	# Voice Network minutes per FTE
sK221	% Data network availability
sK671	% Computer diffusion rate
sK783	# Propagation delay
sK790	% Web server availability
sK795	# Host latency
sK796	# Network latency
sK801	# TCP round-trip time (RTT)
sK838	# Watts per active port
sK839	$ Hardware equipment value
sK840	# Printers to employees ratio
sK842	% Network packet loss
sK843	% Network bandwidth used
sK845	# Network round trip latency
sK846	% Data packets retransmission
sK847	# Minimum bandwidth guarantee
sK849	% Storage volume utilization
sK850	% Central Processing Unit (CPU) utilization
sK851	% Inoperative servers
sK852	# Server to system administration ratio
sK854	# Maximum memory usage
sK856	# Critical business processes supported by obsolete IT infrastructure
sK859	% Users affected by network failures
sK861	# Data access methods used
sK864	% Mainframe availability
sK866	# Network traffic usage
sK869	% Bit error rate (BER)
sK871	# Server response time
sK872	# Retransmission delay
sK873	# Network connection time
sK875	# Refused sessions by server
sK876	# Unfulfilled TCP/IP session requests
sK877	# Byte volumes
sK878	# Connection setup time
sK879	# Data rate in bits/second
sK881	# Propagation speed of data packages
sK882	# Link transmission time
sK883	# Bandwidth of a network link
sK884	# Flow capacity of a network path
sK885	# Maximum flow capacity of an IP cloud
sK886	# Instantaneous route of a network path
sK887	# Hop count of a route
sK888	# Buffer size of router

sKPI #	Key Performance Indicator name
sK889	# Instantaneous queue size of a router interface
sK890	# Instantaneous connectivity of an Internet path
sK891	# Maximum jitter along an internet path
sK893	% Local area network (LAN) server availability
sK895	% File servers backed up and restored
sK896	% Severe network attacks
sK1039	# Critical time outage
sK1144	# Web services response time

Service Management

IT - Service Management is a process - focused function, centered towards delivering high qualitative IT services. KPIs in IT Service Management refer to the support services offered by IT, within the company and towards their clients, in terms of covering needs and requirements.

sKPI #	Key Performance Indicator name
sK98	# Time for service request fulfillment
sK129	$ Unit cost of IT services
sK204	% Usage of old technology causing breached SLAs
sK228	# Incidents per PC
sK229	# Days for lease refresh/upgrade fulfillment
sK582	% Facility efficiency (FE)
sK624	% Software licenses in use
sK625	% Unauthorized software licenses used
sK626	% Licenses purchased and not accounted for in repository
sK627	# Deviations between configuration repository and actual asset configurations
sK628	% Compliance issues caused by improper configuration of assets
sK629	% Critical time failures
sK630	# Exceeding alerts capacity threshold
sK631	% Repeated IT incidents
sK632	% Incidents not closed within the established time frame
sK655	# Time to detect incident
sK656	% False detection rate
sK658	# Incident response time
sK660	% Incidents backlog
sK661	% Incidents solved by first point of contact
sK662	% Incidents resolved remotely
sK663	# Incidents processed per service desk workstation
sK667	% IT incidents solved within agreed response time
sK668	% IT incidents fixed before users notice
sK678	# IT service desk availability
sK792	% Service Improvement Initiatives (SIP) completed on time
sK811	% Virtual server availability
sK841	# Email service requests created
sK909	% User accounts classified as obsolete

sKPI #	Key Performance Indicator name
sK985	$ Software support cost
sK986	% Successful software installations
sK989	% Outage due to incidents
sK990	% Outage due to changes
sK991	% Service outage duration
sK992	% Incidents with a root cause analysis
sK993	# Incident closure duration
sK994	% Reopened service requests
sK995	% Escalated service requests
sK996	% Infrastructure components with automated availability monitoring
sK997	# Change propagation time
sK999	# New service requests arrival rate
sK1000	% Critical changes
sK1002	% Problems with available workaround
sK1003	% Reopened incidents
sK1004	% Changes applied without authorization
sK1005	$ Problem resolution average cost
sK1006	$ Cost to solve an incident
sK1007	% Changes proposed by customers
sK1010	% Reassigned incidents
sK1011	% Incidents incorrectly assigned
sK1012	% Problems resolved within the scheduled time
sK1013	% Problems with root cause analysis
sK1014	% Implementations non-authorized
sK1015	% Response time of Service Level Agreements (SLAs) not met
sK1016	% Availability SLAs (Service Level Agreements) met
sK1018	% Changes that required backup
sK1019	% Software work outsourced
sK1020	% Backed out changes
sK1021	# SLA issues logged
sK1022	# Time to implement SLA requests
sK1023	% Service Level Agreements (SLAs) reviewed
sK1024	# Incidents produced by hardware failures
sK1025	% Changes that result in incidents
sK1026	% SLA targets missed
sK1027	% Overdue changes
sK1028	% SLA targets threatened
sK1029	# IT service requests backlog
sK1030	$ Cost per customer for delivery of services
sK1031	$ Cost of change implementation
sK1033	% Workarounds applied to service requests
sK1034	# Planned to unplanned system downtime
sK1035	% First line email resolution rate
sK1037	# Incidents caused by deficient user training
sK1041	# Email backlog

Organizational » Functional Areas

sKPI #	Key Performance Indicator name
sK1042	# Underpinning Contract issues logged
sK1043	# Operational Level Agreement (OLA) issues logged
sK1044	# Service Level Agreements (SLA) breaches due to poor performance
sK1046	# Business compliance issues caused by improper configuration of assets
sK1047	% Routine changes
sK1048	% Changes completed before deadline
sK1050	% Repeated major incidents that caused downtime
sK1051	% Operational Level Agreements (OLAs) not yet agreed upon
sK1052	% Incidents caused by changes
sK1053	# Downtime
sK1055	% Agreed Service Level Agreements (SLAs) not supported by OLAs/Ucs
sK1056	# Time required for incident impact assessment
sK1057	% Expenditure on IT investments
sK1059	% Incidents cleared up within Service Level Agreement (SLA) timeframe
sK1060	# Time lag between software releases
sK1061	# Open service requests
sK1062	# Incidents not closed within time limits
sK1063	# Delivered services not available in the company service offer
sK1065	$ SLA delivery penalties paid
sK1066	# Outstanding actions against last Service Level Agreement (SLA) review
sK1068	# Configuration Item (CI) attribute errors found in CMDB
sK1069	# Incidents that breach the SLA
sK1070	# Time to provision (TTP)
sK1072	% Incidents resolved before customer notice
sK1075	% Incidents incorrectly categorized
sK1077	% Emails replied within service level target
sK1078	% First line resolution of service request
sK1079	# Service requests per agent
sK1080	$ Service desk operating costs
sK1088	% Incidents by-passing the service desk
sK1091	% Incidents assigned to a higher level of support
sK1098	% Releases implemented without adequate testing
sK1105	# Time for problem closure
sK1111	% Key stakeholders satisfied with suppliers
sK1115	% Services covered by Service Level Agreements (SLAs)
sK1116	# Email customer wait time
sK1117	% Infrastructure components acquired outside the acquisition process
sK1118	% Configuration Items successfully audited
sK1120	% Service Level Agreement (SLA) with automated reports
sK1121	# Time for data restoration

sKPI #	Key Performance Indicator name
sK1122	% Successful data restorations
sK1123	% Critical processes monitored
sK1126	# Time to configure infrastructure components
sK1127	# Incidents where sensitive data was retrieved after media were disposed
sK1133	% Timely implementation of new technology in line with business requirements
sK1134	# Service requests logged
sK1135	# Web call-backs handled
sK1137	# Emails received
sK1138	# Emails replied
sK1139	# Emails composed
sK1140	# Frequency of email replies
sK1145	# Size of file downloads
sK1176	% Tickets associated with SOA related services
sK1260	% Incidents caused by lack of required support skills
sK1273	# Service Improvement Initiatives (SIP) established
sK1410	# Downtime reaction time
sK1478	% Variance in service errors attributable to wrong Configuration Item information
sK1807	# Service Improvement Initiatives (SIPs) not yet staffed
sK1948	% Variance in the number of missing or duplicate Configuration Items (CIs)
sK2035	# Unauthorized changes detected
sK2621	% Business critical systems unplanned service downtime
sK2926	% SLAs in renegotiation
sK2927	% SLAs requiring changes
sK2936	% Service Level Agreement (SLA) breaches caused by third party support contracts
sK2938	% Fully documented Service Level Agreements in place
sK3555	% Accuracy of forecasts of business trends
sK3556	% Workload forecasts produced on time
sK3557	# Incidence of operational reviews uncovering security and reliability exposures in application designs
sK3558	% Timely production of management reports
sK3559	# Time taken to complete an availability plan
sK3561	# Time taken to review system resilience
sK3562	# Time taken to complete a risk analysis
sK3563	$ Cost of unavailability
sK3564	% Timely completion of regular cost-benefit analysis established for infrastructure Component Failure Impact Analysis (CFIA)
sK3565	% Timely completion of regular risk analysis and system review
sK3566	% End-to-end availability of services
sK3567	% Service Level Agreements (SLAs) with effective review and follow-up
sK3570	% Outstanding Service Level Agreements (SLAs) for annual renegotiation

sKPI #	Key Performance Indicator name
sK3572	# Time to respond to a Service Level Agreement (SLA) request
sK3573	# Time to develop a Service Level Agreement (SLA)
sK3574	$ Cost of monitoring and reporting of SLAs
sK3576	% Undiagnosed problems
sK3578	% Known incidents and problems encountered
sK3580	# Incidents and problems affecting service to customers
sK3581	% Incidents resolved by first line operatives on first response
sK3582	$ Cost of handling a release
sK3585	% Identified vulnerabilities with remediation plans
sK3586	# Releases backed out
sK3587	% Service unavailability caused by releases
sK3588	% Releases built and implemented on schedule and within budget
sK3592	% High priority releases requested without the appropriate business case
sK3596	% Releases implemented without being tested
sK3598	% Releases causing incidents
sK3599	% On time implementation of releases at all sites
sK3601	% Urgent releases
sK3602	% Failed distributions of releases to remote sites
sK3605	# New releases planned and controlled by Release Management
sK3606	% Hardware and software unauthorized use
sK3610	% Software and hardware releases not passing the required quality checks
sK3613	% Failed changes
sK3619	$ Cost of failed changes
sK3682	# Change overtime
sK3686	$ Cost of handling a change
sK3689	% Accuracy of change estimates
sK3691	% Failed changes not having recorded back-out plan
sK3693	% Changes not referred to a Change Advisory Board (CAB) or Change Advisory Board Emergency Committee (CAB/EC)
sK3694	% Changes activated outside core service time and SLA service hours
sK3700	% Changes impacting core service time and SLA service hours
sK3702	% Unsuccessful changes
sK3703	% Scheduled and unscheduled service unavailability caused by changes
sK3704	% High priority changes submitted without business case to justify decision

sKPI #	Key Performance Indicator name
sK3705	% Urgent changes requiring back-up
sK3706	% Changes implemented without being tested
sK3708	% Urgent changes causing incidents
sK3712	# Urgent changes
sK3715	% Change reports produced on schedule
sK3717	# Changes required by previous change failures
sK3718	% Changes backed out because of testing failures
sK3719	# Changes backed out because of testing failures
sK3720	# Change backlog
sK3860	% SLA breaches due to either poor service performance or poor component performance
sK3934	% Time variance to complete requested changes
sK3936	# Time needed to make requested changes
sK3945	% Services not covered by IT Service Continuity (ITSC) plan
sK3966	$ Lost business due to inadequate IT capacity
sK4050	% Change requests implemented on time
sK4630	# Active enhancement requests by type
sK4631	# Scope changes per business request
sK4632	# Enhancement completion
sK4636	# Defects introduced from changes
sK4637	# Issues from missed requests
sK4799	# Transactions completed in the application server
sK4970	$ Capacity plan production cost
sK5573	% Recommendations made by Capacity Management that are acted upon
sK5580	% New services implemented which match Service Level Requirements (SLRs)
sK5855	# System downtime
sK5876	# Report processing time
sK6039	% Subscribers enrolled for automated notifications services
sK6108	# Software installation time
sK6109	# Software application download time
sK6110	# User load capacity
sK6113	% Accounts with weak or default passwords
sK6114	% Inactive user accounts
sK6228	# Days to install a mid-range server
sK6229	# Time to complete a mainframe migration
sK6929	% Planned application changes
sK6946	% IT support service desk channel usage
sK14093	# Down-time of the computer system

Knowledge and Innovation

Knowledge and Innovation represent the support areas that facilitates the organization to have access, retain and efficiently use the expertise, know-how, skills, internal capabilities, as well as converting this knowledge and ideas into ways of improving the business: products, services, processes, added value of the organization to its stakeholders.

Innovation

Innovation refers to applying knowledge in order to develop new methods, technology or ways for improving organizational processes, products, services or overall performance. KPIs track new ideas and innovative approaches that contribute to the organizational objectives, structure or processes.

sKPI #	Key Performance Indicator name
sK24	% Employees involved in the innovation process
sK25	# Ideas put forward by individuals to team leaders
sK109	% Customer focused innovations
sK200	# Expenditure saved ratio by introducing innovations
sK201	% Time saved with innovations
sK202	% Training programs for newly introduced innovations
sK210	% Evaluated ideas
sK315	# Ideas for new or improved products
sK385	% Revenue generated from new products
sK622	% Idea conversion rate
sK623	# Time to respond to ideas
sK2146	% Design cycle time reduction due to innovation
sK2148	# Engineering changes in design due to innovation
sK2150	% Part-count reduction time
sK2185	# Hours spent developing innovations
sK2186	% Ideas receiving positive evaluations from teams
sK2187	% Ideas from outside the organization
sK2191	% Employees who have received innovation training
sK2193	% Dedicated resources for radical innovation
sK2216	# Innovation trainings
sK2217	# Time spent for innovation training
sK2218	# New-to-company opportunities in new markets
sK2220	% Hours spent developing new innovations
sK2221	% Corrective actions as result of innovation process
sK2223	% Parts reused due to product innovation
sK2224	$ Funding allocated to innovative ideas
sK2225	$ Resources invested in continuous innovation
sK2230	# Innovation recognitions received by the organization
sK2231	% Innovations that significantly advance existing business
sK2232	% Idea submissions rewarded
sK2450	# Ideas submitted per employee
sK3447	$ Savings due to employee suggestions
sK3818	% New projects launched based on customer input
sK4550	# New services launched
sK4657	# Ideas for new or improved services
sK4702	# Time spent with legal research and writing activities

sKPI #	Key Performance Indicator name
sK6098	# Time to market (TTM)
sK6691	% Ideas implemented from the suggestion log
sK6699	$ Savings from implemented employee suggestions
sK6746	% Ideas for new products put forward by customers
sK6751	# Rewards and recognition for innovation ideas
sK7049	% Ideas approved for implementation
sK7054	# Ideas for new or improved service from suppliers
sK14055	# Continuous improvement initiatives generated by team and implemented
sK14212	# Innovations

Knowledge Management

Knowledge Management identify, create, represent, distribute and enable the knowledge embodied in individuals or embedded in organizational processes. KPIs refer to Knowledge Management practices used within the organization, their efficacy and efficiency.

sKPI #	Key Performance Indicator name
sK74	% Savings due to Knowledge Management initiatives
sK75	# Knowledge Management briefings facilitated
sK76	% Employees trained in Knowledge Management (KM) practices
sK111	# Paper documents to electronic format ratio
sK112	# Steps to modify a document
sK113	% Use of intranet or groupware
sK196	# Knowledge materials distributed to employees
sK197	% Adjustment in administrative and operational cost due to KM
sK198	% Searches intensification per knowledge repository
sK382	% Electronic files backup
sK599	% Staff involved in Communities of Practice
sK600	# Community of Practice meetings
sK601	# Members per Community of Practice
sK602	# Experts to practitioners to novices ratio
sK603	# Divisions represented per Community of Practice
sK604	% Community of Practice meetings involving external experts
sK606	% Unnecessary data duplicates
sK607	% Documents archived in digital format
sK609	# Drop in time due to Knowledge Management
sK610	% Adjusted time to correct the loss due to mismanagement of data
sK611	% Time saved for data gathering
sK616	% Documents in non-enterprise repositories

sKPI #	Key Performance Indicator name
sK617	% Documents accessible through search engine
sK618	% Documents rarely accessed
sK619	$ Document storage costs
sK620	% Duplicate customer contact information in the database
sK1096	% Company documents accessible by the search engines
sK1999	% Documents classified incorrectly
sK2144	% KM initiatives successfully implemented
sK2152	# Time to implement a KM initiative
sK2153	% Lessons learned reviewed periodically
sK2154	# Best Practices files shared
sK2158	# Knowledge repositories eliminated due to the KM initiatives
sK2162	# Knowledge base users
sK2164	% Cross-functional teams
sK2165	# Experts contacted from the expertise directory
sK2166	% Time saved due to KM initiative, for submitting required regulatory forms by clients
sK2167	# Reports on lessons learned
sK2168	# Partnerships or strategic alliances to acquire knowledge
sK2169	% Standard operating procedures written
sK2170	% Knowledge sharing recognized and rewarded
sK2171	# External experts participating in project teams
sK2173	% Staff contributing documents
sK2174	% Employees that access the knowledge base
sK2175	# External sources of knowledge
sK2176	# Internal centers of excellence
sK2177	# Knowledge repositories introduced due to KM initiatives
sK2180	# Knowledge base document views
sK2181	# Frequency of use of knowledge base documents
sK2182	% Searches resulting in a document being opened
sK2183	$ Cost of KM initiative
sK2194	% Procedures reviewed and updated
sK2205	% KM initiatives positively evaluated
sK2228	# Knowledge management initiatives
sK2462	# Rewards for knowledge sharing
sK2463	# Questions asked on the internal forum
sK2464	# Answers per question on the internal discussion forum
sK2465	# Internal knowledge sharing platforms
sK2466	% Employees that contribute to the knowledge base
sK2467	# Publications on the corporate intranet
sK3087	% Documents filled according to standards
sK4694	# Age of documents in knowledge repository
sK4695	# Documents entered into knowledge repositories
sK4696	# Time saved through use of existing knowledge repositories

sKPI #	Key Performance Indicator name
sK4697	# Times distinct documents in the online knowledge repository are accessed
sK4698	$ Estimated savings through the use of existing knowledge
sK4699	% Legal spend attributable to law library and online research expenses
sK4700	% Employees who contribute to the knowledge repository
sK4701	% Legal matters that receive KM review
sK6152	% Data that meets pre-established department standards
sK6730	% Forms available to staff on the intranet

R & D

R & D sums up the activities centered around research and development, with the purpose of improving current situations and performance within the organization. According to the Organization for Economic Co-operation and Development, R&D refers to "creative work undertaken on a systematic basis in order to increase the stock of knowledge, including knowledge of man, culture and society, and the use of this stock of knowledge to devise new applications."

sKPI #	Key Performance Indicator name
sK18	% R&D projects involving customers
sK71	% New academic research recruits in R&D
sK72	# Employees in R&D
sK73	% R&D budget from total budget
sK110	% Products meeting cost target
sK117	% Market share increase due to R&D
sK118	# Time to break-even
sK119	% Academic scientific staff
sK199	% R&D budget spent on new innovations
sK207	# Patents per researcher
sK208	% R&D staff involved in customer contacts
sK209	# Ideas submitted per researcher
sK456	# Prototypes per new product
sK459	% R&D budget allocated to new product development
sK461	# Concept approval cycle time
sK462	$ Development costs per new product
sK772	# Patents
sK2135	# Age of patents rights
sK2136	# Improvements made to existing products
sK2137	# Profitable new products
sK2138	% Patents incorporated into products
sK2139	% New product development projects
sK2140	% R&D intensity
sK2141	% R&D time to develop next generation of products
sK2142	% Hours spent on R&D
sK2145	% R&D expenditure as a percentage of output sales
sK2147	# Engineering changes to off-the-shelf system

sKPI #	Key Performance Indicator name	sKPI #	Key Performance Indicator name
sK2151	# Research papers	sK2226	% New products failure rate
sK2184	% Patents granted	sK2227	% Patented inventions not yet published
sK2188	% Senior executive time spent on strategic innovation	sK2229	% New product success rate
sK2189	# Time to register a patent	sK2454	% Patented inventions commercially used
sK2190	% R&D hours spent to new product development	sK2455	% Patented inventions
sK2192	$ New product introduction cost	sK2456	% Patented inventions involved in disputes
sK2195	# Inventions disclosed	sK2457	% Patented inventions licensed to others
sK2196	% Disclosed inventions internally evaluated	sK2458	% Income from licensing patent rights
sK2197	# First patent filings	sK2459	% New-to-market products / services protected by patent rights
sK2198	# Patent applications per researcher	sK2460	% Sales protected by patent rights
sK2199	# Time from idea disclosure to evaluation by management	sK2461	% Sales protected by patent rights per R&D expenditure
sK2200	# Days from invention to first patent filing	sK3812	# Projects leveraged from existing platforms
sK2201	% Patents pending	sK4655	$ Research and development costs
sK2202	% Patents rejected	sK4813	% Design cost from revenue
sK2203	% Current-year percentage sales due to new products released in the past six years	sK4993	$ Cost per patent reviewed
sK2204	% R&D cost to revenue of a new product	sK4994	# Patent pendency
sK2206	% R&D projects involving universities / research institutes	sK5117	# Research papers online hits
sK2207	% R&D projects involving pre-competitive research with competing companies	sK5930	# Publications in high impact journals
sK2208	% R&D projects involving non-competing companies	sK6370	# Payback period of new products
sK2209	# Time to create a first prototype	sK6371	# Patents per million dollars of R&D investment
sK2210	% Concepts to actual products	sK6592	% Product development projects completed
sK2211	# Time for patent application	sK6742	# Products / services co-developed in partnership with customers
sK2212	% R&D projects at end of research pipeline per year	sK6743	# First to market products
sK2213	% R&D projects successfully transferred to business areas	sK6789	$ Cost per researcher
sK2214	% Patents for sale out from first filings	sK6790	# New products per researcher
sK2215	# New product introduction time	sK6792	% Staff with PhD degrees
sK2222	% Invention patent rights lost	sK6797	$ Maintenance cost per R&D laboratory surface
		sK6799	$ Cost savings due to R&D

Management

Management involves analysis, decisions and actions of an organization for the purpose of creating and sustaining competitive advantages. Management includes effective strategy formulation, planning decisions and processes, execution and control.

sKPI #	Key Performance Indicator name	sKPI #	Key Performance Indicator name
sK7051	% Active KPIs	sK14249	# Proposed strategic initiatives
sK7068	% KPIs with reliable data	sK14254	% Documented KPIs
sK14115	% Employees whose key performance appraisal are linked to strategic objectives	sK14255	% Employee objectives linked to BSC
sK14215	% KPIs with green status	sK14256	% Employees performance evaluations performed on time
sK14216	% KPIs with red status	sK14257	% Employees that accessed performance management eLearning courses
sK14217	% KPIs with yellow status	sK14258	% Employees that attended trainings on performance management subjects
sK14244	% Objectives with green status	sK14259	% Employees understanding of Strategy Map
sK14245	% Objectives with red status	sK14260	% Employees with individual performance plans constructed
sK14246	% Objectives with yellow status		

sKPI #	Key Performance Indicator name
sK14261	% Employees with individual performance plans updated
sK14263	% Functional departments objectives aligned with the organizational strategy
sK14264	% Initiatives thoroughly documented
sK14265	% KPIs allocated to data custodians
sK14266	% KPIs below target
sK14267	% KPIs on target
sK14268	% KPIs reviewed / changed / replaced
sK14269	% KPIs thoroughly documented
sK14270	% KPIs visualized through dedicated instruments
sK14271	% KPIs with automated data collection process
sK14272	% KPIs with data collection process thoroughly mapped
sK14273	% KPIs with identified responsible
sK14274	% Performance review meetings attendance
sK14275	% Performance review meetings held as planned

sKPI #	Key Performance Indicator name
sK14276	% Staff who can identify organization's strategic priorities
sK14277	% Staff engagement with strategy
sK14278	% Staff with incentive aligned with strategy
sK14279	% Staff with objectives and incentives linked to the Balanced Scorecard
sK14280	% Strategic awareness
sK14281	% Strategic initiatives approved
sK14282	% Strategic initiatives documented
sK14283	% Strategic job readiness
sK14285	% Strategic objectives with approved initiatives
sK14286	% Targeted measures, data and statistics accessible across organization
sK14287	% Personnel aligned with strategy
sK20163	% Operational performance reviews conducted
sK22983	# Performance measurement maturity level

Marketing & Communications

Marketing and Communications activities create the basic interaction with potential clients, through different methods of informing, communicating, persuading and attracting the prospect customers.

Advertising

Advertising is the form of promotion of an organization's products or services, in order to attract new customers and increase sales. Without advertising, the average consumer would not be able to be told what to buy.

sKPI #	Key Performance Indicator name
sK36	% Share of voice (SoV)
sK38	# Exposure to advertisement
sK39	% Inquiries growth due to advertising campaign
sK70	% Coupon conversion
sK101	$ Cost per broadcast hour
sK103	# Gross rating points (GRPs)
sK325	# Advertisement viewers
sK326	% Audience share
sK327	% Consumer retention of commercial messages
sK407	$ Cost per exposure
sK408	# Target rating points (TRPs)
sK409	$ Cost per mille (CPM)
sK1412	% Advertising recall
sK1413	# Media exposures in a given period
sK1414	% Advertising spending
sK1415	% Effective reach
sK1416	$ Campaign cost
sK1417	# Ratio of successful to mediocre to unsuccessful campaigns
sK1418	% Ad awareness
sK1419	% Carryover effect

sKPI #	Key Performance Indicator name
sK1421	# Creative awards
sK1422	# Opportunities-to-see (OTS)
sK1423	# Wear-in
sK1424	# Wear-out
sK1425	# Effective frequency
sK1429	$ Cost per thousand impressions
sK3611	% Player buzz in the social media
sK4803	$ Advertising expenditure
sK5797	% Reach (Rating Point)
sK5798	% Target Rating Points (TRPs)
sK5805	$ Outdoor advertising generated revenue
sK5820	% Change in broadcast network advertising
sK5821	% Change in TV station local advertising spot revenue
sK13974	# Ads placed

Marketing

Marketing represents the activity of informing, communicating or persuading diverse potential customers that certain products and services may satisfy their needs and wants. Marketing KPIs refer to marketing campaigns results, as well as the support of this area within the customer relationship management process and outcomes.

sKPI #	Key Performance Indicator name
sK3	% Customer retention
sK19	% Customer attrition
sK20	$ Marketing spend per customer
sK37	% Brand awareness

Organizational » Functional Areas

sKPI #	Key Performance Indicator name
sK108	% Customer satisfaction with new products and services
sK138	% Repeat customers
sK144	% Dormancy rate
sK154	$ Customer profitability
sK155	$ Lifetime value of a customer
sK187	% Customer acquisition
sK188	# New customers
sK189	# Time lag between customer purchases
sK254	% Response rate
sK1278	% Customers with key attributes
sK1279	$ Customer size by category
sK1280	# Brand image index
sK1281	# Direct communications to key customers
sK1282	% Market share
sK1283	# Customer referrals
sK1285	# Client relationships producing significant net profit
sK1286	# Visits made to core customers in a week
sK1287	% Customer satisfaction of top 10% of customers
sK1288	# Time elapsed since repeat business with category A customers
sK1289	% Key customer satisfaction
sK1290	% In-house customer satisfaction
sK1291	% Category A customers covered by partnership projects
sK1292	% Top ten customers' business
sK1293	$ Product-line profitability
sK1294	# Dealer satisfaction survey
sK1295	$ Marketing expense per new customer
sK1296	# New business by occurrence type
sK1297	% Profitable customers
sK1298	$ Investment in development of new markets
sK1299	% Unprofitable customers
sK1300	% Brand dominance in market
sK1301	% Pricing accuracy
sK1302	$ Investment in new product support and training
sK1303	% Net promoter score
sK1304	% Stakeholder awareness of marketing services
sK1305	% Stakeholder usage of marketing services
sK1306	% Stakeholder intent to use marketing
sK1307	% Customers participating in loyalty programs
sK1308	% Active loyalty program members
sK1309	# Member purchase frequency of program members
sK1310	$ Purchase volume relative to non loyalty program members
sK1311	% Non loyalty program members' share of wallet
sK1312	% Non loyalty program member satisfaction
sK1313	% Marketing spend of marketing budget
sK1314	# Hours required to service clients and prospects

sKPI #	Key Performance Indicator name
sK1315	$ Spend by communication channel
sK1316	$ Brand equity
sK1317	$ Costs of brand building
sK1318	% Brand association
sK1319	% Brand perception
sK1320	$ Cost of new customer acquisition
sK1322	# Stakeholder satisfaction index
sK1324	# New customers added
sK1325	% Increase in new customers per quarter
sK1326	# Frequency of purchases to opportunity to purchase
sK1327	# Moving average of customer purchases over six-month period
sK1329	% Return on marketing investment
sK1331	# Ratio of new to existing to lapsed customers
sK1332	# Share of voice relative to share of market
sK1333	% Unit market share
sK1334	# Relative market share
sK1335	# Brand development index
sK1336	# Category development index
sK1337	% Market penetration
sK1338	% Share of requirements
sK1339	# Heavy usage index
sK1340	% Willingness to search
sK1341	% Willingness to recommend
sK1342	# Brand likeability
sK1343	% Brand penetration
sK1344	% Penetration share
sK1345	% Intention to purchase
sK1346	% Market concentration
sK1347	# Herfindahl-Hirschman index
sK1348	# Market share rank
sK1349	% Share of category
sK1350	# Active customers
sK1351	% Acceptors
sK1352	% Rejectors
sK1353	% Ever-tried
sK1354	% Sole usage
sK1355	# Brands purchased
sK1356	% Repurchase rate
sK1357	% Top of mind
sK1358	% Brand knowledge
sK1359	% Served market
sK1361	% Target market fit
sK1362	% Effective market share
sK1363	# Relative price
sK1364	% Durability

sKPI #	Key Performance Indicator name
sK1365	# Brand equity (Moran)
sK1366	# Purchase recency
sK1367	$ Customer acquisition cost
sK1368	$ Customer retention cost
sK1369	% Visits made to customers in comparison to competition
sK1370	% Callbacks by comparison to competition
sK1371	# Compliments to complaints
sK1372	% Customer defection rate
sK1373	# Customer engagement
sK1374	% Marketing campaign effectiveness
sK1375	# Brand strength
sK1376	$ Revenue generation capabilities of the brand
sK1395	# Analyst calls attended
sK2320	% Price premium
sK2321	% Good value
sK2322	$ Reservation price
sK2323	# Price elasticity
sK2324	# Residual price elasticity
sK3432	% Concentration ratio
sK4647	% New customers from existing clients' referrals
sK4660	% New clients
sK4671	% Account expansion
sK4991	$ Cost per trademark registered
sK6220	% New customer acquisition through alliances
sK6744	# New market segments entered
sK6992	% Member attrition rate
sK13992	# Articles written
sK14018	# Campaigns implemented within operational plan time frames
sK14052	# Contacts per collector
sK14053	# Contacts with customer during project and post-project success
sK14144	# Financial assistance programs implemented within advertised schedules
sK14238	# Loyalty programs
sK14242	# Marketing focus group scores

Public Relations

Public Relations (PR) refers to managing the organization's relations with the public, in terms of building and managing relationships and communication with those who influence an organization's audience and public. KPIs refer not only to the PR activities, but also to their impact within the company's goals.

sKPI #	Key Performance Indicator name
sK1323	% Marketing spend of revenues
sK1379	# Community satisfaction index
sK1381	% Local residents in total workforce
sK1382	# Entries to environment / community awards
sK1385	# Media coverage events
sK1386	# Photos in papers
sK1387	# Sponsorship projects
sK1389	% Marketing projects that are environmentally friendly
sK1390	% Trade show participation
sK1391	# Industry analysts coverage volume
sK1392	# Industry analyst recommendations
sK1393	# Keynote speeches
sK1394	# Media coverage quality
sK1396	# Special events
sK1397	% Negative buzz
sK1398	% Positive buzz
sK1399	# Media mentions
sK1400	# Visibility
sK1401	$ Advertising value equivalents (AVEs)
sK1402	% Recall events
sK1403	% Awareness of messages via PR
sK1404	# Inquiries generated
sK1405	% Opinions changed
sK1406	% Target audience that receives messages
sK1407	% Press releases picked up by media outlets
sK1408	# Press releases picked up by media
sK1409	# Negative media stories
sK1411	# Positive to negative editorial feedback comments
sK6908	% Aggregated rating in review sites
sK14129	# Entries to awards
sK22660	$ Cost per information product

Online Presence - eCommerce

Online Presence - eCommerce reflects all supporting activities and processes relating to one business online presence. KPIs track eCommerce transactions, email marketing campaigns , online advertising and marketing efficiency, search engine optimization related matters and web analytics.

eCommerce

eCommerce comprises the electronic sale by online stores of downloadable 'soft merchandise' such as music, e-books, e-newsletters, photos and video recordings, software and documents (direct e-commerce), the electronic ordering of tangible products (indirect e-commerce), online securities transactions as well as the provision of financial or other services. It also includes the subscription to and use of an internet service provider (ISP) or an online service provider (OSP) and has also been held to cover electronic data interchange (EDI), electronic fund transfers (EFT) and all credit and debit card activity. E-commerce transactions can be 'business-to-business' (B2B) or 'business-to-consumer' (B2C). KPIs refer to the process efficiency, the customer satisfaction and the means to do eCommerce.

sKPI #	Key Performance Indicator name
sK10	% On-time delivery
sK70	% Coupon conversion
sK78	$ Order value (OV)
sK79	# Visits to purchase
sK240	# Items per order
sK434	# New customer on first visit ratio
sK435	% Revenue from new visitors
sK1431	$ Cost per order (CPO)
sK2469	# Shopping carts abandoned
sK2475	# Unique online buyers
sK2490	% Revenue from first time online customers
sK2491	% Shopping cart session
sK2492	% Shopping cart conversion rate
sK2495	# Revenue from first time customers to repeated customers ratio
sK2501	$ Cost per conversion
sK2502	% Returning costumers on the site
sK2503	% New customers on site
sK2504	% Shopping cart start rate
sK2511	% Browser session product page
sK2517	# Product views per session
sK2519	# Shopping session length
sK2521	# Shopping carts started
sK2522	% Level of shipping errors
sK2529	% Revenue from repeat online customers
sK2537	% Level of stock-outs
sK2538	# Channel specific products and services
sK2542	$ Revenue per visitor
sK2547	$ Revenue per visit
sK2548	$ Per visit value
sK2549	# Problems with customer order processing

sKPI #	Key Performance Indicator name
sK2551	% Checkout completion rate
sK2553	% Order session
sK2554	% Shopping cart abandonment rate
sK2555	% On site search conversion
sK2556	# Frequency of sales transactions
sK2558	% Checkout start rate
sK2560	% Cart completion rate
sK2564	# Unique purchases
sK2575	% Level of customer cost savings achieved
sK2579	# New features added to the site
sK2589	# Visits prior to conversion
sK2591	# Days to purchase
sK2593	# Orders from first time customers to repeated customers ratio
sK2638	# Shopping cart transactions completed
sK2733	$ Revenue per unique customer
sK6425	% Customer transactions via the Internet
sK7064	# Active paying accounts (APA)
sK7066	$ Transaction revenue

Email Marketing

E-mail Marketing is a form of direct marketing which uses electronic mail for promoting a brand or product to prospective or current customers. KPIs for e-mail marketing refer to the frequency of e-mails, their types, impact, purpose and techniques used.

sKPI #	Key Performance Indicator name
sK1136	# Email leads created
sK1272	$ Cost per email message
sK1716	# Newsletter sign-ups
sK2505	% Opened email rate
sK2506	% Email response rate
sK2507	% Bounce email rate
sK2508	% Opt-out rate
sK2509	% Opt-in rate
sK2512	% Out of office replies received
sK2513	% Invalid email addresses
sK2514	% Abuse complaint rate
sK2515	% Soft bounced email rate
sK2516	% Email deliverability rate
sK2518	# Newsletter click through
sK2520	% Newsletter click through rate
sK3177	# Email referrals through forwarded email messages

sKPI #	Key Performance Indicator name
sK3179	% Email list hurdle rate
sK3210	# Email list size
sK3221	# Auto-response emails to customer inquiries
sK3222	$ Order size per email
sK3224	# Orders per email
sK3226	% Click to open (CTO)
sK3227	# Personalization errors in emails
sK3228	# Email tests conducted per email marketing campaign
sK3230	% Email conversion rate

Online Advertising

Online Advertising is a form of promotion that uses internet in order to inform, communicate and persuade the message receiver to become a customer of a product or service. KPIs refer to its costs, frequency, outcomes and efficiency of the means used.

sKPI #	Key Performance Indicator name
sK2470	% Advertising response rates
sK2471	# Ad units per visit
sK2472	# Ads served
sK2473	% Video ads expense rate
sK2484	% Ad click through ratio (CTR)
sK2485	# Ads clicked per visit
sK2486	% Video ads overlay click through rate
sK2487	% Click through rates for standard overlays
sK2488	% Animated overlays click-through rates
sK2489	% Click through rates from overlay initiated video ads to advertiser websites
sK2493	% Impression rate
sK2497	$ Effective cost per mile (eCPM)
sK2498	$ Cost per click (CPC)
sK2499	$ Cost per action (CPA)
sK2534	% Close-out rates for overlays
sK2535	% Completion rate for overlay initiated video ads
sK2544	$ Ad revenue per visit
sK2546	$ Online advertising revenue
sK3234	% Video advertisements completion rate
sK3235	% Interaction rate (IR)
sK3239	# Power ratio of online advertising
sK3240	$ Cost per revenue (CPR) of online advertising
sK3241	# Customer touch points of an online advertisement
sK3242	# Visits generated by online advertisements
sK3247	# Requests for information generated by online advertisements
sK3249	# Interaction time per online advertisement
sK3250	# Online advertisement display time
sK3252	# Expansion rate of expandable advertisements
sK3259	# Video view time
sK3261	# Customer events of online advertisements

sKPI #	Key Performance Indicator name
sK3263	$ Lead generation advertising
sK3265	# Catalog requests generated by an online advertisement
sK3266	% Online ad abandonment rate
sK3272	# Rich media manual closes

Online Publishing - Weblogs

Online Publishing refers to digital publication of e-books and electronic articles, as well as developing digital libraries and catalogues, while using blogs. KPIs outline not only the efficacy, impact and usage of online publishing, but also aspects related to online readers.

sKPI #	Key Performance Indicator name
sK1718	% Newsletter unsubscribe rate
sK2474	# Blog post trackbacks
sK2476	% New blog commentators
sK2477	# Frequency of blog posts
sK2481	# RSS blog subscribers
sK2482	# Comments per blog post
sK2601	# Visitors per blog post
sK2609	# Blog subscribers conversion ratio
sK3135	# Video access sales
sK3138	# Video downloads completed
sK3143	% Video download errors
sK3167	# Views per video
sK3168	# Time for video buffering
sK3171	# Likes per video
sK3175	# Social shares per post
sK3176	# Time spent per post
sK4213	# Time to subscribe
sK4334	% Subscription renewal rate

Search Engine Optimization (SEO)

SEO (Search Engine Optimization) represents the process whereby web pages are designed, built and modified so as to improve the search engine results. KPIs refer to placement in the organic listings of search engines, as well as to the efficiency of the process and the methods used.

sKPI #	Key Performance Indicator name
sK2526	% Website visitors exiting the site after viewing search results
sK2530	# Indexed pages
sK2531	# Index to crawl ratio
sK2571	# External search engine referrals
sK2572	# Google referrals
sK2573	% Google referrals
sK2577	% Natural traffic from keyword search
sK2578	# Keywords per page yield
sK2580	% Share of search

sKPI #	Key Performance Indicator name
sK2583	# Search results viewed per search
sK2584	% Users conducting multiple searches during their visits
sK2608	% Visits that use site search
sK2610	# Visits per keyword
sK2611	% Pages yielding traffic
sK2615	% Change in visits from organic search

Web Analytics

Web analytics represents the study and analysis of website traffic and activity. It is a vey useful tool to identify issues that can be improved so as to increase the website's performance. KPIs indicate visitors' profile, accessibility of the website, costs of conversions as well as revenues generated.

sKPI #	Key Performance Indicator name
sK77	% Conversion rate
sK114	% New visitors
sK115	# Visits per visitor
sK116	$ Cost per lead
sK203	# Web traffic concentration
sK205	# Unique authenticated visitors
sK206	% Visits under one minute
sK438	% Bounce rate
sK449	# Time on site
sK450	# Time on page
sK451	# Page views per session
sK452	% Page exit rate
sK453	# Visitor recency
sK454	# Website success rate
sK798	# Page redirect latency
sK799	# Page idle time
sK800	# Session think time
sK1427	# Page views
sK2494	% Conversion of RSS subscribers to blog readers
sK2500	$ Maintenance cost of the website
sK2523	% Error pages served
sK2527	# Page exits due to inactivity
sK2533	# Incoming backlinks
sK2536	# Search depth
sK2561	# Search exits

sKPI #	Key Performance Indicator name
sK2562	# Unique searches
sK2563	% Website downtime
sK2565	# Search refinements
sK2566	% Task completion rate
sK2567	# Stickiness
sK2568	% Subscription rate
sK2570	# Depth of visits
sK2574	% Referral traffic
sK2581	% On site searches
sK2582	# Searches leading to website (by keyword)
sK2586	% Page requests growth rate
sK2587	# Daily page requests
sK2588	# Page views per visitor
sK2590	# Time on site after search (TOSAS)
sK2592	# Session times
sK2596	% Heavy user share
sK2597	% Committed visitors
sK2598	% Unique browsers
sK2599	# Unique browsers
sK2602	% Site reach
sK2603	# Visitor loyalty and recency
sK2604	# Page depth
sK2605	# Returning visitors
sK2606	% Returning visitors
sK2607	# Visitors per conversion
sK2612	# Website visits per day
sK2613	% One page visits
sK2614	# Unique visitors
sK3238	# In-stream advertisements
sK3248	% Recommendation rate on social networks
sK3264	# Pass-along rate
sK3267	% Scanning visitors
sK3938	% New versus returning visitors
sK6851	# Followers on social media platforms
sK6852	% Online positive comments
sK6904	# Website visits
sK7063	# Daily active users (DAU)
sK7065	# Trial accounts

Portfolio and Project Management

Portfolio and Project Management aims to determine the optimal mix of projects in a portfolio to best achieve the organization's overall goals, through analyzing and collectively managing a group of current or proposed projects, based on numerous key characteristics. KPIs focus on outlining the profitability and status of projects, as well as the resources' allocation.

Benefits Realization Management

The benefits of a project are more than outputs or deliverables, they consist in the added value brought by the project to the business, reflected in the outcomes, motivating the organization in a certain direction. KPIs refer to the end benefits a project brings for the organization and its customers.

sKPI #	Key Performance Indicator name
sK118	# Time to break-even
sK262	$ Cost avoidance savings
sK2664	$ Project net present value (NPV)
sK2667	$ Cash flow generated by the project
sK2699	# Earned revenue to total project expenses
sK6433	% Projects with predefined benefits
sK21264	# Benefits identified
sK21265	% Benefits assessed
sK21266	# Monetary benefits
sK21267	% Benefit-cost ratio
sK21268	% Discount rate

Portfolio Management

Project Portfolio Management (PPM) is a coordinated set of management processes and decisions designed to help organizations deliver the change required by their business plans. It involves acquiring and reviewing information about all projects, sorting (based on strategic value, impact on resources and cost among others), prioritizing and coordinating their delivery. KPIs refer to the diversity, structure and impact of the portfolio.

sKPI #	Key Performance Indicator name
sK158	# Milestones per project plan
sK412	% Successful projects
sK416	% Profitable projects
sK1076	% Projects linked to business objectives
sK1087	% Budget allocated for new initiatives
sK1099	% Projects with post implementation audits
sK1104	% Projects meeting stakeholder expectations
sK1106	% Projects with post project review
sK1107	% Projects with the quality assurance review completed
sK1108	% Projects with a quality assurance provider
sK1215	% Strategic business initiatives driven by IT
sK1221	% Time spent on new projects development
sK1223	% Projects on time
sK1224	% Projects on budget
sK2616	# Projects per project manager
sK2617	# Project managers to staff ratio

sKPI #	Key Performance Indicator name
sK2618	# FTEs assigned per project
sK2620	% Understaffed projects
sK2622	% Projects prioritized according to business needs
sK2629	# Project managers experience in the field
sK2636	$ Project deviation from planned budget
sK2637	$ Project budget size
sK2639	% Projects with scope changes
sK2643	% Project cost predictability
sK2649	% Completion cost of best in class projects
sK2655	% Projects rejected
sK2657	% Projects without a business case
sK2658	% Projects with at least one milestone missed
sK2660	% Projects with insufficient resources
sK2663	% Aborted projects
sK2666	# Project break even time
sK2674	% Projects that completed quality assurance review
sK2677	% Projects completed on time and on budget
sK2683	% Projects in control
sK2684	% Projects completed
sK2690	% Completed projects compliant to quality specifications
sK2702	% High risk projects
sK2703	% Projects with risk assessment overview
sK2706	# Project approval time
sK2707	# Project duration
sK2708	# Project schedule deviation
sK2709	% Completion time of best in class project
sK2863	% Active running projects on time, on budget and according to specifications
sK4658	$ Profit per project
sK4662	% Project budget overruns rate
sK4996	% Projects completed on time, on budget and compliant with the quality specifications
sK5219	% Design projects completed early or on time
sK6240	% Transformation initiatives where to-be state is defined
sK6427	# Changes per project
sK6428	# Issues raised per project
sK6429	# Risks identified per project
sK6430	# Active projects
sK6431	% Projects that never get materialized
sK6432	% Projects related to business

Project Management

Project Management refers to the planning, organizing and managing of resources to successfully achieve the goals of the project, within a specific timeframe. KPIs refer to the efficiency of the implementation processes, as well as the quantitative outputs and outcomes of the project.

sKPI #	Key Performance Indicator name
sK27	% Project budget variance
sK28	# Conflicts arising during the project
sK29	# Project issues addressed ratio
sK54	% Project or program budget spent on training
sK159	% Overdue project tasks
sK347	# Earned man-hours
sK410	# Time per project task
sK411	% Time spent as planned
sK478	% Progress reports submitted as planned
sK483	$ Estimate at completion (EAC)
sK484	$ Estimate to complete
sK485	# Cost performance index (CPI)
sK486	# Schedule performance index (SPI)
sK487	# Cost schedule index (CSI)
sK488	% Project schedule variance
sK489	# To complete schedule performance index (TSPI)
sK492	$ Cost variance
sK493	# To complete performance index (TCPI)
sK1049	% Proposed changes without impact analysis
sK1236	% Stakeholders satisfied with the accuracy of the project feasibility study
sK2070	% Requirements changed during project execution
sK2623	# Project issues identified
sK2624	% Project resource utilization
sK2633	% Conflicts positively resolved during the project
sK2644	$ Actual cost of work performed (ACWP)
sK2645	$ Budgeted cost of work performed (BCWP)

sKPI #	Key Performance Indicator name
sK2646	$ Budgeted cost of worked scheduled (BCWS)
sK2651	% Cost of rectifying major defects before project completion
sK2653	% Partnering development cost of project
sK2654	$ Project cost savings from innovation
sK2661	% Project milestones missed
sK2662	# Third party non-conformity identified during inspections
sK2671	# Unique project requirements
sK2692	# Initiatives for improvement of the project introduced
sK2695	% Overdue project status reports
sK2696	% Progress reports submitted
sK2697	# Non conformance reports generated per month
sK2704	# Project delay
sK2718	% Project completion predictability
sK3256	$ Cost to complete
sK3558	% Timely production of management reports
sK4684	% Requirements stability
sK5901	# Man-hours per occurrence spent locating problems
sK6203	% Critical path activities
sK6257	% Project cost contingency
sK6358	% Delivery deadlines met
sK6486	# Inactive projects
sK6758	# Requests for time extension submitted
sK6865	% Order value variance from original contract value
sK7052	% Planned projects that have started
sK14049	# Completed projects reviewed
sK14071	# Cycle time to close projects
sK14168	# Goals achieved versus goals set
sK14203	# Infrastructure projects facilitated
sK14204	# Infrastructure projects facilitated within an agreed time frame
sK14248	# Offshore projects roll-up

Production & Quality Management

Production and Quality Management refer to a set of activities that aim to assure the planned and systematic production processes for providing confidence in a product's suitability, in quantity and quality for its intended purpose. KPI's refer to the efficiency of production processes and compliance with quality standards.

Maintenance

Maintenance refers to the technical and administrative actions for keeping an equipment or item, in proper functioning conditions. KPIs in this subcategory refer to maintenance efficiency, quality and plan tracking.

sKPI #	Key Performance Indicator name
sK396	# Time between failures (TBF)
sK442	% Downtime
sK597	# Time spent performing preventive maintenance (PM) work

sKPI #	Key Performance Indicator name
sK644	$ Maintenance, repair and operating supplies (MRO)
sK1607	# Waste caused by maintenance
sK1618	# Effective equipment productivity
sK1619	# Equipment effectiveness
sK1645	% Maintenance time
sK1654	% Preventive maintenance cost
sK1656	% Corrective maintenance cost
sK1663	$ Maintenance cost per unit output

sKPI #	Key Performance Indicator name
sK1704	% Maintenance rework
sK1732	# Preventive to corrective costs
sK1733	% Maintenance effectiveness
sK1748	% Emergency repairs
sK1749	# Maintenance backlog
sK1755	% Maintenance cost
sK1756	% Maintenance quality index
sK3304	% Maintenance cost from equipment cost
sK6362	# Machine breakdowns per week
sK6561	# Preventive to breakdown maintenance time
sK6562	# Preventive repair to preventive inspection time
sK6563	% Scheduled maintenance compliance
sK6951	% Work requests reviewed and validated within a maximum of 5 days
sK6952	% Work orders with all the planning fields completed
sK6953	% Work orders in planning status' for less than 5 days
sK6954	% Accuracy of work order man-hour estimates
sK6955	% Planned, scheduled and assigned work orders delayed
sK6956	% Work orders completed and returned with all the recording data fields completed
sK6957	% Maintenance work orders closed within a maximum of 3 days
sK6958	# Asset failures by area of consequence
sK6959	# Maintenance cost and replacement value ratio
sK6960	# Maintenance cost to sales ratio
sK6962	# Shutdown overrun for maintenance related reasons

Production

Production is the functional area defining the processes and methods used to create from tangible and intangible inputs, final products as goods or services. Production KPIs refer to assuring efficiency and productivity of production, as well as the desired quantity and quality of products realized.

sKPI #	Key Performance Indicator name
sK84	# Unit production time
sK181	$ Energy costs per unit of production
sK182	# Energy used per unit of production
sK335	$ Fixed production overhead volume capacity variance
sK443	# Units per man-hour
sK497	% Time yield
sK503	# Piece variance
sK504	# Average cycle time (ACT)
sK505	# Takt time
sK507	# Startup rejects
sK509	# Production rejects
sK521	% Production losses
sK522	# Production lead time
sK591	% Hazardous operational waste

sKPI #	Key Performance Indicator name
sK638	# Working stock
sK639	# Decoupling stock
sK651	% Slow moving stock
sK707	% Boomerang return rate
sK754	% Residual value
sK1597	$ Fixed production overhead total variance
sK1600	# Emissions from production
sK1601	$ Direct labor efficiency variance
sK1603	% Production delays due to raw material shortage
sK1604	% Production uptime
sK1605	% Work in progress days
sK1606	% Unplanned maintenance
sK1608	% Value of finished products
sK1609	$ Value of work in progress
sK1610	$ Material cost per product
sK1611	% Schedule cycle variances
sK1614	$ Labor costs per unit production
sK1615	# Small stops
sK1617	# Production volume
sK1620	% Idle time
sK1621	# Material consumption per product
sK1623	% Production orders finished late
sK1624	% Production orders finished ahead time
sK1627	% Production schedule adherence
sK1628	$ Production costs per unit
sK1629	# Actual to projected unit production costs
sK1631	% Machine utilization in production
sK1633	# Product line extensions
sK1634	# Production lot size
sK1636	# Manufacturing process steps
sK1637	# Work in progress
sK1639	$ Variable overhead expenditure variance
sK1640	% Floor space utilized
sK1643	$ Fixed production overhead volume efficiency variance
sK1644	$ Fixed overhead volume variance
sK1646	% Production within takt time
sK1647	% On time value rate
sK1658	# Production processes out of control
sK1666	$ Downtime costs
sK1672	# Production downtime per occurrence
sK1675	% Unplanned downtime in production
sK1676	$ Production cost
sK1678	% Production cost variance
sK1679	$ Direct material total variance
sK1680	$ Direct labor rate variance
sK1681	$ Direct material usage variance

sKPI #	Key Performance Indicator name
sK1686	$ Direct labor cost variance
sK1687	$ Variable production overhead variance
sK1688	$ Variable production overhead efficiency variance
sK1689	# Changeover time
sK1693	$ Direct materials price variance
sK1695	$ Fixed overhead expenditure variance
sK1703	% Downtime due to operator lack of training
sK1706	$ Incremental cost
sK1707	# Production operating time
sK1734	% Production equipment performance
sK1735	% Equipment availability
sK1736	% Equipment quality rate
sK1737	# Ideal cycle time
sK1738	# Ideal run rate
sK1739	% Production performance efficiency
sK1740	% Production net operating rate
sK1741	% Speed loss
sK1742	% Loss ratio of material
sK1743	% Labor handling material damage
sK1744	% Production schedule attainment
sK1750	# Production capacity
sK1752	% Production capacity utilization
sK1753	$ Unused production capacity costs
sK1754	# Unused production capacity
sK3707	$ Penalties cost due to unsatisfied demand
sK6363	# Frequency of production delays due to inventory shortages or supply delays
sK6365	% Products for which common production processes are used
sK6600	% Recovery yield rate of returned products
sK6834	# Production plants
sK13973	# Activity processing time
sK13975	# Age of equipment
sK13976	# Age of plant
sK13999	# Availability Index
sK14051	# Condensate production
sK14072	# Cycle time
sK14162	# Full day supply of raw material in stock
sK14230	# Level of automation

Quality Management

Quality Management is focused on controlling the products so that the desired quality standards are achieved, but also the methods to obtain it. KPIs refer to the efficiency of implementing and maintaining quality control systems by a specialized team.

sKPI #	Key Performance Indicator name
sK395	# Failure rate
sK397	# Regression testing

sKPI #	Key Performance Indicator name
sK441	# Breakdowns
sK496	% Production first time yield (FTY)
sK498	% Defects per million opportunities (DPMO)
sK499	$ Cost of poor quality (COPQ)
sK500	% Final products which do not meet quality criteria
sK556	$ Price of non-conformance
sK745	% Scrap rate
sK1583	# Waste per product
sK1602	% Processes under statistical control
sK1641	# Duration of quality control inspection
sK1642	# Production failures by type of defect
sK1648	% Production conformance to preset quality standards
sK1649	% Quality assurance processes based on 'Best Practices'
sK1650	# Quality control stages
sK1651	# Production quality improvement methods used
sK1652	% Quality assurance processes that need 'Improvement Measures'
sK1655	# Quality awareness programs
sK1657	$ Rework costs
sK1659	# Preventive actions
sK1660	# Defect density
sK1662	% Final product problems due to lack of quality assurance and control
sK1664	% Planned quality control reviews conducted
sK1665	# Defects per unit
sK1667	% Quality control costs
sK1668	% Quality control costs within warranty costs
sK1669	% Quality control personnel ratio
sK1670	% Reworked items
sK1671	% Quality assurance cost
sK1673	% Quality assurance time
sK1674	# Sample size
sK1677	# Out of specification products per quality review
sK1682	% Review efficiency
sK1683	$ Cost of quality inspection per sample
sK1684	% Utilization of Quality Assurance instruments
sK1685	# Time spent on Quality Assurance (QA) activities to non-QA activities
sK1690	# Corrective actions
sK1691	# Quality assurance reviews
sK1692	% Reports for quality control reviews
sK1694	# Production quality control projects
sK1696	# Rework time per item
sK1698	# Time between two quality inspections
sK2149	% Quality problems attributable to design
sK2284	% Processes optimized
sK3305	% Error and rework rate

sKPI #	Key Performance Indicator name
sK3808	# Process completion time
sK3819	# Non-value added processes eliminated
sK3823	# Ideas for quality and process improvement shared
sK3991	% Employee process improvement suggestions adopted
sK4008	% Employees trained in quality management techniques
sK4163	# Omissions of allergens in list of ingredients
sK4450	# Informative inspections
sK5869	% Process efficiency ratio
sK5878	# Time to notify
sK5879	# Collection time
sK5882	% Deficiencies improvement
sK6141	# Deficiencies per manufacturing plant inspection

sKPI #	Key Performance Indicator name
sK6215	% Automated contacts per full-time equivalent (FTE)
sK6355	$ Cost for administrative error per revenue
sK6364	% Production delays due to substandard materials or parts
sK6366	$ Cost of rejected materials
sK6367	% Improvement recommendations by vendor implemented
sK6369	% Rework cost
sK6424	# ISO certifications acquired
sK6843	% Processes mapped
sK7060	% Beverage quality index
sK13998	# Audit action overdue
sK14086	# Defects or repairs that require action not rectified in the scheduled time frames

Sales and Customer Service

Sales and Customer Service refer to the activities conducted to actually exchange the organization's goods and/or services for financial value and provide a series of additional services to customers pre-, during and post-sales.

Customer Service

Customer Service stands for an organization's capability in offering specific services for their customers, at their required qualitative level to satisfy their needs and wants. KPIs refer to the time efficiency responsiveness as perceived by the customers, as well as the quality of the services and responses offered.

sKPI #	Key Performance Indicator name
sK4	% Orders delivered with damaged products
sK10	% On-time delivery
sK31	# Service calls to travel time
sK32	% Customer calls answered in the first minute
sK105	# Completion to billings
sK165	# Call handling time
sK166	% Call completion rate
sK168	% Call abandon rate
sK292	% Unique received calls
sK380	# Response time to business partner request
sK383	% Reports submitted on-time
sK384	% Timeliness of issues resolution
sK433	# Time to rectify defects
sK598	% Work orders closed within the specified time period
sK621	% Customer complaints due to poor service or product quality
sK701	# Pick-to-ship cycle time for customer orders
sK751	# Complaints received
sK1001	% Overdue service requests
sK1017	% Call transfer rate
sK1079	# Service requests per agent
sK1081	# After call work time
sK1113	# Speed of answer (SA)
sK1114	% Calls answered within service level time

sKPI #	Key Performance Indicator name
sK1360	% Agent availability rate
sK1380	% Repeat calls
sK2351	# Actual delivery date versus promised date
sK2352	# Time from inquiry to response
sK2353	# Time to resolve complaints
sK2354	# Defect goods on installation
sK2355	% Order entry error rate
sK2356	$ Service expense per customer
sK2357	% Calls on hold longer than X seconds
sK2358	% Complaints not resolved in X hours
sK2359	% Complaints not resolved on first call
sK2360	# Credit request processing time
sK2362	% Complete and on time delivery
sK2363	# Service requests outstanding
sK2365	% Sales invoices issued on time
sK2366	% Resolution of queries the same day
sK2367	# Orders processed
sK2370	% Correspondence replied to on time
sK2371	# Time taken from order to delivery
sK2372	# Longest call hold
sK2373	# Longest delay in queue
sK2374	# Busy signals
sK2375	# On-hold time
sK2377	% Complaints resolved
sK2378	# Talk time
sK2379	% Customer satisfaction with service levels
sK2380	% Right answers or advice the first time
sK2381	# Support requests
sK2382	% Consistency of advice

Organizational » Functional Areas

sKPI #	Key Performance Indicator name
sK2383	% Customer service representatives (CSR) occupancy
sK2385	% Interactive voice response (IVR) completion rate
sK2386	% Blockage
sK2387	% Service level
sK2388	% Customer service representatives (CSR) quality rating
sK2389	% Information requests not repeated
sK2390	% Interactions routed properly
sK2391	% Kept promises
sK2392	% Computer telephony integration (CTI)
sK2393	% Customer emails with no response
sK2394	% Email response in one day
sK2395	# Service time
sK2396	% Responses as promised
sK2397	% Acknowledge emails
sK2398	# Wait
sK2399	% Customer satisfaction with complaints handling
sK2400	% Customers without service contract
sK3456	% Claims frequency rate
sK3566	% End-to-end availability of services
sK3567	% Service Level Agreements (SLAs) with effective review and follow-up
sK3570	% Outstanding Service Level Agreements (SLAs) for annual renegotiation
sK3572	# Time to respond to a Service Level Agreement (SLA) request
sK3573	# Time to develop a Service Level Agreement (SLA)
sK3574	$ Cost of monitoring and reporting of SLAs
sK4030	% Customers who can track order status online
sK4682	% Service charges of profits
sK5787	$ Penalties paid for poor performance
sK5795	$ Loss due to piracy
sK5854	% Accounts never activated
sK5880	% Inaccurate client updates
sK5886	# Paperwork turnaround time
sK5887	% Not in good order account applications (NIGO)
sK5888	# Account opening time
sK6125	% New account processes that utilize automated document routing
sK6144	% First contact resolution rate
sK6178	% Time spent by case managers securing authorizations
sK6186	# Time to process a customer account transfer
sK6354	# Time spent on customer relations related issues
sK6357	% Customer complaints resolved on the first contact
sK6454	# Queue length at service points
sK6692	# Duration of customer relationship
sK6700	# Time spent visiting customers
sK6740	# Time to process customer returns
sK6747	# Time spent with customers understanding their needs

sKPI #	Key Performance Indicator name
sK6748	# Jointly developed service level agreements
sK6752	$ Customer care funding per resolved complaint
sK6754	# Text-Chat volume
sK6773	# Customer focus groups
sK6780	# Time spent on customer relations
sK6852	% Online positive comments
sK6857	% Complaints responded to within standard time
sK6899	% Customer loyalty
sK6900	# Reviews available online
sK7000	% Customer satisfaction
sK7064	# Active paying accounts (APA)
sK13991	# Appointments not met within 2 hours of scheduled time
sK14010	# Call times
sK14012	# Calls answered within 30 seconds
sK14013	# Calls by day of week
sK14014	# Calls by time of day
sK14015	# Calls received
sK14017	# Calls to call center fault line
sK14041	# Complaint logs
sK14042	# Complaints
sK14043	# Complaints and compliments received
sK14044	# Complaints per 1,000 transactions
sK14045	# Complaints received and completed
sK14046	# Complaints received and not completed
sK14047	# Complaints received in a week
sK14048	# Complaints within categories advised by the Director of Gas
sK14062	# Customer arranged appointments
sK14063	# Customer complaints
sK14064	# Customer feedback
sK14065	# Customer plan migration
sK14066	# Customer reported problems in the first 90 days of an application deployment
sK14067	# Customer satisfaction levels
sK14068	# Customer satisfaction scores
sK14069	# Customer success factor
sK14070	# Customers
sK14092	# Distance between the service and the user measured either in physical distance or in time
sK14094	# During project surveys measuring top 5 customer quality standards
sK14127	# Enforcement notices served for customer related incidents
sK14135	# Evaluation performed on prospective clients
sK21489	% Rating "5" (Excellent) on survey items
sK22473	# Frequency of customer complaints
sK22597	% Visit customers served within 3 minutes
sK5	$ Revenue per successful call

sKPI #	Key Performance Indicator name
sK21	$ Revenue per sale
sK22	% First appointment-to-sales proposal ratio
sK23	% Closing ratio

Sales

Sales is the activity of goods commercialization or services in return for money or other compensations. KPIs refer to the amount of sales, the productivity and efficiency of sales agents, the retention of customers and their satisfaction.

sKPI #	Key Performance Indicator name
sK66	# Days in accounts receivable
sK68	% Sales quota attainment
sK70	% Coupon conversion
sK116	$ Cost per lead
sK118	# Time to break-even
sK148	$ Activated new business value
sK156	% Cannibalization rate of new product offering
sK157	% Repurchases of services following project completion
sK164	% Lead conversion rate
sK187	% Customer acquisition
sK317	% Sell-through
sK331	# Selling opportunities
sK332	$ Sales by department
sK333	# Sales as a result of the average purchase
sK420	% Markdown goods
sK421	% Store conversion rate
sK422	$ Sales revenue per hour
sK712	$ Sales turnover
sK829	# Sales orders filled per FTE
sK835	# Sales orders filled per unit time
sK1136	# Email leads created
sK1428	% Attempted contact of potential customers in database
sK1699	% Sales growth in stores open at least 12 months
sK2233	$ Revenue gained from top customers
sK2234	# Successful to unsuccessful tenders
sK2236	# Order frequency
sK2237	% Orders canceled by reason
sK2238	# Time people wait in line
sK2239	% Sales from cross-selling among business units
sK2241	% Revenue from new products
sK2242	$ Profits from new products or business operations
sK2243	$ Sales by manager
sK2244	% Sales growth by market segment
sK2245	$ Potential revenue in sales pipeline
sK2246	# Selling costs to sales ratio
sK2247	% Timeliness and accuracy of requests for samples
sK2249	# Leads generated by agents

sKPI #	Key Performance Indicator name
sK2250	% Bids for proposals accepted
sK2254	% Sales with discounts from total sales
sK2255	# Purchase frequency
sK2256	# Repeat purchase volume
sK2257	% Time on deal
sK2258	% Pass-through rate
sK2259	# Product samples dispensed
sK2260	% Vendors participating in promotional campaigns
sK2261	# Promotions conducted
sK2262	% Revenue as a percentage of the average market sales revenue
sK2263	% Unit sales as a percentage of average market unit sales
sK2264	# Stock keeping units in portfolio
sK2265	# Category sales in a specific geographic area
sK2266	# Items sold per transaction
sK2269	$ Sales goal per catalog
sK2270	$ Sales goal per page
sK2271	# Sales channel density ratio
sK2272	$ Sales compensation per unit
sK2273	$ Sales compensation per value of sales
sK2274	$ Sales value productivity
sK2275	# Sales volume productivity
sK2276	$ Customer repeat purchase value
sK2277	$ Telemarketing cost per sales lead
sK2279	% Revenue market share by segment
sK2280	% Share of wallet
sK2281	% Conversation to appointment rate
sK2282	% Sales from newly launched products or services
sK2283	% Cross sale rate
sK2285	$ Revenue per sales representative
sK2286	$ Net income per sales representative
sK2287	# Sales cycle duration
sK2288	$ Allowable cost per order
sK2289	$ Unit margin
sK2290	% Margin
sK2291	% Sales channel margin
sK2292	$ Price per unit
sK2293	$ Price per statistical unit
sK2294	$ Contribution margin per unit
sK2297	$ Channel margin
sK2298	$ Selling price
sK2299	% Trial users in the market
sK2300	# Sales penetration
sK2301	# Projection of sales
sK2302	% Adjusted trial rate
sK2303	% Repeat purchase rate

sKPI #	Key Performance Indicator name
sK2304	# Trial population
sK2305	% Repeat buyers
sK2306	# Trial volume
sK2307	# Sales volume
sK2308	% Sales growth
sK2309	% Compound annual growth rate (CAGR)
sK2310	$ Sales potential forecast
sK2311	% Numeric distribution
sK2312	$ Sales force effectiveness
sK2313	% All commodity volume (ACV) distribution
sK2314	% Product category volume (PCV) distribution
sK2315	% Category performance ratio
sK2316	% Share of shelf
sK2317	% Out-of-stocks
sK2318	% Markdown
sK2319	% Gross margin return on investment (GMROI)
sK2326	$ Cost per redemption
sK2327	$ Coupon cost
sK2328	% Sales with coupon
sK2329	% Rebates breakage rate
sK2330	$ Incremental sales from marketing
sK2331	$ Baseline sales
sK2332	$ Cost of incremental sales
sK2333	% Lift from promotion
sK2334	% Sales on deal
sK2335	% Price waterfall effect
sK2336	% Return on sales (ROS)
sK2337	% Missed sales opportunities
sK2338	% Sales representatives with sales quota attainment
sK2339	# New-hire time to quota attainment
sK2340	# Sales forecast reports frequency
sK2341	% Delayed sales opportunities
sK2342	% Customer winback rate
sK2343	% Completely automated sales orders level
sK2344	# Closed deals in the sales pipeline
sK2345	$ Sales-to-date
sK2346	% Voluntary customer churn
sK2347	% Involuntary customer churn
sK2348	# Cycle time to open account
sK2349	# Tenders attended
sK2350	% Rotting leads
sK2369	% Up sale rate
sK3406	# Business development to administrative expenditure ratio
sK3537	% Electronic tickets sold
sK3975	$ Commission earned per sales agent

sKPI #	Key Performance Indicator name
sK3976	$ Commission per transaction
sK3977	% Commission margin
sK4048	% Sales to new customers
sK4096	$ Revenue per client
sK4489	$ Revenue by product
sK4546	$ Sales per customer
sK4548	% Sales by product category
sK4549	$ Sales per labor hour
sK4586	# Financial services outreach
sK4756	% Sales from repeat customers
sK4807	% Sales discounts
sK4810	% Broker-executed trades
sK5884	% Qualified prospects to total leads ratio
sK6196	% Sales accounts with open and pending status
sK6356	# Sales that had to be declined
sK6359	% New business done with repeat customers
sK6360	% Sales from products whose patents are about to expire within 12 months
sK6581	$ First purchase sales
sK6582	% Cost of sales force from sales
sK6586	$ Discount per booking
sK6587	$ Booking discounts offered
sK6589	# Customers per salesperson
sK6590	# Contacts per sale closed
sK6688	# Time from customer contact to sales response
sK6689	# Sales contacts to sales closed ratio
sK6741	% Unprofitable customers transformed
sK6749	$ Revenue from post sale services
sK6762	% Sales revenue mix by location
sK6765	% Time spent with key customers
sK6767	# Staff to clients ratio by nationality
sK6768	# Active clients to staff ratio
sK6781	$ Revenue from new business operations
sK6876	$ Earnings (revenue)
sK6907	% Sales enquiry conversion rate
sK6916	# Potential new clients contacted
sK6917	# New business proposals submitted
sK7045	$ Revenue at restaurants open at least a year
sK7061	% Pipeline coverage
sK7065	# Trial accounts
sK7066	$ Transaction revenue
sK13965	# Account expansion
sK14027	# Clients by target market segment
sK14074	# Days for contract staff to develop contracts
sK14136	# Failed contracts not reviewed
sK14228	# Leads per day

Supply Chain, Procurement, Distribution

Supply Chain/Procurement and Distribution's role is to optimize the purchase, storage and distribution of raw materials, work-in-progress or final products.

Contract Management

Contract Management is the process of contract creation, administration and execution, as well as analyzing the potential benefit maximization and minimizing risks. It includes establishing terms and conditions, ensuring compliance with them, but also documenting and agreeing any changes that may arise during its implementation or execution.

sKPI #	Key Performance Indicator name
sK145	# Contract variations
sK146	% Retention rate of active contracts
sK147	$ Contract value
sK149	$ Value of activated contract renewals
sK150	$ Contract terminated billed value with contractors
sK151	# Identified contract breaches
sK152	% Cancelled and suspended contracts
sK261	% Contract compliance
sK294	% Contracts reviewed
sK295	% Contracts delivered within original budget
sK296	# Contract complaints
sK761	$ Terminated contract remaining value
sK908	% Claims recovery rate
sK1095	$ Transaction cost with new service providers
sK2798	% Contracts awarded through competitive tendering process
sK2917	% Contracts due to expire in the next X days
sK2918	$ Contract expired value
sK2920	# Contracts renewed
sK2921	% Contract renewals growth rate
sK2922	$ Contract renewals value uplift
sK2923	% Changes to contract specifications
sK2924	# Contracts up for renewal
sK2925	$ Contract value
sK2928	$ Contract value per client
sK2929	$ Annualized contract value
sK2930	$ Annual contracts value
sK2931	# Contract negotiation time
sK2932	% Contract response times not met
sK2933	% Contracts completion on-time
sK2934	% Cost reimbursement contracts
sK2935	% Contract breaches due to non-compliance
sK2937	$ Penalty payments for contract failures
sK2941	# Contract time to completion
sK2943	% Contract penalties
sK2944	# Frequency of contract renewals
sK2945	% Contracts that fail to deliver direct agreements

sKPI #	Key Performance Indicator name
sK2946	$ Estimated value of contract extension
sK2948	$ Contract variation value
sK2949	% Requirements contracts
sK2951	% Changes to contract milestone dates
sK2952	# Contract duration
sK2954	# Length of contract extensions
sK2955	# Contract reports
sK2958	% Variations of supply quantity
sK3033	$ Bid and proposal costs
sK4537	$ Vendor fraud
sK6231	# Policies, agreements and contracts updated
sK6690	% Contracts filled without error
sK6865	% Order value variance from original contract value
sK7055	# Contract concessions

Inventory Management

Inventory Management represents the activities of administration and replenishment of physical stock, in order to insure an adequate supply without generating costs through excessive or under supply. KPIs outline the stock level and the costs incurred by supply's procurement.

sKPI #	Key Performance Indicator name
sK425	$ Stock value
sK426	$ Surplus inventory
sK427	# Inventory turnover
sK428	% Sales order cancellation rate
sK503	# Piece variance
sK557	% Obsolete items in inventory
sK558	% Spoilage rate
sK566	% Pilferage rate
sK633	# Stock rotations
sK634	# Safety stock
sK635	# Reorder point (ROP)
sK636	# Anticipation stock
sK637	# Pipeline stock
sK638	# Working stock
sK639	# Decoupling stock
sK640	% Distressed stock
sK641	$ Beginning inventory (BI)
sK642	# Days sales of inventory (DSI)
sK643	% Inventory quality ratio (IQR)
sK644	$ Maintenance, repair and operating supplies (MRO)
sK645	# Theoretical inventory
sK646	$ Ending inventory
sK647	# Consignment stock

sKPI #	Key Performance Indicator name
sK649	$ Obsolete stock
sK650	# Stock level
sK651	% Slow moving stock
sK900	# Dock to stock cycle time
sK913	% Inventory space utilization
sK1008	$ Inventory value per revenue earned
sK1208	# Damaged goods received to total receipts ratio
sK1212	# Pallets processed per day
sK1242	# Cross docking utilization
sK1598	# Stock outs
sK1625	% Damaged goods while handling
sK1745	# Quality of purchasing receipts
sK1747	$ Dollar value of inventory per purchasing employee
sK2319	% Gross margin return on investment (GMROI)
sK2433	# Inventory days of supply
sK2440	% Inventory management cost
sK2642	# Warehouse damage
sK2723	$ Inventory value
sK2737	% Inventory carrying rate
sK2806	# Exits from stock
sK2807	# Return to stock
sK2808	% Surplus inventory to total inventory value
sK2809	$ Consumption value
sK2810	$ Value of stock at third parties
sK2811	% Stock at third parties value
sK2812	% Forecast to actual inventory consumption variance
sK2813	% Return to stock value to total stock value
sK2814	% Third party warehousing cost
sK2815	% Obsolete stock value
sK2816	# Surplus items
sK2817	# New stock items created
sK2818	% Inventory efficiency
sK2819	# Removed stock items
sK2820	# Stock at third parties
sK2821	# Reception stock at warehouse
sK2823	% Stock to sales ratio
sK2825	% Markdowns/margin loss from write-downs
sK2826	% Write-downs from costs
sK2828	% Inventory accuracy
sK2830	$ Inventory carrying costs
sK2833	# Months on hand
sK2836	# Physical counts of items in inventory
sK2838	# Accurate logistics management information system reports
sK2839	% Accuracy of logistics data for inventory management
sK2840	% Facilities with accurate logistics data for inventory management

sKPI #	Key Performance Indicator name
sK2841	% Facilities with up-to-date reports of the logistics management information system
sK2842	% Facilities with optimal stock levels to ensure near-term product availability
sK2843	% Damaged inventory
sK2844	# Planned stock
sK2845	# Inventory visibility
sK2846	% Inventory shrinkage of throughput
sK2847	$ Full inventory reduction value
sK2848	$ Cash flow inventory reduction improvement
sK2850	% Consumption value to total inventory value
sK2851	% Inventory holding costs from total sales
sK2852	% Inventory holding costs from inventory value
sK2869	# Inventory risk
sK3982	% Out of stock items
sK4808	# Inventory to sales ratio (ISR)
sK6368	% Stored products damaged by employee mistakes
sK6601	$ Inventory holding cost per unit item
sK14150	# Frequency of use of stock

Logistics / Distribution

Logistics/Distribution is the combination of movement of goods and warehousing operation, responsible for storing and delivering products. It involves the physical distribution of the company's products to other distributors or directly to the final customer. KPIs monitor the time efficiency of the distribution, as well as the quality of movement and warehousing operation of the goods.

sKPI #	Key Performance Indicator name
sK4	% Orders delivered with damaged products
sK10	% On-time delivery
sK56	% Orders delivered with complete and accurate documentation
sK143	# Fuel consumption per 100 kilometers
sK160	# Stops per trip
sK235	% Transport capacity utilization
sK236	% Order fill rate
sK237	$ Backorder costs
sK238	% Time spent picking back orders or stock-outs
sK239	# Orders picked per hour
sK240	# Items per order
sK264	# Baggage transfer time
sK265	$ Fuel cost
sK267	$ Freight revenue per ton-mile
sK482	% Packaging to product ratio
sK700	% Distribution cost
sK701	# Pick-to-ship cycle time for customer orders
sK703	$ Internal logistics costs
sK704	% Outsourced logistics costs
sK705	$ Value of goods returned
sK706	% Cross-docking operations

sKPI #	Key Performance Indicator name
sK707	% Boomerang return rate
sK708	# Warehouse network surface
sK716	% Orders with wrong items shipped
sK717	% Orders shipped to wrong destinations
sK743	$ Repair cost per return
sK744	% Warranty claims rate
sK746	# Warranty claims per item
sK747	% Warranty expenses
sK748	$ Warranty cost per item sold
sK749	% Deliveries on behalf of other branches
sK750	% Orders shipped with price errors
sK755	# Warehouses operated
sK766	$ Value of damaged goods per shipment
sK812	% Cost of logistics for shipped orders
sK826	% Premium freight charges
sK848	% Sales orders shipped as part of full load shipments
sK858	% Cost of damaged products from total sales
sK894	% Reverse logistics costs
sK898	# Customer shipment to delivery cycle time
sK901	# Trucks loaded per unit time
sK902	% Orders picking error rate
sK905	% Orders shipped with quantity errors
sK920	$ Cost of logistics per logistics FTE
sK1435	# Pallets loaded per unit time
sK1513	# Packaging consumption
sK1514	# Packaging recycling rate
sK1577	# Packaging weight per product
sK1697	% Delays duration at collection points
sK2155	# Duration of delays
sK2159	# Shipment inspections duration
sK2160	% Transportation cost to delivered sales value
sK2161	# Post-shipment inspections
sK2163	# Pre-shipment inspections
sK2172	$ Operating cost per vehicle
sK2179	% Physically inspected containers
sK2435	% Electronically scanned containers
sK2447	% Product repairs performed
sK2449	% Product repairs performed internally
sK2734	# Warehouse storage space
sK2764	$ Revenue per ton shipped to customer
sK2771	% Orders delivered with errors during installation
sK2781	# Transit borders crossed
sK2784	# Loading points for vehicles
sK2788	# Vehicle load capacity
sK2799	# Loading time per vehicle
sK2802	# Unloading time per vehicle

sKPI #	Key Performance Indicator name
sK2805	% Loading cost
sK2853	$ Operating cost per warehouse
sK2854	# Pallets unloaded per hour of dock time
sK2855	% Hours of machine use in logistics and distribution
sK2856	# Vehicles loaded per hour
sK2857	# Vehicles unloaded per hour
sK2858	# Units unloaded per machine hour
sK2860	# Loss and damage claims
sK2861	% Orders with no damaged line items
sK2865	# Signatures per trade transaction
sK2866	# Border wait times
sK2867	# Transit countries crossed
sK2868	# Agencies inspecting goods
sK2870	# Time for distribution procedures
sK2871	$ Cost per procedure type
sK2872	$ Warehouse rental per stock unit
sK2873	$ Warehouse rental per stock value
sK2874	% Returned items due to shipping damage
sK2876	% Reverse logistics cost to delivered sales value
sK2879	% Travel time with full load
sK2880	% Transit time variability
sK2882	# Line items per order
sK2883	$ Cost per ton-mile
sK2885	# Nodal efficiency
sK2886	$ Delivery cost per order
sK2888	% Vehicle fill
sK2889	% Time spent on driving when delivering
sK2890	% Time utilization
sK2891	# Frequency of delays at collection points
sK2893	% Fuel savings in distribution
sK2894	$ Savings per vehicle
sK2895	$ Fuel cost savings
sK2896	% Deck area utilization
sK2898	% Warehouse capacity use rate
sK2899	$ Warehouse rental
sK2900	% Warehousing discrepancies
sK2903	$ Value of goods in warehouse
sK2904	# Cartons shipped per hour
sK2905	# Units processed per hour
sK2906	# Orders packed per hour
sK2908	% Conveyors downtime
sK2911	$ Losses due to damage
sK2912	# Weight per order
sK2913	$ Warehouse cost per tons shipped
sK2914	# Time from receipt to put away
sK2915	# Weight stored

sKPI #	Key Performance Indicator name
sK2916	% Warehouse labor cost
sK2919	# Warehouse storage space per location
sK2939	# Warehouse storage systems
sK2940	% Distribution cost variance per order
sK2942	$ Distribution cost per ton shipped to customer
sK2947	% Perfect order delivery rate
sK2953	# Deliveries
sK2956	$ Distribution cost per cubic meter shipped to customer
sK2957	$ Revenue per order delivered
sK3474	% Net asset recovery
sK3648	% Damage-free shipments
sK3679	% On time pick-ups
sK3707	$ Penalties cost due to unsatisfied demand
sK3776	% Shipment traceability
sK3785	# Transit time
sK4529	% On-time and accurate raw material orders
sK4613	% Port labor cost to terminal operating cost
sK6358	% Delivery deadlines met
sK6361	$ Delivery cost per truckload shipment
sK6599	% Refurbishment cost from reverse logistics cost
sK6600	% Recovery yield rate of returned products
sK14162	# Full day supply of raw material in stock
sK14232	# Loading docks
sK14234	# Logistic center capacity
sK14243	# Maturity of the logistics process

Procurement / Purchasing

Procurement and Purchasing is the process of material and services acquisition in order to assure the necessary supplies to create and deliver its own service or product. KPIs refer to the quality of cost - benefit report, compliance to the Procurement/Purchasing procedures, as well as assuring the needed supplies on time.

sKPI #	Key Performance Indicator name
sK153	% Key suppliers accounting for 80% of spending
sK253	$ Negotiated cost reduction savings
sK274	# Requisition, purchase order, or invoice transaction volume
sK283	% Local suppliers
sK829	# Sales orders filled per FTE
sK835	# Sales orders filled per unit time
sK1103	% Goods purchased from certified suppliers
sK1109	% Procurement requests satisfied by preferred suppliers
sK1110	% Procurements in compliance with standing procurement policies and procedures
sK1217	# Receipts processed per full working hour
sK1231	% Active suppliers that are certified
sK1240	% Key suppliers visited regularly
sK1612	% Supplier on-time delivery

sKPI #	Key Performance Indicator name
sK1622	% Raw material conformance
sK1653	% Transactions handled by the purchasing department
sK1820	$ Purchase dollars spent per active supplier
sK1822	$ Purchase operating expense per active supplier
sK2157	% Non-contract purchases
sK2439	$ Material acquisition cost
sK2442	% Cost of material acquisition within supply chain
sK2742	% Purchase spend from sales revenue
sK2743	% Purchase operating expense from sales
sK2744	% Purchase operating expense from purchase spend
sK2745	$ Purchase spend per purchasing employee
sK2746	% Payable invoices not matched to a purchase order
sK2747	% Purchase spend controlled by purchasing
sK2748	# Purchase orders
sK2749	% Purchase spend offshore
sK2750	% Purchase spend onshore
sK2751	% Cost avoidance savings in procurement
sK2752	% Cost reduction savings in procurement
sK2753	% Active suppliers who are e-Procurement enabled
sK2754	% Purchase spend via e-Auctions
sK2755	% Purchase spend via procurement cards
sK2756	% Purchase spend via strategic alliances
sK2757	% Purchase spend with diversity suppliers
sK2758	% Inactive suppliers
sK2759	% Procurement return on investment
sK2760	% Invoice accuracy
sK2761	% Purchase spend under management
sK2762	$ Purchase order value
sK2763	$ Purchase price variance
sK2765	# Purchase order cycle time
sK2766	# Days to pay
sK2767	% Customer invoices past due
sK2768	# Customers past due
sK2769	% Vendor invoices past due
sK2770	% Vendors on hold
sK2772	# Vendor invoices due today
sK2773	# Customer invoices due today
sK2774	$ Warehouse cost per order
sK2775	# Planned purchase orders
sK2776	% Purchase orders not sent
sK2777	% Unconfirmed purchase orders
sK2778	# Approved purchase requisitions released
sK2780	# Requests for quote
sK2782	% Purchase return
sK2783	$ Invoiced purchase amount
sK2785	% Delayed purchases

sKPI #	Key Performance Indicator name
sK2786	% Pending purchase order invoices
sK2787	% Purchase amount rate
sK2789	# Procurement training hours per employee
sK2790	% Purchase spend aggregated through corporate contracts
sK2792	# Load handling time
sK2793	% Invoices received electronically
sK2794	$ Purchase spend per supplier
sK2795	% Company invoices paid electronically
sK2796	$ Invoice value
sK2797	% Undisputed supplier invoices paid within 30 days
sK2800	# Suppliers managed by purchasing employee
sK2801	% Supplier purchase orders in full
sK2803	% Supplier rejections
sK2804	$ Variable cost of placing order with supplier
sK2875	% Returned to suppliers
sK2960	% Perfect purchase order rate
sK3961	$ Activity-based cost of acquiring materials and services
sK6745	% Relationship established with certified suppliers
sK7053	# Value added suppliers
sK7056	# Rating of supplier performance
sK7059	$ Life cycle cost (LCC)
sK13980	# Amortization period in months
sK14056	# Cost improvement plan
sK14079	# Days to execute purchase orders
sK14233	# Local suppliers attending quarterly procurement workshops

Supply Chain Management

Supply Chain Management refers to managing the interconnected process of movement and storage of materials (raw, work-in-progress and final goods), from the point of origin until consumption point. KPIs refer to the efficiency of processes and their qualitative management.

sKPI #	Key Performance Indicator name
sK555	% Product return rate
sK699	% Empty running
sK1599	% Delivered In-Full, On-Time
sK1613	% Order entry accuracy
sK1616	# Supply chain response time
sK1626	# Order processing time
sK1630	# Order fulfillment lead time
sK1632	# Order receipt to order entry complete time
sK1635	% Scheduled orders to customer request
sK2425	% Delivery to request date
sK2426	% Delivery to commit date
sK2427	# Time from customer authorization to order receipt
sK2428	# Order entry complete to start manufacture time
sK2429	# Start manufacture to order complete manufacture time
sK2430	# Order complete manufacture to customer receipt of order

sKPI #	Key Performance Indicator name
sK2431	# Customer receipt of order to installation complete time
sK2432	# Cash-to-cash cycle time
sK2434	# Days sales outstanding (DSO)
sK2436	% Cost of goods sold
sK2437	$ Supply chain management cost
sK2438	$ Order management cost
sK2441	% IT cost for supply chain
sK2443	% Supply chain related order management cost
sK2444	% Supply chain related finance and planning cost
sK2445	# Re-plan cycle time
sK2446	% Returns management costs
sK2448	# Make response time
sK2722	# Lines per order
sK2729	% Fill rate for ship-from-stock
sK2732	# Upside supply chain flexibility
sK2735	% Adherence to delivery schedule
sK2738	% Unsaleable stock
sK2740	$ Cost per line dispatched
sK2741	# Software used to support supply chain
sK2864	# Documents per trade transaction
sK2950	# Customers errors placing orders
sK3345	% Employees allocated to order processing
sK3749	$ Freight cost per ton shipped
sK4363	# Interruptions in raw material supply
sK4812	# Processing time in days
sK6950	# Relative asset utilization frequency
sK23024	# Order cycle time
sK23025	# Customer order path
sK23026	# Length of haul
sK23027	# Empty miles factor
sK23028	# Age of revenue equipment
sK23029	% Equipment utilization rate
sK23030	# Tractor operating life
sK23031	# Trailer operating life
sK23032	# Tractors in service
sK23033	# Trailers in service
sK23034	# Hundredweight
sK23035	# Loaded miles per load
sK23036	# Pounds per shipment
sK23037	$ Revenue per hundredweight
sK23038	$ Revenue per loaded mile
sK23039	$ Revenue per shipment
sK23040	# Shipments
sK23041	# Shipments per business day
sK23042	# Railcars on line
sK23043	# Terminal dwell time

Industries

Agriculture

Agriculture includes two basic activities, namely the production of crops and animal raising. Also included are service activities incidental to agriculture, as well as hunting, trapping and related activities.

Crops

Crops includes the production of crop products, covering also the forms of organic agriculture and the growing of genetically modified crops. Agricultural activities exclude any subsequent processing of the agricultural products, except the preparation of products for the primary markets witch is included.

sKPI #	Key Performance Indicator name
sK58	% Irrigation application efficiency
sK445	# Area of land cultivated
sK455	% Land prepared for cultivation
sK561	% Farmers using conservation farming methods
sK585	% Irrigation system efficiency
sK608	$ Cost of harvesting
sK612	# Fruits per plant
sK613	# Canopy volume
sK614	# Weight of fruit production per plant
sK615	# Fruit weight
sK659	# Fruit density
sK666	# Weight harvest rate per picker
sK669	# Tractors per hectare
sK677	% Agricultural machinery availability
sK1492	# Depth to groundwater
sK1497	# Fertilizer consumption
sK1516	# Pesticides consumption
sK2701	$ Cost of pasture production
sK4018	# Hours of operation per hectare of irrigated land
sK4070	# Hours of maintenance per hectare of irrigated land
sK4082	# Operational hours per water depth applied
sK4092	# Energy per unit volume of water pumped
sK4094	# Irrigation supply reliability
sK4345	# Crop yield
sK5021	% Pest introductions detected before spread
sK5291	% Irrigation system hydraulic efficiency
sK5294	% Headworks efficiency
sK5299	# Irrigation return interval
sK5300	# Irrigation application depth
sK5301	# Water infiltration rate
sK5308	% Irrigated farming land
sK5311	# Irrigation hours per day
sK5312	% Irrigation application uniformity
sK5314	# Irrigation application rate
sK5315	% Adequacy of irrigation

sKPI #	Key Performance Indicator name
sK5996	# Rainfall
sK6410	% Agricultural water intensity
sK6411	# Pesticide regulation compliance
sK6870	# On-farm trials and demonstrations
sK22606	# Benefit cost ratio
sK22608	% WA crop area sown to crop varieties developed by the Department
sK22609	# Season hectares planted
sK22610	# Strawberry exports
sK22611	$ Strawberry exports
sK22612	# Carrot exports
sK22613	$ Carrot exports
sK22614	# Exports of seed potatoes
sK22615	$ Exports of seed potatoes
sK22616	% Wheat grades delivered to AWB
sK22617	# Wheat yields
sK22618	# Fibre diameter
sK22619	# Diameter of wool sold at auction
sK22620	$ Cost per unit of knowledge
sK22621	# Planted non-irrigated perennial pasture species
sK22622	# Planted saltland pasture species
sK22623	# Planted trees for commercial production
sK22624	# Stubble retention or mulching practices
sK22625	# Farmed to soil type
sK22626	# Tree/shrub planting
sK22627	# Preserve or enhanced areas of conservation value
sK22628	# Excluded stock from areas impacted by land degradation
sK22629	# Protected river or creek frontages from grazing animals
sK22630	# Regular soil testing for nutrient levels
sK22631	# Regular soil testing for pH
sK22632	# Regular soil testing for compaction
sK22633	# Regular monitoring of the water table
sK22635	# Regular monitoring of pasture/vegetation cover on sandy/light soils
sK22636	# Water on sloping land
sK22637	# Water on the valley floors using surface drains
sK22638	# Water on the valley floor using deep drains
sK22639	% Permanent control methods on stock water supplies
sK22640	% Rotational pasture spelling during plant growth season

sKPI #	Key Performance Indicator name
sK22641	% Fencing to land systems
sK22642	% Conduct a prescribed burn for management purposes
sK22643	% Preserve or enhanced areas of conservation value
sK22644	% Excluded stock from areas impacted by land degradation
sK22645	% Protected river or creek frontages from grazing animals
sK22646	% Formal monitoring of vegetation/ pasture conditions
sK22647	% Specifically spelled pasture for subsequent use by export cattle
sK22656	% Primary producers participating in training that undertook formal training in the FarmBis programme
sK22659	% Primary producers who have adopted a Quality Assurance, Environmental Management System or Code of Practice
sK22661	$ Cost per hectare assessed for risks, options and impacts
sK22662	# Hectare assessed for risks, options and impacts
sK22665	$ Cost per Landcare grant administered
sK22666	# Landcare grants processed
sK22667	$ Administrative cost per participant in farm business and rural community (FB/RC) development activities
sK22668	# Participants in FB/RC development activities
sK22669	# Farms
sK22670	# Pest interceptions by interstate and international barrier quarantine activities
sK22673	# Interceptions of significant pests, diseases and weeds
sK22674	# Pests
sK22675	# Removal of properties from quarantine
sK22676	$ Cost per freight consignment cleared or certified
sK22677	$ Passenger quarantine checking cost per passenger
sK22679	$ Cost per diagnostic samples processed
sK22680	# Legal provisions allowing for ownership and transfer of water
sK22681	% Share of agricultural area equipped for irrigation
sK22682	% Per-capita availability of surface and groundwater resources
sK22683	# Prevalence of volumetric pricing of irrigation water
sK22684	# Command area of irrigation schemes that have undergone turnover under Irrigation Management Transfer (IMT) programs
sK22685	% Irrigation schemes under farmer control/ management
sK22686	$ Expenditures on irrigation, as share of total agricultural expenditure
sK22687	% Irrigation expenditures on O&M versus capital investments
sK22688	% Irrigation cost recovered in user fees
sK22689	$ Irrigation water delivery per unit irrigated area
sK22690	# Surface water storage capacity in the region
sK22691	% Crop evapotranspiration met by available precipitation

sKPI #	Key Performance Indicator name
sK22692	% Prevalence of volumetric pricing of irrigation water
sK22693	% Water charge per hectare to average agricultural revenue per hectare
sK22694	% Prevalence of non-monetized payments for irrigation services
sK22695	% Irrigated area that is waterlogged
sK22696	# Depth to groundwater table
sK22697	% Irrigated area experiencing salinization
sK22698	# Levels of water salinity in available surface water sources
sK22699	% Variability of precipitation
sK22700	% Station coverage of climate data
sK22701	# Water stressed countries
sK22702	% Projected water scarcity

Forestry and Logging

Forestry and logging includes the production of round wood for the forest-based manufacturing industries, as well as the extraction and gathering of wild growing non-wood forest products. Besides the production of timber, forestry activities result in products that undergo limited processing, such as fire wood, charcoal, wood chips and round wood used in an unprocessed form (e.g. pit-props, pulpwood). These activities can be carried out in natural or planted forests. KPIs measure efficiency and diversity of the forestry activities.

sKPI #	Key Performance Indicator name
sK515	# Trees and shrubs species
sK553	% Authorized removal of firewood
sK1527	% Area covered by woodland
sK1535	# New woodland creation
sK1567	# Loss of woodland
sK1571	% Woodland area by species
sK1572	# Tree density
sK1574	% Woodland area certified
sK1575	# Lying deadwood per hectare of forest
sK1576	# Standing deadwood per hectare of forest
sK1580	# Wind thrown timber
sK1581	# Woodland surface affected by wind blow
sK1582	# Volume of growing trees stock
sK1585	% Trees with mammal damage
sK1592	% Trees with common or abundant damage from fungi
sK1593	% Trees with common or abundant damage from insects
sK1701	% Land area covered by forest
sK1758	# Allowable cut (AC)
sK2068	% Tree crown density
sK2077	% New woodland creation by natural regeneration
sK3854	# Forest land protected from wildfires
sK3855	% Land burned through prescribed burning
sK3862	# Wildfires detected and suppressed

sKPI #	Key Performance Indicator name
sK3864	# Wildfires caused by humans
sK3940	% Wildfires caused by human actions
sK3944	% Acres of protected forest and wild lands burned by wildfire
sK5013	$ Cost per acre of environmentally important forest protected
sK6352	% Cases of alleged illegal felling investigated
sK6372	# Woodland area under approved grant schemes
sK6373	% Woodland area that has been thinned
sK6406	% Forest cover
sK6407	# Wood stock volume

Livestock, Hunting and Fishing

Livestock, hunting and fishing includes raising (farming) and breeding of all animals, breeding support services, such as stud services, farm animal boarding and care. It also includes capture fishery and aquaculture, covering the use of fishery resources from marine, brackish or freshwater environments, with the goal of capturing or gathering fish, crustaceans, mollusks and other marine organisms and products (e.g. aquatic plants, pearls, sponges). Also included are activities that are normally integrated in the process of production for own account (e.g. seeding oysters for pearl production). Hunting refers to hunting and trapping activities on a commercial basis, taking of animals (dead or alive) for food, fur, skin, or for use in research, in zoos or as pets, production of fur skins, reptile or bird skins from hunting or trapping activities. KPIs focus on resources consumed to feed the animals, outputs of their use and breeding-related aspects (such as survival or diseases).

sKPI #	Key Performance Indicator name
sK102	# Rams to sheep ratio
sK107	% Farrowing rate
sK120	% Stillborn piglets
sK121	% Piglet survival
sK216	$ Artificial insemination cost per mating
sK286	$ Price per kilogram of meat sold
sK318	% Prime carcasses
sK346	$ Supplementary feed cost per lamb
sK439	% Preweaning mortality
sK508	# Live weight at slaughter
sK552	# Milk yield per cow
sK696	# Piglets born dead per farrowing
sK727	% Milk quota delivered
sK784	# Milk production per kilogram body weight
sK1321	# Dressed weight at slaughter
sK1432	# Animal deaths in transit
sK1433	# Meat sold per sow
sK1434	# Pigs weight gained
sK1466	# Fertilizer to milk price ratio
sK1479	# Milk solids production per cow
sK1489	# Milk solids production per hectare

sKPI #	Key Performance Indicator name
sK1491	# Milk flow rate
sK1506	# Lamb carcass weight
sK1507	# Wool production per sheep
sK1508	% Stalls idle
sK1584	# Piglets born alive per farrowing
sK1778	% 80 days submission rate
sK1780	$ Concentrate cost per liter milk produced
sK1809	# Concentrate use per liter of milk produced
sK1811	# Cows in milk
sK1815	% Cows in calf from second round of mating
sK1817	$ Cost per weight gained by calves
sK1818	# Calving to conception interval
sK1821	# Calf body weight gained per day
sK1827	$ Cost to rear from birth to sale
sK1839	$ Cost to rear a calf from weaning to 12 weeks or 300 Kg
sK1899	$ Cost to rear a calf from birth to weaning
sK1947	% 100 day in calf rate
sK2156	% Piglets fit for rearing
sK2295	% Oestrous rate
sK2368	# Piglets weaned per litter born
sK2468	% 200 day not in calf rate
sK2478	% Heat detection rate
sK2479	$ Cow replacement cost
sK2480	$ Cow pregnancy value
sK2483	# Dry days
sK2496	# Calf weight gained at weaning
sK2525	# Calves weaning weight
sK2532	% Cow pregnancy rate
sK2539	# Concentrate mixture used per head
sK2541	% Dairy calves deaths under 1 month old
sK2543	$ Concentrate mixture cost per tonne
sK2545	% Herd replacement rate
sK2550	% 21 day service submission rate
sK2552	# Cows milking days lost
sK2559	% 6 weeks in calf rate
sK2569	# Cows per hectare
sK2576	% Dry cows
sK2585	% Milk lactose
sK2594	# Feed conversion ratio
sK2595	# Milk yield per hectare
sK2600	# Calves live weight at x months
sK2672	# Sow age at first farrowing
sK2678	% Heifers first lactation milk yield
sK2679	% Non pregnant heifers
sK2680	$ Operating profit per cow
sK2681	$ Replacement cost per cow

sKPI #	Key Performance Indicator name
sK2682	$ Gross margin per cow
sK2685	# Suckling calves
sK2689	# Rejected milk per delivery
sK2691	% Calf mortality up to weaning
sK2693	# Artificial inseminations per conception
sK2694	# Age at first calving
sK2698	# Stocking capacity
sK2700	$ Feed cost per 100 liters of milk
sK2701	$ Cost of pasture production
sK2705	$ Medicine cost per cow
sK2711	% Feed cost of total cost
sK2712	# Milk production per cow lifespan
sK2713	# Cows managed per person employed
sK2714	# Mastitis incidents
sK2715	$ Return over feed per cow
sK2716	# Milkings per cow per day
sK2717	# Milkings undertaken by the robotic system per day
sK2719	# Cows milked per robotic unit per hour
sK2720	# Process time for robotic milking per cow
sK2721	# Cows in herd
sK2730	# Somatic cell counts
sK3074	% Milk collected in the first minute
sK3078	% Time milking units were attached
sK3352	% Time spent in low milk flow
sK3417	% Time spent in high milk flow
sK3435	# Feed ratio
sK3440	# 305 days milk yield per cow
sK3446	# Silage fed
sK3535	% First service conception rate
sK3620	% Milking cows in lactation
sK4214	# Litters per sow
sK4239	# Egg weight
sK4246	% Eggs failed to hatch
sK4277	% Eggs hatching success
sK4338	% Eggs fertility
sK4341	% Broken eggs
sK4342	# Egg production
sK4344	# Egg production per bird
sK4467	$ Profit margin per kilogram of clean wool
sK4468	# Lambs lost from 3 days to weaning per 100 ewes
sK4471	% Ewe deaths around lambing time
sK4472	# Lambs per 100 ewes
sK4473	$ Supplementary feed cost per hectare

sKPI #	Key Performance Indicator name
sK4622	# Milk yield per cow
sK4815	% Culling rate
sK4818	% Mean milk fat of calving cows
sK4819	# Lactation period
sK4823	% Bull conception rate
sK4826	# Calvings per cow
sK4830	% 365 days re-appearance rate
sK4835	# Calving interval
sK4836	# Born calves per cow
sK4850	% Mean milk protein of calving cows
sK4851	% Low to low cows over two consecutive lactations
sK4852	% Low to high cows over two consecutive lactations
sK4856	% High to low cows over two consecutive lactations
sK4857	% High to high cows over two consecutive lactations
sK4862	% Chronic cows with high somatic cell counts (SCC) at milk recording
sK4868	% Cows with repeated high somatic cell counts (SCC) at milk recording
sK4869	% New cows with high somatic cell counts (SCC) at milk recording
sK4888	% Cows with somatic cell counts (SCC) below threshold level
sK5433	% Cows with somatic cell counts (SCC) above threshold level
sK5937	% Wool clip yield
sK5939	# Wool clip fiber diameter
sK5946	# Wool cut per grazed hectare
sK5948	% Ewes fecundity
sK5950	% Ewes fertility
sK6410	% Agricultural water intensity
sK22671	# Identifications of notifiable animal diseases
sK22672	# Animal diseases
sK22678	$ Cost per property management plan for animal disease
sK22703	# New or expanded aquaculture permits per annum
sK22704	% Aquaculture farms providing Department of Primary Industries with "acceptable" compliance reports on time per annum
sK22705	# Surface area of estuary pond farms per estuary
sK22706	% Designated development proposals
sK22707	# Years since review (if not triggered for other reasons)
sK22708	% Branding
sK22709	% Turn-off
sK22710	% Branding to turn-off difference
sK22711	% Sex turn-off difference

Arts and Culture

Arts and culture includes a wide range of activities that meet the diversified cultural, entertainment and recreational interests of the general public, including live performances, operation of museum sites, gambling and recreation services.

Event Production and Promotion

Event production and promotion refers to the conception, organization and promotion of events of arts, live performances and exhibitions. KPIs focus on public-related performance, such as attendance, impressions, but also on the profitability of the events.

sKPI #	Key Performance Indicator name
sK1702	# Gross impressions
sK5926	# Partners for recurring campaigns and events
sK5953	# Event participants
sK5972	% Annual recurrent events
sK6778	% Event seats filled

Libraries and Archives

Libraries and archives include all types of archives (academic, church, national) and libraries (national library, local public library, school library). KPIs are related to the quality in serving and guiding customers, managing and preserving the archives and books, as well as the efficiency in organizing and structuring them.

sKPI #	Key Performance Indicator name
sK349	% Use of public libraries
sK350	% Public libraries open over 45 hours per week
sK2985	# Items per registered borrower
sK3022	# PCs per 1,000 registered library borrowers
sK3035	# Borrowers from other jurisdictions
sK3042	% Registered borrowers by borrowing criteria
sK3051	# Size of population served
sK3061	% Students that agree the library resources suit their needs
sK3233	% Library borrowers from total population
sK3237	$ Library operating cost per capita
sK4267	# Students per networked library computer workstation
sK4409	# Queue time at the self-issue units
sK4411	$ Cost per open hour
sK4423	$ Cost per circulation
sK4444	# Circulation per capita
sK4563	# Circulation per FTE staff hour
sK5253	# Response time to historical photo requests
sK5254	# Photographic reproduction requests received
sK5255	% Archives capacity available for new accessions
sK5256	% Vital library record requests responded to within the established time frame
sK5257	# Response time to vital record requests
sK5293	# Library materials borrowed
sK5296	# Library card holders
sK5307	# Public library Internet terminals available for access
sK5425	% Library users who found the book(s) they wanted

sKPI #	Key Performance Indicator name
sK5657	# Loans per volume held
sK5658	# Locations served by mobile libraries
sK5664	$ Library expenditure on electronic resources
sK5681	# Loans per full-time equivalent (FTE) library staff member
sK5730	% Library service points with Internet terminals
sK5746	# Operational library service points
sK5747	# Population served per library service point
sK5752	$ Library materials expenditure
sK5756	$ Library materials expenditure per capita
sK5906	# Circulation per hour
sK6195	# Visits to the library
sK6204	# Circulation per visit
sK6214	# Visits to the library per capita
sK6219	# Throughput at self-service units
sK6222	% Accuracy of web links in the library catalogue
sK6223	# Reshelving time lapse
sK6224	% Items returned from loan reshelved within standard time
sK6226	% Open hours from total advertised opening hours
sK6227	% Librarians that are full time employees
sK6232	% Library staff by position type
sK6233	# Library branches
sK6234	# Staff per 1,000 FTE students
sK6235	# Items held in collections by type of items
sK6236	# Items added to collections by type of items
sK6237	% Expenditure on electronic resources
sK6242	% Expenditure on information resources
sK6243	$ Library expenditure per FTE student
sK6244	# Downloads from electronic journals per FTE student
sK6246	# Items loaned per FTE student
sK6248	# Visits to the library per FTE student
sK6275	# Visits per registered borrower
sK6276	# Items loaned to other libraries
sK6277	# Items borrowed from other libraries
sK6278	# Circulation per registered borrower
sK6279	% Turnover rate of circulating materials
sK6280	# In-library use of non-print materials
sK6281	# Instanced of access to electronic products and services per registered borrower
sK6282	# Access instances through the gateway or portal to external resources per registered borrower
sK6283	# Circulation breakdown
sK6284	# Acquisitions per capita per annum

sKPI #	Key Performance Indicator name
sK6285	% Library collection age ratio
sK6286	# Requests for service
sK6287	# Reader education and training programs offered
sK6288	% Attendance of library customers at public reader education and other training programs
sK6289	% Discards from total stock
sK6290	# Items in the local history collection
sK6291	# Times local history resources are accessed
sK6292	# Exhibitions of local studies collections/materials
sK6293	# Oral history interviews conducted
sK6294	% Cataloged materials according to the recommended standards
sK6295	# Library item turnaround time
sK6296	% Items digitized from library's collection
sK6297	% Outages for all library electronic services
sK6298	# Designated library services for people with disabilities
sK6320	% National publications acquired by the national library
sK6321	% Borrower required titles in the collection
sK6322	% Unique titles in the collection
sK6323	% Rare materials cataloged
sK6324	% Shelving accuracy
sK6325	% Virtual visits of all library visits
sK6326	# Content units downloaded per document digitized
sK6327	% Correct answer fill rate
sK6328	% Information requests submitted electronically
sK6329	% Public seating occupancy rate
sK6330	% Items that have received preservation treatment
sK6331	% Collection in stable condition
sK6332	$ Cost per title cataloged
sK6711	# Online catalog searches
sK6713	# Catalog records created
sK6715	# Visits to reading rooms
sK6716	# Cataloging backlogs
sK6911	# Time lag for inter-library lending
sK6912	# Online materials accessed
sK6913	% Relevant publications acquired based on requests
sK6914	# Registered borrowers
sK6915	$ Library expenditure
sK14150	# Frequency of use of stock
sK14155	# FTE library staff
sK14355	# Academic libraries
sK14356	# Academic libraries with branches
sK14357	# Academic libraries with branches with FTE enrollment less than 1,000
sK14358	# Academic libraries with documents digitized by library staff
sK14359	# Academic libraries with electronic theses and dissertations produced

sKPI #	Key Performance Indicator name
sK14360	# Academic libraries with FTE enrollment from 1,000 to 2,999
sK14362	# Academic libraries with FTE enrollment less than 1,000
sK14363	# Academic libraries with online library reference services
sK14364	# Academic libraries with technology to assist patrons with disabilities
sK14365	# Academic libraries without branches
sK14366	# Academic libraries without branches with FTE enrollment less than 1,000
sK14394	# Acquired monographs per capita
sK14437	# Adults using library cards
sK14566	# Audio materials per 1,000 visitors served
sK14567	# Audiovisual materials added in academic libraries
sK14568	# Audiovisual materials added per FTE enrollment in academic libraries
sK14569	# Audiovisual materials held in academic libraries
sK14570	# Audiovisual materials held per FTE enrollment in academic libraries
sK14617	# Bibliographic utilities, networks, consortia at academic libraries
sK14643	# Book acquisitions
sK14644	# Book processing time
sK14646	# Books per 1,000 visitors served
sK14647	# Books, serial backfiles, and other paper materials including government documents added in academic libraries
sK14648	# Books, serial backfiles, and other paper materials including government documents added per FTE enrollment in academic libraries
sK14649	# Books, serial backfiles, and other paper materials including government documents held in academic libraries
sK14650	# Books, serial backfiles, and other paper materials including government documents held per FTE enrollment in academic libraries
sK14693	# Campus students per networked workstation
sK14758	# Children using library cards
sK14767	# Circulation in academic libraries
sK14836	# Computer hardware and software at academic libraries
sK14878	# Content units downloaded per database
sK14937	# Current Serial Subscriptions added in academic libraries
sK14938	# Current Serial Subscriptions added per FTE enrollment in academic libraries
sK14939	# Current Serial Subscriptions held in academic libraries
sK14940	# Current Serial Subscriptions held per FTE enrollment in academic libraries
sK14941	# Current subscriptions per capita
sK14967	# Customers using Bookmobile Services
sK15084	# Digital downloads performed by the public

sKPI #	Key Performance Indicator name
sK15116	# Documents digitized per 1,000 titles in the collection
sK15143	# E-Books added in academic libraries
sK15144	# E-Books added per FTE enrollment in academic libraries
sK15145	# E-Books held in academic libraries
sK15146	# E-Books held per FTE enrollment in academic libraries
sK15156	# Elapsed time between the receipt of a request for an item and the receipt of the requested item through the inter-library loan system
sK15170	# Electronic reference sources and aggregation services added in academic libraries
sK15171	# Electronic reference sources and aggregation services added per FTE enrollment in academic libraries
sK15172	# Electronic reference sources and aggregation services held in academic libraries
sK15173	# Electronic reference sources and aggregation services held per FTE enrollment in academic libraries
sK15190	# Employee productivity in media processing
sK17220	# Video materials per 1,000 visitors served
sK17246	# Waiting time for access to items stored where they are not accessible to users
sK17360	# Full text articles downloaded from various full text databases from publishers
sK17361	# Full text articles downloaded per capita
sK17362	# Full time equivalents in the department funded by outside sources
sK17364	# Full time equivalent (FTE) librarians at academic libraries
sK17365	# Other full time equivalent (FTE) paid staff at academic libraries
sK17366	# Other full time equivalent (FTE) professional staff at academic libraries
sK17367	# Full time equivalent (FTE) staff at academic libraries
sK17368	# Full time equivalent (FTE) student assistants at academic libraries
sK17387	# General collection circulation in academic libraries
sK17634	# Interlibrary loan received from commercial services in academic libraries
sK17635	# Interlibrary loan received from other libraries in academic libraries
sK17636	# Interlibrary loan requests received, articles
sK17637	# Interlibrary loan requests received, books
sK17638	# Interlibrary loan transactions in academic libraries
sK17671	# Items catalogued, acquired or processed per staff or per technical services FTE staff
sK17672	# Items catalogued, acquired or processed relative to dollars expended
sK17673	# Items used in the library
sK17782	# Libraries having public service hours less than 20
sK17783	# Libraries in bachelor degree-granting institutions
sK17784	# Libraries in doctoral degree-granting institutions
sK17785	# Libraries in institutions with less than 4-year degree granting status

sKPI #	Key Performance Indicator name
sK17786	# Libraries in institutions with total 4-year and above degree granting status
sK17787	# Libraries in master degree-granting institutions
sK17788	# Libraries with branches in bachelor degree-granting institutions
sK17789	# Libraries with branches in doctoral degree-granting institutions
sK17790	# Libraries with branches in institutions with less than 4-year degree granting status
sK17791	# Libraries with branches in institutions with total 4-year and above degree granting status
sK17792	# Libraries with branches in master degree-granting institutions
sK17793	# Libraries without branches in bachelor degree-granting institutions
sK17794	# Libraries without branches in doctoral degree-granting institutions
sK17795	# Libraries without branches in institutions with less than 4-year degree granting status
sK17796	# Libraries without branches in institutions with total 4-year and above degree granting status
sK17797	# Libraries without branches in master degree-granting institutions
sK17798	# Library materials in circulation
sK17799	# Library equipment and systems
sK17800	# Library items loaned
sK17801	# Library items photocopied
sK17802	# Library materials in circulation to local residents
sK17803	# Library materials in circulation to local residents per capita
sK17804	# Library users
sK17805	# Library visits
sK17806	# Library visits per FTE staff
sK17807	# Library visits relative to dollars expended
sK17829	# Loan period of materials
sK17830	# Loans
sK17831	# Loans and interlibrary loan requests
sK17832	# Loans per capita
sK17839	# Local residents newly registered for library cards each year
sK17840	# Local residents using library cards each year
sK17877	# Materials available per capita
sK17892	# Time of document processing
sK17893	# Time of document retrieval from closed stacks
sK17926	# Microform units added in academic libraries
sK17927	# Microform units added per FTE enrollment in academic libraries
sK17928	# Microform units held in academic libraries
sK17929	# Microform units held per FTE enrollment in academic libraries
sK17932	# Miles per gallon of state library bookmobiles

sKPI #	Key Performance Indicator name
sK18022	# New patrons in three months following each campaign
sK18054	# Non-returnable interlibrary loan from other libraries in academic libraries
sK18055	# Non-returnable interlibrary loan transactions in academic libraries
sK18090	# Opening hours
sK18091	# Opening hours of full services only
sK18092	# Opening hours per week
sK18297	# Person-hours of staff assistance available during open hours
sK18407	# Printed and electronic journals
sK18412	# Private academic libraries
sK18413	# Private academic libraries with branches
sK18414	# Private academic libraries without branches
sK18418	# Processed books per FTE book processing
sK18492	# Public wireless internet sessions that happen in the library system
sK18493	# Public academic libraries
sK18494	# Public academic libraries with branches
sK18495	# Public academic libraries without branches
sK18496	# Public internet sessions using computers excluding wireless internet sessions
sK18517	# Questions posed at the information desk
sK18566	# Reference queries per library visitor
sK18567	# Reference transactions per staff or per public services staff
sK18568	# Reference transactions relative to dollars expended
sK18569	# Referrals to other libraries
sK18591	# Reported circulation figures in academic libraries
sK18594	# Reported interlibrary loan received from other libraries in academic libraries
sK18595	# Reported interlibrary loan transactions in academic libraries
sK18605	# Requests
sK18614	# Reserve circulation in academic libraries
sK18649	# Returnable interlibrary loan received from other libraries in academic libraries
sK18650	# Returnable interlibrary loan transactions in academic libraries
sK18745	# Searches in the local databases
sK18784	# Service level of instructional and informational
sK18785	# Service level of library facilities maintenance and support
sK18786	# Service level of room booking
sK18787	# Service level of study and community access
sK18814	# Size of the collection
sK18834	# Speed of interlibrary lending
sK18843	# Staff FTEs per 1,000 borrowers
sK18844	# Staff FTEs per 1,000 circulation
sK18845	# Staff FTEs per 1,000 reference transactions

sKPI #	Key Performance Indicator name
sK18905	# Study places or workstations in the library for users
sK18909	# Subscriptions per 1,000 visitors served
sK18919	# Supply time interlibrary loan article requests
sK18920	# Supply time interlibrary loan book requests
sK18933	# Surveys of customer training relevance
sK18951	# Teens using library cards
sK18998	# Time taken between the receipt of a requested item by the library and the user gaining access to the item
sK18999	# Time taken to answer reference queries
sK19000	# Time taken to process a loan plus the time the user spent waiting to be served
sK19016	# Times queries can be anticipated
sK19131	# Unique visitors to library website
sK19165	# Use made of current awareness services
sK19166	# Use made of interlibrary loans
sK19167	# Use made of subscriptions
sK19174	# User rating for perceived accessibility of library services and activities
sK19175	# User rating for perceived availability of library services and activities
sK19176	# User rating for perceived quality of library services and activities
sK19177	# User rating for perceived timeliness of library services and activities
sK19178	# User population by age groups
sK19179	# User population by first language
sK19180	# User population by gender
sK19181	# User population by geographical location
sK19182	# User population by grades within occupational groups
sK19183	# User population by occupations
sK19184	# User ratings of importance of accessibility
sK19185	# User ratings of importance of availability
sK19186	# User ratings of importance of comprehensiveness
sK19187	# User ratings of importance of scope
sK19188	# User ratings of importance of timeliness of services
sK19189	# User satisfaction rating for accessibility
sK19190	# User satisfaction rating for availability
sK19191	# User satisfaction with: Comprehensiveness
sK19192	# User satisfaction rating for scope
sK19193	# User satisfaction with: Timeliness of services
sK19350	$ Bibliographic utilities, networks, consortia at academic libraries
sK19370	$ Collection expenditure
sK19373	$ Computer hardware and software at academic libraries
sK19393	$ Cost of library collection use
sK19434	$ Costs per title catalogued
sK19451	$ Download per electronic resource
sK19461	$ Expenditure on collection per capita

sKPI #	Key Performance Indicator name
sK19462	$ Expenditure on training and instruction per FTE library employee
sK19561	$ Information resources expenditures at academic libraries
sK19586	$ Loans relative to dollars expended
sK19703	$ Processing costs of library stock items
sK19712	$ Purchase price per Bibliographic Equivalent Unit
sK19811	$ Staff costs per loan
sK19922	% Academic libraries
sK19923	% Academic libraries with institution-wide committee to implement strategic plan for information literacy
sK19924	% Academic libraries that formally recognize the library's role in information literacy instruction
sK19925	% Academic libraries reporting defined information literacy or information literate student
sK19926	% Academic libraries reporting incorporated information literacy into institution's mission
sK19927	% Academic libraries reporting incorporated information literacy into institution's strategic plan
sK19941	% Accuracy of answers to reference queries
sK19944	% Accurate links in library catalogue identified by monthly link checking program
sK20007	% Advertised hours that the library opened
sK20148	% Blind Services Patron Usage
sK20336	% Collection expenditures on print materials
sK20337	% Collection housed in the appropriate environment
sK20403	% Cost of resources per item viewed by customers
sK20501	% Document delivery transactions per document acquired
sK20502	% Documents digitized per special collection
sK20503	% Documents entered in repository out of documents registered
sK20615	% Expenditure devoted to library materials
sK20616	% Expenditure on collection to library expenditure
sK20617	% Expenditure on electronic resources to expenditure on printed and electronic resources
sK20618	% Expenditure on serials to expenditure on monographs and serials
sK20644	% Fill loan rate of interlibrary loan requests for articles
sK20645	% Fill loan rate of interlibrary loan requests for books
sK20685	% Full text articles downloaded out of journals with available use statistics
sK20805	% Hours the library catalogue available during core service hours
sK20836	% Income generated to library expenditure
sK20905	% Items returned from loan reshelved within 24 hours
sK20938	% Library collection use
sK20939	% Library expenditure allocated for salaries and wages
sK20940	% Library expenditure spent for foreign literature
sK20941	% Library expenditure to university expenditure
sK20942	% Library facility access

sKPI #	Key Performance Indicator name
sK20943	% Library staff providing electronic services
sK20944	% Library stock that is directly accessible to users
sK20945	% Library users satisfied with library facilities and equipment
sK20946	% Library users satisfied with the quality of library service
sK20947	% Library visitor needs filled to needs identified
sK20957	% Loans last year out of books acquired in the last five years
sK20983	% Materials needing conservation treatment that received such treatment
sK21079	% New entries in the national bibliography
sK21080	% New entries in the national bibliography that refer to publications of the last 2 years
sK21124	% Operating expenditures on collection
sK21133	% Orders received by the report date that are placed by staff in the Information Resources Division
sK21466	% Public library customers usage
sK21482	% Queries been satisfied from the library's resources
sK21523	% Relevance of collection
sK21525	% Relevance of on-line search outputs
sK21537	% Requested material or notice of its availability sent within one working day of receipt
sK21538	% Requests dispatched to first potential supplier within one working day of receipt
sK21539	% Requests resolved or forwarded for action
sK21540	% Required titles in the collection
sK21662	% Staff in national and international cooperation and projects
sK21709	% Students agree that library services are readily accessible
sK21790	% Successful interlibrary loans
sK21947	% Use of serviced population
sK21950	% Users to serviced population
sK22020	% Library items mis-shelved
sK22021	% Library stock on loan
sK5734	# Library service points per 100,000 residents

Museums

Museums include all types of institutions collecting and preserving artifacts of all kinds (history, art, science, archeology, maritime). Specific KPIs refer to managing collections and expositions, managing equipment, supplies and services of the museum institutions.

sKPI #	Key Performance Indicator name
sK352	# Visits to museums or galleries
sK353	% Museums operated or supported by government authorities
sK4285	% Operating expenses paid from endowment proceeds
sK4404	# Museum subscriptions
sK4441	# Tourists to museum

sKPI #	Key Performance Indicator name
sK6299	% Awareness of museum
sK6300	# Temporary exhibitions held
sK6301	# Museum club members
sK6302	# Volunteer hours achieved
sK6303	# Exhibition catalogues published
sK6331	% Collection in stable condition
sK6374	% Collection stored in controlled environment
sK6375	% Items from the collection described and recorded
sK6376	# New items added to the museum collection
sK6377	# Museum collection renewal ratio
sK6378	$ Museum collection valuation
sK6379	# Exhibition space available
sK6380	# Museum objects cataloged
sK6381	# Items per collection
sK6382	# Museum collections
sK6383	% Collection items exhibited
sK6384	% Exhibitions held outside the museum
sK6385	% Collection additions by type
sK6386	% Free museum admissions
sK6387	# Paid entries to the museum
sK6388	# Items that have undergone conservation treatment
sK6389	# Items that have undergone restoration work
sK6416	% Exhibition space always opened to the public
sK6417	# Participants in visiting groups
sK6418	# Museum visiting groups

sKPI #	Key Performance Indicator name
sK6419	# Visits to temporary exhibitions with separate entrance fees
sK6420	% Collection ownership
sK17228	# Visits to museums per 1,000 population
sK18506	# Pupils visiting museums and galleries in organised school groups
sK22712	# Visitors to programmes, events and performances
sK22713	# Students to theatre learning programmes in Wellington at theatre and region
sK22714	# Students to SoundHouse-TM NZ and OnTV learning programmes
sK22715	% Visitors rate their visit as very good, good or satisfactory
sK22716	# Visitors to the museum
sK22717	% Awareness of museum by residents
sK22718	# Public open day held
sK22719	# Students to education programmes
sK22720	# Temporary exhibitions
sK22721	# Foundation club members
sK22723	# Vistors to the gallery exhibitions
sK22724	# Exhibitions in main galleries
sK22725	% International festival of art exhibitions
sK22726	# Exhibition catalogues
sK22727	# Partnerships with other national and international institutions
sK22728	# Gallery friends
sK22729	# Positive media profile maintained

Construction & Capital Works

Construction and capital works include general construction and specialized construction activities for buildings and civil engineering works. It includes new work, repair, additions and alterations, the erection of prefabricated buildings or structures on the site and also constructions of a temporary nature.

Civil Engineering

Civil engineering includes general construction for civil engineering objects such as motorways, streets, bridges, tunnels, railways, airfields, harbors and other water projects, irrigation systems, sewerage systems, industrial facilities, pipelines and electric lines, outdoor sports facilities. KPIs measure resources consumption, process efficiency and cost benefit analysis.

sKPI #	Key Performance Indicator name
sK4417	% Cost of construction
sK5220	% Civic construction projects completed early or on time
sK5369	% Active capital projects in construction phase on schedule
sK5454	# Construction related incidents, injuries and fatalities reported
sK5606	$ Committed costs
sK6088	% Time for construction
sK6089	% Time predictability for design
sK6090	% Time predictability for construction

sKPI #	Key Performance Indicator name
sK6091	% Time predictability for design and construction
sK6092	% Construction design scope specifications met in full
sK6213	# Unapproved change orders
sK6304	% Cost to rectify defects in the maintenance period
sK6305	% Cost predictability at design
sK6306	% Cost predictability at construction
sK6307	% Cost predictability at design and construction
sK6308	# Quality issues found in constructions ready for use
sK6309	$ Cost of rework
sK6310	# Procedural audits
sK6311	# Accident prediction techniques in place
sK6312	% Quality control tests passed
sK6333	% Cost predictability at construction due to project manager change orders
sK6334	% Cost predictability at construction due to client change orders

sKPI #	Key Performance Indicator name
sK6335	% Time predictability at construction due to client change orders
sK6336	% Time predictability at construction due to project manager change orders
sK6337	% Predictability of the construction project profit
sK6758	# Requests for time extension submitted
sK22733	# Road and bridge construction contractor

Construction of Buildings

Construction of buildings includes general construction of buildings of all kinds, new work, repair, additions and alterations. KPIs focus on costs, schedule adherence and conformity of the buildings with user requirements.

sKPI #	Key Performance Indicator name
sK348	% Cost predictability
sK433	# Time to rectify defects
sK773	% Construction cost in use
sK3256	$ Cost to complete
sK4417	% Cost of construction
sK5454	# Construction related incidents, injuries and fatalities reported
sK5606	$ Committed costs
sK5902	% Man hours spent for punch items
sK6089	% Time predictability for design
sK6090	% Time predictability for construction
sK6091	% Time predictability for design and construction
sK6092	% Construction design scope specifications met in full
sK6093	# Time to rectify defects in maintenance period
sK6257	% Project cost contingency
sK6304	% Cost to rectify defects in the maintenance period
sK6305	% Cost predictability at design
sK6306	% Cost predictability at construction
sK6307	% Cost predictability at design and construction
sK6308	# Quality issues at Available for Use
sK6309	$ Cost of rework
sK6310	# Procedural audits
sK6311	# Accident prediction techniques in place
sK6312	% Quality control tests passed
sK6333	% Cost predictability at construction due to project manager change orders
sK6336	% Time predictability at construction due to project manager change orders
sK6337	% Predictability of the construction project profit
sK6758	# Requests for time extension submitted
sK6865	% Order value variance from original contract value
sK6869	$ Corrective work value

sKPI #	Key Performance Indicator name
sK6878	% Construction project value represented by punch list items
sK6972	% Proactive inspections that identified violations
sK6973	% Construction sites or locations with reoccurring complaints
sK6974	% Complaints received that were followed by an onsite check
sK6975	# Quotes accepted for major construction projects
sK6976	# Building orders opened to closed ratio
sK6977	% Existing building re-used
sK6978	% Building material re-used on site
sK6979	% Building appliances and fittings that have an energy and water ratings
sK6980	# Days to complete first plan review
sK6981	% Jobs professionally certified in compliance with local regulations
sK6982	% Construction sites proactively checked for compliance with permit conditions
sK6983	# Impact on the environment
sK6984	# Impact on biodiversity
sK6985	% Area of habitat created or retained
sK22730	# General construction contractor
sK22731	# House construction contractor
sK22732	# Non-residential building construction contractor
sK22734	# Construction trade services contractor
sK22735	# Building structure services contractor
sK22736	# Building completion services contractor
sK22737	# Building construction contractor
sK22738	# Residential building construction contractor
sK22739	# Non-building construction contractor
sK22741	# Site preparation services contractor
sK22742	# Installation trade services contractor
sK22743	$ Spending on new buildings
sK22744	$ Spending on refurbishment
sK22745	$ Spending on repairs and maintenance
sK22746	# New projects commissioned
sK22747	# New build projects commissioned
sK22748	# New refurbishment projects commissioned
sK22749	# New repair and maintenance projects commissioned
sK22750	# Defects
sK22751	% Client satisfaction index for construction products
sK22752	% Clients satisfaction index for construction services
sK22753	% Defects on handover
sK22754	% Safety accidents
sK22755	% Predictability of construction cost
sK22756	% Predictability of construction time

Education & Training

Education and training refers to assuring educational preparation at any level or for any profession, oral or written, as well as by radio and television or other means of communication.

Academic Education

Academic education refers to the national or international educational systems, their way of work and their results. It includes education offered by different institutions in the regular school system at its different levels, as well as the literacy programs available. The indicators relate to the quality and effectiveness of the academic education system.

sKPI #	Key Performance Indicator name
sK33	% Student acceptance rate
sK34	$ Academic activity cost per student
sK35	% Nationally accredited study programs
sK273	% Graduation rate
sK275	# Students to professor ratio
sK276	% Drop-out rate
sK278	% International students
sK282	% Student repetition rate
sK297	% Student scholarships
sK298	% Students participating in research activities
sK299	% Students in a preferred student group targeted for enrollment
sK328	% Attendance rate per course
sK330	# Students to computer ratio
sK334	% Students involved in extracurricular activities
sK702	$ Cost per graduate
sK2822	% Ethnic minority student grants
sK2824	# Students transferred from other schools
sK2827	% School revenue from private donors
sK2832	% School revenue received from the government
sK2834	$ School revenue from governmental sources
sK2837	% Students receiving grants
sK2849	% Student satisfaction rate
sK2859	$ School spending on scholarships
sK2862	$ School private donations
sK4285	% Operating expenses paid from endowment proceeds
sK4494	# National examination score
sK4495	# Students per class
sK4496	# Student grades
sK4497	# Time to graduate
sK4498	# Extracurricular activities per student
sK4499	# Male to female student ratio
sK4500	# Teaching experience
sK4502	# Students enrolled
sK4503	% Ethnic minority students
sK4505	% Teaching hours delivered
sK4506	% Drop rate of web-based course

sKPI #	Key Performance Indicator name
sK4507	% Early graduation rate
sK4508	% Student expulsion rate
sK4509	$ Expenditure with extracurricular activities
sK4511	% Graduate employment rate
sK4512	% Graduates employed in their field of study
sK4513	% Extended graduation rate
sK4514	% Parents satisfied with education programs and school service
sK4515	% Student housing room occupied
sK4516	% Students satisfaction with teaching skills
sK4517	% Satisfaction with curriculum
sK4518	% School spending on educational resources
sK4519	% Student enrollment rate growth
sK4520	% Enrolled students applying for scholarships
sK4521	# Scholarship types
sK4522	% Students transferring to another school
sK4523	% Web-based or web enhanced academic courses
sK4801	% Entering students through transfer
sK4802	% Degrees conferred by distance education programs
sK5025	# Academic staff winning Nobel Prizes and Fields Medals
sK5117	# Research papers online hits
sK5118	# Citations in top journals
sK5119	# H-index
sK5595	# University alumni winning Nobel Prizes and Fields Medals
sK5810	% Graduates that demonstrate field leadership after graduation
sK5849	% Vocational Education and Training (VET) unit enrollments that use e-learning
sK5852	# Collaborations with other education agencies
sK5857	# Contracted partnerships with industry
sK5858	% Leaning programs that ensure family participation
sK5922	# Time to submit grant applications
sK5929	% Alumni that offer their support
sK5930	# Publications in high impact journals
sK6638	# Immediacy index
sK6639	# Citation trend line
sK6640	% Articles not cited
sK6656	% Eigenfactor score
sK6657	# Article influence score
sK6658	# Source normalized impact per paper (SNIP)
sK6660	# Citation potential
sK6665	% Academic programs with identified learning objectives
sK6666	% Academic programs with a formal assessment plan

sKPI #	Key Performance Indicator name
sK6667	% Full time faculty personnel on fixed term appointments
sK6668	$ Extramural research awards received
sK6669	# Academic programs that have been eliminated or consolidated
sK6670	# Graduate assistantship positions available
sK6671	# Students enrolled in education programs abroad
sK6672	# Students enrolled in exchange programs
sK6673	# Incoming to outgoing exchange students ratio
sK6674	# Mean duration of sponsored exchange programs
sK6675	# International visiting faculty scholars
sK6676	% Students who study advanced foreign languages
sK6677	% Students receiving need based institutional scholarship
sK6678	$ Scholarship award from internal funds
sK6679	% Students whose financial need was fully met
sK6680	$ Student loan debt
sK6681	$ Education financing need unmet
sK6682	# Online learning course offerings
sK6683	% Students enrolled in online learning courses
sK6684	% Classroom utilization rate
sK6685	% Research space utilization rate
sK6686	% Education programs that are under-enrolled
sK6687	% Academic offerings that incorporate sustainability into the curriculum
sK6757	% Courses requiring technology access
sK6791	% Academic staff with PhD degrees
sK6802	$ Research grants for academic staff
sK6804	# Postgraduate students to academic staff ratio
sK6806	# Research experience
sK6809	# Postgraduate fellowships from prestigious bodies
sK6812	# Academic recognitions by professional bodies
sK6813	# Research facilities
sK6814	% Research assistantships
sK6836	% Students meeting or exceeding standards
sK6837	# Student transportation complaints
sK6838	% Student satisfaction with guidance and counseling
sK6839	% Freshman retention rate
sK6840	% Campus housing occupancy rate
sK6841	% Job placement rate within 'x' months of graduation
sK6858	% Alumni satisfaction level
sK6859	% Quality of campus environment
sK6860	% Faculties offering doctoral degrees
sK6864	# Time from graduation to employment in major field of study
sK6866	% Punch list items completion
sK6930	% Courses with e-learning components
sK6931	% Trainers who have included e-learning in the design, development and delivery of units

sKPI #	Key Performance Indicator name
sK6932	% Trainers promoting e-learning
sK6938	% Actual training tracks that follow intended industry training plans
sK14898	# Countries of origin of students
sK19244	% Take-up rate of resources, facilities and services
sK20532	% Employees agree that adequate software is available at their school
sK20533	% Employees agree that athletic facilities are safe and attractive
sK20534	% Employees agree that bus drivers treat students fairly and with respect
sK20535	% Employees agree that the code of conduct is clear and consistently enforced - ca sa nu fie chiar la fel cu urmatorul
sK20536	% Employees agree that bus rules are clear and consistently enforced
sK20537	% Employees agree that buses are clean and well maintained
sK20538	% Employees agree that drills are conducted during the school year
sK20539	% Employees agree that guidance and counseling services meet identified student needs
sK20540	% Employees agree that opportunities are provided for parent and teacher interaction
sK20541	% Employees agree that opportunities are provided for parents to become involved in the school
sK20542	% Employees agree that playground and PE areas are safe and well maintained
sK20543	% Employees agree that programs for special needs students are of high quality
sK20544	% Employees agree that requests for service and maintenance on buses are handled in a professional and efficient manner
sK20545	% Employees agree that requests made to the technology specialist in their school are answered
sK20546	% Employees agree that school administrators are supportive of bus drivers and their discipline efforts
sK20547	% Employees agree that school buildings are kept neat and clean
sK20548	% Employees agree that school meetings and activities are effective methods of encouraging parental involvement
sK20549	% Employees agree that students here understand why they are in school
sK20550	% Employees agree that students show an acceptable degree of responsibility toward their school assignments
sK20551	% Employees agree that teachers and students enjoy an attitude of mutual trust and respect
sK20552	% Employees agree that teachers feel safe in the school buildings before and after school
sK20553	% Employees agree that technology tools are available at their school
sK20554	% Employees agree that the administration accepts and supports decisions made by committees comprised of all stakeholders
sK20555	% Employees agree that the administration has a visible presence within the school

sKPI #	Key Performance Indicator name
sK20556	% Employees agree that the administration provides recognition for the work of the teachers
sK20557	% Employees agree that the administration strongly encourages teachers to consistently implement standards based strategies in the classroom
sK20558	% Employees agree that the administration treats all staff members equally without showing bias to a particular group
sK20559	% Employees agree that the curriculum at their school is based on clearly defined learning standards
sK20560	% Employees agree that the meals that are prepared to the guidelines are suitable to the needs of the students and adults
sK20561	% Employees agree that the media program supports the learning needs of all students and adults
sK20562	% Employees agree that the principal addresses issues and concerns in a timely manner
sK20563	% Employees agree that the principal clearly defines expectations and shares these expectations with the staff
sK20564	% Employees agree that the principal employs data-driven instructional decision making to improve student learning
sK20565	% Employees agree that the principal makes school improvement and student learning a top priority
sK20566	% Employees agree that the principal's expectations are reasonable and obtainable
sK20567	% Employees agree that the school celebrates and acknowledges achievements
sK20568	% Employees agree that the school grounds are neat and attractive
sK20569	% Employees agree that the school has effective and efficient assessments for daily learning
sK20570	% Employees agree that the transportation director and staff are visible and available to drivers and staff on a daily basis
sK20571	% Employees agree that the transportation director's expectations are reasonable and attainable
sK20572	% Employees agree that the transportation staff acknowledges and shows appreciation for the work of all drivers and transportation employees
sK20573	% Employees agree that the transportation staff addresses concerns in a timely manner
sK20574	% Employees agree that the transportation staff treats all staff members equally without showing bias to a particular group
sK20575	% Employees agree that their curriculum is successfully preparing students for the next level of learning
sK20576	% Employees agree that their school and administration value progress monitoring and the Response to Intervention (RTI) process
sK20577	% Employees agree that their school buses and Board of Education vehicles are clean, safe and well maintained
sK20578	% Employees agree that their school effectively promotes school-home communication through newsletters, flyers, telephone notification, web page, and local media
sK20579	% Employees agree that there is a clear set of rules for students to follow in their school
sK20580	% Employees agree that they agree with the reduction of fat, salt, and sugar in the meals
sK20581	% Employees agree that they can effectively use the software available in their school
sK20582	% Employees agree that they can effectively use the technology tools available to them
sK20583	% Employees agree that they feel supported by administration and transportation staff
sK20584	% Employees agree that they feel supported by the administration
sK20585	% Employees agree that they get an adequate meal for the money they pay
sK20586	% Employees agree that they have an overall level of satisfaction with security and maintenance
sK20587	% Employees agree that they have an overall level of satisfaction with student responsibility and discipline in our school
sK20588	% Employees agree that they have an overall level of satisfaction with the curriculum and their job tasks
sK20589	% Employees agree that they have an overall satisfaction with the level of parental involvement at our school
sK20590	% Employees agree that they would agree to pay more for a larger meal
sK20591	% Employees agree that they would encourage students and parents to participate in the lunchroom program
sK21160	% Parents agree that athletic facilities are safe and attractive
sK21161	% Parents agree that bus drivers treat students fairly and with respect
sK21162	% Parents agree that bus rules are clear
sK21163	% Parents agree that buses are clean and well maintained
sK21164	% Parents agree that parent volunteers are encouraged and appreciated at the school
sK21165	% Parents agree that playground and PE areas are safe and well maintained
sK21166	% Parents agree that school activities for parents help them support their child's learning
sK21167	% Parents agree that school personnel treat their child in a fair and consistent manner
sK21168	% Parents agree that students see a relationship between what they are studying and their everyday lives
sK21169	% Parents agree that teachers give their child extra individual help when needed
sK21170	% Parents agree that teachers have high expectations for child's academic performance
sK21171	% Parents agree that the bus rules are consistently enforced
sK21172	% Parents agree that the faculty and staff are responsive to their concerns
sK21173	% Parents agree that the school does a good job teaching academic subjects
sK21174	% Parents agree that the school does a good job teaching electives/enrichment courses
sK21175	% Parents agree that their child's school gives them information about programs, events, and workshops

sKPI #	Key Performance Indicator name
sK21176	% Parents agree that the school has a sufficient amount of technology
sK21177	% Parents agree that the school is clean, well maintained and attractive
sK21178	% Parents agree that the school provides high quality programs for special needs students
sK21179	% Parents agree that the school provides training and opportunities for them to volunteer at school
sK21180	% Parents agree that the School System provides high quality programs for gifted students
sK21181	% Parents agree that the school keeps them well informed of their child's progress
sK21182	% Parents agree that the school's rules and behavioral expectations for students have been made clear
sK21183	% Parents agree that the teachers use a variety of strategies and learning activities to help students learn
sK21184	% Parents agree that their child enjoys the food prepared by the school nutrition program
sK21185	% Parents agree that their child has enough time to eat meals during school
sK21186	% Parents agree that their child has opportunities to use technology for learning at school
sK21187	% Parents agree that their child is challenged to reach his/her full potential
sK21188	% Parents agree that their child learns good work habits at school
sK21189	% Parents agree that their child's school does a good job teaching respect
sK21190	% Parents agree that their child's school has a clear focus on academic learning and success for each student
sK21191	% Parents agree that there should be more food choices for their child in the School Nutrition Program
sK21192	% Parents agree that they believe their child has a safe and secure bus ride
sK21193	% Parents agree that they feel that their child is safe and secure at this school
sK21427	# Academic staff per 100 students
sK21490	% Ratio of students to full-time faculty
sK21695	% Student perform above average on end of course tests
sK21703	% Students agree that athletic facilities are safe and attractive
sK21704	% Students agree that bus drivers treat students fairly and with respect
sK21705	% Students agree that bus rules are clear and consistently enforced
sK21706	% Students agree that buses are clean and well maintained
sK21707	% Students agree that guidance and counseling services meet the needs of students
sK21708	% Students agree that guidance counselors are accessible and available to meet with students
sK21710	% Students agree that playground and PE areas are safe and well maintained
sK21711	% Students agree that school rules and policies are clear, fair, and enforced consistently

sKPI #	Key Performance Indicator name
sK21712	% Students agree that the atmosphere in the lunchroom is conducive to an enjoyable meal
sK21713	% Students agree that the lunchroom employees are friendly
sK21714	% Students agree that the media center/program supports the learning needs of all students
sK21715	% Students agree that the school provides numerous opportunities for them to be involved in extra-curricular activities
sK21716	% Students agree that their school is clean and well maintained
sK21717	% Students agree that their teachers exhibit passion for learning, enthusiasm, and inspire me to be successful
sK21718	% Students agree that their teachers have high expectations for students
sK21719	% Students agree that their teachers provide them with opportunities to use technology for learning
sK21720	% Students agree that their teachers use a variety of methods (hand-on activities, group activities, graphic organizers, technology, etc.) to help them understand the subject matter
sK21721	% Students agree that there is a significant problem with substance abuse (drugs and/or alcohol problems) among the students at my school
sK21722	% Students agree that they are recognized and rewarded for success and good behavior at this school
sK21723	% Students agree that they are treated with respect by adults at my school
sK21724	% Students agree that they believe learning is very important at my school
sK21725	% Students agree that they feel comfortable sharing their ideas with teachers and other adults at this school
sK21726	% Students agree that they feel confident with the information and direction provided by the guidance and counseling department at their school
sK21727	% Students agree that they feel safe and secure in their school
sK21728	% Students agree that they feel safe and secure when riding a school bus
sK21729	% Students agree that they have enough food choices in the lunchroom
sK21730	% Students agree that they have enough time to eat their meal when they eat in the lunchroom
sK21731	% Students agree that they have heard or seen the vision, mission, and beliefs in their school
sK21732	% Students agree that they like the lunchroom food
sK21733	% Students agree that they would like more fresh fruits and vegetables

Colleges and Universities

A college or university is an educational institution that facilitates learning, issues degrees in various majors and conducts academic research activities.

sKPI #	Key Performance Indicator name
sK14441	# Advanced degrees granted
sK14507	# Alumni engagement

sKPI #	Key Performance Indicator name
sK14522	# Anticipated RAE grade point
sK14571	# Audit grade
sK14768	# Citations
sK14769	# Citations per faculty of research
sK14899	# Course completion index
sK15028	# Degree classes awarded
sK15029	# Degrees granted in engineering and computer sciences
sK15071	# Departments in top quartile of National Research Council rankings
sK15220	# Economic impact of research
sK17233	# Volunteers associated with Statewide Public Services programs per FTE faculty in SWPS
sK17281	# Withdrawals
sK17395	# Global level research index
sK17409	# Graduate entry standards
sK17410	# Graduate student placement
sK17411	# Graduates admitted to the graduate school
sK17412	# Graduates employed in the chosen field out of graduates
sK17414	# Grants
sK17471	# Higher degree courses
sK17628	# Institutional Grants Scheme (IGS)
sK17629	# Institutional processes and funding plans implemented
sK17644	# International alliances
sK17646	# International esteem of research
sK17650	# International students
sK17657	# Invention disclosures
sK17670	# Gaps between expectations reported
sK17814	# Licenses
sK17975	% Nationally accredited programs
sK18181	# Participations in international publications and presentations
sK18277	# Perceived teaching quality
sK18348	# Position in League Tables
sK18354	# Postgraduate applications per place
sK18355	# Postgraduate research students intake
sK18356	# Postgraduate research students volume
sK18357	# Postgraduate taught students intake
sK18358	# Postgraduate taught volume
sK18504	# Publications
sK18508	# Qualitative assessment of new programme proposals submitted
sK18512	# Academic staff's assessment of quality of student assignments produced
sK18577	# Reinvestment in university activities
sK18602	# Representation among influential regional bodies
sK18603	# Reputation with students in League Tables
sK18604	# Reputation with Students from NSS survey

sKPI #	Key Performance Indicator name
sK18607	# Research awards
sK18608	# Contributions for research awards
sK18609	# Research degrees awarded
sK18610	# Research publications
sK18611	# Research publications per 10 FTE academic staff
sK18612	# Research students
sK18734	# Science and technology campus partnerships
sK18741	# Score in learner surveys
sK18842	# Staff and student satisfaction with facilities
sK18860	# Start-up/spin-off companies per $100M research expenditures
sK18879	# Students admitted in diploma and certification courses
sK18887	# Students participated in research activities
sK18890	# Students per faculty
sK18893	# Students satisfied with instruction level
sK18894	# Students satisfied with the post-graduation instruction level
sK18912	# Successful research grants
sK18942	# Tariff points score
sK18950	# Technology transfer of research
sK19116	# Undergraduate intake
sK19117	# Undergraduate intake quality
sK19118	# A level scores among undergraduate intake
sK19126	# Undergraduate applications per place
sK19334	$ Analysis of income and grants profile for all other funding sources
sK19335	$ Analysis of income and grants profile
sK19352	$ Biological/medical waste cost per kg of biological/medical waste managed
sK19377	$ Contingency funds
sK19382	$ Cooperative Research Centre (CRC) funding
sK19458	$ Equipment expenditure
sK19470	$ External funds generated invested in Statewide Public Services (SWPS)
sK19472	$ External grants and contracts
sK19537	$ Hazardous chemical waste cost per kg of hazardous chemical waste managed
sK19580	$ License income per $100M research expenditures
sK19630	$ Non-HEFCE income per staff member
sK19726	$ Research funding
sK19727	$ Research funding per 10 FTE academic staff
sK19728	$ Research grant income
sK19729	$ Research income and grants profile by funding body
sK19730	$ Research income and grants profile for EU Government
sK19731	$ Research income and grants profile for research councils
sK19732	$ Research income and grants profile for state charities

Organizational » Industries

sKPI #	Key Performance Indicator name
sK19733	$ Research income and grants profile for State Government
sK19809	$ Sponsored research and development supported by external fund sources
sK19810	$ Sponsored research dollars per faculty at research/ doctoral universities
sK19827	$ Teaching and learning expenditure per successful EFTSL
sK19928	% Academic staff engaged in knowledge transfer activities
sK19940	% Acclamation ratio
sK20041	% Facilities operations, maintenance and physical plant expenditures of current replacement value
sK20098	% Attendance against college average
sK20099	% Attendance pay for a resident undergraduate less grant aid as a percent of median income
sK20127	% Bachelor's graduates completing an internship
sK20158	% Budget devoted to development and support of faculty and staff
sK20338	% College transfers completing a bachelor's degree at an university
sK20400	% Cost of attendance at university covered by federal and state needbased aid for resident undergraduate financial aid recipients
sK20402	% Cost of attendance for a resident undergraduate out of family income
sK20466	% Deferred maintenance backlog of current replacement value
sK20529	% Employed graduates working in local
sK20595	% Employment and study destinations of new first degree graduates
sK20622	% External evaluators satisfied with the institution
sK20629	% Facilities renewal requirements of current replacement value
sK20632	% Faculty and staff from diverse backgrounds
sK20650	% First destinations to employment performance
sK20675	% Fractional staff out of teaching team
sK20689	% Full-time freshmen returning for the second year
sK20691	% Full-time staff out of teaching team
sK20693	% Funds granted by the Government
sK20714	% Graduate productivity rate
sK20715	% Graduates continuing education
sK20716	% Graduates employed
sK20761	% High grades against national benchmarks
sK20804	% Hourly paid staff out of teaching team
sK20894	% International conference fraction
sK20896	% International study exchange initiatives
sK21149	% Overseas students of total student body
sK21394	% Postgraduate conversion rates
sK21395	% Postgraduate research intake of EU students
sK21396	% Postgraduate taught intake of EU students

sKPI #	Key Performance Indicator name
sK21499	% Recruitment to full-time provision
sK21500	% Recruitment to part-time provision
sK21541	% Research expenditure of total income
sK21542	% Research higher degree enrolments of total enrolments
sK21543	% Research income out of operating revenue
sK21633	% Sessional staff out of teaching team
sK21663	% Staff undertaking research at or approaching international level
sK21744	% Student's engagement with faculty
sK21770	% Students retained and achieving following ALS
sK21772	% Students supported by scholarship schemes
sK21773	% Students that took part in academic enhancement activities
sK21775	% Students who are successfully placed by the education provider
sK21785	% Subject load pass rate
sK21847	% Teaching and learning expenditure per EFTS of total expenditure
sK21848	% Teaching hours delivered as overtime by fractional staff
sK21849	% Teaching hours delivered as overtime by full-time staff
sK21850	% Teaching space utilisation
sK21851	% Teaching staff against teaching positions
sK21879	% Top-school leavers enrolled in the university
sK21915	% UG intake of home to EU
sK21919	% Undergraduate completion rate
sK21920	% Undergraduate conversion rates
sK21986	% Web based courses offered
sK14592	# Bachelor's degrees granted
sK15030	# Degrees granted in engineering and computer sciences
sK15205	# Entering first- time freshmen
sK15346	# Freshman participation rate in institutions
sK15394	# Gifts from philanthropic sources
sK15659	# Inventions disclosed per year
sK16540	# Rating of overall quality of experience by recent bachelor's graduates
sK16543	# Rating of overall quality of engineering/computer science graduates by employers
sK16623	# Residents participating in activities sponsored through SWPS programs per FTE faculty in SWPS
sK16898	# Students who are new community college transfers
sK17004	# Time to degree for community college transfers
sK17006	# Time to degree for students entering as full-time freshmen
sK18859	# Start-up or spin-off companies per $100M research expenditures
sK19346	$ Attendance pay for a resident undergraduate
sK20401	% Cost of attendance for a resident undergraduate
sK20687	% Full-time freshmen starting and completing a bachelor's degree at an university

sKPI #	Key Performance Indicator name
sK20717	% Graduates employed and/or continuing education
sK21880	% Cost of attendance at university covered by federal and state needbased aid for resident undergraduates

Primary and Secondary Schools / K-12

A school is an administrative unit dedicated to and designed to impart skills and knowledge to students. K-12 schools is a designation of primary and secondary schools that enroll students from 4 to 19 years of age. KPIs in this context reflect students' performance, as well as administrative aspects.

sKPI #	Key Performance Indicator name
sK14335	# 11th and 12th graders enrolled in dual enrollment courses
sK14336	# 11th and 12th graders who earn 10 or more college credits
sK14337	# 11th graders taking ACT
sK14338	# 11th graders taking SAT
sK14348	# Advanced Placement (AP) students taking AP tests
sK14354	# Academic achievement rating for extracurricular activities
sK14393	# Achievement test scores and basic learning competencies in Language, Mathematics and Social Studies
sK14408	# Activities in extracurricular activities
sK14537	# Ascendancy in extracurricular activities
sK14557	# Attendees
sK14560	# Self-rating of attitude in extracurricular activities
sK14760	# Children enrolled in ECBG preschools
sK14761	# Children enrolled in head start or early head start programs
sK14762	# Children enrolled in voluntary, state-funded, full-day kindergarten
sK14838	# Computers per classroom
sK14927	# CTE completers
sK15186	# Emotional Stability in extracurricular activities
sK15240	# Students, parent and other community members' customer service index
sK15243	# Extra-curricular activities conducted
sK17305	# Focus walks
sK17392	# Gifted students being served
sK17423	# Gross enrollment in early childhood development programs
sK17469	# High school students enrolled in Advanced Placement courses
sK17470	# High school students enrolled in Advanced Placement courses who achieved a score above 3
sK17641	# Principals, teachers and other staff's customer service index
sK17722	# Rating of learning attitude in extracurricular activities
sK17931	# Middle school students enrolled in courses
sK18073	# Offered sessions

sKPI #	Key Performance Indicator name
sK18565	# Reduction of students identified as needing intervention
sK18638	# Responsibility in extracurricular activities
sK18710	# Safe schools violations
sK18729	# Scholarships awarded
sK18730	# School's overall academic rank in the province
sK18731	# Schools accredited
sK18732	# Schools achieving Adequate Yearly Progress (AYP)
sK18733	# Schools in school improvement
sK18743	# Scores on SAT as compared to national averages
sK18757	# Secondary students engaged in over 30 hours of service learning each year
sK18818	# Sociability in extracurricular activities
sK18846	# Staff hours attending per teacher
sK18848	# Staff with bachelors degrees
sK18849	# Staff with doctorate degrees
sK18850	# Staff with masters degrees
sK18852	# Staff with specialist degrees
sK18873	# Strategy management meetings
sK18877	# Student contact hours delivered
sK18878	# Student discipline in "X" grade
sK18880	# Students above range on PALS-PreK assessment
sK18881	# Students eligible for specialized services enrolled in private day placements
sK18883	# Students getting scores of 3 or above in AP exam
sK18884	# Students identified on Fall PALS as needing intervention
sK18885	# Students involved in CTE student organizations
sK18886	# Students meeting AYP as a district
sK18888	# Students participating in SAT
sK18891	# Students receiving industry certification
sK18892	# Students receiving specialized services enrolled in private day placements to support appropriate educational services
sK18895	# Students scoring 'Advanced Proficient'on one or more SOL tests
sK18896	# Students scoring in the upper range on the PALS assessment
sK18901	# Students with disabilities receiving state-sanctioned diplomas by diploma type
sK18902	# Students with disabilities who have exited special education services
sK18903	# Students employed and/or enrolled in postsecondary education within 1 year of leaving high school
sK18904	# Students who have had IEPs after secondary school
sK18931	# Community's assessment of student achievement
sK18940	# Targeted community groups addressed
sK18941	# Targeted community groups addressed by Superintendent and Cabinet
sK18946	# Teachers' effective implementation of the Teaching Expectations

sKPI #	Key Performance Indicator name
sK18947	# Teaching skill satisfaction level
sK18969	# Test security incidents
sK18970	# Testing irregularities reported
sK18997	# Time spent reported by oneself in extracurricular activities
sK19313	$ Actual spending of budget
sK19424	$ Cost per student
sK19436	$ Child care center charge
sK19482	$ Federal dollars received
sK19530	$ Grants awarded
sK19549	$ Early childhood education teachers' wage
sK19662	$ Parental employment income in student families
sK19688	$ Per pupil cost elementary
sK19689	$ Per pupil cost secondary
sK19707	$ Public current expenditure on primary education
sK19803	$ Spending on books and other educational resources
sK19872	% 11th and 12th graders who earn 10 or more college credits
sK19873	% 11th graders taking ACT
sK19874	% 11th graders taking SAT
sK19909	% Advanced Placement (AP) students taking AP tests
sK19919	% Absenteeism
sK19929	% Academic staff with doctorate degree
sK19962	% Administrator attendance
sK20079	% APS by stakeholders
sK20080	% APS/State student achievement gap in English/Language Arts for grades 11, first-time test takers
sK20081	% APS/State student achievement gap in English/Language Arts for grades 3, 5 and 8
sK20082	% APS/State student achievement gap in Mathematics for grades 11, first-time test takers
sK20083	% APS/State student achievement gap in Mathematics for grades 3, 5 and 8
sK20084	% APS/State student achievement gap in Reading for grades 3, 5 and 8
sK20086	% Armed Forces after graduation
sK20095	% Accessibility to instructional technology
sK20100	% Attendance Rate
sK20109	% Audit corrective action plans completed
sK20146	% Births to mothers with less than a 12th grade education
sK20252	% Children meeting the basic grade in reading assessment
sK20335	% Coefficient of efficiency to Grade 5
sK20451	% Daily participation of eligible students in free/reduced breakfast
sK20452	% Daily participation of eligible students in free/reduced lunch
sK20475	% Gender difference in Language Arts test marks for grade 6 students

sKPI #	Key Performance Indicator name
sK20493	% District first time test takers who passed in at least 4 out of 5 GHSGT subjects
sK20494	% District sites migrated to new Wide Area Network (WAN)
sK20495	% District staff who completed ethics training
sK20496	% District targets met
sK20509	% Drop out rate
sK20512	% Early childhood education teachers on the job less than 2 years
sK20513	% Early childhood education teachers with a bachelor degree
sK20522	% Elementary grades students who were absent 10 or more days during the school year
sK20531	% Employee with goals and objectives aligned to the district Balanced Scorecard
sK20596	% Employment option after graduation
sK20603	% Entering 4 year colleges and universities after graduation
sK20604	% Entering less than 4 year schools after graduation
sK20686	% Full time employees responding to charitable giving campaign
sK20692	% Fund balance in compliance with state accounting requirements
sK20697	% Gender parity index
sK20698	% General education teachers receiving inclusion professional development
sK20699	% General Fund resources spent toward instruction
sK20713	% Grade-3 and grade-6 achievement tests in Language Arts and Mathematics
sK20719	% Gross enrollment rate for grades 1-5
sK20720	% Gross intake rate in Grade 1 of the population of official entry age
sK20762	% High School ACT Scores
sK20763	% High school completion rate
sK20764	% High school Grad Test to state average
sK20765	% High School Grad Writing Test TC/State Average
sK20767	% High School SAT Scores Math
sK20768	% High School SAT Scores Verbal
sK20769	% High school seniors will average at or above the state on the SAT
sK20770	% High school students enrolled in Advanced Placement courses who achieved a score above 3
sK20772	% Highly qualified paraprofessionals
sK20773	% Highly qualified teachers
sK20774	% Highly qualified teachers employed by KRSD
sK20823	% Improvement in learning rate of students
sK20824	% Improvement of public relationships with business partners
sK20825	% Improvement of public relationships with newspaper articles
sK20826	% Improvement of public relationships with websites visitors

sKPI #	Key Performance Indicator name
sK20891	% Instructional employees satisfied with relevance of trainings received
sK20909	% Job related training for district instructional employees
sK20910	% Job related training for district non-instructional employees
sK20919	% Kindergarten students perform on or above grade level in English Language Arts
sK20920	% Kindergarten students perform on or above grade level in Math
sK20921	% Kindergarten students perform on or above grade level in Personal/Social Development
sK20923	% KRHS receiving unconditional NEASC approval
sK20935	% Literacy rate of population aged 15 to 24
sK20949	% Licensed child care facilities that are accredited
sK20954	% Literacy rate of population 15+ years old
sK20971	% Lower-Income children entering kindergarten with "benchmark" literacy-related skills
sK21016	% Middle grades students who were absent 10 or more days during the school year
sK21017	% Middle school students enrolled in courses
sK21073	% Net enrollment rate for grades 1 to 5
sK21077	% New entrants to primary Grade 1 of the official primary school entrance age
sK21078	% New entrants to primary Grade 1 who attended early childhood development programs
sK21102	% Novice classroom teachers who were retained
sK21157	% Parent calls returned within designated time
sK21158	% Parent conference attendance
sK21159	% Parent resource center checkouts
sK21194	% Parents satisfactied with educational programs and services
sK21215	% Participants using parent suggestion box
sK21255	% PASS training participation
sK21328	% Peer acceptance in extracurricular activities by those by whom students were being led by
sK21329	% Peer acceptance in extracurricular activities by those with whom students participated in activities
sK21330	% Peer acceptance in extracurricular activities of those by whom students are sitting with
sK21331	% Peer acceptance in extracurricular activities of those by whom students are studying with
sK21364	% Planned process improvements implemented
sK21415	% Primary school teachers having the required academic qualifications
sK21416	% Primary school teachers who are certified to teach according to national regulations
sK21423	% Principals, assistant principals, academy leaders, and LLS certified on the state teacher evaluation tool
sK21463	% Public expenditure on primary education of total public expenditure on education
sK21515	% Reduction of students identified on PALS as needing intervention

sKPI #	Key Performance Indicator name
sK21535	% Repetition rates at Grade 5
sK21602	% Scheduled hours assessed and passed
sK21606	% School Nutrition Services profitability
sK21607	% School partnerships meeting agreed objectives
sK21608	% Schools accredited
sK21609	% Schools achieving Adequate Yearly Progress (AYP)
sK21610	% Schools meeting Adequate Yearly Progress (AYP)
sK21611	% Schools receiving state unconditional approval
sK21612	% Schools satisfaction with targeted district business units
sK21613	% Schools that made Adequate Yearly Progress (AYP)
sK21620	% Secondary students who were absent 10 or more days during the school year
sK21653	% Special education planned recommendations initiated
sK21654	% Special education recommendations initiated
sK21655	% Special education teachers receiving inclusion professional development
sK21658	% Spending directed to classroom instruction
sK21659	% Staff attendance (certified)
sK21660	% Staff attendance (classified)
sK21684	% Strategic projects on schedule and within budget
sK21690	% Student attendance in "X" grade
sK21691	% Student breakfast participation
sK21692	% Student enrolment rate
sK21693	% Student participation Elem/MS/HS
sK21694	% Student participation in PSAT
sK21696	% Student perform on or above grade level on the GHSGT English
sK21697	% Student perform on or above grade level on the GHSGT Math
sK21698	% Student perform on or above grade level on the GHSGT Science
sK21699	% Student perform on or above grade level on the GHSGT Social Studies
sK21700	% Student to teacher ratio
sK21701	% Student who supports the Tech Plan
sK21702	% Students achieving VA On-Time Graduation Rate overall
sK21734	% Students at levels 2 and 3 perform on or above grade level in English Language Arts
sK21735	% Students at levels 2 and 3 perform on or above grade level in Mathematics
sK21736	% Students at levels 2 and 3 perform on or above grade level in Reading
sK21737	% Students at levels 2 and 3 perform on or above grade level in Science
sK21738	% Students at levels 2 and 3 perform on or above grade level in Social Studies
sK21739	% Students ranking in top quintile in test results
sK21740	% Students above range on PALS-PreK assessment

sKPI #	Key Performance Indicator name
sK21741	% Students at stage 4, 5 or 6 perform on or above grade level in Grade 5 Writing
sK21742	% Students at stage 6 perform above grade level in Grade 5 Writing
sK21746	% Students enrolled in student support services
sK21748	% Students identified eligible for special education services
sK21749	% Students identified on Fall PALS as needing intervention
sK21752	% Students in traditional schools who met or exceeded state standards on the English/Language Arts CRCT in grades 3 through 8
sK21753	% Students in traditional schools who met or exceeded state standards on the Mathematics CRCT in grades 3 through 8
sK21754	% Students in traditional schools who met or exceeded state standards on the Reading CRCT in grades 3 through 8
sK21755	% Students in traditional schools who met or exceeded state standards on the Science CRCT in grades 3 through 8
sK21756	% Students in Voyager Schools identified as emergent
sK21757	% Students in Voyager Schools identified as on track
sK21758	% Students in Voyager Schools identified as struggling
sK21759	% Students meeting growth target
sK21760	% Students meeting promotional requirements
sK21761	% Students participating in after school active
sK21762	% Students participating in honors options
sK21763	% Students participating in SAT
sK21765	% Students perform above grade level in Grade 8 Writing
sK21766	% Students perform on or above grade level in Grade 8 Writing
sK21767	% Students proficient and above in NECAP
sK21768	% Students proficient on eighth grade Technology Literacy Test
sK21769	% Students proficient to NECAP
sK21771	% Students scoring in the upper range on the PALS assessment
sK21776	% Students who reported they feel they can be successful
sK21777	% Students who graduated with a regular diploma within 4 years
sK21778	% Students who report school as a welcoming and friendly place
sK21781	% Students with disabilities receiving state-sanctioned diplomas by diploma type
sK21782	% Students with disabilities who have exited special education services
sK21783	% Students with IEPs spending 80% of time or more in general education classrooms
sK21784	% Students with Parent Portal Login Accounts
sK21819	% Survival rate to Grade 5
sK21827	% Taking up of duties in extracurricular activities
sK21843	% Teacher positions vacant at the end of each quarter

sKPI #	Key Performance Indicator name
sK21844	% Teacher to pupil
sK21845	% Teachers' effective use of techonology
sK21846	% Teachers with educational attainment level of masters and above
sK21852	% Tech Plans that meet standard established
sK21866	% Tests that could have been completed by the school's students but were not assigned a score
sK21884	% Traffic safety training in elementary schools
sK21931	% Unknown career path after graduation
sK21937	% Unqualified audit opinions

Training and Other Education

Training and other education refers to the teaching, examination, graduation and learning activities and their outcomes. It includes other means of education than the ones offered by the academic field and they can require or not, an accreditation. A difference is made between vocational education, mostly undertaken at the workplace and frequently related to up skilling, and non-formal adult education including the learning for personal development. KPIs focus on the quality and attractiveness of the educational offer and act.

sKPI #	Key Performance Indicator name
sK1237	% Business owners satisfied with training program and support materials
sK3072	% Distance learning courses from the whole course portfolio
sK3073	# Updates made to the course materials
sK3079	% Courses delivered with training follow-up completed
sK3095	% Course participants providing feedback at the end of the course
sK3110	% Course participants involved in follow-up X months after the course
sK3137	# Student contact hours (SCH) generated by e-learners
sK3294	% Training session actual attendance rate
sK3297	% E-learners who achieve improved techniques and skills
sK3298	% Course attendees who have or expect to have improved employment outcomes
sK3324	% Client satisfaction with the e-learning experience
sK3342	% Online learning module completion rate
sK3359	% Referrals from previous training attendees
sK3360	# Rating of attendee support
sK3361	# Training participant satisfaction reports available to training managers and course designers
sK3363	% Training participants that have completed pre-course evaluation tests
sK3371	% Training participants that have completed post-course evaluation tests
sK3386	# Meetings with course designers, trainers and evaluators
sK3411	# Follow-up visits conducted after the training
sK4506	% Drop rate of web-based course
sK5616	% Participants who paid to attend the training course

sKPI #	Key Performance Indicator name
sK5796	# Course content partners
sK5804	# Training courses offered
sK5808	% Training courses updated compared to the previous edition
sK5809	% Training sessions updated compared to the previous edition
sK6871	% Employees reaching competence after training
sK6872	# Post training evaluations
sK6873	% Training objectives met
sK6930	% Courses with e-learning components
sK6932	% Trainers who believe increased access to e-learning resources has improved teaching and learning outcomes
sK14288	$ Further education funds invested per trainer
sK14289	# Surveys of employer satisfaction

sKPI #	Key Performance Indicator name
sK14290	# Training providers
sK14291	# Industry training needs
sK14292	% Shares of training market
sK14294	# Demand for existing certifications
sK14322	% Employers of a given sector who are satisfied with programme completers
sK17721	# Learners enrolled in units on providers' online delivery platforms
sK17767	# Length of time for trainees to gain certifications
sK18934	# Surveys of trainee satisfaction
sK19953	% Actual training tracks
sK20930	% Learners enrolled in units on providers' online delivery platforms
sK21887	% Trainers participating at accredited in-service training programmes

Financial Institutions

Financial institutions includes all the activities that take place in an institution that provides financial services, such as deposit-taking institutions, insurance companies and pension funds, brokers, underwriters and investment funds.

Banking and Credit

Banking's core activities include borrowing and lending money. Banks provide almost all payment services, issue debt securities such as banknotes and bonds, and invest in marketable debt securities and other forms of money lending. KPIs consist of specific financial indicators (risk, reserves), as well as measures of efficiency in performing banking operations.

sKPI #	Key Performance Indicator name
sK285	$ Soft prepayment penalty
sK343	% Efficiency ratio
sK344	% Debt service ratio (DS)
sK345	% Gross debt service ratio (GDS)
sK399	% Adjusted return on equity
sK401	% Adjusted return on assets (AROA)
sK402	% Capital adequacy ratio (CAR)
sK403	% Portfolio at risk
sK404	% Financial self-sufficiency
sK405	% Operating self-sufficiency (OSS)
sK406	% Portfolio yield
sK413	% Price-to-income ratio
sK506	% Net interest spread
sK516	% Annual equivalent rate
sK518	% Gross interest rate
sK648	$ Hard prepayment penalty
sK2063	# Debt-service coverage ratio (DSCR)
sK2065	% Loan-to-value (LTV)
sK2066	% Debt-to-income ratio (DTI)
sK2076	% Securitized loans
sK2079	% Probability of default (PD)

sKPI #	Key Performance Indicator name
sK2081	% Estimated rate of recovery
sK2083	$ Unexpected loss (UL)
sK2095	% Unsecured recovery rate
sK2126	% Expected loss given default (ELGD)
sK2451	% Loss given default (LGD)
sK2452	$ Exposure at default (EAD)
sK2453	$ Expected loss from exposure at default (EL)
sK2978	# Corporate credit rating
sK2979	% Credit loss ratio
sK3001	% Maximum loan-to-value ratio
sK3015	% Risk-adjusted capital ratio
sK3060	$ Net interest income (NII)
sK3090	$ Value of loans and investments
sK3105	% Combined loan to value ratio (CLTV ratio)
sK3117	% Front-end ratio
sK3120	% High ratio loans
sK3122	# Liquidity ratio
sK3159	% Operating costs
sK3231	# Years debt
sK3251	# Amortization term
sK3307	$ Prepayment penalty
sK3392	% Reserve ratio
sK3419	% McDonough ratio
sK3426	# Texas ratio
sK3453	% Cooke ratio
sK4016	# Loan officer productivity
sK4526	# Cost per dollar loaned

sKPI #	Key Performance Indicator name
sK4558	# Participatory radio programs airing over a period of 6 months
sK4564	% Operating costs of credit operations
sK4583	$ Client poverty level
sK4586	# Financial services outreach
sK4588	% Cost of funds rate
sK4620	$ Portfolio value per loan officers
sK4640	% Risk coverage ratio
sK4641	% Large credit exposure
sK4806	# Incoming credit applications to branch sales staff
sK5844	% Account rejection rate
sK5867	# Deposits per depositor
sK5885	% Account opening rate
sK5887	% Not in good order account applications (NIGO)
sK5905	% Returned items as a percentage of total transactions
sK5907	% Transactions with incorrect settlement requirements
sK5909	% Shares debited to Depository Trust and Clearing Corporation (DTCC)
sK5910	% Straight through processing
sK5961	$ Cost per loan
sK5962	% Cash collection rate
sK6783	# Deposit accounts per staff member
sK6784	$ Loan balance per borrower
sK6785	# Active loan borrowers
sK6786	# Active loan borrowers per branch
sK6787	# Loan officers employed
sK6810	$ Credit limit per account
sK6811	% Credit applications accepted
sK6815	% Past due accounts
sK6816	# Past due time on delinquent accounts
sK6817	$ Amount past due on delinquent accounts
sK6818	% Available credit line used
sK6819	# New credit inquiries
sK6820	# Length of credit history
sK14404	# Active depositor to dormant depositor
sK14651	# Borrowing risk
sK14775	# Closed bank accounts
sK14784	# Collective bonus potential to provisions
sK14789	# Combined ratio
sK14895	# Cost account surplus to provisions
sK14909	# Credit card cancelling
sK14911	# Credit card replacement
sK14912	# Credit cards issued by the retail bank
sK14966	# Customers served in a day
sK15014	# Default borrowers
sK15015	# Default risk
sK15074	# Depositors per retail bank branch

sKPI #	Key Performance Indicator name
sK15210	# Equity to provisions
sK15221	# Excess solvency to provisions
sK15230	# Expense ratio in health and accident insurance
sK17282	# Withdrawals made by each depositor
sK17844	# Loss ratio
sK17845	# Loss ratio in health and accident insurance
sK18098	# Operating ratio
sK18336	# Policyholders' funds to provisions
sK18427	# Profit on risk elements to provisions
sK18546	# Ratio of expenses to provisions
sK19441	$ Deposits
sK19465	$ Expenses per policyholder
sK19742	$ Return on customers' funds after expenses but before tax
sK19743	$ Return on equity
sK19744	$ Return on investments after tax on pension returns
sK19745	$ Return on investments before tax on pension returns
sK19746	$ Return on members accounts before tax
sK19748	$ Return on subordinated loan capital before tax
sK19749	$ Return on type A bonus provisions before tax
sK20956	% Loan delinquency
sK21598	% Savings out of GDP
sK21878	% Times rates are "better" compared with major banks on mortgages
sK22386	$ New deposit
sK22387	$ Long-term bonds
sK22388	$ Medium-term bonds
sK22389	$ Bonds for individuals
sK22390	# Trusts sold
sK22402	$ Liquid deposits
sK22403	$ Time deposits
sK22404	# Certificates of deposit
sK22405	$ Loans on notes
sK22406	$ Loans on deeds
sK22407	$ Overdrafts
sK22408	$ Notes discounted
sK22409	$ Government bonds
sK22410	$ Local government bonds
sK22411	$ Short-term corporate bonds
sK22412	$ Corporate bonds
sK22413	$ Stock
sK22414	$ Foreign bonds
sK22415	$ Foreign stock
sK22416	$ Investment trust sales
sK22417	# Investment trust sales
sK22418	$ Investment trust accounts
sK22419	# Investment trust accounts

sKPI #	Key Performance Indicator name
sK22420	$ Over-the-counter sales of Japanese government bonds
sK22421	# Mutual remittances sent
sK22422	# Mutual remittances received
sK22423	$ Mutual remittances sent
sK22424	$ Mutual remittances received
sK22425	$ Transfer deposits inpayment
sK22426	$ Transfer deposits outpayment
sK22427	$ Transfer deposits

Insurance

Financial institutions includes all the activities that take place in an institution that provides financial services, such as deposit-taking institutions, insurance companies and pension funds, brokers, underwriters and investment funds.

sKPI #	Key Performance Indicator name
sK161	% Policy renewal rate
sK162	% Missed payments or lapses
sK163	$ Insurance policy value
sK440	# Policy sales
sK446	% Not taken up (NTU) ratio
sK532	% Combined ratio
sK554	% Insurance loss ratio
sK573	# Insurance claim processing time
sK579	# Insurance underwriting time
sK580	# New insurance policies issued
sK581	# Insurance claims processed
sK2994	% Free asset ratio (FAR)
sK3015	% Risk-adjusted capital ratio
sK3090	$ Value of loans and investments
sK3122	# Liquidity ratio
sK3145	# Burning cost ratio
sK4552	$ Incurred but not reported reserve
sK4568	# Profit on risk elements to provisions ratio
sK4574	% Insurance solvency ratio
sK4575	# Claim denials
sK4576	# Claims reported
sK4577	$ Cash claims
sK4578	$ Claims in course of settlement
sK4579	$ Incurred claims
sK4580	% Claims rejection ratio
sK4582	% Promptness of claims settlements
sK4587	# Claim settlement time
sK4590	# Funding expense ratio
sK4593	% Benefits from premium
sK4595	% Expense ratio per line of insurance
sK4597	% Expenses to provisions
sK4598	% Incurred expense ratio

sKPI #	Key Performance Indicator name
sK4605	$ Face value of policies sold
sK4606	% Lapsed policies from sold
sK4607	% Policies that lapsed within the first two years
sK4609	% Policyholders' liabilities to shareholders' funds ratio
sK4610	% Women policy holders
sK4611	% Premium collection rate
sK4616	$ Premium income
sK4617	$ Premium rate charged to clients
sK4619	$ Unearned premium reserve
sK4623	# Ratio of collective bonus potential to provisions
sK4624	% Return on customer funds
sK4639	% Interest rate risk
sK5887	% Not in good order account applications (NIGO)
sK6121	% Screening of uninsured inpatients and high-dollar outpatients for financial assistance
sK6156	# Time to process medicare supplement insurance billing
sK6171	% Denial rate (clinical and technical) out of gross revenue
sK6174	% Additional collection for underpayments
sK6175	% Appeals overturned
sK6176	% Electronic eligibility rate
sK6181	% Underpayments overturn
sK6183	# Medical claim denial reason codes per claim
sK6188	% Overturn denial rate
sK6189	# Clean claim payment duration
sK6208	% Claim denials value from gross revenue
sK14771	# Claims ratio
sK15229	# Expense ratio
sK16822	# Solvency ratio
sK17983	# Net income ratio
sK19332	$ Amount of any additional dollar-based management costs
sK19428	$ Cost per year for the amount of cover
sK19794	$ Service fees
sK20390	% Contribution fee
sK20977	% Management costs for investment option to account
sK21865	% Termination fee
sK21991	% Withdrawal fee
sK22391	# Policies sold
sK22428	# Foreign exchange transactions
sK22429	# Policies in force
sK22430	# Insurance for individuals
sK22431	# Annuities for individuals
sK22432	$ Policies in force
sK22433	$ Insurance for individuals
sK22434	$ Annuities for individuals

Investments

Investments includes legal entities organized to pool securities or other financial assets, without managing, on behalf of shareholders or beneficiaries. The portfolios are customized to achieve specific investment characteristics, such as diversification, risk, rate of return and price volatility. KPIs focus on the achievement of the desired results in the management of portfolios.

sKPI #	Key Performance Indicator name
sK406	% Portfolio yield
sK3002	% Member short-sales ratio
sK3003	% Modified Sharpe ratio
sK3004	# Mutual fund liquidity ratio
sK3012	# Profit/loss ratio
sK3014	# Put-call ratio
sK3015	% Risk-adjusted capital ratio
sK3018	# Sharpe ratio
sK3019	# Short interest ratio
sK3026	# Treynor ratio
sK3090	$ Value of loans and investments
sK3096	% Return on net asset value
sK3119	# Hedge ratio
sK3122	# Liquidity ratio
sK3133	# Up-down capture ratio
sK3139	# After reimbursement expense ratio
sK3288	% Management expense ratio (MER)
sK3319	% Expense ratio (ER)
sK3403	% Administrative expense per gross premium
sK3415	# Information ratio (IR)
sK3416	# K-ratio
sK3420	# Nova/Ursa ratio
sK3425	# Sortino ratio
sK3426	# Texas ratio
sK3428	# Appraisal ratio
sK3431	# Calmar ratio
sK5839	# Account funded to committed account value
sK5840	# Commitments to purchase the security
sK5842	$ Firm exposure
sK5846	% Broker-executed profitable trades
sK5848	# Time of order execution
sK5856	% Rejected trades
sK5859	$ Trades to be settled
sK5861	% Wire transactions under investigation
sK5864	% Unsettled trades
sK5865	% Shares credited to the Depository Trust and Clearing Corporation (DTCC)
sK5870	% Funds transacted by customers
sK5872	% Trades cleared
sK5881	$ Gain or loss on securities lending activity

sKPI #	Key Performance Indicator name
sK5893	% Final bid against published offering
sK5896	% Trades matched on trade date
sK5900	$ Settlement of matched financial trades
sK5903	% On-time trade settlement rate
sK5910	% Straight through processing
sK5962	% Cash collection rate
sK6941	$ Prospective investments in pension funds
sK7043	# Active members of the pension fund
sK14401	# Active clients per loan officer
sK14402	# Active clients per staff member
sK14896	# Cost of funds ratio
sK18096	# Operating Expense ratio
sK18347	# Portfolio yield
sK18660	# Risk coverage ratio
sK19402	$ Cost per borrower
sK19602	$ Median stock price
sK21389	% Portfolio at risk (PAR)
sK22435	$ Underwriting risk
sK22436	$ Assumed interest rate return risk
sK22437	$ Asset management risk
sK22438	$ Business management risk
sK22439	$ Minimum guarantee risk
sK22440	$ Insurance risk for third-sector insurance
sK4810	% Broker-executed trades

Mortgages

Mortgages reflect operations of charging of real (or personal) property by a debtor to a creditor as security for a debt (especially one incurred by the purchase of the property), on the condition that it shall be returned on payment of the debt within a certain period. KPIs reflect mortgage operations efficiency and effectiveness.

sKPI #	Key Performance Indicator name
sK14340	# 30-59 days delinquent government-guaranteed mortgages
sK14341	# 30-59 days delinquent mortgages held by reporting banks and thrift
sK14342	# 30-59 days delinquent mortgages in the portfolio
sK14344	# 60-89 days delinquent mortgages held by reporting banks and thrift
sK14345	# 60-89 days delinquent mortgages in the portfolio
sK14346	# 90 or more days delinquent mortgages held by reporting banks and thrift
sK14347	# 90 or more days delinquent mortgages in the portfolio
sK14503	# Alt-A mortgages in the portfolio
sK14594	# Bankruptcy 30 or more days delinquent mortgages held by reporting banks and thrift
sK14595	# Bankruptcy 30 or more days delinquent mortgages in the portfolio
sK14704	# Capitalization of loans

sKPI #	Key Performance Indicator name
sK14705	# Capitalization of loans for HAMP modifications
sK14746	# Changes in loan terms for modifications made
sK14747	# Changes in loan terms for modifications made by risk category
sK14748	# Changes in terms for combination modifications
sK14788	# Combination modifications
sK14830	# Completed foreclosures
sK14831	# Completed foreclosures and other home forfeiture actions
sK14930	# Current and performing government-guaranteed mortgages
sK14931	# Current and performing mortgages held by reporting banks and thrift
sK14932	# Current and performing mortgages in the portfolio
sK16006	# New home HAMP modifications
sK16008	# New home modifications
sK16010	# New home retention actions
sK16776	# Seriously delinquent mortgages in the portfolio
sK17309	# Foreclosures in process
sK17310	# Foreclosures in process for Alt-A loans
sK17311	# Foreclosures in process for prime loans
sK17312	# Foreclosures in process for subprime loans
sK17313	# Foreclosures in process mortgages held by reporting banks and thrift
sK17314	# Foreclosures in process mortgages in the portfolio
sK17407	# Government-guaranteed mortgages
sK17431	# GSE mortgages
sK17446	# HAMP modifications resulting changes in monthly principal and interest payments
sK17447	# HAMP modifications to Alt-A mortgages
sK17448	# HAMP modifications to Fannie Mae mortgages
sK17449	# HAMP modifications to Freddie Mac mortgages
sK17450	# HAMP modifications to government-guaranteed mortgages
sK17451	# HAMP modifications to portfolio mortgages
sK17452	# HAMP modifications to prime mortgages
sK17453	# HAMP modifications to private mortgages
sK17454	# HAMP modifications to subprime mortgages
sK17948	# Modifications resulting in changes in monthly principal and interest payments
sK17949	# Modifications resulting in a decrease in monthly principal and interest payments
sK17950	# Modifications resulting in an increase in monthly principal and interest payments
sK17951	# Modifications that do not affect the monthly principal and interest payments
sK17957	# Mortgage modification actions implemented by state
sK17958	# Mortgages held by reporting banks and thrift
sK18001	# New deed-in-lieu-of-foreclosure actions
sK18007	# New home HAMP trial-period plans

sKPI #	Key Performance Indicator name
sK18009	# New home payment plans
sK18011	# New home trial-period plans
sK18028	# New short sales
sK18032	# Newly initiated foreclosures
sK18033	# Newly initiated foreclosures for Alt-A loans
sK18034	# Newly initiated foreclosures for prime loans
sK18035	# Newly initiated foreclosures for subprime loans
sK18058	# Not reported changes in loan terms for HAMP modifications
sK18059	# Not reported changes in loan terms for modifications made
sK18402	# Prime mortgages in the portfolio
sK18403	# Principal deferral of loans
sK18404	# Principal deferral of loans for HAMP modifications
sK18405	# Principal reduction of loans
sK18406	# Principal reduction of loans for HAMP modifications
sK18533	# Rate freeze of loans
sK18534	# Rate freeze of loans for HAMP modifications
sK18535	# Rate reduction of loans
sK18536	# Rate reduction of loans for HAMP modifications
sK18774	# Seriously delinquent mortgages held by reporting banks and thrift
sK18793	# Servicing loans
sK18906	# Subprime mortgages in the portfolio
sK18964	# Term extension of loans
sK18965	# Term extension of loans for HAMP modifications
sK19367	$ Variance in monthly payments resulting from HAMP modifications
sK19368	$ Variance in monthly payments resulting from modifications
sK19796	$ Servicing mortgage
sK19892	% 30-59 days delinquent government-guaranteed mortgages
sK19893	% 30-59 days delinquent mortgages held by reporting banks and thrift
sK19894	% 30-59 days delinquent mortgages in the portfolio
sK19895	% 30-59 days delinquent mortgages modified
sK19899	% 60-89 days delinquent mortgages held by reporting banks and thrift
sK19900	% 60-89 days delinquent mortgages in the portfolio
sK19901	% 90 or more days delinquent mortgages held by reporting banks and thrift
sK19902	% 90 or more days delinquent mortgages in the portfolio
sK20037	% Alt-A mortgages 30 to 59 days delinquent
sK20038	% Alt-A mortgages in the portfolio
sK20131	% Bankruptcy 30 or more days delinquent mortgages held by reporting banks and thrift
sK20132	% Bankruptcy 30 or more days delinquent mortgages in the portfolio
sK20187	% Capitalization of loans

sKPI #	Key Performance Indicator name
sK20188	% Capitalization of loans for HAMP modifications
sK20241	% Changes in loan terms for modifications made
sK20242	% Changes in loan terms for modifications made by risk category
sK20243	% Changes in terms for combination modifications
sK20364	% Completed foreclosures relative to mortgages in that risk category
sK20365	% Completed mortgage foreclosures
sK20418	% Current and performing government-guaranteed mortgages
sK20419	% Current and performing mortgages held by reporting banks and thrift
sK20420	% Current and performing mortgages in the portfolio
sK20422	% Current mortgages modified
sK20670	% Foreclosures in process mortgages held by reporting banks and thrift
sK20671	% Foreclosures in process mortgages in the portfolio
sK20672	% Foreclosures in process relative to mortgages in that risk category
sK20710	% Government-guaranteed mortgages
sK20723	% GSE mortgages
sK20729	% HAMP modifications
sK20730	% HAMP modifications resulting changes in monthly principal and interest payments
sK20731	% HAMP mortgage modifications of state total
sK21022	% Modification actions in combination actions
sK21023	% Modifications resulting in changes in monthly principal and interest payments
sK21024	% Modifications resulting in a decrease in monthly principal and interest payments
sK21025	% Modifications resulting in an increase in monthly principal and interest payments
sK21026	% Modifications that do not affect the monthly principal and interest payments
sK21054	% Mortgage foreclosures in process
sK21055	% Mortgage modifications of state total
sK21056	% Mortgage modifications that reduced payments by 10% or more
sK21057	% Mortgage modifications that reduced payments by less than 10%
sK21058	% Mortgages held by reporting banks and thrift
sK21059	% Mortgages modified
sK21060	% Mortgages no longer in the portfolio
sK21061	% Mortgages paid off
sK21081	% New home retention actions relative to forfeiture actions, by risk category
sK21082	% New home retention actions relative to newly initiated foreclosures
sK21100	% Not reported changes in loan terms for HAMP modifications
sK21101	% Not reported changes in loan terms for modifications made

sKPI #	Key Performance Indicator name
sK21417	% Prime mortgages 30 to 59 days delinquent
sK21418	% Prime mortgages in the portfolio
sK21419	% Principal deferral of loans
sK21420	% Principal deferral of loans for HAMP modifications
sK21421	% Principal reduction of loans
sK21422	% Principal reduction of loans for HAMP modifications
sK21485	% Rate freeze of loans
sK21486	% Rate freeze of loans for HAMP modifications
sK21487	% Rate reduction of loans
sK21488	% Rate reduction of loans for HAMP modifications
sK21501	% Re-default rates for Fannie Mae loans
sK21502	% Re-default rates for Freddie Mac loans
sK21503	% Re-default rates for government-guaranteed loans
sK21504	% Re-default rates for loans
sK21505	% Re-default rates for loans 12 months after modification
sK21506	% Re-default rates for loans 3 months after modification
sK21507	% Re-default rates for loans 6 months after modification
sK21508	% Re-default rates for loans 9 months after modification
sK21509	% Re-default rates for portfolio loans
sK21510	% Re-default rates for private loans
sK21511	% Re-default rates of loans modified by change in payment
sK21512	% Re-default rates of loans modified by decrease in payment
sK21513	% Re-default rates of loans modified by increase in payment
sK21624	% Seriously delinquent government-guaranteed mortgages
sK21625	% Seriously delinquent mortgages held by reporting banks and thrift
sK21626	% Seriously delinquent mortgages in the portfolio
sK21628	% Seriously delinquent mortgages modified
sK21786	% Subprime mortgages 30 to 59 days delinquent
sK21787	% Subprime mortgages in the portfolio
sK21861	% Term extension of loans
sK21862	% Term extension of loans for HAMP modifications

Pension Funds

A pension fund is an investment company that manages the assets of employees of a company and disburses the assets to employees upon retirement. Contributions to the fund by both employer and employee finance the pension fund assets.

sKPI #	Key Performance Indicator name
sK14731	# Cases requiring intervention at a senior level
sK14936	# Current pensioners (including spouses' and children's pensions)
sK15005	# Deaths in service
sK15024	# Deferred members

sKPI #	Key Performance Indicator name
sK15025	# Deferred pensioners
sK15073	# Dependents receiving allowances
sK15227	# Expected tracking error
sK17480	# Hits to the pension website
sK17702	# Late notification of previous year leavers
sK17703	# Late notifications
sK17901	# Member satisfaction surveys
sK17902	# Members with access to the pension website
sK18025	# New retirement pensions
sK18029	# New starter opted out before contributions made
sK18030	# New starters
sK18110	# Options pending
sK18151	# Participants in the pension system
sK18265	# Pensioners
sK18371	# Potential prospects in the pension system
sK19315	$ Additional voluntary contributions (AVCs)
sK19348	$ Benefits payable
sK19380	$ Contributions receivable
sK19439	$ Deferred benefits
sK19449	$ Dividends from equities
sK19516	$ Fund manager fees
sK19521	$ Global custody
sK19538	$ Holdings of bank bonds
sK19539	$ Holdings of covered bonds
sK19557	$ Income from fixed-interest securities
sK19558	$ Income from property unit trusts and managed funds
sK19560	$ Individual transfers from other schemes
sK19564	$ Interest on cash deposits
sK19567	$ Investment advisers
sK19569	$ Investment income
sK19570	$ Investment management expenses

sKPI #	Key Performance Indicator name
sK19571	$ Investments in pension funds
sK19588	$ Lump sum death grants
sK19589	$ Lump sum retirement grants
sK19596	$ Market value of investments
sK19597	$ Market value of the Government Pension Fund
sK19618	$ Net additions from dealings with members
sK19619	$ Net assets of the fund
sK19624	$ Net purchases of bank bonds
sK19625	$ Net purchases of covered bonds
sK19626	$ Net returns on investments
sK19631	$ Normal contributions
sK19686	$ Payments to and on account of leavers
sK19690	$ Performance and risk measurement expenses
sK19710	$ Purchase of added years
sK19711	$ Purchase of annuities
sK19719	$ Recapitalisation of financial institutions
sK19721	$ Refunds of contributions
sK19741	$ Retirement and dependents' pensions
sK19802	$ Special contributions
sK19838	$ Transfer values received
sK19839	$ Transfers
sK19882	% 1-year return
sK19920	% Absolute volatility
sK20612	% Excess return
sK21074	% Net real return
sK21148	% Overseas equity
sK21150	% Ownership of equity markets
sK21562	% Return
sK21868	% Three-year rolling annualized excess return
sK21869	% Three-year rolling annualized return

Government - Local

Local public administration includes activities of a governmental nature, normally carried out by the public administration at a local level. This includes the enactment and judicial interpretation of laws and their pursuant regulation, as well as the administration of programs based on them, legislative activities, taxation, public order and safety, immigration services, and the implementation of government programs. KPIs focus on the quality and impact of the service delivery to the local community.

Budget and Finance

Budget and Finance covers matters relating to the local administration's budget execution and also fiscal-related issues such as local tax management. KPIs in this area focus on the efficiency and effectiveness of the local budget management and implementation of the fiscal policies.

sKPI #	Key Performance Indicator name
sK356	% Tax collected on time
sK357	$ Net cost of tax collection

sKPI #	Key Performance Indicator name
sK2791	% Purchasing share of public sector spending
sK5222	$ Revenue generated from the sale of local community surplus goods
sK5229	% Family homes market value from sales price
sK5230	# Time to record a property interest from transfer date
sK5232	% Increase in tax liability as a result of audits
sK5235	# Time to issue a property tax refund

Organizational » Industries

sKPI #	Key Performance Indicator name
sK5236	# Time to issue a business tax refund
sK5240	% City debt resolved
sK5241	% Property taxes paid on time
sK5242	# Time to render tax conciliation decisions
sK5245	$ Financial recoveries to the city ordered / agreed
sK5246	$ Financial recoveries to the city collected
sK5268	$ Net expenditure per head of population
sK5269	# Time for processing new claims for council tax benefit
sK5270	# Time for processing new claims for housing benefit
sK5271	# Time for paying new claims for rent allowance
sK5272	% Renewal claims for rent allowance paid on time
sK5273	# Benefit claimants
sK5275	% Amount of benefit overpayment
sK5276	% Recoverable overpayment recovered
sK5277	% Council tax received by the authority
sK5278	% Business rates collected
sK5279	$ Net cost of collecting council tax per chargeable dwelling
sK5280	$ Net spending per resident
sK5282	% Council tax collection rate
sK5397	$ Net spending per capita on environmental health and consumer protection
sK5556	# Changes in Housing Benefit and/or Council Tax Benefit entitlements
sK5935	$ Funding per individual reached
sK14438	# Adults and older people receiving direct payments
sK19806	$ Spent by the local authority on advice and guidance services provided by external organisations
sK19807	$ Spent on Advice and Guidance in the areas of housing, welfare benefits and consumer matters which is provided directly by the authority to the public
sK21027	% Monies spent on advice and guidance services provision which was given to organisations holding the CLS Quality Mark at "General Help" level or above
sK22787	$ GVA (Gross value added)
sK22788	$ GVA (Gross value added) per capita
sK22792	% Void rate across all stock
sK22793	% Properties in council tax bands to H in the inner score

Community - Quality of Life

Community – Quality of Life covers all essential community demographics, growth trends, age, gender race, marital status, but also the community quality of life or well being status. KPIs focus on population's main characteristics, such as: life expectancy, standard of living, wealth and employment, general physical and mental health, as well as general aspects related to social being, becoming and belonging.

sKPI #	Key Performance Indicator name
sK340	% Civic participation in the local area
sK3926	# Adults with a severe and persistent mental illness in the community served
sK4149	% Under-five child mortality rate

sKPI #	Key Performance Indicator name
sK4217	# Orphans
sK4365	# Children with a disability
sK5260	# Citizens
sK5575	# Child abuse and/or neglect allegation rate
sK5583	# Suicide reports
sK5609	% Adult population smoking rate
sK5628	% Perceptions that residents of the reference area treat one another with respect and dignity
sK5629	% People satisfaction with the way the police and local council dealt with anti-social behavior
sK5632	% Understanding of local concerns about anti-social behavior and crime by the local council and police
sK5661	% Children adoption rate
sK5702	# Deaths due to drug abuse
sK5705	# New adults AIDS cases diagnosed
sK5706	# New syphilis cases diagnosed
sK5707	# New tuberculosis cases diagnosed
sK5714	% Infant mortality rate
sK5938	# Public recognition awards within the community
sK5951	# Children and youth participating in community projects
sK5998	% Local population of working age who are economically inactive
sK5999	% People with mental health problems in employment
sK6002	% People with mental health problems who have maintained paid employment for more than one year in lifetime
sK22797	% Improved street and environmental cleanliness
sK22798	# Level of litter
sK22799	# Detritus
sK22801	# Households living in temporary accommodation
sK22802	% People satisfied with cleanliness standards
sK22813	% Satisfaction of people over 65 with both home and neighbourhood
sK22814	% People who feel they can influence decisions in their locality
sK22815	% People who believe people from different backgrounds get on well together in their local area
sK22818	# Children in care
sK22831	% Inequality gap in the achievement of a level 3 qualification by the age of 19
sK22832	% Inequality gap in the achievement of a level 2 qualification by the age of 20

Culture, Recreation and Entertainment

Culture, Recreation and Entertainment covers all leisure and recreational activities and events that are organized and managed in the local community. KPIs in this area focus on the impact of cultural and recreational activities on the citizens, level of involvement and participation, as well as community ability to offer a high quality of life outside the workplace.

sKPI #	Key Performance Indicator name
sK3064	% Design integrity index (DII)
sK5292	% Libraries open 6 days per week
sK5295	# Local community libraries attendance
sK5296	# Library card holders
sK5306	# Library Internet terminals available per 10,000 people
sK5307	# Public library Internet terminals available for access
sK5336	# Recreation center attendance
sK5337	# Swimming pools attendance
sK5338	# Time recreation centers are open per week
sK5364	% Utilization of community centers by youngsters
sK5365	# Attendance in community centers by category age
sK5378	# Swims and other leisure visits per 1,000 population
sK5380	# Public playgrounds and play areas per 1,000 children
sK5381	# Sports pitches available to the public
sK5382	$ Net spending per capita on sport, recreation and entertainment activities
sK5383	# Museums operated or supported by the authority
sK5385	# Museum visits in person per 1,000 population
sK5386	$ Cost per visit at museum
sK5420	# Items loaned by public libraries per head of population
sK5421	# Public libraries visits per population
sK5422	# Books and recordings available in the public libraries per head of population
sK5423	# Public libraries open 45 hours or more per week
sK5424	# Operational mobile libraries
sK5425	% Library users who found the book(s) they wanted and/or the information they needed
sK5426	% Patrons satisfied with library staff and opening hours
sK5524	# Attendance at special events and festival
sK5657	# Loans per volume held
sK5658	# Locations served by mobile libraries
sK5662	# Active professionally qualified librarians
sK5664	$ Library expenditure on electronic resources
sK5673	$ Public library expenditure per resident
sK5681	# Loans per full-time equivalent (FTE) library staff member
sK5708	# Locations served on average by mobile library
sK5730	% Library service points with Internet terminals
sK5734	# Library service points per 100,000 residents
sK5746	# Operational library service points
sK5747	# Population served per library service point

sKPI #	Key Performance Indicator name
sK5752	$ Library materials expenditure
sK5756	$ Library materials expenditure per capita
sK5933	% Amusement attractions found in compliance with safety requirements on first inspection

Economic & Business Affairs

Economic & Business Affairs concerns all activities that support and manage the economic development of the local community. KPIs in this area focus on efficiency, effectiveness and productivity of the local economy, development of commercial parks, employment and support of the business community development.

sKPI #	Key Performance Indicator name
sK135	% Hotel occupancy
sK4991	$ Cost per trademark registered
sK4993	$ Cost per patent reviewed
sK4997	# Jobs created and retained in distressed communities
sK5220	% Civic construction projects completed early or on time
sK5281	# Violations issued at public wholesale markets
sK5288	# Public wholesale market registrations approved
sK5353	% Medallions confiscated as a result of inspections
sK5369	% Active capital projects in construction phase on schedule
sK5395	% Food premises inspections carried out
sK5396	# Consumer protection visits per high and medium risk premise
sK5455	# Construction inspections per inspector day
sK5461	# Time to approve carting licenses
sK5462	# Time to approve carting registrations
sK5463	# Age of pending carting applications
sK5465	% Carting license applications denied
sK5466	% Carting registration applications denied
sK5467	# Violations for unlicensed business activity
sK5468	# Time to approve public wholesale markets registrations
sK5469	% Public wholesale markets applications denied
sK5470	% Complaints resolved to the satisfaction of the businesses and consumers
sK5471	# Business or consumer complaints processing time
sK5472	# Complaints resolved to the satisfaction of the businesses and consumers
sK5473	$ Restitution awarded to consumers and businesses in complaint cases
sK5474	# Processing time of basic license applications
sK5475	# Licensing center wait time
sK5476	% Inspected stores complying with tobacco regulations
sK5477	% Stores complying with tobacco regulation on a follow-up inspection after a previous tobacco violation
sK5478	% License law compliance rate
sK5479	% Fines collected within 45 days of assessment
sK5480	$ New private investment related to sale and long lease of city owned property

sKPI #	Key Performance Indicator name
sK5481	# Projected jobs created or retained in connection with the sale and/or long term lease of city owned property
sK5482	# Projected jobs created in connection with industrial development contracts
sK5483	$ City tax revenue generated by closed industrial development contracts
sK5484	% Unemployment rate
sK5485	% Minority and women owned business enterprise re-certification rate
sK5486	# Minority and women owned business enterprises certified
sK5487	# City contracts awarded
sK5488	# Workforce system wide job placements
sK5490	# Business development loans awarded to businesses through city programs
sK5491	# Unique businesses receiving public loans
sK5492	# Recruit to hire ratio for job placements
sK5493	# Businesses awarded city training funds
sK5495	# City blocks receiving supplemental sanitation services
sK5498	# Days to receive a for-hire vehicle driver's license from initial application
sK5503	% Car stop compliance rate
sK5504	$ Public and private reinvestment in the local community
sK5505	# Net new businesses generated in the local community
sK5506	$ Cost per new business created in the local community
sK5507	$ Reinvestment per community
sK5508	# Net new jobs generated in the local community
sK5509	$ Ratio of reinvestment into the community
sK5510	$ Cost per job created in the local community
sK5514	# Restaurants operating in the local community
sK5515	# Personal services businesses operating in the local community
sK5516	# Location neutral businesses operating in the local community
sK5517	# Chain stores operating in the local community
sK5518	$ Retail sales volume of local community businesses
sK5519	# Retail businesses operating in the local community
sK5521	# Housing units developed in the local community
sK5522	% Businesses in the local community with websites
sK5523	# Franchise businesses in the local community
sK5526	# Quick stop shopping opportunities present in the local community
sK5527	# New housing development projects initiated in the local community
sK5528	# Residential redevelopments completed through local administration incentive programs
sK5530	$ New downtown construction value
sK5531	# Employees working downtown
sK5533	$ Local administration revenues from short term parking
sK5534	% Street front retail vacancy
sK5536	# Community development initiatives embarked on

sKPI #	Key Performance Indicator name
sK5537	$ Shop rents collected
sK5540	% Working age people from ethnic minorities
sK5542	# New homes build on brown field sites
sK5544	# Working age people receiving out of work benefits
sK5545	% Working age people on out of work benefits
sK5546	% Working age people claiming out of work benefits in economically challenged neighborhoods
sK5550	% Supply of ready to develop housing sites
sK5551	% Previously developed land vacant or derelict for more than 5 years
sK5552	# Business registrations rate per 10,000 adult population
sK5553	% Value Added Tax (VAT) registered businesses showing growth
sK5554	# Surface of previously developed land vacant or derelict
sK5555	% Level of skills gaps reported in the current workforce by employers
sK5558	% Satisfaction of businesses with local authority regulation services
sK5560	% Food establishments compliant with food hygiene law
sK5778	% Unemployment rate of working age people from ethnic minorities
sK5779	# Working age people with disabilities
sK5782	# Working age people from ethnic backgrounds
sK5783	$ Loans awarded to businesses through city programs
sK20961	% Local Development Scheme (LDS) milestones met by the Local Planning Authority
sK20962	% Local Development Scheme (LDS) programs up-to-date
sK21038	% Monitoring reports published on time by the local planning authority
sK22791	% New business registration rate

Environment

Environment covers all essential activities linked with the nurture, protection and management of the community natural physical assets, such as water, air, parks, energy or street. KPIs focus on the ability to manage a sustainable, clean and environmental friendly local community.

sKPI #	Key Performance Indicator name
sK359	$ Spending per head of population on street cleaning
sK1973	% Public water bodies in which invasive aquatic plants are under maintenance control
sK2736	% Population exposed to ozone levels above standards
sK5221	# Estimated greenhouse gas emissions reduction due to local administration energy conservation projects
sK5223	% Citywide fleet that is hybrid or uses alternative fuel
sK5227	# Time to complete environmental review applications
sK5228	% Environmental review applications completed within the established time frame
sK5310	# Catch basin complaints received
sK5320	# Chlorofluorocarbon or freon appliance recoveries
sK5321	# Days to close air quality complaints

sKPI #	Key Performance Indicator name
sK5322	# Noise complaints received
sK5323	# Days to close noise complaints
sK5324	$ Paper recycling revenue per tonne
sK5325	# Days to close asbestos complaints
sK5326	$ Recycling collection cost per tonne
sK5327	% Missed refuse collection rate
sK5328	$ Waste disposal cost per tonne
sK5329	$ Refuse collection cost per tonne
sK5333	# Trees planted in parks
sK5334	# Public service requests received for forestry work
sK5335	# Street trees removed in response to a service request
sK5339	# Snow overtime incurred
sK5340	% Streets rated acceptably clean
sK5341	# Graffiti sites cleaned
sK5342	# Refuse tons collected per truck shift
sK5343	# Trucks dumped on shift
sK5344	# Recycling waste collected per shift
sK5345	% Curbside and containerized recycling diversion rate
sK5346	% Recycling diversion rate
sK5348	# Quantity of waste disposed
sK5350	% Dual bin collection trucks outage rate
sK5351	% Front load collection truck outage rate
sK5355	# Surface of graffiti removed
sK5357	% Archeology applications reviewed within the established time
sK5368	# Archeology applications received
sK5371	# Household waste collections missed per 100,000 collections
sK5372	% Missed collections solved by the end of the next working day
sK5373	$ Net cost of refuse collection per household
sK5379	% Monuments receiving annual maintenance
sK5387	% Highways length that are of a high standard of cleanliness
sK5388	% Highways length of an acceptable standard of cleanliness
sK5389	# Time taken to remove fly-tips from public land
sK5390	$ Net spending per capita on street cleaning
sK5437	% Tonnage of household waste which has been recycled
sK5439	% Tonnage of household waste sent for composting
sK5442	# Waste quantity collected per household
sK5443	# Waste collections missed per 100,000 households
sK5450	% Carbon dioxide (CO2) reduction from local authority operations
sK5451	# CO2 emissions per capita
sK5453	% Municipal waste land filled
sK5563	# Days the sewage treatment plant didn't operate at required standards
sK5565	# Air quality complaints received

sKPI #	Key Performance Indicator name
sK5566	# Asbestos complaints received
sK5775	# Tonnage of household waste sent for composting
sK6395	# Outdoor air pollution
sK6396	# Sulfur dioxide emissions per populated land area
sK6397	# Nitrogen dioxide emissions per populated land area
sK6399	# Ecosystem ozone
sK6400	# Water quality index
sK6401	% Water stress index
sK6402	# Water scarcity index
sK6404	% Marine protected area
sK6413	# Industrial greenhouse gas emissions intensity
sK6414	# Greenhouse gas emissions per capita
sK6415	# Carbon dioxide emissions per kilowatt of electricity generated
sK17528	# Household waste arisings which have been landfilled
sK17529	# Household waste arisings which have been used to recover heat, power and other energy sources
sK17530	# Household waste arisings which have been sent by the Authority for recycling
sK17531	# Household waste collected per head of the population
sK17532	# Household waste sent by the Authority for composting or treatment by anaerobic digestion
sK19866	$ Waste disposal per tonne for municipal waste
sK20809	% Household waste arisings which have been used to recover heat, power and other energy sources
sK20810	% Household waste arisings which have been landfilled
sK20811	% Household waste arisings which have been sent by the Authority for recycling
sK21029	% Monitored freshwater species not at risk: other fish
sK21030	% Monitored freshwater species not at risk: other organisms (amphibs, molluscs)
sK21031	% Monitored freshwater species not at risk: salmonids
sK21032	% Monitored marine species not at risk: fish
sK21033	% Monitored marine species not at risk: other (mammals only - plant data n/a)
sK21034	% Monitored marine species not at risk: shellfish
sK21035	% Monitored terrestrial species not at risk: invetebrates
sK21036	% Monitored terrestrial species not at risk: plants
sK21037	% Monitored terrestrial species not at risk: vertebrates
sK21983	% Waste sent by the Authority for composting or treatment by anaerobic digestion
sK21984	% Wastewater discharge permits issued within the target time period or less
sK22757	# Emissions from utility boilers
sK22758	# Petrol and diesel used by staff and van hire fleet
sK22759	# General office waste, which includes a mixture of paper, card, wood, plastics and metals
sK22760	# General office waste recycled, primarily cardboard
sK22761	# Directly purchased electricity, which generates Greenhouse Gases including CO2 emissions

sKPI #	Key Performance Indicator name
sK22762	% Conversion of tonnes of oil used in heating boilers to tonnes of CO_2 emitted
sK22763	% Conversion of Combined Heat and Power kWh to tonnes of CO_2 emitted
sK22764	% Electricity conversion factors
sK22765	# Typical process emissions
sK22766	% Greenhouse gas conversion protocols
sK22767	% Conversion of miles travelled in medium-sized petrol car to tonnes of CO_2 emitted
sK22768	# Acid rain and smog precursors
sK22769	# Dust and particles
sK22771	# Volatile organic compounds
sK22773	# Nutrients and organic pollutants
sK22775	# Pesticides and fertilizers
sK22777	# Acids and organic pollutant emissions to land
sK22778	# Waste (recycling, recovery and landfill)
sK22781	# Natural gas
sK22782	# Agricultural produce
sK22796	% Household waste sent for reuse, recycling and composting
sK22849	# Doublesides printing
sK22850	# Photocopiers doublesiding
sK22851	% Waste diverted from landfill
sK22852	% Contamination
sK22853	# Litter at hot spots and target areas
sK22854	# Plastic bag consumption

General Local Administration

General Local Administration concerns all activities that relate to establishing and managing policies by the local administration. KPIs in this area focus on aspects that include the efficiency, effectiveness and productivity of the local public administration departments.

sKPI #	Key Performance Indicator name
sK177	$ Government land action cost
sK388	# e-Public sector as an active partner in the innovation system
sK391	% Online public procurement
sK392	% Public authorities' online presence
sK393	% e-Authentication across population
sK3657	# Daily number of passengers arriving in the city
sK3912	# Journey distance by main mode
sK3928	# Journey time to work
sK5216	# Days from civil service exam administration to list establishment
sK5218	% Local administration building space that receives acceptable ratings for cleanliness and maintenance
sK5225	# Time to refer land use applications
sK5226	% Land use applications referred within a specific time frame

sKPI #	Key Performance Indicator name
sK5233	# Turnaround time for in person parking ticket hearings
sK5237	# Time to issue refunds for parking tickets, appeals and towing charges
sK5238	% Parking tickets issued that are paid within the established time frame
sK5239	% Parking tickets that are dismissed within the established time frame
sK5243	# Time to issue decision for parking tickets appeals
sK5244	% Parking tickets appeals granted a reversal
sK5252	# Response time to agency requests for records stored in the public archive
sK5253	# Response time to historical photo requests
sK5254	# Photographic reproduction requests received
sK5255	% Archives capacity available for new accessions
sK5256	% Vital library record requests responded to within the established time frame
sK5257	# Response time to vital record requests
sK5259	# State of town center environmental quality
sK5261	# Authority's buildings open to the public
sK5262	# Buildings in which all public areas are suitable for and accessible to disabled persons
sK5263	% Householder planning applications decided within the established time frame
sK5264	% Non-householder planning applications decided within the established time frame
sK5265	# Decisions on planning appeals reported
sK5266	% Successful appeals to planning decision appeals
sK5267	% Local community population covered by a unitary local development plan
sK5274	$ Cost of administration per claimant
sK5284	# Time to process new claims
sK5285	% Responsive repairs completed within established time frame
sK5286	# Time taken to process reports of abandoned vehicles
sK5287	# Abandoned vehicles reported
sK5354	# Individual landmarks and historic buildings designated
sK5384	% Public administration online forms available
sK5419	# Tenderers registered per public tender
sK5496	# Time to process a hearing decision
sK5497	# Days to issue a medallion driver's license
sK5499	# Time to conduct a safety and emissions inspection of a licensed vehicle
sK5500	% Vehicles safety inspection failure rate
sK5502	# Time from a consumer's request for a hearing to the hearing close date
sK5547	# Public administration online forms submitted monthly by the public
sK5712	# Response time for mailed requests for birth certificates
sK5713	# Response time for mailed requests for death certificates

sKPI #	Key Performance Indicator name
sK6732	% Elections turnout
sK6733	% Eligible population who voted online
sK17780	# Level of the CRE Standard for local government to which the authority conforms
sK18341	# Population of the city
sK20517	% Economically active population from ethnic minority communities in the authority area
sK20518	% Economically active population who have a disability
sK20958	% Local authority employees from ethnic minority communities in the authority area
sK20959	% Local authority employees with a disability
sK22845	# Presentations, support from councillors, senior management
sK22846	# Team members and departmental representation
sK22847	# Strategic action plan developed
sK22848	# Consistent signage introduced contracts implemented

Public Safety

Local Public Safety concerns the protection and prevention from events that can endanger the security and safety of the citizens. KPIs in this area focus on the effectiveness and ability of the authorities to prevent and fight against crime, significant damage, injury and harm and natural or manmade disasters, such as terrorist attacks

sKPI #	Key Performance Indicator name
sK211	% Crimes against visitors
sK358	# Domestic burglaries per 1,000 households
sK1094	% Incidents satisfactorily managed
sK2728	% Suicide rate
sK3994	# Public safety cases by category
sK4012	# Active missing children cases
sK4013	% Registered sexual offenders identified to the public
sK4021	% Youth who remain crime free one year after release
sK4062	# Population in home detention
sK4080	% Random inmate drug tests that are negative
sK4343	# Domestic violence incidents
sK4368	# Civil protection orders
sK4967	% Fugitives apprehended or cleared
sK5071	# Properties provided with storm water drainage facilities
sK5258	% Perception of safety and occurrence of crime
sK5283	# Case closures per investigator
sK5305	# Inmates involved in vocational skills training programs
sK5309	# Inmate health clinic visits
sK5330	# Fire safety education presentations completed
sK5347	# Counter terrorism training hours conducted
sK5349	# Gang motivated incidents
sK5352	# Fire weapons seized during arrests
sK5366	# Major felony crimes in public housing developments

sKPI #	Key Performance Indicator name
sK5435	# Incidents of unsafe facade conditions and falling debris resulting in injuries
sK5444	# Complaints for unsafe facade conditions and falling debris received
sK5501	% Medallion safety and emissions inspections completed on time
sK5529	# Traffic monitoring cameras installed
sK5535	# Speed humps installed near schools
sK5561	% Samples testing positive for coliform bacteria
sK5562	# Drinking water tests above maximum contaminant level
sK5567	$ Daily cost per juvenile in detention
sK5568	# Population in detention
sK5569	# Combined average length of stay in secure and non secure detention
sK5570	# Escapes from secure detention facilities
sK5571	# Youth on youth assaults and altercations resulting in injury
sK5572	# Youth on staff assaults and altercations resulting in injury
sK5574	# Abscond rate in non-secure detention
sK5577	% Residents in detention seen within 24 hours of sick call report
sK5579	% Youth with previous admissions to detention
sK5581	# Stabbings and slashing reports
sK5582	# Assaults on staff by service category
sK5584	% Pre-sentence investigation reports on adults cases submitted 24 hours prior to scheduled hearing
sK5585	% Family court juvenile cases with investigations and reports submitted on time
sK5586	% Rearrest rate of adults on probation
sK5587	% Adult police arrest that are probationers
sK5588	% Juvenile delinquency cases diverted from court through adjustment
sK5589	% Juvenile probationer rearrest rate
sK5590	% Juvenile police arrests that are probationers
sK5591	# Time to respond to traffic signal defects and make the traffic safe
sK5592	# Citywide traffic fatalities
sK5593	# Traffic crashes
sK5594	# Major felonies in parks
sK5596	# Response time to life threatening medical emergencies by ambulance units
sK5597	# Combined response time to life threatening medical emergencies by ambulance and fire units
sK5598	# Response time to structural fires
sK5599	# Civilian fire fatalities
sK5600	# Critical fires per 1000 structural fires
sK5602	# Firefighter burns and injuries while on duty
sK5604	# Major felony crime by category
sK5608	# Women who die from intimate partner homicide per 100,000 women

sKPI #	Key Performance Indicator name
sK5612	# Major felony crimes in housing developments
sK5613	# Major felony crime in transit system
sK5614	# Response time to all crimes in progress
sK5615	# Public safety field exercises or drills held
sK5617	% Emergency response training goal met
sK5618	# Community Emergency Response Team (CERT) volunteer hours
sK5619	# Racial incidents per 100,000 residents
sK5621	% Racial incidents that resulted in further action
sK5622	# Violent crimes per 1000 residents
sK5623	# Serious acquisitive crimes per 1000 population
sK5624	% Perceptions of anti-social behavior
sK5625	% Adult re-offending rates for those under probation supervision
sK5626	% Proven re-offending rate by young offenders
sK5627	# Assault with less serious injury offenses per 1000 population
sK5628	% Perceptions that residents of the reference area treat one another with respect and dignity
sK5629	% People satisfaction with the way the police and local council dealt with anti-social behavior
sK5631	% Specialist support to victims of a serious sexual offense
sK5632	% Understanding of local concerns about anti-social behavior and crime by the local council and police
sK5633	# Serious violent knife crimes per 1000 residents
sK5634	# Gun crimes per 1000 residents
sK5635	% Re-offending rate of prolific and priority offenders
sK5636	% Re-offending rate of registered sex offenders
sK5637	% Repeat incidents of domestic violence
sK5638	# Domestic violence homicide victims
sK5639	# Protection level against terrorist attacks
sK5640	% Awareness of civil protection arrangements in the local area
sK5641	% Drug-related offending rate
sK5642	# Hospital admissions for alcohol related harm per 100,000 residents
sK5644	% Perception of drunk or rowdy behavior as a problem
sK5645	% Perceptions of drug use or drug dealing as a problem
sK5646	% Young people within the youth justice system being sentenced to custody
sK5648	% Young offender engagement in suitable education, employment or training
sK5649	% Young offenders access to suitable accommodation
sK5652	# Primary fires per 100,000 population
sK5697	# Weapons recovered per day
sK5784	# Non fatal casualties per 100,000
sK5785	# Fatalities due to primary fires per 100,000 population
sK6040	% Victims killed or injured by released offenders
sK6755	# Intervention response time
sK6756	% Property crimes clearance rate

sKPI #	Key Performance Indicator name
sK14757	# Children killed or seriously injured (KSI) in road traffic collisions
sK14990	# Days of temporary traffic controls or road closure on traffic sensitive roads
sK17225	# Violent crime per year 1,000 population in the local authority area
sK17836	# Local bus passenger journeys originating in the authority area undertaken each year
sK18269	# People killed or seriously injured (KSI) in road traffic collisions
sK18273	# People slightly injured in road traffic collisions
sK18676	# Robberies per year, per 1,000 population in the local authority area
sK19203	# Vehicle crimes per 1,000 population
sK20248	# Children in road traffic collisions
sK20249	% Children killed or seriously injured (KSI) in road traffic collisions since previous year
sK21155	% Panning applications determined within 13 weeks
sK21335	% People killed or seriously injured (KSI) in road traffic collisions
sK21336	% People slightly injured in road traffic collisions
sK22804	% Proven re-offending by young offenders
sK22805	% Serious violent crime rate
sK22806	# ASB incidents reported per 1,000 population to the police
sK22807	# Repeat incidents of domestic violence
sK22808	% Re-offending rate of prolific and other priority offenders
sK22809	% Gun crime rate
sK22810	% People who strongly agree or tend to agree that the police and local authority are dealing with anti-social behavior and crime in their area
sK22842	# Sworn Officers
sK22843	# Violent Crimes
sK22844	# Property Crimes

Public Services

Local Public Services refers to all activities performed by the local administration directly or indirectly, by financing private provision of services for the benefit of the citizens. KPIs in this area focus on aspects of efficiency, effectiveness and productivity of services, such as general commodities provision, public transportation, telecommunication, environment protection, access to public libraries and archives, or town planning.

sKPI #	Key Performance Indicator name
sK260	% Ground crew trained
sK351	# Building rehabilitation projects
sK354	% Pedestrian crossings with facilities for people living with disabilities
sK373	# Frequency of public transport services
sK374	% On-time performance for public transport services
sK389	% Government basic services available online
sK390	% Maturity of online public service delivery

sKPI #	Key Performance Indicator name
sK394	% Citizens satisfied with the public service responsiveness
sK3577	$ Road rehabilitation expenditure per paved mile
sK3623	% Functional traffic signs
sK3640	# Footbridges under administration
sK3641	# Urban accessibility to public transport
sK3645	# Lane kilometers of arterial roads per 1000 residents
sK3684	# Repair time for road defects
sK3685	# Time for the repair of broken street lights
sK3688	% Congested intersections for which a solution has been designed
sK3882	% Coverage of public transport network
sK3892	% Main streets lengths that have been aesthetically customized
sK3893	% Planned public transport investment for which land is allocated
sK3894	% Planned public transport investment for which funding is allocated
sK3895	% Planned public transport investment completed
sK3905	% Journeys made on foot
sK3909	% Motorised trips to work by public transport
sK3911	# Distance for residents to the closest public transport station
sK3919	% Vehicles complying with the safety public transportation standards
sK3925	% Residents satisfied with roads quality and ease of travel
sK3927	% Satisfaction with public transport
sK3929	# Days of traffic disruption for public roads and highways infrastructure works
sK3932	# Travel time for work trips by public transport
sK4083	# Emergency medical services providers licensed
sK4978	# Daily metered water consumption per capita
sK4979	# Gross volume of water resource available
sK4980	% Water connection rate
sK5010	% Population with access to piped water
sK5012	# Population residing in the utility service area
sK5040	$ Revenue per cubic meter of water billed
sK5044	$ Operating expenses per cubic meter of water billed
sK5046	$ Connection charge for water
sK5047	$ Connection charge for sewerage
sK5049	# Water wells installed
sK5050	% Water coverage
sK5053	% Sewerage services coverage
sK5056	# Population supplied with water
sK5061	# Operational sewage treatment plants
sK5063	# Population with sewerage connections
sK5155	% Urban properties without sewerage service
sK5169	# Frequency of unplanned interruptions per 1000 properties
sK5197	% Waste disposed via landfill

sKPI #	Key Performance Indicator name
sK5251	% Inspected public phones deemed operable
sK5316	# Street cave-in complaints received
sK5317	# Time to respond to street cave-in complaints
sK5319	% Intersections operating above capacity
sK5331	% Spray showers in service
sK5332	% Drinking fountains in service
sK5356	% Investigations resulting in enforcement actions
sK5358	# Elevator related fatalities
sK5359	% Elevator outages due to vandalism
sK5360	# Time to resolve elevator outages
sK5361	# Outage per elevator per month
sK5362	# Alleged elevator injuries reported
sK5363	# Public housing apartments available for occupation
sK5367	% Elevator service uptime rate
sK5370	# Buildings rehabilitation completed
sK5375	% Relevant repairs completed within government time limits
sK5376	% Repair jobs for which an appointment was both made and kept by the authority
sK5391	# Public conveniences opened for more than 12 hours a day
sK5392	# Public conveniences opened for less than 12 hours a day
sK5393	# Public conveniences providing access for people living with disabilities
sK5398	% Children under five in public maintained schools
sK5399	# Students permanently expelled from local authority schools per 1,000 students
sK5400	% Permanently expelled pupils attending less than ten hours a week of alternative tuition
sK5401	# Absences per pupil in secondary schools
sK5402	% Unauthorized absences in secondary schools
sK5403	% Unfilled places in schools
sK5404	% Pupils in excess of school capacity in secondary schools
sK5405	% School classes below standard number of pupils
sK5406	$ Expenditure per pupil in local authority schools
sK5407	% Pupils in local authority schools passing national tests
sK5408	# Points score per local authority secondary pupil in national exams
sK5409	% Primary pupils in local authority schools where meals are available to all full-time pupils
sK5410	% Human remains recovered following a disaster or mass fatality incident
sK5411	$ Price per primary school meal
sK5412	% Pupils with statements of special educational need
sK5413	# Statements of special education needs issued
sK5414	% Pupils placed by a government authority in special schools
sK5415	# Enrollments in adult education courses per 1,000 adult residents

sKPI #	Key Performance Indicator name
sK5416	# Hours adult students are enrolled in for adult education classes per 1,000 adult population
sK5417	% Human remains identified following a disaster
sK5418	$ Adult education spending per head of adult resident
sK5427	% Streetlights not working as planned
sK5428	% Critical roads and pavements damage repairs which were carried out within 24 hours
sK5430	% Principal roads that reached the point at which repairs to prolong their future life should be considered
sK5431	# Days of major roadworks per mile of busy road
sK5434	% Signposted footpaths and other rights of way
sK5436	$ Net expenditure per resident by service category
sK5438	% Public services to citizens delivered electronically
sK5440	% Length of footpaths easy to use by the public
sK5441	% Principal roads not needing major repairs
sK5446	% Schools judged as having good or outstanding standards of behaviour
sK5447	% Persistent absence rate for school pupils
sK5448	# Time spent by a school subjected to special measures
sK5449	# Schools in special administrative or performance related supervision measures
sK5456	# Congestion journey time per mile during morning peak
sK5457	# Parking meters installed
sK5458	# Local bus and light rail passenger journeys originating in the authority area
sK5459	% Electronic parking meters
sK5460	% Local authority tenants' satisfaction with landlord services
sK5489	% Traffic signals installed within scheduled time from approval
sK5494	# Bicycle racks available
sK5495	# City blocks receiving supplemental sanitation services
sK5512	# Bicycle lane length installed
sK5532	# Time to repair priority regulatory signs after notification
sK5538	$ New school construction cost per square foot
sK5541	# New schools and additions built
sK5559	# Students no longer in need of special education services
sK5564	# Time to repair or replace high priority broken or inoperative hydrants
sK5601	# Time to process cremation requests
sK5603	# Dog licenses issued
sK5605	# Pest control exterminations performed
sK5607	% Adults without a family doctor
sK5647	% Primary school pupils who took a free meal
sK5653	$ Cost per stray dog collected
sK5759	% Public conveniences opened for less than 12 hours a day
sK5760	# Stray dogs collected
sK5762	% Public conveniences providing access for people living with disabilities

sKPI #	Key Performance Indicator name
sK5776	% Buildings in which all public areas are suitable for and accessible to people living with a disability
sK6392	% Access to sanitation
sK6393	% Access to water
sK6529	$ Parking revenue per transaction
sK6540	% Street lights in working order
sK7003	# Time for processing new claims
sK7004	% New claims outstanding over 50 days
sK7005	# Time for processing changes of claim circumstances
sK7006	% Case calculation accuracy
sK7007	% New claims decided within 14 days of receipt of the local authority receiving all necessary information
sK7008	% Government allowance claims paid where the first payment was made on time
sK7009	# Cases referred to local authority for further action
sK14367	# Acceptable waiting time for assessment
sK14368	# Acceptable waiting time for care packages
sK14840	# Conceptions to females aged under 18
sK14843	# Condition of surface footways
sK14994	# Days taken to repair a street lighting fault, which is under the control of the local authority
sK15149	# Education and training for care leavers
sK15151	# Educational qualifications of children looked after
sK18415	# Problem drug misusers in treatment per thousand head of population aged 15-44
sK19001	# Time taken to repair a street lighting fault, where response time is under control of a DNO
sK19875	% 14 year old pupils in schools maintained by the local education authority achieving Level 5 or above in Key Stage 3 tests in English
sK19876	% 14 year old pupils in schools maintained by the local education authority achieving Level 5 or above in the Key Stage 3 tests in ICT Assessment
sK19877	% 14 year old pupils in schools maintained by the local education authority achieving Level 5 or above in the Key Stage 3 tests in Mathematics
sK19878	% 14 year old pupils in schools maintained by the local education authority achieving Level 5 or above in the Key Stage 3 tests in Science
sK19879	% 15 year old pupils in schools maintained by the authority achieving 5 GCSEs at grade A*- G and above or equivalent including English and Maths
sK19880	% 15 year old pupils in schools maintained by the authority achieving 5 or more GCSEs at grades A* - C or equivalent
sK20110	% Authority buildings open to the public in which all public areas are suitable for and accessible to disabled people
sK20251	% Children looked after at 31 March with 3 or more placements during the year
sK20370	% Compliance against the public library service standards (PLSS)
sK20727	% Half days missed due to total absence in secondary schools maintained by the authority

sKPI #	Key Performance Indicator name
sK20728	% Half days missed due to total absence in primary schools maintained by the authority
sK20892	% Interactions with the public through electronic service delivery and other paperless methods
sK20928	% Leaders of integrated early education and childcare settings funded or part funded by the local authority
sK20929	% Leads of integrated early education and childcare settings funded or part-funded by the local authority with a qualification at Level 4 or above
sK20934	% Length of footpaths and other rights of way
sK20960	% Local authority principal road network where structural maintenance is considered
sK21091	% Non-principle classified road network where maintenance is considered
sK21342	% Permanently excluded pupils offered full-time alternative educational provision of 21 hours or more
sK21474	% Pupils achieving level 5 or above in Key Stage 2: English
sK21475	% Pupils achieving level 5 or above in Key Stage 2: Maths
sK21476	% Pupils in schools maintained by the authority achieving Level 4 or above in the Key Stage 2 English test
sK21477	% Pupils in schools maintained by the authority achieving Level 4 or above in the Key Stage 2 Mathematics test
sK21669	% Statements of Special Educational Needs prepared within 18 weeks excluding those affected by "Exceptions to the Rule" under the SEN Code of Practice
sK21670	% Statements of Special Educational Needs prepared within 18 weeks including those affected by "Exceptions to the Rule" under the SEN Code of Practice
sK21916	% Unclassified road network where structural maintenance are considered
sK22001	% Young people aged 13-19 gaining a recorded outcome compared to the percentage of young people in the Local Authority
sK22002	% Young people aged 13-19 gaining an accredited outcome compared to the percentage of young people in the local authority area
sK22785	% Access to services and facilities by public transport walking and cycling
sK6528	$ Revenue per parking space

Social Services

Local Social Services includes all activities that have as the main purpose to sustain quality of life, social justice and the development of the full potential for each individual. KPIs in this area focus on aspects regarding the efficient delivery of assistance, such as health care, housing, insurance or subsidizing to poor, elderly, disabled or children.

sKPI #	Key Performance Indicator name
sK2648	# Households receiving social services assistance
sK3583	% Adults employed upon discharge from substance abuse treatment services
sK3887	% Children with substance abuse problems who are drug free during the 12 months following completion of treatment

sKPI #	Key Performance Indicator name
sK3889	% Children with substance abuse problems who complete treatment
sK3913	# Emotionally disturbed children served
sK3922	% Children with emotional disturbances who improved their level of functioning
sK4371	# Programs for disabled children
sK5374	% Lettings to new tenants arranged by the local authorities to homeless households
sK5377	% New social services tenancies given to vulnerable people excluding elderly people
sK5445	# Effectiveness of child and adolescent mental health services
sK5452	% People receiving income based benefits living in homes with a low energy efficiency rating
sK5548	# New social homes delivered
sK5549	% Non decent council homes
sK5576	% Youth who received medical screening within 24 hours of admission
sK5578	$ General healthcare cost per youth per day
sK5611	$ Administrative cost per cash assistance case
sK5630	# People receiving cash assistance
sK5654	% Abuse and/or neglect reports responded to within 24 hours of receipt
sK5655	% Children with repeat substantiated investigations
sK5656	# Caseload per child protective specialist ratio
sK5659	# Children placed in foster care
sK5660	# Children who re-enter foster care within a year of discharge to a family
sK5663	# New cases entering purchased preventive services
sK5665	# Children using vouchers for child care
sK5666	# Enrollment in subsidized child care
sK5667	% Contracted child care capacity filled
sK5668	# Hours of home care services provided
sK5669	# Recipients of home care services
sK5670	$ Contracted cost per hour of home care
sK5671	# Home delivered meals served
sK5672	# Caregivers who received assistance services or training
sK5674	% Senior centers operating at a minimum of 90% capacity
sK5675	# Registered users of senior centers
sK5676	# Meals served to poor people
sK5677	% Adults receiving preventive services who did not enter the shelter system
sK5678	# Single adults entering the shelter services system
sK5679	# Single adults sheltered per day
sK5680	# Safety, maintenance and cleanliness deficiencies noted on independent inspections of adult shelters
sK5682	# Single adults placed into permanent housing
sK5683	# Unsheltered individuals who are estimated to be living on the streets

sKPI #	Key Performance Indicator name
sK5684	% Adult families receiving preventive services who did not enter the shelter system
sK5685	# Adult families entering the shelter services system
sK5686	# Adult families in shelter per day
sK5687	# Length of stay for adult families in shelter
sK5688	# Critical incidents in the adult family shelter per 1000 residents
sK5689	% Adult families placed in permanent housing
sK5690	% Families with children receiving preventive services who did not enter the shelter system
sK5691	# Families with children entering the shelter services
sK5692	# Families with children in shelters per day
sK5693	# Length of stay for families with children in shelter
sK5694	# Critical incidents involving families with children per 1000 residents in the shelter system
sK5695	% Families with children placed into permanent housing
sK5696	# Families with children placed into permanent housing who return to the shelter services system within one year
sK5698	$ General healthcare cost per youth entering the juvenile justice system per day
sK5699	% In care youth who were referred for and received mental health services
sK5700	% In-care youth who were referred for mental health services
sK5701	# Inmates transported directly to community based service sites
sK5703	% Children in the public schools who have completed required immunization
sK5704	# Individuals tested for HIV
sK5709	% Food service establishments that fail initial inspection
sK5710	# Pest control complaints received
sK5711	% Compliance inspections failed due to signs of active rats
sK5716	% Utilization rate for independent living beds
sK5717	% Youth reunited with family or placed in a suitable environment from crisis shelter
sK5718	% Out of school time programs meeting target enrollment
sK5719	% Adult basic education participants meeting standards of improvement in literacy
sK5728	% Child support cases with orders of support
sK5729	% Current obligations collected for child assistance
sK5731	% Cash assistance family cases participating in work or work related activities in compliance with standard guidelines
sK5732	% Cash assistance applicants and recipients placed into jobs
sK5733	% Cash assistance cases that remained closed for half year time due to employment
sK5735	% Food stamp estimated payment error rate
sK5736	# Days to approval or denial of enhanced housing benefits

sKPI #	Key Performance Indicator name
sK5737	# Days to issue enhanced housing-related benefits following the application approval
sK5738	% Serious personal care complaints resolved within the specified time frame
sK5739	% Cash assistance application timeliness rate
sK5740	% Cash assistance approval rate
sK5741	% Public health insurance application processing timeliness
sK5742	% Responses to Public Health Insurance renewal notices mailed to clients
sK5748	# Homeless individuals in temporary accommodation
sK5749	# Length of stay in bed & breakfast accommodation as temporary shelter
sK5750	# Time taken to decide whether to accept people as homeless
sK5751	# Adults aged 65 and over whom the local authorities provides home care, per 1,000 adults aged 65 and over
sK5753	# People whom the local authority supports in residential care per 1,000 people in the relevant age category
sK5754	% Single adults going into residential care housed in single rooms
sK5755	% Inspections of adults residential homes
sK5757	# Children being looked after by the local authority per 1,000 children
sK5758	% Children being looked after placed in foster care
sK5761	% Children being looked after by the local authority with 3 or more placements during the year
sK5763	# Children on the child protection register per 1,000 children
sK5764	% Children on the child protection register who have been on the register for two years or more
sK5765	% Children on the child protection register whose cases were reviewed
sK5766	% Children on the child protection register visited by their social worker
sK5767	% Children on the child protection register who had previously been on the register
sK5768	% Inspections of children residential homes that were carried out
sK5769	% Inspections of children day care facilities that were carried out
sK5770	$ Net expenditure on social services per head of population
sK5771	% Care leavers in education, training, employment
sK5772	% Children in care who are emotionally and behaviorally healthy
sK5773	% Initial assessments for children's social care performed within 7 working days of referral
sK5774	% Core assessments for children's social care that were performed within 35 working days of their commencement
sK5777	% Stability of placements of looked after children - length of placement
sK5780	% Looked after children cases which were reviewed within required timescales

smartKPIs.com
The smart choice in performance management

sKPI #	Key Performance Indicator name
sK5781	% Child protection cases which were reviewed within required timescales
sK5786	# People supported to live independently through social services
sK5915	# Non-profit community projects
sK5917	% Community volunteers participation
sK5925	# Community volunteers
sK5936	$ Value of a volunteer work
sK5954	# Field visits within affected communities
sK5955	# Dialogues conducted with affected communities
sK5965	# Community families reached
sK5966	$ Dollars mobilized by community actions
sK6000	% Adults in contact with specialized mental health services who are in paid work
sK6001	% Adults in contact with specialized mental health services who report having received help with finding work
sK6137	% Foster emancipating youth homeless for one day or more after emancipation
sK6142	% Adults formerly in foster care employed at age of 21
sK6159	# Youth emancipated from foster care
sK6160	% Children in foster care who have chronic medical problems
sK6161	# Licensed foster homes
sK6172	# Placements per child
sK6173	# Stay in foster care
sK6179	# Age of children in foster care
sK6180	% Children adopted from foster care
sK7002	# Client bed-nights during the reporting period
sK14433	# Adoptions of children looked after
sK17533	# Households receiving intensive home care per 1000 population aged 65 or over
sK18082	# Older people aged 65 or over helped to live at home per 1000 population
sK18740	# Score against a checklist of enforcement best practice for trading standards
sK22794	% Social housing meeting the decent homes standard
sK22795	# Net additional homes provided
sK22816	% Turnover of social workers in Safeguarding Support teams
sK22817	# Children with a child protection plan

sKPI #	Key Performance Indicator name
sK22819	# Referrals made to children's social care
sK22821	% People on self-directed support achieving outcomes
sK22822	# Social care clients receiving self-directed support per 100,000 population
sK22823	% Carers receiving needs assessment or review and a specific carer's service, or advice and information
sK22825	% Adult safeguarding referrals resulting in a positive outcome
sK22826	% Adult safeguarding referrals resulted within target timescale
sK22827	% People with long term condition supported to be independent and in control of their condition
sK22829	# Placements of looked after children
sK22830	% Working age people claiming out of work benefits in the worst performing neighbourhoods
sK22833	% Young offenders' engagement in suitable education, training and employment

Sports

Sports covers all sports activities and events that are organized and managed in the local community.

sKPI #	Key Performance Indicator name
sK22811	% Children participating in 5 hours of physical activity per week
sK21270	# Clubmark accredited clubs
sK21271	$ Government grants
sK21272	% Fund allocation
sK21273	# Sports centers built
sK21274	# Sports facilities renovated
sK21275	% Sports facilities usage
sK21315	% Population participation in sports
sK21317	% Satisfaction with government sports programmes
sK21320	# Volunteers involved in sports
sK21387	# Local sports authorities
sK21960	# Sports awareness programmes
sK22005	% Physical Education classes in public schools
sK14490	# Sports associations
sK19355	$ Public spending per sports event participant
sK19865	% Drop-off rate among sports participants
sK19870	# Satisfaction surveys regarding quality of sports activities in the local area

Government - State/Federal

The State / Federal Government sector includes the exercise of public policy or authority over a state or federal political unit. State public administration includes activities of a governmental nature, such as enactment and judicial interpretation of laws and their pursuant regulation, as well as the administration of programs based on public policy, through legislative activities, taxation, public safety and order, immigration services, foreign affairs and the administration of government programs and departments. KPIs are used to monitor the quality of state administration, through its interventions in the core social-economic areas mentioned above.

Agriculture, Fisheries and Forestry

Agriculture, Fisheries and Forestry includes two basic activities, namely the production of crops and animal raising. Also included are service activities incidental to agriculture, as well as hunting, trapping and related activities. KPIs usually focus on the efficiency, effectiveness and productivity of agricultural activities and associated processes, relevant at central state administration level.

sKPI #	Key Performance Indicator name
sK445	# Area of land cultivated
sK457	# Farm size
sK559	# Food production per capita
sK560	$ Value of agricultural exports
sK669	# Tractors per hectare
sK675	# Agricultural mechanization level
sK1505	# Herd size
sK1527	% Area covered by woodland
sK1574	% Woodland area certified
sK1581	# Woodland surface affected by wind blow
sK1978	# Acres where plant pest and disease eradication or control efforts were undertaken
sK1985	# Sterile med flies released
sK1986	# Commercial citrus acres surveyed for citrus canker
sK1987	% Commercial citrus acres free of citrus canker
sK1988	% Newly introduced pests and diseases prevented from infesting plants
sK1989	# Animals tested or vaccinated
sK1992	# Animal site inspections performed
sK1994	# Shellfish processing plant inspections
sK1995	# Tonnes of fruits and vegetables inspected
sK3822	# Milk products inspections conducted
sK3854	# Forest land protected from wildfires
sK3855	% Land burned through prescribed burning
sK3862	# Wildfires detected and suppressed
sK3864	# Wildfires caused by humans
sK3940	% Wildfires caused by human actions
sK3943	% Threatened structures not burned by wildfires
sK3944	% Acres of protected forest and wild lands burned by wildfire
sK3947	% State managed forestry
sK3951	% State forest timber producing acres adequately stocked
sK4227	# Cattle per household
sK4235	% Households with cattle

sKPI #	Key Performance Indicator name
sK4463	# Seasonal workers demand
sK5297	# Pesticide sample determinations made in the pesticide laboratory
sK5298	% Feed, seed and fertilizer inspected products in compliance with quality standards
sK5952	# Dairy establishment inspections
sK5997	% People who made at least one recreational visit from home to woodlands
sK6069	# Home visits to woodland
sK6250	% Home grown timber consumption
sK6397	# Nitrogen dioxide emissions per populated land area
sK6400	# Water quality index
sK6403	# Biome protection
sK6404	% Marine protected area
sK6405	% Critical habitat protection
sK6408	# Marine trophic index
sK6409	% Trawling intensity
sK6411	# Pesticide regulation compliance
sK6412	$ Agriculture subsidies
sK19583	$ Livestock production
sK19587	$ Losses in the livestock sector

Education

Education at national level includes activities related to the educational system, research, analysis, through monitoring the capability and viability of the national educational sector: the support of learning and teaching, compliance with national education standards, funding or sponsorship of professional development programs, assurance of students' achievements and participation. KPIs in this area focus on the efficiency and effectiveness of the educational system activities, policies and programs at national level.

sKPI #	Key Performance Indicator name
sK35	% Nationally accredited study programs
sK273	% Graduation rate
sK276	% Drop-out rate
sK281	% Apparent intake rate
sK329	# Educational institutions
sK336	% Population projections of young persons
sK2143	% Investment in research
sK2178	# Public research organizations
sK2829	$ Federal and state funds granted for education

sKPI #	Key Performance Indicator name
sK3207	# Time for trainees to gain qualifications
sK3208	% Teachers and trainers participating in in-service training programs
sK3209	$ Funds invested in the formation of teachers and trainers
sK3311	% Trainees who value interdisciplinary training
sK4499	# Male to female student ratio
sK4504	$ Expenditure on teaching materials
sK4510	# Government student financial aid programs
sK5250	# Academic degrees granted
sK5394	# Certified teachers employed in the education system
sK5398	% Children under five in public maintained schools
sK5399	# Students permanently expelled from local authority schools per 1,000 students
sK5400	% Permanently expelled pupils attending less than ten hours a week of alternative tuition
sK5401	# Absences per pupil in secondary schools
sK5402	% Unauthorized absences in secondary schools
sK5403	% Unfilled places in schools
sK5404	% Pupils in excess of school capacity in secondary schools
sK5405	% School classes with fewer than the established standard number of of pupils
sK5406	$ Expenditure per pupil in local authority schools
sK5407	% Pupils in local authority schools passing national tests
sK5408	# Points score per local authority secondary pupil in national exams
sK5409	% Primary pupils in local authority schools where meals are available to all full-time pupils
sK5412	% Pupils with statements of special educational need
sK5413	# Statements of special education needs issued
sK5414	% Pupils placed by a government authority in special schools
sK5415	# Enrollments in adult education courses per 1,000 adult residents
sK5416	# Hours adult students are enrolled in for adult education classes per 1,000 adult population
sK5418	$ Adult education spending per head of adult resident
sK5446	% Schools judged as having good or outstanding standards of behaviour
sK5447	% Persistent absence rate for school pupils
sK5448	# Time spent by a school subjected to special measures
sK5449	# Schools in special administrative or performance related supervision measures
sK5538	$ New school construction cost per square foot
sK5539	% Scheduled new school seats constructed in time
sK5541	# New schools and additions built
sK5543	# New seats created in schools
sK5557	% Professionally certified teachers
sK5559	# Students no longer in need of special education services
sK5719	% Adult basic education participants meeting standards of improvement in literacy

sKPI #	Key Performance Indicator name
sK5815	% Trainees with cultural competence in their curricula
sK5849	% Vocational Education and Training (VET) unit enrollments that use e-learning
sK5850	# Schemes used to improve access to a training program
sK5851	% Accredited education and training providers
sK5852	# Collaborations with other education agencies
sK5857	# Contracted partnerships with industry
sK5858	% Leaning programs that ensure family participation
sK5860	% Education and training providers offering units that use e-learning
sK6591	% Education and training workplace delivery
sK6671	# Students enrolled in education programs abroad
sK6673	# Incoming to outgoing exchange students ratio
sK6684	% Classroom utilization rate
sK6933	$ Industry funding for training programs
sK6934	% Education providers applying internal quality assurance systems defined by law or at own initiative
sK6935	# Mechanisms used to update the VET offer to the future labour market needs
sK6936	# Qualifications gained to total trainees employed in the industry
sK6937	% Trainees who proceed to high level qualifications within the industry
sK6938	% Actual training tracks that follow intended industry training plans
sK6939	# Trainees that engage in policy development, implementation and evaluation
sK14592	# Bachelor's degrees granted
sK14880	# Continuing education (CE) activities evaluated for continuing education providers
sK15030	# Degrees granted in engineering and computer sciences
sK15205	# Entering first-time freshmen
sK15346	# Freshman participation rate in institutions
sK15394	# Gifts from philanthropic sources
sK15659	# Inventions disclosed per year
sK16540	# Rating of overall quality of experience by recent bachelor's graduates
sK16543	# Rating of overall quality of engineering/computer science graduates by employers
sK16623	# Residents participating in activities sponsored through SWPS programs per FTE faculty in SWPS
sK16898	# Students who are new community college transfers
sK17004	# Time to degree for community college transfers
sK17006	# Time to degree for students entering as full-time freshmen
sK17776	# Level of Ministry of Education employee morale as measured by an annual employee survey
sK18859	# Start-up or spin-off companies per $100M research expenditures per year
sK19346	$ Attendance pay for a resident undergraduate minus grant aid out of median income
sK19961	% Administrative rules reviewed for clarity annually

sKPI #	Key Performance Indicator name
sK19963	% Administrators-In-Training (AIT) that report a satisfactory training experience/program
sK19988	% Adult citizens with intermediate literacy skills (document)
sK19989	% Adult citizens with intermediate literacy skills (prose)
sK19990	% Adult citizens with intermediate literacy skills (quantitative)
sK19994	% Adults (25+) who have an Associates degree or other occupation-related credential
sK19995	% Adults (25+) who have completed some college
sK20363	% Completed applications processed in 20 days
sK20401	% Cost of attendance for a resident undergraduate
sK20485	% Discipline-related workshops provided to educators annually compared to the target of 15
sK20597	% Employment rate of vocational secondary graduates that enter the labor market after graduation
sK20687	% Full-time freshmen starting and completing a bachelor's degree at an university
sK20717	% Graduates employed and/or continuing education
sK20766	% High school graduates who attain a Certificate of Initial Mastery
sK20902	% Investigated cases resolved in 180 days
sK21350	% Phone calls and email responded to within 3 days
sK21880	% Cost of attendance at university covered by federal and state needbased aid for resident undergraduate financial aid recipients
sK22803	# First time entrants into the youth justice system aged 10-17
sK22835	% Looked after children achieving five A*-C GCSEs (or equivalent) at key stage 4 (including English and maths)
sK22836	% Secondary school persistent absence rate
sK22837	% Population aged 19-64 for males and 19-59 for females qualified to at least Level 2 or higher
sK22838	% Population aged 19-64 for males and 19-59 for females qualified to at least Level 3 or higher
sK22839	% 16 to 18-year-olds who are not in education, training or employement (NEET)
sK22840	% Achievement of 5 or more A*-C grades at GCSE or equivalent including English and Maths
sK22841	% Achievement of at least 78 points across the Early Years Foundation Stage with at least 6 in each of the scales in Personal Social and Emotional Development and Communication, Language and Literacy

Employment and Workplace Relations

Employment and Workplace Relations includes all activities linked with the labor market development, career and employment services, youth support and engagement for finding jobs, income support services and immigration aspects. KPIs in this area focus on the efficiency, effectiveness and quality of services provided for the support of employers, employees, youth or unemployed people in developing and reaching their full potential.

sKPI #	Key Performance Indicator name
sK179	% Entered employment rate
sK336	% Population projections of young persons

sKPI #	Key Performance Indicator name
sK338	% Employment rate
sK339	% Youth unemployment rate
sK361	% Working age people with disabilities
sK1483	% Child dependency ratio
sK1550	% Aged dependency ratio
sK3454	% Dependency ratio
sK3459	# Jobs birth/death ratio
sK5484	% Unemployment rate
sK5486	# Minority and women owned business enterprises certified
sK5488	# Workforce system wide job placements
sK5540	% Working age people from ethnic minorities
sK5544	# Working age people receiving out of work benefits
sK5545	% Working age people on out of work benefits
sK5555	% Level of skills gaps reported in the current workforce by employers
sK5778	% Unemployment rate of working age people from ethnic minorities
sK5779	# Working age people with disabilities
sK5782	# Working age people from ethnic backgrounds
sK5967	% Participants in community action employment initiatives who seek and obtain jobs
sK6003	% Employers who know whom to approach for advice on training and skills
sK6004	% Employment rate over the age of 50
sK6005	% Employment rate among lone parents
sK6006	% Employment rate of people with disabilities
sK6007	% Employment rate of ethnic minority people
sK6008	% Employment rate of low qualified
sK6009	$ Employer investment in learning and development
sK6010	$ National GVA per person employed
sK6011	# Organizations with 10 or more HPW (high performing work) practices
sK6066	% Nonresident hire rate
sK6067	% Individuals exiting the vocational rehabilitation program employed
sK6068	% Workplace lost time due to injuries and illness
sK6070	% Resident hire rate
sK6071	$ Unemployment benefits paid
sK6072	# Work-related deaths per 100,000 workers
sK6073	# Work-related illnesses and injuries resulting in hospitalization per 100,000 workers
sK6074	# Work days lost due to work-related illnesses and injuries per worker
sK6075	# Industry representatives trained in health and safety
sK6076	% Employer participation in industry accreditation programs
sK6077	% Central government agencies participating in workplace safety management programs
sK6078	# Employment by industry

sKPI #	Key Performance Indicator name
sK6079	% Unemployment by industry
sK6080	% Job losses by industry
sK7044	% Excessive arbitration claims
sK14452	# Agency employees divided by number of payroll staff
sK14688	# Calendar days from the date HR receives an approved recruitment request to the date the first job offer is extended
sK17467	# High school students enrolled in community college credit programs
sK17972	# National rank for new Employer Identification Numbers per 1000 workers
sK18426	# Professional-technical degrees and certificates awarded
sK18531	# Rank for college tuition and fees among all states
sK19343	$ Payroll per worker covered by unemployment insurance in rural area
sK19344	$ Payroll per worker covered by unemployment insurance in urban area
sK19871	% GED certificate applicants successful
sK20276	% Citizens employed outside the urban area
sK20305	% Clients served in adult workforce programs who obtained employment upon exiting the program
sK20345	% Community college transfer students who demonstrate progress by returning for the second year
sK20356	% Companies ranking training they received through community college Business and Industry Training System (BITS) as good or better
sK20360	% Complaints resolved by means other than formal administrative hearing within a year
sK20417	% Current and incumbent workers who retained employment after exit
sK20492	% Dislocated workers who obtained employment with at least 80% of prior earnings
sK20601	% Enrolled at-risk youth who remained in or returned to school
sK20602	% Enrolled older at-risk youth who obtained employment upon exiting the program
sK20950	% Licensees meeting continuing education requirements
sK20951	% Licensing applications processed within target
sK21599	% SBDC pre-venture/start-up entrepreneurs with a completed business plan who start a business
sK21743	% Students attending an Oregon community college during one academic year who transfer to an OUS institution the following academic year
sK21745	% Students enrolled in a basic skills or ESL program who complete successfully
sK21750	% Students in a community college pass for national licensing tests compared to national pass rates
sK21751	% Students in Associates degree programs who obtain an Associates degree
sK21774	% Students who successfully complete a Nursing program
sK22783	# Jobs in knowledge economy sectors
sK22786	% Small businesses in an area showing employment growth

sKPI #	Key Performance Indicator name
sK22789	# Jobs safeguarded from investment
sK22790	# New jobs created from investment
sK22855	% Local population who are employed
sK22856	% Local population who are unemployed
sK22857	% Local population of working age who are economically inactive
sK22858	% Local population whose qualifications are equivalent to NVQ Level 2 or above
sK22860	% People with mental and behavioural disorders who are in current receipt of Incapacity Benefit / Severe Disablement Allowance
sK22863	% Adults in contact with specialized mental health services who would have liked to receive help in finding work but did not
sK22864	% Adults in contact with specialized mental health services who report being unable to work because of mental health problems
sK22865	% People in contact with specialized mental health services at time of referral
sK22866	% Recency of any kind of paid employment
sK22867	% People who have maintained any paid employment for more than one year in lifetime
sK22868	% People in receipt of employment-related long-term benefits
sK22869	# People with mental health problems known to be in contact with specialized mental health services placed in paid employment
sK22870	% People in contact with specialized mental health services who are currently employed
sK22871	% People in contact with specialized mental health services who are currently unemployed, but actively seeking employment
sK22872	% People in contact with specialized mental health services moving into education/ training, unpaid voluntary work, or retirement in year
sK22873	% People in contact with specialized mental health services where care plan contains clear actions regarding placement in paid employment
sK22874	% People in contact with specialized mental health services and currently employed where care plan contains clear actions regarding job retention
sK22875	% New recruits to local mental health trust declaring 'mental health condition' on the confidential equal opportunities monitoring section of the new NHS Standard Application Form

Finance/Treasury

Finance covers matters relating to economic policy, central government budget, fiscal, banking, security, and insurance policies as well as the capital markets of the state. KPIs in this area focus on the efficiency and effectiveness of the state financial system.

sKPI #	Key Performance Indicator name
sK172	$ Managed expenditure (ME)
sK174	% National public spending expenditure on services
sK356	% Tax collected on time

sKPI #	Key Performance Indicator name
sK546	# Sacrifice ratio
sK2791	% Purchasing share of public sector spending
sK2902	$ Gross National Product (GNP) per capita
sK2976	% Consumer price index
sK3058	$ Net capital outflow (NCO)
sK3422	% Placement ratio
sK3441	$ Tax collected
sK3659	$ Road user charge collected
sK4171	% Approved funding applications
sK5174	% Uncollected penalties
sK5268	$ Net expenditure per head of population
sK5382	$ Net spending per capita on sport, recreation and entertainment activities
sK5556	# Changes in Housing Benefit and/or Council Tax Benefit entitlements
sK5927	$ Per capita donations
sK5963	$ Charitable expenditure
sK6890	# Terms of trade
sK14134	# Equity financing
sK14146	# Fixed asset financing
sK14310	$ Household income
sK15283	# Fiscal impact statements corrected and reissued
sK19519	$ Gross Domestic Product (GDP)
sK19523	$ Gross National Income (GNI) per capita (Atlas method)

Foreign Affairs and Trade

Foreign affairs and Trade includes all activities from the national level linked with international trade, including imports and exports, free level agreements and global negotiation, and foreign affairs such as environmental issues and treaties, international conventions and organizations, security and global cooperation. KPIs in this area focus on the efficiency and effectiveness of national foreign affairs and trade activities.

sKPI #	Key Performance Indicator name
sK3536	% Refugee cases closed
sK3674	# Non containerized seaport traffic
sK3930	# Containerized seaport trade
sK5116	% Potential Net Migration Index (PMMI)
sK19555	$ Imports
sK20406	% Country share of world exports
sK20619	% Exports by commodity
sK20646	% Findings in compliance with established state policies and CBA's
sK21640	% Share of world trade

General State Administration

General State Administration concerns all activities that relate to establishing and managing policies within ministries and other state operational departments. KPIs in this area focus on aspects that include the efficiency, effectiveness and productivity of the state public administration departments and ministries, but also general national statistics.

sKPI #	Key Performance Indicator name
sK389	% Government basic services available online
sK391	% Online public procurement
sK3144	% Propensity to consume (PC)
sK4379	% Urbanized population
sK5260	# Citizens
sK5397	$ Net spending per capita on environmental health and consumer protection
sK5940	# Non-profit organizations
sK6732	% Elections turnout
sK6733	% Eligible population who voted online
sK6823	# Beer consumption per capita
sK14396	# Acres of state-owned parks per 1,000 citizens
sK14398	# Actions completed within deadline
sK14399	# Actions initiated or completed
sK14425	# Adjudicated claims upheld
sK14618	# Bidders per solicitation
sK14764	# Children under 18, who are neglected/abused or at a substantial risk of being neglected/abused
sK14772	# Claims resolved before adjudication (BOLI, EEOC, Tort, ERB)
sK14813	# Comparison of average incomes of top 5th families to lowest 5th families with national rank
sK14829	# Complaints resolved by means other than from formal administrative hearings within a year
sK14995	# Days to file opening brief
sK15091	# Disciplinary actions preserved as issued
sK17235	# Voter turnout for presidential elections in national rank
sK17405	# Governing magazine's ranking of public management quality
sK17955	# Months from approved KPM receipt of a new complaint to completion of the investigation
sK17959	# Most threatening invasive species not successfully excluded or contained since 2000
sK17970	# Municipal solid waste landfilled or incinerated per capita
sK17973	# National ranking for state and local taxes and charges as a percent of personal income
sK18267	# People employed by the regulatory body
sK18339	# Population by cities
sK18564	# Records lost or accessed without authorization
sK18829	# Species populations that are protected in dedicated conservation areas: species found in streams or rivers
sK18830	# Species populations that are protected in dedicated conservation areas: species not found in streams or rivers

sKPI #	Key Performance Indicator name
sK18861	# State/Region's national rank in traded sector strength
sK18863	# State's national rank in economic diversification
sK18864	# State's national rank in new companies
sK18865	# State's national rank in per capita state arts funding
sK19298	# Years earning the State Controller's Division Gold Star Certificate
sK19812	$ State's national rank in venture capital investments
sK19987	% Adult citizens who volunteer time to civic, community or nonprofit activities
sK20028	% Air contaminant discharge permits issued within the target time period or less
sK20033	% All Automatic Call Distributor (ACD) calls answered by a live representative and not abandoned by the caller
sK20036	% Allotment plan reports submitted to BAM on time during the year
sK20065	% Application development projects completed on time as per the "approved" project plans
sK20135	% Best practices met by the Board
sK20189	% Carbon dioxide emissions as of 1990 emissions
sK20201	% Cases investigated and referred to Board within 120 days of receipt of complain
sK20278	% Citizens who demonstrate knowledge of state's main revenue sources and main expenditure categories
sK20279	% Citizens who feel they are a part of their community
sK20280	% Citizens who speak a language in addition to English
sK20281	% Citizens who have high-speed Internet access
sK20359	% Complaints determined to be unfounded or resulting in final order within nine months
sK20361	% Complaints resolved by means other than from formal administrative hearings within a year
sK20377	% Conditional releases maintained in community
sK20405	% Counties that have completed a strategic cooperative policing agreement
sK20408	% Covered workers with earnings of 150% or more of the poverty level for a family of four
sK20421	% Current child support paid on time
sK20430	% Customers rating their satisfaction with the agency's customer service as "good" or "excellent" on timeliness
sK20431	% Customers rating their satisfaction with the agency's customer service as "good" or "excellent" on availability of information
sK20432	% Customers rating their satisfaction with the agency's customer service as "good" or "excellent" on accuracy
sK20433	% Customer safaction with the agency's customer service as "good" or "excellent" on expertise
sK20434	% Customers rating their satisfaction with the agency's customer service as "good" or "excellent" on helpfulness
sK20435	% Customers rating their satisfaction with the agency's customer service as "good" or "excellent" on overall customer service
sK20484	% Disciplined licensees with a new complaint within one year of Board closing original case with a disciplinary action

sKPI #	Key Performance Indicator name
sK20516	% E-commerce RN renewals compared to total RN renewals
sK20620	% Exports traded with non-primary partners (Primary partners are Canada, Japan and South Korea)
sK20635	% Families with incomes below the state median income for whom child care is affordable
sK20712	% Grade 9-12 students who report carrying weapons in the last 30 days
sK20818	% Identified State hazardous substance sites cleaned up or being cleaned up
sK20864	% Initial and renewal license and limited permit applications from qualified applicants that are processed within 10 business days
sK20918	% Key streams meeting minimum flow rights at 9 or more months a year
sK20964	% Local suppliers shortlisted for tenders
sK21334	% People keen to be involved in local delivery
sK21384	% Population growth
sK21385	% Population living below $1 a day
sK21425	% Procurement staff holding a state and/or national procurement certification
sK21494	% Receivables collected by state agency staff within unstated time period
sK21623	% Seniors (over 75) living independently outside of nursing facilities
sK21664	% State counties and communities prepared for emergencies or disasters with hazard data and risk reduction and with response and recovery capabilities
sK21665	% State cropland not converted to urban or rural development
sK21666	% State households with limited or uncertain access to enough food for all household members to live a healthy and active life
sK21667	% State other agricultural land not converted to urban or rural development
sK21668	% State's non-federal forest land still preserved for forest use
sK21671	% State's concentration in professional services relative to the national concentration in professional services
sK21974	% Voter turnout for presidential elections

Healthcare

Healthcare covers the medical government programs dealing with prevention of illnesses and diseases, as well as other healthcare related policies and activities. KPIs in this area refer mostly to the accessibility of preventive services and their impact.

sKPI #	Key Performance Indicator name
sK310	% Hospitals national accreditation rate
sK337	% Birth rate for unmarried women
sK760	# Patients on the semi-urgent surgery list that waited longer than the 90 days government benchmark
sK1661	# Frequency of dentist visits
sK2647	% Population with no hospital stay
sK2668	% Health insurance coverage

sKPI #	Key Performance Indicator name
sK2673	# Registered nurses to population ratio
sK2710	# Emergency rescuers service organizations
sK2724	# Mental health services
sK2725	# Healthcare facility capacity ratio
sK2731	# Health service facilities
sK2739	# Physicians to population ratio
sK2892	% Government expenditure on health service facilities
sK2901	# Hospital admission rate per 10,000 inhabitants
sK2910	% Government expenditure on medical R&D
sK4083	# Emergency medical services providers licensed
sK4091	# Emergency medical technicians and paramedics certified
sK4143	# Public health research initiatives
sK4144	# Animal sterilizations
sK4145	% National immunization coverage
sK4146	# Healthy life expectancy
sK4147	# Life expectancy at birth
sK4149	% Under-five child mortality rate
sK4150	# Health service utilization
sK4151	% Premature mortality
sK4152	% Maternal mortality
sK4153	% Mortality amenable to healthcare
sK4156	% Alcohol abuse rate
sK4157	# Public hospitals
sK4159	% ER admissions by clinical condition
sK4160	$ Health spending per capita
sK4162	% Ability to see doctor same/next day when sick or need medical care
sK4164	# Hospital admissions to ER visits
sK4167	$ Pharmaceutical expenditure per capita
sK4168	% Health expenditure from GDP
sK4172	# School days missed because of illness or injury per child
sK4173	% Children that missed 11 or more school days due to illness or injury
sK4178	% National health expenditures spent on health insurance administration
sK4180	% Public institutions with a written HIV and AIDS workplace policy
sK4183	$ National health expenditure
sK4185	# Public to private patients ratio
sK4190	# Research centers for medical engineering
sK4191	% Suicide rate among mental health patients
sK4193	# Ambulances available
sK4199	# Ambulance responses to population ratio
sK4253	$ Ambulance service expenditure to population ratio
sK4278	$ Uncompensated care
sK4280	# Sub-acute care centers
sK4290	# Medical laboratory accredited

sKPI #	Key Performance Indicator name
sK4301	# Prescriptions filled
sK4309	% Pharmaceutical expenditure to total expenditure on health
sK4315	# Physicians
sK4340	# Child health facilities
sK4350	# Injecting drug users
sK4351	% Population living with HIV
sK4354	# Fertility rate
sK4358	# Health education programs in public schools
sK4366	% Adults with depression who received treatment
sK4373	# AIDS mortality
sK4374	# Auditory screenings in public schools
sK4376	# Dental examinations completed
sK4385	% Infants with low birth weight
sK4387	$ Cost of diabetes
sK4394	% Voluntary counseling and testing for HIV/AIDS population
sK4395	% Health incidents by disease category
sK4397	% Children severe underweight
sK4398	% Patients that discontinue antidepressant treatment
sK4400	% Households consuming iodized salt
sK4986	# Cases of vaccine-preventable diseases
sK5224	% Children with mental retardation restored to competency
sK5234	% Children with mental illness restored to competency
sK5247	% Hospitals that fail to report serious incidents
sK5248	% Ambulatory surgical centers with deficiencies that pose a serious threat to patients life
sK5249	% Clinical laboratories with deficiencies that pose a serious threat for patients life
sK5290	$ Cost of ambulance tours per day
sK5417	% Human remains identified following a disaster
sK5583	# Suicide reports
sK5607	% Adults without a family doctor
sK5609	% Adult population smoking rate
sK5610	% People who received a flu shot in the last 12 months
sK5643	% Registered drug users in effective treatment
sK5702	# Deaths due to drug abuse
sK5703	% Children in the public schools who have completed required immunization
sK5704	# Individuals tested for HIV
sK5705	# New adults AIDS cases diagnosed
sK5706	# New syphilis cases diagnosed
sK5707	# New tuberculosis cases diagnosed
sK5714	% Infant mortality rate
sK5715	% Prevalence of smoking
sK5720	# Length of stay in general care
sK5721	% Prenatal patients retained in care through delivery

sKPI #	Key Performance Indicator name
sK5722	% HIV patients using dedicated HIV clinics
sK5723	# Time spent for a primary care visit
sK5724	% Emergency room revisits for adult asthma patients
sK5725	% Emergency room visits for asthma patients
sK5726	% Eligible women receiving a mammogram screening
sK5727	# Uninsured patients served
sK5895	# ER visits to 1,000 population
sK5970	# Hospital beds to population ratio
sK6130	% Healthcare facilities compliance
sK6131	# Inspections of care
sK6160	% Children in foster care who have chronic medical problems
sK6193	% Children with special healthcare needs
sK6194	% Children with special healthcare needs receiving referrals when needed
sK6198	% Children with a medical home
sK6201	% Children with a preventive medical care visit in the last year
sK6202	% Premium for employer based family health insurance coverage by median income
sK6391	# Environmental burden of disease
sK6750	# New cures and treatments for diseases discovered
sK18005	# New HIV diagnoses among citizens aged 13 and older
sK20275	% Citizens 18 and older who report that they do not currently smoke cigarettes
sK21401	% Pregnancy per 1,000 females at ages 10-14
sK21402	% Pregnancy per 1,000 females atages 15-17
sK21403	% Pregnant women who report not using alcohol and tobacco
sK22000	% Years of life lost before age 70 per 1,000 people
sK22824	% Hospital admission per 100,000 for alcohol related harm
sK22834	# Emotional health and behavior of children in care
sK4181	% Cost of preventive screening from national healthcare spending

Human/Social Services

Human / Social Services includes all activities with a national impact that have as main purpose to sustain quality of life, social justice and the development of the full potential for each individual. KPIs in this area focus on aspects regarding the efficient delivery of assistance such as health care, housing, insurance or subsidizing to people unemployed, poor, elderly, disabled or children.

sKPI #	Key Performance Indicator name
sK178	% Vulnerable people who are supported to maintain independent living
sK3960	# Price-to-income ratio for typical housing units
sK4217	# Orphans
sK5578	$ General healthcare cost per youth per day
sK5630	# People receiving cash assistance
sK5669	# Recipients of home care services

sKPI #	Key Performance Indicator name
sK5770	$ Net expenditure per head of population on social services
sK5772	% Children in care that are emotionally and behaviorally healthy
sK5777	% Stability of placements of looked after children - length of placement
sK5780	% Looked after children cases which were reviewed within required timescales
sK5781	% Child protection cases which were reviewed within required timescales
sK6101	% Population in long term care
sK6123	# Days in nursing home
sK6128	# Nursing home residents
sK6136	% Nursing home residents with pressure sores
sK6137	% Foster emancipating youth homeless for one day or more after emancipation
sK6155	% Adults formerly in foster care with a bachelor degree
sK6159	# Youth emancipated from foster care
sK6392	% Access to sanitation
sK14897	# Council wide redundancy cases
sK15252	# Families leaving the National Aid Fund (NAF) rolls as a result of productive families assistance
sK17766	# Time for completion of Safeguarding Inspections
sK17777	# Level of officer performance as determined by their agency after successful completion of Basic Training
sK19435	$ Council wide redundancy cases
sK19881	% Population groups by age who are not in education, employment or training
sK20102	% Attendees who ranked the usefulness of DPSST criminal justice regional training courses at or above "6" on a scale of 1-7
sK20103	% Attendees who ranked the usefulness of DPSST fire service regional training courses at or above "6" on a scale of 1-7
sK20186	% Capital programme approved using the authority's agreed governance arrangements
sK20937	% LGSS Project milestones met
sK21363	% Planned Pride workshops delivered by Pride leaders in their directorate
sK21544	% Residential and nursing customers placed in homes rated as 2 star or above
sK21565	% Revocation or denial actions appealed that are upheld at the appellate level

Law and Justice

Law and Justice refers to the activity of the legal and judicial bodies that are responsible for the enforcement of laws. KPIs measure the efficiency and effectiveness in dealing with aspects from the civil law, land rights, family law, intellectual property, births, deaths and marriages registries and law reform.

sKPI #	Key Performance Indicator name
sK767	# Patents issued
sK1509	% Guilty verdicts obtained
sK1510	# Cautions offered

sKPI #	Key Performance Indicator name
sK1519	# Fraud visits to claimants per 1,000 caseload
sK3967	# Default concealed weapon/firearm licensees with prior criminal histories
sK3971	% Parole release decisions granted
sK3972	# Revocation determinations made
sK3988	# Conditional release cases handled
sK3992	% Conviction rate where the commission has found probable cause
sK3995	% Legal cases that are closed within 12 months
sK4003	% Lemon law cases resolved in less than one year
sK4005	% Citizens expressing satisfaction with civil enforcement legal services
sK4006	# Disposition records added to the criminal history file
sK4009	# Criminal history errors corrected
sK4011	# Arrest records created and maintained
sK4014	% Requests for criminal history record checks responded to
sK4015	% Criminal history records compiled accurately
sK4017	% Criminal investigations closed resulting in an arrest
sK4019	% Closed criminal investigations resolved
sK4020	# Youths served daily per juvenile probation officer
sK4062	# Daily population in home detention
sK4064	% Youth who remain crime free while in secure detention
sK4068	$ Cost per case for case preparation
sK4069	# Inmates receiving substance abuse services
sK4081	# Inmates receiving major disciplinary reports per 1,000 inmates
sK4297	# Officer terminations
sK4709	$ Cost to resolve matter
sK5302	$ Detention cost per inmate
sK5303	# Inmates delivered to court
sK5304	% On trial inmates delivered to court on time
sK5305	# Daily inmates involved in vocational skills training programs
sK5309	# Inmate health clinic visits
sK5313	# Jail based arrests for inmates misconduct
sK5356	% Investigations resulting in enforcement actions
sK5567	$ Daily cost per juvenile in detention
sK5568	# Daily population in detention
sK5569	# Combined average length of stay in secure and non secure detention
sK5581	# Stabbings and slashing reports
sK5584	% Pre-sentence investigation reports on adults cases submitted 24 hours prior to scheduled hearing
sK5585	% Family court juvenile cases with investigations and reports submitted on time
sK5586	% Rearrest rate of adults on probation
sK5620	# Fraud investigations per 1000 caseload
sK5650	# Prosecutions and sanctions per 1,000 caseload
sK5651	# Fraud investigators per 1,000 caseload

sKPI #	Key Performance Indicator name
sK6012	% Court user satisfaction
sK6013	# Village courts of law
sK6014	% Confidence in the village courts of law
sK6015	# Prisoners
sK6016	% Remandees
sK6017	# Escapees from prison
sK6018	# Rehabilitating prisoners
sK6019	# Public corruption complaints
sK6020	# Officers suspended
sK6021	# Reported crimes by type of offense
sK6022	# Arrests by type of offense
sK6023	% Frequency of household victimization
sK6024	# Arrest warrants
sK6025	# Cases cleared using the new technology
sK6026	# Automated information exchanges in use
sK6027	% Crimes cleared by arrest
sK6028	% Case dispositions recorded in repository
sK6029	% Homicide cases refused by the district attorney (DA)
sK6030	# Minutes required to complete a jail intake booking
sK6031	# Emergency calls answered per officer per shift
sK6032	% Criminal cases brought to trial in less than 180 days
sK6033	% Emergency calls with officer on-scene within 15 minutes
sK6034	% Citizens "satisfied" or "very satisfied" with law enforcement service
sK6035	% Prison records with significant clerical errors
sK6036	% Events that the responsible agency has posted to the state criminal history repository within 30 days of occurrence
sK6037	% Felony cases reaching disposition within established time standards
sK6038	% Arrestees accurately identified before release
sK6040	% Victims killed or injured by released offenders
sK6041	# Officers killed or injured at dispatched locations
sK6042	% Personnel who log on a Court Management System module each day
sK6043	% Documents exchanged non-electronically among criminal justice agencies in the jurisdiction
sK6044	# Interagency phone requests for information
sK6045	# Domestic violence homicides committed by individuals restrained by orders of protection
sK6046	# People successfully completing drug rehabilitation program
sK6047	# People in drug rehabilitation program
sK6048	% Drug court clients who are arrested in 12 months following release from the program
sK6049	# Full time personnel responsible for the management of case-related records
sK6050	# Erroneous jail releases due to court paperwork errors
sK6051	# Arrested probationers released prior to notification of the probation officer

sKPI #	Key Performance Indicator name
sK6052	# Gun sales denied through use of instant check system
sK6053	# Time to conduct a gun purchase background check
sK6054	# Gun checks that are delayed/unresolved
sK6055	# Warrant arrests resulting from notification by gun check personnel
sK6056	# Inmates killed or injured from assaults by other inmates or in suicide attempts
sK6057	# Correctional officers injured or killed by inmate assaults
sK6058	# Days from incident to arrest
sK6059	# Time from initial submission of evidence to laboratory report availability
sK6060	# Cases where chain of custody breaches are recorded
sK6061	# Final reports requiring revision
sK6062	# Time from incident to arrest in cases requiring a crime lab report
sK6063	# Time from screening decision to trial
sK6064	# Convictions
sK6065	# Outstanding warrants
sK6734	% Vehicles exceeding speed limit
sK6735	% Motorists using seat belts
sK6736	% Motorists driving under influence
sK14894	# Corruption Perception Index
sK19297	# Years out of last five that Financial Services earns State Controller Division Gold Star Certificate for the Legislative agencies it serves
sK20045	% Annual voluntary turnover rate of the Legislative Administration continuing workforce
sK20341	% Commission recommendations to the Supreme Court upheld versus the total number of recommendations forwarded to the Supreme Court
sK20429	% Customers rating overall satisfaction with problem solution as above average or excellent
sK20741	% Hearings scheduled within statutory timeframes
sK20912	% Judges prosecuted by the Commission who are not exonerated
sK20916	% Juveniles released from detention centers who have no conflict with the law for one year after release
sK21460	% Prosecutions completed within two years of first review through date of final Commission action before the Supreme Court
sK21483	% Racial/ethnic diversity in Legislative Administration as compared to the total State diversity
sK21673	% Stipulated agreements unchanged and approved by the Supreme Court

Military, Security and Defense

Military, security and defense includes administration, supervision and operation of military defense affairs and land, sea, air and space defense forces. KPIs focus on the adequacy of the forces and other resources to community needs and the quality of their interventions.

sKPI #	Key Performance Indicator name
sK4281	# Officers charged with criminal offenses
sK4297	# Officer terminations

sKPI #	Key Performance Indicator name
sK4539	# Disciplinary offenses
sK4594	# Warnings from superior officers
sK4889	% Armed forces reputation
sK4900	# Suicides and suspected suicides of military personnel
sK4907	# Fatalities attributed to training designed to simulate combat conditions
sK4913	% Women in the military
sK4924	# Reserve military forces
sK4959	# Military trained strength
sK4960	% Canceled military training events
sK4961	# Military training exercises completed
sK4966	# Military training exercises scheduled
sK4992	% Relocated military forces
sK5011	% Manning balance
sK5014	% Military forces readiness
sK5018	% Military armed forces deployment breakdown
sK5020	% Armed forces deployed on operations and undertaking military tasks
sK5464	# Officer intake to military forces from civilian life
sK5639	# Protection level against terrorist attacks
sK14730	# Cases in the Appellate Division backlog

Resources and Energy

Resources and energy includes all activities linked to the management of the national energy supply, procurement of energy at reasonable prices, promotion of competition within the private sector, the provision of alternative and renewable sources of energy for citizens, such as wind energy, conduction of research and development in energy and coordination of energy relating affairs at international level. KPIs in this area focus on the efficiency and effectiveness of the energy related activities at the national level.

sKPI #	Key Performance Indicator name
sK59	# Energy consumption
sK60	% Energy dependency
sK1952	% Petroleum contaminated sites with cleanup completed
sK2361	% Petroleum products meeting quality standards
sK4816	% Electricity demand growth
sK4820	% Energy consumption breakdown
sK4821	% Villages with access to electricity
sK4829	# Domestic electricity demand
sK4831	% Electricity demand met by domestic generation
sK4832	% Net electricity imports
sK4858	# Electricity consumption intensity
sK4859	# Electricity consumption per capita
sK4917	# Daytime energy consumption
sK4918	# Nighttime energy consumption
sK4919	# Length of overhead network
sK4920	# Length of underground cables
sK5024	# Water production

Organizational » Industries

sKPI #	Key Performance Indicator name
sK5026	# Water consumption
sK5077	# Mining hazards reported
sK5078	# Mining hazards requiring emergency response
sK5081	# Underground ore or coal production
sK5082	# Surface mining production
sK5083	# Operational surface mines
sK5084	# Underground operational mines
sK5085	# Closed mines
sK5093	# Fatal mining accidents
sK5099	# Tonnes of coal mined
sK5100	# Coal reserves
sK5103	# Mineral waste produced
sK5105	# Non mineral waste produced
sK5110	# Accidental discharges of hydrocarbons
sK5114	# Reserves proved
sK5115	# Reserves probable
sK5120	# Measured resources
sK5121	# Indicated resources
sK5122	# Inferred resources
sK5140	# Mine entries inspected
sK5141	# Non fatal mining accidents
sK5194	# Rig drilling offshore oil spills
sK5199	# Exploration drilling meters completed
sK5200	# Area held under exploration license
sK5203	# Exploration permits granted
sK5211	# Lands available for oil and gas exploration
sK6394	% Use of solid fuels indoors
sK6396	# Sulfur dioxide emissions per populated land area
sK6398	# Non-methane volatile organic compound emissions per populated land area
sK6399	# Ecosystem ozone
sK6401	% Water stress index
sK6402	# Water scarcity index
sK17267	# Water losses from well water
sK5015	% Households with access to safe water

Tourism

National tourism represents the tourism industry development, statistics and programs for leisure, cultural, religious or business purposes. KPIs in this area focus on the efficiency, effectiveness and quality of the national tourism programs, policies and services provided.

sKPI #	Key Performance Indicator name
sK132	# Tourists
sK133	% Domestic tourism
sK134	% Tourists entering through airports
sK135	% Hotel occupancy

sKPI #	Key Performance Indicator name
sK137	$ Tourist spending
sK212	# Tourism inquiries
sK213	# Nights of hotel stays sold
sK214	% Tourism employment
sK4405	# Annual touristic events
sK4408	# Length of stay per tourist
sK4410	# Concerts
sK4412	# Day tours available
sK4413	# Facilities available at tourist information centers
sK4414	# First time visitors
sK4415	# Free-access attractions and sites
sK4416	# Domestic annual overnight trips per capita
sK4418	# Inquiries answered by the visitor information center
sK4419	# International hospitality companies planning hotel development in the country
sK4420	# International visitor arrivals (Ingoing tourists)
sK4421	# Media visitors
sK4422	# Museums
sK4424	# Outbound tourism
sK4425	# Foreign tourists overnight trips
sK4426	# Paid-access attractions and sites
sK4427	# Registered hotels
sK4428	# Registered hotel rooms
sK4429	# Registered travel agencies
sK4430	# Safaris
sK4431	# Skiing touristic areas
sK4432	# Mountaineering tourists
sK4433	# National tourists
sK4434	# Tour operators offering touristic services
sK4435	# Tourism employees
sK4436	# Tourist information centers
sK4437	# Tourist visas
sK4439	# Tourists (bed nights)
sK4440	# Tourist resorts
sK4441	# Tourists to museum
sK4442	# Travel agents
sK4443	# Water tourist attractions
sK4445	$ Income per visitor per day
sK4446	$ Day trip spend
sK4447	$ Income in foreign currency
sK4448	$ International tourism expenditure
sK4452	% Days in which hotels 95% or above occupancy
sK4453	% First-time visitors
sK4454	% National tourism employees
sK4455	% Outbound tourism expenditure
sK4456	$ Overnight trip spend

sKPI #	Key Performance Indicator name
sK4457	% Residents as outgoing tourists
sK4458	% Residents' tourism spending from total personal spending
sK4460	% Tourism receipts from GDP
sK4461	% Tourism foreign earnings from world exports
sK4462	% Share of global tourism
sK4464	% Tourist satisfaction with the attractions, transport and accommodation facilities
sK4465	% Tourists arrived by land
sK4466	% Tourists departed by land
sK4469	% Visitors by type of purpose
sK4470	% Tourism budget spent by destination
sK4483	$ Cost per day of vacation
sK4777	# Guest rooms in operation
sK4785	# Hotel industry pulse index (HIP)
sK5525	# Tourists drawn to downtown
sK5992	% Spas by category
sK5993	$ Treatment revenue per spa
sK5994	# Daily visits per spa
sK5995	% International visitors in spas
sK15206	# Entry of travellers
sK18138	# Overnight stays
sK19082	# Travel price index
sK20125	% Awareness of situation involving sport fishing and visitation
sK20828	% Inbound Tourism by region of origin
sK20898	% International tourist arrival by mode of transport
sK20982	% Market share of international tourist arrival
sK21895	% Travel and Tourism economy aggregate as of employment
sK21943	% Usage of visitor centers

Transportation and Infrastructure

Transportation includes the provision of passenger or freight transport, whether scheduled or not, by rail, pipeline, road, water or air and associated activities, such as terminal and parking facilities, cargo handling, and storage. KPIs in this area focus on the efficiency, effectiveness and productivity of transportation activities at national level. Infrastructure operations consist of activities related to the administration and operation of the national infrastructure assets. Infrastructure assets administered by operators acting in this industry include airports, ports, roads, toll roads and parking assets among others.

sKPI #	Key Performance Indicator name
sK360	% Streets and highways expenditure variation
sK1073	% Incidents classified as major
sK1729	# Highway network length
sK3577	$ Road rehabilitation expenditure per paved mile
sK3579	$ Government expenditure per kilometer of primary road network constructed
sK3584	% Investment in road transport infrastructure

sKPI #	Key Performance Indicator name
sK3612	# Road network density per square kilometer of land
sK3614	% Primary network length from total network length
sK3615	% Length of the road network by type
sK3616	% Rural population living within 2 kilometers of a paved road
sK3617	% Rural population living within 2 kilometers of gravel road
sK3621	# Rail lines density per square kilometer
sK3622	# Kilometers of new road network built
sK3625	% Road network length constructed to full standard
sK3626	$ Household spending on public transport
sK3632	% Rural population accessibility to road network infrastructure
sK3647	# Rural accessibility to public transport
sK3662	# Fatalities per ten thousand vehicles
sK3663	# Traffic fatalities per hundred thousands inhabitants
sK3666	% Roads in good condition
sK3667	% Eligible traffic safety and efficiency upgrades completed
sK3669	% Multi-tracked rail lines route length
sK3673	% Transport freight share
sK3674	# Non containerized seaport traffic
sK3675	% Transport passenger share
sK3676	# Road maintenance effectiveness
sK3677	# Motor traffic
sK3681	# Road salt usage
sK3710	% Households owning private cars
sK3711	# Households owning private cars
sK3923	% Rural population living within 2 kilometers of a public transport station
sK3930	# Containerized seaport trade
sK3933	# Vehicle kilometers
sK4297	# Officer terminations
sK4557	# National ports equipped to international standards
sK5031	% Rural telecommunication subscribers receiving new or improved service
sK5201	$ Road network rehabilitation expenditure per capita
sK5318	# Time freeways operate above capacity
sK5387	% Highways length that are of a high standard of cleanliness
sK5388	% Highways length of an acceptable standard of cleanliness
sK5428	% Critical roads and pavements damage repairs which were carried out within 24 hours
sK5429	# Serious accidents per 1,000,000 miles traveled by a vehicle on principal roads
sK5432	$ Cost of highway maintenance per 100 miles traveled by a vehicle
sK5454	# Construction related incidents, injuries and fatalities reported

sKPI #	Key Performance Indicator name
sK5513	$ Cost per lane mile resurfaced
sK5520	$ Cost per tonne of asphalt used
sK5593	# Traffic crashes
sK6532	% Participants in traffic experiencing a delay
sK6552	% Roads with access to hub airports and ports
sK19776	$ Revenues from transport sector taxation

sKPI #	Key Performance Indicator name
sK20277	% Citizens who commute during peak hours by means other than driving alone
sK21575	% Roads in fair or better condition in county
sK21576	% Roads in fair or better condition in state
sK21639	% Share of the world traffic

Healthcare

Healthcare includes prevention services, medical diagnosis or treatment for an illness, provided by trained medical professionals in healthcare facilities, to both humans and animals. KPIs refer to the availability, efficiency and quality of healthcare services for patients.

Emergency Response/Ambulance Services

Emergency response and ambulance services includes all specific services for dealing with healthcare emergency cases. KPIs in this area are used to monitor the efficiency and the quality of services.

sKPI #	Key Performance Indicator name
sK306	# Length of stay in ER
sK2675	% Non -operational ambulances due to breakdowns and accidents
sK4193	# Ambulances available
sK4194	# Medical rescuers
sK4195	% Ambulances with advanced medical equipment
sK4196	% Ambulances with basic medical equipment
sK4197	% Emergency cases which receive a paramedic medical treatment
sK4198	% Survival rate from out-of-hospital cardiac arrest
sK4199	# Ambulance responses to population ratio
sK4200	# Call response time for ambulance services
sK4203	# Ambulance response time
sK4204	$ Expenditure per urgent and non-urgent response
sK4205	% Abandoned calls for ambulance services
sK4206	% Activation times within X minutes
sK4209	# Ambulance time on scene
sK4210	# Ambulance case cycle time
sK4211	# Inpatient falls
sK4219	% Emergency Department visits resulting in hospital admissions
sK4231	# Repeated Emergency Room visits
sK4265	# Trolley wait
sK4273	% Patients waiting more than X hours
sK4326	% Reusable medical devices properly decontaminated
sK4327	# Patient wait time
sK4328	% Patients who leave without being seen
sK5290	$ Cost of ambulance tours per day
sK5596	# Response time to life threatening medical emergencies by ambulance units
sK5724	% Emergency room revisits for adult asthma patients

sKPI #	Key Performance Indicator name
sK5725	% Emergency room visits for asthma patients
sK5895	# ER visits to 1,000 population
sK5897	% Semi-urgent ER visits
sK5898	# Cost per ER visit to cost per primary care visit
sK5899	% ER visits that could have been treated by a primary care physician
sK5971	# Ambulance activation time
sK6146	# Emergency room patient wait time
sK6148	% Collection of emergency room payment balances prior to patient departure
sK6151	# Outpatient per registrar per shift

Healthcare Support Services

Healthcare support services include specific programs and associations in healthcare, not covered by the other subcategories. KPIs in this subcategory measure the outcomes of healthcare programs, association membership, efficiency, capability, accessibility of such programs and their impact.

sKPI #	Key Performance Indicator name
sK760	# Patients on the semi-urgent surgery list that waited longer than the 90 days benchmark
sK1705	# Epidemiologists per 100,000 population
sK4339	# AIDS home care treatment
sK4347	# Pre-abortion counseling
sK4352	# Abortion related services
sK4372	# Access to alcohol counseling
sK6118	# Elective services to urgent care patients ratio
sK6119	% Scheduling rate for ambulatory surgery patients
sK6120	% Scheduling rate for high-dollar diagnostic outpatients
sK6122	% Prompt payment discount
sK6124	% Overall insurance verification rate of scheduled patients
sK6129	% Copay or deductibles requests rate
sK6130	% Healthcare facilities compliance
sK6132	% Screening of uninsured inpatients for financial assistance
sK6133	% Payment arrangements made for high-dollar inpatients or outpatients

sKPI #	Key Performance Indicator name
sK6136	% Nursing home residents with pressure sores
sK6145	# Inpatient and outpatient wait time
sK6158	% Medicare claims denied
sK6793	# Units of whole blood collected
sK6794	# Whole blood donors
sK6795	% Blood cells shipped to whole blood collected
sK6796	# Blood product recalls per 10,000 collections
sK6798	$ Cost per blood product unit shipped
sK6800	% Hospitals satisfied with the blood service provided
sK6801	% Donors satisfied with the donation process
sK6803	% Order fill rate by blood product type
sK6805	# Potential donors in registry
sK6807	# Hospital red blood cell outdated
sK6808	# New donors
sK6162	% In-house inpatient A/R days
sK6149	% Collection of elective service deposits
sK6157	# Time to process the secondary COB billing
sK6212	% Referrals and net fees of total collection agency recoveries
sK6215	% Automated contacts per full-time equivalent (FTE)

Hospitals

Hospitals include healthcare institutions for both inpatients and outpatients, providing treatment by specialized personnel, for shorter or longer patient stays. KPIs in this area monitor the administration and management activities of hospitals. They complement the indicators for medical practice, by measuring the bed related - inpatient care, the surgical treatment and the discharge procedure performance.

sKPI #	Key Performance Indicator name
sK40	# Hospital bed capacity
sK41	% Hospital bed occupancy rate
sK42	% Unplanned readmission rate
sK305	% Outpatient surgeries
sK307	% Length of stay variance
sK308	% Cases classified as May Not Require Hospitalization (MNRH)
sK309	% Alternate level of care days (ALC)
sK311	% Medication error rate
sK312	% Surgical site infection rate
sK322	% Inpatient mortality
sK323	% Peri-operative mortality
sK324	# Hospital-acquired infections
sK2877	% Outpatient revenue
sK2884	$ Hospital operating profit per bed
sK2897	$ Revenue per physician
sK4159	% ER admissions by clinical condition
sK4186	% Retreatment ratio
sK4192	% Medical residents employed after residency

sKPI #	Key Performance Indicator name
sK4201	# Operating time on bypass
sK4202	% Patient falls that result in a fracture
sK4207	# Daily census
sK4212	# Length of stay (LOS)
sK4215	# Throughput per bed
sK4216	% Available hospital beds
sK4218	% Patient visits resulting in transfer
sK4219	% Emergency Department visits resulting in hospital admissions
sK4220	% Time that hospital beds are occupied
sK4221	# Adverse events prevalence
sK4224	# Medical ancillary services
sK4226	# Caseload per physician
sK4229	# Surgeries performed
sK4230	# Discharges
sK4232	# Nurses per physician
sK4233	# Full Time Equivalents per occupied bed
sK4236	# Medical residency positions opened
sK4237	# Medical specialties covered
sK4240	# Medical residents work hours
sK4241	# Patients on the waiting list for admission to long-term care
sK4242	$ Revenue per patient per day
sK4243	$ Medical support staff cost per Full Time Equivalent physician
sK4245	% Compliance before patient contact
sK4250	# Post discharge complications
sK4251	% Repeat prescriptions
sK4252	% Successful surgeries of critical diseases
sK4254	# Cases where a foreign body was left in during procedure
sK4255	% Post operating hematoma
sK4256	# Anesthesia cases
sK4257	# Waiting time for planned surgical care
sK4259	% Deaths within a month of a bypass surgery
sK4260	% Postoperative sepsis incidence
sK4261	% Readmission to hospital within a month of discharge
sK4262	% Readmission for complication or infection
sK4263	% Risk-adjusted mortality
sK4264	# Surgical infection prevention procedures
sK4266	# Cycle time to discharge patients
sK4268	% Delayed inpatient discharges
sK4269	% Heart failure patients discharged home with written instructions
sK4271	# Inpatients waiting longer than the standard
sK4272	% Patients leaving against medical advise
sK4273	% Patients waiting more than x hours
sK4274	# New patients per physician
sK4275	$ Cost per discharge

sKPI #	Key Performance Indicator name
sK4276	% Successful completion rate of medical treatment
sK4279	% Inpatient revenue
sK4282	% Plan adherence of hospital bed occupancy
sK4283	# Patients treated
sK4284	# Non-physician practitioners (NPP)
sK4285	% Operating expenses paid from endowment proceeds
sK4286	% Patients with a self-pay liability
sK4287	# Follow-up visits per physician
sK4288	% Accuracy of discharge predictions
sK4289	% Hospital revenue from charitable sources
sK4302	# Patients experiencing medical errors
sK4304	# Patient consultation time
sK4305	% Patient complication rate
sK4313	# Hygienic precautions measures
sK4314	# Paid hours per discharge
sK4323	% Patient oriented time
sK4326	% Reusable medical devices properly decontaminated
sK4327	# Patient wait time
sK4328	% Patients who leave without being seen
sK4329	# Clinical negligence cases
sK4331	% Patient satisfaction
sK4332	% Patient willingness to return
sK5720	# Length of stay in general care
sK5727	# Uninsured patients served
sK5898	# Cost per ER visit to cost per primary care visit
sK6121	% Screening of uninsured inpatients and high-dollar outpatients for financial assistance
sK6126	% Insurance verification rate of unscheduled inpatient admissions
sK6127	% Insurance verification rate of unscheduled high-dollar outpatient admissions
sK6134	# Final bills or claims that are in the backlog
sK6150	# Inpatient registrations per shift
sK6153	% Advanced beneficiary notifications obtained
sK6154	% Master patient index (MPI) duplicates
sK6163	# Discharged not final billed
sK6176	% Electronic eligibility rate
sK6184	# Time to post cash payment
sK6187	% Third party payer underpayments and overpayments
sK6192	% Self pay A/R of medical bill aged more than 90 days from placement date
sK6206	% Patient cash net revenue
sK6207	% HIPAA-compliant electronic payments posted
sK6827	% Hospital initiated cancellations
sK6828	# Surgery cancellations on surgery day
sK6829	% Same diagnostic early readmission cases
sK6835	% Patient complaints

sKPI #	Key Performance Indicator name
sK6861	# Patients transferred to another hospital, with the same pathology type, in a 72 hour period
sK6862	% Patients transferred due to insurance reasons or patient preference
sK6863	% Hospitalized patients who reside in other counties
sK6886	% Visits that require the use of scans or tests available in the practice
sK7010	% Patients without medical cover who have been hospitalized
sK14339	# 28-day emergency readmission rates
sK14343	# 30-day perioperative mortality data
sK14349	# Abdominal aortic aneurysm repair
sK14350	# Abnormal mammogram turnaround time
sK14372	# Access to primary dental services
sK14379	# Accidental puncture or laceration
sK14391	# ACEI or ARB for LVSD
sK14417	# Acute ALOS
sK14418	# Acute CMI
sK14419	# Acute LOS
sK14420	# Acute patient days
sK14426	# Adjusted length of stay
sK14428	# Admissions per 1,000 members
sK14429	# Admissions
sK14430	# Adolescent immunization
sK14431	# Adolescent well-care visit
sK14439	# Adults registered with an NHS dentist
sK14440	# Adults' access to ambulatory health services
sK14442	# Adverse drug reactions
sK14444	# Advising smokers to quit
sK14449	# Age of hospitals buildings
sK14494	# All age all cause mortality rate per 100,000 population (females)
sK14495	# All age all cause mortality rate per 100,000 population (males)
sK14499	# ALOS
sK14500	# ALOS medicare
sK14501	# ALOS non-medicare
sK14509	# Ambulatory care service types
sK14512	# Annual dental visit
sK14516	# HbA1c testing
sK14523	# Anticoagulation therapy for atrial fibrillation/flutter thrombolytic therapy
sK14524	# Antithrombolytic therapy by end of second day of hospitalization
sK14529	# Appropriate initial empiric antibiotic selection
sK14544	# Aspirin administration within 24 hours post- MI
sK14545	# Aspirin at arrival
sK14546	# Aspirin prescribed at discharge
sK14548	# Assessed for rehabilitation

sKPI #	Key Performance Indicator name
sK14585	# Avoidable hospitalizations by selected conditions
sK14586	# Avoidable mortablity by selected conditions
sK14587	# Avoidance of sublingual nifedipine
sK14597	# Bed days per 1,000 members
sK14600	# Beds available in long term care facilities
sK14602	# Beds in service
sK14603	# Beds per 1000 sq m built-up area
sK14606	# Benzodiazepines
sK14614	# Beta blocker treatment after a heart attack
sK14615	# Beta-blocker prescribed at discharge
sK14616	# Beta-blocker therapy
sK14620	# Lipid profile
sK14621	# Mammography screening
sK14622	# Retinal exam
sK14624	# Bilateral cardiac catheterization
sK14628	# Births
sK14629	# Births of newborns
sK14638	# Blood culture before antibiotics administration
sK14639	# Blood cultures performed prior to initial antibiotic received
sK14640	# Blood cultures performed within 24 hours from arrival for patients admitted to ICU
sK14658	# Breast cancer screening
sK14659	# Breastfeeding at 6-8 weeks
sK14667	# Built-up area
sK14687	# Caesarean sections
sK14692	# CAMHS
sK14696	# Cancer registrations
sK14708	# Cardiac surgery patients with controlled 6 a.m. postoperative blood glucose
sK14709	# Care coordination at hospitals discharge
sK14710	# Care provided in public programs
sK14711	# Care transition record transmitted
sK14726	# Carotid endarterectomy
sK14740	# Central line-associated blood infection
sK14742	# Cervical cancer screening
sK14752	# Charity Care
sK14755	# Check-ups after delivery
sK14756	# Childhood immunisation
sK14763	# Children registered with an NHS dentist
sK14765	# Chlamydia screening
sK14766	# Chronic disease under control
sK14774	# CLI rate per 1000 central line days
sK14781	# Code response time
sK14833	# Complications of anesthesia
sK14835	# Computed tomography (CT) wait times
sK14837	# Computerized physician order entry
sK14854	# Consistent messages from multiple providers
sK14888	# Coordination of care
sK14889	# Co-pay
sK14892	# Coronary artery bypass graft surgery
sK14893	# Correlation between pathology reports and autopsy findings
sK14910	# Credit card collections
sK14920	# Crisis resolution services
sK14921	# Crude length of stay
sK14928	# Cultural competence training programs
sK14974	# Census
sK14984	# Data quality on ethnic group
sK14989	# Days of occupancy
sK14996	# Days to next appointment
sK15000	# Death in low-mortality DRGs
sK15001	# Death within 30 days of surgery per 100,000 patients
sK15002	# Deaths from 'avoidable' diseases
sK15003	# Deaths from cancer per 100,000
sK15004	# Deaths from heart disease per 100,000
sK15007	# Deaths per 100 Medicare beneficiaries
sK15009	# Decayed, missing and filed teeth in five year olds
sK15013	# Decubitus ulcer
sK15048	# Delayed discharge from Hospitals for people by age group
sK15053	# Delayed transfers
sK15054	# Delayed transfers of care per 100,000 population
sK15068	# Denied Claims
sK15086	# Discharge for females in maternity care
sK15087	# Discharged on antithrombotic
sK15088	# Discharged on antithrombotic therapy
sK15089	# Discharged on statin medication
sK15090	# Discharged on warfarin
sK15096	# Discussion of advance directives
sK15097	# Disease-specific mortality
sK15125	# Drug users in effective treatment
sK15126	# Drug users recorded as being in effective treatment
sK15138	# Early intervention in psychosis services
sK15140	# Ease of use of translation services
sK15147	# ED visits
sK15153	# Time between scheduling and account resolution
sK15154	# Time between scheduling and completing financial resolution
sK15155	# Time between scheduling and completing insurance verification
sK15159	# Elective surgery clearance time
sK15176	# Emergency admissions to hospitals for people aged 75 or over, per 1000 population
sK15177	# Emergency department wait times for admitted patients

sKPI #	Key Performance Indicator name
sK15180	# Emergency department waiting times
sK15183	# Emergency readmission to hospital within 28 days of discharge following hip fracture
sK15184	# Emergency room visits
sK15188	# Employee exposures to blood and bodily fluids
sK15195	# Employees with an individual development implemented or revised
sK15201	# Enrolment years by payer
sK15209	# Equiseps
sK15211	# ER visits
sK15212	# Esophageal resection (cancer)
sK15231	# Experience of patients
sK15244	# Eye exams for people with diabetes
sK15248	# Failure to rescue
sK15249	# Falls per quarter
sK15250	# Falls reported
sK15276	# Fibrinolytic therapy received within 30 minutes of Hospitals arrival
sK15601	# Influenza vaccinations
sK15614	# Inpatient mortality
sK17759	# Length of stay for general inpatients
sK16126	# Outpatient visits
sK16294	# Perioperative mortality
sK16333	# Pneumococcal vaccinations
sK17236	# VRE blood stream infection cases per quarter
sK17237	# VTE patients receiving unfractionated heparin with dosages/platelet count monitoring by protocol
sK17238	# VTE patients with anticoagulation overlap therapy
sK17239	# VTE prophylaxis
sK17240	# VTE warfarin therapy discharge instructions
sK17242	# Wait time
sK17243	# Wait time for pain medication
sK17244	# Wait times
sK17249	# Waiting times for elective surgery
sK17275	# Weeks of pregnancy at time of enrolment
sK17277	# Well child care visits in the first 15 months of life
sK17278	# Well child care visits in the third, fourth, fifth and sixth year of life
sK17304	# Flu shots for older adults
sK17306	# Follow up after hospitalization for mental illness
sK17315	# Foreign body left in
sK17319	# Four week smoking quitters
sK17333	# Frequency of attacks
sK17337	# Frequency of ongoing prenatal care
sK17338	# Frequency of selected procedures
sK17351	# FTEs per bed
sK17352	# FTEs per discharge
sK17369	# Full-time equivalent staff per adjusted occupied bed

sKPI #	Key Performance Indicator name
sK17466	# Herfindahl index
sK17468	# High risk families receiving home visiting services
sK17473	# High-occurrence DRGs
sK17474	# High-risk delivery
sK17476	# Hip fractures
sK17477	# Hip operations per 100,000
sK17478	# Hip replacements
sK17483	# Home care patient loyalty index
sK17484	# Home Management Plan of Care (HMPC) document given to patient/caregiver
sK17493	# Hospitals acquired CDI cases per month
sK17494	# Hospitals acquired MRSA blood stream infection cases
sK17495	# Hospitals admissions for ambulatory care-sensitive conditions
sK17496	# Hospitals initiated postponements per 100 scheduled admissions from the waiting list
sK17497	# Hospitals outpatient ACEI or ARB for LVSD
sK17498	# Hospitals outpatient activity recommendations
sK17499	# Hospitals outpatient aldosterone receptor antagonists for LVSD
sK17500	# Hospitals outpatient assessment of functional status for heart failure
sK17501	# Hospitals outpatient beta-blocker therapy for LVSD
sK17502	# Hospitals outpatient cardiac resynchronization therapy
sK17503	# Hospitals outpatient discussion of advance directives
sK17504	# Hospitals outpatient icd counseling for LVSD
sK17505	# Hospitals patients' beds
sK17506	# Hospitals-acquired infections
sK17507	# Hospitalizations
sK17508	# Hospitals-standardized mortality ratios
sK17512	# Hours of emergency room diversion
sK17516	# Hours of physical restraint use
sK17517	# Hours of seclusion
sK17518	# Hours per weighted case
sK17537	# Iatrogenic pneumothorax
sK17539	# ICU hours
sK17540	# ICU staffing by intensivist physicians
sK17541	# ICU VTE prophylaxis
sK17545	# Immunization
sK17546	# Implementation of the stroke strategy
sK17548	# In hospital hip fracture for elderly
sK17564	# Incidence of infectious diseases
sK17598	# Infant mortality
sK17599	# Infection control
sK17600	# Influenza vaccination
sK17603	# In hospital mortality
sK17604	# Initial antibiotic dose within 8 hours of hospital arrival

sKPI #	Key Performance Indicator name
sK17605	# Initial antibiotic selection for CAP in immunocompetent of ICU patient
sK17606	# Initial antibiotic selection for CAP in immunocompetent of non ICU patient
sK17607	# Initial antibiotic selection for CAP in immunocompetent patient
sK17608	# Initiation of prenatal care
sK17611	# Inpatient days
sK17612	# Inpatient loyalty index
sK17615	# Inpatient paid per employee
sK17616	# Inpatient paid per member
sK17617	# Inpatient payer mix
sK17618	# Inpatient surgical operations
sK17620	# Inpatients waiting per head of population
sK17621	# Inpatients waiting times
sK17687	# Knee replacements
sK17700	# Language translation services of health care services
sK17758	# Length of stay for females in maternity care
sK17761	# Length of stay in ED
sK17762	# Length of stay of newborns
sK17771	# Length of visit with nurse practitioner
sK17772	# Length of visit with physician
sK17851	# Low birth-weight babies
sK17852	# Low birth-weight deliveries at facilities for high-risk deliveries and neonates
sK17856	# Magnetic resonance imaging (MRI) wait times
sK17895	# Medicare case-mix
sK17896	# Medicare outpatient payer mix
sK17897	# Medication error rate or adverse drug events due to medication errors
sK17898	# Medication errors
sK17899	# Medicine error severity ratio
sK17903	# Membership of the health plan
sK17942	# Minutes before possible heart attack patients were transferred to another hospital
sK17943	# Minutes before possible heart attack patients received an ECG
sK17956	# Mortality amenable to health care, deaths per 100,000 population
sK17981	# Neonatal immunization after X days
sK18012	# New hospital acquired CLI cases
sK18013	# New hospital acquired VAP cases
sK18037	# NHS staff survey scores-based measures of job satisfaction
sK18038	# NHSLA PCT standards, risk management assessment levels
sK18061	# Nursing home readmissions
sK18062	# Nursing home residents with pressure sores
sK18063	# Nursing homes
sK18064	# Nursing homes admissions

sKPI #	Key Performance Indicator name
sK18066	# Nursing Task Force Recommendations implemented
sK18067	# Nursing-sensitive adverse event for medical conditions
sK18068	# Nursing-sensitive adverse event for surgical conditions
sK18070	# Occupation time of hospital bed
sK18111	# Order sets
sK18118	# Outpatient mix
sK18119	# Outpatient mortality
sK18120	# Outpatient occasions of service
sK18121	# Outpatient paid per employee
sK18122	# Outpatient paid per member
sK18123	# Outpatient Surgeries
sK18124	# Outpatient surgical operations
sK18127	# Outpatient waiting time for first appointment
sK18128	# Outpatient waiting times
sK18141	# Paid hours per Adjusted Patients Days (APD)
sK18142	# Pancreatic resection (cancer)
sK18221	# Patients with early readmission to hospital
sK18222	# Patient care hours
sK18223	# Patient days
sK18224	# Patient due A/R
sK18225	# Patient due aging
sK18227	# Patient satisfaction score for admission not through ED
sK18228	# Patient satisfaction score for admission through hospitals ED
sK18229	# Patient satisfaction score for hospitals with 1-50 beds
sK18230	# Patient wait time in admissions
sK18231	# Patient wait time in pharmacy
sK18232	# Patient-centered hospital care score
sK18233	# Patients admitted to emergency departments
sK18234	# Patients admitted to hospitals
sK18235	# Patients on the elective surgery waiting list
sK18236	# Patients' overall rating for hospital
sK18237	# Patients referred outside of the network
sK18238	# Patients served in free clinical service programs
sK18239	# Patients who wait less than 2 hours for emergency admissions through A&E
sK18240	# Patients staying in the emergency department over 24 hours
sK18241	# Patients with infections
sK18242	# Patients with operations cancelled for non-medical reasons
sK18243	# Patients with vaccinations
sK18263	# Pediatric heart surgery
sK18270	# People on hospital waiting lists
sK18281	# Percutaneous coronary interventions
sK18284	# Perinatal mortality
sK18303	# PHealth promotion
sK18304	# Physician FTEs

sKPI #	Key Performance Indicator name
sK18305	# Physician practices
sK18306	# Physician satisfaction score
sK18307	# Physician satisfaction score with ease of practice
sK18308	# Physician satisfaction score with overall assessment
sK18309	# Physician satisfaction score with patient care
sK18310	# Physician satisfaction score with relationship with leaders
sK18311	# Physicians, including specialists per capita
sK18312	# Physicians' visits
sK18321	# Planned day only patients admitted to overnight stay
sK18335	# Pneumonia and flu hospitalization of persons over 64
sK18349	# Positive blood cultures in NICU
sK18350	# Possible outpatients
sK18352	# Post-discharge appointment for heart failure patients
sK18353	# Post-discharge evaluation for heart failure patients
sK18359	# Postnatal women breastfeeding at discharge
sK18360	# Postoperative abdominopelvic wound dehiscence
sK18361	# Postoperative espsis
sK18362	# Postoperative hemorrhage or hematoma
sK18363	# Postoperative metabolic derangement
sK18364	# Postoperative physiologic derangement
sK18365	# Postoperative respiratory failure
sK18366	# Postoperative stay
sK18367	# Postoperative thromboembolism
sK18370	# Potential overuse or waste
sK18372	# Potential years of life lost from cancer and heart disease
sK18383	# Prenatal care visits in the first trimester
sK18388	# Prevalence of daily physical restraints
sK18389	# Preventable admissions
sK18391	# Preventive care
sK18394	# Price to revenue
sK18395	# Primary care physicians joining primary care reform
sK18396	# Primary care sites where reform is implemented
sK18401	# Primary pci received within 90 minutes of hospital arrival
sK18416	# Problems in communication
sK18486	# Provider mix reflective of community(ies) served
sK18511	# Quality of life
sK18550	# Readmission for chemical dependency
sK18551	# Readmissions for specified mental health disorders
sK18592	# Reported consumer complaints
sK18598	# Reported patient incidents
sK18600	# Reported staff incidents
sK18637	# Responses from staff survey on satisfaction with employer
sK18651	# Returning home within 28 days of emergency admission to hospital for fractured hip
sK18725	# Scheduled patients

sKPI #	Key Performance Indicator name
sK18726	# Scheduled patients with a self-pay liability
sK18742	# Score of respect for patient preferences
sK18762	# Selected infections due to medical care
sK18763	# Self reported experience of patients
sK18772	# Separations per 1,000 population
sK18828	# Specialists per 100,000
sK18853	# Staffed beds
sK18856	# Stage of cancer at diagnosis
sK18874	# Stroke education
sK18875	# Stroke patients cared for in a dedicated unit
sK18876	# Stroke patients with VTE prophylaxis
sK18925	# Surgery patients on beta-blocker therapy prior to arrival who received a beta-blocker during the perioperative period
sK18926	# Surgery patients who received appropriate venous thromboembolism prophylaxis 24 hours before and after surgery
sK18927	# Surgery patients with appropriate hair removal
sK18928	# Surgery patients with recommended venous thromboembolism prophylaxis ordered
sK18929	# Surgery wait times
sK18930	# Surgical-wound infections
sK18981	# TIA patients scanned and treated within 48 hours
sK18982	# Time between patient entering ED and seeing physician
sK18987	# Time in A&E
sK19012	# Time to reperfusion
sK19065	# Transfusion reaction
sK19093	# Treating children's ear infections
sK19094	# Treatments
sK19125	# Uncompensated care
sK19129	# Unique Medicaid members
sK19140	# Unplanned and unexpected hospital readmissions
sK19153	# Unplanned return to the operating room during the same admission
sK19155	# Unsafe drug use
sK19163	# Urinary catheter removed within two days of surgery
sK19164	# Urinary catheter-associated UTI
sK19168	# Use of angiography following AMI
sK19169	# Use of dangerous abbreviations in medication orders
sK19195	# Vaginal birth after caesarean
sK19196	# Vancomycin-resistant-enterococcus (VRE) infection
sK19199	# Variation from expected length of stay
sK19201	# Variations in intervention rates
sK19209	# Ventilator-associated pneumonia
sK19210	# Ventilator-associated pneumonia (VAP)
sK19295	# Years in business of the health plan
sK19394	$ Cost of medications prescribed
sK19398	$ Cost per adjusted discharge

sKPI #	Key Performance Indicator name
sK19404	$ Cost per case
sK19405	$ Cost per casemix-adjusted separation
sK19408	$ Cost per discharge for patients aged 1-17
sK19414	$ Cost per non-admitted occasion of care
sK19423	$ Cost per RUG-III weighted patient day
sK19447	$ Direct cost per case
sK19448	$ Direct cost per RUG-III weighted patient day
sK19464	$ Expense per discharge
sK19536	$ Handling costs
sK19568	$ Investment in research programs
sK19576	$ Labor cost per adjusted discharge
sK19577	$ Labor cost per casemix-adjusted separation
sK19591	$ Maintenance budget per bed
sK19603	$ Medicare costs for chronic diseases
sK19604	$ Medicare costs for COPD
sK19605	$ Medicare costs for diabetes
sK19606	$ Medicare costs for heart failure
sK19607	$ Medicare costs of care
sK19608	$ Medicare outlays
sK19609	$ Medicare revenue per day
sK19613	$ Monthly drug cost
sK19623	$ Net patient revenue
sK19644	$ Operating expense per APD
sK19659	$ Packaging costs
sK19660	$ Paid per admission
sK19676	$ Patient deductions
sK19691	$ Pharmacy cost
sK19702	$ Price per bed
sK19760	$ Revenue per discharge
sK19765	$ Revenue per physician FTE
sK19789	$ Sales by therapy area
sK19818	$ Supply expense per APD
sK19851	$ Unit cost of caring for patients in receipt of specialized mental health services
sK19852	$ Unit cost of maternity
sK19855	$ User cost of capital per casemix-adjusted separation
sK19883	% 28 day emergency readmission
sK19884	% 28-day readmission after AMI
sK19885	% 28-day readmission after asthma
sK19886	% 28-day readmission after hysterectomy
sK19887	% 28-day readmission after prostatectomy
sK19888	% 28-day readmission after stroke
sK19889	% 30 day mortality rates following myocardial infarction for patients ages 50 and over
sK19890	% 30 day perioperative mortality rate
sK19896	% 30-day in-hospitals mortality following AMI
sK19897	% 30-day in-hospitals mortality following stroke

sKPI #	Key Performance Indicator name
sK19898	% 5 day mortality following major surgery
sK19903	% 90-day readmission after hip replacement
sK19904	% 90-day readmission after knee replacement
sK19911	% Ability to see a doctor when needed
sK19912	% Able to get an appointment fairly quickly
sK19932	% Access to dental services
sK19934	% Access to primary care
sK19943	% Accuracy of transfusion protocols
sK19946	% ACE-inhibitor at discharge for low LVF
sK19956	% Acute myocardial infarction
sK19958	% Adequacy of follow-up for antidepressant treatment
sK19967	% Admissions, discharges and transfers index
sK19968	% Admissions, discharges and transfers index of cardiovascular unit
sK19969	% Admissions, discharges and transfers index of critical care unit
sK19970	% Admissions, discharges and transfers index of emergency department
sK19971	% Admissions, discharges and transfers index of intensive care unit
sK19972	% Admissions, discharges and transfers index of medical unit
sK19973	% Admissions, discharges and transfers index of medical/surgical unit
sK19974	% Admissions, discharges and transfers index of neonatal intensive care unit
sK19975	% Admissions, discharges and transfers index of neurology unit
sK19976	% Admissions, discharges and transfers index of oncology unit
sK19977	% Admissions, discharges and transfers index of operating room
sK19978	% Admissions, discharges and transfers index of orthopedics unit
sK19979	% Admissions, discharges and transfers index of pediatric intensive care unit
sK19980	% Admissions, discharges and transfers index of pediatrics unit
sK19981	% Admissions, discharges and transfers index of psychiatric unit
sK19982	% Admissions, discharges and transfers index of rehabilitation unit
sK19983	% Admissions, discharges and transfers index of respiratory unit
sK19984	% Admissions, discharges and transfers index of surgical unit
sK19985	% Admissions, discharges and transfers index of telemetry unit
sK19986	% Admissions, discharges and transfers index of women's and children's unit
sK19996	% Adults over 18 assisted to live independently
sK19997	% Adults over 18 receiving direct payments and/or individual budgets per 100,000 population

sKPI #	Key Performance Indicator name
sK19998	% Adults received recommended screening and preventive care
sK19999	% Adults under 65 insured all year
sK20000	% Adults under 65 limited in any activities because of physical, mental, or emotional problems
sK20001	% Adults under 65 not underinsured
sK20002	% Adults under 65 with accessible primary care provider
sK20003	% Adults under 65 with no medical bill problems or medical debt
sK20004	% Adults with chronic conditions given self-management plan
sK20005	% Adults with no access problem due to costs
sK20006	% Adverse drug reactions
sK20015	% Age standardised admission rates for asthma
sK20016	% Age standardised admission rates for diabetes
sK20017	% Age standardised admission rates for epilepsy
sK20018	% Age standardised admission rates for heart failure
sK20019	% Age standardised admission rates for kidney/urinary tract infection
sK20020	% Age standardised admission rates for severe ENT infection
sK20021	% Agency nursing/midwifery staff to hospital staff
sK20032	% All age all cause mortality
sK20047	% Antibiotic discontinued within 24 hours from surgey
sK20048	% Antibiotic prophylaxis within 1 hour before surgery
sK20051	% Antibiotics started within 4 hours of hospital arrival
sK20066	% Appropriate antibiotics choice
sK20068	% Appropriate initial antibiotic choice
sK20078	% Appropriate use of ACEI at discharge
sK20085	% Area around the patient rooms always kept quiet at night
sK20091	% Aspirin at arrival
sK20092	% Aspirin at discharge
sK20096	% Assessment of oxygenation at admission
sK20112	% Autopsy rate
sK20113	% Availability of dentists
sK20114	% Availability of foreign-language written materials
sK20115	% Availability of general practice doctors and specialists province-wide and in under-serviced areas
sK20117	% Availability of language interpretation services
sK20119	% Availability of mental health/chemical dependency providers
sK20120	% Availability of obstetrical/prenatal care providers
sK20121	% Availability of primary care providers
sK20124	% Availability of use of translation services
sK20126	% Babies born by Caesarean section
sK20129	% Bacteraemia infection rates
sK20133	% Bed occupancy
sK4330	% Hospital bed occupancy by category of stay
sK20136	% Beta blocker after acute mi

sKPI #	Key Performance Indicator name
sK20137	% Beta-blocker at arrival
sK20138	% Beta-blocker at discharge
sK20142	% Birth trauma
sK20143	% Birth trauma-injury to neonate
sK20144	% Birth trauma among high risk women
sK20150	% Blood cultures before antibiotics
sK20154	% Board certified surgeons
sK20155	% Bowel cancer surgeries completed within priority access target wait times
sK20156	% Breast cancer surgeries completed within priority access target wait times
sK20165	% CABG mortality rates
sK20166	% CABG surgery using internal mammary artery
sK20167	% Caesarean section
sK20168	% Caesarean section and vaginal birth after caesarean (VBAC)
sK20176	% Cancer mortality rate
sK20177	% Cancer mortality rate for people aged 75 or less
sK20178	% Cancer surgeries completed within the recommended priority access target wait times
sK20179	% Cancer surgeries completed within priority access target wait times
sK20191	% Cardiac surgery/conditions discharges
sK20192	% Cardiovascular disease (CVD) mortality rate for people aged 75 or less
sK20193	% Carers receiving a 'carer's break'
sK20200	% Casemix adjusted length of stay
sK20203	% Category 1 patients admitted within 30 days
sK20204	% Category 2 elective surgery patients waiting 90 days or less
sK20205	% Category 3 elective surgery patients waiting 365 days or less
sK20208	% Census disparity index of cardiovascular
sK20209	% Census disparity index of critical care
sK20210	% Census disparity index of emergency department
sK20211	% Census disparity index of intensive care
sK20212	% Census disparity index of medical
sK20213	% Census disparity index of medical/surgical
sK20214	% Census disparity index of neonatal intensive care
sK20215	% Census disparity index of neurology
sK20216	% Census disparity index of oncology
sK20217	% Census disparity index of orthopedics
sK20218	% Census disparity index of pediatric intensive care
sK20219	% Census disparity index of pediatrics
sK20220	% Census disparity index of psychiatric
sK20221	% Census disparity index of rehabilitation
sK20222	% Census disparity index of respiratory
sK20223	% Census disparity index of surgical
sK20224	% Census disparity index of telemetry

sKPI #	Key Performance Indicator name
sK20225	% Census disparity index of women's and children's
sK20226	% Central line infection (CLI)
sK20227	% Central line-associated primary bloodstream infection (BSI)
sK20228	% Central line-associated primary bloodstream infection (BSI) - burn
sK20229	% Central line-associated primary bloodstream infection (BSI) - cardiothoracic
sK20230	% Central line-associated primary bloodstream infection (BSI) - combined medical/surgical (all hospitalss other than major teaching)
sK20231	% Central line-associated primary bloodstream infection (BSI) - combined medical/surgical (major teaching hospitals)
sK20232	% Central line-associated primary bloodstream infection (BSI) - coronary care
sK20233	% Central line-associated primary bloodstream infection (BSI) - medical
sK20234	% Central line-associated primary bloodstream infection (BSI) - neurosurgical
sK20235	% Central line-associated primary bloodstream infection (BSI) - respiratory
sK20236	% Central line-associated primary bloodstream infection (BSI) - surgical
sK20237	% Central line-associated primary bloodstream infection (BSI) - trauma
sK20238	% Central venous catheter infection rates
sK20239	% Cesarean delivery
sK20245	% Chemical dependency utilization
sK20246	% Childhood immunization rates
sK20250	% Children and their caregivers receiving a home management health plan of care, while hospitalized for asthma
sK20253	% Children who missed 11 or more school days due to illness or injury
sK20254	% Children receiving recommended immunizations and preventive care
sK20255	% Children who complete immunization by recommended ages
sK20256	% Children receiving reliever medication while hospitalized for asthma
sK20257	% Children receiving systemic corticosteroid medication while hospitalized for asthma
sK20258	% Children's access to primary care providers
sK20261	% Chlamydia screening
sK20262	% Chronic patients in physical restraints daily
sK20263	% Chronic patients on antipsychotic medication without a diagnosis of psychosis
sK20264	% Chronic patients who became more depressed or anxious
sK20265	% Chronic patients who declined in their ability to communicate
sK20266	% Chronic patients who declined in their ability to walk or wheel themselves

sKPI #	Key Performance Indicator name
sK20267	% Chronic patients who fell within 30 days prior to assessment
sK20268	% Chronic patients whose bladder continence worsened
sK20269	% Chronic patients with indwelling catheters
sK20270	% Chronic patients with new stage II or greater skin ulcers
sK20271	% Chronic patients with pain
sK20272	% Chronic patients with pressure sores
sK20273	% Chronic patients with rehabilitation potential who improved in the performance of activities of daily living
sK20284	% Clear documentation of informed surgical and anesthesia consent
sK20331	% Clostridium Difficile
sK20332	% Clostridium difficile infection (CDI)
sK20342	% Commissioning a comprehensive child and adolescent mental health service (CAMHS)
sK20354	% Community-acquired pneumonia
sK20372	% Computed tomography (CT) completed within the recommended priority access target wait times
sK20376	% Conceptions below age 16
sK20378	% Congestive heart failure
sK20396	% Cost effective prescribing NIC/DDD of inhaled corticosteroids
sK20397	% Cost effective prescribing NIC/PU of combination products
sK20398	% Cost effective prescribing NIC/PU of drugs of limited clinical value
sK20399	% Cost effective prescribing NIC/PU of modified release products
sK20412	% C-section infection rates
sK20413	% C-section rates
sK20414	% C-sections
sK20443	% CVD mortality rate
sK20444	% D&Cs performed in women under 40
sK20445	% Bed occupancy for ENT surgery
sK20446	% Bed occupancy for general medicine and its associated sub -specialties
sK20447	% Bed occupancy for gynecology
sK20448	% Bed occupancy for ophthalmology
sK20449	% Census of acute beds
sK20450	% Census of swing-SNF beds
sK20454	% Day case rate
sK20456	% Days net patient revenue in accounts receivable
sK20457	% Days patients spend in acute care hospitals, when another type of facility would be more appropriate
sK20458	% Death rates from all circulatory diseases
sK20459	% Death rates from all malignant neoplasms
sK20460	% Death rates from suicide
sK20461	% Death rates from undetermined injury
sK20463	% Deaths that occur at home
sK20465	% Deep vein thrombosis (DVT)

Organizational » Industries

sKPI #	Key Performance Indicator name
sK20469	% Delay to hip fracture surgery
sK20471	% Deliberate or unintended injuries to young people aged under 19
sK20473	% Diabetic retinopathy
sK20476	% Digestive system discharges
sK20479	% Discharge instructions documented and given to patient
sK20480	% Discharge within 28 days of emergency admission with a fractured neck of femur for patients aged over 65
sK20481	% Discharge within 56 days of emergency admission with a stroke for patients aged over 50
sK20491	% Disenrollment of a health plan
sK20497	% Doctors recognized as always giving explanations to patients
sK20498	% Doctors recognized as always listening to patients
sK20499	% Doctors recognized as always showing respect to patients
sK20500	% Doctors recognized as spending enough time with patients
sK20508	% Dose
sK20510	% Ear, nose and throat surgeries completed within the recommended priority access target wait times
sK20514	% Hospitals recognized as easily providing after hours care
sK20523	% Emergency admissions
sK20525	% Emergency patient readmission rate
sK20526	% Emergency patients transferred to an inpatient bed within 8 hours
sK20527	% Emergency psychiatric readmission
sK20630	% Facilities that were accredited according to national healthcare standards
sK20634	% Families spending less than 10% of income on medical costs
sK20648	% First / follow-up attendances in emergency room
sK20651	% First outpatient appointments for which patient did not attend
sK20653	% Five-year survival rates for specific cancers
sK20701	% General surgeries completed within the recommended priority access target wait times
sK20703	% Generic prescribing
sK20705	% Glycosylated hemoglobin testing for diabetics
sK20711	% GP practices with validated registers of patients without symptoms of cardiovascular disease
sK20724	% GUM Access
sK20725	% Gynecology surgeries completed within the recommended priority access target wait times
sK20726	% Haema/Inf. Diseases discharges of all discharges
sK20732	% Hand hygiene
sK20733	% Hand hygiene after contact with the patient and patient environment for all health care providers
sK20734	% Hand hygiene before initial contact with the patient and patient environment for all healthcare providers
sK20739	% Health insurance administration of national health expenditures

sKPI #	Key Performance Indicator name
sK20740	% Health plan provider turnover
sK20742	% Heart attack care composite
sK20744	% Heart attack mortality rate
sK20745	% Heart attack patients given ACE Inhibitor or ARB for Left Ventricular Systolic Dysfunction
sK20746	% Heart attack patients given aspirin at arrival
sK20747	% Heart attack patients given aspirin at discharge
sK20748	% Heart attack patients given beta blocker at discharge
sK20749	% Heart attack patients given fibrinolytic medication within 30 minutes of arrival
sK20750	% Heart attack patients given PCI within 90 minutes of arrival
sK20751	% Heart attack patients given smoking cessation advice
sK20752	% Heart attack readmission rate
sK20753	% Heart attack survival
sK20754	% Heart failure mortality rate
sK20755	% Heart failure patients given ACE Inhibitor or ARB for Left Ventricular Systolic Dysfunction
sK20756	% Heart failure patients given an evaluation of left ventricular systolic function
sK20757	% Heart failure patients given smoking cessation advice
sK20758	% Heart failure readmission rate
sK20759	% Heart surgery patients whose blood sugar was kept under control after surgery
sK20771	% High-cost DRGs
sK20775	% Histories and physicals charted within 24 hours
sK20776	% HMO penetration
sK20784	% Hospitals acquired CDI per 1,000 patient days
sK20785	% Hospitals acquired CDI per month
sK20786	% Hospitals acquired infection rate
sK20787	% Hospitals acquired MRSA blood stream infections per 1,000 patient days
sK20788	% Hospitals acquired MRSA blood stream infections per quarter
sK20789	% Hospitals admissions of home health
sK20790	% Hospitals admissions per 100,000 population for alcohol related harm
sK20791	% Hospitals standardized mortality ratio (HSMR)
sK20792	% Hospitals stays accounted for by Medicaid
sK20793	% Hospitals stays accounted for by Medicare
sK20794	% Hospitals stays accounted for by patients 65-84 years old
sK20795	% Hospitals stays accounted for by private insurance
sK20796	% Hospitals stays accounted for by uninsured
sK20797	% Hospitalizations generated by local residents
sK20799	% Hospitalized patients receiving recommended care for heart attack, heart failure and pneumonia
sK20800	% Hospitals-level complication rate
sK20801	% Hospitals-level infection rate
sK20802	% Hospitals-level mortality rate
sK20835	% Incidental appendectomy for people aged over 65

sKPI #	Key Performance Indicator name
sK20846	% Infants breastfed at 6 - 8 weeks
sK20848	% Influenza screen or vaccination for people aged over 50
sK20850	% Influenza vaccination rates
sK20854	% In-hospital mortality
sK20855	% In-hospital mortality after abdominal aortic aneurysm repair
sK20856	% In-hospital mortality after coronary artery by pass graft surgery
sK20857	% In-hospital mortality after craniotomy
sK20858	% In-hospital mortality after esophageal resection (cancer)
sK20859	% In-hospital mortality after pancreatic resection (cancer)
sK20860	% In-hospital mortality after pediatric heart surgery repair
sK20861	% In-hospital mortality after percutaneous coronary interventions
sK20862	% In-hospital mortality after total hip arthroplasty
sK20863	% In-hospital neonatal mortality
sK20866	% Inpatient admission rates
sK20867	% Inpatient capitated revenue
sK20868	% Inpatient commercial revenue
sK20869	% Inpatient HMO revenue
sK20870	% Inpatient medicaid revenue
sK20871	% Inpatient nursing productivity
sK20873	% Inpatient revenue
sK20874	% Inpatient RN earned hours
sK20875	% Inpatient satisfaction
sK20876	% Inpatient satisfaction with caring of staff
sK20877	% Inpatient satisfaction with cleanliness
sK20878	% Inpatient satisfaction with courtesy of staff
sK20879	% Inpatient satisfaction with follow up education and instrution
sK20880	% Inpatient satisfaction with pain management
sK20881	% Inpatient satisfaction with parking
sK20882	% Inpatient satisfaction with quality of meals
sK20883	% In-patient self-pay revenue
sK20884	% Inpatient rating for satisfaction with coordination of care
sK20885	% Inpatient utilization of general hospitals/acute care
sK20886	% Inpatient utilisation of non-acute care
sK20887	% Inpatient
sK20900	% Interventions provided
sK20913	% Junior doctors complying with new deal on working hours
sK20926	% Laparoscopic to open cholecystectomy
sK20967	% Low birthweight
sK20969	% Low birthweight birth rate
sK20974	% Magnetic resonance imaging (MRI) completed within the recommended priority access target wait times

sKPI #	Key Performance Indicator name
sK20980	% Market share by patient
sK20984	% Maternal mortality for patients ages 15-44
sK20987	% Medicare hospitals 30-day readmission rates
sK20988	% Medicare outpatient cost to charge
sK20989	% Medication reconciliation completed within 24 hours of admission
sK20992	% Members receiving inpatient, day/night care and ambulatory services
sK20993	% Mental health utilization
sK21015	% Methicillin-resistant staphylococcus aureus (MRSA)
sK21021	% Mammography rates
sK21040	% Mortality for colon cancer
sK21041	% Mortality for heart attacks
sK21042	% Mortality for hip fractures
sK21043	% Mortality from appendicitis, abdominal hernia, cholelithiasis and cholecystitis for people aged 5 to 64
sK21044	% Mortality from CHD of people aged over 65
sK21045	% Mortality from chronic rheumatic heart disease for people aged 5 to 44
sK21046	% Mortality from Hodgkin's disease for people aged 5 to 64
sK21047	% Mortality from hypertensive and cerebrovascular disease for people aged 35 to 64
sK21048	% Mortality from peptic ulcer for people aged 25 to 74
sK21049	% Mortality from tuberculosis for people aged 5 to 64
sK21050	% Mortality rate
sK21051	% Mortality rate from fracture of skull and intracranial injury
sK21052	% Mortality rates for injury and suicide
sK21053	% Mortality ratios from accidents and adverse effects
sK21065	% Multiple antipsychotic medications at discharge
sK21066	% Multiple antipsychotic medications at discharge with appropriate justification
sK21071	% Needed mental health care and received treatment
sK21072	% Nervous system discharges
sK21086	% NHS staff satisfaction
sK21089	% Non-admitted emergency patients who stayed less than 4 hours
sK21098	% Non-use of ACEI at discharge
sK21099	% Nosocomial Pressure Ulcers
sK21103	% Nurse response rate
sK21104	% Nurses recognized as always communicating well with patients
sK21106	% Obesity among primary school aged children (reception year)
sK21107	% Obstetrical trauma - vaginal delivery with instrument
sK21108	% Obstetrical trauma - vaginal delivery without instrument
sK21115	% One month cancer diagnosis to treatment
sK21126	% Operating time on Hospitals bypass

sKPI #	Key Performance Indicator name
sK21130	% Ophthalmic surgeries completed within the recommended priority access target wait times
sK21131	% Oral and dental surgeries completed within the recommended priority access target wait times
sK21134	% Orthopedic surgeries completed within the recommended priority access target wait times
sK21136	% Outpatient drug utilization
sK21137	% Out-patient Medicaid revenue
sK21138	% Outpatient revenue
sK21139	% Outpatients receiving an antibiotic the right time before surgery
sK21140	% Outpatients having surgery who received the right kind of antibiotic
sK21141	% Outpatients seen within 13 weeks of GP referral
sK21142	% Outpatients with possible heart attack receiving aspirin within 24 hours of hospital arrival
sK21143	% Outpatients with possible heart attack receiving drugs to break up blood clots within 30 minutes of arrival
sK21145	% Satisfaction with patient care index
sK21152	% Pediatric surgeries completed within the recommended priority access target wait times
sK21153	% Pain assessed at specified intervals
sK21252	% Participation of consumers in decision making and advisory processes
sK21276	% Patient functionality
sK21277	% Patient reported medical error
sK21278	% Patient reported medication error
sK21279	% Patient rooms and bathrooms kept clean
sK21280	% Patient safety issues
sK21281	% Patient-reported satisfaction with cancelled operations
sK21282	% Patient-reported satisfaction with continuity
sK21283	% Patient-reported satisfaction with delayed discharge
sK21284	% Patient-reported satisfaction with patient-rated access to support networks during care
sK21285	% Patient-reported satisfaction with patient-rated autonomy and confidentiality
sK21286	% Patient-reported satisfaction with patient-rated choice of care provider
sK21287	% Patient-reported satisfaction with patient-rated dignity of treatment
sK21288	% Patient-reported satisfaction with patient-rated promptness of attention
sK21289	% Patient-reported satisfaction with patient-rated quality of basic amenities
sK21290	% Patient-reported satisfaction with physician-patient communication
sK21291	% Patient-reported satisfaction with privacy
sK21292	% Patient-reported satisfaction with provision of information
sK21293	% Patient-reported satisfaction with waiting times
sK21294	% Patient-reported satisfaction
sK21295	% Patient-reported satisfaction with appearance of facilities

sKPI #	Key Performance Indicator name
sK21296	% Patient-reported satisfaction with caring and compassion
sK21297	% Patient-reported satisfaction with communication
sK21298	% Patient-reported satisfaction with control of pain or other symptoms
sK21299	% Patient-reported satisfaction with ease of access
sK21300	% Patient-reported satisfaction with expected results achieved
sK21301	% Patient-reported satisfaction with food
sK21302	% Patient-reported satisfaction with parking
sK21303	% Patient-reported satisfaction with technical quality of care
sK21304	% Patient-reported satisfaction with wait times
sK21305	% Patient-reported satisfaction with frequency of help from hospital staff
sK21306	% Patient-reported likeliness to recommend the hospital
sK21307	% Patients given information about what to do during their recovery at home
sK21308	% Patients on waiting list waiting 12 months or more
sK21309	% Patients' pain well controlled
sK21310	% Patients seen within 13 weeks of GP referral for first outpatient appointment
sK21311	% Patients seen within 18 weeks for admitted pathways
sK21312	% Patients in emergency that could have been treated by regular doctor
sK21313	% Patients waiting no more than 31 days for subsequent cancer treatments
sK21314	% Patients waiting six months or less for an inpatient admission
sK21316	% Patients who received treatment within 24 hours before or after surgery to help prevent blood clots after certain types of surgery
sK21318	% Patients' families who declared they would recommend hospital
sK21321	% Patients with suspected cancer who wait less than 62 days from referral to treatment
sK21338	% Percutaneous intervention within 120 mins
sK21353	% Physician satisfaction
sK21354	% Physicians recognized as always communicating well with patients
sK21355	% Physicians using electronic medical records
sK21369	% Plastics and reconstructive surgeries completed within the recommended priority access target wait times
sK21372	% Pneumococcal screen or vaccination for people aged over 65
sK21374	% Pneumonia 30-day mortality rate
sK21375	% Pneumonia care composite
sK21377	% Pneumonia patients assessed and given influenza vaccination
sK21378	% Pneumonia patients assessed and given pneumococcal vaccination
sK21379	% Pneumonia patients given initial antibiotics within six hours after arrival
sK21380	% Pneumonia patients given smoking cessation advice

sKPI #	Key Performance Indicator name
sK21381	% Pneumonia patients given the most appropriate initial antibiotics
sK21382	% Pneumonia patients whose initial emergency room blood culture was performed prior to the administration of the first hospital dose of antibiotics
sK21383	% Pneumonia readmission rate
sK21391	% Post discharge continuing care plan
sK21392	% Post discharge continuing care plan transmitted
sK21398	% Post-operative wound infection (LSCS) infection rates
sK21404	% Prenatal care in first trimester
sK21406	% Preoperative blood type screening and antibody testing
sK21408	% Prescription utilization
sK21409	% Pre-term birth rate
sK21413	% Primary caesarean
sK21428	% Profit margin of investor-owned hospitals
sK21429	% Profit margin of Non-profit / Non-governmental hospitals
sK21441	% Prophylactic antibiotic received within one hour prior to surgical incision
sK21442	% Prophylactic antibiotic selection for surgical patients
sK21443	% Prophylactic antibiotics discontinued within 24 hours after surgery end time
sK21445	% Proportion of elective admissions for ENT surgery
sK21446	% Proportion of elective admissions for general medicine and its associated sub-specialties
sK21447	% Proportion of elective admissions for gynecology
sK21448	% Proportion of elective admissions for ophthalmology
sK21449	% Proportion of emergency admissions for ENT surgery
sK21450	% Proportion of emergency admissions for general medicine and its associated sub-specialties
sK21451	% Proportion of emergency admissions for gynecology
sK21452	% Proportion of emergency admissions for ophthalmology
sK21455	% Proportion of transfer admissions for ENT surgery
sK21456	% Proportion of transfer admissions for general medicine and its associated sub-specialties
sK21457	% Proportion of transfer admissions for gynecology
sK21458	% Proportion of transfer admissions for ophthalmology
sK21461	% Prostate cancer surgeries completed within priority access target wait times
sK21493	% Readmissions to Hospitals for congestive heart failure and chronic obstructive pulmonary disease
sK21519	% Registration error rates
sK21529	% Relievers for asthma inpatients aged 2 to 17
sK21533	% Repeat rates for clinical and radiological services
sK21549	% Respiratory syncytial virus infection rates
sK21550	% Respiratory system discharges
sK21555	% Restraint use rates
sK21570	% Risk-adjusted 3rd or 4th degree perineal laceration
sK21571	% Risk-adjusted in-hospital mortality

sKPI #	Key Performance Indicator name
sK21581	% Rotavirus infection rates
sK21596	% Satisfaction with physical
sK21642	% Short-stay patients with pain
sK21643	% Sickness absence rate
sK21649	% Smoking cessation advice given to patients aged over 18
sK21650	% Smoking quit rates
sK21656	% Specific medical errors
sK21657	% Specimen rejection rates
sK21661	% Staff recognized as explaining about medicines before giving them to patients
sK21672	% Stillbirth rates
sK21686	% Stress ulcer disease (SUD) prophylaxis
sK21793	% Suicide and injury of undetermined intent mortality rate
sK21798	% Surgery for hernia recurrence
sK21799	% Surgery patients needing their hair removed from the surgical area before surgery, who underwent hair removal using a safe method
sK21800	% Surgery patients who were given an antibiotic at the right time
sK21801	% Surgery patients who were given the right kind of antibiotic to prevent infection
sK21802	% Surgery patients who were taking beta blockers before coming to the hospital and were kept on beta blockers before and after their surgery
sK21803	% Surgery patients whose physicians ordered treatments to prevent blood clots after certain types of procedures
sK21804	% Surgery patients whose preventive antibiotics were stopped at the right time
sK21805	% Surgery patients whose urinary catheters were removed within 2 days from surgery
sK21806	% Surgery rates for CABG and PTCA
sK21807	% Surgery rates for cataract replacement
sK21808	% Surgery rates for hip replacement for people aged over 65
sK21809	% Surgery rates for knee replacement for people aged over 65
sK21811	% Surgical care composite
sK21813	% surgical intervention for glue ear (grommet surgery)
sK21814	% Surgical safety checklist compliance
sK21815	% Surgical site infection prevention
sK21818	% Surgical site nosocomial infection rates
sK21820	% Survival rates from breast cancer for people aged 15 to 99
sK21821	% Survival rates from cancer
sK21822	% Survival rates from cervical cancer for people aged 15 to 99
sK21823	% Survival rates from dialysis and transplants
sK21825	% Systemic corticosteroids for asthma inpatients aged 2 to 17
sK21835	% Target patient enrolment rate achieved
sK21837	% Target population screened for breast cancer

sKPI #	Key Performance Indicator name
sK21838	% Target population screened for cervical cancer
sK21839	% Target population vaccinated
sK21854	% Teenage pregnancy rates
sK21870	% Thrombolytic agent within 30 mins
sK21875	% Timeliness of admit registration
sK21876	% Timeliness of social care assessment
sK21877	% Timeliness of social care packages
sK21891	% Transfusions having reactions
sK21901	% Triage Category 1 patients seen immediately
sK21902	% Triage Category 2 patients seen within 10 minutes
sK21903	% Triage Category 3 patients seen within 30minutes
sK21917	% Uncomplicated caesarean
sK21918	% Conception rate for females aged 15 to 17
sK21921	% Unexpected return to surgery
sK21934	% Unplanned return to theatre
sK21935	% Unplanned returns to ER
sK21936	% Unplanned returns to OR
sK21941	% Urinary/Male Repro discharges
sK21942	% Urologic surgeries completed within the recommended priority access target wait times
sK21946	% Use of relievers for asthma inpatients aged under 18
sK21948	% Use of systemic steroid for asthma inpatients aged under 18
sK21957	% Vaccination rates
sK21958	% Vaginal birth after cesarean delivery
sK21959	% Vaginal births after Caesarean section
sK21961	% VAR per 1000 mechanically ventilated days
sK21962	% Vascular surgeries completed within the recommended priority access target wait times
sK21965	% Ventilator-associated pneumonia (VAP) prevention-patient positioning
sK21972	% Voluntary labor turnover
sK21975	% VRE blood stream infections per 1,000 patient days
sK21992	% Women aged 53 to 70 who were screened for breast cancer
sK21993	% Women who have seen a midwife or a maternity healthcare professional by 12 completed weeks of pregnancy
sK21994	% Workload contribution factor
sK21995	% Workload contribution factor of day shift
sK21996	% Workload contribution factor of evening shift
sK21997	% Workload contribution factor of night shift
sK6147	% Collection of outpatient payment balances before service rate for copays and deductibles
sK6148	% Collection of patient balances prior to departure
sK7013	% Asset utilization frequency

Medical Laboratory

Medical laboratory includes all facilities where tests are done on clinical subjects in order to get information about the health of a patient, for supporting either the prevention, the diagnosis, or the treatment of an illness. KPIs in this area measure the performance of the administrative operations, service efficiency and quality.

sKPI #	Key Performance Indicator name
sK4270	% Blood culture contamination rate
sK4291	# Laboratory test results errors
sK4292	# Laboratory test turn-around time (TAT)
sK4293	% Laboratory test accuracy
sK4295	# Laboratory procedures
sK4296	# Radiology procedures
sK4298	$ Cost per x-ray
sK4300	% Test results received the same day
sK4326	% Reusable medical devices properly decontaminated
sK5744	# Time to complete toxicology cases
sK5745	# Time to complete DNA testing cases
sK5837	% Trainees working on interdisciplinary tasks
sK6121	% Screening of uninsured inpatients and high-dollar outpatients for financial assistance
sK6176	% Electronic eligibility rate
sK6187	% Third party payer underpayments and overpayments
sK6192	% Self pay A/R of medical bill aged more than 90 days from placement date
sK6750	# New cures and treatments for diseases discovered
sK6835	% Patient complaints

Medical Practice

Medical practice includes all specialized healthcare institutions for outpatients, where the medical staff diagnoses, treats and prevents diseases using clinical judgment. KPIs in this area generally monitor the performance of the medical clinics in terms of patients treated and service quality, the administration operations and the medical diagnosis and treatment.

sKPI #	Key Performance Indicator name
sK305	% Outpatient surgeries
sK311	% Medication error rate
sK323	% Peri-operative mortality
sK2897	$ Revenue per physician
sK4186	% Retreatment ratio
sK4226	# Caseload per physician
sK4229	# Surgeries performed
sK4242	$ Revenue per patient per day
sK4243	$ Medical support staff cost per Full Time Equivalent physician
sK4245	% Compliance before patient contact
sK4251	% Repeat prescriptions
sK4273	% Patients waiting more than X hours
sK4276	% Successful completion rate of medical treatment

sKPI #	Key Performance Indicator name
sK4283	# Patients treated
sK4287	# Follow-up visits per physician
sK4294	# Days taken to patient recall
sK4302	# Patients experiencing medical errors
sK4303	% Errors related to laboratory test
sK4304	# Patient consultation time
sK4305	% Patient complication rate
sK4306	# Time to establish a medical appointment
sK4311	# Clinic locations
sK4313	# Hygienic precautions measures
sK4317	$ Cost of missed appointments
sK4318	% Patient canceled appointments
sK4319	% Board-certified or board-eligible physicians
sK4320	% Case acceptance by patients
sK4322	% Patient missed appointment rate
sK4323	% Patient oriented time
sK4324	% Prescriptions not collected by patients
sK4325	% Primary health care physicians using electronic medical records
sK4326	% Reusable medical devices properly decontaminated
sK4327	# Patient wait time
sK4328	% Patients who leave without being seen
sK4329	# Clinical negligence cases
sK4331	% Patient satisfaction
sK4332	% Patient willingness to return
sK4335	$ Cost of treatment
sK4336	$ Disposal and recycling of medical waste cost per tonne
sK4337	% Revenue from returning patients
sK4384	# Time spent per new patient visit
sK5721	% Prenatal patients retained in care through delivery
sK5723	# Time spent for a primary care visit
sK5743	# Time to complete autopsy reports
sK6117	% Scheduling rate of potentially eligible patients
sK6119	% Scheduling rate for ambulatory surgery patients
sK6121	% Screening of uninsured inpatients and high-dollar outpatients for financial assistance
sK6176	% Electronic eligibility rate
sK6187	% Third party payer underpayments and overpayments
sK6192	% Self pay A/R of medical bill aged more than 90 days from placement date
sK6199	% HIPAA compliant electronic claim submissions
sK6206	% Patient cash net revenue
sK6209	% Pending patient accounts
sK6827	% Hospital initiated cancellations
sK6828	# Surgery cancellations on the day
sK6829	% Same diagnostic early readmission cases
sK6835	% Patient complaints

sKPI #	Key Performance Indicator name
sK6874	# Forthcoming appointments in the scheduling system
sK6875	% Visits resulting in a reappointment
sK6877	# Time to complete scans or tests available in the practice
sK6879	% Patient returns from recalls
sK6880	# Instances of medical information system unavailability
sK6881	% Patient files up to date
sK6882	% Appointments reconfirmed by staff with patients
sK6883	% Appointment slots coverage over the next 30 days
sK6885	% Staff working hours delivered
sK6886	% Visits that require the use of scans or tests available in the practice
sK14489	# Alcohol and other drug use disorder treatment at discharge
sK14491	# Alcohol use brief intervention provided or offered
sK14492	# Alcohol use brief intervention treatment
sK14493	# Alcohol use screening
sK14496	# Allied health outpatient attendances
sK14549	# Assessing status of alcohol and drug use after discharge
sK14556	# Attendances of accident and emergency services
sK14736	# Catheter-associated urinary tract infections (UTI) for intensive care unit (ICU) patients
sK14739	# Central line catheter-associated blood stream infections for ICU and NICU patients
sK14985	# Day patients treated
sK14999	# Death among surgical inpatients with treatable serious complications
sK15251	# Falls with injury
sK17248	# Waiting time of patients booking new cases
sK17388	# General outpatient attendances
sK17391	# Geriatric outreach attendances
sK17486	# Home visits by community nurses
sK17619	# Inpatients treated
sK17666	# IOD case per 100 FTE
sK17667	# IOD leave day per 100 FTE
sK17873	# Manpower position by staff groups
sK17894	# Medical staff on resignation
sK17993	# New case booking for specialist outpatient service by major specialty
sK18060	# Nursing care hours per patient day
sK18065	# Nursing staff on resignation
sK18226	# Patient falls
sK18377	# Practice environment scale-nursing work index (PES-NWI)
sK18387	# Hospital-acquired pressure ulcer prevalence
sK18490	# Psychiatric day hospitals attendances
sK18491	# Psychiatric outreach attendances
sK18640	# Restraint prevalence

sKPI #	Key Performance Indicator name
sK18754	# Seclusion in hours per 1,000 patient hours
sK18755	# Seclusion in hours per 1,000 patient hours by age group
sK18804	# Sick leave day per staff member
sK18827	# Specialist outpatient attendances
sK18858	# Standardized admission rate for patients of emergency department
sK19211	# Ventilator-associated pneumonia for ICU and NICU patients
sK19311	$ Accrued medical fee income
sK19891	% 30 degree head up maintained on ITU ventilated patients
sK19905	% A&E patients of critical cases with target waiting time
sK19906	% A&E patients of emergency cases with target waiting time
sK19907	% A&E patients of urgent cases with target waiting time
sK19908	% A&E patients with target waiting time
sK19913	% Absence of CSF leak after neurosurgery
sK19914	% Absence of missed eardrum injury
sK19915	% Absence of missed injury found at relaparotomy
sK19916	% Absence of missed penetrating/sight-threatening ocular injury
sK19917	% Absence of unplanned admission to critical care
sK19918	% Absence of unplanned relaparotomies or rethoracotomies
sK19945	% ACEI or ARB at discharge
sK19950	% Activity counseling for osteoporosis
sK19955	% Acute compartment fasciotomies performed less than 1 hour of arrival in ED
sK19965	% Admission screening
sK19966	% Admission screening by age group
sK20034	% All wounds ICRC scored at initial surgery
sK20035	% All wounds photographed before and after debridement with copies available country-wide
sK20046	% Antenatal steroids
sK20049	% Antibiotic within six hours of arrival
sK20050	% Antibiotics given less than 1 hour of wounding
sK20052	% Antibiotics to ICU patients
sK20053	% Antibiotics to non-ICU patients
sK20054	% Antibiotics within one hour before the first surgical cut
sK20055	% Antibiotics within one hour before the first surgical cut for CABG surgery
sK20056	% Antibiotics within one hour before the first surgical cut for cardiac surgery (other than CABG)
sK20057	% Antibiotics within one hour before the first surgical cut for colon surgery
sK20058	% Antibiotics within one hour before the first surgical cut for hip joint replacement surgery
sK20059	% Antibiotics within one hour before the first surgical cut for knee joint replacement surgery
sK20060	% Antibiotics within one hour before the first surgical cut for vascular surgery

sKPI #	Key Performance Indicator name
sK20061	% Antibiotics within one hour before the first surgical cutf for hysterectomy surgery
sK20062	% Anticoagulation therapy for atrial fibrillation/flutter
sK20064	% Antithrombolytic therapy within 2 days of hospitalization
sK20067	% Appropriate antibiotics administered in less than 6 hours from open fracture
sK20069	% Appropriate initial wound surgery performed in less than 6 hours from injury
sK20070	% Appropriate prophylactic antibiotics
sK20071	% Appropriate prophylactic antibiotics for CABG surgery
sK20072	% Appropriate prophylactic antibiotics for cardiac surgery
sK20073	% Appropriate prophylactic antibiotics for colon surgery
sK20074	% Appropriate prophylactic antibiotics for hip joint replacement surgery
sK20075	% Appropriate prophylactic antibiotics for hysterectomy surgery
sK20076	% Appropriate prophylactic antibiotics for knee joint replacement surgery
sK20077	% Appropriate prophylactic antibiotics for vascular surgery
sK20090	% Aspirin at arrival
sK20094	% Assessed for rehabilitation
sK20130	% Bacteriologic test results available to clinicians before and after debridement
sK20140	% Beta-blocker patients who received beta-blocker perioperatively
sK20141	% Betadine-soaked dressings applied to wounds in less than 1 hour of ED arrival
sK20149	% Blood administration documentation
sK20151	% Blood cultures in ED
sK20152	% Blood cultures in ICU
sK20153	% BMD testing of glucocorticoid patients
sK20157	% BSA, location, depth estimate, and fluid resuscitation begun less than 1 hour of burn
sK20190	% Cardiac patients with 6 a.m. postoperative blood glucose
sK20198	% Case discussed at periodical meetings focused on the topics of morbidity and mortality
sK20199	% Case discussed at a weekly MDT meeting
sK20202	% Casualties with continuing haemorrhage from injury with shock taken to theatre less than 30 minutes from arrival in ED
sK20240	% Cesarean section
sK20259	% Children's asthma care composite
sK20282	% CK measured for crush and burns patients or when tourniquet applied for more than 1 hour
sK20333	% Closure of penetrating head injuries performed less than 6 hours of injury
sK20386	% Continuing care plan
sK20387	% Continuing care plan by age group
sK20388	% Continuing care plan transmitted

smartKPIs.com
The smart choice in performance management

sKPI #	Key Performance Indicator name	sKPI #	Key Performance Indicator name
sK20389	% Continuing care plan transmitted by age group	sK20914	% Justification for multiple antipsychotic medications
sK20415	% CT head performed within 1 hour of arrival in the ED for isolated closed head injury	sK20915	% Justification for multiple antipsychotic medications for patients aged 1 to 12 years
sK20453	% Damage control laparotomy performed in less than 90 minutes	sK20927	% Laparotomy, if performed, therapeutic
sK20455	% Day surgery	sK20953	% Limb salvage scoring for performed preamputation
sK20464	% Decompressive craniotomy/craniectomy performed less than 4 hours of a blunt head injury	sK20955	% LMWH started less than 24 hours of admission
sK20474	% Dietary education for osteoporosis	sK20966	% Long bone fractures stabilized in less than 1 hour from injury
sK20478	% Discharge instructions	sK20973	% LVS assessment
sK20482	% Discharged on antithrombotic therapy	sK21019	% Minimum monitoring standards followed during anesthesia
sK20483	% Discharged on statin medication	sK21020	% MIST handover performed at the ED
sK20521	% Elective delivery	sK21064	% Multiple antipsychotic medications
sK20528	% Emergency thoracotomy for patients in extremis less than 10 minutes of arrival in the ED	sK21067	% Multiple antipsychotic medications for patients aged 1 to 12 years
sK20607	% Escharotomy occured in less than 4 hours of burn	sK21084	% Newborn bloodstream infections
sK20608	% ETCO2 measured if the patient was intubated	sK21085	% NG feeding begun within 6 hours of burnsmore
sK20609	% ETCO2 recorded less than every 10 minutes in all patients ventilated in ED	sK21105	% Nutritional assessment plan documented postsurgery
sK20611	% Excess beds to 1,000 in-use beds	sK21113	% Off-table temperature more than 34 degrees Celsius
sK20613	% Exclusive breast milk feeding	sK21114	% Old aged homes covered by outreach service
sK20633	% Fall risk and personal safety education	sK21154	% Pain score maintained under 4 in pre-hospital and ED phases
sK20636	% Fasciotomies performed for confirmed vascular injuries	sK21319	% Patients with appropriate hair removal
sK20643	% Fibrinolytic therapy	sK21324	% PCI therapy within 90 minutes
sK20673	% Formal burn assessment performed less than 4 hours following burn	sK21332	% Penetrating abdominal injury with systolic BP less than 90
sK20683	% Full spinal immobilization used where appropriate	sK21333	% Penetrating extremity wounds x-rayed predebridement
sK20684	% Full tertiary survey carried out within 24 hours from arrival in ED	sK21341	% Perinatal care composite
sK20695	% GCS measured prior to intubation	sK21349	% Pharmacotherapy
sK20700	% General outpatient attendances for chronic diseases with pre-scheduled appointment	sK21351	% Physical restraint in hours per 1,000 patient hours
sK20704	% Glycaemic level 4-8 mmol/L sustained during admission and AEROMED	sK21352	% Physical restraint in hours per 1,000 patient hours by age group
sK20736	% Hb maintained over 8 g/dl during hospital admission and AEROMED	sK21368	% Plasma transfusion indication
sK20778	% Home management plan of care	sK21370	% Platelet transfusion indication
sK20803	% Hospitals achieving composite rates greater than 90 percent for accountability measures	sK21373	% Pneumococcal vaccination
sK20816	% Hypothermia mitigation equipment used where appropriate	sK21397	% Postoperative temperature maintained more than 34 degrees Celsius
sK20829	% Incidence of potentially preventable VTE	sK21405	% Preoperative anemia screening
sK20844	% Indications for novel hemostatic use documented	sK21407	% Prescribing VTE medicine or treatment
sK20849	% Influenza vaccination	sK21492	% RBC transfusion indication
sK20853	% Inhalation/airway injuries identified less than 1 hour following burn	sK21495	% Receiving VTE medicine/treatment
sK20872	% Inpatient psychiatric services composite	sK21528	% Relievers for inpatient asthma
sK20906	% ITU patients evacuated within 48 hours of admission to ITU	sK21530	% Relievers for inpatient asthma for children aged 2 to 4
		sK21534	% Repeat vital signs recorded less than every 10 minutes in first hour
sK20907	% IV fluid boluses given to maintain radial pulse	sK21563	% Revascularisation surgeries performed within less than 6 hours from injuries
		sK21569	% Risk assessment and treatment after fracture

sKPI #	Key Performance Indicator name
sK21583	% RSI/ETT completed within 10 minutes of arrival for those GCS less than 9
sK21591	% Same day surgery
sK21614	% Screening of females at risk
sK21618	% Secondary causes
sK21644	% Significant events fed back to the theatre of operation
sK21647	% Smoking and alcohol education
sK21648	% Smoking cessation advice
sK21674	% Stopping antibiotics within 24 hours
sK21675	% Stopping antibiotics within 24 hours for CABG surgery
sK21676	% Stopping antibiotics within 24 hours for cardiac surgery
sK21677	% Stopping antibiotics within 24 hours for colon surgery
sK21678	% Stopping antibiotics within 24 hours for hip joint replacement surgery
sK21679	% Stopping antibiotics within 24 hours for hysterectomy surgery
sK21680	% Stopping antibiotics within 24 hours for knee joint replacement surgery
sK21681	% Stopping antibiotics within 24 hours for vascular surgery
sK21688	% Stroke care composite
sK21689	% Stroke education
sK21810	% Surgical airway secured in less than 10 minutes from arrival in the ED
sK21824	% Systemic corticosteroids for inpatient asthma
sK21826	% Systemic corticosteroids for inpatient asthma for children aged 2 to 4
sK21853	% TED stockings fitted
sK21855	% Temperature at arrival in the ED above 36 degrees Celsius
sK21867	% Tetanus IgG given in less than 4 hours from arrival in ED in heavily contaminated wounds
sK21871	% Thrombolytic therapy
sK21873	% Time from point of wounding to appropriate surgical care is less than 2 hours
sK21882	% Tourniquet cases reviewed by a surgeon in less than 2 hours of application
sK21890	% Transfusion consent
sK21933	% Unplanned readmission rate for general inpatients
sK21939	% Urgent thoracotomy performed for shocked patients with penetrating chest injury within 1 hour from arrival to ED
sK21940	% Urinary catheter removed
sK21964	% Venous thromboembolism (VTE) care composite
sK21969	% Vital signs recorded on arrival
sK21970	% Vital signs recorded to a minimum standard
sK21973	% Voluntary turnover
sK21976	% VTE medicine/treatment
sK21977	% VTE medicine/treatment in ICU
sK21978	% VTE patients with overlap therapy

sKPI #	Key Performance Indicator name
sK21979	% VTE patients with UFH monitoring
sK21980	% VTE prophylaxis
sK21981	% VTE warfarin discharge instructions
sK21985	% Waterlow score performed on admission to the ward
sK22533	# Employees in Nurses Union

Preventive Healthcare

Preventive healthcare represents the area of medicine dealing with prevention of illnesses and diseases, through prevention measures and programs. KPIs in this area refer to the accessibility of preventive services, and their impact.

sKPI #	Key Performance Indicator name
sK2726	# Teen births
sK2727	% Birth rate among teenage women
sK2901	# Hospital admission rate per 10,000 inhabitants
sK4353	# HIV/AIDS mother to child transmissions
sK4355	# Condoms distributed within sexual education programs
sK4357	# Family planning services
sK4359	# HIV prevention counseling services
sK4360	% HIV prevalence
sK4362	% Mortality due to sudden infant death syndrome (SIDS)
sK4364	# Preventive health services
sK4367	# Promotion campaigns for preventive healthcare
sK4369	# Access to sexual and reproductive health services
sK4370	# Voluntary counseling and testing programs
sK4375	% Contraceptive use
sK4376	# Dental examinations completed
sK4377	# Families involved in dietary counseling
sK4378	% Participation in regular physical activity
sK4380	# Flu vaccine uptake
sK4381	% Mammography screenings
sK4382	% AIDS orphans
sK4383	% Teenagers pregnancy rate
sK4386	# Tobacco cessation counseling programs
sK4388	% Preventive screening coverage
sK4389	$ Cost savings due to preventive healthcare
sK4390	% Adolescents informed on sexual education
sK4391	% Use of family planning services
sK4392	% Childhood obesity rate
sK4393	% Population suffering of diabetes
sK4396	% Prevalence of obesity
sK4399	% Smokers who attempt to quit for one day or longer
sK4401	% Use of preventive services
sK4986	# Cases of vaccine-preventable diseases

Veterinary Medicine

Veterinary medicine refers to medical diagnose and treatment services specialized for farm or pet animals. These activities are carried out by qualified veterinarians within veterinary clinics, as well as when visiting farms, kennels or private households. It also includes activities of veterinary assistance or other auxiliary veterinary personnel, clinic-pathological and other diagnostic activities pertaining to animals and animal ambulance activities. KPIs in this area monitor efficiency and quality of veterinary services, as well as administration of veterinary clinics.

sKPI #	Key Performance Indicator name
sK1708	# Veterinary visits per household
sK1725	$ Veterinary expenses per pet household
sK1726	# Households that own a pet
sK1727	% Companion pets registered to a veterinarian
sK1728	# Companion pets owned
sK4144	# Animal sterilizations
sK4326	% Reusable medical devices properly decontaminated

Hospitality & Tourism

Hospitality and tourism includes tourism activities for leisure, cultural, religious or business purposes, providing accommodation, food and beverage service to customers (tourists or not).

Food and Beverage Service

Food and beverage service includes the provision of complete meals or drinks fit for immediate consumption, whether in traditional restaurants, self-service or take-away restaurants, whether as permanent or temporary stands, with or without seating. It also includes the service of food and beverages to a group as part of an organized event, where services occur to all guests within a specific time frame. KPIs focus on resources consumption, customer satisfaction with the quality of service and process flows within the food and beverage serving facility.

sKPI #	Key Performance Indicator name
sK81	% Positive feedback from guests
sK222	% Canceled reservations
sK458	$ Revenue per table
sK460	# Complaints per restaurant order
sK477	# Time per table turn
sK752	# Absent days per employee during peak operational periods
sK1330	% Food costs from food sales
sK1724	% Duplicate bookings
sK2235	% Front of house labor
sK2240	% Food loss
sK2251	# New menu items
sK2325	# Guests
sK2364	% Customers satisfied with the time to be served
sK4549	$ Sales per labor hour
sK4730	% Reserved tables
sK4732	$ Spent on equipment
sK4736	% Restaurants that apply principles of managing the purchasing process
sK4737	% Restaurants that apply principles of menu planning
sK4738	% Restaurants that apply principles of workplace safety and sanitation
sK4739	# Additional services provided by restaurant
sK4740	# Menu items
sK4741	# Product quality uniformity
sK4742	% Unavailability of menu items

sKPI #	Key Performance Indicator name
sK4743	# Guests per table
sK4744	# Order count
sK4745	# People per party (catering)
sK4746	# Cars served over a span of time
sK4747	# Length of time for which a given car waits at a drive-through menu sign
sK4748	# Length of time between a car leaving the drive-through menu sign and arriving at the pick-up window
sK4749	# Times the server speaks with the customer, while the customer is at the drive-through menu sign
sK4750	# Times employees speak with each other while servicing a drive-through customer
sK4751	$ Amount of dining
sK4752	$ Restaurant revenue per employee
sK4753	$ Revenue per available seat hour (RevPASH)
sK4755	% Beverage loss
sK4757	% Food service strike rate
sK4758	% Tips from total collected
sK4760	# Tables served per waiter
sK4762	% Workforce considered to master "Cafe latte art"
sK4771	% No show rate
sK4781	# Weight of linen laundered
sK4788	$ Revenue per available square meter (RevPAM)
sK6891	$ Drinks revenue
sK6892	$ Food revenue
sK6893	$ Revenue per head
sK6894	% Satisfaction with food quality
sK6895	$ Cost of food material
sK6896	% Satisfaction with amenities
sK6897	# Customers per waiter
sK6898	# Visits by top 100 guests
sK6900	# Reviews available online
sK6901	# Waiting time between placing the order and being served
sK6902	# Order serving mistakes

sKPI #	Key Performance Indicator name
sK6903	% Complaints with workplace safety and sanitation
sK6905	# Kitchen hours
sK6906	# Value for money assessment by customers
sK6908	% Aggregated rating in review sites
sK7045	$ Revenue at restaurants open at least a year
sK14613	# Best selling items
sK14743	# Chain restaurants failed
sK14949	# Customer traffic
sK15085	# Dining time
sK17245	# Waiting guests
sK17247	# Waiting time for walk-in guests
sK17253	# Walk-in guests
sK17265	# Water consumed per dish served
sK17347	# Front of house labor hours
sK17370	# Function inquiries
sK17371	# Function labor charge-out
sK17413	# Grams of residual waste per dish served
sK17432	# Guaranteed reservations
sK17436	# Guests who will stay an additional night
sK17572	# Independent restaurants failed
sK17573	# Independent to chain restaurants
sK17622	# In-process segment of a meal
sK17661	# Inventory perishes
sK17685	# Kitchen labor hours
sK17686	# Kitchen size
sK17688	# Electricity used per dish served
sK17705	# Late shows
sK17765	# Length of time a party stays once it is seated
sK18039	# No shows
sK18368	# Post-process time of a meal
sK18384	# Pre-process time of a meal
sK18386	# Press mentions
sK18420	# Product lines carrying information about food provenance (including Fair Trade)
sK18421	# Product lines carrying information about sustainability
sK18505	# Published policies and procedures which facilitate access to approved lists for small suppliers
sK18553	# Reconfirmed reservations
sK18613	# Reservations
sK18639	# Restaurant density by zip code
sK18753	# Seats
sK18803	# Short shows
sK18811	# Sites that are enrolled into associations where energy consumption can be measured directly
sK18825	# Sources of sea fish used that feature on the Marine Conservation Society's Black list of locations
sK18854	# Staffing level

sKPI #	Key Performance Indicator name
sK18866	# Stock turnover
sK18868	# Stock take discrepancies
sK18918	# Suppliers engaged in environmental initiatives
sK18983	# Time during which a seat or table is available
sK19133	# Units registered with an environmental management system, e.g. ISO14001
sK19134	# Units which are recycling glass, cooking oil and steel cans as a minimum
sK19341	$ Annual cost of food waste
sK19349	$ Beverage sales per head
sK19362	$ Carrying cost of stock
sK19365	$ Cash over
sK19366	$ Cash short
sK19369	$ Check per person
sK19442	$ Deposits for reservations
sK19443	$ Dessert sales per head
sK19453	$ Drink expense
sK19496	$ Food costs
sK19497	$ Food costs per head
sK19498	$ Food sales per head
sK19573	$ Labor Costs
sK19582	$ Linen costs
sK19599	$ Marketing and advertising costs
sK19661	$ Paper expense
sK19687	$ Payroll taxes
sK19790	$ Sales per head
sK19797	$ Shift manager wages
sK19847	$ Uniforms
sK19942	% Accuracy of POS system
sK20008	% Advertising response rate
sK20206	% Catering outlets offering a seasonal menu choice
sK20340	% Commercial retail food loss
sK20393	% Convenience stores food loss
sK20416	% Cumulative Restaurant Ownership Turnover (ROT)
sK20477	% Dining guests satisfaction
sK20637	% Fast food restaurants food loss
sK20652	% Fish supplied which is certified by the Marine Stewardship Council
sK20665	% Food by specified commodity group purchased that is local sourced
sK20666	% Food cost
sK20667	% Food supplied from local sources
sK20668	% Food supplied that meets criteria for assured standards
sK20682	% Full service restaurants food loss
sK20808	% Household food loss
sK20922	% Kitchen labor
sK20924	% Labor cost

sKPI #	Key Performance Indicator name
sK20963	% Local purchasing in emerging countries
sK21132	% Order transactions under 60 seconds to drive-thru order transactions
sK21151	% Packaged edible food losses
sK21156	% Paper expense to actual sales
sK21362	% Planned drink to actual sales
sK21478	% Purchases of approved products out of total products
sK21480	% Purchases sourced from approved suppliers
sK21552	% Restaurant Ownership Turnover (ROT)
sK21553	% Restaurant Ownership Turnover (ROT) per year
sK21554	% Restaurants food loss
sK21566	% RevPASH (Revenue per available seat-hour)
sK21589	% Sales inquiry conversion rate
sK21590	% Sales of product lines carrying information about sustainability from all sales
sK21615	% Seat occupancy
sK21617	% Seating efficiency
sK21645	% Sites offering sustainable choices, e.g. organic or Fair Trade
sK21682	% Stores achieved service target order transactions
sK21683	% Stores achieved service target window transactions
sK21796	% Suppliers which follow a recognized sustainable trading code of practice
sK21927	% Units providing information about food provenance to consumers
sK21928	% Units registered with an environmental management system, e.g. ISO14001
sK21929	% Units which are recycling glass, cooking oil and steel cans as a minimum
sK21930	% Units which operate in accordance with corporate environmental policies on energy, waste and water
sK21989	% Window transactions under 70 seconds to drive-thru order transactions

Hotel/Accommodation

Hotel / Accommodation includes the provision of short-stay accommodation for visitors and other travelers. Also, included is the provision of longer-term accommodation for students, workers and similar categories. Some units may provide only accommodation, while others provide a combination of accommodation, meals and/or recreational facilities. KPIs focus on the efficiency in operating the accommodation unit (reservation management, cleaning, staffing) and on customer-related performance (occupancy, satisfaction, complaints).

sKPI #	Key Performance Indicator name
sK80	$ Unrealized potential revenue
sK81	% Positive feedback from guests
sK82	% Internet bookings
sK135	% Hotel occupancy
sK136	% Stays of 2+ nights
sK139	% Room occupancy

sKPI #	Key Performance Indicator name
sK213	# Nights of hotel stays sold
sK215	# Length of stay in hotel
sK218	% Rooms with maintenance problems
sK222	% Canceled reservations
sK676	$ Revenue per available room (RevPAR)
sK697	# Guests per employee
sK738	$ Cleaning cost per room
sK739	$ Average daily room rate (ADR)
sK740	$ Gross operating profit per available room (GOPPAR)
sK741	% Rooms booked through own reservation channels
sK742	% Reservation channel revenue
sK752	# Absent days per employee during peak operational periods
sK1722	$ Revenue per booking
sK1724	% Duplicate bookings
sK2325	# Guests
sK4490	# Overseas to local customer travel bookings
sK4492	% Favorable customer reviews
sK4763	$ Booking value
sK4764	% Bookings conversion rate
sK4765	% Wages costs from total sales
sK4766	# Available customer nights
sK4767	# Occupied rooms per employee
sK4769	% Equivalent occupancy
sK4770	% Hotel bed occupancy
sK4771	% No show rate
sK4772	# Hotel-to-chain ratio
sK4773	# Hotel-to-city ratio
sK4774	# Hotel-to-market ratio
sK4775	# Hotel-to-region ratio
sK4776	# Occupied rooms per receptionist
sK4777	# Guest rooms in operation
sK4778	# Hotel waste per occupied bed night
sK4779	# Tonnes of hotel waste per year per employee
sK4780	# Area of catering division
sK4781	# Weight of linen laundered
sK4782	$ Catering division production value per employee
sK4783	% Perceived hotel cleanliness
sK4784	% Guests dining in-house
sK4786	# Monthly room revenue divided by total payroll and benefits
sK4787	$ Room rate
sK4788	$ Revenue per available square meter (RevPAM)
sK4789	$ Profitability per accommodation unit
sK4790	$ Revenue per available customer (RevPAC)
sK4791	$ Total revenue per available room (TRevPAR)
sK4792	$ Total revenue per client (TRevPEC)

sKPI #	Key Performance Indicator name	sKPI #	Key Performance Indicator name
sK4793	% Room rate achievement factor	sK18015	# New hotel/accommodation services
sK4794	% Identical yield occupancy	sK18282	# Performance-to-market
sK4795	% Hotel non-room revenue	sK18417	# Process improvement initiatives
sK4797	% Rooms sold at rack rate	sK18532	# Rate achievement factor
sK4798	% Accommodation yield	sK18537	# Rate spread
sK5974	% Capture rate of hotel guests	sK18678	# Room nights sold
sK5975	$ Gross margin by treatment	sK18679	# Room rate achievement factor
sK5976	% Sales contribution by treatment category	sK18847	# Staff to guest ratio
sK5977	$ Spa revenue per treatment room	sK19374	$ Consolidated PrePAR
sK5978	$ Spa revenue per treatment delivered	sK19437	$ Daily rate per guest
sK5979	$ Spa revenue per occupied hotel rooms	sK19440	$ Departmental expenses
sK5980	% Treatment payroll from treatment revenues	sK19524	$ GOPPAR (gross operating profit per available room)
sK5981	$ Operating expenses per guest	sK19541	$ Hotel/accommodation revenue
sK5982	# Treatment rooms	sK19551	$ House profit
sK5983	# Variety of spa services	sK19699	$ Potential double rate
sK5984	$ Treatment revenue	sK19700	$ Potential single rate
sK5985	% Therapist productivity	sK19706	$ Profit PAR (per available room)
sK5986	% Treatment room utilization	sK19759	$ Revenue per available square foot (RevPAS)
sK5987	# Treatments per guest visit	sK19767	$ Revenue per room
sK5988	$ Revenue per guest visit	sK19791	$ Sales per seat
sK5989	$ Revenue per available treatment room (RevPAT)	sK19792	$ Sales PAR (per available room)
sK5990	# Days between clients' appointments	sK20134	% Beds in destination
sK5991	% Retail sales from spa revenue	sK20159	% Budgeted occupancy
sK6896	% Satisfaction with amenities	sK20368	% Completion of capital projects
sK6898	# Visits by top 100 guests	sK20373	% Computer use in reservations
sK6900	# Reviews available online	sK20391	% Contribution to reforecast
sK6906	# Value for money assessment by customers	sK20626	% F & B expenses
sK6908	% Aggregated rating in review sites	sK20627	% F & B sales
sK14353	# Absent days per employee	sK20663	% Flow-through index
sK14599	# Beds	sK20798	% Hospitality beds
sK14776	# Clothing and textiles	sK20806	% House profit to budget
sK14900	# Covers	sK21068	% Multiple occupancy percentage
sK14946	# Customer payment time	sK21323	% Payroll from revenue
sK14981	# Daily seat turnover	sK21399	% Pour to cost
sK15016	# Defects by Area	sK21577	% Room expenses
sK15099	# Disposable nappies	sK21578	% Room revenue potential
sK15193	# Employees in hotel/accommodation activities	sK21579	% Room sales
sK17348	# FTE per room	sK21580	% Rooms in destination
sK17349	# FTE F&B Employees	sK21795	% Supplementary beds
sK17350	# FTE hotel/accommodation employees	sK21999	% Year-on-year growth
sK17434	# Guest satisfaction score	sK18922	# Supportive housing units made available for emergency hostel users
sK17435	# Guests per room		
sK17643	# Internal process audit index		
sK17681	# Kilograms of waste per night per occupied bed space		
sK17971	# Mystery guests in the hotel/accommodation		
sK18014	# New hotel/accommodation products		

Tour Operator

Tour operator includes activities of assembling and promoting visit tours that are sold through travel agencies or directly by agents, as well as other travel-related services, like leisure reservations. KPIs in this subcategory complete the indicators from travel agency, by adding the specific products and services aspects, such as the tour and vacation packages assembled.

sKPI #	Key Performance Indicator name
sK82	% Internet bookings
sK222	% Canceled reservations
sK1722	$ Revenue per booking
sK1724	% Duplicate bookings
sK4148	% Mass market holidays sold at brochure price
sK4165	% Controlled tour booking distribution
sK4474	# Complaints received per tour
sK4475	# Events and programs offered
sK4476	# Tour packages sold per tour consultant
sK4477	# Tours offered
sK4478	# Types of tour services offered
sK4479	# Vacation packages
sK4480	$ Selling price per tour package sold
sK4481	$ Revenue from tours per tour directors / consultants
sK4482	$ Revenue from tour packages
sK4484	# Tour packages sold
sK4486	% Tour packages sold growth rate
sK4490	# Overseas to local customer travel bookings
sK4492	% Favorable customer reviews
sK4764	% Bookings conversion rate
sK4771	% No show rate
sK6900	# Reviews available online
sK6908	% Aggregated rating in review sites

Travel Agency

Travel agency include all related activities to selling travel-related products and services, by representing third part suppliers, such as airlines, hotels, car rentals or sightseeing tours. KPIs in this industry focus on customer service, productivity, booking services, in terms of quality and efficiency.

sKPI #	Key Performance Indicator name
sK82	% Internet bookings
sK222	% Canceled reservations
sK1720	# Booking channels
sK1721	# Booking requests
sK1722	$ Revenue per booking
sK1723	# Ancillary facilities offered for tourists
sK1724	% Duplicate bookings
sK3444	% Written confirmations including relevant information issued to travelers
sK3449	% Compliance with national travel industry policies
sK3451	# Days before first online purchase of travel products
sK3797	# Packaged to independent bookings ratio
sK3798	# Group bookings to independent bookings ratio
sK4175	# Days since last online purchase of travel products
sK4485	# Package tour bookings
sK4487	# Response time to confirm reservation
sK4488	# Tours and vacation packages sold per travel consultant
sK4490	# Overseas to local customer travel bookings
sK4491	% Bookings confirmed
sK4492	% Favorable customer reviews
sK4764	% Bookings conversion rate
sK6585	# Travel bookings processed per day
sK6588	# Customer interaction time to bookings ratio
sK6900	# Reviews available online
sK6908	% Aggregated rating in review sites

Infrastructure Operations

Infrastructure operations consists of activities related to the administration and operation of infrastructure assets by operators serving various secondary industries. Infrastructure assets administered by operators acting in this industry include airports, ports, roads, toll roads and parking assets among others.

Airports

Airports includes all facilities and infrastructure necessary to operate the airline services and traffic. KPIs focus on airport infrastructure parameters, such as landing and takeoff installation efficiency, aircraft maintenance quality and refueling, as well as accommodation for passengers and cargo capacity. The indicators also measure airport activity, such as passenger transfers and boarding effectiveness, traffic control and airport security.

sKPI #	Key Performance Indicator name
sK3461	# Aircraft density
sK3462	# High speed turnoffs
sK3463	# Air bridges

sKPI #	Key Performance Indicator name
sK3465	# Aircraft movements
sK3466	% Airport activity
sK3470	% Electronic checked baggage screening equipment availability
sK3475	# Airmail tonnes handled
sK3483	$ Aircraft landing fee
sK3505	# Daily international flights to country
sK3508	# Flights per week during off-season
sK3517	# Frequency of air flights
sK3519	# International passenger traffic

sKPI #	Key Performance Indicator name
sK3520	# Domestic passenger traffic
sK3521	# Passenger transfers between flights
sK3522	# Arriving passenger capacity
sK3523	# Departing passenger capacity
sK3528	% Revenue from non-aviation activities
sK3542	# Minutes delayed for all flights
sK3549	# Arrival processing time
sK4572	# Pollutant emissions
sK6441	# Waste per passenger
sK6442	% Aircraft on track for departure
sK6443	# Population within specified noise counter
sK6444	# Populated area surrounding airport affected by noise
sK6445	# Noise limit infringements
sK6446	# Engine testing rules infringements
sK6447	% Airplanes that meet the international noise standard
sK6448	% Airport passengers using public transport
sK6449	% Operational deicing trucks
sK6450	# Deicing assignments per truck
sK6451	# Deicing truck refill time
sK6452	# Time to complete a deicing assignment
sK6453	# Fluid used per deicing assignment
sK6455	# Deiced airplanes per weather event
sK6468	$ Cost of snow removal
sK6469	% Cost of preventive maintenance
sK6470	% Cost of corrective maintenance
sK6480	% Damaged baggage
sK6481	% Delayed baggage
sK6482	% Rescheduled flights
sK6483	% Aircraft experiencing delays on tarmac before take off
sK6484	# Aircraft waiting time before take off
sK6485	# Aircraft waiting time at arrival before receiving a boarding gate
sK6487	# Process time for the turn-around activities
sK6488	% Turn around flights scheduled
sK6489	# Airport safety code violations
sK6490	$ Airline rental cost per gate
sK6491	$ Hangar rental rate per surface area
sK6492	% Airport hangar space that is leased
sK6493	% Leased airport terminal space
sK6494	$ Airport fees per passenger
sK6495	# Runway capacity utilization in peak hour operations
sK6496	% Runway availability
sK6497	# Flights operated per hour
sK6498	# Time from passengers entering to plane take off
sK6500	# Private aircraft flights operated
sK6501	# Loading bridges available

sKPI #	Key Performance Indicator name
sK6502	# Air traffic movements per employee
sK6503	# Aircraft movements per runway
sK6504	# Aircraft movements per length of runway
sK6505	# Passengers per aircraft movements
sK6506	% Baggage handling system reliability
sK6507	# Baggage handling system events causing penalty for the supplier
sK6508	# Baggage handling system stoppages per day
sK6509	$ Airport cost per passenger
sK6510	# Landings / take offs per day
sK6511	$ Landing fee revenue per aircraft movement
sK6512	$ Airport revenue per passenger
sK6513	% Airport aeronautical revenue
sK6514	# Terminal gates available
sK6515	# Boardings per gate per day
sK6516	# Boarding gate changes per day
sK6517	# Flights per air traffic controller
sK6518	# Night flights operated
sK6519	# Night flights operated per air traffic controller
sK6520	$ Rental car revenue per destination passenger
sK6521	# Aircraft departures per gate
sK6522	# Passengers per terminal area
sK6524	# Fuel volume supplied to airlines
sK6525	# Airport based pilots
sK6526	# On airport parking spaces available
sK6527	# Daily utilized parking spaces
sK6528	$ Daily revenue per parking space
sK6529	$ Parking revenue per transaction
sK6530	# Vehicles parked per departing passenger
sK14447	# Noise affected population
sK14461	# Air route traffic control centers
sK14462	# Air traffic control facilities
sK14463	# Air traffic control towers
sK14464	# Air traffic controller hiring
sK14465	# Air traffic controllers on board
sK14483	# Airport capacity (VMC)
sK14484	# Airport traffic control towers
sK14486	# Airports passengers handled
sK14487	# Airspace segregated
sK14502	# ALS (Approach Lighting System)
sK14504	# Alternating take-off and landing traffic
sK14536	# Arriving passenger capacity of the terminal building
sK14550	# ATC tactical interventions
sK14551	# ATCO error in providing runway entry instructions
sK14554	# ATM functions related occurrences
sK14578	# Automated flight services stations

sKPI #	Key Performance Indicator name
sK14579	# Automation facilities
sK14580	# Available airport slots
sK14815	# Competitors in the aeronautical services sector
sK14816	# Competitors in the air traffic control sector
sK14817	# Competitors in the airport management sector
sK14818	# Competitors in the commercial services sector
sK14819	# Competitors that are operating in airport infrastructure sector
sK14844	# Conflict in the TMAs
sK14845	# Conflict in uncontrolled airspace
sK14977	# IFR flights in Europe
sK14978	# IFR flights that can be accommodated at airport level
sK15039	# Delay of delayed flights as a consequence of the business trajectory full re-definition at airport level
sK15040	# Delay of delayed flights at airport level
sK15041	# Delay of delayed flights due to a business trajectory update at the airport
sK15081	# Difference between addition of arrival delays and departure delays
sK15082	# Difference between airport capacity (VMC) and airport capacity (IMC)
sK15083	# Difference between mean throughput (VMC) and mean throughput (IMC)
sK15161	# Electronic cargo screening machines available
sK15162	# Electronic carry-on screeners
sK15163	# Electronic carry-on screeners available
sK15164	# Electronic carry-on screeners being used
sK15165	# Electronic carry-on screeners in working order
sK15166	# Electronic checked baggage screeners
sK15167	# Electronic checked baggage screeners available
sK15168	# Electronic checked baggage screeners being used
sK15169	# Electronic checked baggage screeners in working order
sK15189	# Employee in traffic control
sK15191	# Employees in airport security
sK15192	# Employees in fire services
sK15199	# En route controller staffing
sK15202	# En-route delay
sK15214	# Estimated airspace volume capacity
sK15217	# Estimated overall system capacity
sK15558	# Inadequate separation instructions
sK17212	# Vertical resolutions
sK17227	# Visibility in feet
sK17543	# IFR flight hours per controller
sK17551	# Inadequate communication of instructions to pilot
sK17552	# Inadequate communication with pilot
sK17553	# Inadequate ground movement clearance
sK17554	# Inadequate pilot response to ATC
sK17555	# Inadequate runway entry instructions by ATCO

sKPI #	Key Performance Indicator name
sK17556	# Inadequate separation by pilot
sK17559	# Inadequate separation instructions to pilot
sK17560	# Inadequate take-off instructions by ATCO
sK17588	# Ineffective collision avoidance
sK17589	# Ineffective conflict warning
sK17590	# Ineffective runway entry procedures
sK17591	# Ineffective STCA warning
sK17592	# Ineffective tactical separation by pilot
sK17593	# Ineffective tactical separation of ATCO induced conflict
sK17594	# Ineffective take-off procedures
sK17595	# Ineffective traffic synchronization
sK17596	# Ineffective visual avoidance on commercial aircraft
sK18040	# Noise contours around the airport
sK18041	# Noise footprint area within the noise contours
sK18042	# Noise footprints
sK18084	# On-airport weather observation stations
sK18093	# Operating air bridges
sK18097	# Operating public airports in the country
sK18202	# Passenger terminal buildings
sK18203	# Passenger terminal doors
sK18204	# Passenger terminals
sK18400	# Primary methods of access to airport
sK18487	# Proving flights
sK18519	# R/T contacts
sK18520	# R/T contacts per 10 minutes
sK18521	# Radar vectors
sK18529	# Range of primary radar coverage in nautical miles
sK18530	# Range of secondary radar coverage in nautical miles
sK18545	# Ratio between maximum throughput (IMC) and maximum throughput (VMC)
sK18576	# Regulatory bodies (RBs) governing the airport sector
sK18578	# Release of airspace
sK18625	# Resolution complexity
sK18626	# Resolutions
sK18631	# Resource utilization
sK18687	# Runway approach type
sK18688	# Runway collisions
sK18689	# Runway confusion
sK18690	# Runway crossing movement
sK18691	# Runway entry at intermediate location
sK18692	# Runway excursion
sK18693	# Runway exit location in km
sK18694	# Runway exit speed
sK18695	# Runway incursion
sK18697	# Runway incursions per million operations
sK18698	# Runway surface material types

Organizational » Industries

sKPI #	Key Performance Indicator name
sK18699	# Runway usable length
sK18700	# Runway usable length for landing
sK18701	# Runway usable length for takeoff
sK18770	# Separation minima infringements
sK18812	# Size of cargo terminals
sK18833	# Speed clearances
sK18855	# Stage length
sK18862	# State-owned utilities in airport sector that are commercialized and corporatized
sK18937	# Takeoff roll time
sK18944	# Taxi-out additional time
sK18945	# Taxiway collisions
sK19061	# Training in non-segregated airspace
sK19063	# Trajectory instructions result in conflict
sK19121	# Unauthorized penetration of airspace
sK19128	# Unguarded gates
sK19172	# Used air bridges
sK19194	# Utilization of airspace
sK19320	$ Air traffic control costs
sK19321	$ Air transport freight
sK19322	$ Aircraft and traffic servicing
sK19324	$ Airport fees per international passenger
sK19326	$ Airport operation costs
sK19327	$ Airport user charges
sK19329	$ Airways turnover
sK19378	$ Contract maintenance costs
sK19379	$ Contract tower costs
sK19389	$ Cost of air operations
sK19656	$ Operations and network control center costs
sK20030	% Airspace designated segregated
sK20392	% Controller error
sK21087	% Nighttime use of runways
sK21096	% Non-scheduled delayed flights at the airport
sK21125	% Operating runway edge lighting
sK21327	% Pedestrian or vehicle error
sK21339	% Perimeter fence
sK21340	% Perimeter road closed to the public
sK21414	% Primary radar coverage
sK21584	% Runway side drainage
sK21619	% Secondary radar coverage
sK21842	% Taxiways in parallel with runways
sK21863	% Terminals designated for international travel
sK21864	% Terminals handling domestic travel
sK21872	% Time controlled item over-runsafety
sK21966	% VFR-IFR change requests accommodated without penalties
sK21967	% VFR-IFR change success

sKPI #	Key Performance Indicator name
sK21982	% Walk-up capability by the public of cargo terminals
sK22008	# Ineffective avoidance warning by ATCO
sK22876	# Runway
sK22877	# Apron
sK22878	# Terminal
sK22879	# Terminal capacity in passengers per year
sK22880	# Runway capacity in passengers per year
sK22881	# Terminal space per passenger
sK22882	# Level of airport charges
sK22883	# Airport operational time
sK22884	# Aggregate evaluation of service competitive strength
sK22885	$ Net profit per unit throughput
sK22886	$ Sales per unit throughput
sK22887	# Level of induced force of demand
sK22888	% Airport accessibility
sK22889	# Air transport movement (ATM) rate per hour
sK22890	% Noise track deviations
sK22891	# Contamination events
sK22892	% Journeys that use public transport
sK22893	% Scheduled operations by chapter 2 aircraft
sK22894	# Area affected by aircraft noise
sK22895	# Breaches of noise limits
sK22896	# Community complaints about airport activity
sK22897	$ Landing fees
sK22899	$ Aircraft parking fees
sK22900	$ Handling fees (if handling is provided by the airport operator)
sK22901	$ Aeronautical revenue
sK22902	$ Air traffic control fees
sK22903	$ Lighting fees
sK22904	$ Airbridge fees
sK22905	$ Car park revenue (if provided by the airport operator)
sK22906	$ Visitor and business service revenue
sK22907	$ Non-aeronautical revenue
sK22908	% Availability of lifts
sK22909	% Availability of escalators
sK22910	% Availability of moving walkways
sK22911	% Availability of trolleys
sK22912	# Waiting time per queue at check-in
sK22913	# Waiting time per queue at security check
sK22914	# Waiting time per queue at immigration catering
sK22915	# Baggage delivery time
sK22916	% Taxi availability
sK22917	# Waiting time for taxi
sK22918	% Passenger arriving who answered "excellent" or "good" to the overall assessment of airport

sKPI #	Key Performance Indicator name
sK22919	% Passenger departing and transfering who answered "excellent" or "good" to the overall assessment of airport
sK22920	% Airlines and handling agents who rated the airport as 'excellent' or 'good' in the client satisfaction survey
sK22921	# Mark awarded by tenants for the rented space and associated facilities
sK22922	% Convenient layout of terminal
sK22923	% Waiting facilities near gates
sK22924	% Satisfaction with lounges' atmosphere
sK22925	% Departures delayed more than 15 minutes
sK22926	% Arrivals delayed more than 15 minutes
sK22927	% Time available at stands
sK22929	% Passengers pier served
sK22930	# Cars available at transit system
sK22931	% Additional security test less than 10 minutes
sK22932	% Baggage arrivals reclaim
sK22933	% Availability of aircraft parking stands
sK22934	% Availability of airbridges
sK22935	% Availability of electro-mechanical equipment
sK22936	% Availability of luggage carousels
sK22937	% Availability of flight information systems
sK22938	# Parking stands in contact with terminal
sK22939	# Passenger satisfaction on direction signs and information on flights
sK22940	% Arriving passengers using an airbridge
sK22941	% Departing passengers using an airbridge
sK22942	% Hours with more than 80% check-in desks in use
sK22943	# Arriving passengers per inbound immigration desk during peak hour
sK22944	# Arriving passengers per baggage inspection desk during peak hour
sK22945	# Departing passengers per outbound migration desk during peak hour
sK22946	# Departing passengers per security clearance system during peak hour
sK22947	# Departing passengers per seat in gate lounges during peak hour
sK22948	# Density of departing passengers in lounge area during peak hour
sK22949	# Throughput of outbound baggage system, bags per hour
sK22950	# Passengers per baggage trolley during peak hour
sK22951	# Passengers per flight information display screen during peak hour
sK22952	# Passengers per flight information point during peak hour
sK22953	# Baggage inspection waiting time
sK22954	% Security clearance
sK22955	% Seating availability in gate lounges
sK22956	# Seating quality in gate lounges
sK22957	% Airport use of biometric identification
sK22958	% Airport use of self-service kiosks

sKPI #	Key Performance Indicator name
sK22959	# Quality of signage
sK22962	# Indirect employment related to airports
sK22963	# Propensity to fly in return trips per person
sK22964	# Surface distance to airport for domestic end-to-end trips
sK22965	# Surface time to airport for domestic end-to-end trips
sK22966	# Time between airport shut down and reopening due to breach of security
sK22967	# Time for business operations to begin after the incidents
sK22968	% Resolving the incident in such a manner that everything returns to normal with minimal destruction within the shortest possible time
sK22969	# Attack on airport facilities or installations
sK22970	# Destructive or criminal behavior by passenger on board aircraft
sK22971	# Destructive or criminal behavior directed at cargo on board aircraft
sK22972	$ Traffic income per passenger
sK22973	$ Traffic income per WLU
sK22974	$ Depreciation cost per WLU Traffic income per turnover %
sK22975	$ Commercial income per passenger
sK22976	$ Concession income per passenger
sK22977	$ Duty and tax-free revenue per international departing passenger
sK22978	$ Property income per passenger
sK22979	$ Property income per WLU
sK22980	# Public airports
sK22981	# Private airports
sK22982	# Part private -part public airports
sK22994	% Homes subjected to a specified noise level
sK22995	% Passenger trips to the airport by public transport

Ports

Ports includes all facilities and infrastructure required for the efficient and effective handling of passengers and cargo. KPIs focus on accommodation and trans boarding of passengers, as well as cargo handling capacity. Indicators also cover cargo handling equipment efficiency and availability, freight access in port from land and containerization capabilities, vessels docking capacity and additional port infrastructure parameters.

sKPI #	Key Performance Indicator name
sK191	# Major shipping lines in port
sK263	# Turnaround time
sK3007	# Tonnage handled per ship day in port
sK3089	# Idle time due to rain
sK3104	% Berth utilization rate
sK3215	# Container freight stations
sK3273	# Punitive measures in force due to delays in submission of documents
sK3487	# Port state control (PSC) inspected ships
sK3721	# Job dependency directly and indirectly on the port

sKPI #	Key Performance Indicator name
sK3722	# Gross dredge volume
sK3724	# Operational spills
sK3725	# Cargo handled in the port
sK3726	# Bulk goods handled
sK3729	# Non containerized trade
sK3731	% Trade by cargo type breakdown
sK3732	# Container dwell time
sK3733	# Container truck processing time
sK3734	# Container vessel pre-berth time
sK3735	# Container vessel berth productivity
sK3736	# Gross container crane productivity
sK3741	# Container throughput
sK3742	# Overseas containerized imports volume
sK3743	# Overseas containerized exports volume
sK3744	# Twenty-foot equivalent units (TEUs) moved by rail
sK3745	% Twenty-foot equivalent units (TEUs) moved by rail
sK3746	% Container trade growth
sK3747	# Containers lifted per hour
sK3748	# Containers handled at gate per hour
sK3752	# Port capacity
sK3753	# Port area
sK3757	# Ocean going vessel quay walls
sK3758	# Ocean going vessel berths
sK3759	# Port public roads length
sK3760	# Bridges in the port
sK3761	# Port railway track network length
sK3780	# Ship turn around time (ASTA)
sK3781	# Truck turnaround time gate to gate
sK3786	$ Seaport dues per vessel
sK3789	# Ocean going vessels received
sK3791	% Increase in the number of ships visiting the port
sK3792	# Chargeable vessel visits
sK3816	% Passenger vessels
sK3916	$ Port handling cost per TEU (twenty foot equivalent unit)
sK3921	$ Cargo handling cost per tonne of general cargo
sK4154	% Cargo handling equipment utilization rate
sK4158	$ Revenue per unit of cargo
sK4161	# Unproductive port time
sK4166	# Waiting time of ships
sK4170	# Customs in port
sK4174	% Port operations computerized
sK4176	$ Cost of ship waiting time per hour
sK4179	# Vessel calls per berth
sK4184	$ Ship congestion cost
sK4187	# Vessel repairs
sK4223	$ Berth occupancy revenue per tonne of cargo
sK4247	# Terminal operators
sK4258	$ Labor cost per hour per tonne handled
sK4299	# Ship waiting ratio
sK4310	# Logistics activities with a high dependency on short-sea shipping
sK4312	# Static storage capacity
sK4349	% Container yard capacity utilization
sK4361	$ Profit margin per tonne of cargo
sK4530	% Berth occupancy rate
sK4531	% Capacity of vessel calls per category
sK4532	$ Cost of explosion incidents
sK4542	# Vessel time outside
sK4559	% Container yard to gross acreage
sK4560	$ Lost cargo units value
sK4565	# Twenty-foot equivalent units handles per FTE
sK4566	# Deficiencies in the container handling
sK4567	# Import to export containers ratio
sK4570	# Twenty-foot equivalent units handled per acre
sK4572	# Pollutant emissions
sK4573	# Drayage truck vehicle miles traveled
sK4581	% Vessel calls per category
sK4584	# Vessel time at berth
sK4585	# Tonnes per gang hour
sK4589	# Re-handles per import pickup
sK4591	# Free flow time
sK4596	# Trips to and from the port terminals
sK4599	# Marine environmental deficiencies
sK4600	$ Cost per unit of cargo
sK4601	# Container oriented logistics parks
sK4602	$ Revenue per berth
sK4603	# Dry-docking time per vessel
sK4613	% Port labor cost to terminal operating cost
sK4614	% Turn rate per 10 000 liquid barges
sK4615	$ Operating surplus to cargo handled
sK4618	$ Expenditure per net registered tonnage
sK4625	# Port shipping trades
sK5866	# Twenty-foot equivalent units per crane hour
sK5892	$ Income per gross register tonnage
sK5908	# Throughput handled per berth
sK6245	# Tonnage handled per man hour
sK6435	# Tonnage per vessel day handled
sK6436	# Vessels handled per day
sK6437	# Hours of work stoppage due to poor weather conditions
sK6438	# Gangs employed per ship per shift
sK6439	# Vessels berthed
sK6469	% Cost of preventive maintenance
sK6470	% Cost of corrective maintenance

sKPI #	Key Performance Indicator name	sKPI #	Key Performance Indicator name
sK6579	# Trains handled per day	sK14991	# Days per year operation
sK6580	$ Port charges per throughput tonnes	sK15127	# Dry docks
sK6583	# Incidents involving ships while in the port	sK17213	# Vessel dwell time in port waters
sK6584	% Empty containers handled in the port	sK17214	# Vessel related dwell time
sK6633	# Throughput per linear meter of berth	sK17215	# Vessel turn around time
sK6634	$ Cargo handling revenue per tonne of cargo	sK17264	# Water areas
sK6635	% Fraction of time berthed ships worked	sK17300	# Flood barrages, gates and flash locks
sK6641	# Tonnes per ship hour in port	sK17355	# Fuel consumed in freight service
sK6642	# Tonnes per ship hour at berth	sK17374	# Gang labor productivity
sK6643	# Ship arrival rate	sK17375	# Gantry cranes
sK6644	# Quay transfer throughput	sK17384	# Gate fluidity indicator
sK6645	# Container yard throughput	sK17385	# Gate throughput
sK6646	# Receipt/delivery throughput	sK17386	# General break bulk cargo handled
sK6647	% Unproductive container moves	sK17422	# Gross dredged volume
sK6648	# Containers exchanged per container vessel	sK17424	# Gross productivity per hour
sK6649	% Vessels affected by berths unavailability	sK17425	# Gross tonnes railed
sK6650	# Delay time per vessel	sK17426	# Gross truck turnaround time
sK14534	# Area of water	sK17526	# Hours worked per day
sK14607	# Berth length	sK17623	# Inspected ships
sK14608	# Berth Length Utilization Rate	sK17624	# Inspected ships found having deficiencies
sK14609	# Berth productivity	sK17625	# Inspected ships which were detained
sK14610	# Berth utilization	sK17633	# Inter-island vessels
sK14611	# Berths	sK17651	# International vessels
sK14654	# Boxes moved	sK17678	# Jobs depending directly or indirectly on the port
sK14668	# Bulk cargo productivity	sK17689	# Land area utilization rate
sK14706	# Car capacity	sK17690	# Land areas
sK14707	# Car load	sK17695	# Land utilization
sK14715	# Cargo dwell time	sK17723	# Leased-out land in the port
sK14721	# Cargo or container related dwell time	sK17824	# Diesel production per tonne of wet lignite
sK14729	# Cars per freight train	sK17842	# Long wharves and waterfront structures
sK14869	# Container in	sK17883	# Maximum sailing draft (msd)
sK14871	# Container trade	sK17933	# Military vessels
sK14872	# Containers full out	sK17934	# Million tonnes railed per employee
sK14873	# Containers handled in 1000 TEU	sK17969	# Moves per crane-hour
sK14874	# Containers out empty	sK17985	# Net tonne-miles per train-hour
sK14875	# Containers shifted	sK17986	# Net truck turnaround time
sK14876	# Containership turnaround time	sK18044	# Non working time of vessels at berth
sK14877	# Containership waiting time	sK18080	# Oil jetties
sK14902	# Covered storage	sK18129	# Output per ship berth day
sK14907	# Crane productivity	sK18343	# Port productivity
sK14908	# Crane utilization	sK18344	# Port railway track network and facilities
sK14922	# Cruise	sK18346	# Port surface
sK14923	# Cruise passengers	sK18379	# Pre-berthing detention time (pbd)
sK14924	# Cruise passengers in the seaports	sK18497	# Public roads in the port
sK14925	# Cruise ships in the seaports	sK18516	# Quay length
sK14970	# D.W.H tonnage	sK18528	# Railway length

sKPI #	Key Performance Indicator name
sK18656	# Revenue tonne-miles per gallon of fuel consumed
sK18668	# Road length
sK18792	# Service Time Vessel Service Time
sK18797	# Shipment containers
sK18802	# Shore areas
sK18871	# Storage productivity
sK18938	# Tanker
sK18966	# Terminal area
sK18967	# Terminals
sK18973	# Throughput
sK18974	# Throughput by category of assets in the port
sK18975	# Throughput in the port
sK18976	# Throughput of agribulk
sK18977	# Throughput of coal
sK18978	# Throughput of containers
sK18979	# Throughput of oil products
sK18980	# Throughput of sand, gravel and minerals
sK19018	# Tonnage in
sK19020	# Tonnage out
sK19021	# Tonnage transshipped
sK19033	# Trade by cargo type
sK19056	# Train load
sK19062	# Trains per day to port and back to mines
sK19294	# Yachts D.W.H.
sK19314	$ Added vessel cost from berth waiting
sK19376	$ Container inventory cost
sK19385	$ Cost differential from inefficiency
sK19388	$ Cost from port cost model
sK19413	$ Cost per move
sK19509	$ Freight revenue tonne-miles per employee
sK19510	$ Freight revenue tonne-miles per employee-hour
sK19566	$ Inventory cost on the goods
sK19695	$ Port costs
sK19772	$ Revenue tonne-miles
sK19773	$ Revenue tonne-miles per carload
sK19815	$ Subsidies granted
sK19862	$ Vessel costs from port charges
sK19863	$ Vessel costs from vessel and berth waiting
sK20467	% Degree of containerization of the general cargo handled
sK21147	% Oversea containerized exports by region
sK21601	% Schedule integrity
sK23045	# Calls (all vessels)
sK23046	# Capacity of all calls
sK23047	# Tanker vessel calls
sK23048	# Product vessel calls
sK23049	# Crude oil vessel calls

sKPI #	Key Performance Indicator name
sK23050	# Container ship calls
sK23051	# Dry bulk cargo vessel calls
sK23052	# Ro-ro (roll-on roll-off container) vessel calls
sK23053	# Motor vehicle vessel calls
sK23054	# Gasoline carrier vessel calls
sK23055	# Combination vessel calls
sK23056	# General cargo vessel calls
sK23057	# Stationary days for covered hoppers
sK23058	# Turn rate per 10,000 liquid barges
sK23070	# Hazardous liquid pipeline spills in unusually sensitive areas (USAs)
sK23071	# Serious incidents
sK23072	# Pipeline incidents caused by corrosion
sK23073	# Pipeline incidents caused by excavation damage
sK23074	# Time required to close a Corrective Action Order after a safety sensitive incident
sK23075	# Unrecovered oil spill costs per costs for implementing IMP (Integrity Management Programs) in USAs
sK23076	# Barrels per day
sK23077	# Haul (miles)
sK23078	# Barrel-miles
sK23079	# Inland terminal throughput (in millions of barrels)
sK23080	# Marine terminal average storage capacity utilized per month
sK23081	# Transportation barrels shipped
sK23082	# Transportation revenue per barrel shipped
sK23083	# Rehandling productivity
sK23084	# Ships
sK23085	# Throughput volume
sK23086	# Port related employment
sK23087	% Port value added out of regional GDP
sK23088	# Establishments of new companies in port area
sK23089	# First port of call services
sK23090	$ Goods passing through the port
sK23091	% EDI use in port
sK23092	# Warehouse area
sK23093	# Time to major customer
sK23094	# Environmental accidents
sK23095	$ Economic impact of a port
sK23096	# Ship turn around time
sK23097	# Connectivity index
sK23098	# Throughput per square meter
sK23099	% Goods to which value is added in port region
sK23100	$ Housing prices in vicinity of port
sK23101	# Inland transport providers
sK23102	# Port operators
sK23103	# Shipping lines
sK22928	% Time available at jetties

Railways

Railways includes all equipment and infrastructure necessary to facilitate a fluent and efficient transportation of passengers and freight on railroads. KPIs focus on railway infrastructure quality, network size and density, as well as on network development and improvement capabilities and efficiency. KPIs also cover all additional installations parameters, such as traffic signs, railroad lights, freight terminals capacity, as well as railway security efficiency.

sKPI #	Key Performance Indicator name
sK3637	# Traffic lights
sK3643	# Rail length built
sK4572	# Pollutant emissions
sK6458	# Wheel sets replaced
sK6459	% Railway infrastructure capacity utilization
sK6460	% Train delays due to infrastructure
sK6461	# Delayed trains at the final destination due to infrastructure
sK6462	# Hours of train delays due to infrastructure
sK6463	# Train service disruptions
sK6464	$ Maintenance cost per track length
sK6465	% Railway infrastructure availability
sK6466	% Railway infrastructure performance
sK6467	# Energy consumption per kilometer of electrified rail lane
sK6468	$ Cost of snow removal
sK6469	% Cost of preventive maintenance
sK6470	% Cost of corrective maintenance
sK6471	$ Investment in track renewals
sK6472	# Accidents at level crossing
sK6473	# Train accidents per million train kilometers
sK6475	# Train delay per incident
sK6476	# Length of rail renewal completed
sK6477	# Derailments
sK6478	# Railway segments with speed restrictions imposed
sK6479	% Broken or parked railroad cars
sK6577	% Train incidents without derailment
sK6578	# Derailments per million train miles

Roads

Roads includes all equipment and infrastructure necessary to facilitate a fluent and efficient transportation of passengers and freight on roads. KPIs focus on road infrastructure quality, network size and density, as well as on network development and improvement capabilities and efficiency. KPIs also cover all additional installations parameters, such as traffic signs and road marking, as well as road security efficiency.

sKPI #	Key Performance Indicator name
sK3627	% Planned maintenance and repair programs completed to standards
sK3628	% Asphalt surfacing projects with defects within 3 years of completion
sK3631	% Major road network covered by controlled traffic management system

sKPI #	Key Performance Indicator name
sK3633	# Road network length
sK3634	# Flyovers
sK3635	# Vehicular bridges
sK3636	# Vehicular underpasses
sK3637	# Traffic lights
sK3638	# Pedestrian overhead bridges
sK3639	# Pedestrian underpasses built
sK3640	# Footbridges under administration
sK3642	# Public street lights
sK3644	# Area lane kilometers of freeway per 1000 population
sK3646	% City road network in good conditions
sK3659	$ Road user charge collected
sK3697	# Speed during peak hours
sK3899	# Distance between bus stops
sK4572	# Pollutant emissions
sK5318	# Time freeways operate above capacity
sK5432	$ Cost of highway maintenance per 100 miles traveled by a vehicle
sK5512	# Bicycle lane length installed
sK5513	$ Cost per lane mile resurfaced
sK5520	$ Cost per tonne of asphalt used
sK6468	$ Cost of snow removal
sK6469	% Cost of preventive maintenance
sK6470	% Cost of corrective maintenance
sK6527	# Daily utilized parking spaces
sK6528	$ Daily revenue per parking space
sK6529	$ Parking revenue per transaction
sK6531	% Length of marked bicycle paths
sK6533	% Delays caused by roadworks
sK6534	# Delays caused by traffic volume
sK6535	# Length of traffic congestion
sK6536	# Duration of traffic congestion
sK6537	% Road defects reported and repaired within x hours
sK6538	% Road inspections carried out within established frequency
sK6539	% Road network where maintenance work should be considered
sK6540	% Street lights in working order
sK6541	# Distance traveled with plow down
sK6542	# Distance traveled by plowing vehicle per snow event
sK6543	# Distance traveled to plow down distance ratio
sK6544	# Quantity of salt/sand mixture applied per distance traveled
sK6545	# Quantity of salt/sand mixture applied per vehicle
sK6546	# Time to bare pavement
sK6547	# Time to wet pavement
sK6548	# Time to provide one wheel track friction

sKPI #	Key Performance Indicator name
sK6549	% Roads returned to reasonably near normal winter condition within 24 hours
sK6550	# Time for traffic volume to return to normal after a snow event
sK6551	# Time lost due to traffic congestion
sK6552	% Roads with access to hub airports and ports
sK6553	% Roads with electronic tolls installed
sK6554	# Electronic toll points installed
sK6555	% Toll points with electronic system
sK6556	$ Money spent on roads safety improvement programs
sK6557	# Length of resurfaced roads by category
sK6564	% Length of road meeting pavement marking standards
sK6565	# Road length congested during weekday peak periods

sKPI #	Key Performance Indicator name
sK6566	# Clearance time for road incidents
sK6567	# Distance covered by the road incidents response safety team
sK6568	% Scheduled bridge preventive maintenance completed
sK6569	# Length patched on roads
sK6570	# Length of highway newly constructed
sK6571	% Signalized intersections
sK6572	% Roundabout intersections
sK6573	$ Cost of winter service salting per salted distance
sK6574	# Paved to unpaved roads ratio
sK6575	# Length of tunnels under administration
sK6576	# Road tunnels under administration

Manufacturing

Infrastructure operations consists of activities related to the administration and operation of infrastructure assets by operators serving various secondary industries. Infrastructure assets administered by operators acting in this industry include airports, ports, roads, toll roads and parking assets among others.

sKPI #	Key Performance Indicator name
sK26	# Time to manufacturing
sK84	# Unit production time
sK414	$ Cost of goods sold (COGS)
sK425	$ Stock value
sK428	% Sales order cancellation rate
sK494	# Altman Z-Score
sK596	% Critical equipment availability
sK634	# Safety stock
sK635	# Reorder point (ROP)
sK636	# Anticipation stock
sK638	# Working stock
sK639	# Decoupling stock
sK640	% Distressed stock
sK649	$ Obsolete stock
sK745	% Scrap rate
sK1569	# Electricity consumption per manufactured product
sK1573	# Hazardous raw material per kilogram of product
sK1609	$ Value of work in progress
sK1628	$ Production costs per unit
sK1638	% Lost manufacturing capacity
sK1655	# Quality awareness programs
sK2436	% Cost of goods sold
sK3304	% Maintenance cost from equipment cost
sK3952	$ Value added per manufacturing employee
sK4163	# Omissions of allergens in list of ingredients
sK4244	% Label accuracy
sK4346	% Manufacturing plant inspections with zero deficiencies

sKPI #	Key Performance Indicator name
sK4356	% Bulk containers with obvious signs of internal rusting
sK4363	# Interruptions in raw material supply
sK4450	# Informative inspections
sK4571	% Manufacturing containers not used
sK5882	% Deficiencies improvement
sK6141	# Deficiencies per manufacturing plant inspection
sK6177	% Bulk containers compliance
sK6600	% Recovery yield rate of returned products
sK6830	$ Manufacturing floor space utilization
sK6831	# People productivity
sK6832	% Not right first time
sK6833	% Delivered on time and in full
sK6834	# Production plants
sK17663	# Inventory turns
sK19666	$ Parts ordered
sK22022	# Calendar time
sK22023	# Planned downtime
sK22024	# Scheduled operation time
sK22025	# Set-up and change of coils
sK22026	# Tests
sK22027	# Defects of machines
sK22028	# Defects of transfer
sK22029	# Defects of tools
sK22030	# Defects in material and faults in disposition
sK22031	# Faults in logistics
sK22032	# Container not available
sK22033	# Operators not available

sKPI #	Key Performance Indicator name
sK22034	# Preventive maintenance
sK22035	# Faults in organisation
sK22036	# Inventory levels
sK22037	$ Fixed management costs
sK22038	# Cycle times
sK22039	# Scrap and rework
sK22040	$ Variable management costs
sK22041	% Profitability of product mix across sites
sK22042	# Raw material quality
sK22043	# Finished good quality
sK22044	# Demand variance
sK22045	% Management line scheduling visibility
sK22046	# Transportation logistics schedules
sK22047	% Management line capacity visibility
sK22048	# Supplier on-time delivery
sK22049	# Statistical process control
sK22050	# Schedule cycle variances
sK22051	# First pass yield
sK22052	# Variability of cycle times
sK22053	# Asset availability maintenance
sK22055	# Downtime events
sK22057	% OEE availability

sKPI #	Key Performance Indicator name
sK22058	# Slow cycles
sK22060	# OEE performance
sK22063	# OEE quality
sK22065	# Performance to takt time
sK22067	# Estimated time to completion
sK22068	% Run rate
sK22069	# Piece per labor hour
sK22070	# Effective equipment productivity (EEP)
sK22072	# Waste of overproduction
sK22073	# Waste of waiting
sK22074	# Waste of transporting
sK22075	# Waste of inappropriate processing
sK22076	# Waste of unnecessary inventory
sK22077	# Waste of unnecessary motions
sK22078	# Waste of defects
sK22079	# Waste of not utilising everyone's talents
sK22080	# Working time lost by the employee
sK22081	# Time lost indirectly to assist the injured party
sK22082	# Time lost to determine the cause of the accident
sK22083	$ Cost of interrupting the process and of equipment repairings or safety modifications
sK22084	$ Potentially large compensation payments and legal procedures following any pay-outs

Media

Media (audio/video) includes all activities aiming at creating content, motion pictures, movies, music and broadcasting them using different technologies. Also included are gambling and betting activities, which all have the purpose of entertainment. KPIs focus on the efficiency of the technologies used, and the impact of the entertainment activities over the customers.

Broadcasting (TV and Radio)

TV and Radio includes the activities of creating content or acquiring the right to distribute content and subsequently broadcasting that content, such as radio, television and data programs of entertainment or news. The broadcasting can be performed using different technologies, over-the-air, via satellite, via a cable network or via Internet.

sKPI #	Key Performance Indicator name
sK100	# Audience reach
sK101	$ Cost per broadcast hour
sK325	# Advertisement viewers
sK326	% Audience share
sK327	% Consumer retention of commercial messages
sK408	# Target rating points (TRPs)
sK409	$ Cost per mille (CPM)
sK927	# Quarter hour (QH) audience
sK935	% Quarter hour rating
sK941	% Radio station share
sK947	# Cumulative audience (cume)

sKPI #	Key Performance Indicator name
sK980	# Audience turnover
sK998	# Time spent listening (TSL)
sK1226	% Cumulative rating
sK1713	$ Film budget
sK4189	% National broadcast content
sK4225	% Output broadcast hours by genre
sK4234	$ Cost per viewer
sK4248	% Full episodes available on the website
sK4249	% Online audience to total reach of a TV or radio program
sK4348	# Hours produced in house
sK4451	# Repeated broadcast hours
sK4533	# Live broadcast hours
sK4553	# First-run syndicated programs by the radio station or television station
sK4554	% Fully advertiser funded programs or series
sK4555	# Digital platforms that form partnerships with the broadcaster

sKPI #	Key Performance Indicator name
sK4561	# Broadcast programs for specific audience
sK4562	# Journalists trained via informal channels
sK4569	# Journalists trained in formal qualification programs
sK5797	% Reach (Rating Point)
sK5801	% HDTV household penetration
sK5803	% Homes outside the area of available media services
sK5819	$ Television station revenue
sK5820	% Broadcast network advertising cost variance
sK5821	% Advertising expenditures on TV local stations
sK5823	% Network compensation to revenue
sK5824	$ Basic cable license fees
sK5825	% Carriage fees to broadcast revenue
sK5833	% Households watching a free-to-air TV program
sK5834	# Household TV share ratio
sK5835	% Cable television households watching a broadcast
sK7012	$ Cost per listener
sK22085	% National Content
sK22087	% Output hours (broadcast) by genre
sK22088	$ Cost per production hour
sK22089	% Overheads against total expenditure
sK22091	$ Cost per consumed hour
sK22094	% Utilisation of production resources
sK22095	# Output per employee
sK22096	# Daily readership
sK22097	# Sunday readership
sK22098	# Pulitzer Prize
sK22099	# Commercial ratings
sK22100	# Session quality
sK22101	# Session engagement
sK22102	# Viewing behavior
sK22103	# Opt-in activity
sK22104	# Consumer participation
sK22105	# Sales impact

Film and Music

Film and music includes all the activities of recording and producing motion pictures and music. Copyright measures and indicators are not included here.

sKPI #	Key Performance Indicator name
sK1709	# Movie attendance
sK1711	% Frequency of movie-going
sK1713	$ Film budget
sK1715	$ Worldwide movie box office
sK2080	# Movie awards received
sK2101	# Movie award nominations
sK2103	% Movie award success rate
sK2107	$ International movie box office

sKPI #	Key Performance Indicator name
sK2118	$ Domestic movie box office
sK2120	# Movie position in all time worldwide box office
sK2133	$ Movie domestic grosses adjusted for ticket price inflation
sK5789	% Box office receipts from total income
sK5790	# Tickets sold
sK5791	$ Price of admission
sK5792	# DVD to box office revenue ratio
sK5793	% Households owning DVD players
sK5794	$ DVD rental revenue
sK5795	$ Loss due to piracy
sK5800	% DVR market penetration
sK5802	% Pay-TV household penetration
sK5806	$ Income from album sales
sK5807	$ Recorded music market revenue
sK5814	# Mobile music subscribers
sK5816	% Album losses due to piracy
sK5817	% Film marketing costs as a percentage of window of exhibition revenue
sK5818	% Online rental subscriptions revenue
sK5822	% Music publishing revenue
sK5826	% Single sales
sK5827	% DVD audio sales
sK5828	% DVD video sales
sK5829	% Home video units returned to distributor by retailer
sK5830	% Actual returns
sK5831	% Worldwide home video units returned
sK5832	$ Cost of media unit shipped
sK5836	% Royalty expenses
sK5875	# Movies rented
sK6963	# Movie releases
sK6964	# Movie screens
sK6965	# Movie admissions
sK6966	# Cam-cording incidents detected
sK6967	# Artists attached to the company
sK6968	# Artists per artist manager
sK6969	# Performance tours
sK6970	% Paid artists
sK6971	# Partnerships with media platforms

Social Media

Form of electronic communication (as web sites for social networking and microblogging) through which users create online communities to share information, ideas, personal messages and other content.

sKPI #	Key Performance Indicator name
sK14403	# Active contributors
sK14636	# Blog posts
sK14637	# Blog subscribers

sKPI #	Key Performance Indicator name	sKPI #	Key Performance Indicator name
sK14655	# Brand evangelists	sK18658	# Reviews
sK14792	# Comments	sK18766	# Sentiment negative
sK14885	# Contributors	sK18767	# Sentiment neutral
sK15142	# E-books	sK18768	# Sentiment positive
sK15245	# Facebook updates	sK18819	# Social bookmarks
sK15254	# Fans	sK18820	# Social media sharing
sK17221	# Videos	sK18995	# Time spent on site
sK17307	# Followers	sK19046	# Traffic from social networking sites
sK17317	# Forum posts	sK19114	# Tweets
sK17318	# Forward to a friend	sK19762	$ Revenue per follower
sK17563	# Inbound links	sK19763	$ Revenue per lead
sK17817	# Likes	sK19799	$ Social media development costs
sK17904	# Mentions	sK19800	$ Social media marketing budget
sK17984	# Net Promoter	sK19801	$ Social media staff payroll
sK18140	# Page views	sK19819	$ Support cost per customer in social channels
sK18385	# Presentations	sK19837	$ Transaction value per customer
sK18548	# Reach	sK21594	% Satisfaction
sK18573	# Registered users	sK21635	% Share of conversation vs competitors
sK18634	# Response time	sK21638	% Share of repeat customers
sK18652	# Retweets		

Non-profit / Non-governmental

Non-profit organizations (NPOs) include all entities where funds are not distributed to owners, but are used in pursuing the organization's reasons of existence. Several examples would be charitable organizations, trade unions and public arts organizations. Most governments and government agencies meet this definition, but in most countries they are considered a separate type of organization and not counted as non-profit organizations. Non-governmental organizations (NGOs), sometimes called civil society organizations, are entities where there is no governmental participation. KPIs measure the efficiency in raising the resources needed and the impact of their redistribution.

sKPI #	Key Performance Indicator name	sKPI #	Key Performance Indicator name
sK368	% Appeal Coverage	sK5919	% Revenue from donations
sK369	% Items donated delivered	sK5920	# New volunteers recruited in the last three months
sK370	# Donation to delivery time	sK5921	$ Revenue from grants obtained
sK371	% Donor financial efficiency	sK5922	# Time to submit grant applications
sK372	% Donation transportation cost efficiency	sK5923	# Meeting frequency with volunteers
sK376	% Assessment accuracy	sK5924	# Governance steering groups
sK377	% Mentored youth who improved their academic results	sK5926	# Partners for recurring campaigns and events
sK378	% Mentored youth who establish themselves in employment	sK5929	% Alumni that offer their support
sK379	% Improved alliances in the community	sK5931	# Mechanisms used for feedback and complaints
sK653	$ Donation per donor	sK5932	# Stakeholder groups involved regarding NGO policies
sK654	$ Cost per dollar raised	sK5935	$ Funding per individual reached
sK5911	# Volunteers	sK5936	$ Value of a volunteer work
sK5913	# Volunteers to paid employees ratio	sK5938	# Public recognition awards within the community
sK5914	# Sources of revenue	sK5940	# Non-profit organizations
sK5915	# Non-profit community projects	sK5941	# Partnerships with non-profit organizations
sK5916	# Sponsors per project	sK5942	# Community awareness campaigns
sK5917	% Community volunteers participation	sK5943	# Internal reports to members

sKPI #	Key Performance Indicator name
sK5944	$ In-kind contributions
sK5947	% Annual loan loss rate
sK5949	# Fund raising events for charity
sK5953	# Event participants
sK5954	# Field visits within affected communities
sK5955	# Dialogues conducted with affected communities
sK5956	# International joint activities and cooperation
sK5957	% Donations collection rate
sK5958	% Projects financially sustainable
sK5959	% Volunteers attracting funding
sK5960	% Projects addressing community needs
sK5964	$ Grants payable in furtherance of the charity's objects
sK5965	# Community families reached
sK5966	$ Dollars mobilized by community actions
sK5968	# Monthly volunteers hours
sK5969	% Youth volunteering
sK5972	% Annual recurrent events
sK5973	# Volunteers involved on average in community projects
sK6993	# Competitive bids solicited for selecting outside professional fundraisers
sK6994	% Administration costs from donations
sK6995	% Services offered at no charge
sK6996	% Supporters who are considered active
sK6997	% Legislators who are aware of the issue
sK6998	% Clients who reported immediate needs were met as a result of assistance
sK6999	% Volunteer satisfaction
sK7001	# Applications received for certain assistance services
sK7067	# NGO Stakeholder groups involved in selecting programs
sK14422	# Additional fulltime employees employed by the client organizations for which the assistance played a significant role in the increase
sK14434	# Adult participants who attend parent meetings or attend school activities
sK14435	# Adult participants who read to their children daily
sK14436	# Adult participants who regularly help children with their school work
sK14519	# Annual subscriptions
sK14525	# Applications for housing received from targeted population
sK14559	# Attendence at events by type of event
sK14562	# Audience reporting enhanced attitude, feeling, after arts performance
sK14563	# Audience, by population type, reporting increased appreciation of arts from the programs
sK14564	# Audience, by population type, who report gaining increased knowledge of local culture as a result of attendance
sK14565	# Audience, population type X, deciding to pursue additional arts programs after performance

sKPI #	Key Performance Indicator name
sK14589	# Awards
sK14598	# Bed-nights in the shelter program during the reporting period
sK14664	# Building code violations in the project, broken out by severity of the violations
sK14678	# Businesses provided with assistance
sK14796	# Community aware of the particular performing arts opportunities
sK14797	# Community business in the area reporting a positive image towards the housing complex
sK14798	# Community members seeking information on issue X through calls to hotline
sK14799	# Community members seeking information on issue X through website hits
sK14800	# Community organization partnerships
sK14801	# Community partnerships
sK14802	# Community reporting that performances are inaccessible for disabled people
sK14803	# Community reporting that performances are too costly
sK14804	# Community reporting that performances are too hard to reach
sK14805	# Community residents in the area reporting a positive image towards the housing complex
sK14806	# Community residents providing funding to support the cause
sK14807	# Community residents satisfied with services of community organizing or policy
sK14809	# Community residents, by population type, reporting increased appreciation of arts from the performances
sK14810	# Community, by population type, who report that they believe the particular performing art is sensitive to their culture
sK14828	# Complaints received and satisfactorily resolved
sK14918	# Crimes in the housing neighborhood
sK15150	# Educational levels advanced per program participant
sK15158	# Elected officials who publicly support the campaign
sK15196	# Employer partners
sK15222	# Ex-offenders applying for program
sK15223	# Ex-offenders mandated to program
sK15264	# Favorable awards given by the media
sK15265	# Favorable critic reviews given by peers
sK15266	# Favorable critic reviews given by the media
sK15267	# Favorable legislation measures passed related to program goals or development
sK15268	# Favorable policy measures passed
sK15269	# Favorable reform measures passed related to program goals or development
sK15270	# Favorable reviews
sK15730	# Legislative votes in favor of the program's position on issue X
sK15823	# Litigation in favor of the program's position on issue X
sK17274	# Weeks continued

sKPI #	Key Performance Indicator name
sK17322	# Free tickets provided
sK17487	# Homebuyers in disability groups
sK17488	# Homebuyers in minority ethnic groups
sK17489	# Homebuyers receiving housing subsidies
sK17490	# Homebuyers with low incomes
sK17491	# Homeowners rating their feeling of safety in and around their homes as satisfactory
sK17492	# Homeowners satisfied with application process and other processes in obtaining affordable housing
sK17527	# House vacancy
sK17534	# Households who complete the shelter program
sK17535	# Housing projects having joint funding
sK17536	# Housing projects receiving joint funding
sK17580	# Individuals enrolled in program
sK17581	# Individuals taking part in the actions
sK17582	# Individuals, population type X, attending arts performances at least once per month
sK17675	# Job interviews per client
sK17676	# Job offers per client within the first 3 months of program completion
sK17727	# Legislative contacts
sK17728	# Legislative policies passed to create or protect long-term housing opportunities
sK17768	# Length of time in program
sK17833	# Loans received per year to support the program
sK17853	# Low income families housed in affordable, well-maintained units
sK17855	# Low-income units in market-rate neighborhood
sK17891	# Media outlets that publish material developed by organization
sK17905	# Mentored youth participants who are enrolled in college the first year after high school graduation
sK17906	# Mentored youth participants who establish themselves in employment within 5 years of graduating from high school
sK17907	# Mentored youth participants who graduate from high school
sK17908	# Mentored youth who have refrained from their involvement in gangs over the 12 months since entry into the program
sK17909	# Mentored youth who improved substantially on tests since entering the program
sK17910	# Mentored youth who improved their grade point average (GPA) since entering the program
sK17911	# Mentored youth who increased their weekly hours of doing homework since entering the program
sK17912	# Mentored youth who increased weekly hours spent reading since entering the program
sK17913	# Mentored youth who refrained from committing crimes since entering the program
sK17914	# Mentored youth who showed a decrease in times they skipped class since entering the program

sKPI #	Key Performance Indicator name
sK17915	# Mentored youth who showed a reduction in substance abuse since entering the program
sK17916	# Mentored youth who showed a reduction in times they skipped a day of school since entering the program
sK17917	# Mentored youth who showed decreased levels of anger since entering the program
sK17918	# Mentored youth who showed improved relationships with family members since entering the program
sK17919	# Mentored youth who showed improved self-worth since entering the program
sK17996	# New clients accepted for services during the reporting period
sK17997	# New clients applying for transitional housing during the reporting period
sK18016	# New households enrolling in transitional shelter during the reporting period
sK18019	# New leaders and volunteers taking part in the campaign for issue X
sK18020	# New leaders recruited
sK18021	# New leaders trained
sK18023	# New persons enrolling in transitional shelter during the reporting period
sK18056	# Non-ticketed performances
sK18109	# Options
sK18114	# Organizations attending meeting
sK18115	# Organizations involved in coalition for issue X
sK18130	# Outside programs offered by arts group
sK18131	# Outside services offered by arts group
sK18146	# Participants (who at time of enrollment are not registered to vote) who register to vote
sK18147	# Participants (who at time of enrollment are not registered to vote) who vote for the first time
sK18148	# Participants (who upon program entry were enrolled in TANF) whose grant is reduced or eliminated due to employment or increased income
sK18149	# Participants abusing alcohol X months after release from prison
sK18150	# Participants articulating or speaking about the issue
sK18152	# Participants involved in education or training the year after their release from prison
sK18153	# Participants providing funding to support the cause
sK18154	# Participants reporting greater understanding of issue X
sK18155	# Participants that are receiving support from family to meet basic needs X days after release from prison
sK18156	# Participants that engage in high-risk behaviors (see notes) X months after their release
sK18157	# Participants who are charged with misdemeanor offences after their release from prison
sK18158	# Participants who are convicted of serious crime after their release from prison
sK18159	# Participants who are convicted of violent after their release from prison
sK18160	# Participants who are law-abiding and supported by family after their release from prison

sKPI #	Key Performance Indicator name
sK18161	# Participants who are law-abiding and self-sufficient after their release from prison
sK18162	# Participants who are placed in jobs X days after their release from prison
sK18163	# Participants who are reunited with family members upon or as of X days after their release from prison
sK18164	# Participants who attend in-house and referral programs X days after release from prison
sK18165	# Participants who complete their service plan
sK18166	# Participants who completed the program
sK18167	# Participants who contribute to the support of family members
sK18168	# Participants who develop a service plan with a counselor within 30 days of program application
sK18169	# Participants who enrolled in adult education program
sK18170	# Participants who have maintained safe and stable housing for six consecutive months (see notes) after leaving the program
sK18171	# Participants who have steady earnings above minimum wage after their release from prison
sK18172	# Participants who participated in job placement activities after their release from prison
sK18173	# Participants who pass citizenship exam
sK18174	# Participants who retained employment for X days or months after most recent job placement
sK18175	# Participants who return to prison after their release
sK18176	# Participants who tested positive for drug abuse X months after their release from prison
sK18177	# Participants who tested positive for HIV after their release from prison
sK18178	# Participants with a post-release health plan that connects them with community-based health service providers
sK18179	# Participants with appropriate housing X months after their release from prison
sK18180	# Participants with mental health issues who remain free of psychiatric hospitalizations after their release from prison
sK18268	# People increasing participation in the actions overtime
sK18271	# People participating in event
sK18272	# People reached through communications
sK18274	# People targeted with information on issue X
sK18275	# People volunteering
sK18342	# Population type X placed in jobs
sK18428	# Program participants accepted for services during the reporting period
sK18429	# Program participants applying for services during the reporting period
sK18430	# Program participants attending program
sK18431	# Program participants attributing the training to their ability to find work
sK18432	# Program participants being assisted with training type X
sK18433	# Program participants enrolling for the training program

sKPI #	Key Performance Indicator name
sK18434	# Program participants in need of mental health treatment who enter into such treatment within X days of shelter entry
sK18435	# Program participants in need of mental health/ addiction treatment who enter into such treatment within X days of shelter entry
sK18436	# Program participants in same job after X months of being placed
sK18437	# Program participants indicating improved attitudes towards changing their behavior
sK18438	# Program participants indicating improved confidence towards changing their behavior
sK18439	# Program participants provided with assistance
sK18440	# Program participants receiving health care benefits, as part of their wage package
sK18441	# Program participants reporting a substantial improvement in their behavior after the end of service
sK18442	# Program participants reporting being satisfied with the job at X months
sK18443	# Program participants reporting being satisfied with the services of employment training courses/ organization
sK18444	# Program participants reporting feeling healthier than before the service
sK18445	# Program participants satisfied with business assistance services in courses
sK18446	# Program participants satisfied with business assistance services in organization
sK18447	# Program participants still enrolled after the first week of training
sK18448	# Program participants still in business, 2 years after start
sK18449	# Program participants that attributed increased sales revenue/profits to program assistance
sK18450	# Program participants that attributed new business operations or methods to program assistance after the assistance was received
sK18451	# Program participants that attributed solving of a significant operational problem to program assistance after the assistance
sK18452	# Program participants that began a business after the assistance
sK18453	# Program participants that expand existing business after the assistance
sK18454	# Program participants that made a positive change in their business or markets at least in part because of the assistance
sK18455	# Program participants who accept a job offer
sK18456	# Program participants who are healthy, or have improved health
sK18457	# Program participants who attain economic stability
sK18458	# Program participants who began a business within 12 months after assistance and reported the assistance as a contributing factor
sK18459	# Program participants who complete or advance at least one educational level
sK18460	# Program participants who complete service plan

smartKPIs.com
The smart choice in performance management

sKPI #	Key Performance Indicator name
sK18461	# Program participants who complete shelter program
sK18462	# Program participants who complete the training
sK18463	# Program participants who develop a recovery/treatment/service plan by the end of their Xth day of shelter at that site
sK18464	# Program participants who do not re-enter the homeless system within one year of obtaining permanent housing
sK18465	# Program participants who dropped out of service before the service was completed
sK18466	# Program participants who enroll in postsecondary education or occupational skills training program
sK18467	# Program participants who have met with counselor and developed a treatment/recovery/service plan within X days of entry
sK18468	# Program participants who move to a transitional shelter, long-term housing, a rehabilitative setting (excluding prison), or the home of a friend or family member
sK18469	# Program participants who moved to safe and permanent housing within 24 months of program entry
sK18470	# Program participants who obtain a job within 3 months of program completion
sK18471	# Program participants who obtain safe and permanent housing within 24 months of program entry and maintain that housing for 6 months or more
sK18472	# Program participants who receive a secondary school diploma or GED
sK18473	# Program participants who remain employed 12 months after program completion
sK18474	# Program participants who remain in the shelter three or more days and utilize services
sK18475	# Program participants who report their immediate shelter needs are met
sK18476	# Program participants who, as a result of their service plan, make use of programs (in-house or by referral) within X days of shelter entry
sK18477	# Program participants who, as a result of their service plan, participate in supportive services (in-house or by referral to community resources) within X days of entry
sK18478	# Program participants with improved knowledge about how to reduce risk behaviors
sK18479	# Program participants with improved knowledge of the nature and consequences of risk behaviors
sK18575	# Regulations changed in favor of issue X
sK18583	# Renwed subscription
sK18589	# Repeat hires by employer partners
sK18633	# Respondents that strongly agreed that their business functions better as a result of assistance
sK18748	# Seasonal subscriptions
sK18773	# Series subscriptions
sK18791	# Service requests per month
sK18823	# Sought actions taken by the government agency
sK18857	# Stakeholders convened
sK18882	# Students enrolled in tutoring

sKPI #	Key Performance Indicator name
sK18889	# Students participating in tutoring
sK18899	# Students who showed a reduction in times they skipped a day of school since entering the program
sK18900	# Students who showed a reduction in times they skipped class since entering the program
sK18907	# Subscriptions
sK18908	# Seasonal subscriptions
sK18917	# Supplemental support hours utilized per client (on coaching, counseling)
sK18939	# Target population in jurisdiction X without access to affordable housing
sK18958	# Tenants in disability groups
sK18959	# Tenants in minority ethnic groups
sK18960	# Tenants rating their feeling of safety in and around their homes as satisfactory
sK18961	# Tenants receiving housing subsidies
sK18962	# Tenants satisfied with application process and other processes in obtaining affordable housing
sK18963	# Tenants with low incomes
sK18996	# Time spent planning
sK19106	# Turnover of residents
sK19107	# Tutored students who are enrolled in college the first year after high school graduation
sK19108	# Tutored students who improved their grade point average (GPA) since entering the program
sK19109	# Tutored students who increased their weekly hours of doing homework since entering the program
sK19110	# Tutored students who increased weekly hours spent reading since entering the program
sK19111	# Tutored students whose parents and teachers reported improved attitudes and motivation for their child/student towards school work since entering the program
sK19112	# Tutored youth who graduated from high school or passed the GED or other high school graduation equivalent
sK19113	# Tutored youth who improved substantially on tests from entry to program completion
sK19132	# Unit vacancy
sK19305	# Youth enrolled in mentoring
sK19306	# Youth participating in mentoring
sK19307	# Youth recruited in relation to number of mentors recruited
sK19550	$ Hourly wage of clients who became employed after training
sK19585	$ Loan fund available to support the program
sK19930	% Acceptance rate
sK19991	% Adult participants who attend parent meetings or attend school activities
sK19992	% Adult participants who read to their children daily
sK19993	% Adult participants who regularly help children with their school work
sK20101	% Attendance rate at events

sKPI #	Key Performance Indicator name
sK20104	% Audience reporting enhanced attitude after arts performance
sK20105	% Audience, by population type, reporting being very satisfied with their performing arts experience
sK20106	% Audience, by population type, reporting increased appreciation of arts from the programs
sK20107	% Audience, by population type, who report gaining increased knowledge of local culture as a result of attendance
sK20108	% Audience, population type X, deciding to pursue additional arts programs after performance
sK20160	% Building code violations in the project, broken out by severity of the violations
sK20180	% Capacity enrolled
sK20181	% Capacity filled at event
sK20182	% Capacity registered
sK20285	% Clients who do not re-enter the homeless system within one year of obtaining permanent housing
sK20286	% Clients accepted for services during the reporting period
sK20287	% Clients attributing the training to their ability to find work
sK20288	% Clients being assisted with training type X
sK20289	% Clients enrolling for the training program
sK20290	% Clients in need of mental health treatment who enter into such treatment within X days of shelter entry
sK20291	% Clients in need of mental health/ addiction treatment who enter into such treatment within X days of shelter entry
sK20292	% Clients in same job after X months of being placed
sK20293	% Clients indicating improved attitudes towards changing their behavior
sK20294	% Clients indicating improved confidence towards changing their behavior
sK20295	% Clients passing job skill competency exams on initial attempt after completing course
sK20297	% Clients placed in X jobs
sK20298	% Clients receiving health care benefits, as part of their wage package
sK20299	% Clients reporting a substantial improvement in their behavior after the end of service
sK20300	% Clients reporting being satisfied with the job at X months
sK20301	% Clients reporting being satisfied with the services of employment training courses/organization
sK20302	% Clients reporting feeling healthier than before the service, 6 months after the end of service
sK20303	% Clients satisfied with business assistance services in courses
sK20304	% Clients satisfied with business assistance services in organization
sK20306	% Clients still enrolled after the first week of training
sK20307	% Clients that attributed increased sales revenue/profits to program assistance
sK20308	% Clients that attributed new business operations or methods to program assistance after the assistance was received

sKPI #	Key Performance Indicator name
sK20309	% Clients that attributed solving of a significant operational problem to program assistance after the assistance
sK20310	% Clients that began a business after the assistance
sK20311	% Clients that expand existing business after the assistance
sK20312	% Clients that made a positive change in their business or markets at least in part because of the assistance
sK20313	% Clients who accept a job offer
sK20314	% Clients who are healthy, or have improved health after the end of service
sK20315	% Clients who attain economic stability after training
sK20316	% Clients who began a business within 12 months after assistance and reported the assistance as a contributing factor
sK20317	% Clients who complete service plan
sK20318	% Clients who complete shelter program
sK20319	% Clients who complete the training
sK20320	% Clients who develop a recovery/ treatment/service plan by the end of their Xth day of shelter at that site
sK20321	% Clients who dropped out of service before the service was completed
sK20322	% Clients who have met with counselor and developed a treatment plan with in X days of entry
sK20323	% Clients who move to a transitional shelter, long-term housing, a rehabilitative setting (excluding prison), or the home of a friend or family member
sK20324	% Clients who moved to safe and permanent housing after program entry
sK20325	% Clients who remain in the shelter three or more days and utilize services
sK20326	% Clients who report their immediate shelter needs are met
sK20327	% Clients who, as a result of their service plan, make use of services/programs (in-house or by referral) within X days of shelter entry
sK20328	% Clients who, as a result of their service plan, participate in supportive services (in-house or by referral to community resources) within X days of entry
sK20329	% Clients with improved knowledge about how to reduce risk behaviors
sK20330	% Clients with improved knowledge of the nature and consequences of risk behaviors
sK20343	% Community aware of the particular performing arts opportunities
sK20344	% Community business in the area reporting a positive image towards the housing complex
sK20347	% Community reporting that performances are inaccessible for disabled people
sK20348	% Community reporting that performances are too costly
sK20349	% Community reporting that performances are too hard to reach
sK20350	% Community residents in the area reporting a positive image towards the housing complex

sKPI #	Key Performance Indicator name
sK20351	% Community residents providing funding to support the cause
sK20352	% Community residents satisfied with services of community organizing or policy
sK20353	% Community, by population type, who report that they believe the particular performing art is sensitive to their culture
sK20369	% Completion rate
sK20380	% Constituent satisfaction rate
sK20381	% Constituents renewing
sK20382	% Constituents satisfied
sK20383	% Constituents utilizing multiple services
sK20385	% Continue with program past initial experience
sK20411	% Crimes in the housing neighborhood
sK20594	% Employer partners offering jobs to clients
sK20631	% Facility capacity filled per performance
sK20639	% Favorable awards given by the media
sK20640	% Favorable critic reviews given by the media (or peers)
sK20641	% Favorable critic reviews given by the peers
sK20642	% Favorable policy measures passed
sK20706	% Goals achieved
sK20779	% Homebuyers in disability groups
sK20780	% Homebuyers in minority ethnic groups
sK20781	% Homebuyers receiving housing subsidies
sK20782	% Homebuyers with low incomes
sK20783	% Homeowners rating their feeling of safety in and around their homes as satisfactory
sK20807	% House vacancy
sK20815	% Households who complete the shelter program
sK20820	% Improvement
sK20821	% Improvement as reported by parent, teacher, and co-worker
sK20822	% Improvement as reported by participant
sK20830	% Incidence rate
sK20838	% Increase in investment dollars in neighborhood re-development
sK20839	% Increase in knowledge
sK20841	% Increase in scores after attending
sK20843	% Increase in turnout
sK20845	% Individuals, population type X, attending arts performances at least once per month
sK20917	% Key stakeholders as partners
sK20932	% Legislative policies passed to create or protect long-term housing opportunities
sK20933	% Legislators aware of issue
sK20970	% Low income families housed in affordable, well-maintained units
sK20972	% Low-income units in market-rate neighborhood
sK20994	% Mentored youth participating for 12 months who are enrolled in college the first year after high school graduation

sKPI #	Key Performance Indicator name
sK20995	% Mentored youth participating for 12 months who establish themselves in employment within 5 years of graduating from high school
sK20996	% Mentored youth participating for 12 months who graduate from high school
sK20997	% Mentored youth who have refrained from, or decreased, their involvement in gangs over the 12 months since entry into the program
sK20998	% Mentored youth who improved substantially on tests as of 12 months of entering the program
sK20999	% Mentored youth who improved their grade point average (GPA) as of 12 months of entering the program
sK21000	% Mentored youth who increased their weekly hours of doing homework over the 12 months since entering the program
sK21001	% Mentored youth who increased weekly hours spent reading over the 12 months since entering the program
sK21002	% Mentored youth who refrained from, or showed a reduction in, crimes committed over the 12 months since entering the program
sK21003	% Mentored youth who showed a decrease in or absence of times they skipped class over the 12 months since entering the program
sK21004	% Mentored youth who showed a reduction in substance abuse, or no abuse of substances, as of 12 months since entering the program
sK21005	% Mentored youth who showed a reduction in, or absence of, times they skipped a day of school over the 12 months since entering the program
sK21006	% Mentored youth who showed decreased levels of anger as of 12 months since entering the program
sK21007	% Mentored youth who showed improved relationships with family members (see note) as of 12 months of entering the program
sK21008	% Mentored youth who showed improved self-worth as of 12 months since entering into the program
sK21110	% of mentored youth who felt that the mentoring they received from the program had helped them in feeling good about themselves as of 12 months since entering the program
sK21111	% of subscribers who are donors
sK21195	% Paricipants that change over time
sK21197	% Participants (who at time of enrollment are not registered to vote) who register to vote
sK21198	% Participants (who at time of enrollment are not registered to vote) who vote for the first time
sK21199	% Participants (who upon program entry were enrolled in TANF) whose grant is reduced or eliminated due to employment or increased income
sK21200	% Participants abusing alcohol X months after release from prison
sK21201	% Participants articulating/speaking about the issue
sK21202	% Participants considered active
sK21203	% Participants enrolled in education programs
sK21204	% Participants feeling well-prepared for a particular task
sK21206	% Participants involved in education or training during the 12 months after their release from prison

sKPI #	Key Performance Indicator name
sK21207	% Participants meeting minimum qualifications for next level
sK21208	% Participants moving to next level
sK21209	% Participants providing funding to support the cause
sK21210	% Participants reporting greater understanding of issue X
sK21211	% Participants that are receiving support from family to meet basic needs X days after release from prison
sK21212	% Participants that believe skills were increased after attending
sK21213	% Participants that do not reenter the program
sK21214	% Participants that engage in high-risk behaviors (see notes) X months after their release
sK21216	% Participants who are charged with misdemeanor offenses within 12 months of their release from prison
sK21217	% Participants who are convicted of serious crime within 12 months of their release from prison
sK21218	% Participants who are convicted of violent within 12 months of their release from prison
sK21219	% Participants who are law abiding and supported by family 12 months after their release from prison
sK21220	% Participants who are law-abiding and self-sufficient 12 months after their release from prison
sK21221	% Participants who are placed in jobs X days after their release from prison
sK21222	% Participants who are reunited with family members upon or as of X days after their release from prison
sK21223	% Participants who attend in-house and referral programs X days after release from prison
sK21224	% Participants who avoid undesirable course of action
sK21225	% Participants who complete their service plan
sK21226	% Participants who continue to next level
sK21227	% Participants who contribute to the support of family members, especially child support, as of 12 months in the program
sK21228	% Participants who develop a service plan with a counselor within 30 days of program application
sK21229	% Participants who establish career
sK21230	% Participants who graduate
sK21231	% Participants who have steady earnings above minimum wage 12 months after their release from prison
sK21232	% Participants who maintain current level
sK21233	% Participants who maintain safe and permanent housing
sK21234	% Participants who move to long term housing
sK21235	% Participants who move to next condition
sK21236	% Participants who participated in job placement activities during the 12 months after their release from prison
sK21237	% Participants who pass citizenship exam
sK21238	% Participants who report immediate needs met
sK21239	% Participants who retain employment
sK21240	% Participants who retained employment for X days or months after most recent job placement

sKPI #	Key Performance Indicator name
sK21241	% Participants who return to prison within 12 months of their release from prison
sK21242	% Participants who successfully complete program
sK21243	% Participants who tested positive for drug abuse X months after their release from prison
sK21244	% Participants who tested positive for HIV during the 12 months after their release from prison
sK21245	% Participants with a post-release health plan that connects them with community-based health service providers
sK21246	% Participants with appropriate housing X months after their release from prison
sK21247	% Participants with immediate positive response
sK21248	% Participants with improved relationships
sK21249	% Participants with increased earnings
sK21250	% Participants with mental health issues who remain free of psychiatric Hospitalsizations during the 12 months after their release from prison
sK21251	% Participants with reduced incidence of health problem
sK21253	% Participation rate
sK21257	% Past clients still working after 12 months
sK21337	% People who enroll for multiple services
sK21386	% Population type X placed in jobs
sK21431	% Program participants still in business, 2 years after start
sK21432	% Program participants who complete or advance at least one educational level
sK21433	% Program participants who enroll in postsecondary education or occupational skills training program
sK21434	% Program participants who obtain a job within 3 months of program completion
sK21435	% Program participants who receive a secondary school diploma or GED
sK21436	% Program participants who remain employed 12 months after program completion
sK21437	% Programs that report positive response post-90 days
sK21462	% Public aware of issue
sK21467	% Public taking precautions
sK21496	% Recidivism rate
sK21514	% Reduction in reported behavior frequency
sK21516	% Referral rate
sK21521	% Relapse
sK21531	% Renewal rate
sK21536	% Reporting improved attitude
sK21551	% Respondents that strongly agreed that their business functions better as a result of assistance
sK21595	% Satisfaction with conditions and maintenance of housing units
sK21652	% Sought actions taken by the government agency
sK21764	% Students participating in tutoring for a 12 month period
sK21779	% Students who showed a reduction in, or absence of, times they skipped a day of school over the 12 months since entering the program

sKPI #	Key Performance Indicator name
sK21780	% Students who showed a reduction in, or absence of, times they skipped class over the 12 months since entering the program
sK21788	% Subscribers who are donors
sK21789	% Success rate
sK21797	% Supporting votes secured
sK21828	% Target constituency aware of service
sK21829	% Target constituency enrolled
sK21830	% Target constituents aware of issue
sK21831	% Target constituents reporting significant barriers to entry
sK21832	% Target constituents served
sK21833	% Target constituents taking desirable action
sK21834	% Target constituents turned away
sK21836	% Target population in jurisdiction X without access to affordable housing
sK21856	% Tenants in disability groups
sK21857	% Tenants in minority ethnic groups
sK21858	% Tenants rating their feeling of safety in and around their homes as satisfactory
sK21859	% Tenants receiving housing subsidies
sK21860	% Tenants with low incomes

sKPI #	Key Performance Indicator name
sK21907	% Turnover of residents
sK21908	% Tutored students participating for 12 months who are enrolled in college the first year after high school graduation
sK21909	% Tutored students who improved their grade point average (GPA) over the 12 months since entering the program
sK21910	% Tutored students who increased their weekly hours of doing homework over the 12 months since entering the program
sK21911	% Tutored students who increased weekly hours spent reading over the 12 months since entering the program
sK21912	% Tutored students whose parents and teachers reported improved attitudes and motivation for their child/student towards school work over the 12 months since entering the program
sK21913	% Tutored youth participating for 12 months who graduated from high school or passed the GED or other high school graduation equivalent
sK21914	% Tutored youth who improved substantially on tests from entry to program completion over the 12 months since entering the program
sK21922	% Unit vacancy
sK22003	% Youth enrolled in mentoring over a 12 month period
sK22004	% Youth participating in mentoring for a 12 month period

Other

General KPIs that don't fit under any other of the industries in the smartKPIs.com taxonomy.

sKPI #	Key Performance Indicator name
sK4529	% On-time and accurate raw material orders
sK5945	$ Payroll tax paid by the employer
sK6039	% Subscribers enrolled for automated notifications services
sK6095	$ Coding cost per line of code (LOC)
sK6096	% Cost of testing and debugging
sK6097	# Bugs per 1,000 lines of code (KLOC)
sK6098	# Time to market (TTM)
sK6099	# Software process execution time in seconds
sK6102	# Software defects per testing minute
sK6103	% Single-user licenses sold
sK6104	% Multi-user licenses sold
sK6105	% Software sales from revenue
sK6106	$ Single-user license price
sK6110	# User load capacity
sK6115	% User inputs with improper error handling
sK6116	% Encrypted servers
sK6164	# Net account receivable days
sK6440	% Expense of temporary staffing to labor cost
sK22456	% Staff attendance rate
sK22470	# Ratio of production staff to administrative and supervisory staff

sKPI #	Key Performance Indicator name
sK22471	# Work hours lost to accidents
sK22472	# Hours of training per FTE
sK22473	# Frequency of customer complaints
sK22474	# Clerks
sK22523	# Employees by union code
sK22593	% Cheques cleared to standard
sK22597	% Visit customers served within 3 minutes
sK22598	# Staff key competencies
sK22983	# Performance management maturity level
sK22984	# Benchmarking capability maturity level
sK22985	# Total Quality Management (TQM) maturity level
sK22986	# Activity Based Costing maturity level
sK22987	# Environmental Management System maturity level
sK22988	% Balanced Scorecard maturity level
sK22989	# Business Process Re-engineering maturity level
sK22990	# Quality Management System maturity level
sK22991	# EFQM maturity level
sK22992	# Value Based Management maturity level
sK22993	# Malcolm Baldridge Award assessment level
sK22996	# Vehicles loaded or unloaded per labor hour
sK22997	# Weight loaded or unloaded per labor hour

sKPI #	Key Performance Indicator name	sKPI #	Key Performance Indicator name
sK22998	# Miles driven	sK23021	# Operation time
sK22999	# Driving hours	sK23022	# Haulage time
sK23000	# Miles per driving hour	sK23023	# Crowd indexes
sK23001	# Labor hours used	sK23024	# Order cycle time
sK23002	# Transit hours per trip	sK23025	# Customer order path
sK23003	$ Equivalent cost of outside substitute	sK23026	# Length of haul
sK23004	# Fuel use per mile	sK23027	# Empty miles factor
sK23005	# Fuel use per tonne-mile	sK23028	# Age of revenue equipment
sK23006	# Fuel use per stop	sK23029	% Equipment utilization rate
sK23007	# Miles driven per gallon	sK23030	# Tractor operating life
sK23008	# Lines, cases, orders or units per labor hour	sK23031	# Trailer operating life
sK23009	# Weight unloaded per dock door per day	sK23032	# Tractors in service
sK23010	# Equivalent vehicles unloaded per dock door per day	sK23033	# Trailers in service
sK23011	# Weight, orders, lines or units throughput per labor hour	sK23034	# Hundredweight
sK23012	# Weight, units or pallets throughput per total warehouse cost	sK23035	# Loaded miles per load
sK23013	# Lines, units or orders per square foot	sK23036	# Pounds per shipment
sK23014	# Units, weight, lines, orders or dollars throughput per square foot	sK23037	$ Revenue per hundredweight
sK23015	# Replenishment cycle time	sK23038	$ Revenue per loaded mile
sK23016	# Weight of transported goods	sK23039	$ Revenue per shipment
sK23018	$ Transport tariff revenue	sK23040	# Shipments
sK23019	# Transported units	sK23041	# Shipments per business day
sK23020	# Vehicles	sK23042	# Railcars on line
		sK23043	# Terminal dwell time

Postal and Courier Services

Postal and Courier Services refers to postal and courier activities, such as pickup, transport and delivery of letters and parcels under various arrangements. Local delivery and messenger services are also included. KPIs in postal and courier services measure the efficiency in operations and customer satisfaction with delivery.

sKPI #	Key Performance Indicator name	sKPI #	Key Performance Indicator name
sK235	% Transport capacity utilization	sK3804	% Delivery routes completed each day
sK263	# Turnaround time	sK3805	% Special delivery by next day
sK265	$ Fuel cost	sK3806	# Residential deliveries
sK898	# Customer shipment to delivery cycle time	sK3807	# Business deliveries
sK3476	# Express services tonnes	sK3809	# Post office (PO) boxes
sK3776	% Shipment traceability	sK3811	% Collection points served each day
sK3785	# Transit time	sK3813	# Public mail collection points
sK3787	# Mail volume processed per hour	sK3814	# Delivery points
sK3795	# Inhabitants served by post office	sK3815	% Stamped and metered mail sent by first class
sK3796	# Post offices	sK3817	# Electronic sorting machines
sK3799	# Distance traveled by postal vehicles	sK3820	% Parcels posted at the post offices
sK3800	% Mail delivered by next working day	sK3821	% Parcels posted in the post offices that were the origin of a complaint
sK3801	% Outgoing international mail shipped by next working day	sK3824	# Mail volume processed per day
sK3802	% Mail delivered by postcode area	sK3825	# Mail volume handled
sK3803	# Postal address changes processed	sK3826	% Advertising mail out of domestic letter posts

sKPI #	Key Performance Indicator name
sK3827	% Advertising mail - share of international letter-post
sK3828	# Letter-post items
sK3829	# Letter-post items sent per capita
sK3830	# Letter-post items distributed per person employed
sK3831	% Ordinary letters and postcards
sK3832	% Reserved area from total letter-post services
sK3833	% Registered letters with erratic delivery time planned
sK3834	# Mail items posted per day
sK3836	% Domestic mail posted
sK3837	% Mail received by businesses
sK3838	% Mail received by residential addresses
sK3839	% Business to business mail
sK3840	% Stamped and metered mail sent to second class
sK3842	% Growth in eParcel volumes
sK3843	% Express post revenue variance
sK3844	# Mail weight shipped
sK3845	# Mail shipping services
sK3846	% Inbound international mail
sK3847	% Outbound international mail
sK3850	% Mail correctly delivered
sK3851	$ Mail shipping services revenue
sK3852	$ Stamped envelope and card revenue
sK3853	$ Post office box rent revenue
sK3856	% Large parcels delivered on time or earlier
sK3857	% Express post items delivered on time or earlier
sK3858	% Domestic letters delivered on time or earlier
sK3859	% Bulk mail delivered on time or earlier
sK3861	# Mail delivery delays
sK3863	% Delivery delayed at mail centers
sK3865	% Parcels delivered on time
sK3866	% On-time postal services by type
sK3867	% Priority letters delivered on time
sK3868	# Delivery time by type of item delivered
sK3869	% Incoming mail received before 8pm at airport, delivered by next working day
sK14820	# Complaints on delivery completion delay
sK15062	# Delivery time for delivery registered letters receipt
sK15063	# Delivery time for industrial mail
sK15064	# Delivery time for intra-regional priority letters
sK15065	# Delivery time for newspapers
sK17857	# Mail boxes with last time deposit before 1pm
sK18036	# Next day delivery
sK18826	# Special delivery
sK19200	# Variation of last time deposit for mail boxes
sK19720	$ Recompense paid
sK19933	% Access to post offices

sKPI #	Key Performance Indicator name
sK20162	% Business and social collections from all access points at or after the final advertised time of collection
sK20472	% Delivered on the first working day after receipt
sK20505	% Domestic parcels inside US scope delivered on time
sK20904	% Items correctly delivered
sK20975	% Mail boxes with last time deposit before 1pm
sK21144	% Outward European mail delivered on time
sK21393	% Postcode area delivered
sK21424	% Priority single piece letters delivered on time according to national performance indicators
sK21518	% Registered letters with erratic delivery times
sK22326	% Bills of first-class volume
sK22327	% Invoices of first-class mails
sK22328	% Statements of first-class mails
sK22329	% Payments of first-class mails
sK22330	% Advertising content of first-class mails
sK22331	% Legal and financial papers of first-class mails
sK22332	% Membership cards of first-class mails
sK22333	% ID cards of first-class mails
sK22334	% Credit cards of first-class mails
sK22335	% Debit cards of first-class mails
sK22336	% Publications of first-class mails
sK22337	% Newsletters of first-class mails
sK22338	% Merchandise of first-class mails
sK22339	% Forms of first-class mails
sK22340	% Orders of first-class mails
sK22341	% Business correspondence of first-class mails
sK22342	% B2B mail by class CAGR
sK22343	# Business email boxes
sK22344	# Business email boxes (corporate)
sK22345	# Business email boxes (hosted businesses)
sK22346	# B2B email messages
sK22347	# B2B mail
sK22348	% B2B first-class mail by size of establishments
sK22349	# Overnight air shipments
sK22350	# Ground packages
sK22351	# USPS E&PS
sK22352	% USPS E&PS share
sK22353	# Business-generated first-class mails by destination
sK22354	% Business-generated first-class mails to households
sK22355	% Business-generated first-class mails to other organizations
sK22356	% Business-generated first-class mails to other location of their organizations
sK22357	# FedEx
sK22358	# Daily express package volume
sK22359	# FedEx U.S. overnight

sKPI #	Key Performance Indicator name
sK22360	# Daily volume of FedEx U.S. overnight
sK22361	# Weight of priority mail services
sK22362	# Weight of non-priority mail services
sK22363	# Weight of a standard parcel service
sK22364	# Items posted
sK22365	# Addresses posted
sK22366	# Licensed operators of postal service
sK22367	# End-to-end mail items
sK22368	# Items delivered under an access agreement
sK22369	# Postal customer complaints by region
sK22370	# Postal customer complaints by population
sK22371	# Postal customer complaints by compensation
sK22372	$ Compensation for delay
sK22373	$ Compensation for loss
sK22374	$ Compensation for damage
sK22375	$ Compensation for first-class mail
sK22376	$ Compensation for second-class mail
sK22377	$ Compensation for special delivery
sK22378	$ Compensation for standard parcels
sK22379	# Collection points
sK22380	# Delivery routes completed
sK22382	% Postcode area services
sK22383	$ Fine for lost, stolen or damaged mail
sK22384	% Fine for lost, stolen or damaged mail out of operating profit
sK22385	$ Fine for missing Royal Mail performance standards
sK22392	# Domestic mails
sK22393	# New year's postcards
sK22394	# Election mails
sK22395	# Special mails
sK22396	# International mails
sK22397	# EMS
sK22398	# Parcels
sK22399	# Yu-Pack
sK22400	# Yu-Mail
sK22401	# Private-sector parcel delivery
sK22441	# Delivery delayed
sK22442	# Articles delivered after 5pm
sK22443	% Basic letters
sK22444	% Large parcels (TOPS)
sK22445	% Bulk letters
sK22446	% Express post
sK22447	% Non-round sorted mail to delivery on last drop
sK22448	% Articles received by delivery by 3.30am
sK22449	% On time service
sK22450	% Round sorted SL to target metro DCs

sKPI #	Key Performance Indicator name
sK22451	# CFC production rate
sK22452	# MLOCR production rate
sK22453	# BCS production rate
sK22454	% Manual sort
sK22457	$ Cost per piece by class of mail
sK22458	# Mail sort rate
sK22459	# Pieces of mail handled per full time equivalent (FTE)
sK22460	% Internal mail delivered on time
sK22461	% Incoming USPS mail delivered on time
sK22462	% Accountable mail delivered on time
sK22463	% Internal and USPS mail sorted correctly
sK22464	# Customer satisfaction
sK22465	$ Work-sharing savings
sK22466	% Express mail expense out of postage
sK22467	% Meter postage and stamps that are spoiled
sK22468	% Outgoing mail that is moved to the USPS on the same day it is received in the mail center
sK22469	% Outgoing mail that is returned as undeliverable as addressed
sK22475	# City carriers
sK22476	# Mail handlers
sK22477	# Rural carriers
sK22478	# Area offices
sK22479	# Postmasters
sK22480	# Installation heads
sK22481	# Supervisors
sK22482	# Professional administrative technical personnel
sK22483	# City delivery carriers
sK22484	# Motor vehicle operators
sK22485	# Rural delivery carriers-full time
sK22486	# Building and equipment maintenance personnel
sK22487	# Vehicle maintenance personnel
sK22488	# Field career employees
sK22490	# Classified stations and branches
sK22491	# Contract stations and branches
sK22492	# Community post offices
sK22493	# Residential delivery points
sK22494	# Business delivery points
sK22495	# Highway contract delivery points
sK22496	# Priority mail
sK22497	# Express mail
sK22498	# Mailgrams
sK22499	# Standard mails
sK22500	# Periodicals
sK22501	# Package services
sK22502	# International economy mail
sK22503	# International airmail

sKPI #	Key Performance Indicator name
sK22504	# Free matter for the blind
sK22505	# Priority mail in weight
sK22506	# Express mail in weight
sK22507	# Mailgrams in weight
sK22508	# Standard mails in weight
sK22509	# Periodicals in weight
sK22510	# Package services in weight
sK22511	# International economy mail in weight
sK22512	# International airmail in weight
sK22513	# Free matter for the blind in weight
sK22514	$ Revenue from priority mail
sK22515	$ Revenue from express mail
sK22516	$ Revenue from mailgrams
sK22517	$ Revenue from standard mails
sK22518	$ Revenue from periodicals
sK22519	$ Revenue from package services
sK22520	$ Revenue from international economy mail
sK22521	$ Revenue from international airmail
sK22522	$ Revenue from free matter for the blind
sK22524	# Employees in American Postal Workers Union
sK22525	# Employees in Fraternal Order of Police-Postal
sK22526	# Employees in National Association of Letter Carriers
sK22527	# Employees in National Postal Mail Handlers Union
sK22528	# Employees in National Rural Letter Carrier Association
sK22529	# Employees in National Association of Postal Supervisors
sK22530	# Employees in National Association of Postmasters
sK22531	# Employees in National League of Postmasters
sK22532	# Employees in National Postal Professional Nurses
sK22534	# Employees in National Alliance Postal Employees
sK22536	# Countries defining Universal Service
sK22537	# Countries having split operational and regulatory functions
sK22538	# Countries having independent regulatory authority
sK22539	# Countries participating in UPU continuous testing
sK22540	% Items delivered in J+5
sK22541	# Countries using bar codes (parcels)
sK22542	# Countries having track and trace systems installed
sK22543	# Countries with a postcode system
sK22544	# Active standards
sK22545	# Countries connected to e-Maria
sK22546	# Countries receiving security related training
sK22547	% Advertising mails out of domestic letter-post
sK22548	% Advertising mails out of international letter-post
sK22549	# Countries exchanging dispatch data (PREDES/RESDES)

sKPI #	Key Performance Indicator name
sK22550	# Countries exchanging parcels data at item level
sK22551	# UPU members participating in WNS
sK22552	# WNS members registering their stamps
sK22553	# Countries connected to IFS/IFS light/STEFI
sK22554	# Bilateral IFS corridors
sK22555	# Members signatory of UPU PPSA
sK22556	# Bamako initiative
sK22557	# RDPs formulated and presented
sK22558	# IPDPs formulated and presented
sK22559	# MIPs regional projects
sK22560	# MIPs national projects
sK22561	# Permanent post offices
sK22562	# Inhabitants served per office
sK22563	# Letter post (domestic service)
sK22564	# Letter post (international service)
sK22565	# Items per inhabitant
sK22566	# Postal parcels
sK22567	# Postal employees
sK22568	# Inhabitants served per employee
sK22569	# Establishments
sK22570	# Enterprises
sK22571	# Letter-post services
sK22572	# Ordinary letters and postcards
sK22573	$ List price of standard letter
sK22574	# People served by one post office
sK22576	# Letter post items distributed per employee
sK22577	% Ordinary letters and postcards out of the letter-post services
sK22578	% Priority letters delivered on-time
sK22579	$ List price for a standard (1st class) letter weighting less than 20 g (universal service) for domestic services
sK22580	$ Prices related to Purchasing Power Parities for a standard (1st class) letter weighting less than 20 g (universal service) for domestic services
sK22581	# Postal agencies
sK22582	# Postal outlets
sK22583	# Postal mobile offices
sK22584	# Letter boxes
sK22586	# Points that only sell stamps
sK22588	# PO Box letters
sK22594	% Passport error rate
sK22595	% Passport error rate for renewals
sK22596	% PO Box mail delivered on time
sK22599	# Standard retail parcels
sK22600	# European international delivery
sK22602	% Postcode area target delivered

Professional Services

Specialized service, provided by groups of individuals (professionals) who are accepted as possessing special knowledge and skills in a widely recognized, organized body of learning, and who are prepared to exercise this knowledge and these skills in the interest of others.

Accounting Services

Accounting services includes the provision of accounting, bookkeeping, audit and tax returns services to both private and public organizations. Also included can be the provision of advisory and assistance with financial and fiscal-related issues. KPIs are used to measure accountants' expertise, quality of operations and the impact on clients' activity.

sKPI #	Key Performance Indicator name
sK104	% Chargeable ratio
sK106	$ Backlog of commissioned projects
sK313	$ Bill rate
sK320	% Employee utilization rate
sK321	% Realization rate
sK415	% Consultant retention by client
sK416	% Profitable projects
sK417	$ Hourly fee
sK2253	% Successful financial audits
sK4642	$ Fines received by clients
sK4643	% Reduction in mistakes
sK4644	% Successful fiscal controls
sK4645	% Tax returns submitted in specified time
sK4646	% Clients with more than one service provided
sK4648	% Certified accountants
sK4649	% Knowledge of accounting and fiscal regulations
sK4650	$ Cost of services delivered
sK4651	$ Delivery overhead costs
sK4654	% Adherence to schedule estimate
sK4656	# Project assignment or work package duration
sK4658	$ Profit per project
sK4664	$ Net revenue per technical staff
sK4665	$ Revenue by practice
sK4672	# Labor multiplier
sK4703	# Billable hours
sK4710	$ Blended rate
sK4713	$ Net fees
sK4714	$ Net fees per FTE
sK4715	$ Billable fees write-downs
sK6763	% Research and preparation from chargeable time
sK6764	% Travel time from chargeable time
sK6916	# Potential new clients contacted

Business Consulting

Business consulting includes the provision of advice and assistance to businesses and other organizations on various organizational issues, such as corporate finance, marketing & PR, strategy, operations or change management. KPIs focus on both consulting operations (billing, time management) and performance at project, type of service or consultant level.

sKPI #	Key Performance Indicator name
sK104	% Chargeable ratio
sK106	$ Backlog of commissioned projects
sK313	$ Bill rate
sK320	% Employee utilization rate
sK321	% Realization rate
sK415	% Consultant retention by client
sK416	% Profitable projects
sK417	$ Hourly fee
sK418	% Consultants generating revenue
sK419	% Consulting hours generating revenue
sK4650	$ Cost of services delivered
sK4651	$ Delivery overhead costs
sK4652	$ Load costs
sK4653	$ Seminar & collateral materials costs
sK4654	% Adherence to schedule estimate
sK4656	# Project assignment or work package duration
sK4658	$ Profit per project
sK4663	% Budgeted time against actual time
sK4664	$ Net revenue per technical staff
sK4665	$ Revenue by practice
sK4666	$ Solution revenue
sK4667	$ Services revenue
sK4669	% Chargeable work non recoverable
sK4670	$ Solution margin
sK4672	# Labor multiplier
sK4703	# Billable hours
sK4710	$ Blended rate
sK4713	$ Net fees
sK4714	$ Net fees per FTE
sK4715	$ Billable fees write-downs
sK6763	% Research and preparation from chargeable time
sK6764	% Travel time from chargeable time
sK6766	# Days of consulting
sK6779	# Consulting hours sold
sK6916	# Potential new clients contacted
sK14405	# Active engagements

sKPI #	Key Performance Indicator name
sK14750	# Chargeable hours per week from professional staff
sK14968	# Customers who increase consulting per quarter
sK14992	# Days rework
sK14993	# Days spent as stock in hand
sK14997	# Days warrant
sK15066	# Delivery tools
sK15363	# Full-time employees
sK17251	# Walk ratio
sK17511	# Hours in contact with client
sK18182	# Partner mix
sK18424	# Professional staff
sK18483	# Projects meeting milestones
sK18484	# Projects with all progress payments paid
sK18588	# Repeat business
sK18601	# Reports not rewritten or reworked
sK19007	# Time to engage
sK19009	# Time to implement
sK19011	# Time to productivity
sK19292	# Working hours per week for professional staff
sK19330	$ Alliances costs
sK19347	$ Backlog
sK19375	$ Consultant and media relations costs
sK19438	$ Deal size
sK19487	$ Fee revenue
sK19488	$ Field costs
sK19489	$ Field gross margin
sK19547	$ Hourly rate factor
sK19665	$ Partnering costs
sK19704	$ Professional salaries
sK19725	$ Repeat business
sK19755	$ Revenue outstanding to date
sK19766	$ Revenue per practice
sK19787	$ Salary of professional staff
sK19793	$ Seminars and collateral material costs
sK19844	$ Unbilled work in progress
sK19869	$ Work in progress
sK20097	% Attach rates
sK20244	% Chargeable projects
sK20296	% Clients paying cash up front
sK20423	% Customer balance to fees
sK20489	% Discount given on standard rates
sK20664	% Follow through for meetings
sK21083	% New projects where payment up front received
sK21426	% Professional salaries out of expenses
sK21646	% Skills matrix gap progress

Engineering

Engineering consists of the design and production of materials, structures, machines, devices, systems and processes that safely realize a desired objective by the means of applying technical, scientific and mathematical knowledge. KPIs focus on results quality and process productivity.

sKPI #	Key Performance Indicator name
sK104	% Chargeable ratio
sK106	$ Backlog of commissioned projects
sK313	$ Bill rate
sK320	% Employee utilization rate
sK321	% Realization rate
sK397	# Regression testing
sK415	% Consultant retention by client
sK416	% Profitable projects
sK417	$ Hourly fee
sK418	% Consultants generating revenue
sK4650	$ Cost of services delivered
sK4651	$ Delivery overhead costs
sK4654	% Adherence to schedule estimate
sK4656	# Project assignment or work package duration
sK4658	$ Profit per project
sK4664	$ Net revenue per technical staff
sK4665	$ Revenue by practice
sK4666	$ Solution revenue
sK4670	$ Solution margin
sK4672	# Labor multiplier
sK4674	# Generations of product family concurrently worked on
sK4675	# Projects simultaneously worked on by a single person
sK4676	# Units of work signed off
sK4677	# Break-even time
sK4678	% Planned to actual product development cycle time
sK4679	% Product development completion dates met
sK4680	% Planned jobs executed using the specified amount of labor
sK4683	% Automation delivered by the product
sK4685	# Review rate
sK4686	# Ratio of design engineers to manufacturing engineers
sK4687	# Ratio of engineering support staff to value-adding engineers
sK4710	$ Blended rate
sK4713	$ Net fees
sK4714	$ Net fees per FTE
sK4715	$ Billable fees write-downs
sK6764	% Travel time from chargeable time
sK6779	# Consulting hours sold
sK22106	# Package quality changes
sK22107	# Engineering technical adequacy
sK22108	# Organizational quality clock
sK22109	% Plant engineering personnel error rate
sK22110	# Unplanned change package revisions due to design errors

Legal Practice

Legal practice includes legal advisory, drafting of legal documentation and representation in different fields of law of one party's interest against another one, whether or not before courts or other judicial bodies. KPIs measure the quality of legal advice, cost compliance and legal knowledge management.

sKPI #	Key Performance Indicator name
sK104	% Chargeable ratio
sK106	$ Backlog of commissioned projects
sK313	$ Bill rate
sK320	% Employee utilization rate
sK321	% Realization rate
sK342	$ Cost to litigate a lawsuit
sK365	# Legal dispute cycle time
sK366	% After action review usage (AAR)
sK367	# Caseload
sK415	% Consultant retention by client
sK417	$ Hourly fee
sK418	% Consultants generating revenue
sK1976	# Cases per lawyer
sK2252	# Litigation to non-litigation matters
sK2524	# Lawyers per case
sK3782	% Lawyers generating revenue
sK3835	% Lawyer retention by client
sK4650	$ Cost of services delivered
sK4651	$ Delivery overhead costs
sK4654	% Adherence to schedule estimate
sK4656	# Project assignment or work package duration
sK4658	$ Profit per project
sK4664	$ Net revenue per technical staff
sK4665	$ Revenue by practice
sK4668	% Billing contribution
sK4672	# Labor multiplier
sK4688	# Copyright registrations filed
sK4689	# Copyright registrations submitted and accepted
sK4690	# Patents filed
sK4691	# Patents submitted and accepted
sK4692	# Trademark registrations filed and accepted
sK4693	# Trademark registrations filed
sK4699	% Legal spend attributable to law library and online research expenses
sK4701	% Legal matters that receive KM review
sK4702	# Time spent with legal research and writing activities
sK4703	# Billable hours
sK4706	# Matters handled per attorney
sK4707	# Matters handled per paralegal / legal assistant
sK4709	$ Cost to resolve matter
sK4710	$ Blended rate

sKPI #	Key Performance Indicator name
sK4713	$ Net fees
sK4714	$ Net fees per FTE
sK4715	$ Billable fees write-downs
sK4716	# Active litigation matters
sK4717	# Litigation matters closed
sK4718	# New litigation matters
sK4719	# Active non-litigation matters
sK4720	# Non-litigation matters closed
sK4721	# New non-litigation matters
sK4722	# Non-partners to partners
sK6763	% Research and preparation from chargeable time
sK6764	% Travel time from chargeable time
sK6779	# Consulting hours sold
sK14510	# Anecdotal perception of the firm and its strengths after the media coverage
sK14561	# Attorney and the firm's Google rankings before and after the campaign
sK14625	# Billable hours per full-time equivalent timekeeper (FTE)
sK14626	# Billable hours per legal assistant FTE
sK14627	# Billed-to-work rate
sK14849	# Connection requests the attorney received on Facebook or LinkedIn
sK14887	# Conversations the attorney had with prospects before and after the campaign
sK17562	# Inbound calls from reporters to the attorney seeking his opinion
sK17712	# Lawyers per client
sK17713	# Lawyers with time on matters connected to this client
sK17878	# Matters opened
sK17879	# Matters per client
sK18003	# New followers the attorney attracted on Twitter
sK18375	# Practice areas per client
sK18376	# Practice areas that serve clients
sK18636	# Responses from clients and prospects to media clips sent by the attorney
sK18836	# Spikes in the attorney's profile and the firm's website on days in which the attorney appeared in the news or spoke at an event
sK19123	# Unbilled days
sK19124	# Uncollected days
sK19289	# Work rate
sK19351	$ Billings per FTE
sK19429	$ Cost recovery revenue per matter
sK19483	$ Fee per client
sK19484	$ Fee per matter
sK19485	$ Fee per new client
sK19486	$ Fee per new matter
sK19764	$ Revenue per matter

sKPI #	Key Performance Indicator name
sK20507	% Dormant client
sK20901	% Interviews with the attorney to articles in which he was quoted
sK20931	% Legal counsel attains clients' planned results
sK21254	% Partner hours
sK21631	% Services at point of billing
sK22111	# Paralegals per lawyer
sK22112	# Assistants per lawyer
sK22113	# Legal staff per lawyer
sK22114	# Lawyers per billion in revenue
sK22115	$ Inside spend per lawyer
sK22116	$ Outside counsel spend per lawyer
sK22117	# Inside to outside spend
sK22118	$ Spend per lawyer
sK22119	$ Fully loaded cost per lawyer hour
sK22120	$ Internal cost to litigate each lawsuit
sK22121	$ External cost to litigate each lawsuit
sK22122	# Cycle time to resolve matters
sK22123	# Cycle time for internal lawsuit
sK22124	# Cycle time for outside counsel
sK22125	# Internal hours billed for each lawsuit
sK22126	# Outside counsel hours billed for each lawsuit
sK22127	# Cases per legal assistant
sK22128	# Cases per attorney
sK22129	# Hours spent by internal attorneys and legal assistants
sK22130	# Hours spent by external attorneys and legal assistants
sK22131	% Pre-discovery resolution rate for internal lawsuits
sK22132	% Pre-trial resolution rate for internal lawsuits
sK22133	% Pre-discovery resolution rate for external lawsuits
sK22134	% Pre-trial resolution rate for external lawsuits
sK22135	$ Law department's budget
sK22136	% Law-related expense of total revenue
sK22137	$ Expense of temporary staffing (for internal positions)
sK22138	# Litigation matters
sK22141	# Closed litigation matters
sK22142	# Cycle time to resolve matters
sK22143	# Non-litigation matters
sK22146	# Closed non-litigation matters
sK22147	# Intellectual property matters
sK22148	# Active intellectual property matters
sK22149	# New intellectual property matters
sK22150	# Closed intellectual property matters
sK22151	$ External legal spending
sK22152	$ Law department's fees for outside counsel
sK22153	# Non-management in-house attorneys to in-house management attorneys
sK22154	# Cycle time to resolve ethics Line

sKPI #	Key Performance Indicator name
sK22155	# Cycle time to resolve hotline reports
sK22156	# Department procedures
sK22157	# Ethics line
sK22158	# Time to conclude disputes
sK22159	# Time to conclude transactions
sK22160	# Time to resolve disputes
sK22161	# Time to resolve transactions
sK22162	$ Cost to resolve matter (excluding liability)
sK22163	$ Cost to resolve matter (law-firm specific)
sK22164	$ Estimated dollar savings through use of existing knowledge (electronic or hard copies of documents research, know-how, etc.)
sK22165	$ External spending on Intellectual property matters
sK22166	$ External spending on litigation matters
sK22167	$ External spending on non-litigation matters (other than intellectual property)
sK22169	$ Law department's fees for legal research
sK22170	$ Law department's fees for outside legal vendors and suppliers (excluding law firms)
sK22171	$ Law-related expense relative to corporate revenues
sK22172	$ Outside legal expense per in-house attorney
sK22173	% Budgeted matters handled within budget
sK22174	% Client satisfaction rate
sK22175	% Cost of resolving a matter associated with non-professional staff time
sK22176	% Disputed matters resolved by ADR
sK22177	% Employees to whom code of conduct distributed
sK22178	% Employees to whom code of conduct/ethics distributed
sK22179	% Employees who contributed to knowledge repository
sK22180	% Employees who know identity of Chief Compliance Officer
sK22181	% Employees who know identity of Chief Compliance Officer and Compliance Program
sK22182	% Geographic dispersion of law-related costs as compared to geographic dispersion of company revenues
sK22183	% In-house time devoted to counseling/proactive risk-reduction efforts
sK22184	% Legal matters that receive a KM-specific post-mortem review
sK22186	% Legal research assigned to inside counsel
sK22187	% Legal research assigned to outside counsel
sK22188	% Legal writing assigned to inside counsel
sK22189	% Legal writing assigned to outside counsel
sK22190	% Matters for which budget prepared
sK22191	% Matters for which prior work product located and applied
sK22192	% Matters handled entirely consistently with established law

sKPI #	Key Performance Indicator name
sK22193	% Matters handled purely by means of data and information sharing extranet
sK22194	% Matters handled under alternative fee arrangements
sK22195	% Time devoted to review and improve the existing practices and procedures
sK22196	% Time devoted to strategic planning to time devoted to specific liability matters
sK22197	% Time devoted to substantive legal matters as compared to operational and administrative tasks
sK22198	% Transactions closed with no unscheduled post-closing items
sK22199	% Workforce that believes there is an open environment to raise issues and questions
sK22200	% Workforce that confirms understanding of Code of Conduct
sK22201	% Workforce that have performance evaluation incentives aligned with compliance objectives
sK22202	% Workforce that is tested to confirm understanding of Code of Conduct
sK22203	% Workforce that receives Code of Conduct
sK22204	% Workforce that understands how to use the hotline
sK22205	% Workforce trained regarding compliance/ethics responsibilities by geography
sK22206	% Workforce trained regarding compliance/ethics responsibilities by job family
sK22207	% Workforce trained regarding compliance/ethics responsibilities by level of emplyoee
sK22208	% Workforce trained regarding compliance/ethics responsibilities by department
sK22209	% Lawyers evaluated on their KM participation
sK22210	% Legal assistants evaluated on their KM participation
sK22211	% Lawyers expected to engage in KM activities
sK22212	% Legal assistants expected to engage in KM activities
sK22214	# Budget to actual legal expense ratio per lawsuit handled by outside
sK22215	$ Cost of discovery for each lawsuit for matters handled internally
sK22216	$ Cost of legal research for each lawsuit for matters through outside counsel
sK22217	$ Cost of trial for each lawsuit for matters handled internally
sK22218	$ Cost of trial for each lawsuit for matters handled through outside counsel
sK22219	$ Cost per filing to handle filings and registrations internally
sK22220	$ Cost per filing to handle filings externally using alternative fee
sK22221	$ Cost per filing to handle filings externally using standard billing
sK22222	$ Cost to resolve disputes using alternative dispute resolution
sK22223	# Cycle time for each lawsuit handled by outside counsel
sK22224	# Cycle time for each lawsuit handled internally
sK22225	# Cycle time to resolve disputes using alternative dispute resolution

sKPI #	Key Performance Indicator name
sK22228	$ External cost to litigate each lawsuit using alternative fee arrangement
sK22230	# Cases handled by each law department attorney
sK22231	# Cases handled by each law department legal assistant
sK22232	# Filings per responsible attorney for filings handled internally
sK22233	# Filings per responsible per legal assistant for filings handled
sK22234	# General corporate matters per attorney for matters handled
sK22235	# General corporate matters per legal assistant for matters
sK22236	# Filing time per attorney
sK22237	# Filing time per legal assistant
sK22238	# Filing time per responsible attorney
sK22239	# Filing time per responsible legal assistant
sK22240	# Time per attorney for general corporate matters
sK22241	# Time per legal assistant for general corporate matters
sK22242	# Time per attorney for transactional matters
sK22243	# Time per legal assistant for transactional matters
sK22246	# Transactional matters per attorney for matters handled internally
sK22247	# Transactional matters per legal assistant for matters handled
sK22248	# Transactional matters per responsible attorney for matters
sK22249	# Time to process each legal invoice
sK22250	# Time to respond to company request for legal advice/ work product
sK22251	# Budget to actual internal and external expenses ratio
sK22255	$ Costs due to reputational damage
sK22256	# Cycle time to resolve ethics line and hotline reports
sK22258	# Estimated time saved using existing knowledge
sK22260	% Inside expense out of expense
sK22261	$ Law department's budget for compensation
sK22263	# Law firm legal assistants
sK22264	# Legal invoices processed per accounts payable FTE
sK22265	# Ethics line calls
sK22267	# Matters handled per paralegal
sK22268	# Matters handled per legal assistant
sK22269	# Times distinct documents in an online knowledge repository are accessed
sK22270	$ Outsourcing expenses (excluding outside law firms and temporary staffing)
sK22271	% Pre-discovery resolution rate of lawsuits handled by outside counsel
sK22272	% Pre-discovery resolution rate of lawsuits handled internally
sK22273	% Pre-trial resolution rate of lawsuits handled by outside counsel
sK22274	% Pre-trial resolution rate of lawsuits handled internally

sKPI #	Key Performance Indicator name
sK22275	% Pre-trial resolution rate of lawsuits handled through alternative dispute resolution
sK22276	# Ratio of amount budgeted for filings versus actual costs
sK22277	# Ratio of amount budgeted for general corporate matters versus actual costs
sK22278	# Ratio of amount budgeted for transactional matters versus actual costs
sK22279	# Ratio of costs of patent filings under alternative fee arrangements and those of
sK22280	# Ratio of filings and registrations versus those issued
sK22281	# Ratio of hours spent per general corporate matter by attorneys compared to legal
sK22282	# Ratio of hours spent per intellectual property matter by attorneys compared to legal
sK22283	# Ratio of hours spent per lawsuit by law departments attorneys compared to law
sK22284	# Ratio of hours spent per lawsuit by outside law firm attorneys compared to outside
sK22285	# Ratio of hours spent per transactional matter by attorneys compared to legal
sK22286	# Ratio of law department business processes undergoing quality improvement
sK22287	# Ratio of law department FTE time spent on preventive/training versus other legal
sK22288	# Ratio of legal work awarded through competitive bidding versus non-competitive
sK22290	$ Spend per employee for ethics training by subject area
sK22291	$ Spend per employee for ethics training by geography
sK22292	$ Spend per employee for ethics training by department
sK22293	$ Spend per employee for ethics training by job family
sK22294	$ Spend per employee for ethics training by level of employee
sK22295	$ Spend per employee for compliance training by subject area
sK22296	$ Spend per employee for compliance training by geography
sK22297	$ Spend per employee for compliance training by department
sK22298	$ Spend per employee for compliance training by job family
sK22299	$ Spend per employee for compliance training by level of employee
sK22300	$ Technology spending per law department FTE
sK22301	$ Cost to handle filings internally
sK22302	$ Cost to manage intellectual property assets internally
sK22306	% Law-related expense out of revenue
sK22307	$ Liability of matters handled by law department
sK22309	# Copyright registrations issued
sK22310	# Filings handled internally
sK22312	# Hours to manage intellectual property assets externally
sK22313	# Patents filed last year

sKPI #	Key Performance Indicator name
sK22314	# Patents issued last year
sK22316	# Trademark registrations issued
sK22318	$ Training spending per law department FTE
sK22319	# under standard hourly billing arrangements
sK22321	% Annual legal research/writing spend attributable to law
sK22322	% Inside counsel routinely and systematically submitted
sK22323	% Legal research/writing conducted routinely and systematically
sK22324	% Outside counsel routinely and systematically submitted
sK22325	% Legal spend attributable to legal research and

Recruitment/Employment Activities

Recruitment and employment activities includes the search and placement of permanent or temporary staff. Clients can be both organizations that have outsourced these human resources processes, integrally or for specific vacancies, and individuals in search for a job. KPIs focus on both process efficiency (planning, interviewing, selecting, hiring) and suitability with the client's needs.

sKPI #	Key Performance Indicator name
sK104	% Chargeable ratio
sK106	$ Backlog of commissioned projects
sK243	# Recruiter to open requisitions ratio
sK313	$ Bill rate
sK320	% Employee utilization rate
sK321	% Realization rate
sK415	% Consultant retention by client
sK674	% Interviews from submitted CVs
sK688	# Time to fill a vacant position
sK1819	$ Interviewing cost
sK4650	$ Cost of services delivered
sK4651	$ Delivery overhead costs
sK4654	% Adherence to schedule estimate
sK4656	# Project assignment or work package duration
sK4658	$ Profit per project
sK4661	$ Recruitment costs per position
sK4664	$ Net revenue per technical staff
sK4665	$ Revenue by practice
sK4672	# Labor multiplier
sK4713	$ Net fees
sK4714	$ Net fees per FTE
sK4715	$ Billable fees write-downs
sK4723	# Requisitions handled per recruiter
sK4724	% Hires achieving satisfactory appraisal at first assessment
sK4725	% Screened candidates
sK4727	# Inquiries per open job positions
sK4728	% Recruitment projects meeting hiring plan

sKPI #	Key Performance Indicator name	sKPI #	Key Performance Indicator name
sK4729	% Job vacancies filled within x time	sK6927	% Labor hire margin rate
sK6916	# Potential new clients contacted	sK14712	# Career path
sK6917	# New business proposals submitted	sK17674	# Job category
sK6918	# Permanent to labor hire revenue ratio	sK18004	# New hire failure factor
sK6919	# Administrative staff per recruiter	sK18771	# Separation reason
sK6920	# Permanent placements completed	sK19008	# Time to fill
sK6921	# Client interviews to hire ratio	sK19620	$ Net fees per consultant
sK6922	# Candidates database size	sK21112	% Offer acceptance rate
sK6923	# Live labor hire placements	sK21390	% Positions without ready candidate rate
sK6924	% Candidate files up to date in database	sK21561	% Retention Rate
sK6925	# Labor hire placements within x months of expiring	sK21792	% Successor pool growth rate
sK6926	$ Labor hire margin revenue	sK21956	% Vacancy Rates

Publishing

Publishing is the industry whose reason of existence is making information available for public view, this including the services and activities of production and dissemination of literature or information. Publishing activities and operations include material acquisition, copy-editing, graphic design, production – printing, marketing and distribution of newspapers, magazines, books, literary works, musical works, software and other works dealing with information, including the electronic media. KPIs focus on the publishing services' efficiency and the behavior of the consumers of the publishing outputs.

sKPI #	Key Performance Indicator name	sKPI #	Key Performance Indicator name
sK1710	# Subscription length	sK6345	# Publication circulation breakdown
sK1712	% Increase in subscriptions	sK6346	# Circulation per issue
sK1714	% Online purchases of books	sK6347	% Publication returns
sK2878	% Publications sold through subscriptions	sK6348	# Subscription copies served
sK2881	# Pages per issue	sK6349	# Subscriptions sold
sK2907	# Publication issues per subscription	sK6350	$ Price of publication
sK2909	# Readers per copy	sK6351	# Copies served on subscriptions not more than three months after expiration
sK3055	$ Revenue per article published	sK6622	# News articles per journalist
sK4213	# Time to subscribe	sK6623	$ Cost per article reading (CPR)
sK4307	$ Profit per subscription	sK6624	$ Cost per article published
sK4308	# Publication frequency	sK6625	$ Pay rate per word
sK4316	% Online news consumption	sK6626	# Pages per article
sK4321	# Print circulation	sK6627	$ Price per citation
sK4333	% Revenue from print ads	sK6636	$ Cost per page
sK4334	% Subscription renewal rate	sK6637	# Citations per article
sK4459	% Readership	sK6638	# Immediacy index
sK4493	% Publications available online	sK6639	# Citation trend line
sK6338	% Newsprint costs	sK6640	% Articles not cited
sK6339	% Advertising revenue	sK6656	% Eigenfactor score
sK6340	% Advertising revenue by source	sK6657	# Article influence score
sK6341	# Online unique readers	sK6658	# Source normalized impact per paper (SNIP)
sK6342	# Advertorials sold	sK6659	# Raw impact per paper
sK6343	% Subscriptions exceeding the average length	sK6660	# Citation potential
sK6344	# Publication audience		

Real Estate/Property

The Real Estate Industry includes activities related to the sale and leasing of real estate properties (land and other improvements to the land, such as buildings or fences), as well as providing services such as escrow, appraisal or development.

Property Management

Property management refers to the management of commercial, industrial and/or personal property, equipment and physical capital assets that are acquired and used to build, repair and maintain end item deliverables. KPIs focus on the processes, systems and work intensity required to maximize the revenues generated by real estate properties.

sKPI #	Key Performance Indicator name
sK319	% Vacancy rate
sK3103	% Capitalization rate
sK3332	% Cash-on-Cash Return (CCR)
sK3941	# Available rentable area
sK3946	# Rented space usage quality
sK3953	% Rental rate growth
sK3959	# Properties listed for rent
sK3962	$ Rent per square meter
sK3963	# Premium rent per square meter
sK3964	% Appraisal capitalization rate
sK3968	# Gross rent multiplier
sK3970	$ Rental revenue per square foot
sK3986	# Rental transactions completed
sK4033	% Current tenants in serious arrears
sK4034	$ Arrears of tenants
sK4035	% Vacant properties
sK4036	$ Arrears per tenant in arrears
sK4037	% New tenants visited within 6 weeks of tenancy start date
sK4039	% Alleged tenancy breach complaints responded to within 2 weeks
sK4040	% Proven tenancy breach complaints responded to within 1 week
sK4041	% Warning letters sent within the targeted time frame after decision on breach of tenancy
sK4042	% Cases where enforcement action was taken within 1 week of failure to comply with warning
sK4043	# Tenants under contract
sK4046	% Occupancy rate
sK4051	% Maintenance expenditure as proportion of rent collection
sK4053	$ Net recurrent cost per unit
sK4054	# Lease term
sK4057	# Tenants whose leases expire
sK4058	# Aggregate space covered by expiring leases
sK4059	$ Rental revenue from leases expiring
sK4060	% Leases expiring from total annualized rental revenue
sK4063	# Aggregate space covered by expired leases
sK4065	% Dwellings upgraded
sK4066	# Renovated to unrenovated average rent ratio

sKPI #	Key Performance Indicator name
sK4067	# Maintenance requests
sK4071	# Maintenance requests per managed property
sK4072	% Emergency repairs completed on time
sK4074	% Appointments kept on first visit
sK4075	# Time from receipt of keys to repairs ordered
sK4076	# Time from repairs ordered to keys returned to contractor
sK4077	# Time from completion of repairs to letting of the property
sK4078	% Unplanned repairs completed on time
sK4079	% Routine repairs completed on time
sK4084	% Tenants retention rate
sK4085	# Space covered by new lettings, reviews and renewals
sK4086	% Properties compliant with security standards
sK4087	% Vacancy rate by rental value
sK4088	# Properties vacant
sK4089	% Rent due in arrears
sK4090	# Tenancies managed per property manager
sK4095	% Rent collection rate
sK4097	# New leases signed
sK4099	% Leases renewed before expiry
sK4100	# Repairs per managed property
sK4101	% Rent subject to upwards rent review
sK4102	# Tenancies within 3 months of rent review
sK4105	$ Rent per tenancy
sK4106	% Increase in the number of successful lease transactions
sK4107	% Maintenance expenditure as proportion from rent collected
sK4109	% Rental revenue from total revenue
sK4110	# Time to re-let
sK4112	$ Rent lost due to vacant properties
sK4113	% Rent loss from empty properties
sK4115	% Relets rate
sK4116	% Dwellings vacant and available for rent
sK4117	% Dwellings vacant and not available for let
sK4118	# Length of time in rent arrears
sK4120	$ Rental income
sK4124	$ Management fee per tenancy
sK4125	$ Annualized revenue per leased square foot
sK4126	% Property management fee
sK4127	$ Property management income per property manager
sK4129	% Tenants satisfied with the overall repairs and maintenance services

sKPI #	Key Performance Indicator name
sK4130	% Tenants satisfied with landlord services
sK4132	# Apartment size
sK4133	# Square feet under management
sK4139	# Properties under management
sK4140	% New tenancies which failed within 12 months
sK4538	# Gross Leasable Area (GLA) per shopping center
sK4541	% Gross leasable area to gross floor area
sK4621	% Net rentable area to gross floor area
sK5511	# Ground-floor retail sales area available for rent
sK6661	% Street-frontage vacancy

Real Estate Development

Real estate development includes activities that contribute to the development of residential complexes or construction projects. KPIs focus on the management of the construction projects, acquisitions of materials or real estate facilities promotion.

sKPI #	Key Performance Indicator name
sK423	% Real estate capital ratio
sK3103	% Capitalization rate
sK3993	$ Development cost per square meter
sK3996	# Lease space developed
sK3997	# Land surface with development approval
sK3998	# Residential estate lots developed
sK3999	# Land under development
sK4000	# Square foot office building developed
sK4001	# Land surface developed
sK4002	# Land surface undeveloped
sK4004	# Residential units under contract
sK4007	# Development projects in pipeline
sK4010	# Presentations made to investors and potential investors
sK4022	# Space under refurbishment
sK4023	# Vacant commercial spaces under development
sK4026	% Portfolio total property return
sK4027	$ Developed property sales
sK4028	$ Undeveloped or off the plan property sales
sK4031	$ Equity in real estate property
sK14397	# Acres preserved through minimal or dense development
sK14451	# Age of the property in years
sK14605	# Benefits to CRA area
sK14662	# Brownfield
sK14665	# Building energy intensity.
sK14666	# Building water intensity
sK15069	# Density of floor-area
sK15102	# Distance to bus stop
sK15105	# Distance to subway stop
sK15106	# Distance to train stop

sKPI #	Key Performance Indicator name
sK15213	# Essential services
sK17232	# Voluntary certification
sK17241	# Vulnerable location
sK17283	# Within a mile of nearest fixed rail transit station in a CBD
sK17284	# Within a mile of nearest fixed rail transit station in a suburb
sK17302	# Floors
sK17303	# Floors squared
sK17419	# Grievances related to human rights filed, addressed and resolved through formal grievance mechanisms.
sK17519	# Hours per year in philanthropic activity encouraged and coordinated by a given company and its partners
sK17549	# In or near CBD regeneration area
sK17550	# In or near suburban regeneration area
sK17677	# Jobs created in a given area associated with investment in property development or management
sK17838	# Local citizenship
sK18048	# Non-profit / non-governmental or public purpose tenants
sK18498	# Public space
sK18659	# RIDDOR accidents at managed properties
sK18839	# Square feet of the building
sK18956	# Tenant satisfaction
sK18957	# Tenant satisfaction survey
sK19291	# Worker and tenant well-being
sK19466	$ Expenses per square foot
sK19598	$ Market value of the property at the end of the quarter
sK19622	$ Net operating income per square foot per year
sK19714	$ Quarterly return for all office properties
sK19724	$ Rental income per square foot over the past year including expense reimbursements
sK20346	% Community engagement
sK20985	% Mean quarterly occupancy for all office properties
sK21092	% Non-profit / non-governmental or public purpose tenants
sK21439	% Properties located in neighborhoods with area median incomes at 80% of regional average
sK21440	% Property occupancy
sK21444	% Proportion of completed developments on brownfield land
sK21453	% Proportion of EPCs rated "C" or above (UK)
sK21454	% Proportion of properties rated as "moderate risk" or better (UK)
sK21567	% RIDDOR accident rate for shopping centers
sK21923	% Units for purchase affordable to people with 30-80% of area median income
sK21924	% Units for purchase affordable to people with 80-120% of area median income
sK21925	% Units for rent affordable to people with 30-80% of area median income
sK21926	% Units for rent affordable to people with 80-120% of area median income

Real Estate Transactions

Real estate transactions includes all the activities related to selling or buying real estate properties, including appraisal, escrow, marketing and sales. KPIs reflect performance of real estate agencies and agents in terms of financial results, transaction parameters, transaction volume, sales process, property parameters and sales pipeline.

sKPI #	Key Performance Indicator name
sK126	# Price-to-rent ratio
sK3103	% Capitalization rate
sK3452	% Real estate absorption rate
sK3848	% Properties re-listed
sK3849	% Properties sold through organized auctions
sK3939	% Successful auctions
sK3942	# Visits per real estate sale
sK3948	# Properties sold per real estate agent
sK3949	# Real estate demand
sK3950	% Real estate transactions completed successfully
sK3954	$ Property transaction value
sK3955	# Real estate transactions completed
sK3956	% Property listings that switched from private treaty to organized auctions
sK3957	$ Variance between initially listed price and negotiated price

sKPI #	Key Performance Indicator name
sK3958	$ Price per square meter sold
sK3965	% Listing to sale price ratio
sK3973	$ Value of residential lots sold
sK3974	# Real estate properties listed for sale
sK3978	% Transaction discount rate
sK3979	# Residential lots sold
sK3980	% Commercial real estate properties sold
sK3981	$ Value of office building sold
sK3983	$ Properties acquired
sK3984	$ Value of properties sold through organized auction
sK3985	$ Value of real estate transactions completed
sK3987	# New listings in the pipeline
sK3989	% Real estate residential sales
sK3990	% Real estate non residential sales
sK4024	% Vacant commercial spaces under offer
sK4098	# Days on market
sK4132	# Apartment size
sK4188	% Sale agreed properties
sK6738	$ Revenue per square meter sold
sK6739	# Properties advertised per real estate agent

Resources

Resources includes the activities of extracting and refining of natural resources such as gas, oil, coal and others. Also included here are KPIs for the production of energy from sustainable sources, such as solar, water, wind or geothermal power.

Coal and Minerals Mining

Mining includes the extraction of minerals occurring naturally as solids (coal and ores). Extraction can be achieved by different methods, such as underground or surface mining, seabed mining. This section also includes supplementary activities aimed at preparing the crude materials for marketing, for example crushing, grinding, cleaning, drying, sorting, concentrating ores and agglomeration of solid fuels. These operations are often carried out by the units that extract the resource and/or others located nearby. KPIs measure the consumption of resources and the outputs in extracting and preparing the minerals.

sKPI #	Key Performance Indicator name
sK819	# Tonnes per shovel operating shift
sK821	% Mining heavy equipment availability
sK824	% Mineral waste disposed off site
sK825	% Non mineral waste produced
sK868	# Tonnes of ore per day
sK953	# Tonnes mined per day
sK967	% Mineral grade
sK974	% Sampling equipment and weightometers satisfactorily operating
sK1222	# Explosives consumption per tonne rock mined

sKPI #	Key Performance Indicator name
sK1548	# Primary energy consumption
sK5077	# Mining hazards reported
sK5078	# Mining hazards requiring emergency response
sK5079	% Field engineer on site within 24 hours
sK5080	% Mine location secured within 6 hours
sK5081	# Underground ore or coal production
sK5082	# Surface mining production
sK5083	# Operational surface mines
sK5084	# Underground operational mines
sK5085	# Closed mines
sK5087	% First inspection of residential subsidence claims within a specific period in time
sK5088	# Unplanned mine inundations
sK5089	# Unplanned ignitions or explosions
sK5090	% Unplanned mine fire not extinguished within 30 minutes
sK5091	# Unplanned ignitions or explosions of a blasting agent at a mine
sK5092	# Unplanned roof falls at or above the anchorage zone
sK5093	# Fatal mining accidents

sKPI #	Key Performance Indicator name
sK5094	# Tonnes of rock mined
sK5095	# Tonnes of ore milled
sK5097	# Cooper concentrates produced
sK5098	# Concentrate smelted on site
sK5100	# Coal reserves
sK5102	# Employees exposed to an 8 hours noise dose of more than 85 dB
sK5103	# Mineral waste produced
sK5104	% Mineral waste disposed on site
sK5105	# Non mineral waste produced
sK5106	# Hazardous mineral waste produced
sK5107	# Hazardous non mineral waste produced
sK5108	% Hazardous mineral waste recycled and reused
sK5109	% Explored land area rehabilitated
sK5114	# Reserves proved
sK5115	# Reserves probable
sK5120	# Measured resources
sK5121	# Indicated resources
sK5122	# Inferred resources
sK5123	$ Cash cost per gold equivalent ounce
sK5124	# Gold to silver equivalency ratio
sK5125	# Mill processing capacity
sK5126	# Secured years of open pit ore reserves exploration
sK5127	# Operating strip ratio
sK5128	# Metal grade
sK5140	# Mine entries inspected
sK5141	# Non fatal mining accidents
sK5142	# Fuel consumption per tonne of rock mined
sK5143	# Tonnes per shovel operating shift
sK5144	# Energy consumption per tonne milled
sK5148	# Mining productivity per man
sK5149	$ Mining cost per tonne mined
sK5151	$ Mining cost per ton of ore processed
sK5152	# Mining depth
sK5157	$ Leaching costs per ore tonne
sK5158	$ Mining cost per tonne milled
sK5161	# Tonnage mined per shift
sK5162	# Truck productivity per shift
sK5163	# Trucks loaded per shift
sK5164	# Truck fleet size
sK5165	# Productive minutes per 8 hours shift
sK5166	# Operational shovels in fleet
sK5170	$ Operating cost per effective shift hour
sK5171	$ Operating cost for non productive shift
sK5172	# Machine mining rate
sK5175	# Rate of coal removal

sKPI #	Key Performance Indicator name
sK5176	# Ore hoisting time
sK5177	# Frequency of mining equipment inspection
sK5178	# Waste hoisting time
sK5179	# Materials and supply hoisting time
sK5181	% Hoist utilization rate
sK5182	# Daily hoisting time
sK5183	# Tonnes per cut
sK5184	# Cuts per shift
sK5200	# Area held under exploration license
sK5207	% Mine entries inspections that required follow up actions
sK14352	# Aboriginal Economic Development projects facilitated
sK14369	# Access deferred
sK14370	# Access in full
sK14371	# Access refused
sK14375	# Accidental discharges
sK14456	# Agreements granted
sK14506	# Alumina production
sK14513	# Domestic coal leases and licenses
sK14514	# Drilling length
sK14531	# Area mined
sK14532	# Area of disturbance
sK14535	# Area rehabilitated
sK14572	# Audited conformance scores against management standards
sK14574	# Audits high impact function
sK14575	# Audits of dangerous goods
sK14576	# Audits of management safety system
sK14577	# Audits of technical reviews
sK14596	# Bauxite reserves
sK14623	# Biennial survey
sK14633	# Block tonnage to mill tonnage
sK14635	# Block tonnage to Blast-hole mined tonnage
sK14703	# Capital strip
sK14741	# Certificates of competency
sK14749	# Chargeable hours of time involved in provision of services
sK14777	# Coal output
sK14790	# Commence site works to remediate eight minewater discharges
sK14791	# Commence site works to remediate one minewater discharge
sK14794	# Communicate decision on residential subsidence claims to claimants within three weeks
sK14814	# Competent person informed within one hour
sK14839	# Concentrate or metal grade and penalized impurity levels
sK14862	# Consumption of energy and minerals during a specified time period
sK14865	# Contained molybdenum

sKPI #	Key Performance Indicator name
sK14881	# Contract employment by minerals companies
sK14882	# Contractor monthly safety meeting
sK14883	# Contractor principal monthly safety meeting
sK14890	# Copper reserves
sK14891	# Co-product and by-product inter-dependence
sK14926	# Crush or grind size
sK14983	# Dangerous goods licenses issued and renewed
sK15080	# Diamond reserves
sK15111	# Distribution of gridding
sK15114	# Disturbance and rehabilitation over three years
sK15148	# Edited Access
sK15208	# Environmental regulatory weighted units of service provided to the minerals industry
sK15233	# Exploration rights held
sK15235	# Explosives
sK15236	# Explosives consumption per tonne rock mined
sK15271	# Feed size
sK15277	# Field engineer on site within 24 hours
sK15282	# First inspection of residential subsidence claims within four weeks
sK15308	# Footprint
sK15389	# General waste disposal methods
sK17217	# Vessels to transport commodities
sK17226	# Virgin to recycled minerals
sK17262	# Washing efficiency
sK17263	# Waste disposed
sK17266	# Water consumption per tonne milled
sK17316	# Formal audit programs for PPE compliance
sK17358	# Fuel consumption per tonne rock mined
sK17396	# Gold equivalent ounces
sK17397	# Gold grade
sK17398	# Gold ounces
sK17399	# Gold produced
sK17400	# Gold produced combined
sK17401	# Gold produced surface
sK17402	# Gold produced underground
sK17403	# Gold sold
sK17408	# Grade of ores produced
sK17420	# Grinding
sK17421	# Grinding media consumption per tonne milled
sK17459	# Hazards reported
sK17460	# Hazards requiring emergency response
sK17461	# Head grades
sK17464	# Health and safety weighted units of service provided to the minerals industry
sK17542	# Identified resources
sK17583	# Industry contacts

sKPI #	Key Performance Indicator name
sK17640	# Internal and external audit queries for royalties
sK17664	# Investigation of serious dangerous goods incidents
sK17665	# Investigation of serious incidents
sK17668	# Iron ore production
sK17669	# Iron ore reserves
sK17691	# Land available for rehabilitation
sK17692	# Land newly disturbed
sK17693	# Land rehabilitated
sK17694	# Land requiring rehabilitation
sK17698	# Lands available for access for exploration, development, and protection
sK17724	# Leases applied
sK17725	# Leases granted
sK17726	# Leases in force
sK17752	# Length of railroad track to transport commodities
sK17808	# License applications for internal review
sK17809	# License applications on hand but not yet dealt with
sK17810	# License applications transferred in full to another agency
sK17811	# License applications transferred in part to another agency
sK17812	# License applications withdrawn by the applicant
sK17815	# Licensing applications received
sK17847	# Lost time injury frequency rate by oil and gas companies
sK17848	# Lost time injury frequency rate for the extractive industries
sK17849	# Lost time injury frequency rate for the metalliferous and coal sectors
sK17860	# Main development
sK17864	# Main on-reef
sK17866	# Major equipment installed and operating, including Coal and Minerals Mining fleet
sK17871	# Man shifts per tonne mined and milled
sK17935	# Mined bauxite
sK17936	# Mined copper
sK17937	# Mined diamonds
sK17938	# Mineral titles processed in target time
sK17941	# Coal and Minerals Mining index of industrial production
sK17952	# Molybdenum concentrates produced
sK17954	# Monthly safety report
sK17974	# National supply mix of energy and mineral commodities
sK17994	# New cases of occupational illness per 10,000 employees
sK17995	# New cases of occupational illnesses
sK18017	# New illnesses
sK18031	# New valid license applications
sK18089	# Open-file reports made available for viewing within 24 hours of request

sKPI #	Key Performance Indicator name
sK18113	# Ore milled
sK18295	# Permits granted
sK18298	# Petroleum environmental audits
sK18299	# Petroleum environmental weighted units of audits and assessment
sK18300	# Petroleum environmental weighted units of management plans
sK18301	# Petroleum safety and health weighted units of audits and assessment
sK18302	# Petroleum title operation and resource services
sK18318	# Pipeline and transmission line capacity
sK18369	# Potential investors that consider the resource sector investment attraction programs
sK18374	# Power consumption per tonne milled
sK18380	# Precipitation efficiency
sK18392	# Price index of materials used in open cut mining
sK18393	# Price index of materials used in underground mining
sK18397	# Primary crushing
sK18419	# Produced water
sK18422	# Product size
sK18423	# Productivity
sK18538	# Rating by investors of the quality of resource sector information services delivered
sK18541	# Rating of archive processes by specialized geological survey committee
sK18544	# Rating of product quality by specialized geological survey committee
sK18547	# Ratio of geoscientific papers published compared to submitted to international, peer-reviewed journals
sK18552	# Reagent consumption per tonne milled
sK18570	# Refined copper
sK18582	# Renewal licenses
sK18606	# Requests for coal and minerals mining reports responded to within five working days
sK18615	# Reserves
sK18627	# Resource sector information services delivered
sK18628	# Resource sector information services delivered within an agreed timeframe
sK18629	# Resource sector investment attraction programs completed within an agreed timeframe
sK18630	# Resource sector investment attraction programs delivered
sK18632	# Resources left behind
sK18677	# Rock mined
sK18711	# Safety and health promotions
sK18717	# Safety meetings
sK18719	# Safety visits
sK18756	# Secondary crushing
sK18800	# Shipments of iron ore to major markets
sK18806	# Significant safety incidents by type
sK18807	# Silver grade

sKPI #	Key Performance Indicator name
sK18808	# Silver ounces
sK18809	# Sites inspected within two hours
sK18810	# Sites secured within six hours
sK18867	# Stocks in use
sK18910	# Subsidence projects received by region
sK18923	# Surface hazards projects received by region
sK18924	# Surface mobile equipment significant incidents
sK18984	# Time for production of 1:100,000 maps released during the year
sK19010	# Time to process license applications
sK19022	# Tonnes of solution processed per set time periods
sK19023	# Tonnes per day leached
sK19024	# Tonnes per day mined
sK19025	# Tonnes per day mined and processed
sK19026	# Tonnes per day ore
sK19027	# Tonnes to stockpile
sK19028	# Tonnes milled
sK19029	# Tonnes milled combined
sK19030	# Tonnes milled surface
sK19031	# Tonnes milled underground
sK19104	# Trucks available to transport commodities
sK19288	# Work input
sK19293	# Workshop and field inspections
sK19300	# Yield
sK19302	# Yield combined
sK19303	# Yield surface
sK19304	# Yield underground
sK19331	$ Aluminium group underlying earnings contribution
sK19336	$ Amount budgeted for exploration
sK19363	$ Cash cost per gold ounce
sK19383	$ Copper and diamonds underlying earnings contribution
sK19409	$ Cost per environmental regulatory weighted service
sK19410	$ Cost per health and safety weighted service
sK19411	$ Cost per mineral title service
sK19415	$ Cost per petroleum environmental audit and assessment
sK19416	$ Cost per petroleum safety and health weighted unit of audit and assessment
sK19417	$ Cost per petroleum title operation and resource service
sK19418	$ Cost per resource development project facilitated
sK19419	$ Cost per resource sector information service program delivered
sK19420	$ Cost per resource sector investment attraction program delivered
sK19422	$ Cost per royalty returns verified and audited
sK19426	$ Cost per weighted data transaction unit
sK19427	$ Cost per weighted total published product
sK19572	$ Iron ore underlying earnings contribution

sKPI #	Key Performance Indicator name
sK19590	$ Main on-reef
sK19611	$ Mineral exploration expenditure
sK19612	$ Mineral title service units
sK19616	$ Mozambican spend
sK19632	$ Offshore petroleum exploration expenditure
sK19633	$ Onshore petroleum exploration expenditure
sK19637	$ Operating cost per tonne mined and milled
sK19639	$ Operating costs combined
sK19641	$ Operating costs surface
sK19642	$ Operating costs underground
sK19658	$ Overseas mineral exploration expenditure
sK19786	$ Royalty returns verified and audited
sK19798	$ Silver price
sK19814	$ Subsidence projects expenditure by region
sK19821	$ Surface hazards projects expenditure by region
sK19824	$ Tax expense by mineral companies
sK19826	$ Taxes paid by oil and gas companies
sK19845	$ Underlying earnings contribution
sK19856	$ Value of Coal and Minerals Mining exports
sK19857	$ Value of Coal and Minerals Mining imports
sK20040	% Exploration rig use
sK20147	% Blast-hole drill penetration rates
sK20374	% Concentrate or metal production rate
sK20375	% Concentrate shipping rate
sK20424	% Customer business sector of overall volume of searches
sK20426	% Customer satisfaction with timeliness of petroleum title services
sK20437	% Customers satisfied with mineral titles services
sK20438	% Customers satisfied with petroleum titles services
sK20490	% Discovery rate per dollar of exploration expense
sK20592	% Employees in potential exposures
sK20593	% Employees who completed medical examination
sK20605	% Environmental services meeting quality standards
sK20606	% Environmental services meeting timeliness standards
sK20638	% Fatalities at controlled operations
sK20737	% Health and safety services meeting quality standards
sK20738	% Health and safety services meeting timeliness standards
sK20819	% Idle production capacity as it relates to total
sK20888	% Inspect all operational mines at least once annually
sK20889	% Inspect all operational mines in accordance with the authority's risk based criteria
sK21014	% Metal recovery
sK21070	% Natural gas flared and coal bed methane's emitted
sK21343	% Permit compliance
sK21344	% Petroleum customers satisfied with environmental services
sK21345	% Petroleum customers satisfied with health and safety services

sKPI #	Key Performance Indicator name
sK21346	% Petroleum customers satisfied with the timeliness of environmental services
sK21347	% Petroleum customers satisfied with the timeliness of health and safety services
sK21400	% PPE compliance
sK21582	% Royalty audits completed within target plan
sK21593	% Sampling equipment and weightometers satisfactorily operating and calibrated

Oil and Gas

Oil and gas includes the extraction and refining of gas and oil natural resources. Gas includes the extraction of natural gas through a system of mains. Oil includes the refining and distribution of liquid or gaseous fuels or other products from crude petroleum, bituminous minerals or their fractionation products. KPIs focus on the efficiency of processes (extraction and preparation) and the quality of the final outputs.

sKPI #	Key Performance Indicator name
sK791	# Exploration rig use
sK793	# Drilling length
sK797	% Non productive drilling time (NPT)
sK813	# Well duration
sK817	# Perfect well time
sK988	# Drilling meters
sK1523	# Oil spills
sK1548	# Primary energy consumption
sK3393	# Reserves to production ratio (RPR)
sK4025	# Rig operational drilling days
sK4029	# Rig drilling time
sK4032	# Rig completion rate
sK4038	# Rig drilling frequency
sK4047	$ Drilling cost per meter (foot)
sK4055	# Production per well
sK4056	# Well productivity
sK4061	# Perfect well drilling time
sK5099	# Tonnes of coal mined
sK5185	% Drilling rig utilization rate
sK5186	% Drilling rigs in operation
sK5187	% Drilling success rate
sK5188	$ Drilling well costs
sK5189	# Exploration wells drilled
sK5190	# Drilling penetration rate
sK5191	# Well drilling time
sK5192	# Gas production from deep wells
sK5193	% Drilling rigs availability
sK5194	# Rig drilling offshore oil spills
sK5195	# Amount of oil spilled
sK5196	# Drilling water depth
sK5198	# Mine entries inspections requiring follow up actions

sKPI #	Key Performance Indicator name
sK5199	# Exploration drilling meters completed
sK5200	# Area held under exploration license
sK5204	# Rig moving time
sK5205	# Perfect well time ratio
sK5206	# Drilling crews per rig
sK5208	# Casing running time
sK5209	# Well depth drilled
sK5210	% Non productive drilling time at full capacity
sK5212	# Well drilling length
sK5215	# Pipeline transportation capacity
sK6274	# Gas to oil ratio
sK14373	# Accident action items overdue
sK14377	# Accidental gas spills
sK14378	# Accidental oil spills in barrels
sK14857	# Consumer hours of gas supply lost through unplanned losses of supply
sK14859	# Consumer hours off supply per 1000 customers
sK14861	# Consumers connected to the network
sK15133	# Duration of excursions
sK15225	# Expansion in digital geological map coverage at scales of 1:250,000 and 1:25,000
sK15232	# Exploration licenses issued
sK15284	# Flare efficiency
sK15378	# Gas leaks per 1000 customers reported by third party
sK15380	# Gas leaks per 10km of network reported by third party
sK15382	# Gas leaks reported to network operator by third parties
sK17925	# Meters drilled per day
sK18135	# Overdue technical deviations
sK19198	# Variables of excursions
sK19452	$ Drilling costs
sK19713	$ Quarterly exploration expenditure
sK20981	% Market share of exploration expenditure
sK21685	% Strategic prospectivity zone areas held under exploration license

Sustainability/Green Energy

Green energy includes the provision of energy such that it meets the needs of the present without compromising the ability of future generations to meet their needs. Sustainable energy sources are most often regarded as including all renewable sources, such as biofuels, solar power, wind power, wave power, geothermal power and tidal power. KPIs focus on the use of new ways to generate energy and increase in efficiency.

sKPI #	Key Performance Indicator name
sK61	% Energy produced from renewable sources
sK436	% Energy used from renewable sources
sK758	# Effective residual ink concentration (ERIC)
sK1481	# Acid rain and smog precursors emissions
sK1482	# Land polluted by emissions of acids and organic pollutants

sKPI #	Key Performance Indicator name
sK1484	# Environmental sustainability index (ESI)
sK1494	# Airborne particles
sK1499	% Halogenated volatile organic compounds
sK1500	# Land owned, leased or managed in biodiversity-rich habitats
sK1501	# Mass mortality events
sK1502	# Metal emissions to air
sK1503	# Metal emissions to land
sK1504	# Metal emissions to water
sK1512	# Ozone depleting substances
sK1515	# Pest species
sK1517	# PET bottles recycled
sK1520	# Radioactive waste
sK1522	# Size of contaminated land sites
sK1524	# Stoichiometric oxygen demand (StOD)
sK1526	# Threatened species appearing in the IUCN red list
sK1528	# Organic carbon
sK1529	# Suspended solids
sK1531	% Volatile organic compounds (VOC)
sK1533	# Water recycled and reused
sK1534	# Water sources affected by withdrawal of water
sK1536	% Non-hazardous operational waste
sK1537	# Baseflow salinity
sK1538	% Coral bleached
sK1541	# Groundwater salinity
sK1542	% Intensity of salt affected areas
sK1548	# Primary energy consumption
sK1552	# Soil acidity
sK1553	% Soil carbon content
sK1554	% Soil disturbance
sK1555	% Soil erosion by water
sK1556	% Soil erosion by wind
sK1560	% Timber used in construction from a sustainable managed source
sK1562	# Water abstraction
sK1564	# Aquatic acidity
sK1570	# Eutrophication
sK1578	# Photochemical ozone creation potential (POCP)
sK1579	% Land restoration
sK1731	# Soil alkalinity
sK1746	# Revised universal soil loss equations (RUSLE)
sK1751	# Dust storm index (DSI)
sK1757	# Net area to be reforested (NAR)
sK1761	# Dissolved oxygen (DO)
sK1762	# Stratospheric ozone
sK2121	% Reused grey water
sK3488	# Carbon dioxide vessel efficiency

sKPI #	Key Performance Indicator name
sK4987	% Electricity generated and consumed from renewable sources
sK5101	# Fresh water withdrawn for business use
sK5110	# Accidental discharges of hydrocarbons

sKPI #	Key Performance Indicator name
sK5113	# Quantity of wastewater and effluent discharged
sK5145	% Metal recovery rate
sK21564	% Revenue from products or services fostering eco-efficiency, clean technologies or offsetting climate change or carbon emissions

Retail

Retailing consists of the sale of goods or merchandise, usually in small quantities, directly to end consumers. KPIs focus on measuring the volume of sales, turnover and efficiency in organizing the retail store operations.

sKPI #	Key Performance Indicator name
sK69	% Product shelf-space profitability
sK317	% Sell-through
sK331	# Selling opportunities
sK332	$ Sales by department
sK414	$ Cost of goods sold (COGS)
sK420	% Markdown goods
sK421	% Store conversion rate
sK422	$ Sales revenue per hour
sK425	$ Stock value
sK428	% Sales order cancellation rate
sK536	% Store satisfaction while shopping
sK633	# Stock rotations
sK634	# Safety stock
sK635	# Reorder point (ROP)
sK636	# Anticipation stock
sK638	# Working stock
sK649	$ Obsolete stock
sK782	% Same store sales growth
sK1699	% Sales growth in stores open at least 12 months
sK2264	# Stock keeping units in portfolio
sK3982	% Out of stock items
sK4524	# Stores
sK4525	# Time spent in the store
sK4528	# Gross leasable area per employee
sK4535	$ Employee theft
sK4536	$ Shoplifting
sK4537	$ Vendor fraud
sK4540	# Gross leasable area
sK4543	$ Sales per unit area
sK4544	% Selling space
sK4545	% Top selling items
sK4547	$ Net cash flow per customer
sK4548	% Sales by product category
sK4549	$ Sales per labor hour
sK4608	# Net rentable area
sK4754	$ Size of grocery bill

sKPI #	Key Performance Indicator name
sK4808	# Inventory to sales ratio (ISR)
sK4809	% Perishable items with past due date
sK5788	# Frequency of store visits
sK5799	% Store loyalty
sK6247	# Volume of purchase
sK6313	# Units sold per customer
sK6314	# Customers per day
sK6315	$ Sale value
sK6316	# Out of stock product lines
sK6317	# Product lines sold per transaction
sK6888	$ Product returns
sK6889	% Planned opening hours achieved
sK14432	# Adoption rate ratio
sK14630	# Births of retail secondary locations by employment size
sK14834	# Component development ratio
sK14863	# Consumption of refrigerants
sK14884	# Contracts awarded for supermarket developments
sK14886	# Controlled food products
sK14987	# Days inventory for general merchandise and cigarettes
sK15006	# Deaths of retail secondary locations by employment size
sK15141	# EBITDA to value of equipment and leaseholds
sK15187	# Employee and employees per establishment
sK15198	# Employment size of retail firms
sK17254	# Walk-through audit and mystery shopper ratings of compliance with specific implementation standards
sK17255	# Walk-through audit and mystery shopper ratings of compliance with basic operating standards
sK17286	# Women in the retail workforce
sK17301	# Floor space by selected kind of business
sK17321	# Free disposable plastic check-out bags
sK17482	# Holiday employment
sK17662	# Inventory shrinkage
sK17774	# Level of dialogue with stakeholders
sK17775	# Level of information provided to consumers
sK17779	# Level of quality procedure for controlled food products

sKPI #	Key Performance Indicator name
sK17819	# Listed fair-trade products
sK17820	# Listed own brand organic food products
sK17821	# Listed own brand organic or ecological food products
sK17921	# Merchandise sold by e-shopping and mail-order houses
sK17922	# Merchandise sold by general merchandise stores
sK17923	# Merchandise sold by health and personal care stores
sK17953	# Monthly retail employment
sK18143	# Paper purchased for commercial publications
sK18183	# Part-time employment in retailing
sK18184	# Part-time hours in retailing
sK18351	# Post-adoption state
sK18480	# Project completions in floorspace
sK18509	# Quality line contracts
sK18510	# Quality line products
sK18641	# Retail and food service and drinking establishments per firm
sK18642	# Retail employees by age
sK18643	# Retail employees by education
sK18644	# Retail employees by occupation
sK18645	# Retail firm births and deaths by employment size
sK18646	# Retail projects securing detailed planning approval and starting on site
sK18647	# Retail sector floorspace
sK18720	# Sales size of retail firms
sK18722	# Sample development ratio
sK18801	# Shops and shopping centre project completions
sK18815	# Skill rating of non-management store employees
sK18816	# Skill rating of store managers
sK18824	# Sources of inventory shrinkage
sK19296	# Years manager has been with the store
sK19299	# Years with the store for non-management store employees
sK19339	$ Compensation per full-time equivalent employee in food services and drinking places
sK19340	$ Compensation per full-time equivalent employee in retail trade
sK19345	$ Retail wages
sK19371	$ Compensation paid to retail employees
sK19381	$ Controllable contribution less rental or lease cost
sK19456	$ Economic activity generated by retail sales
sK19517	$ G&A cost per store
sK19540	$ Holiday sales
sK19548	$ Hourly retail earnings
sK19559	$ Income taxes paid by retailers
sK19565	$ Inventory
sK19621	$ Net gross profit from new concepts
sK19708	$ Purchase amount of own brand organic food products

sKPI #	Key Performance Indicator name
sK19709	$ Purchase amount of quality line products
sK19734	$ Retail construction projects starting on site
sK19738	$ Retail sales
sK19740	$ Retail sales per establishment
sK19747	$ Return on sales
sK19846	$ Underlying retail project
sK20039	% Discharge and layoff rate by industry
sK20043	% Quit rate by industry
sK20145	% Openings of retail secondary locations by employment size
sK20362	% Complete order fill rate
sK20379	% Consolidated stores audited on hygiene and quality criteria
sK20439	% Customers stating the store as their primary convenience store
sK20440	% Customers viewing the store as fun and entertaining place to shop
sK20441	% Customers who would recommend the store
sK20442	% Customers who would visit the store soon
sK20462	% Closings of retail secondary locations by employment size
sK20519	% Effects of economic activity of retail sales
sK20647	% Finish goods DOH
sK20669	% Forecast accuracy on product family
sK20676	% Franchise stores audited on hygiene & quality criteria
sK20777	% Holiday sales
sK21039	% Monthly discharge and layoff rate
sK21117	% On-time and accurate raw material order
sK21118	% On-time and accurate sample request
sK21430	% Profitability of large retail corporations
sK21479	% Purchases of own brand food products from local suppliers
sK21517	% Regional manager evaluation of store utilization of front and back-office technology
sK21556	% Retail employees by age
sK21557	% Retail employees by education
sK21558	% Retail employees by occupation
sK21559	% Retail firm births and deaths by employment size
sK21560	% Retail firms by employment size
sK21592	% Sample delivered on-time
sK21944	% Use of loss prevention personnel
sK21945	% Use of loss prevention systems
sK22587	% Return on retail revenue
sK22589	$ Retail product sales
sK22590	$ External retail revenue per customer visit
sK22591	# Leads converted
sK22592	# Days supply of stock

Sport Management

Sport management includes all business aspects of sports such as sport event organization, coaching and training. Sport management can be viewed as a goal oriented social process within the sport field, involving the selection and enactment of the best strategies directed towards monitoring and improving performance of any sport entity and related activity.

Coaching/Training

Coaching and training includes all methods of directing, instructing and training an individual sportsman or a group of persons resembled as a team and involved in a sport activity or competition. Sport coaching involves all aspects of sports from physical up to mental player development and preparation. KPIs focus on both coaching activities and related benefits to sportsmen.

sKPI #	Key Performance Indicator name
sK173	# Qualified coaches actively providing coaching in the sport
sK175	# Individuals gaining sports-related qualifications
sK176	% New athletes
sK665	# Gym capacity
sK1244	% Conversion rate to professional contract of young trainees
sK1248	# Daily training session duration
sK1249	# Certified coaches
sK1764	# International appearances of home grown football players
sK1775	% Players that took anti doping tests
sK6986	# Group fitness studios
sK6987	% Gym members participating in regular fitness classes
sK6988	# Group fitness classes per week
sK6989	# Gym members per personal trainer
sK6990	# Gym attendance
sK19425	$ Cost per unit of policy advice
sK19401	$ Cost per attendees at education and training forums, seminars and/or conferences
sK14558	# Attendees at education and training forums, seminars and conferences
sK14660	# Briefings to the Sport and Recreation Council
sK14933	# Current information education resources available
sK14443	# Advice to government
sK14855	# Consultancy services provided within operational plan schedules
sK21524	% Relevance of consultation and involvement in designing programs and campaigns

Sport Club Management

Sport club management is a set of activities oriented towards administrating an organizational entity active in one or more sports, at either amateur or professional level. Performance measures are used to monitor processes that deal with producing, facilitating, promoting and organizing sports activities at club level.

sKPI #	Key Performance Indicator name
sK664	$ Investment in gym equipment
sK1220	% Sports club membership growth
sK1225	# Game attendance

sKPI #	Key Performance Indicator name
sK1230	# Non match day events
sK1241	# Club membership
sK1246	$ Net transfer spending
sK1247	# Sell on value of a player to purchase value
sK1252	# Season tickets holders
sK1763	% Transfer fee to academy running costs
sK1765	# Game attendance range
sK1767	# Demand seats
sK1768	# Boxes and corporate seats marketed to new businesses
sK3611	% Player buzz in the social media
sK4119	% Level of excitement
sK4131	# Season deviation standard (SD) of top five clubs over the last 15 years
sK4142	% Minimum to maximum media revenue within the league
sK6842	% Players' satisfaction with the quality of the venue
sK6844	% Games covered in media
sK6845	# Players in domestic competitions
sK6846	# Teams in international competitions
sK6847	# Teams in pipeline for future competitions
sK6848	$ Revenue from door fee charges
sK6849	% Planned games that took place
sK6850	% Games with administrative incidents
sK6853	% Games with statistics available on website
sK6854	% Games with online reviews
sK6856	% Games with accurate and updated reporting
sK6991	% Fitness equipment in top condition
sK6992	% Member attrition rate
sK14351	# People selected for national youth and senior teams by ethnic groups
sK14389	# Accredited coaches
sK14518	# Recognition awards for key volunteers
sK15219	# Events conducted in accordance with policies and procedures
sK15272	# Female participants registered
sK17479	# Hits per month on national calendar web site
sK17485	# Home matches that were sold out
sK17875	# Match attendances
sK17900	# Member protection policy endorsed at annual general meeting and circulated to all members
sK18276	# People with a disability registered
sK18746	# Season ticket holders
sK18747	# Season tickets
sK18841	# Stadium with conference and banqueting facilities

sKPI #	Key Performance Indicator name
sK18911	# Successful bid for events
sK18921	# Supporters
sK19317	$ Advertising rate
sK19318	$ Affiliation fees
sK19360	$ Capitation fees
sK19384	$ Corporate hospitality sales
sK19444	$ Development initiatives
sK19467	$ Experiential marketing
sK19529	$ Grants
sK19600	$ Match ball sponsorship
sK19601	$ Match magazine sponsorship
sK19610	$ Merchandising sales
sK19843	$ Travelling support
sK19948	% Achieving international ranking of top 3 for female senior national teams
sK20063	% Anti-doping policy approved by the authority body
sK20334	% Clubs delivering policies to members and local community organizations
sK20371	% Compliance with constitutional requirements
sK21196	% Participant satisfaction with national competition program
sK21622	% Senior national teams receiving access to levels of direct athlete support
sK18266	# People benefiting from sponsorship programs
sK18838	# Sports assisted by sponsorships
sK19403	$ Cost per briefing to Sport and Recreation Council
sK19835	$ Trail funding per region

Sport Event Organization

Sport event organization includes all the activities related to event promotion, organization and management, as well as facility management and informing. It includes the management off all sport activities and competitions from high profile major league and international competitions to local professionals and amateur events. KPIs are employed to reflect administrative aspects (security, costs), as well as participant-related aspects (diversity, attractiveness of the event).

sKPI #	Key Performance Indicator name
sK447	% Accredited clubs within the sport
sK448	# Volunteers supporting the sport
sK1009	% Stadium segmented capacity utilization
sK1228	% Match tickets sold online
sK1232	$ Spending per spectator
sK1233	% Crowd full paying adults

sKPI #	Key Performance Indicator name
sK1235	% Corporate seats used during match days
sK1238	% Match day costs from match day revenues
sK1250	% Sport volunteering
sK1766	$ Profit per non-match day event
sK1769	# Viewers per televised match
sK1770	% Ground facility satisfaction
sK1771	$ Merchandise spend per fan head
sK1772	# Replica shirt sales
sK1773	# Dwell time
sK1776	$ Sponsorships
sK1975	$ Sport event operating costs
sK2528	$ Venue renovation cost
sK2619	# Countries participating in paralympic games
sK2625	# Countries participating in the sport event
sK2630	# Olympic torchbearers
sK2634	# Paralympic athletes and officials attending competition
sK2635	# Accredited media representatives
sK2640	# Event tickets available
sK2641	# Competition venues sites
sK2652	$ Security costs per athlete
sK2665	$ Athlete accommodation facilities development cost
sK2670	# Distance traveled by Olympic torch
sK2676	# Olympic torch relay duration
sK2686	# Athletes and officials attending the competition
sK3540	# Medal events during the competition
sK3546	$ Sport event security cost
sK6778	% Event seats filled
sK6842	% Players' satisfaction with the quality of the venue
sK6844	% Games covered in media
sK6848	$ Revenue from door fee charges
sK6849	% Planned games that took place
sK6850	% Games with administrative incidents
sK6854	% Games with online reviews
sK6855	% Games compliant with organizing standards
sK6856	% Games with accurate and updated reporting
sK21205	% Participants in organised sport and physical activities
sK21410	% Prevalence of sufficient physical activity by age group
sK21411	% Prevalence of inactivity by gender
sK20903	% Involvement in designing programs and campaigns
sK14390	# Accredited officials

Sports

Sports includes all athletic activities requiring physical demand, skills and fitness and often of a competitive nature. The term is also used to include activities that require a mental concentration and effort, such as card games or board games which do not involve elements of luck, or motor sports, where beyond physical shape, the quality of the equipment, as well as the mental acuity play an important role.

American Football

American football is a team sport played between two teams of eleven players, using an oval ball. Known as being a combination of strategy and physical play, the purpose of the game is to score points by advancing with the ball in the end zone of the opponent's rectangular field. Points can be scored in a variety of ways and the team with the most points at the end of the legal time is considered to be the winner.

sKPI #	Key Performance Indicator name
sK892	% Passing accuracy
sK1189	# Passing yards
sK1193	# Touchdowns
sK1194	# Field goals scored
sK1196	# Fumbles
sK1197	# Safety
sK1203	# Rushing yards
sK1205	# Interceptions
sK1213	# Punt returns
sK1229	# Receiving yards

Badminton

Badminton is a game between two players or two pairs of players equipped with light rackets used to volley a shuttlecock over a high narrow net that divides in half a rectangular court.

sKPI #	Key Performance Indicator name
sK2411	# Rallies per game
sK2412	# Shuttle in play
sK2413	# Shots per rally
sK2414	# Shots per game
sK2415	% Game intensity
sK2416	# Distance covered
sK2417	# Drives
sK2418	% Low serve
sK2419	% High serve
sK2420	# Smashes

Baseball

Baseball is a team sport played between two teams of nine players, using a bat and a ball, each team playing alternatively in the field or at the bat. The purpose of the game is to score home runs by hitting a thrown ball by the opposing team with a bat and then running a course of four bases disposed in a diamond pattern in order to score.

sKPI #	Key Performance Indicator name
sK248	% Popups (POP)
sK1853	# Turnovers (TO)

sKPI #	Key Performance Indicator name
sK1882	% Bases on balls rate
sK1883	% Fly balls
sK1886	% Stolen bases
sK1888	% On base (OBP)
sK1913	# Bases
sK1919	# Hits achieved
sK1920	% Slugging (SLG)
sK1924	# Runs batted in (RBI)
sK1926	# Hit by pitch (HBP)
sK1927	# Left on base (LOB)
sK1940	# At bats (AB)
sK1969	# Innings pitched (IP)
sK1970	# Earned run average (ERA)
sK1972	# Putouts (PO)
sK1974	# Strike outs (SO)
sK1981	# Walks and hits per inning pitched (WHIP)
sK1983	# Earned runs (ER)
sK1998	# Save opportunities (SvO)
sK2003	# Games started (GS)
sK2012	% Defense efficiency ratio (DER)
sK2013	% Ground balls (GB)
sK2018	% Batted balls
sK2020	# Home runs
sK2031	# Stolen bases (SB)
sK2034	# Runs
sK2036	# Sacrifices

Basketball

Basketball is a team sport played between two teams of five players, using a spherical ball and fallowing a well defined set of rules. The purpose of the game is to score as many points as possible against one another, by throwing the ball through an elevated hoop on the opponent's side of a rectangular court.

sKPI #	Key Performance Indicator name
sK892	% Passing accuracy
sK904	# Rebounds per game (REB)
sK916	# Free throws made (FTM)
sK951	# Field goals made (FGM)
sK1071	# Three point field goals made (3FGM)
sK1085	% Field goals (FG)
sK1086	# Free throws attempted (FTA)
sK1092	% Free throws (FT)

sKPI #	Key Performance Indicator name
sK1100	# Points scored per game
sK1130	% Three points field goals (3FG)
sK1147	# Assists per game (AST)
sK1153	# Blocks per game (BLK)
sK1159	# Steals per game (STL)
sK1794	# Assists to turnover ratio
sK1810	# Personal fouls
sK1848	# Offensive rebounds per game (OREB)
sK1851	# Defensive rebounds per game (DREB)
sK2022	# Field goals attempted (FGA)
sK1125	# Three point field goals attempted (3FGA)

Cricket

Cricket is a team sport played between two teams of eleven, using a red leather ball and a flat wooden bat. The purpose of the game is to score as many runs as possible. In trying to do so, the teams bat and bowl alternatively with the batting team trying to score runs.

sKPI #	Key Performance Indicator name
sK1032	# Wides bowled
sK1036	# Runs conceded
sK1040	% Boundary shots
sK1132	% Strike rate
sK1258	% Scoring shots
sK1259	# Centuries scored
sK1262	% Boundary balls
sK1268	# Bowling average
sK1269	% Run out conversion
sK1270	# Batting average

Football/Soccer

Football (or Soccer in the USA) is a team sport played between two teams of eleven players using a spherical ball and following a well defined set of rules. It is played on a rectangular field and it has two goal nets in the center of each of the two short ends. The purpose of the game is to score in the opposite goal net as many goals as possible. However, the only players who are allowed to use their hands during the active game are the goalkeepers.

sKPI #	Key Performance Indicator name
sK892	% Passing accuracy
sK921	% Shots on target
sK922	# Minutes per goal scored
sK923	# Chances created per game
sK932	# Goals scored per game
sK933	% Goal conversion rate
sK939	# Minutes per goal conceded
sK957	% Catch success rate
sK1119	% Ball possession
sK1160	# Shots off target

sKPI #	Key Performance Indicator name
sK1700	# Corner kicks
sK2421	# Off sides
sK2422	% Duels won
sK2423	% Duels lost
sK2424	# Goal passes
sK4119	% Level of excitement
sK4121	# Season standard deviation (SD)
sK4122	# Average points obtained per season
sK4123	% Concentration rate (CR)
sK4128	# Ratio of concentration rates (RCR)
sK4131	# Season deviation standard (SD) of top five clubs over the last 15 years
sK4134	# Competition level for the champion title
sK4135	% Qualification success
sK4136	# UEFA Champions League qualification success concentration ratio
sK4137	% Swift relegation rate
sK4138	# Volatility among top five clubs
sK4141	# Volatility among bottom three clubs

Rugby

Rugby is a team sport played between two teams of fifteen players, using an oval ball and following a well defined set of rules. It is played on a rectangular pitch, the purpose of the game being to score as many points as possible by running with the ball across the opponent's goal line, which is considered a try, or kick it to the upper side of the goal posts, which is considered to be an essay.

sKPI #	Key Performance Indicator name
sK387	# Tackles made
sK759	# Scrums lost
sK844	# Season player tries
sK853	# Drop goals
sK855	# Free kicks conceded
sK862	# Mauls won
sK863	# Balls won in open play
sK867	% Penalty try conversion
sK870	% Possessions kicked
sK1759	# Scrums won

Tennis

Tennis is a game played between two players or two pairs of players on a rectangular court of grass, clay, asphalt or carpet, using rackets and a light ball.

sKPI #	Key Performance Indicator name
sK227	% Break points conversion
sK1141	% First serve
sK1143	% Second serve win
sK1146	% First serve win
sK1148	% Service points win

sKPI #	Key Performance Indicator name
sK1151	# Aces served
sK1155	% First serve return points won
sK1161	% Second serve return points won
sK1162	# Double faults
sK1163	# Break points faced
sK1167	% Return points win
sK1175	% Break points saved
sK1185	% Points won
sK1187	# Points won
sK1188	# Breaks won
sK1218	# Punting
sK1219	# Sacks
sK1239	# Forced errors
sK1243	# Unforced errors
sK2401	% Tie-breaks won

sKPI #	Key Performance Indicator name
sK2402	# Tie-breaks played
sK2403	% Points won after net approaches
sK2404	% Matches won
sK2405	# Matches played
sK2406	# Games played
sK2407	# Match time
sK2408	# First serve speed
sK2409	# Second serve speed
sK2410	% Games won
sK4103	# Challenges
sK4104	# Correct challenges
sK4108	# Incorrect challenges
sK4111	# Challenges per match
sK4114	% Overturned

Telecommunications/Call Center

Telecommunications and call centers refers to the industry of transmitting data or information through specific channels, such as cable, radio, television or telephone.

Call Center

Call Center is the industry dealing with receiving and transmitting a large volume of requests or inquiries by telephone. The inbound call center deals with calls initiated by the customer, while an outbound call center regards calls initiated from the organization to the customer. Indicators in this area refer to performance aspects regarding call volumes, contact channels or any other specific operations.

sKPI #	Key Performance Indicator name
sK5	$ Revenue per successful call
sK30	% First call resolution rate
sK32	% Customer calls answered in the first minute
sK55	% Agent utilization
sK164	% Lead conversion rate
sK165	# Call handling time
sK166	% Call completion rate
sK167	# Sales per agent
sK168	% Call abandon rate
sK1017	% Call transfer rate
sK1079	# Service requests per agent
sK1081	# After call work time
sK1113	# Speed of answer (SA)
sK1114	% Calls answered within service level time
sK1131	# Calls on hold longer than X seconds
sK1135	# Web call-backs handled
sK1149	# Call completion time
sK1284	# Longest call length
sK1328	# Call arrival rate

sKPI #	Key Performance Indicator name
sK1360	% Agent availability rate
sK1380	% Repeat calls
sK1383	# Dials per hour
sK1384	% Agent schedule adherence
sK1420	% Accuracy in completion of records
sK1426	% Closed records
sK1428	% Attempted contact of potential customers in database
sK1430	% Calls as requests for information
sK2277	$ Telemarketing cost per sales lead
sK2283	% Cross sale rate
sK2285	$ Revenue per sales representative
sK2339	# New-hire time to quota attainment
sK2372	# Longest call hold
sK2373	# Longest delay in queue
sK2375	# On-hold time
sK2376	# Call volume
sK2378	# Talk time
sK2384	$ Cost per call (CPC)
sK2386	% Blockage
sK2390	% Interactions routed properly
sK3275	# Duration of calls with poor voice quality
sK3276	# Time lost due to technology issues
sK3278	$ Cost with poor monitoring of technical failures
sK3293	% Service recovery meetings after technical failures
sK3295	$ Lost sales opportunities due to call center technical failures

sKPI #	Key Performance Indicator name
sK3296	% Forecasted contact load to actual contact load
sK3301	% Call center self-service accessibility
sK3305	% Error and rework rate
sK3325	# All trunks busy (ATB) time
sK3414	# Callback messaging
sK3423	# Peak hour traffic (PHT)
sK3424	$ Sales per sign-on minute
sK3443	# Quality monitoring (QM) scores
sK6143	% Telephone service calls not resolved within x minutes
sK6144	% First contact resolution rate
sK6593	% Call drop rate (CDR)
sK6753	# Wait time before abandon
sK6754	# Text-Chat volume
sK14453	# Agent tenure
sK14689	# Call quality
sK14864	# Contacts per agent month
sK17455	# Handle time
sK17481	# Hold time
sK17818	# Line item per order
sK18518	# Queue time
sK18788	# Service levels
sK19002	# Time to abandon
sK19406	$ Cost per contact
sK19412	$ Cost per minute of handle time
sK19910	% Abandon rates
sK19959	% Adherence
sK20022	% Agent occupancy
sK20023	% Agent satisfaction
sK20024	% Agent turnover
sK20026	% Agents of FTEs
sK20169	% Call Back
sK20172	% Calls blocked
sK20174	% Calls requiring rework
sK20908	% IVR completion rate
sK21481	% Quality Monitored
sK21588	% Sales Conversion
sK21600	% Schedule adherence

Telecommunications

Telecommunications industry refers to the specific services that support the exchange of information over significant distances by electronic means. It includes the activities of providing telecommunications and related service activities (i.e. transmitting voice, data, text, sound and video). The transmission facilities that carry out these activities may be based on a single technology or a combination of technologies. The commonality of activities classified in this division is the transmission of content, without being involved in its creation. The breakdown in this division is based on the type of infrastructure operated. The indicators regard the data transmission outcomes, process and efficiency, as well as the infrastructure supporting it.

sKPI #	Key Performance Indicator name
sK62	$ Revenue per user (RPU)
sK63	# Network throughput
sK64	# Telephone connections per number of inhabitants
sK206	% Visits under one minute
sK221	% Data network availability
sK269	# Usage per telecom user (UPU)
sK270	$ Telecom subscriber acquisition cost
sK271	$ Telecom subscriber retention cost (SRC)
sK272	% Block error rate (BLER)
sK865	% Call setup success rate (CSSR)
sK2656	% Answer seizure ratio (ASR)
sK5031	% Rural telecommunication subscribers receiving new or improved service
sK5871	# SMS messages sent or received per month by age
sK5873	# Mobile phone web users
sK6094	# Television sets per household
sK6168	% Mobile subscribers with Smartphones
sK6426	# Exclusive handset deals completed
sK6593	% Call drop rate (CDR)
sK6594	% Connection drop rate
sK6595	% Connection establishment success rate
sK6596	% Handover success rate
sK6597	# Post dialling delay (PDD)
sK6598	% SMS delivery failures
sK6602	% Answer bid ratio (ABR)
sK6603	% Overflow bids (OFL)
sK6604	# Bids per circuit per hour (BCH)
sK6605	# Seizures per circuit per hour (SCH)
sK6614	# Holding time per seizure
sK6615	% Busy-flash seizure ratio (BFSR)
sK6616	% Successful backward call setup signal
sK6617	% Calls blocked by network management controls
sK6618	# Seizure of outgoing circuit
sK6619	% Overflow to a next circuit group
sK6620	% Calls not routed due to internal congestion
sK6621	# Invalid digit address

sKPI #	Key Performance Indicator name
sK6628	# Echo path loss (EPL)
sK6629	# Echo path delay (EPD)
sK6630	# Dial tone delay
sK6632	% Speech clipping ratio

sKPI #	Key Performance Indicator name
sK6821	% Mobile phone usage
sK6822	# Prepaid mobile customers
sK6867	# Talk time on mobile phones
sK6868	# Applications installed on smartphones

Transportation

Transportation includes the provision of passenger or freight transport, whether scheduled or not, by rail, pipeline, road, water or air and associated activities, such as terminal and parking facilities, cargo handling or storage. Also included in this section is the renting of transport equipment with driver or operator.

Airlines

Airlines includes the transport of passengers or freight by air or via space. Airline services can be categorized as being intercontinental, intracontinental, domestic or international and may be operated as scheduled services or charters. KPIs focus on flight operations and passenger and cargo characteristics.

sKPI #	Key Performance Indicator name
sK11	% Lost luggage
sK12	% Passenger seats sold
sK57	# Seat availability
sK82	% Internet bookings
sK143	# Fuel consumption per 100 kilometers
sK222	% Canceled reservations
sK235	% Transport capacity utilization
sK255	$ Revenue per available seat mile (RASM)
sK256	$ Cost per available seat mile (CASM)
sK257	# Revenue passenger kilometer (RPK)
sK258	% On-time departure of transport vehicles
sK259	# Delay per flight
sK260	% Ground crew trained
sK263	# Turnaround time
sK264	# Baggage transfer time
sK265	$ Fuel cost
sK266	# Airplane block time
sK267	$ Freight revenue per ton-mile
sK268	$ Airplane maintenance cost
sK592	# Aircraft emissions
sK699	% Empty running
sK1724	% Duplicate bookings
sK3464	# Deferrals per aircraft
sK3467	# Check-in counters per flight
sK3468	# Check-in time
sK3469	% Lost baggage on connecting flights
sK3471	# Terminal handling capacity
sK3472	# Capacity (ATK) per employee
sK3473	% Overnight workload accomplished
sK3476	# Express services tonnes

sKPI #	Key Performance Indicator name
sK3477	# Freight tonnes kilometers (FTK)
sK3478	% Overall load factor
sK3479	% Break-even load factor
sK3480	$ Cost with pilot salaries
sK3481	$ Pilot salaries per block hour
sK3482	$ Controllable crew cost per aircraft block hour
sK3484	$ Cost per flight hour
sK3485	$ Aircraft fleet operating costs
sK3486	# Block speeds
sK3489	# Flight crew per aircraft
sK3490	# Crew complaints
sK3491	# Crew control errors
sK3492	# Crew related delay minutes
sK3493	% Flights delayed due to technical issues
sK3494	% Flights delayed due to weather conditions
sK3495	# Aircraft emissions per payload capacity
sK3498	% Flights departures delayed more than 15 minutes
sK3499	# In flight shutdown rate (IFSD)
sK3500	# Rejected takeoffs
sK3501	% Flight diversion rate
sK3502	# Ground damage rate
sK3504	# Canceled flights
sK3506	% Air operations covered by user charges
sK3507	# Flights per week during peak season
sK3509	# Distance flown
sK3510	# Time flown
sK3511	# Airline network size
sK3512	% Punctuality "ready to go"
sK3513	# Destination cities serviced
sK3514	# Destinations served by direct air services
sK3515	# Flight duration
sK3516	% Passenger injury rate
sK3518	# Fuel consumed per block hour
sK3521	# Passenger transfers between flights
sK3527	% Customer recommendation
sK3530	# Load carried per employee

sKPI #	Key Performance Indicator name
sK3531	# Revenue tonne kilometer (RTK)
sK3532	# Available tonne kilometers (AKTM)
sK3533	# Overall yield
sK3534	# Available seat kilometers (ASKM)
sK3537	% Electronic tickets sold
sK3538	# Attacks on airport facilities or installations
sK3539	# In flight destructive and criminal incidents
sK3541	# Airport security breaches
sK3542	# Minutes delayed for all flights
sK3543	# Block hours per pilot
sK3545	# Aircraft fleet mean age
sK3547	% On time departures
sK3548	% On time arrivals
sK3549	# Arrival processing time
sK3550	% Daily pilot utilization
sK3551	% Crew utilization
sK3552	% Aircraft fleet utilization
sK3553	% Flying simulator utilization rate
sK3554	# Aircraft utilization
sK3575	$ Operating expense per passenger
sK3590	# Fuel consumption
sK3723	% Passengers who purchased return tickets
sK3750	% Freight bill accuracy
sK3784	# Transport capacity available
sK3915	# Passenger boardings per trip operated
sK4228	# Passengers injured
sK6490	$ Airline rental cost per gate
sK6498	# Time from passengers entering to plane take off
sK6523	% Non stop destinations operated
sK14383	# Accidents
sK14386	# Accidents controlled flight into terrain (CFIT)
sK14388	# Accidents per category
sK14392	# A-check downtime
sK14410	# Acts of facility attacks
sK14411	# Acts of unlawful seizure
sK14415	# Actual load factor
sK14424	# Adherence to optimum Airspace Dimension
sK14445	# Aeronautical charges
sK14458	# Air cargo capacity
sK14459	# Air cargo traffic in FTK
sK14466	# Air transport environment scoring
sK14467	# Air transport infrastructure scoring
sK14468	# Air transport passengers per year
sK14469	# Air transport related policy scoring
sK14470	# Aircraft capacity
sK14472	# Aircraft deviation from ATC clearance

sKPI #	Key Performance Indicator name
sK14473	# Aircraft in fleet
sK14476	# Aircraft movements handled by airports
sK14477	# Aircraft payload
sK14478	# Aircraft servicing time
sK14479	# Aircraft taken into account for a resolution
sK14480	# Aircraft turnaround time
sK14481	# Airfield hourly capacity
sK14482	# Airline providing scheduled service
sK14485	# Airports
sK14488	# Airspace utilization
sK14505	# Altitude clearances
sK14511	# Annual airfield service volume
sK14515	# Annual flights accommodated
sK14517	# Annual IFR flights in Europe
sK14520	# Annul IFR flights that can be accommodated at Airport level
sK14527	# Approach control
sK14528	# Approach control procedures
sK14538	# ASM productivity per aircraft
sK14539	# ASM productivity per employee
sK14540	# ASM productivity per flight attendant
sK14541	# ASM productivity per pilot
sK14542	# ASMA additional time
sK14543	# ASMs
sK14552	# ATFM arrival delay
sK14553	# ATK per employee
sK14581	# Available capacity
sK14582	# Available capacity per employee
sK14583	# Available passenger capacity
sK14631	# Block hours
sK14632	# Block hours per route
sK14634	# Block speed
sK14656	# Breakeven load factor
sK14679	# Cabin attendant productivity
sK14680	# Cabin crew
sK14681	# Cabin crew productivity
sK14682	# Cabin factor
sK14694	# Cancelled fleet to handled fleet
sK14695	# Cancelled flights
sK14698	# Capacity (ASMs)
sK14700	# Capacity at passport control
sK14714	# Cargo carried
sK14716	# Cargo handled
sK14723	# Cargo terminals
sK14724	# Cargo traffic (RTK)
sK14744	# Change requests

sKPI #	Key Performance Indicator name
sK14754	# Check-in counters per flight for wide-body aircraft
sK14780	# Cockpit crew productivity
sK14782	# Coefficient of variation of gate-to-gate time intervals
sK14783	# Cold storage size of cargo terminals
sK14793	# Commercial aircraft movement
sK14795	# Communication facilities
sK14971	# Daily aircraft block hours
sK14972	# Daily aircraft departures
sK14973	# Daily aircraft movements
sK14976	# Daily flights accommodated
sK14988	# Days lost
sK14998	# Dead flying
sK15010	# Declared capacity per hour
sK15011	# Declared capacity per peak hour
sK15012	# Declared capacity to service rate
sK15032	# Delay due to BT re-definition
sK15033	# Delay due to BT update
sK15034	# Delay due to disruption
sK15036	# Delay in non-scheduled flights
sK15042	# Delay of delayed non-scheduled flights
sK15043	# Delay of delayed non-scheduled flights at Airport level
sK15044	# Delay of non-scheduled delayed flights
sK15047	# Delay severity because trajectory full re-definition
sK15050	# Delayed flights
sK15051	# Delayed flights due to a business trajectory update
sK15055	# Delays in minutes
sK15058	# Delivery flights
sK15070	# Departing passenger capacity of the terminal building
sK15072	# Departure delay per flight
sK15079	# Destinations
sK15115	# Diverted flights
sK15117	# Domestic cargo traffic
sK15118	# Domestic commercial movement
sK15130	# Duration between off-block time and first-bag by aircraft-type and stand-number
sK15131	# Duration between off-block time and last-bag by aircraft-type and stand-number
sK15132	# Duration of check-in per wide-body aircraft flight
sK15152	# Efficient booking procedure
sK15185	# Emissions
sK15194	# Employees per aircraft
sK15207	# Environment facilities
sK15241	# Extra A-checks required
sK15242	# Extra flight duration
sK15281	# First flight of the day delays
sK15286	# Flight attendants to employees
sK17250	# Wake turbulence

sKPI #	Key Performance Indicator name
sK17256	# Walk-through metal detectors
sK17257	# Walk-through metal detectors available
sK17258	# Walk-through metal detectors being used
sK17259	# Walk-through metal detectors in working order
sK17268	# Weather facilities
sK17276	# Weight load factor
sK17279	# Wide-body aircraft arrivals per day
sK17280	# Wide-body aircraft departures per day
sK17287	# Flight attendants
sK17288	# Flight attendants per aircraft
sK17289	# Flight cancellations
sK17290	# Flight crew
sK17291	# Flight duration extension
sK17292	# Flight service stations
sK17293	# Flight time deviation
sK17294	# Flights able to operate at the requested altitude
sK17295	# Flights delayed due to BT update
sK17296	# Flights per week off season for the point of origin
sK17297	# Flights per week off season for the scheduled destination
sK17298	# Flights per week peak season for the point of origin
sK17299	# Flights per week peak season for the scheduled destination
sK17328	# Freight traffic
sK17329	# Freight traffic in tones
sK17330	# Freight traffic in tonnes over distance
sK17334	# Frequency of BDT delayed because trajectory full re-definition
sK17335	# Frequency of BDT update because trajectory full re-definition
sK17336	# Frequency of clearances
sK17339	# Frequency of the periodic review of tariff structure
sK17340	# Frequency of the periodic review of tariff structure in aeronautical services
sK17341	# Frequency of the periodic review of tariff structure in air traffic control
sK17342	# Frequency of the periodic review of tariff structure in airport management
sK17343	# Frequency of the periodic review of tariff structure in commercial services
sK17344	# Frequency of the periodic review of tariff structure in services
sK17353	# Fuel burnt
sK17354	# Fuel capabilities
sK17359	# Fuel expense to revenue ratio
sK17429	# Ground movement procedures unable to ensure separation
sK17433	# Guarded gates
sK17456	# Handled traffic
sK17457	# Handled traffic to declared capacity

sKPI #	Key Performance Indicator name
sK17458	# Hangars
sK17462	# Heading clearances
sK17475	# High-speed turnoffs
sK17509	# Hourly capacity
sK17510	# Hourly throughput overloads
sK17515	# Hours of operation of air traffic control towers
sK17524	# Hours with excessive ATC task demand
sK17525	# Hours with under loads of ATC task demand
sK17538	# ICAO Aerodrome Usability Factor (AUF)
sK17561	# Inaugural flights
sK17566	# Incidents per million flight hours
sK17570	# Incorrect runway entry point
sK17584	# Ineffective ACAS avoidance
sK17585	# Ineffective avoidance by impeded aircraft
sK17586	# Ineffective avoidance by intruding aircraft
sK17587	# Ineffective avoidance on striking aircraft
sK17639	# International freight traffic
sK17642	# Internal perimeter road
sK17645	# International commercial movement
sK17647	# International experts in the field
sK17648	# International flights to country
sK17654	# Intersecting flight paths
sK17660	# Inventory per aircraft
sK17708	# Lateral resolutions
sK17709	# Laws protecting against abuse of monopoly power
sK17710	# Laws protecting against horizontal mergers
sK17711	# Laws protecting against vertical mergers
sK17764	# Length of term for the head or the commission of the regulatory body
sK17773	# Level bust
sK17828	# Loading time
sK17837	# Local change requests
sK17858	# Mail carried
sK17859	# Mail tonnes
sK17876	# Material service level
sK17881	# Maximum measured throughput per hour
sK17882	# Maximum queuing time for check-in
sK17884	# Maximum simultaneous aircrafts
sK17887	# Maximum weight supported by runway
sK17890	# Mechanics per aircraft
sK17930	# Mid-air collisions (MAC)
sK17976	# Navigation facilities
sK17978	# Near controlled flight into terrain
sK17991	# Network size
sK18043	# Non revenue hours
sK18057	# Normal turnoffs

sKPI #	Key Performance Indicator name
sK18085	# One hour capacity
sK18101	# Operational errors
sK18102	# Operational errors per million operations
sK18103	# Operational facilities
sK18108	# Optimal flight duration
sK18134	# Overall load factor
sK18136	# Overload duration
sK18144	# PAPI (Precisions Approach Path Indicator)
sK18189	# Passenger carried
sK18195	# Passenger movements
sK18196	# Passenger per employee productivity
sK18197	# Passenger per flight attendant productivity
sK18200	# Passenger seat factor
sK18205	# Passenger traffic
sK18216	# Passengers killed per 100 million passenger-kilometers on scheduled services
sK18251	# Pax load time
sK18252	# Pax traffic (RPK)
sK18254	# Peak months
sK18264	# Penetration of controlled airspace
sK18283	# Perimeter inspection frequency
sK18285	# Period throughput
sK18286	# Periodic reviews of tariff structure
sK18287	# Periodic reviews of tariff structure in aeronautical services
sK18288	# Periodic reviews of tariff structure in air traffic control
sK18289	# Periodic reviews of tariff structure in airport management
sK18290	# Periodic reviews of tariff structure in commercial services
sK18291	# Periodic reviews of tariff structure in infrastructure
sK18292	# Periodic reviews of tariff structure in services
sK18313	# Pilot error in runway entry
sK18314	# Pilot failure to follow the take-off instructions
sK18315	# Pilots to employees
sK18316	# Pilots
sK18317	# Pilots per aircraft
sK18340	# Population exposed to noise level
sK18378	# Practice flights
sK18381	# Pre-departure delay
sK18382	# Premature take-offs
sK18549	# Reactionary delay
sK18653	# Revenue hours
sK18654	# Revenue miles per passenger
sK18680	# Round trip miles
sK18681	# Round trips
sK18684	# Revenue Passenger Kilometer (RPKM)

sKPI #	Key Performance Indicator name
sK18685	# Revenue Passenger Mile (RPM)
sK18686	# Revenue Tonne Kilometer (RTKM)
sK18714	# Safety incidents reported by day of week
sK18716	# Safety management scoring
sK18723	# Scheduled foreign airlines
sK18727	# Scheduled services yield
sK18749	# Seat capacity per week off season for the point of origin
sK18750	# Seat capacity per week off season for the scheduled destination
sK18751	# Seat capacity per week peak season for the point of origin
sK18752	# Seat capacity per week peak season for the scheduled destination
sK18758	# Sectors per route
sK18761	# Security incidents reported by day of week
sK18769	# Separation losses in the TMAs
sK18789	# Service rate
sK18936	# Surveillance facilities
sK18948	# Technical cooperation programme implementation
sK18949	# Technical cooperation programmes
sK18968	# Test flights
sK18988	# Time since the last periodic review of tariff structure
sK18989	# Time since the last periodic review of tariff structure in aeronautical services
sK18990	# Time since the last periodic review of tariff structure in air traffic control
sK18991	# Time since the last periodic review of tariff structure in airport management
sK18992	# Time since the last periodic review of tariff structure in commercial services
sK18993	# Time since the last periodic review of tariff structure in infrastructure
sK18994	# Time since the last periodic review of tariff structure in services
sK19060	# Training flights
sK19064	# Transfers
sK19095	# Trip distance
sK19127	# Underload duration
sK19135	# Unloading time
sK19154	# Unpredictable deviation
sK19156	# Unscheduled aircraft out-of-service
sK19197	# Variability of arrivals in ASMA
sK19202	# Visual Approach Slope Indicator (VASI)
sK19301	# Yield (Fills per RTKM)
sK19323	$ Aircraft ownership costs
sK19337	$ Annual budget of the regulatory bodies (RBs)
sK19361	$ Cargo revenue
sK19386	$ Cost from capital to second largest domestic population center

sKPI #	Key Performance Indicator name
sK19387	$ Cost from largest population center to second largest domestic population center
sK19399	$ Cost per aircraft mile
sK19400	$ Cost per ASM
sK19430	$ Cost to European cities
sK19431	$ Cost to neighboring countries
sK19432	$ Cost to use air operations
sK19433	$ Costs per A-check
sK19459	$ Estimated cost per landing
sK19460	$ Estimated cost per passenger
sK19473	$ Facility support service costs
sK19492	$ Flight attendant expense per passenger
sK19493	$ Flight attendant salary
sK19494	$ Flight attendant salary cost per unit mile
sK19495	$ Flight inspection service costs
sK19499	$ Foregone revenue due to A-check
sK19512	$ Fuel expense per passenger
sK19542	$ Hourly costs of crew
sK19543	$ Hourly costs of fuel
sK19544	$ Hourly costs of maintenance
sK19545	$ Hourly hull insurance
sK19546	$ Hourly lease rate
sK19562	$ Insured hull value
sK19574	$ Labor expense including wages and benefits per passenger
sK19575	$ Labor expense per ASM
sK19579	$ Landing fee
sK19594	$ Maintenance planning yield
sK19595	$ Management expense per passenger
sK19614	$ Monthly insurance cost
sK19646	$ Operating expense per passenger less fuel and labor
sK19651	$ Operating profit per available seat mile
sK19654	$ Operating unit costs (CASM)
sK19655	$ Operating unit revenue (RASM)
sK19663	$ Parking fee
sK19668	$ Passenger fare
sK19671	$ Passenger fees
sK19672	$ Passenger revenue
sK19675	$ Passenger yield
sK19692	$ Pilot expense per passenger
sK19693	$ Pilot salary
sK19694	$ Pilot salary cost per unit mile
sK19736	$ Retail revenue by day per week by product group
sK19737	$ Retail Revenue by flight or destination
sK19751	$ Revenue from concessions
sK19752	$ Revenue from landing fees
sK19753	$ Revenue from parking fees

sKPI #	Key Performance Indicator name
sK19754	$ Revenue from passenger fees
sK19756	$ Revenue passengers kilometers flown (RPKM)
sK19757	$ Revenue per aircraft
sK19758	$ Revenue per ASM
sK19761	$ Revenue per employee
sK19768	$ Revenue per RPM
sK19769	$ Revenue productivity per employee
sK19770	$ Revenue productivity per flight attendant
sK19771	$ Revenue productivity per pilot
sK19774	$ Revenue tonne kilometers flown (RPKM)
sK19775	$ Revenue tonne kilometers performed (passenger and cargo)
sK19779	$ Round trip costs per aircraft on commissions
sK19780	$ Round trip costs per aircraft on landing and handling
sK19781	$ Round trip costs per aircraft on navigation and communications
sK19782	$ Round trip costs per aircraft on pax services
sK19783	$ Round trip costs per aircraft on sales and reservations
sK19784	$ Round trip costs per aircraft on station
sK19822	$ System command center costs
sK19823	$ System yield
sK19828	$ Technical operations and maintenance costs
sK19829	$ Telecommunication costs
sK19849	$ Unit cost
sK19850	$ Unit cost (Fills per ATKM)
sK19853	$ Unit costs without fuel and labor expense
sK19854	$ Unit costs without labor expense
sK19957	% Additional fuel consumption for flight of more than 2.5%
sK19960	% Adherence to optimum Airspace Dimension
sK20029	% Air traffic control systems with backup power
sK20087	% Arrival punctuality
sK20111	% Automatic palletizing of cargo terminals
sK20116	% Availability of international air links
sK20118	% Availability of maintenance and repair crews
sK20122	% Availability of qualified air transport employees
sK20123	% Availability of regional air links
sK20164	% Business Trajectory that requested a 4D Trajectory change success
sK20194	% Cargo containerization of cargo terminals
sK20195	% Cargo that get electronic cargo screening
sK20196	% Cargo that get security screened
sK20197	% Cargo traffic
sK20468	% Degree of implementation of the critical elements of a safety oversight system
sK20470	% Delayed flights due to a business trajectory update
sK20506	% Donors contribution to the financing of the regulatory body
sK20511	% Early arrivals

sKPI #	Key Performance Indicator name
sK20625	% External perimeter road
sK20655	% Flight attendant salary out of labor expense
sK20656	% Flight attendant salary to passenger fare
sK20657	% Flight delayed at arrival more than 3 minutes
sK20658	% Flight departure on time
sK20660	% Flight suffering additional fuel consumption of more than 2.5%
sK20661	% Flight with normal flight duration
sK20662	% Flights departing on time
sK20707	% Government contribution to the financing of the regulatory body
sK20721	% Ground damage rate
sK20735	% Hangars
sK20760	% Heavy aircraft maintenance facilities
sK20817	% ICAO standard
sK20847	% In-flight shutdown rate
sK20897	% International tourist arrival
sK20899	% Internet access to weather observation
sK20936	% Levies on companies contributing to the financing of the regulatory body
sK20948	% License fees contributing to the financing of the regulatory body
sK20952	% Light aircraft maintenance facilities
sK20978	% Management salary to passenger fare
sK20990	% MEL and deferred items rates
sK21097	% Non-scheduled flights delayed more than 3 minutes
sK21127	% Operational availability of equipment
sK21356	% Pilot errors
sK21357	% Pilot salary out of labor expense
sK21358	% Pilot salary to passenger fare
sK21371	% PLF
sK21520	% Rejected take-off rate
sK21998	% Worldwide passenger growth
sK22535	# Employees in International Association of Machinists and Aerospace Workers

Land Transport (Road & Rail)

Land transport includes the transport of passengers and freight via road and rail over long distances. Local public transport KPIs are grouped in a separate sub-category.

sKPI #	Key Performance Indicator name
sK12	% Passenger seats sold
sK57	# Seat availability
sK143	# Fuel consumption per 100 kilometers
sK160	# Stops per trip
sK235	% Transport capacity utilization
sK258	% On-time departure of transport vehicles
sK263	# Turnaround time

smartKPIs.com
The smart choice in performance management

sKPI #	Key Performance Indicator name
sK265	$ Fuel cost
sK267	$ Freight revenue per ton-mile
sK699	% Empty running
sK1377	$ Congestion cost
sK1530	# Traffic congestion delay
sK2248	# Excess fuel consumption due to congestion
sK2831	# Congested road distance
sK2835	# Vehicles out of service
sK3473	% Overnight workload accomplished
sK3516	% Passenger injury rate
sK3560	# Distance empty running
sK3568	# Freight transported
sK3569	# Wagon productivity
sK3571	$ Operating expense per vehicle-kilometers
sK3575	$ Operating expense per passenger
sK3589	# Rail track productivity
sK3590	# Fuel consumption
sK3591	# Fuel efficiency
sK3593	$ Vehicle revenue per liter of fuel
sK3594	$ Fuel cost savings per vehicle
sK3595	$ Fuel cost per vehicle
sK3597	# Fuel consumption per four plus wheel road motor vehicle
sK3603	# Wagon reliability
sK3604	# Congestion extent
sK3623	% Functional traffic signs
sK3624	# Traffic signal cycle failures
sK3629	# Locomotive time utilization
sK3630	# Drivers per licensed vehicle
sK3648	% Damage-free shipments
sK3651	# Distance running loaded
sK3653	# Passenger vehicles per household
sK3654	# Railway passenger kilometer by sector
sK3655	# Passenger train kilometer
sK3656	# Passenger rail traffic density
sK3658	# Non-compliance with parking restrictions
sK3660	# Road accidents per ten thousands vehicles
sK3661	# Road accidents per thousand population
sK3664	# Vehicle kilometers per operating employee
sK3665	# Road traffic pedestrian fatalities
sK3668	% Road accidents due to road problems
sK3669	% Multi-tracked rail lines route length
sK3670	# People killed in road accidents
sK3671	# People seriously injured in road accidents
sK3672	# Children killed or seriously injured in road accidents
sK3678	# Locomotive utilization

sKPI #	Key Performance Indicator name
sK3679	% On time pick-ups
sK3680	# Locomotive distance utilization
sK3683	# Delay per vehicle
sK3687	% Travel time in traffic congestion
sK3690	$ Operating expense per vehicle-hour
sK3692	# Locomotive fleet reliability
sK3697	# Speed during peak hours
sK3698	# Locomotive productivity
sK3699	# Vehicle kilometers traveled (VKT)
sK3701	# Traffic travel speed
sK3709	% Peak period train capacity utilization
sK3713	% Locomotive availability
sK3714	# Main line locomotives
sK3716	# Freight wagons per train
sK3723	% Passengers who purchased return tickets
sK3744	# Twenty-foot equivalent units (TEUs) moved by rail
sK3745	% Twenty-foot equivalent units (TEUs) moved by rail
sK3750	% Freight bill accuracy
sK3784	# Transport capacity available
sK3785	# Transit time
sK3904	% Vehicles beyond useful life
sK3915	# Passenger boardings per trip operated
sK4228	# Passengers injured
sK6456	# Train distance covered per track length
sK6457	# Train distance covered per staff
sK6461	# Delayed trains at the final destination due to infrastructure
sK6462	# Hours of train delays due to infrastructure
sK6463	# Train service disruptions
sK6473	# Train accidents per million train kilometers
sK6474	# Incidents that caused train delays
sK6475	# Train delay per incident
sK6532	% Participants in traffic experiencing a delay
sK14323	# Delay in late registration
sK14324	# Delay in late transport end
sK14325	# Delay in late transport start
sK14326	# Delivery time
sK14327	# Duration
sK14328	# Current transport duration
sK14329	# Planned total duration
sK14330	# Planned transport duration
sK14331	# Timed-out for the planned loading time
sK14332	# Timed-out for the planned transport duration
sK14333	# Volume utilization
sK14334	# Web visits of live departure boards
sK14385	# Accidents at level crossings

sKPI #	Key Performance Indicator name
sK14387	# Accidents involving railway vehicles
sK14414	# Actual intermodal transit time
sK14423	# Adequacy of cost recovery
sK14455	# Agreed sector strategy followed
sK14460	# Air quality
sK14555	# Attendance of open days
sK14652	# Bottleneck delay in vehicle-hours
sK14661	# Broken rails
sK14663	# Buffer index
sK14677	# Buses in the city
sK14699	# Capacity adequacy
sK14727	# Carriers per mode
sK14728	# Cars per 1000 persons
sK14770	# City bus supply index
sK14773	# Classified rural road network length
sK14827	# Complaints rate per 100,000 passenger journeys
sK14846	# Congestion burden index
sK14847	# Congestion Index
sK14901	# Coverage of services
sK14934	# Current loading duration
sK14935	# Current loading time
sK14969	# Cycling index
sK15031	# Delay
sK15035	# Delay in late loading start
sK15037	# Delay in person-hours
sK15038	# Delay in vehicle-hours
sK15045	# Delay per person
sK15052	# Delayed freight trains due to infrastructure
sK15057	# Delivery duration
sK15059	# Delivery gross weight
sK15060	# Delivery net weight
sK15067	# Delivery volume
sK15103	# Distance to formal and informal places of work
sK15123	# Double-stacking capability
sK15135	# Dwell time
sK15197	# Employment in transport sector disaggregated by income groups
sK15200	# Energy consumption per area
sK15224	# Expand western bypass
sK15246	# Facilities with maintenance contracts
sK15255	# Fare types for bus services
sK15256	# Fare types for individual motorized transport (IMT) services
sK15257	# Fare types for minibus services
sK15258	# Fare types for taxi services
sK15260	# Fatalities per 100,000 vehicles
sK15826	# Load factor

sKPI #	Key Performance Indicator name
sK16323	# Planned delivery time
sK16337	# Population
sK16523	# Rail lines
sK16986	# Time from moment of ship readiness to unload to final destination for an imported container
sK17088	# Travel time index
sK17103	# Truck turnaround time
sK17231	# Volume to capacity ratio
sK17252	# Walkability Index
sK17260	# WAP visits of live departure boards
sK17261	# WAP visits of online journey planner
sK17269	# Web visits of online journey planner
sK17271	# Weekly intermodal direct city-to-city trains
sK17272	# Weekly intermodal trains on a line segment
sK17273	# Weekly steel trains
sK17320	# Franchised passenger kilometres
sK17323	# Freight
sK17325	# Freight volume
sK17326	# Freight weight
sK17327	# Freight tariff
sK17356	# Fuel consumption per person
sK17357	# Fuel consumption per person during delays
sK17372	# Functional disruptions
sK17415	# Gravel road
sK17416	# Gravel road average age
sK17417	# Gravel road carrying less than 50 vpd
sK17428	# Gross weight of the main send element
sK17513	# Hours of freight train delays due to infrastructure
sK17547	# Imported containers travelling to the given destination
sK17602	# Infrastructure manager's organization size
sK17632	# Interference index
sK17701	# Late loading start
sK17704	# Late registration
sK17706	# Late transport end
sK17707	# Late transport start
sK17746	# Length of gravel roads
sK17753	# Length of road markings
sK17763	# Length of surfaced roads
sK17816	# Light vehicles per person
sK17827	# Load factor of public transport
sK17843	# Long-distance operators
sK17861	# Main diesel line locomotives
sK17862	# Main electric line locomotives
sK17865	# Main operational line locomotives
sK17868	# Major road network length
sK17869	# Major roads in fair condition

sKPI #	Key Performance Indicator name
sK17870	# Major roads in good condition
sK17872	# Managers
sK17874	# Markdowns in current standard
sK17885	# Maximum volume of the main send element
sK17886	# Maximum weight of the main send element
sK17940	# Mini-buses in the city
sK17946	# Modal split of commuters
sK17947	# Mode selection to optimal
sK17963	# Motorized traffic count on major roads
sK17964	# Motorized traffic count on rural classified roads
sK17965	# Motorized traffic count on urban roads
sK17966	# Motorized vehicles
sK17967	# Moto-taxi in the city
sK17982	# Net emissions
sK17987	# Net volume of the main send element
sK17988	# Net weight of the main send element
sK18026	# New road built
sK18071	# Offered capacity on official lines with more than one operator per line over total population
sK18072	# Offered capacity on official lines with one operator per line over total population
sK18083	# On street parking
sK18087	# On-time pickups
sK18099	# Operating vehicles (buses or minibuses) for this operator
sK18104	# Operational freight wagons
sK18105	# Operational passenger coaches
sK18107	# Operators
sK18139	# Packages
sK18145	# Paratransit index
sK18190	# Passenger coaches and freight wagons
sK18198	# Passenger per urban transport ship category
sK18201	# Passenger ships per type
sK18206	# Passenger trips by all modes
sK18210	# Passenger trips per vehicle revenue hour
sK18212	# Passenger trips per vehicle revenue mile
sK18213	# Passengers
sK18217	# Passengers on (sub)urban rail system
sK18219	# Passengers per year
sK18244	# Paved road
sK18245	# Paved road average age
sK18246	# Paved road carrying less than 250 vpd
sK18247	# Paved road network of the city
sK18248	# Paved road network of the city in fair condition
sK18249	# Paved road network of the city in good condition
sK18250	# Paved road network of the city in other condition
sK18255	# Peak period

sKPI #	Key Performance Indicator name
sK18296	# Passenger-distance
sK18324	# Planned duration
sK18326	# Planned loading duration
sK18327	# Planned loading time
sK18331	# Planning time
sK18332	# Planning time index
sK18373	# Potholes
sK18425	# Professional staff (including engineers, managers, accountants) on the gvt payroll
sK18503	# Public transport vehicles per type over total population/area of the metropolis
sK18507	# Q-factor
sK18524	# Rail lines electrified
sK18525	# Rail lines un-electrified
sK18571	# Regional operators
sK18574	# Registered vehicles
sK18661	# Road accidents on non-urban roads
sK18662	# Road accidents on roads
sK18663	# Road accidents on urban roads
sK18664	# Road density
sK18665	# Road fatalities on non-urban roads
sK18666	# Road fatalities on roads
sK18667	# Road fatalities on urban roads
sK18669	# Road length per professional staff
sK18670	# Road network density in the city per type of road and per condition level
sK18682	# Route miles per capita
sK18702	# Rural classified roads
sK18703	# Rural classified roads in fair condition
sK18704	# Rural classified roads in good condition
sK18705	# Rural other roads
sK18706	# Rural other roads in fair condition
sK18707	# Rural other roads in good condition
sK18709	# Rural population living within 2km from a motorable road
sK18715	# Safety index
sK18721	# Same main send elements
sK18724	# Scheduled intermodal transit time
sK18764	# Self service channels
sK18777	# Service accessibility index
sK18778	# Service inquiries
sK18794	# Shifted wheel sets
sK18805	# Signals Passed at Danger (SPADs)
sK18813	# Size of operating vehicles (buses or minibuses) for this operator
sK18817	# Slow moving vehicle index
sK18832	# Speed

sKPI #	Key Performance Indicator name
sK18835	# Speed to formal and informal places of work by mode of transport
sK18869	# Stops
sK18872	# Strategic competence provision index
sK18913	# Suggestions received
sK18932	# Surveys conducted
sK18935	# Surveys on user friendliness of the transport system
sK18943	# Taxi in the city
sK18952	# Telephone enquiries made
sK18953	# Telephone messages of train tracker
sK18971	# Text of train tracker
sK19017	# Timetabled train km
sK19019	# Tonnage km transported per wagon
sK19032	# Track quality
sK19034	# Traffic count of heavy freight vehicles (trucks) on major roads
sK19035	# Traffic count of heavy freight vehicles (trucks) on rural classified roads
sK19036	# Traffic count of heavy freight vehicles (trucks) on urban roads
sK19037	# Traffic count of heavy passenger vehicles (buses) on major roads
sK19038	# Traffic count of heavy passenger vehicles (buses) on rural classified roads
sK19039	# Traffic count of heavy passenger vehicles (buses) on urban roads
sK19040	# Traffic count of IMTs on major roads
sK19041	# Traffic count of IMTs on rural classified roads
sK19042	# Traffic count of IMTs on urban roads
sK19043	# Traffic count of light vehicles on major roads
sK19044	# Traffic count of light vehicles on rural classified roads
sK19045	# Traffic count of light vehicles on urban roads
sK19048	# Traffic signals
sK19049	# Traffic signs
sK19050	# Traffic units per employee
sK19051	# Traffic volume
sK19052	# Train delays due to infrastructure
sK19053	# Train disruptions due to infrastructure
sK19054	# Train flows
sK19055	# Train length
sK19057	# Train speed
sK19058	# Train travel distance on (sub)urban rail system
sK19059	# Train travel distance per year
sK19071	# Transport distance
sK19073	# Transport sections
sK19077	# Transports
sK19083	# Travel speed
sK19089	# Travel time to formal and informal places of work in cities

sKPI #	Key Performance Indicator name
sK19096	# Trips per person by type
sK19097	# Trips per person by foot
sK19098	# Trips per person by individual motorized transport means
sK19099	# Trips per person by individual non-motorized transport means
sK19100	# Trips per person on individual public transport service
sK19101	# Trips per person on shared public transport services
sK19115	# Types of operated lines
sK19136	# Unpaved road network of the city
sK19137	# Unpaved road network of the city in fair condition
sK19138	# Unpaved road network of the city in good condition
sK19139	# Unpaved road network of the city in other condition
sK19158	# Urban road network length
sK19159	# Urban roads
sK19160	# Urban roads in fair condition
sK19161	# Urban roads in good condition
sK19162	# Urgent inspection remarks
sK19170	# Use of environmental hazardous material
sK19171	# Use of non-renewable materials
sK19204	# Vehicle kilometers traveled
sK19208	# Vehicles per day
sK19290	# Worked wheel sets
sK19310	$ Access revenue yield
sK19316	$ Administrative costs of agency responsible for a specific road network
sK19333	$ Amount required for road maintenance
sK19354	$ Budget deviation for permanent way
sK19357	$ Bus fare per passenger-km
sK19358	$ Bus fare per passenger-km on major roads
sK19359	$ Bus fare per passenger-km on rural roads
sK19390	$ Cost of exported good to the buyer (may not be the final user)
sK19391	$ Cost of imported good to final users
sK19392	$ Cost of internally traded good to final users
sK19395	$ Cost of transport of exported good
sK19396	$ Cost of transport of imported good
sK19397	$ Cost of transport of internally traded good
sK19450	$ Domestic trade
sK19468	$ Exports
sK19469	$ External funds (donor and private sectors) funds invested in the road
sK19474	$ Fare for bus services
sK19475	# Fare for individual motorized transport (IMT) services
sK19476	$ Fare for minibus services
sK19477	$ Fare for taxi services
sK19478	$ Fare per kilometer
sK19500	$ Franchised ordinary fares

sKPI #	Key Performance Indicator name
sK19501	$ Franchised passenger revenue
sK19502	$ Franchised season tickets
sK19503	$ Freight cost per unit shipped
sK19504	$ Freight rate per ton-km
sK19505	$ Freight rate per ton-km on major roads
sK19506	$ Freight rate per ton-km on rural roads
sK19507	$ Freight revenue
sK19511	$ Freight tariff
sK19518	$ Gas price
sK19525	$ Government expenditure
sK19526	$ Government expenditure in the road sub-sector
sK19527	$ Government expenditure in the transport sector
sK19528	$ Government spending on road maintenance
sK19531	$ Gravel road average construction cost
sK19553	$ Household spending on transport
sK19592	$ Maintenance cost per distance
sK19615	$ Most recent VOC in economic evaluation of road works
sK19628	$ Network rail profit after tax
sK19679	$ Paved road construction cost
sK19716	$ Rail operation costs
sK19718	$ Rail user charges
sK19777	$ Road assets value
sK19778	$ Road maintenance expenditures
sK19785	$ Routine and periodic maintenance expenditures
sK19788	$ Salary per type of employment
sK19804	$ Spending on the specific road network of which the agency is responsible
sK19817	$ Subsidy spending per capita
sK19825	$ Taxes collected from road users
sK19841	$ Imported container transport cost between unloading from ship to final city of destination for free on board shipping
sK19842	$ Imported container transport cost between unloading from ship to final city of destination
sK19860	$ Vehicle operating costs
sK19939	% Accessorials of total freight
sK19952	% Actual to required maintenance expenditure
sK20010	% Age of land use under Transportation
sK20011	% Age of roads with average speed less than 15kmph
sK20012	% Age of roads with average speed less than 30kmph
sK20013	% Age of VKT with average speed less than 15kmph
sK20014	% Age of VKT with average speed less than 30kmph
sK20027	% Agreed sector strategy followed
sK20042	% Annual government contribution to sector program
sK20044	% Annual review of road maintenance levy per road user charges
sK20170	% Calls abandoned
sK20171	% Calls answered

sKPI #	Key Performance Indicator name
sK20173	% Calls engaged
sK20183	% Capacity restrictions
sK20184	% Capacity utilization
sK20283	% Claims of freight costs
sK20357	% Complaints answered within 20 working days
sK20367	% Completion
sK20384	% Construction completed
sK20394	% Corrective maintenance including stand-by organization for immediate emergency maintenance
sK20407	% Coverage road sector taxation
sK20621	% Extent of infrastructure provision
sK20623	% External funds of road expenditure
sK20708	% Government effectively enforce axle load and traffic regulations
sK20827	% Inbound freight costs of purchases
sK20837	# Ballast
sK20840	# Rail laid
sK20842	# Switches and crossings
sK20976	% Maintenance expenditures covered by in-country resources
sK21028	% Monitor completion of activities
sK21069	% Mystery shopping calls
sK21075	% Network in good and fair condition
sK21135	% Outbound freight costs of net sales
sK21256	% Passengers in excess of capacity
sK21322	% Paved network
sK21464	% Public expenditure on transport out of GDP
sK21465	% Public expenditures on transport out of total expenditures
sK21468	% Public Transport Accessibility Index
sK21484	% Rail, ports and airports operations covered by user charges (or share of public subsidy)
sK21572	% Road administrative cost out of total road expenditure
sK21573	% Road carrying less traffic than the economic threshold of their type (50 vpd for gravel road and 250 vpd for paved road)
sK21574	% Road expenditure of GDP
sK21587	% Rural people who live within 2 km of an all-season passable road out of the total rural population
sK21621	% Semi-autonomous road agency created
sK21634	% Share for renewal to total track budget
sK21641	% Shipment visibility and traceability
sK21651	% Snow removal to cost
sK21885	% Train punctuality
sK21892	% Transit vehicles that arrives on time for its stops
sK21893	% Transport cost element of export/import and internally traded goods
sK21894	% Transport expenditure relative to household income
sK21896	% Travelling to places of work by foot

sKPI #	Key Performance Indicator name
sK21897	% Travelling to work by individual motorized transport means
sK21898	% Travelling to work by individual non-motorized transport means
sK21899	% Travelling to work by individual public transport services
sK21900	% Travelling to work by shared public transport services
sK21906	% Truckload capacity utilized
sK21951	% Utilization of bus fleet
sK21954	% Utilization of taxi fleet
sK21971	% Volume utilization of the main send element
sK21987	% Weight utilization
sK21988	% Weight utilization of the main send element
sK22006	$ Fare revenue per passenger trip
sK22009	% Intercity line segment share in total rail task
sK22010	% Intermodal state-to-state market share
sK22011	$ Operating cost per passenger trip
sK22012	$ Operating cost per vehicle revenue mile
sK22013	# Passenger trips per capita
sK22014	# Rail task, by line segment
sK22015	# Vehicle revenue hours per capita
sK22016	# Findings in compliance with established state policies
sK22017	% Adjudicated claims upheld
sK22018	% Claims resolved before adjudication (BOLI, EEOC, Tort, ERB)
sK22019	% Claims resolved before adjudication
sK18527	# Rail traffic density
sK5591	# Time to respond to traffic signal defects and make the traffic safe

Local Public Transport

Local public transport represents the delivery of local public transport services by public and private service providers. KPI examples in this subcategory reflect the utilization rates, efficiency ratios and infrastructure readiness.

sKPI #	Key Performance Indicator name
sK143	# Fuel consumption per 100 kilometers
sK265	$ Fuel cost
sK267	$ Freight revenue per ton-mile
sK2835	# Vehicles out of service
sK3516	% Passenger injury rate
sK3575	$ Operating expense per passenger
sK3590	# Fuel consumption
sK3591	# Fuel efficiency
sK3593	$ Vehicle revenue per liter of fuel
sK3594	$ Fuel cost savings per vehicle
sK3630	# Drivers per licensed vehicle
sK3649	% Vehicles on maintenance or repair
sK3650	# Passengers per vehicle per day (PPVPD)

sKPI #	Key Performance Indicator name
sK3652	# Passengers carried over road network by public transport
sK3695	# Kilometers traveled per vehicle
sK3696	# Passenger distance traveled per day
sK3723	% Passengers who purchased return tickets
sK3870	# Public transport route capacity
sK3871	# Public transport rolling stock capacity
sK3873	# Bus fleet operated
sK3874	# Bus routes in operation
sK3876	# Public transport network density
sK3877	$ Cost of transport to main tourist sites
sK3878	$ New public transport vehicles acquisition cost
sK3879	$ Daily traffic volume
sK3880	$ Public transport fare
sK3881	$ Monthly cost of work trips by public transport
sK3883	% Public transport share of all motorized trips to work
sK3884	$ Fare subsidy per passenger trip
sK3886	# Operating buses per kilometer of public transport network length
sK3888	# Passenger trips
sK3890	# Daily vehicle kilometers traveled
sK3891	# Ticket controllers per public transport vehicle
sK3896	# Public transport stations in operation
sK3897	# Public transport interchanges
sK3898	# Ticket revenue per operating bus
sK3900	# Taxi stands
sK3901	# Bus stops per square kilometer
sK3902	# Public transport routes
sK3903	# Ticket revenue per operating expense
sK3904	% Vehicles beyond useful life
sK3906	# Daily passenger journeys
sK3907	# Daily passengers
sK3908	# Daily trips per person
sK3909	% Motorized trips to work by public transport
sK3910	# Journey length for a public transport vehicle
sK3914	# In service bus kilometers delivered
sK3915	# Passenger boardings per trip operated
sK3917	% Passenger satisfaction with public transport quality
sK3918	# Age of public transport vehicles
sK3919	% Vehicles complying with the safety public transportation standards
sK3920	% Trips operated in full
sK3924	# Public transport fatalities
sK3927	% Satisfaction with public transport
sK3931	# In service bus hours delivered
sK3932	# Travel time for work trips by public transport
sK3935	% Utilization of public transport fleet

sKPI #	Key Performance Indicator name
sK4228	# Passengers injured
sK5223	% Citywide fleet that is hybrid or uses alternative fuel
sK14293	$ Operating expenditure per passenger km
sK14295	# Lane length of arterials per 1000 population
sK14296	# Stations
sK14297	% Use of fossil energy for all transport
sK14298	# Traffic noise
sK14299	% Efficiency of urban passenger transport
sK14300	# Road traffic fatalities per 100 million vehicle km, by all modes
sK14301	$ Bus subsidy payments for bus trips
sK14302	% Minibus bays at informal ranks
sK14303	% Employment
sK14304	# Overall quality rating
sK14305	% Households spending more than 10% of disposable income on public transport
sK14306	% Transport interchanges under good condition
sK14307	% Land transport freight weight transported by rail
sK14308	% Households within 15 minutes walk from bus stop
sK14309	% Subsidized bus services operating in terms of tendered or negotiated contracts
sK14311	% Network resilience
sK14312	% Public to private transport means
sK14313	$ Road transport user cost
sK14314	# Housing units developed in designated corridors in metropolitan areas
sK14315	# Floor space of housing units developed in designated corridors in metropolitan areas
sK14316	# Customer satisfaction with attributes of public transport modes
sK14317	% Increased trip reliability
sK14318	% Service cancellations
sK14319	% Passenger injury rate per million miles driven
sK14320	$ Expenditure by government in 13 priority rural nodes for infrastructure and operations
sK14321	$ Cost per motor vehicle incident
sK14407	# Active travel options
sK14421	# Additional dedicated scheduled distance
sK14448	# Age of bus fleet
sK14450	# Age of public transport rolling stock by mode
sK14521	# Annulled trips
sK14547	# Assaults per million service hours
sK14619	# Bids per route
sK14641	# Boarded passengers of access transit (including Taxi passengers)
sK14642	# Boarded passengers of conventional systems
sK14669	# Bus accidents involving personal injuries and deaths
sK14670	# Bus and taxi bays
sK14671	# Bus Bays per 1000 population

sKPI #	Key Performance Indicator name
sK14672	# Bus defects per vehicle examination
sK14673	# Bus kilometers operated for the year
sK14674	# Bus patronage
sK14675	# Bus routes operated
sK14676	# Bus shelters
sK14701	# Capacity of public transport facilities
sK14702	# Capacity of roads
sK14753	# Charter to flyer
sK14759	# Children boardings
sK14786	# Collisions and derailments per million kilometers
sK14787	# Collisions per million kms
sK14811	# Commuters of education trips
sK14812	# Commuters of work trips
sK14824	# Complaints of conventional systems
sK14825	# Complaints per 1,000 service hours of conventional systems
sK14826	# Complaints per 100,000 passengers
sK14832	# Complaints handled per million passenger trips
sK14842	# Condition of freeways and arterials
sK14916	# Crime at stations
sK14917	# Crime on trains
sK14979	# Daily public transport trips per person
sK14980	# Daily ridership
sK15027	# Deficiencies that was recorded
sK15075	# Depots held freehold by operators
sK15076	# Depots in use to provide contracted services
sK15077	# Depots owned or controlled
sK15078	# Depots which support the bus network
sK15104	# Distance to station
sK15122	# Door-to-door journey time by main mode
sK15263	# Fatalities for the Total Area
sK15285	# Fleet capacity
sK17085	# Travel time
sK17270	# Weekday ridership
sK17324	# Freight flows
sK17331	# Frequency during off-peak
sK17332	# Frequency during peak
sK17418	# Greenhouse gas emissions from all transport means
sK17574	# Index of emissions from air pollutants from road transport
sK17575	# Index of emissions intensity of the road vehicle fleet
sK17576	# Index of energy intensity of the road vehicle fleet
sK17577	# Index of incidence of injuries and fatalities from road transport
sK17578	# Index of relative household transport costs
sK17579	# Index of the relative cost of urban transit
sK17679	# Journey distance

sKPI #	Key Performance Indicator name
sK17699	# Lane length of freeways per 1,000 population
sK17731	# Length of access to surface
sK17733	# Length of connection to national railway
sK17734	# Length of double railway equivalent
sK17735	# Length of galleries
sK17750	# Length of parking area
sK17751	# Length of paved roads
sK17754	# Length of route built
sK17755	# Length of route in operation
sK17769	# Length of tunnels
sK17770	# Length of underground network lines
sK17813	# Licensed buses
sK17846	# Lost time frequency index per 200,000 hrs
sK17850	# Lost trips
sK17867	# Major injuries per million boarded passengers
sK17888	# Mean distance between failures (MDBF)
sK17939	# Minibus taxi bays per 1000 population
sK17960	# Motorized journeys by main mode
sK17961	# Motorized movement of freight
sK17962	# Motorized movement of people
sK17968	# Movement of light-duty passenger vehicles
sK18094	# Operating bus per km of route length
sK18095	# Operating employee per operating bus
sK18185	# Passenger attitude surveys conducted
sK18186	# Passenger boardings by passenger category
sK18187	# Passenger boardings per in-service vehicle kilometer
sK18188	# Passenger boardings per in-service vehicle hour
sK18192	# Passenger injuries per 1 million boarded passengers of access transit
sK18193	# Passenger injuries per 1 million boarded passengers of conventional systems
sK18199	# Passenger revenue kilometers
sK18207	# Passenger trips per all buses
sK18208	# Passenger trips per available buses
sK18209	# Passenger trips per vehicle hour
sK18211	# Passenger trips per vehicle revenue km
sK18214	# Passengers carried for the year
sK18218	# Passengers per car mile
sK18256	# Peak period Bus passenger departures per1000 population
sK18257	# Peak period passenger departures per 1000 population
sK18258	# Peak period Taxi seat per 1000 population
sK18259	# Peak period train capacity utilization
sK18260	# Peak period train passenger boarding
sK18261	# Pedestrian fatalities per 1000 population
sK18262	# Pedestrian fatalities per area
sK18278	# Perception of noise
sK18279	# Perception of personal safety
sK18280	# Perception of the urban realm
sK18390	# Preventable collisions per million kms
sK18499	# Public transport capacity
sK18500	# Public transport crowding
sK18501	# Public transport fatalities per 100 million vehicle km
sK18502	# Public transport fatalities per area
sK18526	# Rail patronage
sK18572	# Registered buses
sK18655	# Revenue passengers of conventional systems
sK18672	# Road traffic casualties
sK18673	# Road traffic fatalities per area
sK18674	# Road traffic fatalities per vehicle type
sK18683	# Route tender bids which have attracted only one bidder
sK18713	# Safety incidents
sK18728	# Scheduled train hours
sK18735	# Rating for bus cleanliness
sK18736	# Rating for bus ride comfort
sK18737	# Rating for bus temperature
sK18738	# Rating for driver courtesy
sK18739	# Rating for specific passenger facility attributes
sK18765	# Senior boardings
sK18779	# Service Hours of access transit
sK18780	# Service hours of conventional systems
sK18781	# Service improvement items
sK18782	# Service kilometers of access transit
sK18783	# Service kilometers of conventional systems
sK18790	# Service rationalization items
sK18831	# Specified supplier reports delivered within time frames as specified in the contract
sK18837	# Spills per million kms
sK18870	# Stops per km of route length
sK19068	# Transits
sK19069	# Transits per inhabitant for all modes of transport
sK19070	# Transits per inhabitant for mechanized modes of transport
sK19072	# Transport mobility of the population
sK19078	# Travel cost for work and education trips
sK19079	# Travel cost work or education trips per month
sK19080	# Travel demand
sK19081	# Travel modes used for work and education trips
sK19086	# Travel time for work and education trips
sK19090	# Travel time to work
sK19091	# Travel time work trips by public transport
sK19092	# TRE fixed route ridership

sKPI #	Key Performance Indicator name
sK19173	# User group meetings attended during the year
sK19205	# Vehicle revenue km per liter of fuel
sK19206	# Vehicle revenue km per operating bus
sK19207	# Vehicle revenue km per operating employee
sK19338	$ Annual bus subsidy per weekday passenger carried
sK19342	$ Annual operating subsidy per weekday passenger
sK19356	$ Bus fare
sK19364	$ Cash fares
sK19421	$ Cost per revenue car mile
sK19454	$ Dry hire bus payments
sK19463	$ Expenditure target for infrastructure and operations
sK19479	$ Fare per revenue passenger of conventional systems
sK19480	$ Fare revenue per passenger km
sK19481	$ Farebox revenue by time period
sK19490	$ Fixed payments
sK19491	$ Fleet depreciation
sK19513	$ Fuel payments
sK19515	$ Fuel tax concession rebate
sK19554	$ Implementation payments
sK19563	$ Integrated north-west network
sK19578	$ Labor reconciliation payments
sK19617	$ MRT fare
sK19627	$ Net subsidy
sK19629	$ New fleet periodic payment
sK19634	$ Operating cost per passenger kilometer of conventional systems
sK19635	$ Operating cost per revenue passenger of access transit
sK19636	$ Operating cost per service hour of access transit
sK19638	$ Operating cost per total vehicle kilometer of conventional systems
sK19640	$ Operating costs per passenger kilometer
sK19643	$ Operating expenditure per total vehicle km
sK19645	$ Operating expense per operating bus
sK19647	$ Operating expense per passenger trip
sK19648	$ Operating expense per vehicle hour
sK19649	$ Operating expense per vehicle revenue km
sK19653	$ Operating subsidies per area of origin of bus passengers
sK19664	$ Parking sakes
sK19667	$ Pass through lease payments
sK19677	$ Patronage benchmark payments
sK19678	$ Patronage change payments
sK19685	$ Payments for additional M2 services
sK19701	$ Prepaid fares
sK19717	$ Rail transport user cost
sK19750	$ Revenue car miles
sK19795	$ Service payments

sKPI #	Key Performance Indicator name
sK19816	$ Subsidy per passenger
sK19830	$ Ticker revenue per total expense
sK19831	$ Ticket revenue per operating bus
sK19832	$ Ticket revenue per operating expense
sK19833	$ Ticket revenue per passenger trip
sK19834	$ Tolling fees
sK19836	$ Train fares
sK19840	$ Transit revenue
sK19848	$ Union time compensation
sK19858	$ Various STA adjustments
sK19859	$ Vehicle loss cost per million miles driven
sK19861	$ Vehicle revenue per vehicle revenue km
sK19931	% Access of rural people to public transport within 2 km
sK19935	% Access to public transport
sK19936	% Accessibility of rail
sK19937	% Accessibility of road
sK19947	% Achievement of schedule
sK20009	% Affordability
sK20088	% Arterial LOS
sK20089	% Arterials under good condition
sK20355	% Commuters spending out of personal income on work trip
sK20358	% Complaints cleared up within 10 working days
sK20395	% Corridor Efficiency
sK20404	% Cost recovery by metropolitan contract region
sK20410	% Crime rates on public transport
sK20628	% Facilities at stations
sK20654	% Fleet utilization
sK20674	% Formal minibus taxi ranks under good condition
sK20677	% Freeway LOS
sK20678	% Freeways under good condition
sK20696	% Contribution of transport industry to GDP
sK20812	% Households living within 15 min walk from station
sK20813	% Households living within 15 min walk from taxi
sK20814	% Households living within 30 min walk from bus stop
sK20831	% Incident rate based on vehicle mileage
sK20832	% Incident rate by deliveries
sK20833	% Incident rate by loads
sK20834	% Incident rate by vehicles operated
sK20851	% Informal minibus taxi ranks under good condition
sK20852	% Infrastructure in good condition
sK20865	% Injury incident rate based on vehicle mileage
sK20911	% Journey time reliability
sK20986	% Mechanical reliability
sK21009	% Merseyside households with access to public transport

sKPI #	Key Performance Indicator name
sK21010	% Merseyside households within 13 minutes walk of an hourly or better bus service
sK21011	% Merseyside households within 400m of a bus/hail and ride route
sK21012	% Merseyside households within 400m of a public transport network
sK21013	% Merseyside households within 800m of a rail station
sK21018	% Minibus-taxi fleet recapitalized
sK21062	% Motor vehicle injury rates based on work hours
sK21063	% Motor vehicle passenger injury incident rate
sK21088	% NLTSF funding needs sourced from different levels of government
sK21119	% On-time performance
sK21121	% On-time running
sK21123	% Operating Cost Recovery of conventional systems
sK21128	% Operational capacity
sK21129	% Operator capability
sK21146	% Overloaded trucks on national and provincial roads
sK21258	% Households with access to public transport
sK21259	% Households within 13 minutes walk of an hourly or better bus service
sK21260	% Households within 400m of a bus/hail and ride route
sK21261	% Households within 400m of a public transport network
sK21262	% Households within 800m of a railway station
sK21325	% Peak period bus route capacity utilization
sK21326	% Peak period minibus taxi route capacity utilization
sK21367	% Planning capacity utilization
sK21469	% Public transport interchange peak period capacity utilization
sK21470	% Public transport interchanges with more than 95% peak capacity utilization
sK21471	% Public transport reliability
sK21472	% Public transport share of all motorized trips to work
sK21473	% Punctuality
sK21498	% Recovery ratio
sK21526	% Reliability (on time running)
sK21527	% Reliability of urban passenger transport
sK21568	% Ridership growth
sK21585	% Rural households with access to public transport
sK21586	% Rural households within 13 minutes walk of an hourly or better bus service
sK21597	% Public transport satisfaction index
sK21603	% Scheduled trips between 59 seconds before and 4 minutes and 59 seconds after the scheduled departure time at the selected points
sK21604	% Scheduled trips leaving origin stop between 59 seconds before and 4 minutes and 59 seconds after the scheduled departure time
sK21605	% Scheduled trips operated in full
sK21629	% Service hour delivered

sKPI #	Key Performance Indicator name
sK21630	% Service reliability
sK21637	% Share of passenger travel not held by land based public transport
sK21840	% Taxi rank peak period capacity utilization
sK21841	% Taxi ranks with more than 95% peak capacity utilization
sK21883	% Traffic reliability
sK21886	% Train Stations and other Public under good condition
sK21889	% Transferring substantial volumes of work
sK21904	% Trips cancelled
sK21905	% Trips missed
sK21949	% Use of urban land
sK21952	% Utilization of public transport facilities
sK21953	% Utilization of roads

Marine Transport/Shipping

Marine transport and shipping includes the transport of passengers or freight over water, whether scheduled or not. Also included are the operation of towing or pushing boats, excursion, cruise or sightseeing boats, ferries or water taxis. KPIs focus on all transportation operations (embarking, billing, transfer, debarking).

sKPI #	Key Performance Indicator name
sK12	% Passenger seats sold
sK57	# Seat availability
sK143	# Fuel consumption per 100 kilometers
sK235	% Transport capacity utilization
sK263	# Turnaround time
sK265	$ Fuel cost
sK267	$ Freight revenue per ton-mile
sK699	% Empty running
sK2540	# Critical equipment and system failures
sK3473	% Overnight workload accomplished
sK3487	# Port state control (PSC) inspected ships
sK3488	# Carbon dioxide vessel efficiency
sK3490	# Crew complaints
sK3496	# Navigation deficiency ratio
sK3497	# Cargo handling incidents
sK3503	% Port state control (PSC) detention rate
sK3516	% Passenger injury rate
sK3524	# Vessel operational deficiencies
sK3525	# Vessel groundings
sK3526	# Cargo units transported
sK3529	# Crew deficiencies reported
sK3544	# Marine safety deficiency ratio
sK3575	$ Operating expense per passenger
sK3590	# Fuel consumption
sK3727	# Transport volume handled by the port railway

sKPI #	Key Performance Indicator name
sK3728	# Vehicles transported by ferry service
sK3729	# Non containerized trade
sK3730	% Non-containerized trade
sK3731	% Trade by cargo type breakdown
sK3737	# Port state control (PSC) detentions
sK3738	# Vessel deficiencies recorded
sK3739	% Degree of containerization of the general cargo handled
sK3740	# Ballast water discharge violations
sK3741	# Container throughput
sK3746	% Container trade annual growth
sK3749	$ Freight cost per ton shipped
sK3750	% Freight bill accuracy
sK3751	# Vessels found having deficiencies
sK3754	% Inspected ships found having deficiencies
sK3755	% Vessel inspections with no deficiencies detected
sK3756	# Cadets per ship
sK3762	% Cargo damage rate
sK3763	# Coastal passenger transfers
sK3764	# Inland passenger transfers
sK3765	# Passengers transported by ferry service
sK3766	# Port state control (PSC) deficiency ratio
sK3767	% Vessel service reliability
sK3768	% Vessel fleet availability
sK3769	% Vessel reliability
sK3770	# Significant vessel incidents
sK3771	# Vessel collisions
sK3772	# Reportable vessel incidents
sK3773	# Navigational incidents recorded
sK3774	# Security deficiency ratio
sK3775	# Officers months on board
sK3777	# Severe spills of substances
sK3778	# Crew disciplinary issues
sK3779	# Damaged or lost cargo during voyage
sK3783	# Officer tenure
sK3784	# Transport capacity available
sK3785	# Transit time
sK3788	$ Vessel operating cost per hour
sK3790	$ Vessels maintenance cost
sK3793	% Officer retention rate
sK3794	% Vessel availability
sK3816	% Passenger vessels
sK3875	# Officers on board
sK3915	# Passenger boardings per trip operated
sK3916	$ Port handling cost per TEU (twenty foot equivalent unit)
sK3921	$ Cargo handling cost per ton of general cargo

sKPI #	Key Performance Indicator name
sK4155	# Passenger accommodations aboard the vessel
sK4169	$ Actual running cost and accruals per vessel
sK4177	$ Dry-docking costs
sK4222	$ Container shipping cost
sK4228	# Passengers injured
sK4238	% Cargo capacity from dead-weight tonnage
sK4402	# Absconded crew
sK4403	% Unavoidable officer terminations
sK4406	# Vetting deficiencies per inspection
sK4407	# Severe spills of bulk liquid
sK4438	# Vessels under technical management
sK4527	# Crew members sick more than 24 hours
sK4532	$ Cost of explosion incidents
sK4551	# Explosion incidents on-board of the vessel
sK4560	$ Lost cargo units value
sK4592	# Cadets under on board training
sK4599	# Marine environmental deficiencies
sK4603	# Drydocking time per vessel
sK5874	$ Daily cost per ship delayed in port
sK14380	# Accidental releases of substances covered by MARPOL in the environment
sK14381	# Accidental releases of substances
sK14413	# Actual dry-docking duration
sK14416	# Actual off-hire
sK14454	# Agreed dry-docking duration
sK14497	# Allisions
sK14590	# Axle load
sK14593	# Ballast water management violations
sK14604	# Beneficial officer terminations
sK14612	# Best practice initiated
sK14653	# Boxes
sK14683	# Cadets trained
sK14684	# Cadets on board fleet
sK14685	# Cadets per vessel
sK14686	# Cadets under training with the ship manager
sK14713	# Cargo accidents
sK14717	# Cargo handling
sK14718	# Cargo incidents
sK14719	# Cargo incidents during cargo operations
sK14720	# Cargo incidents during voyage
sK14722	# Cargo related incidents
sK14725	# Cargo units/passengers transported
sK14732	# Cases where a crew member is sick for more than hours
sK14733	# Cases where a crew member is sick for more than 24 hours
sK14734	# Cases where crew was not released on time

sKPI #	Key Performance Indicator name
sK14735	# Cases where drugs or alcohol is abused
sK14751	# Charges of criminal offences
sK14778	# Coastal passenger transportation
sK14785	# Collisions
sK14841	# Condition of class
sK14866	# Contained spills
sK14867	# Contained spills of bulk liquid
sK14868	# Containers handled
sK14870	# Container port traffic
sK14913	# Crew accidents
sK14914	# Crew disciplinary frequency
sK14915	# Crew not relieved on time
sK14919	# Criminal offence
sK14982	# Damaged or lost cargo units during cargo handling
sK14986	# Days delayed
sK15026	# Deficiencies per inspection
sK15098	# Dismissed crew members
sK15100	# Distance between origin and destination
sK15124	# Dredging
sK15136	# Dwelling time for containers in ports
sK15137	# Dwelling time of container
sK15139	# Early terminations
sK15234	# Explosion incidents
sK15237	# Exposure hours
sK15247	# Failure of critical equipment and systems
sK15259	# Fatalities
sK15261	# Fatalities due to injuries
sK15262	# Fatalities due to sickness
sK15273	# Marine flights
sK15274	# Marine passenger transportation
sK15275	# Marine shipping vehicle transportation
sK15279	# Fire and explosions
sK15280	# Fire incidents
sK17216	# Vessel under management
sK17218	# Vetting deficiencies
sK17219	# Vetting inspections
sK17222	# Violation of rest hours
sK17223	# Violations of MARPOL
sK17224	# Violations of rest hours
sK17427	# Gross weight of all shipments
sK17430	# Groundings
sK17463	# Health and safety related deficiencies
sK17610	# Inland passenger transportation
sK17626	# Inspections resulting in zero deficiencies
sK17841	# Logged warnings
sK17880	# Max. wet tonnes per wagon

sKPI #	Key Performance Indicator name
sK17977	# Navigational incidents
sK17980	# Near miss incidents
sK17992	# New cadets
sK18002	# New deficiencies identified from externals
sK18018	# New initiations
sK18027	# New ships
sK18074	# Officer days onboard all vessels under technical management (DOC)
sK18075	# Officer experience points
sK18076	# Officer terminations from whatever cause
sK18077	# Officer trainee man days
sK18078	# Officer working days
sK18079	# Officers retention rate
sK18081	# Oil major inspections
sK18086	# On time line count
sK18088	# Open yards
sK18100	# Operational deficiencies
sK18106	# Operational related deficiencies
sK18112	# Orders
sK18116	# Origin points
sK18191	# Passenger exposure hours
sK18194	# Passenger injury ratio
sK18215	# Passengers injured during cargo handling
sK18329	# Planned off-hire
sK18345	# Port state control inspections
sK18488	# PSC inspections resulting in a detention
sK18489	# PSC inspections resulting in zero deficiencies
sK18558	# Recorded external inspections
sK18579	# Releases of substances covered by MARPOL, to the environment
sK18593	# Reported crew deficiencies
sK18599	# Reported safety deficiencies
sK18648	# Retained clients in 3 year window
sK18712	# Safety deficiencies
sK18718	# Safety related deficiencies
sK18744	# Sea cargo transportation
sK18759	# Security deficiencies
sK18795	# Ship turnaround time
sK18796	# Ship waiting time in ports
sK18798	# Shipment visibility
sK18799	# Shipments in m3
sK19066	# Transit shed
sK19075	# Transport work
sK19122	# Unavoidable officer terminations
sK19312	$ Actual dry-docking costs
sK19319	$ Agreed dry-docking costs
sK19328	$ Airway bills

sKPI #	Key Performance Indicator name
sK19353	$ Budget control per vessel
sK19407	$ Cost per crew
sK19445	$ Deviation
sK19446	$ Deviation of repairs and maintenance costs from budget
sK19455	$ Dry-Ice surcharge
sK19514	$ Fuel surcharge
sK19556	$ Inbound freight costs
sK19657	$ Outbound freight costs
sK19696	$ Port fee charged per imported container
sK19697	$ Port operation costs
sK19698	$ Port user charges
sK19705	$ Profit margin
sK19805	$ Transportation spending
sK19808	$ Transportation spending per given time period

sKPI #	Key Performance Indicator name
sK19820	$ Surcharges
sK19864	$ Vessel running cost budget
sK19921	% Absorption
sK19938	% Accessorials
sK19954	% Actual unavailability
sK20161	% Bunker costs to budget
sK20366	% Completed observations
sK20681	% Fuel Efficiency
sK20722	% Growth on profit year on year
sK21120	% On-time pickups
sK21122	% On time value rate
sK21388	% Port state control deficiency rate
sK21459	% Proposed observations initiated
sK21881	% Total Recordable Injury Frequency Rate (TRIFR)
sK3937	# Reefer containers handled per month

Utilities

Utilities refers to providing finished service (generation of electricity, fuel, and power) for commercial, industrial and residential use, consisting of both utility systems construction (generation facilities, distribution lines and related buildings) and distribution.

Electricity

Electricity includes the generation of bulk electric power, transmission from generating facilities to distribution centers and distribution to end users. In more detail, it includes the operation of generation facilities that produce electric energy, including thermal, nuclear, hydroelectric, gas turbine, and diesel; operation of transmission systems that convey the electricity from the generation facility to the distribution system; operation of distribution systems (i.e. consisting of lines, poles, meters, and wiring) that convey electric power received from the generation facility or the transmission system to the final consumer; sale of electricity to the user. KPIs focus on the efficiency and effectiveness of related processes and stakeholders performance.

sKPI #	Key Performance Indicator name
sK918	% Power generation capacity sufficiency
sK1045	# Disputes involving the Energy Ombudsman
sK1102	% Connected households with reliable supply of electricity
sK1128	% Households with formal mains electricity supply
sK1129	% Properties with metered connection to electricity
sK4816	% Electricity demand growth
sK4817	# Power stations upgraded
sK4821	% Villages with access to electricity
sK4822	# Length of electricity lines
sK4824	% Electrical energy losses in transmission cable
sK4825	% Electrical energy losses in transformers
sK4827	# Daily electric power losses between power plant and user

sKPI #	Key Performance Indicator name
sK4828	% Electricity transported on company's distribution network
sK4829	# Domestic electricity demand
sK4831	% Electricity demand met by domestic generation
sK4832	% Net electricity imports
sK4833	% Availability of power generation plants
sK4834	% Availability of transmission lines
sK4837	# Delivery point unavailability (DPUI)
sK4838	# Frequency deviation (FD)
sK4839	# Voltage deviation (VD)
sK4840	# Transformer tripping due to associate failure
sK4841	# Transformer tripping due to external faults or other clauses
sK4842	# Transformer age profile
sK4843	# Transmission line tripping due to associate failure
sK4844	# Transmission line tripping due to external faults or other clauses
sK4845	# Transmission line age profile
sK4846	# Transformer age
sK4847	# Electricity unavailability index
sK4848	# Planned transmission outages
sK4849	# Planned generating units outages
sK4853	# Transmission outages at distribution level
sK4854	# Energy unsupplied due to incidents
sK4855	# Energy supply interruption incidents
sK4858	# Electricity consumption intensity

sKPI #	Key Performance Indicator name
sK4859	# Electricity consumption per capita
sK4860	# Transformers capacity
sK4861	# Electricity substations operational
sK4863	$ Overhead transmission line maintenance cost to network coverage ratio
sK4864	$ Electric power substation maintenance cost
sK4865	# Voltage complaints received
sK4866	% Actual meter readings
sK4867	# Energy not supplied
sK4870	# Applications for a new connection or modification of the existing connection
sK4871	# Connection applications receiving the technical acceptance on time
sK4872	# Applications of contracts for electricity distribution service per categories of users
sK4873	# Applications for electricity distribution contracts favorably solved within the specified period
sK4874	# Incidents per level of voltage
sK4875	# Electricity supplied to national grid
sK4876	# Electricity billed
sK4877	# Low and medium voltage network to high voltage network length ratio
sK4878	# Capacity utilization factor
sK4879	# Power plant load factor
sK4880	% Electricity reserve margin
sK4881	# Self sufficiency of electricity generation ratio
sK4882	# Utility customer density
sK4883	% Transformer failure rate
sK4884	% Utility service bills collection rate
sK4885	# Accounts receivable in days of utility bill equivalent
sK4887	% Share of electricity billed by voltage level
sK4890	$ Revenue billed per kilowatt hour (kWh)
sK4891	$ Operating expense of electricity supplied to national grid
sK4892	$ Capital expenditures per kilowatt hour (kWh) generated
sK4893	$ Cost of electricity generation
sK4894	$ Book value of gross fixed assets per kWh of electricity billed
sK4895	# Electricity sold per employee
sK4896	% Utility electrification rate
sK4897	$ Electricity connection charge
sK4898	% Residential connections with an operating meter
sK4899	% Share of meters offering prepayment facilities
sK4901	# Reaction time to restore power
sK4902	% Share of underground power grid line
sK4903	# Interruptions of electricity supply
sK4904	# System Average Interruption Duration Index (SAIDI)
sK4905	# Customer Average Interruption Duration Index (CAIDI)

sKPI #	Key Performance Indicator name
sK4906	# Voltage excursion events per 1000 km of system length
sK4908	$ Operating and maintenance cost per network kilometer
sK4909	$ Operating and maintenance cost per kW of maximum demand
sK4910	% Transformer utilization rate
sK4911	$ Asset replacement cost per kWh
sK4912	$ Asset replacement cost per network kilometer
sK4914	% Defective meters replaced
sK4915	# Meters per meter reader
sK4916	# Completed meter readings per meter reader
sK4917	# Daytime energy consumption
sK4918	# Nighttime energy consumption
sK4919	# Length of overhead network
sK4920	# Length of underground cables
sK4933	# Consumers hours of supply per 1000 customers
sK4949	# Active utility meters
sK4962	# Utility service disconnection requests
sK4963	# Utility service connection requests
sK4965	# Utility meters consolidation requests
sK5137	# New services installed
sK5139	$ Operating and maintenance cost per megawatt - hour (MWh)
sK5153	$ Operating and maintenance cost of the power grid per customer
sK5213	# System Average Interruption Frequency Index (SAIFI)
sK5214	% Electricity supply not restored within 2 hours
sK14961	# Customers on installment plans
sK14963	# Customers paying refundable advances
sK15128	# Dual-fuel customers
sK15160	# Electricity consumption per GDP
sK15278	# Final consumption
sK17571	# Indigenous production
sK18137	# Overload events
sK18398	# Primary energy supply
sK18399	# Primary energy supply per unit of GDP
sK19735	$ Retail electricity sales
sK19868	$ Wholesale electricity price
sK20599	% Energy efficiency
sK20600	% Energy intensity
sK20702	% Generation by fuel source
sK21636	% Share of electricity from renewable source
sK21938	% Uptake of online billing

Natural Gas

Gas includes the distribution of natural or synthetic gas to the consumer through a system of mains. Gas marketers or brokers, who arrange the sale of natural gas over distribution systems operated by others, are included. KPIs focus on the efficiency and effectiveness of related processes and stakeholders performance.

sKPI #	Key Performance Indicator name
sK1058	% Network leak surveyed
sK1067	# Hours gas pipeline not operational
sK1084	# Duration of gas suppy planned interruptions
sK1090	# Customers affected by gas interruption
sK1093	# Reconnected utility service after payment
sK4882	# Utility customer density
sK4884	% Utility service bills collection rate
sK4885	# Accounts receivable in days of utility bill equivalent
sK4898	% Residential connections with an operating meter
sK4914	% Defective meters replaced
sK4915	# Meters per meter reader
sK4916	# Completed meter readings per meter reader
sK4921	% Gas supply capacity sufficiency
sK4922	% Households with access to the gas network
sK4923	# Gas leaks reported
sK4925	# Gas network pipe length
sK4926	# Quantity of gas entering each gas network
sK4927	# Quantity of gas delivered to custody transfer points
sK4928	# New areas connected to gas supply
sK4929	# Gas leaks reported to network operator by third parties
sK4930	# Reported mechanical damage incidents to gas networks
sK4931	# Consumers connected to the gas network
sK4932	# New customers connected to the utility network
sK4933	# Consumers hours of supply
sK4934	# Unplanned losses of gas supply up to the meter
sK4935	# Instances of poor supply pressure recorded and confirmed
sK4936	# Recorded instances of non compliant gas entering the network
sK4937	# Recorded instances of odorant level out of specification anywhere within the gas network
sK4938	# Gas incidents responded to
sK4939	# Incidents per 1,000 kilometers of gas pipeline
sK4940	# Ignitions per 1,000 kilometers or miles of gas pipeline
sK4941	# Injuries per 1,000 kilometers of gas pipeline
sK4942	# Property damage per 1,000 kilometers of gas pipeline
sK4943	# Field inspections performed
sK4944	# Defects identified to the gas network
sK4945	# Repairs required to the gas network
sK4946	# Gas over pressure events
sK4947	# Gas pipeline temperature excursions

sKPI #	Key Performance Indicator name
sK4948	# Unplanned or abnormal gas incidents
sK4949	# Active utility meters
sK4950	# Reported unplanned outages affecting one customer
sK4951	# Customers affected by unplanned gas supply outages
sK4952	# Customers affected by repeated unplanned gas supply outages
sK4953	# Planned gas interruptions
sK4954	# Unauthorized activities in the vicinity of transmission pipelines
sK4955	# Low pressure gas services replaced with high pressure gas services
sK4956	# Length of low pressure gas mains decommissioned and replaced
sK4957	# Emergency preparedness exercises
sK4958	% Gas emergency jobs responded within the specified time frame
sK4962	# Utility service disconnection requests
sK4963	# Utility service connection requests
sK4964	# Utility service relocation requests
sK4965	# Utility meters consolidation requests
sK5066	# Kilometers of pipe subject to leak assessment
sK5086	# Gas leaks found during gas network leak surveys
sK5096	# Gas leaks per 10 kilometers of gas network surveyed
sK5137	# New services installed
sK5180	# Emergency simulations completed
sK14395	# Acres of land in total will experience significantly elevated soil temperatures
sK14400	# Actions not addressed within the scheduled maintenance program
sK14406	# Active gas meters
sK14412	# Actual disconnections
sK14427	# Administrative processes or customer service complaints
sK14526	# Appointments not met within 15 minutes of scheduled time
sK14530	# Approved regasification projects
sK14691	# Call center calls dispatched to distribution company
sK14697	# Capacities of gas pipelines
sK14737	# Cathodic Protection (CP) units on pipeline
sK14738	# Cathodic Protection (CP) units that have not been operating correctly
sK14821	# Complaints about connection and augmentation
sK14822	# Complaints about other issues
sK14823	# Complaints about quality and reliability of supply
sK14848	# Connection and augmentation complaints
sK14850	# Connections made
sK14853	# Connections not made within 3 days of agreed date
sK14904	# CP units on network
sK14906	# CP units that have not been operating correctly (in accordance with AS28321 criteria)

sKPI #	Key Performance Indicator name
sK14929	# Cumulative existing and proposed regasification
sK14943	# Customer minutes of gas supply lost through unplanned outages
sK14944	# Customer minutes of gas supply lost through unplanned outages for entire company
sK14945	# Customer minutes of gas supply lost due to planned interruptions
sK14951	# Customers affected by 3 or more unplanned outages within the reporting period
sK14955	# Customers affected by repeated unplanned outages
sK14957	# Customers affected by unplanned outages
sK14958	# Customers affected by unplanned outages for entire company
sK14959	# Customers disconnected at the same supply address
sK14960	# Customers disconnected previously on a budget installment plan
sK14962	# Customers on payment plans
sK14964	# Customers reconnected previously on a budget installment plan
sK14965	# Customers reconnected who were previously disconnected at the same supply address and name
sK14975	# Daily demand across the full reporting period
sK15018	# Defects identified requiring attention
sK15019	# Defects identified that require action
sK15020	# Defects identified requiring action not addressed within the scheduled period
sK15023	# Defects that require action not rectified in the scheduled timeframes
sK15092	# Non-residential customers reconnected at the same supply address and name
sK15093	# Residential customers reconnected at the same supply address and name
sK15094	# Disconnection notices dispatched
sK15095	# Disconnection notices issued
sK15101	# Distance from the pipeline at which elevated soil temperature is deemed undetectable
sK15107	# Distribution customers
sK15108	# Distribution customers with domestic active meters
sK15109	# Distribution customers with non-domestic active meters
sK15110	# Distribution mains damages
sK15112	# Distribution outlets per km of gas mains
sK15113	# Distribution services damages
sK15119	# Domestic customer arranged appointments made in the reporting period
sK15120	# Domestic gas as consumption
sK15134	# Duration of unplanned outages
sK15174	# Emergencies responded
sK15175	# Emergencies that were not responded to within 60 minutes of receipt of notification
sK15181	# Emergency exercises or simulations conducted
sK15182	# Emergency exercises performed

sKPI #	Key Performance Indicator name
sK15215	# Estimated gas throughputs
sK15216	# Estimated natural gas reserves
sK15218	# Estimated reserves to production ratio
sK15226	# Expected changes to soil temperature profiles
sK15239	# Extent of excursions
sK15568	# Incidents that were not responded to within 60 minutes of receipt of notification
sK15569	# Incidents which occurred after notification of work being performed
sK15609	# Injuries that occurred in the reporting period
sK17144	# Unplanned outages
sK17229	# Voltage
sK17230	# Voltage excursions
sK17285	# Wobbe Index
sK17376	# Gas accounts subject to payment plans
sK17383	# Gas odorization
sK17406	# Government funded rebate customer reconnected
sK17437	# Guranteed Service Levels (GSL) payments for late arrival for a gas fault or emergency appointment
sK17438	# Guranteed Service Levels (GSL) payments for late establishment of a gas service
sK17439	# Guranteed Service Levels (GSL) payments for more than 4 unplanned interruptions in a calendar year
sK17440	# Guranteed Service Levels (GSL) payments for unplanned interruptions greater than 12 hours continuously
sK17441	# Guranteed Service Levels (GSL) payments payable as a result of interruptions within a calendar year
sK17442	# Guranteed Service Levels (GSL) payments payable for appointment times not met
sK17443	# Guranteed Service Levels (GSL) payments payable to customers for connection delays
sK17444	# Guranteed Service Levels (GSL) payments payable to domestic customers for appointments not met
sK17445	# Guranteed Service Levels (GSL) payments payable to specific customers as a result of 5 unplanned interruptions within a calendar year
sK17465	# Heat flux from the proposed pipeline into the surrounding soil
sK17472	# Demand record within the reporting period
sK17514	# Hours of gas supply lost through unplanned outages
sK17520	# Duration pipelines not operational
sK17521	# Duration pipelines not operational per year
sK17522	# Duration pipelines or a part thereof not operational
sK17523	# Duration pipelines or a part thereof not operational per year
sK17544	# Ignitions that occurred in the reporting period
sK17565	# Incidents in the reporting period
sK17567	# Incidents responded
sK17597	# Inerts
sK17630	# Integrity related actions identified

sKPI #	Key Performance Indicator name
sK17652	# Interruption duration
sK17653	# Interruptions per customer
sK17682	# Kilometers covered by Cathodic Protection (CP) system
sK17683	# Kilometers of pipe subjected to leak surveys
sK17684	# Kilometers pigged
sK17696	# Land owners affected by pipeline
sK17697	# Land owners have changed in area since last contact
sK17714	# Leak repairs
sK17715	# Leak repairs-mains
sK17716	# Leak repairs-meters
sK17717	# Leak repairs-service connections
sK17718	# Leaks detected on mains
sK17719	# Leaks found during leaks surveys
sK17720	# Leaks per 10km of survey
sK17732	# Length of all gas mains installed and in service
sK17736	# Length of gas distribution mains
sK17737	# Length of gas distribution mains constructed from cast iron
sK17738	# Length of gas distribution mains constructed from polyethylene
sK17739	# Length of gas distribution mains constructed from protected steel
sK17740	# Length of gas distribution mains constructed from PVC
sK17741	# Length of gas distribution mains constructed from unprotected steel
sK17742	# Length of gas distribution mains with high pressure
sK17743	# Length of gas distribution mains with low pressure
sK17744	# Length of gas distribution mains with medium pressure
sK17745	# Length of gas transmission pipelines
sK17747	# Length of low pressure gas mains decommissioned and replaced by high pressure gas mains
sK17748	# Length of low pressure gas mains decommissioned and replaced with HP
sK17749	# Length of mains surveyed
sK17778	# Level of over pressure
sK17781	# Ignitions ocurence
sK17834	# LOC events in the reporting period
sK17835	# LOC events in a given period
sK17854	# Low pressure services replaced with high pressure services
sK17889	# Mechanical damage incidents
sK17920	# Mercaptan sulphur
sK17924	# Meter exchanges
sK17944	# Minutes of gas supply lost through planned customer outages
sK17945	# Minutes-off-supply per customer
sK17979	# Near miss events per one thousand kilometres per year

sKPI #	Key Performance Indicator name
sK17989	# Network incident reports
sK17990	# Network pipe length by pressure class
sK17998	# New connection times for the slowest 10%
sK17999	# New connections
sK18000	# New customers connected to the network
sK18024	# New regions connected to gas supply
sK18045	# Non-conformances identified in the Safety and Operating Plan (SOP) Audit
sK18046	# Non-conformances not corrected within a scheduled rectification period
sK18047	# Non-domestic gas consumption
sK18049	# Non-residential customer direct debit plan terminations
sK18050	# Non-residential customers
sK18051	# Non-residential customers disconnected for failure to pay
sK18052	# Non-residential customers on installment plans
sK18053	# Non-residential customers who have lodged security deposits
sK18069	# Objectionable constituents
sK18117	# Original accounts issued
sK18132	# Outstanding leaks
sK18133	# Over pressure events
sK18253	# Peak gas demand
sK18319	# Planned customer interruptions
sK18320	# Duration of planned customer interruptions
sK18325	# Planned interruptions
sK18328	# Duration of planned mains and renewal interruptions
sK18408	# Priority A & B publicly reported leaks of mains repaired
sK18409	# Length of priority A & B publicly reported leaks repaired
sK18410	# Priority A & B publicly reported leaks on services repaired
sK18411	# Priority A & B publicly reported leaks repaired
sK18481	# Projected gas reserves
sK18482	# Projected regasification terminal delivery
sK18485	# Property damages in the reporting period
sK18513	# Quality of supply complaints
sK18514	# Quantity of gas delivered to custody transfer points in each gas network
sK18515	# Quantity of gas entering each gas network system
sK18554	# Reconnections
sK18555	# Reconnections in the same name
sK18556	# Reconnections in the same name after disconnection
sK18557	# Reconnections within 7 days
sK18559	# Recorded instances of odorant level out of specification anywhere within network
sK18560	# Recorded mechanical damage incidents to gas networks

sKPI #	Key Performance Indicator name
sK18561	# Recorded mechanical damage incidents to gas networks by pressure class
sK18562	# Recorded mechanical damage incidents to gas networks by source
sK18563	# Recorded mechanical damage incidents to gas networks by type
sK18580	# Reliability of supply complaints
sK18581	# Reminder notices dispatched
sK18584	# Repairs carried out
sK18585	# Repairs identified that require action
sK18586	# Repairs identified as requiring action and not addressed on time
sK18587	# Repairs required
sK18590	# Reportable frequency excursions
sK18596	# Reported mechanical damage of network per 1,000 customers
sK18597	# Reported mechanical damage of network per 10km
sK18616	# Residential customer direct debit plan terminations
sK18617	# Residential customers
sK18618	# Residential customers disconnected for failure to pay
sK18619	# Residential customers on installment plans
sK18620	# Residential customers that switched from another retailer
sK18621	# Residential customers who have lodged security deposits
sK18635	# Response times to emergencies
sK18914	# Supervised activities around the pipeline area
sK18915	# Supervised activities around the pipeline easement area
sK18916	# Supervised activities per one thousand kilometers
sK18954	# Temperature excursions
sK18955	# Temperature of the proposed pipeline
sK18972	# Third party activities by patrol identified that did not previously contact the operator
sK19015	# Times loss of operations has occurred
sK19076	# Transported in the reporting period
sK19119	# Unaccounted for gas
sK19120	# Unauthorized activities in vicinity of transmission pipelines
sK19141	# Unplanned losses of supply up to the meter where 5 or more consumers were affected
sK19142	# Unplanned or abnormal incidents
sK19145	# Unplanned outages affecting domestic customers
sK19146	# Unplanned outages affecting domestic customers due to damage
sK19147	# Unplanned outages affecting non-domestic customers
sK19148	# Unplanned outages affecting non-domestic customers due to damage
sK19157	# Unsupplied energy
sK19532	$ Guranteed Service Levels (GSL) payments for late arrival for a gas fault or emergency appointment

sKPI #	Key Performance Indicator name
sK19533	$ Guranteed Service Levels (GSL) payments for late establishment of a gas service
sK19534	$ Guranteed Service Levels (GSL) payments for more than 4 unplanned interruptions in a calendar year
sK19535	$ Guranteed Service Levels (GSL) payments for unplanned interruptions greater than 12 hours continuously
sK19584	$ LNG delivered costs
sK19680	$ Payable as Guranteed Service Levels (GSL) payments for appointments not met
sK19681	$ Payable to customers as Guranteed Service Levels (GSL) payments for connection delays
sK19682	$ Payable to customers as Guranteed Service Levels (GSL) payments resulting from interruptions
sK19683	$ Payable to domestic customers as GSL payments for appointments not met
sK19684	$ Guranteed Service Levels (GSL) payments as a result of 5 unplanned interruptions within a calendar year
sK19723	$ Regasification, liquefaction and pipeline to liquefaction
sK19867	$ Wellhead netback
sK19949	% Activities that contacted call center systems
sK19951	% Activity that contacted the Operator
sK20175	% Calls responded within time frame
sK20207	% Cathodic Protection (CP) units operating correctly
sK20274	% Circuit system availability
sK20409	% CP units operating correctly
sK20427	% Customers disconnected at the same supply address
sK20428	% Customers disconnected previously on a budget installment plan
sK20436	% Customers reconnected who were previously disconnected at the same supply address and name
sK20486	% Disconnected government funded rebate customers reconnected
sK20487	% Non-residential customers reconnected at the same supply address and name
sK20488	% Residential customers reconnected at the same supply address and name
sK20504	% Domestic gas consumption change
sK20524	% Emergency jobs responded to within the specified time
sK20614	% Existing and proposed regasification
sK20694	% Gas distribution outlets per km of gas mains from previous year
sK20709	% Government funded rebate customers disconnected
sK20925	% Land owners contacted within a given period
sK21076	% New connections on-time
sK21090	% Non-domestic gas consumption change
sK21093	% Non-residential customers disconnected for failure to pay
sK21094	% Non-residential customers on installment plans
sK21095	% Non-residential customers who have lodged security deposits

sKPI #	Key Performance Indicator name
sK21359	% Pipeline segment covered by Cathodic Protection (CP)
sK21360	% Pipeline segment covered by CP
sK21361	% Pipelines segments that have been pigged in the last 5 years
sK21365	% Planned unavailability
sK21497	% Reconnections on-time
sK21545	% Residential customer direct debit plans terminated
sK21546	% Residential customers disconnected for failure to pay
sK21547	% Residential customers on installment plans
sK21548	% Residential customers who have lodged security deposits
sK21794	% Summer system availability
sK21990	% Winter peak system availability
sK23059	% Accuracy of contracts
sK23060	% Accuracy of scheduled gas volumes
sK23061	% Attitude of continuous improvement
sK23062	% Customer service orientation of company representatives
sK23063	% Ease of contacting right person
sK23064	% Effectiveness of after-hours support
sK23065	% Execution of transportation requests
sK23066	% Expertise of personnel
sK23067	% Reliability of gas transportation
sK23068	% Timeliness of notification prior to restrictions
sK23069	% Timeliness of problem resolution

Water and Sewage

Water and sewage includes the supply of drinking water and waste water including sewage treatment to households and industry. KPIs focus on the efficiency and effectiveness of related processes and stakeholders performance.

sKPI #	Key Performance Indicator name
sK180	# Residual household waste per household
sK184	# Water consumption per capita
sK185	# Supplied water volume per person
sK1101	% Sewage treatment capacity sufficiency
sK1124	% Amount of water lost before arrival to the consumers
sK4882	# Utility customer density
sK4884	% Utility service bills collection rate
sK4885	# Accounts receivable in days of utility bill equivalent
sK4898	% Residential connections with an operating meter
sK4914	% Defective meters replaced
sK4915	# Meters per meter reader
sK4916	# Completed meter readings per meter reader
sK4933	# Consumers hours of supply per 1000 customers
sK4949	# Active utility meters
sK4962	# Utility service disconnection requests
sK4963	# Utility service connection requests
sK4965	# Utility meters consolidation requests

sKPI #	Key Performance Indicator name
sK4968	% Functional meters
sK4969	# Unplanned water interruptions per property
sK4971	% Households with reliable supply of water
sK4972	% Properties that experienced an unplanned water interruption
sK4973	% Water supply continuity
sK4974	% Drinking water compliance rate
sK4975	# Incidents of sewer flooding
sK4976	# Properties affected by low water pressure
sK4977	# Length of sewer pipes renewed
sK4978	# Daily metered water consumption per capita
sK4979	# Gross volume of water resource available
sK4980	% Water connection rate
sK4981	% Urban wastewater treatment rate
sK4982	% Industrial wastewater treatment rate
sK4983	% Properties that experienced a planned water interruption
sK4984	% Solid capture rate for inland sewage treatment plants (STPs) and ocean STPs
sK4985	% Water biosolid residuals produced and reused
sK4988	% Water tests that meet the drinking water guidelines and standards
sK4989	% Compliance with water health guideline values
sK4990	% Compliance with water aesthetic guideline values
sK4995	# Drinking water saved on account of demand management programs
sK4998	% Beach watch and harbor-watch sites complying with swimming water quality guidelines
sK4999	# Mass of phosphorus discharged to rivers from inland sewage treatment plants
sK5000	# Mass of nitrogen discharged to rivers from inland sewage treatment plants
sK5001	# Mass of suspended solids discharged from ocean sewage treatment plants
sK5002	# Mass of grease discharged from ocean sewage treatment plants
sK5003	% Controlled sewage overflows that occur in dry or wet weather
sK5004	# Treated wastewater discharged in the environment
sK5005	# Wastewater reused or prevented from entering waterways
sK5006	# Properties affected by uncontrolled sewage water overflows
sK5007	# Properties affected by repeat sewage overflows
sK5008	# Response time to sewage overflows
sK5009	# Frequency of sewer main breaks and blockages per 1,000 properties
sK5010	% Population with access to piped water
sK5015	% Households with access to safe water
sK5016	# Non residential water connections
sK5017	# Residential sewerage connections
sK5019	# Non residential sewerage connections

sKPI #	Key Performance Indicator name
sK5022	% Samples passing test against relevant standard for residual chlorine
sK5023	% Waste water subject to primary treatment
sK5024	# Water production
sK5026	# Water consumption
sK5027	% Properties below minimum water pressure
sK5028	% Properties below minimum water flow
sK5029	# Odor sewerage complaints per 1,000 connections
sK5030	# Total length of water distribution mains replaced
sK5032	% Wastewater treatment plants that are nonfunctional
sK5033	% Waste water treated
sK5034	% Waste water treated through complex means
sK5035	# Pipe breaks per kilometer of the water distribution network
sK5036	# Pipe blockages per kilometer of water distribution network
sK5037	# Pipe blockages per kilometer of sewers
sK5038	# Staff per thousand water connections
sK5039	$ Total water operating revenue
sK5040	$ Revenue per cubic meter of water billed
sK5041	$ Revenue per water connection
sK5042	# Volume of sewage collected per property
sK5043	$ Revenue per waste water connection
sK5044	$ Operating expenses per cubic meter of water billed
sK5045	% Non revenue water
sK5046	$ Connection charge for water
sK5047	$ Connection charge for sewerage
sK5048	% Water reservoir level
sK5049	# Water wells installed
sK5050	% Water coverage
sK5051	% Piped water network growth
sK5052	# Water production per capita
sK5053	% Sewerage services coverage
sK5054	% Unaccounted for water (UFW)
sK5055	# Water pumping stations in service
sK5056	# Population supplied with water
sK5057	# Properties with a water main available
sK5058	# Quantity of recycled water supplied
sK5059	# Length of sewers owned and operated
sK5060	# Sewage pumping stations in service
sK5061	# Operational sewage treatment plants
sK5062	# Waste water collected for recycling
sK5063	# Population with sewerage connections
sK5064	# Properties with a sewer main available
sK5065	# Length of stormwater channels under management
sK5067	% Customer satisfaction with water quality and distribution performance
sK5068	% Water saving rate

sKPI #	Key Performance Indicator name
sK5069	# Volume of waste water recycled
sK5070	# Volume of wastewater collected and treated
sK5071	# Properties provided with stormwater drainage facilities
sK5072	# Properties experiencing a planned water interruption
sK5073	% Water transmission and distribution losses
sK5074	# Properties experiencing unplanned water interruptions
sK5075	# Planned water interruptions per property
sK5076	# Consumer complaints per 1,000 properties connections
sK5101	# Fresh water withdrawn for business use
sK5111	% Recycled water used
sK5112	% Fresh water used
sK5129	# Volume of water leakage per property
sK5130	# Volume of water leakage per kilometer of water main
sK5131	# Water reservoir capacity
sK5132	# Volume of desalinated water produced
sK5133	# Length of sewer extensions
sK5134	# Sewer mains blockages cleared
sK5135	# Length of water mains inspected for leakages
sK5136	# Length of sewer mains inspected and cleaned
sK5137	# New services installed
sK5138	# Samples collected
sK5146	# Utility services replacements
sK5147	# Water and sewage tests carried out
sK5150	# Properties served per kilometer of sewer main
sK5154	% Sewerage volume treated that complied with standards
sK5155	% Urban properties without sewerage service
sK5156	% Sewerage treatment works compliant at all times
sK5159	# Volume of water sourced by category
sK5160	# Water treatment plants providing full treatment
sK5167	% Sewage service complaints
sK5168	# Sewerage break repair time
sK5169	# Frequency of unplanned interruptions per 1,000 properties
sK5173	# Customers provided with non potable water
sK5202	$ Wastewater operating revenue
sK5561	% Samples testing positive for coliform bacteria
sK5562	# Drinking water tests above maximum contaminant level
sK5563	# Days the sewage treatment plant didn't operate at required standards
sK5564	# Time to repair or replace high priority broken or inoperative hydrants
sK6393	% Access to water
sK6400	# Water quality index
sK6401	% Water stress index
sK6402	# Water scarcity index

Human Development Areas

Administration

Administration represents the management of public affairs, government or large institutions. It may also be defined as the activity of providing goods and services involving financial, commercial and industrial aspects.

Globalization

Globalization implies the replacement of local or nationalistic perspectives with a broader outlook regarding free international transfer of capital, people, goods and services, as well as the integration in economic activity.

sKPI #	Key Performance Indicator name
sK7390	# Cereal imports
sK7689	# Extent of regional integration rating
sK8080	# International tourists
sK8311	# Member States ratifying one of a selected group of safety and health conventions
sK8312	# Member States in which national Safe Work programmes of action for selected industries and hazardous agents are launched
sK8313	# Member States in which tripartite or bipartite institutions, mechanisms or processes address gender equality issues
sK8314	# Member States that have begun implementation of gender-sensitive technical cooperation
sK8315	# Member States that have improved the coverage of their statistics on occupational accidents and diseases
sK8316	# Member States that have improved the coverage of their statistics on occupational safety and health with gender disaggregation
sK8317	# Member States that have ratified at least one Convention in each of the four categories of fundamental principles and rights
sK8318	# Member States that ratify the Minimum Age Convention
sK8319	# Member States that ratify the Worst Forms of Child Labor Convention
sK8320	# Member States where data are generated and used to develop strategies and policies to combat economic and social insecurity
sK8363	# Net migration
sK9265	$ EU exports to Africa
sK9266	$ EU imports to Africa
sK9267	$ EU-27 inward FDI flows from Africa
sK9268	$ EU-27 outward FDI flows to Africa
sK9269	$ EU-27 trade in goods with Africa
sK10738	% 3 years change of the real effective exchange rates based on HICP/CPI deflators
sK11202	% Engagement in international cooperation
sK11368	% Exports plus imports out of GDP
sK11587	% Foreign direct investment of GDP
sK11745	% Incentives for participation in global agreements
sK11980	% Intra-EU trade in goods, from external trade in goods

sKPI #	Key Performance Indicator name
sK11981	% Involvement of major stakeholders in making and applying the rules of the game
sK12245	% Net international investment position at end of year, from GDP
sK12253	% Net migration from population
sK12394	% Participation in global agreements
sK12395	% Participation in regional agreements
sK13111	% Visitors from population

Political Governance

Political governance represents the specific set of legislation, policies and controls, standards and best practices in determining and delivering coordinated political and legislative leadership by governing. Government is a legal system of expressing the public will.

sKPI #	Key Performance Indicator name
sK7405	# Civil liberties rating
sK7434	# Command & control measures
sK7443	# Compliance operations
sK7466	# Control of corruption
sK7472	# Corruption perception index rank
sK7473	# Corruption perception index score
sK7474	# Corruption perception rating
sK7482	# CPIA accountability in the public sector rating
sK7483	# CPIA building human resources rating
sK7484	# CPIA business regulatory environment rating
sK7485	# CPIA corruption in the public sector rating
sK7486	# CPIA debt policy rating
sK7487	# CPIA economic management cluster
sK7488	# CPIA efficiency of revenue mobilization rating
sK7489	# CPIA equity of public resource use rating
sK7490	# CPIA financial sector rating
sK7491	# CPIA fiscal policy rating
sK7492	# CPIA gender equality rating
sK7493	# CPIA macroeconomic management rating
sK7494	# CPIA policies for social inclusion and equity cluster
sK7495	# CPIA policy and institutions for environment sustainability rating
sK7496	# CPIA property rights and rule-based governance rating
sK7497	# CPIA public sector management and institutions cluster
sK7500	# CPIA quality of public administration rating
sK7501	# CPIA social protection rating

sKPI #	Key Performance Indicator name
sK7502	# CPIA structural policies cluster
sK7503	# CPIA trade rating
sK7504	# CPIA transparency in the public sector rating
sK7563	# Disaster risk reduction progress score
sK7600	# Electoral process rating
sK7669	# Errors in the reporting chain
sK7820	# Freedom of the press index
sK7830	# Functioning of government index
sK7837	# Gender inequality index
sK7866	# Global Competitiveness Index (GCI)
sK7872	# Government effectiveness
sK8090	# Job conversion programmes
sK8407	# Open Budget Index Overall Country Score
sK8428	# Outstanding disagreements
sK8573	# PDI-11 Existence of a monitorable performance assessment framework
sK8574	# PDI-12 Existence of a mutual accountability review
sK8575	# PDI-2a Country financial management systems reliability
sK8576	# PDI-2b Country procurement systems reliability
sK8577	# PDI-6 Project implementation units parallel to country structures
sK8683	# Political culture rating
sK8684	# Political democracy index
sK8686	# Political participation rating
sK8687	# Political Stability
sK8855	# Regulatory Quality
sK8868	# Retraining programmes
sK8889	# Rule of law
sK9068	# User fees established
sK9069	# User rights established
sK10741	% Absence of use of property rights
sK10742	% Acceptance by major stakeholders
sK10894	% Capacity to elicit, receive, and use information from all stakeholders
sK11028	% Co-management
sK11033	% Community-based management
sK11035	% Compatibility between local and higher level enforcement
sK11036	% Compatibility with sustainability goals
sK11113	% Degree to which the regional agreement meets sustainable development objectives
sK11149	% Effective communication between stakeholders
sK11620	% Global management regime
sK11681	% Higher level authorities facilitating lower levels of management
sK12405	% PDI-1 Country with operational national development strategies
sK12406	% PDI-10a Donor missions coordinated

sKPI #	Key Performance Indicator name
sK12407	% PDI-10b Country-analysis coordinated
sK12408	% PDI-3 Government budget estimates comprehensive and realistic
sK12409	% PDI-4 Technical assistance aligned and coordinated with country programmes
sK12410	% PDI-5a Aid for government sectors uses country public financial management systems
sK12411	% PDI-5b Aid for government sectors uses country procurement systems
sK12412	% PDI-7 Aid disbursements on schedule and recorded by government
sK12413	% PDI-8 Bilateral aid that is untied
sK12414	% PDI-9 Aid provided in the framework of programme-based approaches
sK12767	% Proportion of seats held by women in national parliaments
sK12789	% Rate of compliance
sK12832	% Regional body with competence to manage
sK12852	% Resources availability at all levels
sK12889	% Seats held by women in national parliaments
sK12940	% Support to associations
sK13061	% Transparency of management
sK13129	% Management plans in place
sK13139	% Women in Parliament

Public Administration

The role of government is to defend population and the country from foreign aggression, represent national interest abroad, deliberate, pass and enforce laws and administer programs for increasing citizens' quality of life.

sKPI #	Key Performance Indicator name
sK7098	# Administrative forms available for download from official website
sK7099	# Administrative forms which can be submitted electronically
sK7469	# Co-operatives branches per 100,000 adults
sK7518	# Days of lead time to export
sK7519	# Days of lead time to import
sK7520	# Days required to build a warehouse
sK7522	# Days required to enforce a contract
sK7523	# Days required to obtain an operating license
sK7524	# Days required to register property
sK7525	# Days required to start a business
sK7529	# Days to export
sK7530	# Days to import
sK7598	# Elected city representatives
sK7599	# Elected city representatives per 1 000 residents
sK8433	# Park and ride parking spaces per 1000 population
sK9079	# Visits to official city Internet website
sK9110	$ Adjustments to foreign scheduled debt service

sKPI #	Key Performance Indicator name
sK9111	$ Adjustments to foreign scheduled principal repayments
sK9160	$ Budgetary investment
sK9165	$ Capital revenue
sK9166	$ Capital transfers
sK9169	$ Cash surplus/deficit
sK9170	$ Cash surplus/deficit of fiscal balance
sK9172	$ Central government arrears on domestic debt
sK9173	$ Central government arrears on external debt
sK9174	$ Central government debt of monetary system credit
sK9175	$ Central government revenue excluding all grants
sK9186	$ Compensation of employees
sK9197	$ Current budget balance including grants
sK9198	$ Current expenditure
sK9199	$ Current revenue excluding grants
sK9201	$ Customs and other import duties
sK9213	$ Defence expenditure
sK9215	$ Direct taxes
sK9367	$ Expense
sK9386	$ External capital grants
sK9387	$ External central government debt service
sK9428	$ Financing including external capital grants
sK9492	$ Goods and services expense
sK9493	$ Government consumption
sK9496	$ Grants and other revenue
sK10086	$ Interest on domestic debt
sK10160	$ Monetary system credit domestic financing
sK10240	$ Net external borrowing
sK10278	$ Non-tax receipts
sK10321	$ Other current transfers
sK10323	$ Other domestic borrowing

sKPI #	Key Performance Indicator name
sK10324	$ Other domestic central government debt
sK10338	$ Overall budget balance including grants
sK10339	$ Surplus/deficit excluding all grants
sK10340	$ Surplus/deficit excluding current grants
sK10400	$ Primary balance excluding interest
sK10484	$ Revenue excluding grants
sK10723	$ Year end external debt
sK10940	% Central government revenues excluding all grants from GDP
sK11158	% Elected city representatives who are women
sK11177	% Eligible electorate registered for city elections
sK11178	% Eligible electorate registered for EU elections
sK11179	% Eligible electorate registered for national elections
sK11625	% Grants and other revenue
sK11682	% Highest marginal tax rate, corporate rate
sK12430	% Perception of the quality of local administration services
sK12833	% Registered electorate voting in city elections
sK12834	% Registered electorate voting in EU elections
sK12835	% Registered electorate voting in national elections
sK12861	% Revenue excluding grants from GDP
sK13148	% Young people voting in city elections
sK23254	# Private enterprises, producers organizations, water users associations, trade and business associations, and community-based organizations (cbos) receiving USG assistance
sK23255	# Women's organizations/associations assisted as a result of USG supported interventions
sK23260	# Public-private partnerships formed as a result of FTF assistance
sK23262	# Jobs attributed to FTF implementation
sK23264	# Vulnerable households benefiting directly from USG assistance

Economics

Economics deals with the production, distribution and consumption of goods and services and with the theory and management of economies or economic systems.

Agriculture

Agriculture is the practice of cultivating land and raising livestock in order to produce commodities which maintain life, including food, fiber, forest products, horticultural crops and their related services.

sKPI #	Key Performance Indicator name
sK7080	# Fertilizer consumption in kilograms per hectare of arable land
sK7081	# Fodder from arable land
sK7082	# Hectares of land under millet production
sK7083	# Kitchen gardens land use
sK7107	# Aggregate direct, trademark applications

sKPI #	Key Performance Indicator name
sK7108	# Agricultural area farmed by owner
sK7109	# Agricultural area farmed by tenant
sK7110	# Agricultural area in less favored area
sK7111	# Agricultural area in mountain area
sK7113	# Agricultural area of holdings with 100 ESU and over
sK7114	# Agricultural area of holdings with 16 to 40 ESU
sK7115	# Agricultural area of holdings with 2 to 4 ESU
sK7116	# Agricultural area of holdings with 4 to 8 ESU
sK7117	# Agricultural area of holdings with 40 to 100 ESU
sK7118	# Agricultural area of holdings with 8 to 16 ESU

sKPI #	Key Performance Indicator name
sK7119	# Agricultural area of holdings with less than 2 ESU
sK7120	# Agricultural area of holdings with mixed cropping
sK7121	# Agricultural area of holdings with mixed crops and livestock
sK7122	# Agricultural area of holdings with mixed livestock holdings
sK7123	# Agricultural area of holdings with specialized field crops
sK7124	# Agricultural area of holdings with specialized granivores
sK7125	# Agricultural area of holdings with specialized grazing livestock
sK7126	# Agricultural area of holdings with specialized horticulture
sK7127	# Agricultural area of holdings with specialized permanent crops
sK7131	# Agricultural population
sK7132	# Agriculture production index
sK7133	# Agriculture value added per worker
sK7146	# Animal populations
sK7147	# Animals for slaughter
sK7155	# Consumption of commercial fertilizers
sK7156	# Consumption of nitrogenous fertilizers
sK7157	# Consumption of phosphate fertilizers
sK7333	# Barley production
sK7334	# Barley yield
sK7348	# Biotechnology patent applications to the EPO per million labor force
sK7349	# Biotechnology patent applications to the EPO per million of inhabitants
sK7351	# Boars
sK7355	# Bovine animals aged between 1 and 2 years
sK7356	# Bovine animals less than 1 year old
sK7357	# Bovines animals of 2 years and over
sK7359	# Breeding pigs with a live weight of 50 kg and higher
sK7361	# Buffaloes
sK7368	# Calves for slaughter
sK7387	# Cattle population
sK7391	# Cereal production
sK7392	# Cereal production index
sK7394	# Cereal yield
sK7411	# CO2 emission from fossil-fuels in thousand tonnes
sK7412	# CO2 emission from liquid fuel consumption in thousand tonnes
sK7414	# CO2 emissions from gas flaring in thousand tonnes
sK7415	# CO2 emissions from gas fuel consumption in thousand tonnes
sK7422	# CO2 emissions from solid fuel consumption in thousand tonnes
sK7462	# Consumption of pesticides
sK7476	# Cotton seed crop production
sK7480	# Covered sows

sKPI #	Key Performance Indicator name
sK7481	# Cows
sK7508	# Crop production index
sK7513	# Dairy cows
sK7573	# Driven intra-regional trips
sK7593	# Economically active female population in agriculture
sK7594	# Economically active male population in agriculture
sK7595	# Economically active population in agriculture
sK7695	# Fallow and green manures land use
sK7702	# Fattening pigs between 50 and 80 kg
sK7703	# Fattening pigs between 80 and 110 kg
sK7704	# Fattening pigs of at least 110 kg
sK7705	# Fattening pigs, including rejected boars and sows of at least 50 kg
sK7707	# Female bovine animals aged between 1 and 2 years
sK7708	# Female bovines animals of 2 years and over
sK7709	# Female calves
sK7788	# Fishers
sK7805	# Fonio production
sK7806	# Fonio yield
sK7808	# Food production index
sK7822	# Fruit trees crop production, excluding olives and citrus fruit
sK7854	# Gilts not yet covered, from sows not covered
sK7867	# Goat population
sK7873	# Grain maize crop production
sK7876	# Gross agriculture production index
sK7877	# Gross cereal production index
sK7878	# Gross crop production index
sK7879	# Gross food production index
sK7880	# Gross livestock production index
sK7881	# Gross nitrogen balance estimates
sK7882	# Gross non-food production index
sK7883	# Gross phosphorus balance estimates
sK7893	# Hectares of agricultural area of holdings with 10 to 20 ha of agricultural area
sK7894	# Hectares of agricultural area of holdings with 20 to 30 ha of agricultural area
sK7895	# Hectares of agricultural area of holdings with 30 to 50 ha of agricultural area
sK7896	# Hectares of agricultural area of holdings with 5 to 10 ha of agricultural area
sK7897	# Hectares of agricultural area of holdings with 50 ha or more of agricultural area
sK7898	# Hectares of agricultural area of holdings with less than 5 ha of agricultural area
sK7901	# Hectares of land under barley production
sK7903	# Hectares of land under cereal production
sK7904	# Hectares of land under fonio production
sK7905	# Hectares of land under maize production

sKPI #	Key Performance Indicator name
sK7906	# Hectares of land under rice production
sK7907	# Hectares of land under sorghum production
sK7908	# Hectares of land under wheat production
sK7910	# Heifers
sK7911	# Heifers for slaughter
sK7923	# Holdings in less favored areas
sK7924	# Holdings in mountain area
sK7925	# Holdings with rye
sK7926	# Holdings with 10 to 20 ha agricultural area
sK7927	# Holdings with 100 ESU and over
sK7928	# Holdings with 16 to 40 ESU
sK7929	# Holdings with 2 to 4 ESU
sK7930	# Holdings with 20 to 30 ha of agricultural area
sK7931	# Holdings with 30 to 50 ha agricultural area
sK7932	# Holdings with 4 to 8 ESU
sK7933	# Holdings with 40 to 100 ESU
sK7934	# Holdings with 5 to 10 ha of agricultural area
sK7935	# Holdings with 50 ha or more agricultural area
sK7936	# Holdings with 8 to 16 ESU
sK7937	# Holdings with barley
sK7938	# Holdings with bovine animals
sK7939	# Holdings with bovine animals under 1 year old
sK7940	# Holdings with common wheat and spelt
sK7941	# Holdings with dairy cows
sK7942	# Holdings with dried vegetables
sK7943	# Holdings with durum wheat
sK7944	# Holdings with female bovine animals 1 year or over but under 2 years
sK7945	# Holdings with flowers and ornamental plants
sK7946	# Holdings with forage plants
sK7947	# Holdings with fresh vegetables, melons and strawberries
sK7948	# Holdings with goats
sK7949	# Holdings with grain maize
sK7950	# Holdings with heifers 2 year old and over
sK7951	# Holdings with industrial plants
sK7952	# Holdings with less than 2 ESU
sK7953	# Holdings with less than 5 ha of agricultural area
sK7954	# Holdings with livestock
sK7955	# Holdings with male bovine animals 1 year or over but under 2 years
sK7956	# Holdings with male bovine animals 2 year old and over
sK7957	# Holdings with mixed cropping
sK7958	# Holdings with mixed crops and livestock
sK7959	# Holdings with mixed livestock holdings
sK7960	# Holdings with oats
sK7961	# Holdings with odder roots and brassica

sKPI #	Key Performance Indicator name
sK7962	# Holdings with other cereal
sK7963	# Holdings with other cows
sK7964	# Holdings with permanent crops
sK7965	# Holdings with permanent pasture and meadows
sK7966	# Holdings with pigs
sK7967	# Holdings with potatoes
sK7968	# Holdings with poultry
sK7969	# Holdings with rice
sK7970	# Holdings with root crops
sK7971	# Holdings with sheep
sK7972	# Holdings with specialized field crops
sK7973	# Holdings with specialized granivores
sK7974	# Holdings with specialized grazing livestock
sK7975	# Holdings with specialized horticulture
sK7976	# Holdings with specialized permanent crops
sK7977	# Holdings with sugar beet
sK7978	# Holdings with vineyards
sK7979	# Holdings with woodland
sK8134	# Livestock production index
sK8140	# Local units
sK8161	# Maize production
sK8162	# Maize yield
sK8163	# Male bovine animals aged between 1 and 2 years
sK8166	# Male bovines animals of 2 years and over
sK8167	# Male calves
sK8329	# Tonnes of barley seed
sK8330	# Tonnes of fonio seed
sK8331	# Tonnes of maize seed
sK8332	# Tonnes of millet seed
sK8333	# Tonnes of rice seed
sK8337	# Millet production
sK8338	# Millet yield
sK8378	# Non-agricultural population
sK8386	# Non-food production index
sK8403	# Oil flax crop production
sK8404	# Oilseeds crop production
sK8405	# Olives land use
sK8413	# Other calves
sK8417	# Other cows
sK8675	# Pig population
sK8676	# Piglets with a live weight of less than 20 kg
sK8677	# Pigs with a live weight of 20 kg and less than 50 kg
sK8731	# Potato crop production
sK8796	# Production of cow's milk on farms
sK8871	# Rice production
sK8872	# Rice yield

sKPI #	Key Performance Indicator name
sK8893	# Rye crop production
sK8897	# Sales pace
sK8909	# Sheep
sK8913	# Soft fruit crop production
sK8916	# Sows
sK8917	# Sows covered for the first time, from covered sows
sK8918	# Sows not covered
sK8919	# Soya bean crop production
sK8937	# Sugar beet crop production
sK8939	# Sunflower seed crop production
sK8962	# Threatened animal species
sK8972	# Tobacco raw crop production, including seedlings enclosures
sK8973	# Tonnes of cereal exports
sK8974	# Tonnes of cereal food aid deliveries
sK8975	# Tonnes of non-cereal food aid deliveries
sK9046	# Total standard gross margin (ESU)
sK9052	# Tractors and combined harvester-threshers in use
sK9054	# Tractors in agricultural machinery
sK9056	# Tractors per 100 sq. km of arable land
sK9062	# Turning rape crop production
sK9076	# Vineyards land use
sK9114	$ Agriculture value added per worker
sK9115	$ Annual growth of value added by agriculture
sK10429	$ Producer price for barley, per tonne
sK10430	$ Producer price for fonio, per tonne
sK10431	$ Producer price for maize, per tonne
sK10432	$ Producer price for millet, per tonne
sK10433	$ Producer price for rice paddy, per tonne
sK10434	$ Producer price for rice, per tonne
sK10435	$ Producer price for wheat, per tonne
sK10775	% Agricultural area farmed or in other modes of tenure
sK10789	% Agriculture, value added from GDP
sK10900	% Catch of mature fish per unit effort (CM/f)
sK11018	% CO2 emissions from fossil fuels
sK11098	% Current effort to MSY ratio (ft/fMSY)
sK11350	% Excess fishing capacity
sK11362	% Export/Harvest value
sK11536	% Fertilizer consumption from fertilizer production
sK11576	% Fishing effort
sK11577	% Fishing rate
sK11578	% Fishing time
sK11613	% Gear used
sK11668	% Growth rate of number of fishers
sK12006	% Landing
sK13005	% Area fished

sKPI #	Key Performance Indicator name
sK13006	% Catch
sK23225	# Individuals who have received USG supported long term agricultural enabling environment training
sK23226	# Rural hectares formalized
sK23227	# Hectares for which males are registrants
sK23228	# Hectares for which females are registrants
sK23229	# Kilometers of roads improved or constructed
sK23247	$ Agricultural GDP
sK23251	# Additional hectares under improved technologies or management practices as a result of USG assistance
sK23252	# Individuals who have received USG supported short-term agricultural sector productivity or food security training
sK23253	# New technologies or management practices made available for transfer as a result of USG assistance
sK23257	$ Gross margin per unit of land or animal of selected product (crops/animals selected varies by country)
sK23258	$ Incremental sales (collected at farm- level) attributed to FTF implementation
sK23259	$ Exports of targeted agricultural commodities as a result of USG assistance
sK23261	$ New private sector investment in the agriculture sector or food chain leveraged by FTF implementation

Commerce

Commerce refers to the exchange of goods and services between members of the industrial world and it includes all activities which directly or indirectly facilitate this exchange.

sKPI #	Key Performance Indicator name
sK7106	# Age of firm in years
sK7203	# Days to clear exports through customs
sK7210	# Time firms spent in meetings with tax officials
sK7362	# Building permits
sK7364	# Business extent of disclosure index
sK7378	# Capital goods Import Volume Index score
sK7440	# Companies with headquarters in city quoted on stock market
sK7455	# Construction labor input index
sK7456	# Construction new orders index
sK7457	# Construction production index
sK7505	# Credit depth of information index
sK7514	# Days of delay in obtaining a mainline telephone connection
sK7515	# Days of delay in obtaining a water connection
sK7517	# Days of delay in obtaining an electrical connection
sK7528	# Days to clear imports from customs
sK7531	# Days to obtain construction-related permit
sK7532	# Days to obtain import license
sK7533	# Days to obtain operating license
sK7537	# Dealing with construction permits rank
sK7538	# Dealing with procedures in construction

sKPI #	Key Performance Indicator name
sK7553	# Difficulty of hiring or employing workers
sK7561	# Director liability index
sK7567	# Documents to export
sK7569	# Documents to import
sK7578	# Duration of Insufficient Water Supply in hours
sK7579	# Duration of phone outages in hours
sK7580	# Duration of power outages
sK7588	# Ease of doing business index
sK7592	# Economic Sentiment indicator
sK7630	# Employing workers rank
sK7666	# Enforcing contracts rank
sK7673	# Export Diversification Index
sK7674	# Export Market Destination Index
sK7675	# Export price index
sK7676	# Export Product Concentration Index
sK7677	# Export products
sK7678	# Export value index
sK7680	# Export Volume Index
sK7682	# Exports of agricultural tractors
sK7683	# Exports of commodity volume index
sK7807	# Food Import Volume Index score
sK7845	# General Agreement on Trade in Services Commitments Index
sK7850	# Getting credit rank
sK7980	# Home Forfeiture Actions
sK8010	# Import price index of goods and services
sK8011	# Import Product Diversification Index
sK8012	# Import products
sK8013	# Import value index
sK8015	# Import volume index
sK8018	# Imports of agricultural tractors
sK8020	# Incidence of Graft index
sK8045	# Individuals who ordered goods or services over the Internet from sellers from other EU countries
sK8046	# Individuals who ordered goods or services over the Internet from sellers from the rest of the world (non-EU)
sK8047	# Individuals who ordered goods or services over the Internet from sellers with unknown country of origin
sK8066	# Intermediate goods Import Volume Index score
sK8067	# Intermediate import goods
sK8068	# Intermediate primary import goods
sK8073	# International air transport of passengers per 1000 population
sK8085	# Investor protection index
sK8109	# Last online purchase: in the 12 months
sK8115	# Legal rights index in getting credit
sK8141	# Logistics performance index: Ability to track and trace consignments

sKPI #	Key Performance Indicator name
sK8142	# Logistics performance index: Competence and quality of logistics services
sK8143	# Logistics performance index: Ease of arranging competitively priced shipments
sK8144	# Logistics performance index: Efficiency of customs clearance process
sK8145	# Logistics performance index: Frequency with which shipments reach consignee within scheduled or expected time
sK8146	# Logistics performance index: Quality of trade and transport-related infrastructure
sK8154	# Trademark applications in the Madrid system
sK8224	# Manufactures Import Volume Index score
sK8225	# Manufactures in Export Volume Index
sK8226	# Manufactures value index
sK8321	# Merchandise Export Price Index
sK8322	# Merchandise export volume index
sK8323	# Merchandise Import Price Index score
sK8324	# Merchandise Import Volume Index score
sK8325	# Merchandise Terms of Trade
sK8360	# Net barter terms of trade index
sK8365	# New business density in registrations per 1,000 people ages 15-64
sK8373	# New residential buildings prices index
sK8382	# Non-factor services Import Volume Index score
sK8383	# Non-factor services in Export Price Index
sK8384	# Non-factor services in Export Volume Index
sK8388	# Non-residents patent applications
sK8391	# Permanent, full time employees
sK8392	# Seasonal/temporary, full-time employees
sK8393	# Skilled production employees
sK8394	# Unskilled production employees
sK8408	# Ores and metals imports from merchandise imports
sK8415	# Other consumer goods Import Volume Index score
sK8416	# Other consumer import goods
sK8423	# Other primary commodities in Export Volume Index
sK8571	# Paying taxes rank
sK8679	# Point-of-sale terminals per 100,000 adults
sK8680	# Petroleum, Oil and Lubricants (POL) and other energy Import Volume Index score
sK8771	# Power outages in firms in a typical month
sK8783	# Primary goods Import Volume Index score
sK8791	# Procedures to enforce a contract
sK8793	# Procedures to register property
sK8814	# Protecting Investors rank
sK8847	# Redundancy (weeks of wages) of employing workers
sK8854	# Registering property rank
sK8866	# Residents patent applications
sK8873	# Rigidity of employment index

sKPI #	Key Performance Indicator name
sK8874	# Rigidity of hours for employing workers
sK8896	# Sales of highly efficient cars/appliances
sK8908	# Shareholder suits index
sK9045	# Reserves in months of imports
sK9049	# Trademark applications
sK9063	# Turnover and volume of sales index
sK9088	# Year-on-year changes in house prices relative to the final consumption price index
sK9089	# Years firms operated without formal registration
sK9092	# Years to close a business
sK9098	# Intermediate manufacture import goods
sK9101	$ International tourism receipts for travel items
sK9163	$ Capital import goods
sK9184	$ Commercial service exports
sK9185	$ Commercial service imports
sK9194	$ Cost to export per container
sK9195	$ Cost to import per container
sK9259	$ Electronic sales of the enterprise to home country, excluding VAT
sK9260	$ Electronic sales of the enterprise to other EU countries, excluding VAT
sK9261	$ Electronic sales of the enterprise to the rest of the world, excluding VAT
sK9264	$ Enterprises' total turnover from e-commerce
sK9368	$ Export cost per container
sK9370	$ Exports of agricultural tractors
sK9375	$ Exports of goods and services
sK9432	$ Food imports
sK10067	$ Imports of agricultural tractors
sK10079	$ Industrial producer prices
sK10096	$ International tourism expenditures
sK10098	$ International tourism expenditures for passenger transport items
sK10100	$ International tourism expenditures for travel items
sK10106	$ Investment in energy with private participation
sK10108	$ Investment in telecoms with private participation
sK10110	$ Investment in transport with private participation
sK10112	$ Investment in water and sanitation with private participation
sK10136	$ Manufactures exports
sK10140	$ Market share of phosphate-free detergents
sK10143	$ Merchandise exports
sK10146	$ Merchandise imports
sK10330	$ Other primary export commodities
sK10331	$ Other retail sale of new goods in specialized stores
sK10334	$ Other wholesale
sK10354	$ POL and other energy imports
sK10401	$ Primary export commodities

sKPI #	Key Performance Indicator name
sK10463	$ Recovery rate of closing a business
sK10477	$ Retail sale in non-specialized stores
sK10478	$ Retail sale not in stores
sK10479	$ Retail sale of automotive fuel
sK10480	$ Retail sale of food, beverages, tobacco in specialized stores
sK10481	$ Retail sale of pharmaceutical, medical goods, cosmetic
sK10482	$ Retail sale of second-hand goods in stores
sK10483	$ Retail trade, except of motor vehicles, motorcycles and repair of personal and household goods
sK10498	$ Sale of motor vehicle parts and accessories
sK10499	$ Sale of motor vehicles
sK10500	$ Sale, maintenance and repair of motor vehicles
sK10501	$ Sale, maintenance and repair of motorcycles and related
sK10502	$ Sales of generics
sK10504	$ Seasonally adjusted export prices
sK10505	$ Seasonally adjusted import prices
sK10676	$ User charges for waste water treatment
sK10708	$ Value of seasonally adjusted goods exports
sK10710	$ Volume growth rate of seasonally adjusted goods exports
sK10715	$ Wholesale and retail trade, repair of motor vehicles, motorcycles and personal and household goods
sK10716	$ Wholesale of agricultural raw materials, live animals
sK10717	$ Wholesale of food, beverages and tobacco
sK10718	$ Wholesale of household goods
sK10719	$ Wholesale of machinery, equipment and supplies
sK10720	$ Wholesale of non-agricultural intermediate products, waste and scrap
sK10721	$ Wholesale on a fee or contract basis
sK10722	$ Wholesale trade and commission trade, except of motor and motorcycles
sK10744	% Access to finance from firms identifying this as a major constraint
sK10745	% Access to land from managers surveyed ranking this as a major constraint
sK10768	% Adults with private credit bureau coverage
sK10770	% Adults with public credit registry coverage
sK10785	% Agricultural raw materials exports from merchandise exports
sK10787	% Agricultural raw materials imports from merchandise imports
sK10885	% Business licensing and permits from firms identifying this as a major constraint
sK10896	% Cars/appliances that contain a label
sK11034	% Companies gone bankrupt
sK11061	% Construction production
sK11071	% Corruption from managers surveyed ranking this as a major constraint
sK11073	% Cost of business start-up procedures from GNI per capita

sKPI #	Key Performance Indicator name
sK11074	% Cost of closing a business from estate
sK11075	% Cost of dealing with construction permit from income per capita
sK11076	% Cost of enforcing contracts from claims
sK11077	% Cost of registering property from property value
sK11084	% Courts from managers surveyed ranking this as a major constraint
sK11088	% Crime from managers surveyed ranking this as a major constraint
sK11100	% Customs & Trade regulations from managers surveyed ranking this as a major constraint
sK11135	% Domestic market products lost due to breakage or spoilage
sK11136	% Domestic market products lost due to theft
sK11139	% Domestic sales
sK11162	% Electricity from firms identifying this as a major constraint
sK11163	% Electricity from generator
sK11164	% Electricity from managers surveyed ranking this as a major constraint
sK11182	% Employees offered formal training
sK11206	% Enterprise ownership by domestic private entities
sK11207	% Enterprise ownership by foreign private entities
sK11208	% Enterprise ownership by other
sK11209	% Enterprise ownership by the government/state
sK11219	% Enterprises having concerns related to confidentiality and security
sK11220	% Enterprises having done electronic sales or purchases in the rest of the world
sK11221	% Enterprises having done electronic sales or purchases to other EU countries
sK11222	% Enterprises having done electronic sales or purchases to their own country
sK11223	% Enterprises having done electronic sales to other EU countries or the rest of the world
sK11224	% Enterprises having done electronic sales to other EU countries or the rest of the world
sK11225	% Enterprises having done electronic sales to their own country
sK11226	% Enterprises having done electronic sales to the rest of the world
sK11227	% Enterprises having encountered blackmail or threats as security problem
sK11228	% Enterprises having encountered unauthorized access as a security problem
sK11236	% Enterprises having Internet sales to other EU countries over the last calendar year
sK11237	% Enterprises having Internet sales of B2B and B2G over the last calendar year
sK11238	% Enterprises having Internet sales of B2C over the last calendar year
sK11239	% Enterprises having Internet sales to their own country
sK11240	% Enterprises having Internet sales to rest of the world
sK11261	% Enterprises not selling to public sector

sKPI #	Key Performance Indicator name
sK11262	% Enterprises not selling to the public sector or having concerns related to confidentiality and security
sK11329	% Enterprises whose Internet purchases over the last calendar year were 1+ % of orders
sK11330	% Enterprises whose Internet over the last calendar year were 10+ %
sK11363	% Exporter firms
sK11540	% Finance from managers surveyed ranking this as a major constraint
sK11542	% Firms believing the court system is fair, impartial and uncorrupted from firms identifying this as a major constraint
sK11544	% Firms expected to give gifts in meeting with tax officials
sK11545	% Firms expected to give gifts to get a construction permit
sK11546	% Firms expected to give gifts to get a phone connection
sK11547	% Firms expected to give gifts to get a water connection
sK11548	% Firms expected to give gifts to get an electrical connection
sK11549	% Firms expected to give gifts to get an import license
sK11550	% Firms expected to give gifts to get an operating license
sK11551	% Firms expected to give gifts to secure a government contract
sK11553	% Firms formally registered when they started operations in the country
sK11554	% Firms identifying corruption as a major constraint
sK11555	% Firms identifying practices of competitors in the informal sector as a major constraint
sK11557	% Firms offering formal training
sK11558	% Firms paying for security
sK11560	% Firms that do not report all sales for tax purposes
sK11561	% Firms that share or own their own generator
sK11562	% Firms that use material inputs and/or supplies of foreign origin
sK11564	% Firms using banks to finance investment
sK11565	% Firms using email to communicate with clients/suppliers
sK11566	% Firms using its own website
sK11567	% Firms using technology licensed from foreign companies
sK11568	% Firms with annual financial statement reviewed by external auditor
sK11570	% Firms with female participation in ownership
sK11571	% Firms with female top manager
sK11573	% Firms with ISO certification ownership
sK11574	% Firms with line of credit or loans from financial institutions
sK11581	% Food exports from merchandise exports
sK11583	% Food imports from merchandise imports
sK11584	% Food production index
sK11585	% Food, beverages and tobacco from value added in manufacturing
sK11606	% Full time female workers

sKPI #	Key Performance Indicator name
sK11607	% Functioning of the courts from firms identifying this as a major constraint
sK11665	% Growth of air freight transport
sK11666	% Growth of maritime transport
sK11683	% Highly efficient cars/appliances in the sales catalogue
sK11684	% High-technology exports from manufactured exports
sK11691	% Household final consumption expenditure etc. from GDP
sK11727	% ICT goods exports from total good exports
sK11728	% ICT goods imports from total good exports
sK11737	% Imports of goods and services from GDP
sK11870	% Individuals who made online purchases for books/magazines/e-learning material
sK11871	% Individuals who made online purchases for books/magazines/e-learning material, delivered or upgraded online
sK11872	% Individuals who made online purchases for clothes, sports goods
sK11873	% Individuals who made online purchases for computer hardware
sK11874	% Individuals who made online purchases for computer software
sK11875	% Individuals who made online purchases for tickets for events
sK11878	% Individuals who ordered goods over the Internet from retailers known from the Internet or found on the Internet
sK11902	% Individuals who haven't bought/ordered goods or services over the Internet for their own private use, because relevant information about goods and services is difficult to find on website
sK11923	% Informal payments to public officials by firms
sK11948	% International tourism expenditures from total imports
sK11949	% International tourism receipts
sK11955	% Internet purchases of the enterprise over the last calendar year, excluding VAT
sK11999	% Labor regulations from firms identifying this as a major constraint
sK12000	% Labor regulations from managers surveyed ranking this as a major constraint
sK12001	% Labor skill level from firms identifying this as a major constraint
sK12002	% Labor skills from managers surveyed ranking this as a major constraint
sK12007	% Largest shareholder ownership
sK12015	% Licenses and permits from managers surveyed ranking this as a major constraint
sK12023	% Loans requiring collateral
sK12030	% Losses due to theft, robbery, vandalism, and arson from sales
sK12124	% Management time dealing with officials, from total management time
sK12125	% Management time spent dealing with officials
sK12127	% Manufactured exports unit value index

sKPI #	Key Performance Indicator name
sK12129	% Manufactured products with binding coverage
sK12131	% Manufactured products with simple mean bound rate
sK12133	% Manufactures exports from merchandise exports
sK12135	% Manufactures imports from merchandise imports
sK12141	% Market share of highly efficient cars/appliances
sK12149	% Merchandise exports to developing economies in Sub-Saharan Africa from total merchandise exports
sK12150	% Merchandise exports to developing economies in the Arab World from total merchandise exports
sK12151	% Merchandise exports to developing economies in East Asia & Pacific from total merchandise exports
sK12152	% Merchandise exports to developing economies in Europe & Central Asia from total merchandise exports
sK12153	% Merchandise exports to developing economies in Latin America & the Caribbean from total merchandise exports
sK12154	% Merchandise exports to developing economies in Middle East & North Africa from total merchandise exports
sK12155	% Merchandise exports to developing economies in South Asia from total merchandise exports
sK12156	% Merchandise exports to developing economies outside region from total merchandise exports
sK12157	% Merchandise exports to developing economies within region from total merchandise exports
sK12158	% Merchandise exports to high-income economies from total merchandise exports
sK12159	% Merchandise imports from developing economies in South Asia from total merchandise imports
sK12160	% Merchandise imports from developing economies in Sub-Saharan Africa from total merchandise imports
sK12161	% Merchandise imports from developing economies in East Asia & Pacific from total merchandise imports
sK12162	% Merchandise imports from developing economies in Europe & Central Asia from total merchandise imports
sK12163	% Merchandise imports from developing economies in Latin America & the Caribbean from total merchandise imports
sK12164	% Merchandise imports from developing economies in Middle East & North Africa from total merchandise imports
sK12165	% Merchandise imports from economies in the Arab World from total merchandise imports
sK12166	% Merchandise imports from high-income economies from total merchandise imports
sK12167	% Merchandise imports to developing economies outside region from total merchandise exports
sK12168	% Merchandise imports to developing economies within region from total merchandise exports
sK12170	% Merchandise trade from GDP
sK12182	% Minimum capital for starting a business from income per capita
sK12304	% Ores and metals exports from merchandise exports
sK12401	% Paying other taxes
sK12402	% Paying profit tax

sKPI #	Key Performance Indicator name
sK12403	% Paying taxes, labour tax and contributions
sK12443	% Policy uncertainty from managers surveyed ranking this as a major constraint
sK12707	% Practices informal sector from managers surveyed ranking this as a major constraint
sK12739	% Primary products with binding coverage
sK12741	% Primary products with simple mean bound rate
sK12761	% Products with binding coverage
sK12762	% Products with simple mean bound rate
sK12846	% Residual merchandise exports by the reporting economy from total merchandise exports
sK12847	% Residual merchandise imports by the reporting economy from total merchandise imports
sK12855	% Retail trade deflated turnover
sK12947	% Tariff lines with international peak, all products
sK12948	% Tariff lines with international peaks, manufactured products
sK12949	% Tariff lines with international peaks, primary products
sK12950	% Tariff lines with specific rates, all products
sK12951	% Tariff lines with specific rates, manufactured products
sK12952	% Tariff lines with specific rates, primary product
sK12953	% Tariff rate applied in most favorite nation to all products
sK12956	% Tariff rate applied in most favorite nation to manufactured products
sK12958	% Tariff rate applied in most favorite nation to primary products
sK12959	% Tariff rate applied to all products
sK12961	% Tariff rate applied to manufactured products
sK12964	% Tariff rate applied to primary products
sK13049	% Trade from GDP
sK13050	% Trade identifying customs and trade regulations from firms identifying this as a major constraint
sK13051	% Trade in services from GDP
sK13066	% Transportation/distribution losses
sK13075	% Turnover or gross premiums written
sK13157	% Firms with a checking or savings account
sK13158	% Ores and metals imports from merchandise imports
sK23124	# Consultative processes with private sector as a result of USG assistance
sK23125	$ Cost to trade goods across borders as a result of U.S. assistance
sK23126	# Days required to trade goods across borders as a result of U.S. assistance
sK23127	# Procedures required to trade goods across borders as a result of U.S. assistance
sK23128	# New requests that are submitted by a host country as part of international trade talks attributable to USG assistance
sK23129	# New offers that are submitted by a host country as part of international trade talks attributable to USG assistance

sKPI #	Key Performance Indicator name
sK23130	# Revised offers that are submitted by a host country as part of international trade talks attributable to USG assistance
sK23131	# Customs harmonization procedures implemented in accordance with internationally accepted standards as a result of U.S. assistance
sK23132	# Legal, regulatory, or institutional actions taken to improve implementation or compliance with international trade and investment agreements due to support from USG-assisted organizations
sK23133	# Participants in trade and investment environment trainings
sK23134	# Public and private sector standards-setting bodies that have adopted internationally accepted guidelines for standard setting as a result of USG assistance
sK23135	# Trade and Investment Environment diagnostics conducted
sK23136	# USG supported training events held that related to improving the trade and investment environment
sK23137	$ Private Financing Mobilized with a DCA Guarantee
sK23138	# Capacity-Building Service Providers receiving USG assistance
sK23139	# Firms receiving capacity building assistance to export
sK23140	# Firms receiving USG assistance that obtain certification with international quality control, environmental and other process voluntary standards or regulations
sK23141	# Participants in USG supported trade and investment capacity building trainings
sK23142	# Women participants in USG supported trade and investment capacity building trainings
sK23143	# Men participants in USG supported trade and investment capacity building trainings
sK23144	# Trade and Investment capacity building diagnostics conducted
sK23145	# Trade-related business associations that are at least 50 percent self-funded as a result of USG assistance
sK23146	# USG supported training events on topics related to investment capacity building and improving trade

Economic Policy & Debt

Economic policy and debt refers to the administrative and legislative decisions made in order to nurture an economic environment suitable for the needs of population.

sKPI #	Key Performance Indicator name
sK7192	# Grace period in years on new external debt commitments
sK7196	# Maturity in years on new external debt commitments
sK7834	# GDP deflator index
sK8019	# Incentives to comply with the global agreements
sK8934	# Strength of legal rights index
sK8936	# Subsidies
sK9103	$ Per capital outstanding and disbursed debt
sK9106	$ Private non-guaranteed net flows on external debt
sK9109	$ Adjustment to arrears

sKPI #	Key Performance Indicator name
sK9112	$ Adjustments to scheduled debt service
sK9113	$ Adjustments to scheduled interest
sK9148	$ Bilateral concessional PPG debt
sK9149	$ Bilateral concessional PPG debt (DOD)
sK9152	$ Bilateral on non-concessional terms disbursements
sK9154	$ Bilateral PPG debt
sK9155	$ Bilateral PPG debt (DIS)
sK9156	$ Bilateral PPG debt (DOD)
sK9157	$ Bilateral PPG debt (INT)
sK9158	$ Bilateral PPG debt (TDS)
sK9159	$ Net bilateral aid flows from United Kingdom DAC donors
sK9164	$ Capital outflows not elsewhere included
sK9176	$ Cereal exports
sK9177	$ Cereal imports
sK9180	$ Changes in net reserves
sK9196	$ Current account balance
sK9200	$ Current transfer receipts
sK9205	$ Debt forgiveness or reductions
sK9206	$ Debt on non-concessional terms
sK9207	$ Debt service not paid
sK9208	$ Debt service not paid, accumulated arrears
sK9209	$ Debt service on external debt
sK9250	$ Disbursements
sK9253	$ Discrepancy in expenditure estimate of GDP in constant LCU
sK9371	$ Exports of food excluding fish
sK9372	$ Exports of forest products
sK9373	$ Exports of goods
sK9376	$ Exports of goods and services in constant 2000
sK9377	$ Exports of goods and services in constant LCU
sK9378	$ Exports of hazardous pesticides
sK9379	$ Exports of income
sK9380	$ Exports of pesticides
sK9381	$ Exports of services
sK9382	$ Exports of workers' remittances
sK9385	$ External balance on goods and services in constant LCU
sK9388	$ External debt stocks
sK9424	$ Final consumption expenditure in constant 2000
sK9425	$ Final consumption expenditure in constant LCU
sK9426	$ Final consumption expenditure plus discrepancy per capita
sK9433	$ Food imports excluding fish
sK9435	$ Foreign direct investment
sK9436	$ Foreign direct investment outflows
sK9439	$ Forest products imports
sK9440	$ GDFI of central government
sK9441	$ GDFI of central government in constant 2000

sKPI #	Key Performance Indicator name
sK9442	$ GDFI of central government in constant LCU
sK9443	$ GDFI of general government
sK9444	$ GDFI of general government in constant 2000
sK9445	$ GDFI of general government in constant LCU
sK9446	$ GDFI of private sector
sK9447	$ GDFI of private sector in constant 2000
sK9448	$ GDFI of private sector in constant LCU
sK9449	$ GDFI of public enterprises
sK9450	$ GDFI of public enterprises in constant LCU
sK9451	$ GDFI of public sector
sK9452	$ GDFI of public sector in constant 2000
sK9453	$ GDFI of public sector in constant LCU
sK9454	$ GDFI of state and local government
sK9455	$ GDFI of state and local government in constant LCU
sK9460	$ GDP based on PPP in constant 2005
sK9461	$ GDP in constant 2000
sK9462	$ GDP in constant LCU
sK9465	$ GDP per capita
sK9468	$ GDP per capita based on PPP in constant 2005
sK9469	$ GDP per capita in constant 2000
sK9470	$ GDP per capita in constant LCU
sK9479	$ General government final consumption expenditure in constant 2000
sK9480	$ General government final consumption expenditure in constant LCU
sK9483	$ GNI based on PPP
sK9484	$ GNI in Atlas method
sK9485	$ GNI in constant 2000
sK9486	$ GNI in constant LCU
sK9489	$ GNI per capita in Atlas method
sK9490	$ GNI per capita in constant 2000
sK9491	$ Gold at year-end London prices
sK9495	$ Grants (disbursements) from new commitments
sK9497	$ Grants excluding technical cooperation
sK9501	$ Gross capital formation in constant 2000
sK9502	$ Gross capital formation in constant LCU
sK9504	$ Gross domestic income in constant LCU
sK9505	$ Gross domestic savings
sK9506	$ Gross domestic savings in constant 2000
sK9507	$ Gross domestic savings in constant LCU
sK9508	$ Gross domestic savings in private sector
sK9509	$ Gross domestic savings in private sector in constant LCU
sK9510	$ Gross domestic savings in public sector
sK9511	$ Gross domestic savings in public sector in constant LCU
sK9514	$ Gross fixed capital formation in constant 2000
sK9515	$ Gross fixed capital formation in constant LCU
sK9516	$ Gross fixed capital formation in private sector

sKPI #	Key Performance Indicator name
sK9517	$ Gross fixed capital formation in public sector
sK9518	$ Gross national disposable income
sK9521	$ Gross national expenditure in constant 2000
sK9522	$ Gross national expenditure in constant lCU
sK9523	$ Gross national income in constant 2000
sK9524	$ Gross national income in constant LCU
sK9525	$ Gross national savings in private sector
sK9526	$ Gross national savings in private sector in constant LCU
sK9527	$ Gross national savings in public sector
sK9528	$ Gross national savings in public sector in constant LCU
sK9529	$ Gross national savings including net current transfers in constant 2000
sK9530	$ Gross national savings including net current transfers in constant LCU
sK9531	$ Gross ODA aid disbursement for action related to debt from DAC donors
sK9532	$ Gross ODA aid disbursement for administrative costs of DAC donors
sK9533	$ Gross ODA aid disbursement for agriculture from DAC donors
sK9534	$ Gross ODA aid disbursement for agriculture, forestry and fishing sector from DAC donors
sK9535	$ Gross ODA aid disbursement for all sectors and functions of DAC donors
sK9536	$ Gross ODA aid disbursement for banking & financial services from DAC donors
sK9537	$ Gross ODA aid disbursement for basic education from DAC donors
sK9538	$ Gross ODA aid disbursement for basic health from DAC donors
sK9539	$ Gross ODA aid disbursement for business & other services from DAC donors
sK9540	$ Gross ODA aid disbursement for commodity and general program assistance of DAC donors
sK9541	$ Gross ODA aid disbursement for communications from DAC donors
sK9542	$ Gross ODA aid disbursement for conflict, peace and security from DAC donors
sK9543	$ Gross ODA aid disbursement for construction from DAC donors
sK9544	$ Gross ODA aid disbursement for developmental food aid/food security assistance of DAC donors
sK9545	$ Gross ODA aid disbursement for disaster prevention & preparedness from DAC donors
sK9546	$ Gross ODA aid disbursement for economic infrastructure from DAC donors
sK9547	$ Gross ODA aid disbursement for education (level unspecified) from DAC donors
sK9548	$ Gross ODA aid disbursement for education from DAC donors
sK9549	$ Gross ODA aid disbursement for emergency response from DAC donors
sK9550	$ Gross ODA aid disbursement for energy from DAC donors

sKPI #	Key Performance Indicator name
sK9551	$ Gross ODA aid disbursement for fishing from DAC donors
sK9552	$ Gross ODA aid disbursement for forestry from DAC donors
sK9553	$ Gross ODA aid disbursement for general budget support of DAC donors
sK9554	$ Gross ODA aid disbursement for general environment protection from DAC donors
sK9555	$ Gross ODA aid disbursement for general government and civil society from DAC donors
sK9556	$ Gross ODA aid disbursement for general health from DAC donors
sK9557	$ Gross ODA aid disbursement for government & civil society from DAC donors
sK9558	$ Gross ODA aid disbursement for health from DAC donors
sK9559	$ Gross ODA aid disbursement for humanitarian aid from DAC donors
sK9560	$ Gross ODA aid disbursement for industry from DAC donors
sK9561	$ Gross ODA aid disbursement for industry, mining and construction from DAC donors
sK9562	$ Gross ODA aid disbursement for mineral resources and mining from DAC donors
sK9563	$ Gross ODA aid disbursement for multisector from DAC donors
sK9564	$ Gross ODA aid disbursement for other commodity assistance of DAC donors
sK9565	$ Gross ODA aid disbursement for other multisector initiatives from DAC donors
sK9566	$ Gross ODA aid disbursement for population programmes and reproductive health from DAC donors
sK9567	$ Gross ODA aid disbursement for post-secondary education from DAC donors
sK9568	$ Gross ODA aid disbursement for production sectors from DAC donors
sK9569	$ Gross ODA aid disbursement for reconstruction relief and rehabilitation from DAC donors
sK9570	$ Gross ODA aid disbursement for refugees in donor countries from DAC donors
sK9571	$ Gross ODA aid disbursement for secondary education from DAC donors
sK9572	$ Gross ODA aid disbursement for social infrastructure & services from DAC donors
sK9573	$ Gross ODA aid disbursement for support to non-governmental organizations from DAC donors
sK9574	$ Gross ODA aid disbursement for total sector allocable from DAC donors
sK9575	$ Gross ODA aid disbursement for tourism sector from DAC donors
sK9576	$ Gross ODA aid disbursement for trade policy and regulations from DAC donors
sK9577	$ Gross ODA aid disbursement for transport and storage from DAC donors
sK9578	$ Gross ODA aid disbursement for unallocated/ unspecified support from DAC donors

sKPI #	Key Performance Indicator name
sK9579	$ Gross ODA aid disbursement for water supply and sanitation from DAC donors
sK9580	$ Gross ODA aid disbursements for social mitigation of HIV/AIDS from all donors
sK9581	$ Gross ODA aid disbursements for STD control including HIV/AIDS from all donors
sK9586	$ Gross value added at factor cost in constant 2000
sK9587	$ Gross value added at factor cost in constant LCU
sK9588	$ Hazardous pesticides imports
sK10023	$ Household final consumption expenditure based on PPP in constant 2005
sK10024	$ Household final consumption expenditure in constant 2000
sK10025	$ Household final consumption expenditure in constant LCU
sK10040	$ IBRD PPG debt (INT)
sK10041	$ IBRD PPG debt (DIS)
sK10042	$ IBRD PPG debt (DOD)
sK10043	$ IBRD PPG debt (NTR)
sK10044	$ IBRD PPG debt (TDS)
sK10048	$ IDA PPG debt (DIS)
sK10049	$ IDA PPG debt (DOD)
sK10050	$ IDA PPG debt (INT)
sK10051	$ IDA PPG debt (NTR)
sK10052	$ IDA PPG debt (TDS)
sK10058	$ IMF disbursements on external debt
sK10062	$ IMF repurchases
sK10068	$ Imports of goods
sK10071	$ Imports of goods and services
sK10073	$ Imports of income
sK10074	$ Imports of services
sK10075	$ Income payments
sK10076	$ Income receipts
sK10078	$ Indirect taxes
sK10080	$ Inflows of foreign direct investment
sK10089	$ Interest payments of long-term debt including IMF credit
sK10091	$ International Bank for Reconstruction and Development Commitments
sK10092	$ International Bank for Reconstruction and Development PPG debt
sK10093	$ International Development Association Commitments
sK10094	$ International Development Association PPG debt
sK10104	$ Inventory in constant LCU
sK10116	$ Long-term and IMF principal repayments on external debt
sK10120	$ Long-term disbursements on external debt
sK10123	$ Long-term interest due including IMF per BOP
sK10133	$ LT principal due, per balance of payments account
sK10148	$ Migrant remittance inflows

sKPI #	Key Performance Indicator name
sK10149	$ Migrant remittance outflows
sK10166	$ Multilateral concessional PPG debt
sK10167	$ Multilateral concessional PPG debt (DOD)
sK10168	$ Multilateral concessional PPG debt (TDS)
sK10174	$ Multilateral PPG debt
sK10175	$ Multilateral PPG debt (DIS)
sK10176	$ Multilateral PPG debt (DOD)
sK10177	$ Multilateral PPG debt (INT)
sK10178	$ Multilateral PPG non-concessioanl creditor disbursements
sK10179	$ Net adjusted errors and omissions
sK10181	$ Net bilateral aid flows from Australian DAC donors
sK10183	$ Net bilateral aid flows from Austrian DAC donors
sK10187	$ Net bilateral aid flows from Canadian DAC donors
sK10188	$ Net bilateral aid flows from DAC donors
sK10189	$ Net bilateral aid flows from Danish DAC donors
sK10191	$ Net bilateral aid flows from Dutch DAC donors
sK10192	$ Net bilateral aid flows from European Union institution DAC donors
sK10196	$ Net bilateral aid flows from French DAC donors
sK10197	$ Net bilateral aid flows from German DAC donors
sK10200	$ Net bilateral aid flows from Greek DAC donors
sK10202	$ Net bilateral aid flows from Irish DAC donors
sK10203	$ Net bilateral aid flows from Italian DAC donors
sK10206	$ Net bilateral aid flows from Japanese DAC donors
sK10208	$ Net bilateral aid flows from Luxembourger DAC donors
sK10213	$ Net bilateral aid flows from Norwegian DAC donors
sK10215	$ Net bilateral aid flows from Portuguese DAC donors
sK10218	$ Net bilateral aid flows from Spanish DAC donors
sK10220	$ Net bilateral aid flows from Swedish DAC donors
sK10221	$ Net bilateral aid flows from Swiss DAC donors
sK10226	$ Net bilateral flows from Finnish DAC donors
sK10234	$ Net current transfers from abroad in constant LCU
sK10241	$ Net flows on external debt
sK10249	$ Net income from abroad in constant LCU
sK10251	$ Net long-term borrowing
sK10256	$ Net ODA received from DAC donors
sK10257	$ Net ODA received from multilateral donors
sK10258	$ Net ODA received from non-DAC donors
sK10259	$ Net ODA received from other donors
sK10260	$ Net ODA received per capita from DAC donors
sK10261	$ Net ODA received per capita from multilateral donors
sK10268	$ Net other long-term inflows
sK10271	$ Net taxes on products in constant LCU
sK10275	$ Net trade in services
sK10279	$ ODA aid disbursements for malaria control from all donors

sKPI #	Key Performance Indicator name
sK10282	$ Official current and capital transfers
sK10283	$ Official current transfer receipts
sK10284	$ Official current transfers
sK10320	$ Other capital outflows
sK10327	$ Other income payments
sK10335	$ Outstanding and disbursed multilateral PPG debt on non-concessional terms
sK10336	$ Outstanding and disbursed PPG and PNG private creditor debt
sK10337	$ Outstanding and disbursed PPG bilateral and non-concessional debt
sK10345	$ Payments of current transfers
sK10346	$ Payments of official current transfers
sK10347	$ Payments of private current transfers
sK10351	$ Pesticides imports
sK10352	$ PNG external debt stocks
sK10361	$ PPG and PNG private creditor disbursements
sK10363	$ PPG debt from bonds
sK10364	$ PPG debt from bonds (DIS)
sK10365	$ PPG debt from bonds (DOD)
sK10366	$ PPG debt from bonds (INT)
sK10367	$ PPG debt from bonds (NFL)
sK10368	$ PPG debt from bonds (TDS)
sK10369	$ PPG debt from commercial banks
sK10370	$ PPG debt from commercial banks (DIS)
sK10371	$ PPG debt from commercial banks (DOD)
sK10372	$ PPG debt from commercial banks (INT)
sK10373	$ PPG debt from commercial banks (NFL)
sK10374	$ PPG debt from official creditors
sK10375	$ PPG debt from official creditors (DIS)
sK10376	$ PPG debt from official creditors (DOD)
sK10377	$ PPG debt from official creditors (INT)
sK10378	$ PPG debt from official creditors (NFL)
sK10379	$ PPG debt from official creditors (TDS)
sK10380	$ PPG debt from private creditors
sK10381	$ PPG debt from private creditors (DIS)
sK10382	$ PPG debt from private creditors (DOD)
sK10383	$ PPG debt from private creditors (INT)
sK10384	$ PPG debt from private creditors (NFL)
sK10385	$ PPG debt service on external debt
sK10386	$ PPG debts from commercial banks (TDS)
sK10387	$ PPG external debt stocks
sK10388	$ PPG from private creditors (TDS)
sK10389	$ PPG principal arrears
sK10405	$ Principal repayments
sK10406	$ Principal repayments from PPG and PNG private creditors

sKPI #	Key Performance Indicator name
sK10408	$ Private capital inflows
sK10413	$ Private current transfer receipts
sK10414	$ Private current transfers
sK10422	$ Private non-guaranteed debt service on external debt
sK10423	$ Private nonguaranteed disbursements on external debt
sK10437	$ Public an publicly guaranteed disbursements on external debt
sK10450	$ Public and publicly guaranteed net flows on external debt
sK10465	$ Reduction in arrears or prepayments in debt service
sK10508	$ Short-term disbursements
sK10574	$ Stocks private sector
sK10576	$ Stocks public sector
sK10679	$ Value added by agriculture
sK10681	$ Value added by banking
sK10683	$ Value added by construction
sK10685	$ Value added by discrepancy in GDP
sK10687	$ Value added by gas, electricity and water
sK10691	$ Value added by industry
sK10695	$ Value added by manufacturing
sK10697	$ Value added by mining and quarrying
sK10699	$ Value added by other services
sK10701	$ Value added by ownership of dwellings
sK10703	$ Value added by public administration and defense
sK10711	$ Wages and salaries
sK10735	% 3 months interest rate
sK10736	% 3 year backward moving average of the current account balance, from GDP
sK10788	% Agriculture value added from GDP
sK10799	% Broad money growth
sK10804	% DP growth
sK10808	% GNI
sK10809	# Claims on other sectors of the domestic economy from broad money
sK10810	# Claims on private sector from broad money
sK10811	# Claims on central government from broad money
sK10816	$ GDP per capita
sK10818	$ GNI per capita
sK10821	$ Household final consumption expenditure
sK10825	$ Money and quasi money
sK10829	$ Value added by industry from GDP
sK10831	$ Value added by services
sK11093	% Current account balance excluding net official capital grants from GDP
sK11096	% Current account balance from GNP
sK11105	% Debt on concessional terms from exports
sK11106	% Debt on concessional terms from GDP
sK11107	% Debt on non-concessional terms from exports

sKPI #	Key Performance Indicator name
sK11108	% Debt on non-concessional terms from GDP
sK11364	% Exports as a capacity to import
sK11365	% Exports of goods and non-financial services
sK11369	% Ex-post debt to export
sK11586	% Foreign direct investment from GDP
sK11612	% GDP PPP conversion factor to market exchange rate ratio
sK11653	% Gross public investment from GDP
sK11692	% Household final consumption expenditure from GDP
sK11921	% Inflows of direct investment from GDP
sK12171	% Merchandise trade to GDP ratio
sK12173	% Migrant remittance inflows of GDP
sK12221	% Net current transfers from GDP
sK12233	% Net income from GDP
sK12255	% Net ODA received from central government expenditure
sK12258	% Net ODA received from DAC donors from recipient's GDI
sK12259	% Net ODA received from DAC donors from recipient's GDP
sK12260	% Net ODA received from exports and imports
sK12262	% Net ODA received from GDP
sK12265	% Net ODA received from GNP
sK12271	% Net ODA received from multilateral donor from GDP
sK12272	% Net ODA received from multilateral donors from gross capital formation
sK12273	% Net ODA received from non-DAC bilateral donors from GDP
sK12274	% Net ODA received from non-DAC bilateral donors from gross capital formation
sK12354	% Outstanding and disbursed debt from GDP
sK12705	% PPG and IMF only debt service on external debt excluding workers' remittances to exports
sK12711	% Present value of debt to nominal value
sK12746	% Private capital inflows from GDP
sK12769	% Public and publicly guaranteed debt service excluding worker's remittances from exports
sK12803	% Real agricultural GDP
sK12804	% Real agricultural GDP per capita
sK12975	% Terms of regional agreements implemented

Energy Production & Use

Energy production and use is the production of electricity, combustible fuels, nuclear and thermonuclear fuels, heating and cooling processes by renewable resources.

sKPI #	Key Performance Indicator name
sK7091	# Accident fatalities per energy produced by fuel chain
sK7102	# Advised measures with acceptable payback times
sK7128	# Agricultural energy intensities
sK7169	# Assigned auditors and their quality
sK7178	# Audits carried out

sKPI #	Key Performance Indicator name
sK7363	# Buildings constructed according to standard
sK7397	# Checks carried out (permits, buildings)
sK7430	# Coal capacity factor
sK7439	# Companies in the sector that signed the agreement and their share
sK7458	# Construction time for coal
sK7459	# Construction time for natural gas
sK7465	# Contingencies with CCS
sK7475	# Costs of energy savings measures implemented and the variety of costs
sK7509	# Crude steel production
sK7521	# Days required to connect to electricity
sK7585	# CO2e per tonne of steel
sK7590	# Economic life of coal
sK7591	# Economic life of natural gas
sK7604	# Electric power consumption per capita
sK7606	# Electric power transmission and distribution losses
sK7608	# Electricity production from coal sources
sK7610	# Electricity production from hydroelectric sources
sK7612	# Electricity production from natural gas sources
sK7614	# Electricity production from nuclear sources
sK7616	# Electricity production from oil sources
sK7617	# Electricity production from renewable sources
sK7618	# Electricity production from renewable sources, excluding hydroelectric
sK7620	# Electricity production
sK7621	# Electricity use per employee
sK7622	# Eligible actors that apply for the scheme
sK7643	# Energy consumption for space heating per floor area
sK7644	# Energy imports in kt of oil equivalent
sK7645	# Energy intensity
sK7646	# Energy per appliance
sK7647	# Energy per pass-km
sK7648	# Energy per tonne of alumina
sK7649	# Energy per tonne of BOF steel
sK7650	# Energy per tonne of clinker
sK7651	# Energy per tonne of primary aluminum
sK7652	# Energy per vehicle
sK7654	# Energy production in kt of oil
sK7655	# Energy reserves-to-production ratio
sK7656	# Energy resources-to-production ratio
sK7658	# Energy use in kg of oil
sK7659	# Energy use in kg of oil per $1,000 GDP
sK7661	# Energy use in kg of oil per capita
sK7662	# Energy use per capita
sK7663	# Energy use per employee
sK7664	# Energy use per household

sKPI #	Key Performance Indicator name
sK7665	# Energy use per unit of GDP
sK7889	# Heat consumption relative to BAT pulp and paper
sK7890	# Heating degree-days
sK7993	# Household energy intensities
sK7994	# Household energy use for each income group and corresponding fuel mix
sK8031	# Indigenous energy production
sK8049	# Industrial energy intensities
sK8326	# Methane emissions in energy sector
sK8327	# Methane emissions
sK8358	# Natural gas capacity factor
sK8361	# Net energy power output with capture
sK8362	# Net energy power output without capture
sK8380	# Non-compliant energy companies
sK8381	# Non-compliant permits/buildings
sK8434	# Participants (buyers, suppliers)
sK8584	# Per capita energy consumption in the residential sector
sK8585	# Per capita energy consumption per floor area
sK8601	# Permits traded, price of permits and liquidity on the market
sK8781	# Primary energy consumption per capita
sK8782	# Primary energy intensity
sK8794	# Production clinker
sK8845	# Recipients that implement recommended improvements
sK8856	# Rejected projects and variety of rejected projects
sK8879	# Road sector diesel fuel consumption in kt of oil
sK8880	# Road sector diesel fuel consumption per capita in kt per oil
sK8881	# Road sector energy consumption in kt per oil
sK8882	# Road sector energy consumption per capita in kt per oil
sK8883	# Road sector gasoline fuel consumption in kt per oil
sK8884	# Road sector gasoline fuel consumption per capita in kt per oil
sK8898	# Sanctions
sK8906	# Service/commercial energy intensities
sK8915	# Solar heaters per capita, for every 1000 inhabitants
sK8921	# Specific power consumption for aluminum smelting
sK9064	# Unit consumption for steel
sK9070	# VA compliance plans
sK9072	# Value added by energy
sK9178	$ Changes in energy tax or other financial incentives or energy prices
sK9193	$ Cost of CO2 avoided
sK9262	$ End-use energy prices by fuel and by sector
sK9263	$ Energy savings achieved with implemented projects
sK9474	$ GDP per unit of energy use based on PPP
sK10113	$ LCOE with capture
sK10114	$ LCOE without capture

sKPI #	Key Performance Indicator name
sK10341	$ Overnight energy cost with capture (USD/kW)
sK10342	$ Overnight energy cost without capture
sK10466	$ Relative increase in overnight cost
sK10503	$ Sales of new product or technology
sK11001	% Changes in product range suppliers
sK11031	% Commercial fuels exported
sK11148	% EEI for (petro) chemicals
sK11153	% Efficiency of power generation
sK11154	% Efficient process
sK11160	% Electric power transmission and distribution losses from output
sK11161	% Electricity demand met by supply
sK11166	% Electricity production from coal sources
sK11168	% Electricity production from hydroelectric sources
sK11170	% Electricity production from natural gas sources
sK11172	% Electricity production from nuclear sources
sK11174	% Electricity production from oil sources
sK11175	% Electricity production from oil, gas and coal sources
sK11176	% Electricity production from renewable sources, excluding hydroelectric
sK11198	% Energy depletion from GNI
sK11199	% Energy losses in energy sector
sK11200	% Energy related methane emissions
sK11537	% Final and primary energy intensity ratio
sK11595	% Fossil fuel energy consumption
sK11596	% Fossil fuel-based electricity generation efficiency, public, including CHP
sK11603	% Fuel shares in energy and electricity
sK11693	% Household income spent on fuel and electricity
sK11712	% Households or population without electricity or commercial energy, or heavily dependent on non-commercial energy
sK12140	% Market share of eligible changes in product range of suppliers to determine free riders and spill-over
sK12222	% Net efficiency with capture, LHV
sK12223	% Net efficiency without capture, LHV
sK12224	% Net energy import dependency
sK12226	% Net energy imports from energy use
sK12276	% Net oil imports
sK12415	% Penetration levels of energy saving measures within the target group(s)
sK12678	% Population with access to electricity
sK12787	% Quality of auditing tools
sK12829	% Reduction potential compared to BAT iron & steel, cement
sK12837	% Relative decrease in net efficiency
sK12838	% Relative increase in LCOE
sK12840	% Reliance on biomass
sK12902	% Sectoral energy consumption accounted for by the participants in the scheme

sKPI #	Key Performance Indicator name
sK12903	% Sectors and energy carriers in total energy
sK12915	% Self-sufficiency of energy production
sK12917	% Share of decentralized power production
sK13031	% Primary energy supply exported
sK13052	% Traditional fuels in energy consumption
sK23166	# Capacity constructed or rehabilitated as a result of USG assistance
sK23167	# People receiving USG supported training in technical energy fields
sK23168	# Men receiving USG supported training in technical energy fields
sK23169	# Women receiving USG supported training in technical energy fields
sK23170	# People with increased access to modern energy services as a result of USG assistance
sK23171	# Policy reforms to enhance sector governance and/or facilitate private sector participation and competitive markets as a result of USG assistance
sK23172	# Regulations to enhance sector governance and/or facilitate private sector participation and competitive markets as a result of USG assistance
sK23173	# Administrative procedures analyzed to enhance sector governance and/or facilitate private sector participation and competitive markets as a result of USG assistance
sK23174	# Policy reforms for public/stakeholder consultation to enhance sector governance and/or facilitate private sector participation and competitive markets as a result of USG assistance
sK23175	# Regulations for public/stakeholder consultation to enhance sector governance and/or facilitate private sector participation and competitive markets as a result of USG assistance
sK23176	# Administrative procedures drafted and presented for public/stakeholder consultation to enhance sector governance and/or facilitate private sector participation and competitive markets as a result of USG assistance
sK23177	# Regulations passed/approved to enhance sector governance and/or facilitate private sector participation and competitive markets as a result of USG assistance
sK23178	# Administrative procedures passed/approved to enhance sector governance and/or facilitate private sector participation and competitive markets as a result of USG assistance
sK23179	# Policy reforms passed/approved to enhance sector governance and/or facilitate private sector participation and competitive markets as a result of USG assistance
sK23180	# Greenhouse gas emissions, measured in tonnes CO2 equivalent, reduced or sequestered as a result of USG assistance in energy, industry, urban, and/or transport sectors
sK23181	$ Public and private dollars leveraged by USG for energy infrastructure projects
sK23182	# Greenhouse gas emissions reduced or sequestered as a result of USG assistance
sK23183	# Energy saved as a result of USG assistance
sK23184	# Carbon intensity of energy use
sK23185	# Operational Renewable Electric Generation Capacity
sK23186	# Solar electric generation capacity

sKPI #	Key Performance Indicator name
sK23187	# Hydro electric generation capacity
sK23188	# Wind electric generation capacity
sK23189	# Energy displaced with lower carbon fuels due to USG project assistance
sK23190	# Energy saved due to energy efficiency/conservation projects as a result of USG assistance
sK23191	# Households implementing energy efficiency measures as a result of USG assistance
sK23192	# People who now have access to modern energy services as a result of renewable energy technologies through USG assistance
sK23193	# People who now have access to solar energy services as a result of renewable energy technologies through USG assistance
sK23194	# People who now have access to wind energy services as a result of renewable energy technologies through USG assistance
sK23195	# People who now have access to hydro energy services as a result of renewable energy technologies through USG assistance
sK23196	$ Funding leveraged from public and private sources for clean energy and/or energy efficiency as a result of USG assistance
sK23197	# Overseas development assistance (official ODA)
sK23198	# Laws addressing clean energy (climate change) proposed, adopted, or implemented as a result of USG assistance
sK23199	# Policies addressing clean energy (climate change) proposed, adopted, or implemented as a result of USG assistance
sK23200	# Agreements addressing clean energy (climate change) proposed, adopted, or implemented as a result of USG assistance
sK23201	# Regulations addressing clean energy (climate change) proposed, adopted, or implemented as a result of USG assistance
sK23202	# People receiving USG supported training in clean energy related topics
sK23203	# Women receiving USG supported training in clean energy related topics
sK23204	# Men receiving USG supported training in clean energy related topics
sK23205	# Clean energy tools, technologies and methodologies developed, tested and/or adopted
sK23206	$ Anticipated energy savings over years as a result of USG assistance
sK23207	# Energy agencies, regulatory bodies, utilities and civil society organizations undertaking capacity assessments as a result of USG assistance
sK23208	# Energy enterprises with improved business operations as a result of USG assistance
sK23209	# People receiving USG supported training in energy related business management systems
sK23210	# Men receiving USG supported training in energy related business management systems
sK23211	# Women receiving USG supported training in energy related business management systems

sKPI #	Key Performance Indicator name
sK23212	# People receiving USG supported training in energy related policy and regulatory practices
sK23213	# Men receiving USG supported training in energy related policy and regulatory practices
sK23214	# Women receiving USG supported training in energy related policy and regulatory practices

Finance

Finance represents the study of how people allocate their assets over a certain period under conditions of certainty and uncertainty. The financial sector is represented by private and public institutions that offer insurance, banking and asset management services.

sKPI #	Key Performance Indicator name
sK7073	% Consumption of fixed capital from GNI
sK7074	% Letters answered within 20 days
sK7096	# Additional amounts assessed from audit
sK7097	# Additional amounts assessed from audit per auditor
sK7103	# Advisory visits
sK7145	# Amounts recovered from assets
sK7179	# Audits completed by tax type
sK7180	# Automated teller machines (ATMs) per 100,000 adults
sK7182	# Age of collection cases
sK7185	# Audits per tax auditor
sK7190	# Days to issue a refund
sK7194	# Length of appeals case
sK7199	# Processing time
sK7202	# Taxpayer wait time for service
sK7205	# Time to complete an investigation
sK7206	# Time to complete audit by type of audit
sK7207	# Time to complete new registration
sK7208	# Time to resolve non-filer case
sK7209	# Time to respond to written taxpayer requests
sK7332	# Banking survey claims on private sector
sK7406	# Claims flow on other official entities
sK7407	# Claims on central government
sK7408	# Claims on governments and other public entities
sK7436	# Commercial banks branches per 100, 000 adults
sK7454	# Confiscation procedures
sK7461	# Consumer price index
sK7467	# Convictions for crimes other than money laundering originating from STRs
sK7468	# Convictions for laundering proceeds of crimes committed abroad
sK7499	# CPIA quality of budgetary and financial management rating
sK7542	# Declarations made in application to the EU Cash Control Regulation
sK7546	# Deposit accounts, commercial banks per 1,000 adults
sK7547	# Deposit accounts, cooperatives per 1,000 adults

sKPI #	Key Performance Indicator name
sK7548	# Deposit accounts, microfinance institutions per 1,000 adults
sK7549	# Deposit accounts, specialized state financial institutions per 1,000 adults
sK7550	# Depth of credit information index
sK7589	# Ease of shareholder suits index
sK7596	# Educational seminars
sK7624	# Emerging Market Bond Index (JPM Total Return Index)
sK7687	# Extent of director liability index
sK7688	# Extent of disclosure index
sK7787	# Firing cost in weeks of wages
sK7798	# Flow of claims on central government
sK7799	# Flow of claims on private sector
sK7800	# Flow of money and quasi money
sK7801	# Flow of net domestic credit
sK7802	# Flow of net domestic credit to government
sK7803	# Flow of net foreign assets
sK7804	# Flow of other liabilities excluding M2
sK7821	# Freezing procedures, based on a court order
sK7992	# Hours to prepare and pay taxes
sK8028	# Incorrect cash declarations or findings as a result of customs controls in the EU at external borders
sK8087	# J.P. Morgan Emerging Market Bond Index (EMBI+)
sK8128	# Listed domestic companies
sK8135	# Loan accounts in commercial banks per 1,000 adults
sK8136	# Loan accounts in cooperatives per 1,000 adults
sK8137	# Loan accounts in microfinance institutions per 1,000 adults
sK8138	# Loan accounts in specialized state financial institutions per 1,000 adults
sK8334	# Microfinancial institutions branches per 100,000 adults
sK8349	# Money laundering investigations carried out independently by law enforcement agencies, without a prior STR
sK8372	# New registrants
sK8377	# Nominal Effective Exchange Rate
sK8385	# Non-filers by tax type
sK8401	# Official average grace period on new external debt commitments
sK8402	# Official average maturity in years on new external debt commitments
sK8572	# Payments processed manually and electronic
sK8593	# Periodicity of GDP growth indicator
sK8604	# Persons or legal entities convicted for money laundering offences
sK8786	# Private average grace period on new external debt commitments
sK8787	# Private average maturity in years on new external debt commitment
sK8788	# Procedures required to start a business

sKPI #	Key Performance Indicator name
sK8844	# Real effective exchange rate index
sK8853	# Refunds issued, by tax type
sK8862	# Requests received for confiscation orders from another EU Member State and the value of confiscated assets
sK8863	# Requests received for freezing orders from another EU Member State and the value of frozen assets
sK8869	# Returns processed, by tax type
sK8899	# Scientific and technical journal articles
sK8905	# Sentences for money laundering offences
sK8920	# Specialized state financial institutions branches per 100,00 adults
sK8922	# Staff dedicated full time or full time equivalent to money laundering in law enforcement agencies
sK8923	# Staff dedicated full time or full time equivalent to money laundering in the FIU
sK8924	# Staff dedicated full time or full time equivalent to money laundering in the judiciary
sK8926	# Start-up procedures to register a business
sK8928	# Stock of net domestic credit to private sector
sK8933	# Strength of investor protection index
sK8935	# STRs sent to law enforcement and on which further analysis was made
sK8942	# Suspicious cash activities at the EU borders reported to the FIU, including those based on declarations and smuggling
sK8943	# Suspicious Transaction Reports (STRs) filled
sK8944	# Tax payments
sK8945	# Tax rebates
sK8946	# Taxpayers assisted
sK8947	# Taxpayers contacted
sK8951	# Technicians in R&D per million people
sK8980	# Collection cases closed
sK9066	# Unsuspended custodial sentences, as principle offence, as predicate offence
sK9085	# Wholesale price index
sK9093	# Years to resolve insolvency
sK9096	# Claims flow on non-monetary financial institutions
sK9097	# Claims flow on private sector and other financial institutions
sK9099	$ International tourism receipts for passenger transport items
sK9102	$ Net national savings from GNI
sK9104	$ PNG from commercial banks and other creditors
sK9105	$ Private nonguaranteed (PNG) net flows on external debt
sK9107	$ Adjusted net errors and omissions
sK9108	$ Adjusted net national income
sK9120	$ Annual collection per person year
sK9147	$ Bilateral concessional PPG
sK9151	$ Bilateral net financial flows

sKPI #	Key Performance Indicator name
sK9153	$ Bilateral PPG
sK9167	$ Car purchase taxes
sK9168	$ Carbon dioxide damage from GNI
sK9171	$ Central bank assets
sK9179	$ Changes in inventory
sK9188	$ Concessional external debt stocks
sK9189	$ Consumption of fixed capital from GNI
sK9202	$ Debt buyback
sK9203	$ Debt forgiveness grants
sK9204	$ Debt forgiveness or reduction
sK9210	$ Debt stock reduction
sK9211	$ Debt stock rescheduled
sK9212	$ DEC alternative conversion factor
sK9214	$ Demand deposits
sK9252	$ Discrepancy in expenditure estimate of GDP
sK9255	$ Domestic net incurrence of liabilities
sK9256	$ Education expenditure from GNI
sK9270	$ Euro-dollar exchange rate
sK9384	$ External balance on goods and services
sK9423	$ Final consumption expenditure
sK9427	$ Financial net return/capitalized value
sK9438	$ Foreign net incurrence of liabilities
sK9459	$ GDP based on PPP
sK9467	$ GDP per capita based on PPP
sK9476	$ GDP PPP conversion factor
sK9478	$ General government final consumption expenditure
sK9482	$ GNI
sK9488	$ GNI per capita based on PPP
sK9498	$ Grants, excluding technical cooperation
sK9500	$ Gross capital formation
sK9503	$ Gross domestic income
sK9513	$ Gross fixed capital formation
sK9520	$ Gross national expenditure
sK9583	$ Gross saving
sK9585	$ Gross value added at factor cost
sK9658	$ High-technology exports
sK10022	$ Household final consumption expenditure based on PPP
sK10027	$ Household final consumption expenditure per capita
sK10028	$ Household final consumption expenditure, etc.
sK10036	$ IAEA net official flows from UN agencies
sK10037	$ IBRD loans and IDA credits
sK10039	$ IBRD net financial loans
sK10045	$ IDA grants
sK10047	$ IDA net financial flows
sK10053	$ IFAD net official flows from UN agencies
sK10054	$ IMF and long-term disbursements on external debt

sKPI #	Key Performance Indicator name
sK10056	$ IMF charges
sK10057	$ IMF concessional net financial flows
sK10059	$ IMF non-concessional net financial flow
sK10061	$ IMF purchases
sK10064	$ IMF repurchases and charges
sK10065	$ Import cost per container
sK10070	$ Imports of goods and services
sK10085	$ Interest forgiven
sK10088	$ Interest payments
sK10090	$ Interest rescheduled (capitalized)
sK10115	$ Long-term + IMF principal repayments on external debt
sK10118	$ Long-term debt service on external debt
sK10119	$ Long-term disbursements on external debt
sK10122	$ Long-term external debt stocks
sK10125	$ Long-term interest payments on external debt
sK10127	$ Long-term net flows on external debt
sK10128	$ Long-term net transfers on external debt
sK10130	$ Long-term principal repayments on external debt
sK10131	$ Long-term private sector external debt stocks
sK10132	$ Long-term public sector external debt stocks
sK10134	$ M2 money and quasi money
sK10138	$ Market capitalization of listed companies
sK10139	$ Market or replacement value
sK10141	$ Maximum charge of on-street parking in the city center per hour
sK10144	$ Merchandise exports by the reporting economy
sK10147	$ Merchandise imports by the reporting economy
sK10152	$ Mineral depletion from GNI
sK10162	$ Money
sK10163	$ Money and quasi money (M2)
sK10165	$ Multilateral concessional PPG
sK10170	$ Multilateral debt service
sK10172	$ Multilateral net financial flows
sK10173	$ Multilateral PPG
sK10180	$ Net bilateral aid flows from Australia DAC donors
sK10182	$ Net bilateral aid flows from Austria DAC donors
sK10185	$ Net bilateral aid flows from Belgium DAC donors
sK10186	$ Net bilateral aid flows from Canada DAC donors
sK10190	$ Net bilateral aid flows from Denmark DAC donors
sK10193	$ Net bilateral aid flows from European Union institutions DAC donors
sK10194	$ Net bilateral aid flows from Finland DAC donors
sK10195	$ Net bilateral aid flows from France DAC donors
sK10198	$ Net bilateral aid flows from Germany DAC donors
sK10199	$ Net bilateral aid flows from Greece DAC donors
sK10201	$ Net bilateral aid flows from Ireland DAC donors
sK10204	$ Net bilateral aid flows from Italy DAC donors
sK10205	$ Net bilateral aid flows from Japan DAC donors
sK10207	$ Net bilateral aid flows from Luxembourg DAC donors
sK10209	$ Net bilateral aid flows from Netherlands DAC donors
sK10211	$ Net bilateral aid flows from New Zealand DAC donors
sK10212	$ Net bilateral aid flows from Norway DAC donors
sK10214	$ Net bilateral aid flows from Portugal DAC donors
sK10216	$ Net bilateral aid flows from Rep. of Korea DAC donors
sK10217	$ Net bilateral aid flows from Spain DAC donors
sK10219	$ Net bilateral aid flows from Sweden DAC donors
sK10222	$ Net bilateral aid flows from Switzerland DAC donors
sK10223	$ Net bilateral aid flows from United Kingdom DAC donors
sK10225	$ Net bilateral aid flows from United States DAC donors
sK10228	$ Net capital account
sK10229	$ Net change in interest arrears
sK10231	$ Net current transfers
sK10233	$ Net current transfers from abroad
sK10236	$ Net domestic credit
sK10237	$ Net domestic credit stock to other official entities
sK10238	$ Net domestic credit stock to other private financial institutions
sK10239	$ Net domestic credit stock to rest of economy
sK10243	$ Net foreign assets
sK10244	$ Net forest depletion from GNI
sK10246	$ Net income
sK10248	$ Net income from abroad
sK10250	$ Net inflows in reporting economy of foreign direct investment
sK10254	$ Net ODA aid received per capita
sK10263	$ Net official aid received
sK10265	$ Net official development assistance and official aid received
sK10267	$ Net official development assistance received
sK10270	$ Net taxes on products
sK10273	$ Net trade in goods
sK10274	$ Net trade in goods and services
sK10280	$ Official creditors commitments
sK10281	$ Official creditors interest arrears
sK10286	$ Official exchange rate
sK10287	$ Official exchange rate (period average)
sK10288	$ Official interest rescheduled
sK10289	$ Official principal rescheduled
sK10290	$ Oil price
sK10311	$ Old age benefits: other lump sum cash benefits means-tested
sK10314	$ Old age benefits: partial pension non-means tested
sK10322	$ Other depository corporations assets
sK10326	$ Other expense

sKPI #	Key Performance Indicator name
sK10328	$ Other liabilities excluding M2
sK10329	$ Other net financial flows
sK10333	$ Other taxes
sK10343	$ Paid workers' remittances and compensation for employees
sK10344	$ Particulate emission damage from GNI
sK10349	$ Payments of royalty and license fees
sK10353	$ PNG from bonds
sK10355	$ Portfolio equity bonds (PPG + PNG)
sK10356	$ Portfolio equity net inflows
sK10358	$ Portfolio investment equity
sK10360	$ Portfolio investment, excluding LCFAR
sK10362	$ PPG bonds
sK10390	$ PPG, commercial banks
sK10391	$ PPG, IBRD
sK10392	$ PPG, IDA
sK10393	$ PPG, official creditors
sK10394	$ PPG, other private creditors
sK10395	$ PPG, private creditors
sK10397	$ Present value of external debt
sK10402	$ Principal arrears owned to official creditors
sK10403	$ Principal arrears owned to private creditors
sK10404	$ Principal forgiven
sK10407	$ Principal rescheduled
sK10410	$ Private consumption PPP conversion factor
sK10411	$ Private creditors commitments
sK10412	$ Private creditors interest arrears
sK10415	$ Private interest rescheduled
sK10416	$ Private non-guaranteed (PNG) debt service on external debt
sK10417	$ Private non-guaranteed (PNG) disbursements on external debt
sK10418	$ Private non-guaranteed (PNG) external debt stocks
sK10419	$ Private non-guaranteed (PNG) net transfers on external debt
sK10421	$ Private non-guaranteed (PNG) principal repayments on external debt
sK10424	$ Private non-guaranteed EBRD
sK10425	$ Private non-guaranteed IFC
sK10427	$ Private non-guaranteed interest payments on external debt
sK10428	$ Private principal rescheduled
sK10436	$ Profit remittances on FDI
sK10438	$ Public and publicly guaranteed (PPG) debt service on external debt
sK10439	$ Public and publicly guaranteed (PPG) disbursements on external debt
sK10440	$ Public and publicly guaranteed (PPG) external debt stocks

sKPI #	Key Performance Indicator name
sK10441	$ Public and publicly guaranteed (PPG) net flows on external debt
sK10442	$ Public and publicly guaranteed (PPG) net transfers on external debt
sK10444	$ Public and publicly guaranteed (PPG) principal repayments on external debt
sK10445	$ Public and publicly guaranteed commitments
sK10447	$ Public and publicly guaranteed interest arrears
sK10449	$ Public and publicly guaranteed interest payments on external debt
sK10451	$ Public and publicly guaranteed principal arrears
sK10456	$ Quasi money
sK10457	$ RDB concessional net financial flows
sK10458	$ RDB non-concessional net financial flows
sK10459	$ Receipts for workers' remittances
sK10461	$ Receipts of royalty and license fees
sK10462	$ Received workers' remittances and compensation for employees
sK10464	$ Recovery rate of resolving insolvency
sK10474	$ Residual, debt stock-flow reconciliation
sK10497	$ Revenue, excluding grants
sK10507	$ Service exports
sK10510	$ Short-term external debt stocks
sK10512	$ Short-term interest payments on external debt
sK10514	$ Short-term net flows on external debt
sK10549	$ Social contributions
sK10578	$ Subsidies and other transfers
sK10603	$ Tax revenue
sK10604	$ Taxes on exports
sK10605	$ Taxes on goods and services
sK10606	$ Taxes on income, profits and capital gains
sK10607	$ Taxes on international trade
sK10608	$ Technical cooperation grants
sK10609	$ Terms of trade adjustment
sK10610	$ Debt rescheduled
sK10613	$ Deflated value (landed price)
sK10619	$ Interest payments on external debt
sK10622	$ Net transfers on external debt
sK10623	$ Reserves minus gold
sK10624	$ Reserves, including gold
sK10625	$ Resources (person years) assigned
sK10626	$ Undisbursed external debt
sK10627	$ Value of stocks traded
sK10628	$ Water productivity from GDP per cubic meter of total freshwater withdrawal
sK10630	$ UNAIDS net official flows from UN agencies
sK10631	$ Undisbursed external debt to official creditors
sK10632	$ Undisbursed external debt to private creditors

sKPI #	Key Performance Indicator name
sK10633	$ UNDP net official flows from UN agencies
sK10634	$ UNECE net official flows from UN agencies
sK10670	$ UNFPA net official flows from UN agencies
sK10671	$ UNHCR net official flows from UN agencies
sK10672	$ UNICEF net official flows from UN agencies
sK10673	$ UNRWA net official flows from UN agencies
sK10674	$ UNTA net official flows from UN agencies
sK10675	$ Use of IMF credit
sK10678	$ Value added by agriculture
sK10690	$ Value added by industry
sK10694	$ Value added by manufacturing
sK10705	$ Value added by services
sK10706	$ Value of arrears collected
sK10707	$ Value of payments processed
sK10709	$ Variable rate debt stocks
sK10713	$ WFP net official flows from UN agencies
sK10714	$ WHO net official flows from UN agencies
sK10739	% 5 years change in share of world exports (export market shares) measured at current prices
sK10746	% Accuracy of responses provided
sK10747	% Accuracy of taxpayer register
sK10766	% Adults who made payments of private current transfers
sK10794	% All products with simple mean bound rate
sK10801	% Consumer prices inflation
sK10806	% GDP deflator inflation
sK10812	# Claims on governments from M2
sK10813	# Claims on private section from M2
sK10819	# Gross capital formation
sK10834	$ Net national income
sK10841	% Appeals case quality
sK10842	% Appeals in favor of taxpayer
sK10843	% Appeals in favor of the tax administration
sK10857	% Audit quality
sK10860	% Grant element on new external debt commitments
sK10861	% Interest on new external debt commitments
sK10865	% Balance of payments manual in use
sK10866	% Bank capital to assets ratio
sK10867	% Bank liquid reserves to bank assets ratio
sK10869	% Bank nonperforming loans to total gross loans
sK10878	% Bond interest rate
sK10881	% Broad money from GDP
sK10882	% Broad money to total reserves ratio
sK10884	% Business extent of disclosure index
sK10897	% Cases resolved within X months
sK10899	% Cash surplus/deficit from GDP
sK10939	% Central bank intervention rate

sKPI #	Key Performance Indicator name
sK11014	% Claims on central government etc. from GDP
sK11015	% Claims on governments and other public entities, from GDP
sK11016	% Claims on other sectors of the domestic economy from GDP
sK11026	% Collection case quality
sK11054	% Concessional debt from total external debt
sK11069	% Corporations - Taxable incorporated businesses that filed their returns on time
sK11070	% Corporations that paid reported taxes on time
sK11078	% Cost of resolving insolvency, from estate
sK11079	% Cost to build a warehouse from income per capita
sK11080	% Cost to enforce a contract from claim
sK11081	% Cost to get electricity, from income per capita
sK11082	% Cost to register property, from property value
sK11083	% Cost to start a business from income per capita
sK11087	% Credit depth of information index
sK11095	% Current account balance from GDP
sK11102	% Customs and other import duties from tax revenue
sK11112	% Degree to which legal deadlines are met
sK11122	% Depreciation
sK11132	% Domestic credit provided by banking sector from GDP
sK11134	% Domestic credit to private sector from GDP
sK11138	% Domestic net incurrence of liabilities from GDP
sK11185	% Employers paying source deductions on time
sK11186	% Employers who filed their returns on time
sK11201	% Enforced collection amounts from large taxpayers
sK11360	% Expense from GDP
sK11367	% Exports of goods and services from GDP
sK11403	% External balance on goods and services from GDP
sK11404	% External debt stocks from exports of goods, services and income
sK11405	% External debt stocks from GNI
sK11539	% Final consumption expenditure from GDP
sK11541	% Financing via international capital markets from GDP
sK11552	% Firms formally registered when operations started
sK11589	% Foreign net incurrence of liabilities from GDP
sK11611	% GDP deflator
sK11615	% General government final consumption expenditure from GDP
sK11622	% Goods and services expense
sK11633	% Gross capital formation from GDP
sK11635	% Gross domestic savings from GDP
sK11642	% Gross fixed capital formation from GDP
sK11644	% Gross fixed capital formation in the private sector from GDP
sK11650	% Gross national expenditure deflator
sK11652	% Gross national expenditure from GDP

sKPI #	Key Performance Indicator name
sK11656	% Gross savings from GDP
sK11659	% Gross savings from GNI
sK11735	% Implicit internal interest rate
sK11768	% Income tax filing rate for individual
sK11879	% Individuals who paid their reported taxes on time
sK11924	% Informal payments to public officials, from firms
sK11932	% Insurance and financial services ,from commercial service exports
sK11933	% Insurance and financial services, from commercial service imports
sK11936	% Interest payments from expense
sK11938	% Interest payments from revenue
sK11939	% Interest payments on external debt from exports of goods, services and income
sK11940	% Interest payments on external debt from GNI
sK11942	% Interest rate spread
sK11990	% Key tax credits and deductions not subject to third-party reporting - Individual
sK12008	% Late penalties assessed
sK12011	% Lending interest rate
sK12020	% Liquid liabilities (M3) from GDP
sK12035	% M2 money and quasi money from GDP
sK12123	% Management cost recovery
sK12139	% Market capitalization of listed companies from GDP
sK12183	% Minimum paid-in capital required to start a business, from income per capita
sK12190	% Money and quasi money (M2) from GDP
sK12191	% Money and quasi money (M2) to total reserves ratio
sK12192	% Money market rate
sK12195	% Multilateral debt from total external debt
sK12197	% Multilateral debt service from public and publicly guaranteed debt service
sK12234	% Net inflows of direct investment from GDP
sK12254	% Net national savings from GNI
sK12257	% Net ODA received from central government expense
sK12264	% Net ODA received from GNI
sK12268	% Net ODA received from gross capital formation
sK12270	% Net ODA received from imports of goods and services
sK12278	% Net outflows of foreign direct investment from GDP
sK12293	% Official grant element on new external debt commitments
sK12294	% Official interest on new external debt commitments
sK12306	% Other expenses
sK12309	% Other taxes from revenue
sK12310	% Other taxes payable by businesses from commercial profits
sK12404	% Payment processing accuracy/error rate
sK12706	% PPP conversion factor (GDP) to market exchange rate ratio

sKPI #	Key Performance Indicator name
sK12712	% Present value of external debt from exports of goods, services and income
sK12714	% Present value of external debt from GNI
sK12744	% Private grant element on new external debt commitments
sK12745	% Private interest on new external debt commitments
sK12764	% Profit tax from commercial profits
sK12765	% Profitability
sK12770	% Public and publicly guaranteed debt service from exports, excluding workers' remittances
sK12772	% Public and publicly guaranteed debt service from GNI
sK12788	% Quasi-liquid liabilities from GDP
sK12805	% Real deposit interest rate
sK12806	% Real interest on time deposit
sK12808	% Real interest rate
sK12809	% Received workers' remittances and compensation for employees, from GDP
sK12843	% Research and development expenditure from GDP
sK12845	% Researchers in R&D per million people
sK12856	% Return processing accuracy/error rate
sK12857	% Returns filed by paper
sK12858	% Returns filed electronically
sK12859	% Revenue collected through enforced collections
sK12860	% Revenue collected versus revenue expected
sK12862	% Revenue, excluding grants from GDP
sK12865	% Risk premium on lending as prime rate minus treasury bill rate
sK12878	% S&P Global Equity Indices from annual change
sK12918	% Short-term debt from exports of goods, services and income
sK12919	% Short-term debt from total external debt
sK12920	% Short-term debt from total reserve
sK12928	% Social contributions from revenue
sK12938	% Subsidies and other transfers from expense
sK12965	% Tax assessments appealed
sK12966	% Tax revenue from GDP
sK12967	% Taxes on exports from tax revenue
sK12968	% Taxes on goods and services from revenue
sK12969	% Taxes on goods and services from value added of industry and services
sK12970	% Taxes on income, profits and capital gains
sK12971	% Taxes on income, profits and capital gains from revenue
sK12972	% Taxes on international trade from revenue
sK13007	% Central government debt from GDP
sK13010	% Debt service from exports of goods, services and income
sK13011	% Debt service from GNI
sK13023	% Natural resources rents from GDP
sK13032	% Private capital flows from GDP
sK13037	% Reserves from external debt

smartKPIs.com
The smart choice in performance management

sKPI #	Key Performance Indicator name
sK13039	% Tax rate from commercial profits
sK13071	% Trend in ratio of outstanding tax debt to gross cash receipt
sK13076	% Turnover ratio of stocks traded
sK13102	% Utility of visits and seminars
sK13114	% Voluntary compliance for payment
sK13115	% Voluntary compliance for returns filing
sK13126	% WEF burden of customs procedure
sK23108	% Net national disposable income out of gross domestic product
sK23109	$ Disposable income
sK23110	$ Social transfers from general government
sK23111	$ Social transfers in real estate
sK23112	$ Social transfers in recreational facilities and activities
sK23113	$ Social transfers in pharmaceuticals
sK23114	$ Social transfers in social work
sK23115	$ Social transfers in health services
sK23116	$ Social transfers in education
sK23117	# Key items of revenue policy work product prepared by the Fiscal Policy Unit
sK23118	% Necessary preconditions for a successful Fiscal Policy Unit (FPU) established through USG assistance
sK23119	# Key personnel in fiscal policy and fiscal administration trained with USG assistance
sK23120	# Policy reforms drafted and presented for public/stakeholder consultation as a result of USG assistance
sK23121	# Regulations drafted and presented for public/stakeholder consultation as a result of USG assistance
sK23122	# Administrative procedures drafted and presented for public/stakeholder consultation as a result of USG assistance
sK23123	# Monetary policy legislative/regulatory actions taken with USG assistance
sK23147	# Automated off-site surveillance systems been installed and made operational this year with USG assistance
sK23148	# Analysts trained in off-site surveillance with USG assistance
sK23149	# Male analysts trained in off-site surveillance with USG assistance
sK23150	# Female analysts trained in off-site surveillance with USG assistance
sK23151	# Financial professionals certified in compliance with international accounting standards as a result of USG assistance
sK23152	# Male financial professionals certified in compliance with international accounting standards as a result of USG assistance
sK23153	# Female financial professionals certified in compliance with international accounting standards as a result of USG assistance
sK23154	# Financial sector supervisors trained with USG assistance
sK23155	# Male financial sector supervisors trained with USG assistance

sKPI #	Key Performance Indicator name
sK23156	# Female financial sector supervisors trained with USG assistance
sK23157	# Financial sector training programs established or supported that meet international standards
sK23158	# Financial sector certification programs established or supported that meet international standards
sK23159	# On-site examinations undertaken this year with USG assistance
sK23160	# Financial sector professionals trained on international standards this year with USG assistance
sK23161	# Male financial sector professionals trained on international standards this year with USG assistance
sK23162	# Female financial sector professionals trained on international standards this year with USG assistance
sK23163	# Material improvements in the infrastructure institutions that reduce market risks made this year with USG assistance
sK23164	# USG supported special funds loans issued this year
sK23165	$ USG supported special funds loans issued this year
sK7697	# Fatalities due to accidents with breakdown by fuel chains

Industrial Production

Industrial production is the total output from all production industries and industrial establishments. It covers mining and quarrying, manufacturing, electricity, gas and water supply.

sKPI #	Key Performance Indicator name
sK8789	# Procedures to build a warehouse
sK8900	# Seasonally adjusted volume of industrial production
sK10506	$ Seasonally adjusted industrial production
sK10830	% Value added by manufacturing
sK11002	% Chemicals from total value added in manufacturing
sK11017	% Class A and B cars
sK11917	% Industrial new orders
sK12036	% Machinery and transport equipment from value added in manufacturing
sK12307	% Other manufacturing from value added in manufacturing
sK12798	% Ratio of female to male wages in manufacturing
sK12925	% Small cars
sK12985	% Textiles and clothing from value added in manufacturing

Material Well-being

Material well-being refers to life standards and it examines poverty and deprivation, as well as the circumstances that significantly affect the wellbeing of people.

sKPI #	Key Performance Indicator name
sK7559	# Direct non-resident trademark applications
sK7560	# Direct resident trademark applications
sK7855	# Gini coefficient
sK8052	# Infant mortality per 1,000 live births

Global » Human Development Areas

sKPI #	Key Performance Indicator name
sK8122	# Life expectancy
sK9673	$ Household consumption expenditure on alcoholic beverages
sK9698	$ Household consumption expenditure on cheese and curd
sK9738	$ Household consumption expenditure on electricity
sK9749	$ Household consumption expenditure on food and non-alcoholic beverages
sK9756	$ Household consumption expenditure on fresh, chilled or frozen meat of bovine animals
sK9809	$ Household consumption expenditure on jams, marmalades
sK9831	$ Household consumption expenditure on medical products, appliances and equipment
sK9845	$ Household consumption expenditure on narcotics
sK9858	$ Household consumption expenditure on other appliances, articles and products for personal care (ND)
sK9871	$ Household consumption expenditure on other milk products
sK9890	$ Household consumption expenditure on other tobacco
sK9898	$ Household consumption expenditure on passenger transport by road
sK10000	$ Household consumption expenditure on tools and equipment for house and garden
sK10153	$ Minimum cost of living guarantee
sK10276	$ Nominal GDP (US$ bn)
sK10277	$ Nominal GDP (US$PPP bn)
sK10470	$ Repair of personal and household goods
sK11062	% Consumers who base their buying decision on the label
sK11063	% Consumers who recognize and understand the label
sK11361	% Experienced financial loss over the Internet and security concerns kept individual from doing ordering/buying goods/services or carrying out banking activities
sK11753	% Income and asset distribution
sK11880	% Individuals who played the lottery or betted over the Internet
sK11903	% Individuals not placing online orders due to price
sK11904	% Individuals not placing online orders due to other reasons
sK11905	% Individuals not placing online orders due to privacy reasons
sK11906	% Individuals not placing online orders due to speed of Internet
sK11907	% Individuals not placing online orders due to lack of suitable payment methods
sK11908	% Individuals not placing online orders due to lack of need
sK11909	% Individuals with Incentive to pay for online audio-visual content because of better quality of paid content than free services
sK11910	% Individuals with incentive to pay for online audio-visual content because of lack of free available content
sK11911	% Individuals with incentive to pay for online audio-visual content because of more advantageous prices compared to offline content

sKPI #	Key Performance Indicator name
sK11912	% Individuals with incentive to pay for online audio-visual content because of more convenient payment methods
sK11913	% Individuals with incentive to pay for online audio-visual content because of other motivations
sK11914	% Individuals with incentive to pay for online audio-visual content because of the right to share legally protected content
sK11915	% Individuals with incentive to pay for online audio-visual content because of wider range of choices, content more easily available
sK11979	% Selling of goods or services on the Internet
sK12300	% Online purchases of electronic equipment
sK12421	% Perception of financial well-being
sK13081	% Unemployment
sK13104	% Value added by industry from GDP
sK13106	% Value added by manufacturing from GDP
sK13107	% Value added by services etc. from GDP
sK13108	% Value lost due to electrical outages, from sales

Resources

Resources represent materials and other assets required to accomplish an activity. They could be means or natural sources of wealth and revenue, as well as natural features that enhance the quality of human life.

sKPI #	Key Performance Indicator name
sK7160	# Arable land
sK7161	# Arable land per person
sK7162	# Area managed for ex situ gene conservation
sK7163	# Area managed for in situ gene conservation
sK7164	# Area managed for seed production
sK7404	# City product Index
sK7810	# Forest - NTF (Non Timber Forest)
sK8008	# IDA resource allocation index
sK8105	# Land area
sK8445	# Pasture land
sK8780	# Primary aluminum production
sK8795	# Production of alumina
sK9181	$ City product (GDP)
sK9182	$ City product per capita
sK10083	$ Intangible capital
sK10350	$ Per capita wealth estimates
sK10475	$ Resource rent (TR-TC)
sK10579	$ Subsoil assets
sK10616	$ Foreign reserves, excluding gold
sK10617	$ Health estimates
sK10629	$ Total Wealth (TW)
sK11592	% Forest rents from GDP
sK11600	% Fuel exports from merchandise exports
sK11602	% Fuel imports from merchandise imports

sKPI #	Key Performance Indicator name
sK12005	% Land area where elevation is below 5 meters from total land area
sK12180	% Mineral depletion from GNI
sK12181	% Mineral rents from GDP
sK12200	% Natural gas rents from GDP
sK12201	% Natural resources depletion from GNI
sK12232	% Net forest depletion from GNI
sK12296	% Oil rents from GDP
sK12848	% Resource rent potential
sK12849	% Resources allocation decision
sK12851	% Resources assessed
sK12853	% Resources co-managed
sK12976	% Terrestrial protected areas from total land area

Tourism

Tourism comprises of services, activities, industries which deliver travel experience and is the sum of interactions between tourists, business suppliers, host governments and host communities.

sKPI #	Key Performance Indicator name
sK8077	# International tourist arrivals
sK8079	# International tourist departures
sK9129	$ Tourist expenditure per night on domestic holiday trips
sK9130	$ Tourist expenditure per night on holiday trips
sK9131	$ Tourist expenditure per night on long domestic holiday trips
sK9132	$ Tourist expenditure per night on long holiday trips
sK9133	$ Tourist expenditure per night on long outbound holiday trips
sK9134	$ Tourist expenditure per night on outbound holiday trips
sK9135	$ Tourist expenditure per night on short domestic holiday trips
sK9136	$ Tourist expenditure per night on short holiday trips
sK9137	$ Tourist expenditure per night on short outbound holiday trips
sK9138	$ Tourist expenditure per trip on domestic holiday trips
sK9139	$ Tourist expenditure per trip on holiday trips
sK9140	$ Tourist expenditure per trip on long domestic holiday trips
sK9141	$ Tourist expenditure per trip on long holiday trips
sK9142	$ Tourist expenditure per trip on long outbound holiday trips
sK9143	$ Tourist expenditure per trip on outbound holiday trips
sK9144	$ Tourist expenditure per trip on short domestic holiday trips
sK9145	$ Tourist expenditure per trip on short holiday trips
sK9146	$ Tourist expenditure per trip on short outbound holiday trips
sK10102	$ International tourist receipts
sK10948	% Variance in tourist expenditure per night on long holiday trips

sKPI #	Key Performance Indicator name
sK10949	% Variance in tourist expenditure per night on long outbound holiday trips
sK10950	% Variance in tourist expenditure per night on outbound holiday trips
sK10951	% Variance in tourist expenditure per night on short domestic holiday trips
sK10952	% Variance in tourist expenditure per night on short holiday trips
sK10953	% Variance in tourist expenditure per night on short outbound holiday trips
sK10954	% Variance in tourist expenditure per trip on domestic holiday trips
sK10955	% Variance in tourist expenditure per trip on holiday trips
sK10956	% Variance in tourist expenditure per trip on long domestic holiday trips
sK10957	% Variance in tourist expenditure per trip on long holiday trips
sK10958	% Variance in tourist expenditure per trip on long outbound holiday trips
sK10959	% Variance in tourist expenditure per trip on outbound holiday trips
sK10960	% Variance in tourist expenditure per trip on short domestic holiday trips
sK10961	% Variance in tourist expenditure per trip on short holiday trips
sK10962	% Variance in tourist expenditure per trip on short outbound holiday trips
sK10963	# Domestic holiday trips made by EU residents
sK10964	# Holiday nights spent by EU residents on domestic holiday trips
sK10965	# Holiday nights spent by EU residents on holiday trips
sK10966	# Holiday nights spent by EU residents on long domestic holiday trips
sK10967	# Holiday nights spent by EU residents on long holiday trips
sK10968	# Holiday nights spent by EU residents on long outbound holiday trips
sK10969	# Holiday nights spent by EU residents on outbound holiday trips
sK10970	# Holiday nights spent by EU residents on short domestic holiday trips
sK10971	# Holiday nights spent by EU residents on short holiday trips
sK10972	# Holiday nights spent by EU residents on short outbound holiday trips
sK10973	# Holiday trips made by EU residents
sK10974	# Long domestic holiday trips made by EU residents
sK10975	# Long holiday trips made by EU residents
sK10976	% Change in number of long outbound holiday trips made by EU residents
sK10977	# Nights spent by non-residents in collective accommodation, in hotel and similar establishments
sK10978	# Nights spent by non-residents in collective accommodation, in other collective accommodation non-residents

sKPI #	Key Performance Indicator name
sK10979	% Nights spent by non-residents in total collective accommodation
sK10980	# Nights spent by residents in collective accommodation, in hotel and similar establishments
sK10981	# Nights spent by residents in collective accommodation, in other collective accommodation
sK10982	# Nights spent by residents in total collective accommodation
sK10983	# Nights spent in collective accommodation, in hotel and similar establishments
sK10984	# Nights spent in collective accommodation, in other collective accommodation
sK10985	# Nights spent in total collective accommodation
sK10986	% Change in number of outbound holiday trips made by EU residents
sK10987	# Short domestic holiday trips made by EU residents
sK10988	# Short holiday trips made by EU residents
sK10989	# Short outbound holiday trips made by EU residents
sK10991	$ Tourist expenditure by EU residents on domestic holiday trips
sK10992	$ Tourist expenditure by EU residents on holiday trips
sK10993	$ Tourist expenditure by EU residents on long domestic holiday trips
sK10994	$ Tourist expenditure by EU residents on long holiday trips
sK10995	$ Tourist expenditure by EU residents on long outbound holiday trips

sKPI #	Key Performance Indicator name
sK10996	$ Tourist expenditure by EU residents on outbound holiday trips
sK10997	$ Tourist expenditure by EU residents on short domestic holiday trips
sK10998	$ Tourist expenditure by EU residents on short holiday trips
sK10999	$ Tourist expenditure by EU residents on short outbound holiday trips
sK11341	# Domestic holiday trips made by residents
sK11342	# Holiday trips made by residents
sK11343	# Long domestic holiday trips (4 or more nights) made by residents
sK11344	# Long holiday (4 or more nights) trips made by residents
sK11345	# Long outbound holiday trips (4 or more nights) made by residents
sK11346	# Outbound holiday trips made by residents
sK11347	# Short domestic holiday trips (1 to 3 days) made by residents
sK11348	# Short holiday trips (1 to 3 days) made by residents
sK11349	# Short outbound holiday trips (1 to 3 days) made by residents
sK13067	% Travel services from commercial service exports
sK13068	% Travel services from commercial service imports
sK13069	% Travel services from service exports
sK13070	% Travel services from service imports

Health

Health is a state of complete physical, social and mental well-being, meaning to be free from illness, injury or pain.

Disease Prevention

Disease prevention covers measures to prevent the occurrence of disease, to stop its progress and to reduce its consequences.

sKPI #	Key Performance Indicator name
sK7100	# Adults (ages 15+) and children (0-14 years) living with HIV
sK7101	# Adults (ages 15+) living with HIV
sK7399	# Children living with HIV
sK8089	# J-Anti-infective for systemic use
sK8153	# M01A-Anti-inflammatory and antirheumatic products non-steroids
sK8164	# Malaria cases reported
sK8341	# M-Musculo-skeletal system
sK8390	# Notified cases of malaria per 100,000 people
sK8596	# Periodicity of Immunization indicator
sK8753	# Potential years of life lost due to external causes
sK8754	# Potential years of life lost due to HIV disease
sK8755	# Potential years of life lost due to infectious and parasitic diseases
sK8859	# Reported clinical malaria cases
sK10839	% Antenatal care coverage provided by a skilled health provider, at least one visit

sKPI #	Key Performance Indicator name
sK10840	% Antenatal care coverage provided by any provider (skilled or unskilled), at least four visits
sK10871	% BCG immunization, from one-year-old children
sK10936	% Cause of death, by communicable diseases and maternal, prenatal and nutrition conditions
sK11013	% Children with fever receiving antimalarial drugs from children under age 5 with fever
sK11058	% Condom use with non-regular partner, from female adults ages 15-49
sK11059	% Condom use with non-regular partner, from male adults ages 15-49
sK11125	% Diabetes prevalence, from population ages 20-79
sK11140	% DPT immunization from children ages 12-23 months
sK11142	% DPT immunization, from children ages 12-23 months
sK11420	% Female adults with HIV from population ages 15+ with HIV
sK11475	% Female prevalence of HIV from population ages 15-24
sK11527	% Females ages 15-24 with good health
sK11528	% Females ages 15-49 having comprehensive correct knowledge about HIV (prevent ways and reject misconceptions)

sKPI #	Key Performance Indicator name
sK11529	% Females ages 25-44 with good health
sK11530	% Females ages 45-64 with good health
sK11531	% Females ages 65+ with good health
sK11533	% Females of all ages with good health
sK11679	% HepB3 immunization, from one-year-old children
sK11716	% Households with one or more insect-treated mosquito
sK11739	% Improved sanitation facilities from population with access
sK11741	% Improved water source from population with access
sK11922	% Influenza vaccination for adults over 65+
sK12095	% Male prevalence of HIV from population ages 15-24
sK12115	% Males ages 15-24 with good health
sK12116	% Males ages 15-49 having comprehensive correct knowledge about HIV (prevent ways and reject misconceptions)
sK12117	% Males ages 25-44 with good health
sK12118	% Males ages 45-64 with good health
sK12119	% Males ages 65+ with good health
sK12121	% Males of all ages with good health
sK12146	% Measles immunization from children ages 12-23 months
sK12172	% Met need for contraception, from married women ages 15-49
sK12285	% Newborns protected against tetanus
sK12452	% Population ages 15-24 with good health
sK12454	% Population ages 25-44 with good health
sK12455	% Population ages 45-64 with good health
sK12457	% Population ages 65+ with good health
sK12675	% Population of all ages with good health
sK12679	% Population with decayed-missing-filled teeth (DMFT)
sK12709	% Pregnant women who took at least 2 doses of intermittent preventative treatment
sK12871	% Rural improved sanitation facilities from rural population with access
sK12873	% Rural improved water source from rural population with access
sK13029	% Prevalence of HIV from population ages 15-49
sK13073	% Tuberculosis case detection rate from all forms of tuberculosis
sK13074	% Tuberculosis treatment success rate from registered cases
sK13092	% Urban improved sanitation facilities from urban population with access
sK13094	% Urban improved water source from urban population with access

Health Services

Health services are activities performed by individuals and organizations and refer to assessing, maintaining or improving individuals' health. It includes diagnosing illnesses, injuries or disabilities and treating them.

sKPI #	Key Performance Indicator name
sK7159	# Appendectomy procedures
sK7170	# Associate nurses employed in hospitals

sKPI #	Key Performance Indicator name
sK7171	# Associate professional nurses licensed to practice
sK7172	# Practicing associate professional nurses
sK7173	# Professionally active associate nurses
sK7174	# Associate professional nursing graduates
sK7189	# Days of stay in hospital
sK7344	# Beds in for-profit privately owned hospitals
sK7345	# Beds in not-for-profit privately owned hospitals
sK7346	# Beds in nursing and residential care facilities
sK7347	# Beds in publicly owned hospitals
sK7354	# Bone marrow transplants
sK7358	# Breast-conserving surgeries
sK7366	# Caesarean section procedures
sK7380	# Cardiac catheterization procedures
sK7386	# Cataract surgeries
sK7402	# Cholecystectomy procedures
sK7444	# Computed Tomography (CT) exams
sK7445	# Computed Tomography (CT) exams in ambulatory care
sK7446	# Computed Tomography (CT) exams in hospitals
sK7447	# Computed Tomography scanners
sK7448	# Computed Tomography scanners in ambulatory sector
sK7449	# Computed Tomography scanners in hospitals
sK7470	# Coronary bypass procedures
sK7471	# Coronary stenting procedures
sK7510	# Curative (acute) care beds
sK7543	# Dentists consultations
sK7544	# Dentists graduates
sK7545	# Dentists licensed to practice
sK7556	# Digital Subtraction Angiography units
sK7557	# Digital Subtraction Angiography units in ambulatory
sK7558	# Digital Subtraction Angiography units in hospitals
sK7565	# Doctors consultations
sK7642	# End-stage renal failure patients
sK7735	# Female physicians
sK7736	# Female physicians aged 35-44 years old
sK7737	# Female physicians aged 45-54 years old
sK7738	# Female physicians aged 55-64 years old
sK7739	# Female physicians aged 65 years old and over
sK7740	# Female physicians under 35 years old
sK7813	# Formal LTC workers
sK7816	# Formal LTC workers (FTE)
sK7817	# Formal LTC workers at home
sK7818	# Formal LTC workers in institutions
sK7819	# For-profit privately owned hospitals
sK7829	# Functioning kidney transplants
sK7831	# Gamma cameras
sK7832	# Gamma cameras in ambulatory sector

sKPI #	Key Performance Indicator name
sK7833	# Gamma cameras in hospitals
sK7846	# General hospitals
sK7847	# General pediatrics physicians
sK7848	# General practice physicians
sK7886	# Health care assistants employed in hospitals
sK7888	# Heart transplants
sK7921	# Hip replacement procedures
sK7985	# Hospital beds per 1,000 people
sK7986	# Hospital employment
sK7987	# Hospitals
sK8054	# Inguinal and femoral hernia procedures
sK8091	# Kidney transplants
sK8100	# Knee replacement procedures
sK8108	# Laparoscopic cholecystectomy procedures
sK8126	# Ligation and stripping of varicose veins procedures
sK8129	# Lithotripters
sK8130	# Lithotripters in ambulatory sector
sK8131	# Lithotripters in hospitals
sK8132	# Liver transplants
sK8147	# Long-term care beds
sK8148	# Long-term care recipients at home
sK8149	# Long-term care recipients in institutions other than hospitals
sK8151	# Lung transplants
sK8155	# Magnetic Resonance Imaging (MRI) exams
sK8156	# Magnetic Resonance Imaging (MRI) exams in ambulatory care
sK8157	# Magnetic Resonance Imaging (MRI) exams in hospitals
sK8158	# Magnetic Resonance Imaging units
sK8159	# Magnetic Resonance Imaging units in ambulatory sector
sK8160	# Magnetic Resonance Imaging units in hospitals
sK8177	# Male physicians
sK8178	# Male physicians aged 35-44 years old
sK8179	# Male physicians aged 45-54 years old
sK8180	# Male physicians aged 55-64 years old
sK8181	# Male physicians aged 65 years old and over
sK8182	# Male physicians under 35 years old
sK8221	# Mammographs
sK8222	# Mammographs in ambulatory sector
sK8223	# Mammographs in hospitals
sK8228	# Mastectomy procedures
sK8308	# Medical graduates
sK8309	# Medical group of specialties physicians
sK8335	# Midwives graduates
sK8336	# Midwives licensed to practice
sK8389	# Not-for-profit privately owned hospitals
sK8396	# Nurses and midwives per 1,000 people
sK8397	# Nurses licensed to practice
sK8398	# Nursing graduates
sK8399	# Obstetrics and gynecology physicians
sK8414	# Other categories of physicians
sK8421	# Other health service providers employed in hospitals
sK8422	# Other hospital beds
sK8424	# Other staff employed in hospitals
sK8427	# Outpatient visits per capita
sK8431	# Pacemaker procedures
sK8570	# Patients undergoing dialysis
sK8588	# Percutaneous coronary interventions (PTCA and stenting procedures)
sK8606	# PET scanners
sK8607	# PET scanners in ambulatory sector
sK8608	# PET scanners in hospitals
sK8611	# Pharmaceutical consumption of A02A-Antacids
sK8613	# Pharmaceutical consumption of A02B-Drugs for peptic ulcer and gastro-esophageal reflux diseases
sK8615	# Pharmaceutical consumption of A10-Drugs used in diabetes
sK8617	# Pharmaceutical consumption of A-Alimentary tract and metabolism
sK8619	# Pharmaceutical consumption of B-Blood and blood forming organs
sK8621	# Pharmaceutical consumption of C01A-Cardiac glycosides
sK8623	# Pharmaceutical consumption of C01B-Antiarrhythmics, Class I and III
sK8625	# Pharmaceutical consumption of C02-Antihypertensives
sK8627	# Pharmaceutical consumption of C03-Diuretics
sK8629	# Pharmaceutical consumption of C07-Beta blocking agents
sK8631	# Pharmaceutical consumption of C08-Calcium channel blockers
sK8633	# Pharmaceutical consumption of C09-Agents acting on the Renin-Angiotensin system
sK8635	# Pharmaceutical consumption of C10-Lipid modifying agents
sK8637	# Pharmaceutical consumption of C-Cardiovascular system
sK8639	# Pharmaceutical consumption of G03-Sex hormones and modulators of the genital system
sK8640	# Pharmaceutical consumption of G-Genito-urinary system and sex hormones
sK8642	# Pharmaceutical consumption of H-Systemic hormonal preparations, excluding sex hormones and insulin
sK8644	# Pharmaceutical consumption of J01-Antibacterials for systemic use
sK8645	# Pharmaceutical consumption of J-Anti-infectives for systemic use

sKPI #	Key Performance Indicator name
sK8646	# Pharmaceutical consumption of M01A-Anti-inflammatory and antirheumatic products non-steroids
sK8647	# Pharmaceutical consumption of M-Musculo-skeletal system
sK8649	# Pharmaceutical consumption of N02-Analgesics
sK8651	# Pharmaceutical consumption of N05B-Anxiolytics
sK8653	# Pharmaceutical consumption of N05C-Hypnotics and sedatives
sK8655	# Pharmaceutical consumption of N-Nervous system
sK8657	# Pharmaceutical consumption of NO6A-Antidepressants
sK8659	# Pharmaceutical consumption of R03-Drugs for obstructive airway diseases
sK8661	# Pharmaceutical consumption of R-Respiratory system
sK8662	# Pharmaceutical consumption of total pharmaceutical sales
sK8663	# Pharmacists graduates
sK8664	# Pharmacists licensed to practice
sK8666	# Physicians by age group
sK8670	# Physicians employed in hospitals
sK8671	# Physicians licensed to practice
sK8673	# Physicians per 1,000 people
sK8772	# Practicing caring personnel
sK8773	# Practicing dentists
sK8774	# Practicing midwives
sK8775	# Practicing nurses
sK8776	# Practicing pharmacists
sK8777	# Practicing physiotherapists
sK8797	# Products not elsewhere classified
sK8798	# Professional nurses and midwives employed in hospitals
sK8799	# Professional nurses licensed to practice
sK8800	# Practicing professional nurses
sK8801	# Professional nurses professionally active
sK8802	# Professional nursing graduates
sK8803	# Professionally active caring personnel
sK8804	# Professionally active dentists
sK8805	# Professionally active midwives
sK8806	# Professionally active nurses
sK8807	# Professionally active pharmacists
sK8808	# Professionally active physicians
sK8813	# Prostatectomies, excluding transurethral
sK8818	# Psychiatric care beds
sK8819	# Psychiatry physicians
sK8823	# Publicly owned hospitals
sK8829	# Radiation therapy equipment
sK8830	# Radiation therapy equipment in ambulatory sector
sK8831	# Radiation therapy equipment in hospitals
sK8861	# Reported malaria deaths

sKPI #	Key Performance Indicator name
sK8941	# Surgical group of specialty physicians
sK8976	# Tonsillectomies with or without adenoidectomy
sK9058	# Transurethral prostatectomy procedures
sK9071	# Vaginal only hysterectomies
sK9272	$ Expenditure on administration and provision of health related cash-benefits
sK9273	$ Expenditure on administration and provision of social services in kind to assist living with disease and impairment
sK9275	$ Expenditure on administration, operation and support activities of social security funds
sK9276	$ Expenditure on miscellaneous ancillary services
sK9277	$ Expenditure on miscellaneous medical durables
sK9278	$ Expenditure on miscellaneous public health services
sK9280	$ Expenditure on services classified under HC.R.6
sK9281	$ Expenditure on specialized health care
sK9282	$ Expenditure on ancillary services to health care
sK9283	$ Expenditure on ancillary services, including in-patient
sK9284	$ Expenditure on basic medical and diagnostic services
sK9287	$ Expenditure on capital formation of health care provider institutions
sK9290	$ Expenditure on clinical laboratory
sK9291	$ Expenditure on day cases of curative and rehabilitative care
sK9292	$ Expenditure on day cases of curative care
sK9293	$ Expenditure on day cases of long-term nursing care
sK9294	$ Expenditure on day cases of rehabilitative care
sK9295	$ Expenditure on diagnostic imaging
sK9296	$ Expenditure on education and training of health personnel
sK9297	$ Expenditure on environmental health
sK9298	$ Expenditure on food, hygiene and drinking water control
sK9299	$ Expenditure on general government administration of health
sK9300	$ Expenditure on general government administration of health (except social security)
sK9301	$ Expenditure on glasses and other vision products
sK9302	$ Expenditure on HC.1-HC.9; HC.R.1
sK9303	$ Expenditure on health administration and health insurance
sK9304	$ Expenditure on health administration and other private health insurance
sK9305	$ Expenditure on health administration and private health insurance
sK9306	$ Expenditure on health administration and social health insurance
sK9307	$ Expenditure on hearing aids
sK9308	$ Expenditure on in-patient curative and rehabilitative care
sK9309	$ Expenditure on in-patient curative care

sKPI #	Key Performance Indicator name
sK9310	$ Expenditure on in-patient long-term nursing care
sK9311	$ Expenditure on in-patient rehabilitative care
sK9312	$ Expenditure on long-term nursing care: home care
sK9315	$ Expenditure on maternal and child health, family planning and counseling
sK9316	$ Expenditure on medical goods dispensed to out-patients
sK9317	$ Expenditure on medico-technical devices, including wheelchairs
sK9318	$ Expenditure on not specified by kind
sK9319	$ Expenditure on occupational health care
sK9320	$ Expenditure on orthopedic appliances and other prosthetics
sK9321	$ Expenditure on other medical non-durables
sK9322	$ Expenditure on other non-health activities of health care providers
sK9324	$ Expenditure on out-patient curative and rehabilitative care
sK9325	$ Expenditure on out-patient curative care
sK9326	$ Expenditure on out-patient dental care
sK9327	$ Expenditure on out-patient rehabilitative care
sK9329	$ Expenditure on patient transport and emergency rescue
sK9331	$ Expenditure on pharmaceutical and other medical non-durables
sK9332	$ Expenditure on pharmaceuticals and other medical non-durables, including in-patient and other ways of provision
sK9334	$ Expenditure on prevention and public health services
sK9335	$ Expenditure on prevention of communicable diseases
sK9336	$ Expenditure on prevention of non-communicable diseases
sK9337	$ Expenditure on research and development in health
sK9338	$ Expenditure on school health services
sK9339	$ Expenditure on services of curative and rehabilitative care
sK9340	$ Expenditure on services of curative care
sK9341	$ Expenditure on services of curative home and rehabilitative home care
sK9342	$ Expenditure on services of curative home care
sK9343	$ Expenditure on services of long-term nursing care
sK9344	$ Expenditure on services of rehabilitative care
sK9345	$ Expenditure on services of rehabilitative home care
sK9346	$ Expenditure on social care activities of health care providers
sK9363	$ Expenditure on social services of LTC, other than HC.3
sK9364	$ Expenditure on therapeutic appliances and other medical durables
sK9365	$ Expenditure on total current expenditure HC.1-HC.9
sK9494	$ Government health expenditure per capita
sK9589	$ Health expenditure

sKPI #	Key Performance Indicator name
sK9590	$ Health expenditure from all other industries as secondary producers of health care
sK9591	$ Health expenditure from all other providers of health administration
sK9592	$ Health expenditure from all other residential care facilities
sK9593	$ Health expenditure from ambulance services
sK9594	$ Health expenditure from blood and organ banks
sK9595	$ Health expenditure from community care facilities for the elderly
sK9596	$ Health expenditure from dispensing chemists in pharmacies
sK9597	$ Health expenditure from dispensing chemists in pharmacies, in the government sector
sK9598	$ Health expenditure from dispensing chemists in pharmacies, in the private sector
sK9599	$ Health expenditure from establishments as providers of occupational health care services
sK9600	$ Health expenditure from establishments as providers of occupational health care services in the government sector
sK9601	$ Health expenditure from establishments as providers of occupational health care services in the private sector
sK9602	$ Health expenditure from general health administration and insurance
sK9603	$ Health expenditure from general health administration and insurance in the government sector
sK9604	$ Health expenditure from general health administration and insurance in the private sector
sK9605	$ Health expenditure from government administration of health
sK9606	$ Health expenditure from hospitals
sK9607	$ Health expenditure from hospitals in the government sector
sK9608	$ Health expenditure from hospitals in the private sector
sK9609	$ Health expenditure from medical and diagnostic laboratories
sK9610	$ Health expenditure from medical and diagnostic laboratories in the government sector
sK9611	$ Health expenditure from medical and diagnostic laboratories in the private sector
sK9612	$ Health expenditure from mental health and substance abuse hospitals
sK9613	$ Health expenditure from nursing and residential care facilities
sK9614	$ Health expenditure from nursing and residential care facilities in the government sector
sK9615	$ Health expenditure from nursing and residential care facilities in the private sector
sK9616	$ Health expenditure from nursing care facilities
sK9617	$ Health expenditure from offices of dentists
sK9618	$ Health expenditure from offices of dentists in the private sector
sK9619	$ Health expenditure from offices of dentists in the government sector

sKPI #	Key Performance Indicator name
sK9620	$ Health expenditure from offices of other health practitioners in the private sector
sK9621	$ Health expenditure from offices of other health practitioners
sK9622	$ Health expenditure from offices of other health practitioners in the government sector
sK9623	$ Health expenditure from offices of physicians
sK9624	$ Health expenditure from offices of physicians in the government sector
sK9625	$ Health expenditure from offices of physicians in the private sector
sK9626	$ Health expenditure from other (private) insurance
sK9627	$ Health expenditure from other industries and from the rest of the economy
sK9628	$ Health expenditure from other providers of ambulatory health care
sK9629	$ Health expenditure from other social insurance
sK9630	$ Health expenditure from out-patient care centers
sK9631	$ Health expenditure from out-patient care centers in the government sector
sK9632	$ Health expenditure from out-patient care centers in the private sector
sK9633	$ Health expenditure from private households as providers of home care
sK9634	$ Health expenditure from providers of all other ambulatory health care services
sK9635	$ Health expenditure from providers of ambulatory health care
sK9636	$ Health expenditure from providers of ambulatory health care in the government sector
sK9637	$ Health expenditure from providers of ambulatory health care in the private sector
sK9638	$ Health expenditure from providers of home health care services
sK9639	$ Health expenditure from providers of private insurance
sK9640	$ Health expenditure from provision and administration of public health programs
sK9641	$ Health expenditure from provision and administration of public health programs in the government sector
sK9642	$ Health expenditure from provision and administration of public health programs in the private sector
sK9643	$ Health expenditure from residential mental retardation, mental health and substance abuse facilities
sK9644	$ Health expenditure from retail sale and other providers of medical goods
sK9645	$ Health expenditure from retail sale and other providers of medical goods in the private sector
sK9646	$ Health expenditure from retail sale and other providers of medical goods in the government sector
sK9647	$ Health expenditure from retail sale and other suppliers of hearing aids
sK9648	$ Health expenditure from retail sale and other suppliers of medical appliances, including all other miscellaneous sale and other suppliers of pharmaceuticals and medical goods

sKPI #	Key Performance Indicator name
sK9649	$ Health expenditure from retail sale and other suppliers of optical glasses and other vision products
sK9650	$ Health expenditure from social security funds
sK9651	$ Health expenditure from specialty, other then mental health and substance abuse hospitals
sK9652	$ Health expenditure from the rest of the world
sK9654	$ Health expenditure per capita
sK9656	$ Health expenditure per capita based on PPP
sK9657	$ Health expenditure provider from general hospitals
sK10467	$ Remuneration of general practitioners
sK10468	$ Remuneration of hospital nurses
sK10469	$ Remuneration of specialists
sK10848	% ARI treatment from children under 5 taken to a health provider
sK10879	% Breast cancer screening
sK10943	% Cervical cancer screening
sK11037	% Compensated absence from work due to illness
sK11040	% Complementary private health insurance coverage
sK11104	% Deaths among children under five years of age due to malaria
sK11143	% Duplicate private health insurance coverage
sK11407	% External resources for health from total expenditure on health
sK11928	% Inpatient admissions rate, from population
sK12290	% Non-health care activities of health care providers
sK12312	% Out-of-pocket health expenditure from private expenditure on health
sK12314	% Out-of-pocket health expenditure from total expenditure on health
sK12423	% Perception of health services
sK12737	% Primary private health insurance coverage
sK12754	% Private health expenditure from GDP
sK12755	% Private health expenditure from total health expenditure
sK12756	% Private health insurance (PHI) coverage
sK12757	% Private prepaid plans, from private expenditure on health
sK12775	% Public expenditure from total health expenditure
sK12777	% Public health expenditure from GDP
sK12779	% Public health expenditure from government expenditure
sK12883	% Satisfaction with health care services
sK12910	% Self reported unmet need for dental care
sK12911	% Self reported unmet need for medical care
sK12914	% Self-reported absence from work due to illness
sK12939	% Supplementary private health insurance coverage
sK11126	% Diarrhea treatment of children under 5 receiving oral rehydration and continued feeding

Mortality

Mortality reflects the incidence of death in a population and it is often measured by the probability that a randomly selected individual in a population at a certain date and location would die in a certain period of time.

sKPI #	Key Performance Indicator name
sK7887	# Healthy life years
sK8124	# Life expectancy at birth, at age 45 and at age 65
sK8733	# Potential years of life lost due to diseases of the blood
sK8734	# Potential years of life lost due to diseases of the musculoskeletal system
sK8735	# Potential years of life lost due to diseases of the nervous system
sK8736	# Potential years of life lost due to ischemic heart diseases
sK8737	# Potential years of life lost due to endocrine, nutritional and metabolic diseases
sK8738	# Potential years of life lost due to mental and behavioral disorders
sK8739	# Potential years of life lost due to (PYLL), females and males
sK8740	# Potential years of life lost due to accident falls
sK8741	# Potential years of life lost due to acute myocardial infarction
sK8742	# Potential years of life lost due to assault
sK8743	# Potential years of life lost due to bronchitis, asthma and emphysema
sK8744	# Potential years of life lost due to cerebrovascular diseases
sK8745	# Potential years of life lost due to chronic liver diseases and cirrhosis
sK8746	# Potential years of life lost due to congenital anomalies
sK8747	# Potential years of life lost due to diabetes mellitus
sK8748	# Potential years of life lost due to diseases of the circulatory system
sK8749	# Potential years of life lost due to diseases of the digestive system
sK8750	# Potential years of life lost due to diseases of the genito-urinary system
sK8751	# Potential years of life lost due to diseases of the respiratory system
sK8752	# Potential years of life lost due to diseases of the skin and subcutaneous tissue
sK8756	# Potential years of life lost due to influenza and pneumonia
sK8757	# Potential years of life lost due to intentional self-harm
sK8758	# Potential years of life lost due to land transport accidents
sK8759	# Potential years of life lost due to malignant neoplasms
sK8760	# Potential years of life lost due to malignant neoplasms of the cervix
sK8761	# Potential years of life lost due to malignant neoplasms of the colon
sK8762	# Potential years of life lost due to malignant neoplasms of the female breast

sKPI #	Key Performance Indicator name
sK8763	# Potential years of life lost due to malignant neoplasms of the lung
sK8764	# Potential years of life lost due to malignant neoplasms of the prostate
sK8765	# Potential years of life lost due to perinatal conditions
sK8766	# Potential years of life lost due to pregnancy, childbirth and the puerperium
sK8767	# Potential years of life lost due to psychoactive substance use
sK8768	# Potential years of life lost due to symptoms and ill-defined conditions
sK8769	# Potential years of life lost-due to all causes
sK10730	% Reduction in potential years of life lost (PYLL)
sK10751	% Acute care occupancy rate
sK10752	% Acute care turnover rate
sK10793	% All cancer mortality rates, males and females
sK10880	% Breast cancer survival rate
sK10902	% Cause of death -Infectious and parasitic disease
sK10903	% Cause of death -Malignant neoplasms
sK10904	% Cause of death -Accidental falls
sK10905	% Cause of death -Acute myocardial infarction
sK10906	% Cause of death -Assault
sK10907	% Cause of death -Bronchitis, asthma and emphysema
sK10908	% Cause of death -Diseases of the blood
sK10909	% Cause of death -Psychoactive substance use
sK10910	% Cause of death -Cerebrovascular diseases
sK10911	% Cause of death -Chronic liver diseases and cirrhosis
sK10912	% Cause of death -Congenital anomalies
sK10913	% Cause of death -Diabetes mellitus
sK10914	% Cause of death -Diseases of the circulatory system
sK10915	% Cause of death -Diseases of the digestive system
sK10916	% Cause of death -Diseases of the genito-urinary system
sK10917	% Cause of death -Diseases of the musculoskeletal system
sK10918	% Cause of death -Diseases of the nervous system
sK10919	% Cause of death -Diseases of the respiratory system
sK10920	% Cause of death -Diseases of the skin and subcutaneous tissue
sK10921	% Cause of death -Endocrine, nutritional and metabolic diseases
sK10922	% Cause of death -External causes
sK10923	% Cause of death -Influenza and pneumonia
sK10924	% Cause of death -Intentional self-harm
sK10925	% Cause of death -Ischemic heart diseases
sK10926	% Cause of death -Land transport accidents
sK10927	% Cause of death -Malignant neoplasms of the cervix
sK10928	% Cause of death -Malignant neoplasms of the colon
sK10929	% Cause of death -Malignant neoplasms of the female breast
sK10930	% Cause of death -Malignant neoplasms of the lung

smartKPIs.com
The smart choice in performance management

sKPI #	Key Performance Indicator name
sK10931	% Cause of death -Malignant neoplasms of the prostate
sK10932	% Cause of death -Mental and behavioral disorders
sK10933	% Cause of death -Perinatal conditions
sK10934	% Cause of death -Pregnancy, childbirth and the puerperium
sK10935	% Cause of death -Symptoms and ill-defined conditions
sK10937	% Cause of death, by injury
sK10938	% Cause of death, by non-communicable diseases
sK10944	% Cervical cancer survival rate
sK11027	% Colorectal cancer survival rate
sK11428	% Female child mortality rate per 1,000 female children age one
sK11920	% Infant mortality rate per 1,000 live births
sK12017	% Lifetime risk of maternal death
sK12034	% Lung cancer mortality rates, males and females
sK12056	% Male child mortality rate per 1,000 male children age one
sK12194	% Mortality rate for children under 5 per 1,000
sK12203	% Neonatal mortality rate per 1,000 live births
sK12913	% Self-perceived limitations in daily activities

Nutrition

Nutrition represents the processes involved in the selection and use of food, which contribute to the nourishment of the body and maintain health, growth and energy.

sKPI #	Key Performance Indicator name
sK7084	# People who are undernourished
sK7085	# Protein intake
sK7095	# Acute care bed days
sK7143	# Alcohol consumption
sK7367	# Calories intake
sK7552	# Depth of hunger in kilocalories per person per day
sK7696	# Fat intake
sK7823	# Fruits and vegetables consumption
sK7824	# Fruits consumption
sK8779	# Prevalence of undernourishment
sK8938	# Sugar consumption
sK8971	# Tobacco consumption
sK9073	# Vegetables consumption
sK11065	% Consumption of iodized salt in households
sK11351	% Exclusive breastfeeding from children under 6 months
sK11678	% Height for age malnutrition prevalence from children under 5
sK13112	% Vitamin A supplementation coverage rate from children ages 6-59 months
sK13128	% Weight for age malnutrition prevalence from children under 5
sK23231	# The healthy eating index (HEI)
sK23232	# Fruit (includes 100% juice)

sKPI #	Key Performance Indicator name
sK23233	# Whole fruit (not juice)
sK23234	# Vegetables
sK23235	# Dark green and orange vegetables and legumes
sK23236	# Grains
sK23237	# Whole grains
sK23238	# Milk
sK23239	# Meat and beans
sK23240	# Oils
sK23241	# Saturated Fat
sK23242	# Sodium
sK23243	# Calories from Solid Fats, Alcoholic beverages, and Added Sugars (SoFAAS)
sK23265	# Children 6-23 months receiving a minimum acceptable diet
sK23267	# People trained in child health and nutrition through USG-supported programs
sK23269	# Health facilities with established capacity to manage acute under-nutrition
sK23270	# Anemia among children 6-59 months
sK23271	# Children under 5 years of age who received vitamin a from USG-supported programs
sK23272	# Children reached by USG-supported nutrition programs

Reproductive Health

Reproductive health addresses the reproductive processes, functions and system at all stages of life. It implies that people have a responsible, satisfying and safe sex life and that they have the capability to reproduce.

sKPI #	Key Performance Indicator name
sK7400	# Children orphaned by HIV/AIDS
sK7851	# G-Genito-urinary system and sex hormones
sK8598	# Periodicity of maternal health indicator
sK10877	% Births attended by skilled health staff
sK11055	% Condom use among married women 15-49 years old
sK11056	% Condom use in female population ages 15-24
sK11057	% Condom use in male population ages 15-24
sK11067	% Contraceptive prevalence from women ages 15-49
sK11535	% Fertility rate
sK11686	% HIV prevalence among 15-to-24-year-old pregnant women in capital city
sK12032	% Low-birth weight babies from total births
sK12186	% Modeled estimate of maternal mortality ratio per 100,000 live births
sK12187	% Modern contraceptive method use among married women 15-49 years old
sK12199	% National estimate of maternal mortality ratio per 100,000 live births
sK12708	% Pregnant women receiving prenatal care
sK12715	% Prevalence of anemia among pregnant women
sK13117	% Wanted fertility rate in births per woman

sKPI #	Key Performance Indicator name
sK23266	# Exclusive breastfeeding of children under 6 months
sK23268	# Anemia among women of reproductive age

Risk Factors

Risk factors are elements which increase a person's chances of developing a disease. They can be behavioral, biomedical, environmental, genetic or demographic.

sKPI #	Key Performance Indicator name
sK7086	# Table-top exercises of the on-site plan per year
sK7135	# AIDS deaths in adults and children
sK7158	# Appearances of same root cause
sK7177	# Audits and technical reviews completed in relation to the number scheduled
sK7181	# Automatic emergency shut-downs
sK7200	# Risk index of processes/syntheses that go through to pilot/commercial scale
sK7369	# Cancer - Malignant neoplasms
sK7370	# Cancer - Malignant neoplasms of the cervix
sK7371	# Cancer - Malignant neoplasms of the colon
sK7372	# Cancer - Malignant neoplasms of the female breast
sK7373	# Cancer - Malignant neoplasms of the lung
sK7374	# Cancer - Malignant neoplasms of the prostate
sK7375	# Capacity of containment for contaminated fire water
sK7435	# Comments received by the public on the information they have received
sK7441	# Complaints about working conditions received from employees
sK7442	# Complaints from the public regarding safety performance of the enterprise
sK7526	# Days since last recordable incident
sK7534	# Days until the implementation of the recommendations applicable to representatives of the community following the emergency exercises
sK7535	# Days until the implementation of the recommendations applicable to the members of the community following emergency response
sK7539	# Deaths due to tuberculosis among HIV-negative people, per 100,000 population
sK7572	# Downstream users/handlers that have had a product stewardship assessment by the producer of the hazardous substances
sK7690	# Extent of time between provision of information that an accident involving hazardous substances has occurred and appropriate information is provided to the public regarding what actions to take to protect themselves
sK7691	# Extent of time between provision of information that an accident involving hazardous substances has occurred and response personnel arriving at the accident
sK7922	# HIV positive pregnant women receiving antiretrovirals
sK7999	# Human development index
sK8021	# Incidence of hepatitis B
sK8022	# Incidence of measles

sKPI #	Key Performance Indicator name
sK8023	# Incidence of pertussis
sK8025	# Incidence of tuberculosis per 100,000 people
sK8026	# Incidents analysis used during risk analyses
sK8027	# Incidents attributed to failure of training as a root or intermediate cause
sK8051	# Inequality-adjusted Human Development Index
sK8053	# Informal LTC workers
sK8055	# Initiatives coming from the public
sK8111	# Leakages attributable to inferior maintenance
sK8310	# Meetings held periodically, with safety as a substantial item on the agenda
sK8367	# New HIV infections
sK8368	# New HIV infections among 0-14 years
sK8379	# Non-compliance as detected by audits or other
sK8406	# On-site emergency response exercises per year
sK8412	# Orphans 0-17 years currently living
sK8583	# People living with HIV/AIDS
sK8589	# Performance indicators that are measured in a timely fashion, in relation to the number scheduled for measurement
sK8839	# Ratio of land-use planning reviews or applications where the members of the community took part
sK8840	# Ratio of planning permission procedures where the members of the community took part
sK8846	# Reduction in numbers of inquiries from the authorities
sK8860	# Reported incidents
sK8875	# Risk reduction actions achieved
sK8876	# Risks, assessed as non-acceptable, that have not been resolved to an acceptable level
sK8894	# Safety proposals per employee
sK8895	# Safety reviews actually performed versus number of laboratory experiments carried out
sK8970	# Time needed for implementation of recommendations resulting from investigations
sK9065	# Unplanned shut-downs attributable to inferior maintenance
sK9077	# Violations of the system
sK9271	$ Expenditure for promoting safety issues to the public and other stakeholders
sK10164	$ Money or other resource spent per year for safety, relative to other expenditures
sK10740	% Abnormal releases from continuous or normal emissions
sK10748	% Action plans or programmes for hazardous installations, developed with input from members of the community
sK10749	% Activities which should have a written procedure or instruction, that are covered by such written documentation
sK10750	% Actual performance of plan and personnel in major test or in real emergency
sK10753	% Adequacy of the training programme for employees

sKPI #	Key Performance Indicator name
sK10844	% Appropriate prevention requirements completed by staff within a given timeframe
sK10858	% Audits/inspections that members of the community have taken part in the year where they have the opportunity to participate and requested to do so
sK10990	% Change in the reporting of accidents involving hazardous substances and near misses
sK11000	% Change requests that are processed as emergency changes
sK11043	% Completeness of reports on accident involving hazardous substances and near-misses
sK11110	% Deficiencies identified by the public at the time of a response that were subsequently addressed
sK11111	% Deficiencies in the off-site preparedness plan highlighted during an incident or test of the plan
sK11124	% Deviations from internal standards discovered when reviewing projects or existing facilities, internally or by personnel from public authorities
sK11151	% Effectiveness of the community's reaction during emergency response
sK11183	% Employees who pass periodic assessment of training
sK11203	% Engineering disciplines covered by updated internal standards, including incorporation of most recent external standards
sK11204	% Engineering documents maintained up-to-date
sK11370	% Extent downstream users/handlers are satisfied with the enterprise's product stewardship policies and procedures
sK11371	% Extent employees are satisfied with their safety situation
sK11372	% Extent employees consider management a trusted source of information on chemical risks at the facility
sK11373	% Extent employees consider management a trusted source of information on safety related information
sK11374	% Extent employees use appropriate safety equipment, as prescribed in procedures
sK11375	% Extent enterprises have implemented recommendations from accident investigations within their hazardous installations
sK11376	% Extent ideas and suggestions from employees on safety are implemented within the enterprise
sK11377	% Extent local authorities have implemented lessons learned and recommendations from accident investigations by adjusting their local emergency plans appropriately
sK11378	% Extent local communities have made adjustments based on land use planning requirements and/or information
sK11379	% Extent management implements the recommendations in the audit reports and technical review reports
sK11380	% Extent management is informed and aware of the opinion of the public
sK11381	% Extent of the open door policy and non-punishment atmosphere relating to communication on safety issues
sK11382	% Extent of employees that have been trained in accordance with the planned training programme

sKPI #	Key Performance Indicator name
sK11383	% Extent of preventive maintenance versus corrective maintenance
sK11384	% Extent of testing of safety devices carried out versus testing planned
sK11385	% Extent overlaps and conflicts in the requirements related to safety of hazardous installations have been eliminated among relevant public authorities
sK11386	% Extent public authorities apply lessons learned from analyses of accident reports
sK11387	% Extent public authorities have identified causes that contributed to a significant accident involving hazardous substances, based on the specified criteria
sK11388	% Extent recommendations from accident investigations are implemented at hazardous installations
sK11389	% Extent staff performed quickly and adequately during tests of the emergency preparedness plans
sK11390	% Extent the areas of vulnerable populations within the hazardous zone of a hazardous installation have been reduced
sK11391	% Extent the installations within the enterprise have completed appropriate hazard identification and risk assessments using proper methods
sK11392	% Extent the number of people residing and working within the hazardous zone of a hazardous installation has been reduced
sK11393	% Extent the potentially effected public clearly understand the chemical risks associated with hazardous installations in their community as a result of information being provided to the public by non-governmental stakeholders
sK11394	% Extent the public considers the public authorities a good source of information on chemical risks
sK11395	% Extent the public is informed about the risks of chemical accidents in their communities
sK11396	% Extent the public seeks access to information via the internet, as exhibited by the number of hits on public authorities websites
sK11397	% Extent to which employees receive adequate safety-related information and understand this information
sK11398	% Extent to which planned safety rounds/inspections are actually implemented
sK11399	% Extent to which safety information is used or applied
sK11400	% Extent to which the workforce perform during emergency situations, based on tests or actual situations
sK11401	% Extent to which the workforce perform during normal operations
sK11474	% Female prevalence of HIV from population aged 15-24
sK11604	% Fulfillment of the enterprise's performance on the scale used in safety audits
sK11605	% Fulfillment of the enterprise's performance on the scale used in technical reviews
sK11608	% Funding for supporting general external safety research
sK11670	% Hazardous installations having been approached by members of the community for acquisition of information on chemical risks and consequences on human health and the environment

sKPI #	Key Performance Indicator name
sK11671	% Hazardous installations in compliance with all appropriate laws, regulations, etc. based on inspections of such installations
sK11672	% Hazardous installations that are cited for violations of the same requirements on more than one occasion
sK11673	% Hazardous installations that are included in off-site emergency preparedness plans
sK11674	% Hazardous installations that have submitted safety reports containing all required information compared to those that are subject to the reporting requirements
sK11675	% Hazardous installations, required to be inspected, which have been inspected
sK11685	% HIV positive pregnant women receiving antiretrovirals, using WHO/UNAIDS methodology
sK11687	% HIV prevalence rate among adult aged 15-49 years
sK11688	% HIV prevalence rate among young men aged 15-49 years
sK11689	% HIV prevalence rate among young women aged 15-49 years
sK11742	% Improvement in response to chemical accidents (reduction of delay and increased efficiency)
sK11743	% Improvement in the community's reaction during emergency exercises (evaluation of the community responses during the exercise by a mixed committee of stakeholders)
sK11744	% Improvement of staff competency
sK11747	% Incidents attributed to management of change as a root or intermediate cause
sK11748	% Incidents attributed to problems related to human resources
sK11749	% Incidents attributed to visitors as a root or intermediate cause
sK11750	% Incidents related to unknown risks
sK11751	% Incidents reported by downstream users, involving the enterprise's products
sK11752	% Incidents that were not identified in risk analyses
sK11926	% Information transmitted to the potentially affected public by the hazardous installations and the public authorities, which was reviewed by the members of the community
sK11927	% Inherently safer processes in the enterprise as measured by appropriate technical methods
sK11929	% Inspection reports obtained from public authorities by members of the community, where these are publicly available
sK11930	% Installations that have completed an appropriate risks assessment
sK11934	% Interaction and collaboration of public authorities, industry, and communities leading to improved safety of hazardous installations and reduction of chemical risks to local communities
sK12013	% Level of knowledge of the procedures by the affected operators, managers and other categories of employees
sK12033	% LTI (Lost Time Incident) rate and equivalent environmental accident rates
sK12038	% Major risks identified as non-acceptable and not tackled yet

sKPI #	Key Performance Indicator name
sK12096	% Male prevalence of HIV from population aged 15-24
sK12126	% Management visibility in daily operations
sK12188	% Modifications necessary after performance of risk assessments
sK12189	% Modifications needed after project completion to arrive at safe and well performing equipment
sK12202	% Negative comments from various authorities when reviewing new projects
sK12284	% New events identified in risk analyses
sK12295	% Off-site emergency plans that were evaluated by members of the community
sK12302	% On-site emergency plans of hazardous installations that were evaluated by members of the community, when the opportunity is available
sK12396	% Participation of members of the community in public hearings of hazardous installations in its area
sK12435	% Permits instituted by public authorities that were overruled by courts
sK12681	% Potentially affected public informed about emergency measures and actions to be taken in the event of accidents involving hazardous substances
sK12682	% Potentially affected public that know and understand chemical risks and consequences on human health and the environment
sK12683	% Potentially affected public who did not take appropriate action during emergency exercises and chemical accidents
sK12718	% Prevalence of HIV from population aged 15-49
sK12722	% Prevalence of overweight from children under 5
sK12725	% Prevalence of undernourishment from population
sK12726	% Prevalence of wasting from children under 5
sK12782	% Public's satisfaction with chemical risk information provided to them by public authorities
sK12791	% Rate of recordable incidents measured as releases
sK12792	% Rate of recordable incidents relating to personal injury
sK12793	% Ratio between employees who know what actions to take when an accident occurs and relevant employees
sK12794	% Ratio between hazardous installations with on-site plans and hazardous installations required to have on-site plans
sK12795	% Ratio between on-site plans tested and hazardous installations with on-site plans
sK12796	% Ratio between on-site plans with all appropriate information and flexibility and on site-plans audited
sK12797	% Ratio between public who know what actions to take when an accident occurs and the public within an area surrounding facility
sK12813	% Reduction in the number of hazardous installations that have required multiple emergency responses by public authorities
sK12814	% Reduction of accidents with similar processes or in similar installations as those which were the subject of accident investigations
sK12815	% Reduction of chemical risks at hazardous installations

sKPI #	Key Performance Indicator name
sK12816	# Complaints by employees relate to failure to receive adequate safety related information
sK12817	# Complaints from employees regarding lack of information on preparedness and response actions and efforts
sK12818	# Complaints from the hazardous installations regarding lack of information on preparedness and response actions and efforts
sK12819	# Complaints from the public and hazardous installations on preparedness and response actions and efforts
sK12820	# Environmental impacts from chemical accidents
sK12821	# Injuries and fatalities from chemical accidents
sK12823	# Multiple emergency response actions by public authorities
sK12824	# Property damage from chemical accidents
sK12825	# Frequency of accidents and near-misses and their severity
sK12826	# Impact distance of chemical accidents
sK12827	# People affected by chemical accidents
sK12828	# Time needed to mitigate an incident as a result of resources provided by nearby enterprises
sK12836	% Regulated industry which consistently goes beyond established requirements to voluntarily improve the safety of hazardous installations and reduce chemical risk as a result of incentive programmes

sKPI #	Key Performance Indicator name
sK12842	% Replacement of inferior components with safer ones
sK12863	% Risk potential or reduction of risk as a result of risk assessments and actions from them
sK12879	% Safety devices that do not function properly when tested
sK12880	% Safety improvements implemented at the hazardous installation as a result of an inspection
sK12881	% Safety reports evaluated by the public authority with specific criteria within a specific time frame
sK12882	% Satisfaction by the employees of a newly built installation
sK12944	% Tanks containing hazardous substances that have overfilling protection systems
sK12945	% Tanks or ware-houses containing hazardous substances that have second containment
sK12946	% Tanks or warehouses with fail-safe loading and unloading equipment
sK13079	% Understanding and retention of information on chemical hazards and the consequences of accidents by the community
sK13080	% Understanding and retention of the information on emergency measures and actions to be taken by the potentially affected public to protect itself in the event of accidents involving hazardous substances
sK13160	% Procedures reviewed and updated before their expiration date

Information Society

Information society refers to the enablement of an interconnected and informed society through the use of technology.

Communications

Communications cover the systems, technologies, professions and processes involved with the transmission of information.

sKPI #	Key Performance Indicator name
sK7360	# Broadband subscribers per 1,000 people
sK7388	# Cellular mobile telephone subscribers
sK7389	# Cellular subscribers per 100 inhabitants
sK7512	# Daily newspapers per 1,000 people
sK7555	# Digital cellular subscribers
sK7780	# Female professional mobile telecommunication staff
sK8074	# International Internet bandwidth in Mbps
sK8083	# Internet users
sK8084	# Internet users per 100 people
sK8342	# Mobile and fixed-line telephone subscribers
sK8343	# Mobile and fixed-line telephone subscribers per 100 people
sK8347	# Mobile cellular subscriptions per 100 people
sK8348	# Mobile phone subscribers per 1,000 people
sK8602	# Personal computers
sK8603	# Personal computers per 1,000 people
sK8821	# Public payphones

sKPI #	Key Performance Indicator name
sK8822	# Public payphones per 1,000 people
sK8832	# Radio sets
sK8833	# Radio sets per 1,000 people
sK8902	# Secure Internet servers
sK8903	# Secure Internet servers per 1 million people
sK8953	# Telephone lines per 100 people
sK9161	$ Business telephone connection charge
sK9162	$ Business telephone monthly subscription
sK9429	$ Fixed broadband Internet connection charge
sK9431	$ Fixed telephone service investment
sK10081	$ Information and communication technology expenditure
sK10082	$ Information and communication technology expenditure per capita
sK10154	$ Mobile cellular monthly subscription
sK10155	$ Mobile cellular of 3-minute local call at off-peak rate
sK10156	$ Mobile cellular of 3-minute local call at peak rate
sK10157	$ Mobile cellular post-paid connection charge
sK10158	$ Mobile cellular prepaid connection charge
sK10159	$ Mobile communication investment
sK10398	$ Price of 3-minute fixed telephone local call, at an off-peak rate

sKPI #	Key Performance Indicator name
sK10399	$ Price of a 3-minute fixed telephone local call at a peak rate
sK10471	$ Residential monthly telephone subscription
sK10485	$ Revenue from data services
sK10486	$ Revenue from fixed (wired) Internet services
sK10487	$ Revenue from fixed telephone service
sK10488	$ Revenue from fixed value-added telecommunication services
sK10489	$ Revenue from fixed-telephone calls
sK10490	$ Revenue from fixed-telephone connection charges
sK10491	$ Revenue from fixed-telephone subscription charges
sK10492	$ Revenue from international inbound roaming
sK10493	$ Revenue from leased lines
sK10494	$ Revenue from mobile communication
sK10495	$ Revenue from mobile networks
sK10496	$ Revenue from other wireless-broadband services
sK10886	% Business sector workforce involved in the ICT sector
sK10887	% Businesses placing orders over the Internet
sK10888	% Businesses receiving orders over the Internet
sK10889	% Businesses using computers
sK10890	% Businesses using the Internet
sK10891	% Businesses with a local area network (LAN)
sK10892	% Businesses with an extranet
sK10893	% Businesses with an intranet
sK11052	% Computer, communications and other services from commercial service exports
sK11053	% Computer, communications and other services from commercial service imports
sK11690	% Homes with a personal computer
sK11697	% Households with a telephone
sK11714	% Households with a radio
sK11717	% Households with a television
sK11771	% Individual use of the Internet
sK11876	% Individuals who make mobile phone calls very often
sK11877	% Individuals who male mobile phone calls to some extent
sK11884	% Individuals who upload photographs or video clips from phones to websites
sK11891	% Individuals who use fixed telephone line (not linked to Internet) to some extent
sK11892	% Individuals who use fixed telephone line (not linked to Internet) very often
sK11893	% Individuals who use online contacts instead of personal contacts with public services and administrations very often
sK11894	% Individuals who used a computer
sK11895	% Individuals who used a mobile cellular telephone
sK11896	% Individuals who used Internet for leisure activities related to obtaining and sharing audio-visual content, in the last 3 months

sKPI #	Key Performance Indicator name
sK11897	% Individuals who used Internet for making an appointment online with a practitioner
sK11898	% Individuals who used Internet for requesting a prescription online from a practitioner
sK11899	% Individuals who used Internet for seeking medical advice online with a practitioner
sK11900	% Individuals who used the Internet for creating or maintaining own weblog or blog
sK11901	% Individuals who used the Internet
sK11925	% Information and communication technology expenditure from GDP
sK11956	% Internet use for sending and receiving e-mails
sK11957	% Internet use for consulting wikis (to obtain knowledge on any subject)
sK11960	% Internet use for interaction with public authorities
sK11962	% Internet use for listening to web radios and/or watching web TV
sK11963	% Internet use for obtaining information from public authorities web sites
sK11965	% Internet use for participating in professional networks (creating user profile, posting messages or other contributions to LinkedIn, Xing, etc.)
sK11966	% Internet use for participating in social networks
sK11967	% Internet use for posting messages to social media sites or instant messaging
sK11968	% Internet use for reading and downloading online newspapers or news
sK11969	% Internet use for seeking health information
sK11970	% Internet use for sending filled forms
sK11971	% Internet use for taking part in on-line consultations or voting to define civic or political issues
sK11972	% Internet use for telephoning or video calls
sK11973	% Internet use for uploading self-created content to any website to be shared
sK11978	% Internet use for reading and posting opinions on civic or political issues via websites
sK12665	% Population coverage of mobile cellular telephony
sK12666	% Population covered by at least a 3G mobile network
sK12885	% Schools with a radio used for educational purposes
sK12886	% Schools with a telephone communication facility
sK12887	% Schools with a television used for educational purposes
sK12888	% Schools with electricity
sK13165	# Internet users
sK13166	# Mobile-cellular numbers ported
sK23215	# Public institutions with access to telecommunication services as a result of USG assistance
sK23216	$ Public and private dollars leveraged by USG for communication infrastructure projects
sK23217	# People with access to cellular service as a result of USG assistance
sK23218	# People with access to internet service as a result of USG assistance

Technology

Technology deals with the creation and use of technical means and their interaction with life, society and the environment, focusing on industrial arts, engineering, applied science and pure science. It represents the ways in which society provides itself with the material objects of its civilization.

sKPI #	Key Performance Indicator name
sK7365	# Cable television subscribers
sK7376	# Capacity of local public switching exchanges
sK7477	# Countries with which there is a roaming agreement
sK7562	# Direct-to-home (DTH) satellite antenna subscriptions
sK7571	# Domestic fixed-to-fixed telephone traffic, in minutes
sK7670	# Estimated facsimile machines
sK7734	# Female mobile telecommunication staff
sK7781	# Female professional telecommunication staff
sK7790	# Fixed broadband Internet subscribers
sK7791	# Fixed broadband Internet subscribers per 100 people
sK7795	# Fixed wireless local loop subscriptions
sK7796	# Fixed-telephone numbers ported
sK7797	# Fixed-to-mobile telephone traffic, in minutes
sK7827	# Full-time telecommunication staff
sK8032	# Individuals accessing Internet through mobile devices away from home or work
sK8033	# Individuals used Internet for playing networked games with others (in the last 3 months)
sK8034	# Individuals using selected mobile devices to access the Internet
sK8036	# Individuals who have carried out computer related activities
sK8037	# Individuals who have carried out Internet related activities
sK8038	# Individuals who have carried out computer related activities, by frequency of activities
sK8039	# Individuals who have carried out Internet related activities, by frequency of activities
sK8044	# Individuals who have used the Internet to subscribe to news services or products to receive them regularly
sK8075	# International outgoing telephone minutes
sK8081	# Internet hosts
sK8086	# ISDN subscribers
sK8114	# Leased-line subscriptions
sK8387	# Non-resident patent applications
sK8864	# Resident patent applications
sK8885	# Roaming by foreign subscribers (inbound roaming), in minutes
sK8886	# Roaming by home subscribers abroad (outbound roaming), in minutes
sK8911	# SMS international
sK8954	# Television receivers
sK8955	# Telex subscribers
sK9048	# Telephone pulses
sK9081	# VoIP traffic, in minutes

sKPI #	Key Performance Indicator name
sK10473	$ Residential telephone connection charge
sK10725	% Households with broadband Internet connection
sK10733	% Individuals who use online contacts instead of personal contacts with public services and administrations, to some extent
sK10851	% At least once a week, but not every day Internet access
sK11046	% Female computer users by age group
sK11051	% Male computer users by age group
sK11103	% Daily Internet access
sK11123	% Desktop or portable computer used as device for Internet access
sK11127	% Digital main lines
sK11210	% Enterprises connecting to the Internet via DSL
sK11211	% Enterprises connecting to the Internet via fixed broadband
sK11213	% Enterprises connecting to the Internet via wireless connection (satellite, mobile phone)
sK11214	% Enterprises experienced any ICT related security incidents excluding disclosure of confidential data in electronic form by employees
sK11215	% Enterprises giving devices for a mobile connection to the Internet to more than 10% of their employees
sK11216	% Enterprises giving devices for a mobile connection to the Internet to more than 20% of their employees
sK11217	% Enterprises giving devices for a mobile connection to the Internet to more than 5% of their employees
sK11218	% Enterprises having access to Internet
sK11229	% Enterprises having encountered virus, worm or Trojan attack as security problem
sK11230	% Enterprises having ERP software package to share information on sales /purchases with other internal functional areas
sK11231	% Enterprises having experienced ICT related security incidents resulting in disclosure of confidential data in electronic form by employees whether on intention or unintentionally
sK11232	% Enterprises having experienced ICT related security incidents that resulted in destruction or corruption of data due to infection or malicious software or unauthorized access
sK11233	% Enterprises having experienced ICT related security incidents that resulted in disclosure of confidential data due to intrusion, pharming, phishing attacks
sK11234	% Enterprises having experienced ICT related security incidents that resulted in unavailability of ICT services due to attacks from outside
sK11235	% Enterprises having had a formally defined ICT security policy with a plan of regular review
sK11241	% Enterprises having IT systems for orders and purchases which link to IT systems of suppliers or customers outside the enterprise group
sK11242	% Enterprises having made staff aware of their obligations in ICT security related issues
sK11243	% Enterprises having made staff aware of their obligations in ICT security related issues through compulsory training or presentations

sKPI #	Key Performance Indicator name
sK11244	% Enterprises having made staff aware of their obligations in ICT security related issues through contract
sK11245	% Enterprises having made staff aware of their obligations in ICT security related issues through voluntary training or generally available information (on the Intranet, newsletters or paper documents)
sK11246	% Enterprises having no remote employed persons who connect to IT systems through electronic networks
sK11247	% Enterprises having ordered via Internet over the last calendar year (excluding manually typed e-mails)
sK11248	% Enterprises having persons employed used computers with access to the www
sK11249	% Enterprises having received orders placed via EDI-type messages
sK11250	% Enterprises having received orders via Internet over the last calendar year (excluding manually typed emails)
sK11251	% Enterprises having regularly sent e-commerce orders via computer networks to suppliers located in the rest of the world
sK11252	% Enterprises having regularly sent e-commerce orders via computer networks to suppliers located in the rest of the world in the last calendar year
sK11253	% Enterprises having remote employed persons who connect to IT systems through electronic networks
sK11254	% Enterprises having sold products via specialized B2B market places over the last calendar year
sK11255	% Enterprises not aware of electronic tendering relevant to them
sK11256	% Enterprises not having experienced any ICT related security incidents excluding disclosure of confidential data in electronic form by employees
sK11257	% Enterprises not having made staff aware of their obligations in ICT security related issues
sK11258	% Enterprises not having ordered via Internet over the last calendar year
sK11259	% Enterprises not having received orders via Internet over the last calendar year
sK11260	% Enterprises not having sold products via specialized B2B market places
sK11263	% Enterprises not using EDI nor networks other than Internet for purchases over the last calendar year
sK11264	% Enterprises not using EDI nor networks other than Internet for sales over the last calendar year
sK11265	% Enterprises not using Internet for accessing tender documents/specifications in electronic procurement systems of public authorities but use Internet for offering goods or services in the systems
sK11266	% Enterprises not using Internet for accessing tender documents/specifications in electronic procurement systems of public authorities nor for offering goods or services in the systems
sK11267	% Enterprises not using Internet to return filled in forms electronically and find electronic procedures are too complicated and/or too time consuming
sK11268	% Enterprises regularly sharing electronically information on the supply chain management with suppliers or customers
sK11269	% Enterprises regularly sharing electronically information with customers on inventories, production plans or demand forecasts
sK11270	% Enterprises regularly sharing electronically information with customers on progress of deliveries
sK11271	% Enterprises regularly sharing electronically information with suppliers and customers
sK11272	% Enterprises regularly sharing electronically information with suppliers on progress of deliveries
sK11273	% Enterprises sharing electronically information on sales with the software used for any internal function
sK11274	% Enterprises sharing electronically information on purchases with the software used for any internal function
sK11275	% Enterprises used strong password authentication (min 8 characters, max 6 months, encrypted transmission and storage)
sK11276	% Enterprises used user identification and authentication via biometric methods
sK11277	% Enterprises used user identification and authentication via hardware tokens, e.g. smartcards
sK11278	% Enterprises using a digital signature in any message sent, i.e. using encryption methods that assure authenticity and integrity of the message
sK11279	% Enterprises using an internal computer network
sK11280	% Enterprises using automated data exchange between your enterprise and ICT systems of customers or suppliers
sK11281	% Enterprises using automated data exchange for receiving e-invoices
sK11282	% Enterprises using automated data exchange for receiving orders from customers
sK11283	% Enterprises using automated data exchange for sending e-invoices
sK11284	% Enterprises using automated data exchange for sending or receiving data to/from public authorities
sK11285	% Enterprises using automated data exchange for sending or receiving e-invoices
sK11286	% Enterprises using automated data exchange for sending or receiving product information
sK11287	% Enterprises using automated data exchange for sending or receiving transport documents
sK11288	% Enterprises using automated data exchange for sending orders to suppliers
sK11289	% Enterprises using automated data exchange for sending payment instructions to financial institutions
sK11290	% Enterprises using computers
sK11291	% Enterprises using dedicated applications for employees to access human resources services
sK11292	% Enterprises using EDI or networks other than Internet for purchases
sK11293	% Enterprises using Extranet
sK11294	% Enterprises using internal home page (Intranet)
sK11295	% Enterprises using Internet for accessing tender documents and specifications in electronic procurement systems of public authorities

sKPI #	Key Performance Indicator name
sK11296	% Enterprises using Internet for accessing tender documents and specifications in electronic procurement systems of public authorities and for offering goods or services in the systems
sK11297	% Enterprises using Internet for accessing tender documents and specifications in electronic procurement systems of public authorities but not for offering goods or services in the systems
sK11298	% Enterprises using Internet for declaration of corporate tax
sK11299	% Enterprises using Internet for declaration of customs/excise
sK11300	% Enterprises using Internet for declaration of social contributions for the persons employed
sK11301	% Enterprises using Internet for offering goods or services in public authorities' electronic procurement systems (eTendering)
sK11302	% Enterprises using Internet for offering goods or services in public authorities' electronic procurement systems (eTendering), in other EU countries
sK11303	% Enterprises using Internet for offering goods or services in public authorities' electronic procurement systems (eTendering), in own country
sK11304	% Enterprises using Internet for returning filled forms but not for declaration of social contributions, corporate tax, VAT or customs/excise
sK11305	% Enterprises using Internet to return filled in forms electronically, but electronic procedures still requiring exchange of paper mail or personal visits limit electronic interaction
sK11306	% Enterprises using Internet to return filled in forms electronically, but having concerns related to data confidentiality and security which limit electronic interaction
sK11307	% Enterprises using Internet to return filled in forms electronically, but lack of awareness of available electronic procedures limits electronic interaction
sK11308	% Enterprises using Internet to return filled in forms electronically, but too complicated and/or too time consuming electronic procedures limit electronic interaction
sK11309	% Enterprises using Internet to treat an administrative procedure completely electronically and for declaration of social contributions for the persons employed
sK11310	% Enterprises using Internet to treat an administrative procedure completely electronically and for declaration of VAT
sK11311	% Enterprises using LAN and (Intranet or Extranet)
sK11312	% Enterprises using RFID for monitoring and control of industrial production
sK11313	% Enterprises using RFID for payment applications
sK11314	% Enterprises using RFID for person identification or access control
sK11315	% Enterprises using RFID for product identification
sK11316	% Enterprises using RFID for service and maintenance information management, asset management
sK11317	% Enterprises using RFID for supply chain and inventory tracking and tracing
sK11318	% Enterprises using RFID instruments

sKPI #	Key Performance Indicator name
sK11319	% Enterprises using secure protocol, such as SSL or TLS, for reception of orders via Internet
sK11320	% Enterprises using the Internet (as a customer) for banking and financial services
sK11321	% Enterprises using third party free or open source operating systems, such as Linux
sK11322	% Enterprises where remote employed persons access during business travel
sK11323	% Enterprises where the remote employed persons access from customers or other external business partners premises
sK11324	% Enterprises where the remote employed persons access from home
sK11325	% Enterprises where the remote employed persons access from other geographically dispersed locations of the same enterprise or enterprise group
sK11326	% Enterprises which have CRM (software for information about clients)
sK11327	% Enterprises which have CRM to analyze information about clients for marketing purposes
sK11328	% Enterprises which have CRM to capture, store and make available to other business functions the information about its clients
sK11335	% Enterprises whose website or home page has a privacy policy statement, privacy seal or certification related to website safety
sK11336	% Enterprises whose website or home page has advertisement of open job positions or online job applications
sK11337	% Enterprises whose website or home page has online ordering, reservation or booking
sK11338	% Enterprises whose website or home page has order tracking available on line
sK11339	% Enterprises whose website or home page has product catalogues or price lists
sK11340	% Enterprises with employees provided with a portable device with at least 3G technology for accessing the Internet
sK11597	% Frequency of safety copies/back up files: Never or hardly ever
sK11598	% Frequency of safety copies/back up files: Sometimes
sK11609	% Games console used as device for Internet access
sK11669	% Handheld computer used as device for Internet access
sK11729	% ICT goods imports, from exports
sK11730	% ICT goods imports, from imports
sK11731	% ICT sector share of gross value added
sK11732	% ICT-qualified teachers in schools
sK11772	% Individuals mildly concerned about abuse of personal information sent on the Internet and/or other privacy violations (e.g. abuse of pictures, videos, personal data uploaded on community websites)
sK11773	% Individuals mildly concerned about catching a virus or other computer infection (e.g. worm or Trojan horse) resulting in loss of information or time

sKPI #	Key Performance Indicator name
sK11774	% Individuals mildly concerned about children accessing inappropriate web-sites or connecting with potentially dangerous persons from a computer within the household
sK11775	% Individuals mildly concerned about financial loss as a result of receiving fraudulent messages('phishing') or getting redirected to fake websites asking for personal information('pharming')
sK11776	% Individuals mildly concerned about financial loss due to fraudulent payment (credit or debit) card use
sK11777	% Individuals mildly concerned about unsolicited emails received ('Spam')
sK11778	% Individuals not at all concerned about abuse of personal information sent on the Internet and/or other privacy violations (e.g. abuse of pictures, videos, personal data uploaded on community websites)
sK11779	% Individuals not at all concerned about any security issue
sK11780	% Individuals not at all concerned about catching a virus or other computer infection (e.g. worm or Trojan horse) resulting in loss of information or time
sK11781	% Individuals not at all concerned about children accessing inappropriate web-sites or connecting with potentially dangerous persons from a computer within the household
sK11782	% Individuals not at all concerned about financial loss as a result of receiving fraudulent messages('phishing') or getting redirected to fake websites asking for personal information('pharming')
sK11783	% Individuals not at all concerned about financial loss due to fraudulent payment (credit or debit) card use
sK11784	% Individuals not at all concerned about unsolicited emails received ('Spam')
sK11786	% Individuals strongly concerned about abuse of personal information sent on the Internet and/or other privacy violations (e.g. abuse of pictures, videos, personal data uploaded on community websites)
sK11787	% Individuals strongly concerned about catching a virus or other computer infection (e.g. worm or Trojan horse) resulting in loss of information or time
sK11788	% Individuals strongly concerned about children accessing inappropriate web-sites or connecting with potentially dangerous persons from a computer within the household
sK11789	% Individuals strongly concerned about financial loss as a result of receiving fraudulent messages('phishing') or getting redirected to fake websites asking for personal information('pharming')
sK11790	% Individuals strongly concerned about financial loss due to fraudulent payment (credit or debit) card use
sK11791	% Individuals strongly concerned about unsolicited emails received ('Spam')
sK11792	% Individuals who browse the Internet
sK11793	% Individuals who did not downloaded, but only listened to music and/or have watched films
sK11794	% Individuals who did not encounter problems when buying/ordering goods or services over the Internet for private use
sK11795	% Individuals who do not download at all films and videos instead of buying/renting a DVD

sKPI #	Key Performance Indicator name
sK11796	% Individuals who do not download at all music files instead of buying a CD
sK11797	% Individuals who do not listen at all to web radios instead of listening to normal radio
sK11798	% Individuals who do not make at all mobile phone calls
sK11799	% Individuals who do not need to take a computer course because their computer skills are sufficient
sK11800	% Individuals who do not need to take a computer course because they rarely use computers
sK11801	% Individuals who do not use at all fixed telephone line (not linked to Internet)
sK11802	% Individuals who do not use at all online contacts instead of personal contacts with public services and administrations
sK11803	% Individuals who don't update security products
sK11804	% Individuals who don't update security products because it's too expensive
sK11805	% Individuals who don't update security products because it's unnecessary, the risk too low
sK11806	% Individuals who don't update security products because the update is effective
sK11807	% Individuals who don't update security products because they don't know how to update
sK11808	% Individuals who don't update security products for other reasons
sK11809	% Individuals who don't use at all e-mail
sK11810	% Individuals who download films and videos instead of buying/renting a DVD
sK11811	% Individuals who download films and videos instead of buying/renting a DVD by download frequency intervals
sK11812	% Individuals who download music files instead of buying a CD
sK11813	% Individuals who download music files instead of buying a CD by download frequency intervals
sK11814	% Individuals who encountered no problems when making purchases over the Internet
sK11815	% Individuals who encountered problems when buying/ordering goods or services over the Internet for private use
sK11816	% Individuals who encountered the following problem when buying/ordering over the Internet: difficulties finding information concerning guarantees, other legal rights
sK11817	% Individuals who encountered the following problem when buying/ordering over the Internet: technical failure
sK11818	% Individuals who encountered the following problem when making purchases over the Internet: Complaints and redress were difficult
sK11819	% Individuals who encountered the following problem when making purchases over the Internet: Complaints and redress were difficult or no satisfactory response received after complaint
sK11820	% Individuals who encountered the following problem when making purchases over the Internet: Damaged goods delivered

sKPI #	Key Performance Indicator name
sK11821	% Individuals who encountered the following problem when making purchases over the Internet: Delivery costs or final price higher than indicated
sK11822	% Individuals who encountered the following problem when making purchases over the Internet: Lack of security of payments
sK11823	% Individuals who have compressed files
sK11824	% Individuals who have connected and installed new devices, e.g. a printer or a modem
sK11825	% Individuals who have connected computers to a local area network
sK11826	% Individuals who have copied or moved a file or folder
sK11827	% Individuals who have created a Web page
sK11828	% Individuals who have created electronic presentations with presentation software, including images, sound, video or charts
sK11829	% Individuals who have detected and solved computer problems
sK11830	% Individuals who have installed a new or replaced an old operating system
sK11831	% Individuals who have modified or verified the configuration parameters of software applications (except Internet browsers)
sK11832	% Individuals who have modified the security settings of Internet browsers
sK11850	% Individuals who have transferred files between computer and other devices
sK11851	% Individuals who have used a mouse to launch programs such as an Internet browser or word processor
sK11852	% Individuals who have used basic arithmetic formulae to add, subtract, multiply or divide figures in a spread sheet
sK11853	% Individuals who have used copy or cut and paste tools to duplicate or move information onscreen
sK11854	% Individuals who have written a computer program using a specialized programming language
sK11855	% Individuals who have experienced the following security problem: Abuse of personal information sent on the Internet
sK11856	% Individuals who have experienced the following security problem: Computer virus resulting in loss of information or time
sK11857	% Individuals who have experienced the following security problem: Fraudulent payment (credit or debit) card use
sK11858	% Individuals who have installed a virus checking program
sK11859	% Individuals who have updated a virus checking program
sK11860	% Individuals who have used on-line authentication (password, PIN, digital signature) on the Internet
sK11863	% Individuals who judge their current computer or Internet skills not to be sufficient to protect their personal data
sK11864	% Individuals who judge their current computer or Internet skills to be sufficient to protect their personal data

sKPI #	Key Performance Indicator name
sK11865	% Individuals who judge their current computer or Internet skills not to be sufficient to communicate with relatives, friends, colleagues over the Internet
sK11866	% Individuals who judge their current computer or Internet skills not to be sufficient to protect their private computer from virus or other computer infection
sK11867	% Individuals who judge their current computer or Internet skills to be sufficient to communicate with relatives, friends, colleagues over the Internet
sK11868	% Individuals who listen to web radios instead of listening to normal radio to some extent
sK11869	% Individuals who listen to web radios instead of listening to normal radio very much
sK11881	% Individuals who update one or more security products at least occasionally
sK11882	% Individuals who update one or more security products every time an update is available
sK11883	% Individuals who update one or more security products occasionally or when remember
sK11885	% Individuals who use a hardware or software firewall
sK11886	% Individuals who use a parental control or a web filtering software
sK11887	% Individuals who use an email filtering to prevent 'Spam'
sK11888	% Individuals who use an IT security software package but don't know the components
sK11889	% Individuals who use e-mail to some extent
sK11890	% Individuals who reported using e-mail very often
sK11950	% Internet access at place of work
sK11951	% Internet access at postal office
sK11952	% Internet access in Internet café
sK11953	% Internet access only at postal office
sK11954	% Internet access only in Internet café
sK11958	% Internet use for downloading software
sK11974	% Internet use: downloading official forms
sK11975	% Internet use: Internet banking
sK11976	% Internet use: never
sK11977	% Internet use: playing and downloading games, images, films or music
sK12009	% Learners enrolled at the post-secondary level in ICT-related fields
sK12024	% Localities with public Internet access centers
sK12184	% Mobile phone (GPRS, UMTS) used as device for Internet access
sK12299	% Once a week (including every day) Internet access
sK12301	% Only games console used as device for Internet access
sK12439	% Employees provided with a portable device with at least 3G technology for accessing the Internet
sK12440	% Employees routinely using computers
sK12441	% Employees routinely using the Internet
sK12904	% Security concerns kept individual from carrying out banking activities such as account management

sKPI #	Key Performance Indicator name
sK12905	% Security concerns kept individual from communicating with public services and administrations
sK12906	% Security concerns kept individual from downloading software, music, video files, games or other data files
sK12907	% Security concerns kept individual from ordering or buying goods or services for private use
sK12908	% Security concerns kept individual from providing personal information to online communities for social and professional networking
sK12909	% Security concerns kept individual from using the Internet with mobile devices via wireless connection from places other than home
sK12986	% The enterprises' ICT security policy addressed the risks of destruction or corruption of data due to an attack or by unexpected incident

sKPI #	Key Performance Indicator name
sK12987	% The enterprises' ICT security policy addressed the risks of destruction or corruption of data, disclosure of confidential data and unavailability of ICT services due to an attack or an accident
sK12988	% The enterprises' ICT security policy addressed the risks of disclosure of confidential data due to intrusion, pharming, phishing attacks or by accident
sK12989	% The enterprises' ICT security policy addressed the risks of unavailability of ICT services due to an attack from outside
sK13077	% TV set with Internet device used as
sK13163	# Frequency of safety copies/back up files - always or almost always

Intellect

Intellect represents the capacity of thinking, understanding and acquiring knowledge.

Culture

Culture refers to the set of values, conventions or social practices shared by people, which are transmitted to succeeding generations.

sKPI #	Key Performance Indicator name
sK7148	# Annual attendance at concerts per resident
sK7149	# Annual attendance at theaters per resident
sK7152	# Annual cinema attendance per resident
sK7153	# Annual visitors to museums per resident
sK7403	# Cinema seats per 1 000 residents
sK7452	# Concert seats per capita
sK7453	# Concerts per 1 000 residents
sK7990	# Hostility to foreigners rating
sK7991	# Hostility to private property rating
sK8016	# Importance of religion in national life rating
sK8139	# Loans of books and other media per resident
sK8820	# Public libraries
sK8957	# Theater seats per capita
sK8958	# Theaters
sK9086	# Willingness to fight rating
sK12428	% Perception of the quality and quantity of cultural facilities

Education

Education refers to all the parts of the process of imparting and acquiring general knowledge, including schooling and results produced by instruction, training or studies.

sKPI #	Key Performance Indicator name
sK7069	# Years of tertiary schooling, age 30-34
sK7072	# Years of schooling, age 30-34, male
sK7075	% Tertiary graduates in services
sK7076	# Years of schooling by age group 15-19

sKPI #	Key Performance Indicator name
sK7212	# Years of primary schooling, age 15+, female
sK7213	# Years of primary schooling, age 15+
sK7214	# Years of primary schooling, age 15-19, female
sK7215	# Years of primary schooling, age 15-19, total
sK7216	# Years of primary schooling, age 20-24, female
sK7217	# Years of primary schooling, age 25+, total
sK7218	# Years of primary schooling, age 25-29, female
sK7219	# Years of primary schooling, age 25-29, total
sK7220	# Years of primary schooling, age 30-34, female
sK7221	# Years of primary schooling, age 30-34, total
sK7222	# Years of primary schooling, age 35-39, female
sK7223	# Years of primary schooling, age 35-39, total
sK7224	# Years of primary schooling, age 40-44, female
sK7225	# Years of primary schooling, age 40-44, total
sK7226	# Years of primary schooling, age 45-49, female
sK7227	# Years of primary schooling, age 45-49, total
sK7228	# Years of primary schooling, age 50-54, female
sK7229	# Years of primary schooling, age 55-59, female
sK7230	# Years of primary schooling, age 65-69, female
sK7231	# Years of primary schooling, age 65-69, total
sK7232	# Years of primary schooling, age 70-74, female
sK7233	# Years of primary schooling, age 70-74, total
sK7234	# Years of primary schooling, age 75+, female
sK7235	# Years of schooling by age group 15-19
sK7236	# Years of schooling by age group 15-19, quintile 1
sK7237	# Years of schooling by age group 15-19, quintile 2
sK7238	# Years of schooling by age group 15-19, quintile 4
sK7239	# Years of schooling by age group 15-19, quintile 5
sK7240	# Years of schooling by female age group 15-19
sK7241	# Years of schooling by male age group 15-19

smartKPIs.com
The smart choice in performance management

sKPI #	Key Performance Indicator name
sK7242	# Years of schooling by rural age group 15-19
sK7243	# Years of schooling by urban age group 15-19
sK7244	# Years of secondary schooling, age 15+, female
sK7245	# Years of secondary schooling, age 15+, total
sK7246	# Years of secondary schooling, age 15-19, female
sK7247	# Years of secondary schooling, age 15-19, total
sK7248	# Years of secondary schooling, age 20-24, female
sK7249	# Years of secondary schooling, age 20-24, total
sK7250	# Years of secondary schooling, age 25+, female
sK7251	# Years of secondary schooling, age 25+, total
sK7252	# Years of secondary schooling, age 25-29, female
sK7253	# Years of secondary schooling, age 25-29, total
sK7254	# Years of secondary schooling, age 30-34, female
sK7255	# Years of secondary schooling, age 30-34, total
sK7256	# Years of secondary schooling, age 35-39, female
sK7257	# Years of secondary schooling, age 35-39, total
sK7258	# Years of secondary schooling, age 40-44, female
sK7259	# Years of secondary schooling, age 40-44, total
sK7260	# Years of secondary schooling, age 45-49, female
sK7261	# Years of secondary schooling, age 45-49, total
sK7262	# Years of secondary schooling, age 50-54, total
sK7263	# Years of secondary schooling, age 55-59, female
sK7264	# Years of secondary schooling, age 55-59, total
sK7265	# Years of secondary schooling, age 60-64, female
sK7266	# Years of secondary schooling, age 60-64, total
sK7267	# Years of secondary schooling, age 65-69, female
sK7268	# Years of secondary schooling, age 65-69, total
sK7269	# Years of secondary schooling, age 70-74, female
sK7270	# Years of secondary schooling, age 70-74, total
sK7271	# Years of secondary schooling, age 75+, female
sK7272	# Years of secondary schooling, age 75+, total
sK7273	# Years of tertiary schooling, age 15+, female
sK7274	# Years of tertiary schooling, age 15+
sK7275	# Years of tertiary schooling, age 15-19, female
sK7276	# Years of tertiary schooling, age 15-19, total
sK7277	# Years of tertiary schooling, age 20-24, female
sK7278	# Years of tertiary schooling, age 20-24, total
sK7279	# Years of tertiary schooling, age 25+, female
sK7280	# Years of tertiary schooling, age 25+, total
sK7281	# Years of tertiary schooling, age 25-29, female
sK7282	# Years of tertiary schooling, age 25-29, total
sK7283	# Years of tertiary schooling, age 30-34, female
sK7284	# Years of tertiary schooling, age 35-39, female
sK7285	# Years of tertiary schooling, age 35-39, total
sK7286	# Years of tertiary schooling, age 40-44, female
sK7287	# Years of tertiary schooling, age 40-44, total

sKPI #	Key Performance Indicator name
sK7288	# Years of tertiary schooling, age 45-49, female
sK7289	# Years of tertiary schooling, age 45-49, total
sK7290	# Years of tertiary schooling, age 50-54, female
sK7291	# Years of tertiary schooling, age 50-54, total
sK7292	# Years of tertiary schooling, age 55-59, female
sK7293	# Years of tertiary schooling, age 55-59, total
sK7294	# Years of tertiary schooling, age 60-64, female
sK7295	# Years of tertiary schooling, age 60-64, total
sK7296	# Years of tertiary schooling, age 65-69, female
sK7297	# Years of tertiary schooling, age 65-69, total
sK7298	# Years of tertiary schooling, age 70-74, female
sK7299	# Years of tertiary schooling, age 70-74, total
sK7300	# Years of tertiary schooling, age 75+, female
sK7301	# Years of tertiary schooling, age 75+, total
sK7302	# Years of schooling, age 15+, female
sK7303	# Years of schooling, age 15+
sK7304	# Years of total schooling, age 15-19, female
sK7305	# Years of total schooling, age 15-19, total
sK7306	# Years of total schooling, age 20-24, female
sK7307	# Years of total schooling, age 20-24, total
sK7308	# Years of total schooling, age 25+, female
sK7309	# Years of total schooling, age 25+, total
sK7310	# Years of total schooling, age 25-29, female
sK7311	# Years of total schooling, age 25-29, total
sK7312	# Years of total schooling, age 30-34, female
sK7313	# Years of total schooling, age 30-34, total
sK7314	# Years of total schooling, age 35-39, female
sK7315	# Years of total schooling, age 35-39, total
sK7316	# Years of total schooling, age 40-44, female
sK7317	# Years of total schooling, age 40-44, total
sK7318	# Years of total schooling, age 45-49, female
sK7319	# Years of total schooling, age 45-49, total
sK7320	# Years of total schooling, age 50-54, female
sK7321	# Years of total schooling, age 50-54, total
sK7322	# Years of total schooling, age 55-59, female
sK7323	# Years of total schooling, age 55-59, total
sK7324	# Years of total schooling, age 60-64, female
sK7325	# Years of total schooling, age 60-64, total
sK7326	# Years of total schooling, age 65-69, female
sK7327	# Years of total schooling, age 65-69, total
sK7328	# Years of total schooling, age 70-74, female
sK7329	# Years of total schooling, age 70-74, total
sK7330	# Years of total schooling, age 75+, female
sK7331	# Years of total schooling, age 75+, total
sK7335	# Barro-Lee: Years of primary schooling, age 20-24
sK7336	# Barro-Lee: Years of primary schooling, age 25+, female

sKPI #	Key Performance Indicator name
sK7337	# Barro-Lee: Average years of primary schooling, age 60-64, female
sK7338	# Barro-Lee: Average years of primary schooling, age 60-64, total
sK7339	# Barro-Lee: Years of secondary schooling, age 50-54, female
sK7582	# Duration of primary education in years
sK7583	# Duration of secondary education in years
sK7668	# Entrance age of primary education
sK7672	# Expected years of schooling
sK7706	# Female adult illiterate population
sK7710	# Female elderly illiterate population
sK7711	# Female enrolment in pre-primary education, public and private, in all programmes
sK7712	# Female enrolment in total secondary, public and private, in all programmes
sK7713	# Female enrolment in total secondary, public and private, in general programmes
sK7714	# Female enrolment in total secondary, public and private, in technical/vocational programmes
sK7715	# Female expected years of schooling
sK7716	# Female graduates in agriculture, in tertiary education
sK7717	# Female graduates in all programmes, in tertiary education
sK7718	# Female graduates in engineering, manufacturing and construction, in tertiary education
sK7719	# Female graduates in general programmes, in tertiary education
sK7720	# Female graduates in health and welfare, in tertiary education
sK7721	# Female graduates in humanities and arts, in tertiary education
sK7722	# Female graduates in science, in tertiary education
sK7723	# Female graduates in services, in tertiary education
sK7724	# Female graduates in social sciences, business and law, in tertiary education
sK7725	# Female graduates in tertiary education
sK7726	# Female graduates in unspecified programmes, in tertiary education
sK7727	# Female gross enrolment ratio in pre-primary education
sK7732	# Female mean performance on the mathematics scale
sK7733	# Female mean performance on the reading scale
sK7742	# Female population age 0-14
sK7743	# Female population age 10-14
sK7744	# Female population age 10-15
sK7745	# Female population age 10-16
sK7746	# Female population age 10-17
sK7747	# Female population age 10-18
sK7748	# Female population age 11-15
sK7749	# Female population age 11-16
sK7750	# Female population age 11-17

sKPI #	Key Performance Indicator name
sK7751	# Female population age 11-18
sK7752	# Female population age 12-15
sK7753	# Female population age 12-16
sK7754	# Female population age 12-17
sK7755	# Female population age 12-18
sK7756	# Female population age 13-16
sK7757	# Female population age 13-17
sK7758	# Female population age 13-18
sK7759	# Female population age 13-19
sK7760	# Female population age 14-18
sK7761	# Female population age 14-19
sK7762	# Female population age 15-24
sK7763	# Female population age 15-64
sK7764	# Female population age 3-5
sK7765	# Female population age 4-6
sK7766	# Female population age 5-10
sK7767	# Female population age 5-11
sK7768	# Female population age 5-9
sK7769	# Female population age 6-10
sK7770	# Female population age 6-11
sK7771	# Female population age 6-12
sK7772	# Female population age 6-9
sK7773	# Female population age 7-10
sK7774	# Female population age 7-11
sK7775	# Female population age 7-12
sK7776	# Female population age 7-13
sK7777	# Female population age 7-9
sK7779	# Female population of primary education graduation age
sK7782	# Female teachers in secondary education
sK7783	# Female teaching staff in pre-primary education, public and private, full and part-time, in all programmes
sK7784	# Female youth illiterate population
sK7838	# Gender parity index for adult literacy rate
sK7839	# Gender parity index for elderly literacy rate
sK7840	# Gender parity index for gross enrolment ratio in primary and secondary education combined
sK7841	# Gender parity index for gross enrolment ratio in primary education
sK7842	# Gender parity index for gross enrolment ratio in secondary education, for all programs
sK7843	# Gender parity index for gross enrolment ratio in tertiary education
sK7849	# General pupils in secondary education
sK7856	# Gini coefficient of years of rural schooling, age 15+
sK7857	# Gini coefficient of years of schooling, age 15+
sK7858	# Gini coefficient of years of schooling, age 15+, female
sK7859	# Gini coefficient of years of schooling, age 15+, male
sK7860	# Gini coefficient of years of schooling, age 15+, quintile 1

smartKPIs.com
The smart choice in performance management

sKPI #	Key Performance Indicator name
sK7861	# Gini coefficient of years of schooling, age 15+, quintile 2
sK7862	# Gini coefficient of years of schooling, age 15+, quintile 3
sK7863	# Gini coefficient of years of schooling, age 15+, quintile 4
sK7864	# Gini coefficient of years of schooling, age 15+, quintile 5
sK7865	# Gini coefficient of years of urban schooling, age 15+
sK8042	# Individuals who have used Internet, in the last 3 months, for doing an online course (of any subject)
sK8043	# Individuals who have used Internet, in the last 3 months, for looking for information about education, training or course offers
sK8048	# Individuals who used Internet, in the last 3 months, for training and education
sK8112	# Learners who have access to the Internet at school
sK8113	# Learners-to-computer ratio in schools with computer-assisted instruction
sK8165	# Male adult illiterate population
sK8168	# Male elderly illiterate population
sK8169	# Male enrolment in pre-primary education, public and private, in all programmes
sK8170	# Male expected years of schooling
sK8171	# Male gross enrolment ratio in pre-primary education
sK8176	# Male performance on the reading scale
sK8184	# Male population age 0-14
sK8185	# Male population age 10-14
sK8186	# Male population age 10-15
sK8187	# Male population age 10-16
sK8188	# Male population age 10-17
sK8189	# Male population age 10-18
sK8190	# Male population age 11-15
sK8191	# Male population age 11-16
sK8192	# Male population age 11-17
sK8193	# Male population age 11-18
sK8194	# Male population age 12-15
sK8195	# Male population age 12-16
sK8196	# Male population age 12-17
sK8197	# Male population age 12-18
sK8198	# Male population age 13-16
sK8199	# Male population age 13-17
sK8200	# Male population age 13-18
sK8201	# Male population age 13-19
sK8202	# Male population age 14-18
sK8203	# Male population age 14-19
sK8204	# Male population age 15-24
sK8205	# Male population age 15-64
sK8206	# Male population age 3-5
sK8207	# Male population age 4-6
sK8208	# Male population age 5-10
sK8209	# Male population age 5-11

sKPI #	Key Performance Indicator name
sK8210	# Male population age 5-9
sK8211	# Male population age 6-10
sK8212	# Male population age 6-9
sK8213	# Male population age 7-10
sK8214	# Male population age 7-11
sK8215	# Male population age 7-12
sK8216	# Male population age 7-13
sK8217	# Male population age 7-9
sK8219	# Male population of primary education graduation age
sK8220	# Male youth illiterate population
sK8231	# Performance on the mathematics scale
sK8232	# Performance on the mathematics scale for female 3rd grade students
sK8233	# Performance on the mathematics scale for female 6th grade students
sK8234	# Performance on the mathematics scale for male 3rd grade students
sK8235	# Performance on the mathematics scale for male 6th grade students
sK8236	# Performance on the mathematics scale for total 3rd grade students
sK8237	# Performance on the mathematics scale for total 4th grade students
sK8238	# Performance on the mathematics scale for total 6th grade students
sK8239	# Performance on the reading scale for female 3rd grade students
sK8240	# Performance on the reading scale for female 6th grade students
sK8241	# Performance on the reading scale for male 3rd grade students
sK8242	# Performance on the reading scale for male 6th grade students
sK8243	# Performance on the reading scale for total 3rd grade students
sK8244	# Performance on the reading scale for total 4th grade students
sK8245	# Performance on the reading scale for total 6th grade students
sK8246	# Performance on the science scale for female 6th grade students
sK8247	# Performance on the science scale for total 6th grade students
sK8249	# Mean years of schooling, age 15+, female
sK8250	# Mean years of schooling, age 15+, male
sK8251	# Mean years of schooling, age 15+, total
sK8252	# Mean years of schooling, age 15-19, female
sK8253	# Mean years of schooling, age 15-19, male
sK8254	# Mean years of schooling, age 15-19, total
sK8255	# Mean years of schooling, age 15-44, female
sK8256	# Mean years of schooling, age 15-44, male
sK8257	# Mean years of schooling, age 15-44, total

sKPI #	Key Performance Indicator name	sKPI #	Key Performance Indicator name
sK8258	# Mean years of schooling, age 15-64, female	sK8304	# Mean years of schooling, age 75-79, total
sK8259	# Mean years of schooling, age 15-64, male	sK8305	# Mean years of schooling, age 80+, female
sK8260	# Mean years of schooling, age 15-64, total	sK8306	# Mean years of schooling, age 80+, male
sK8261	# Mean years of schooling, age 20-24, female	sK8307	# Mean years of schooling, age 80+, total
sK8262	# Mean years of schooling, age 20-24, male	sK8425	# Outbound mobile students in tertiary education
sK8263	# Mean years of schooling, age 20-24, total	sK8586	% Female population aged 20-24 who attained incomplete secondary education
sK8264	# Mean years of schooling, age 25+, female	sK8587	% Female population aged 25+ who attained incomplete tertiary education
sK8265	# Mean years of schooling, age 25+, male	sK8690	# Population age 6-11
sK8266	# Mean years of schooling, age 25+, total	sK8691	# Population age 6-12
sK8267	# Mean years of schooling, age 25-29, female	sK8698	# Population in thousands, age 15+, female
sK8268	# Mean years of schooling, age 25-29, male	sK8699	# Population in thousands, age 15+, total
sK8269	# Mean years of schooling, age 25-29, total	sK8700	# Population in thousands, age 15-19, female
sK8270	# Mean years of schooling, age 30-34, female	sK8701	# Population in thousands, age 15-19, total
sK8271	# Mean years of schooling, age 30-34, total	sK8702	# Population in thousands, age 20-24, female
sK8272	# Mean years of schooling, age 35-39, female	sK8703	# Population in thousands, age 20-24, total
sK8273	# Mean years of schooling, age 35-39, male	sK8704	# Population in thousands, age 25+, female
sK8274	# Mean years of schooling, age 35-39, total	sK8705	# Population in thousands, age 25+, total
sK8275	# Mean years of schooling, age 40-44, female	sK8706	# Population in thousands, age 25-29, female
sK8276	# Mean years of schooling, age 40-44, male	sK8707	# Population in thousands, age 25-29, total
sK8277	# Mean years of schooling, age 40-44, total	sK8708	# Population in thousands, age 30-34, female
sK8278	# Mean years of schooling, age 45-49, female	sK8709	# Population in thousands, age 30-34, total
sK8279	# Mean years of schooling, age 45-49, male	sK8710	# Population in thousands, age 35-39, female
sK8280	# Mean years of schooling, age 45-49, total	sK8711	# Population in thousands, age 35-39, total
sK8281	# Mean years of schooling, age 45-64, female	sK8712	# Population in thousands, age 40-44, female
sK8282	# Mean years of schooling, age 45-64, male	sK8713	# Population in thousands, age 40-44, total
sK8283	# Mean years of schooling, age 45-64, total	sK8714	# Population in thousands, age 45-49, female
sK8284	# Mean years of schooling, age 50-54, female	sK8715	# Population in thousands, age 45-49, total
sK8285	# Mean years of schooling, age 50-54, male	sK8716	# Population in thousands, age 50-54, female
sK8286	# Mean years of schooling, age 50-54, total	sK8717	# Population in thousands, age 50-54, total
sK8287	# Mean years of schooling, age 55-59, female	sK8718	# Population in thousands, age 55-59, female
sK8288	# Mean years of schooling, age 55-59, male	sK8719	# Population in thousands, age 55-59, total
sK8289	# Mean years of schooling, age 55-59, total	sK8720	# Population in thousands, age 60-64, female
sK8290	# Mean years of schooling, age 60-64, female	sK8721	# Population in thousands, age 60-64, total
sK8291	# Mean years of schooling, age 60-64, male	sK8722	# Population in thousands, age 65-69, female
sK8292	# Mean years of schooling, age 60-64, total	sK8723	# Population in thousands, age 65-69, total
sK8293	# Mean years of schooling, age 65+, female	sK8724	# Population in thousands, age 70-74, female
sK8294	# Mean years of schooling, age 65+, male	sK8725	# Population in thousands, age 70-74, total
sK8295	# Mean years of schooling, age 65+, total	sK8726	# Population in thousands, age 75+, female
sK8296	# Mean years of schooling, age 65-69, female	sK8727	# Population in thousands, age 75+, total
sK8297	# Mean years of schooling, age 65-69, male	sK8785	# Primary school starting age
sK8298	# Mean years of schooling, age 65-69, total	sK8825	# Pupils in primary education
sK8299	# Mean years of schooling, age 70-74, female	sK8826	# Pupils in secondary education
sK8300	# Mean years of schooling, age 70-74, male	sK8827	# Pupil-teacher ratio in pre-primary education
sK8301	# Mean years of schooling, age 70-74, total	sK8901	# Secondary school starting age
sK8302	# Mean years of schooling, age 75-79, female	sK8949	# Teachers in primary education
sK8303	# Mean years of schooling, age 75-79, male		

sKPI #	Key Performance Indicator name
sK8950	# Teachers in secondary education
sK8977	# Adult illiterate population
sK8981	# Elderly illiterate population
sK8982	# Enrollment in pre-primary education, public and private, in all programs
sK8983	# Enrollment in secondary, public and private, in all programs
sK8984	# Enrollment in secondary, public and private, in general programs
sK8985	# Enrollment in total secondary, public and private, in technical/vocational programs
sK8986	# Graduates in agriculture, in tertiary education
sK8987	# Graduates in engineering, manufacturing and construction, in tertiary education
sK8988	# Graduates in general programs, in tertiary education
sK8989	# Graduates in health and welfare, in tertiary education
sK8990	# Graduates in humanities and arts, in tertiary education
sK8991	# Graduates in science, in tertiary education
sK8992	# Graduates in services, in tertiary education
sK8993	# Graduates in social sciences, business and law, in tertiary education
sK8994	# Graduates in tertiary education
sK8995	# Graduates in unspecified programs, in tertiary education
sK8996	# Gross enrollment ratio in pre-primary education
sK9002	# Performance on the reading scale
sK9008	# Population age 0-14
sK9009	# Population age 10-14
sK9010	# Population age 10-15
sK9011	# Population age 10-16
sK9012	# Population age 10-17
sK9013	# Population age 10-18
sK9014	# Population age 11-15
sK9015	# Population age 11-16
sK9016	# Population age 11-17
sK9017	# Population age 11-18
sK9018	# Population age 12-15
sK9019	# Population age 12-16
sK9020	# Population age 12-17
sK9021	# Population age 12-18
sK9022	# Population age 13-16
sK9023	# Population age 13-17
sK9024	# Population age 13-18
sK9025	# Population age 13-19
sK9026	# Population age 14-18
sK9027	# Population age 14-19
sK9028	# Population age 15-24
sK9029	# Population age 15-64

sKPI #	Key Performance Indicator name
sK9030	# Population age 3-5
sK9031	# Population age 4-6
sK9032	# Population age 5-10
sK9033	# Population age 5-11
sK9034	# Population age 5-9
sK9035	# Population age 6-10
sK9036	# Population age 6-9
sK9037	# Population age 7-10
sK9038	# Population age 7-11
sK9039	# Population age 7-12
sK9040	# Population age 7-13
sK9041	# Population age 7-9
sK9042	# Population of primary education graduation age
sK9047	# Teaching staff in pre-primary education, public and private, full and part-time, in all programs
sK9050	# Years of school life expectancy from primary to tertiary education
sK9051	# Youth illiterate population
sK9090	# Years of school life expectancy from primary to tertiary education, female
sK9091	# Years of school life expectancy from primary to tertiary education, male
sK9095	% Internet use for post educational courses
sK9257	$ Educational spending
sK9258	$ Educational spending out of GDP
sK10726	% Female population aged 15+ who completed tertiary education
sK10727	% Female population aged 15+ who attained but not completed primary education
sK10728	% Female population aged 15+ who attained but not completed secondary education
sK10729	% Female population aged 15+ who attained but not completed tertiary education
sK10732	% Tertiary graduates in health and welfare
sK10756	% Adult female literacy rate from females ages 15 and above
sK10759	% Adult illiterate, female population
sK10760	% Adult literacy rate
sK10761	% Adult literacy rate from people ages 15 and above
sK10763	% Adult male literacy rate from males ages 15 and above
sK10864	% Bachelor's degrees 3-4 years of duration
sK11012	% Children out of school in primary education
sK11114	% Degrees following the Bologna structures
sK11115	% Degrees following the Bologna structures1 2008
sK11116	% Degrees for less than 3 years but considered to be at tertiary level and part of the Bologna structure
sK11117	% Degrees outside the Bologna structures
sK11147	% Education expenditure from GNI
sK11155	% Literacy rate for females aged 65+
sK11156	% Illiterate elderly female population

sKPI #	Key Performance Indicator name
sK11157	% Literacy rate for males aged 65+
sK11354	% Expenditure per student in primary education from GDP per capita
sK11356	% Expenditure per student in secondary education from GDP per capita
sK11358	% Expenditure per student in tertiary education from GDP per capita
sK11410	% Female 3rd grade students at the highest level of proficiency on the mathematics scale
sK11411	% Female 3rd grade students at the highest level of proficiency on the reading scale
sK11412	% Female 3rd grade students at the lowest level of proficiency on the mathematics scale
sK11413	% Female 3rd grade students at the lowest level of proficiency on the reading scale
sK11414	% Female 6th grade students at the highest level of proficiency on the mathematics scale
sK11415	% Female 6th grade students at the highest level of proficiency on the reading scale
sK11416	% Female 6th grade students at the highest level of proficiency on the science scale
sK11417	% Female 6th grade students at the lowest level of proficiency on the mathematics scale
sK11418	% Female 6th grade students at the lowest level of proficiency on the reading scale
sK11419	% Female 6th grade students at the lowest level of proficiency on the science scale
sK11444	% Female general pupils in secondary education
sK11445	% Female graduates in tertiary education (ISCED 5 and 6)
sK11447	% Female gross primary graduation ratio
sK11459	% Female literacy rate, youth female from females ages 15-24
sK11462	% Female net enrolment rate in pre-primary education
sK11463	% Female net intake in grade 1 from official school-age population
sK11464	% Female net intake rate in grade 1 from official school-age population
sK11465	% Female over-age enrolment ratio in primary education
sK11467	% Female persistence to grade 5 from cohort
sK11469	% Female persistence to last grade of primary from cohort
sK11477	% Female primary completion rate from relevant age group
sK11478	% Female progression to secondary school
sK11479	% Female pupils in primary education
sK11480	% Female pupils in secondary education
sK11481	% Female repeaters in primary education from female enrolment
sK11482	% Female repeaters in secondary education from female enrolment
sK11483	% Female students in pre-primary education
sK11484	% Female students in total secondary, in general programmes

sKPI #	Key Performance Indicator name
sK11485	% Female students in total secondary, in technical/ vocational programmes
sK11488	% Female teachers in pre-primary education
sK11489	% Female teachers in primary education
sK11490	% Female teachers in secondary education
sK11491	% Female tertiary graduates as from all graduates in agriculture
sK11492	% Female tertiary graduates from all graduates in education
sK11493	% Female tertiary graduates from all graduates in engineering, manufacturing and construction
sK11494	% Female tertiary graduates from all graduates in humanities and arts
sK11495	% Female tertiary graduates from all graduates in science
sK11497	% Female tertiary graduates from all graduates in services
sK11498	% Female tertiary graduates from all graduates in social sciences, business and law
sK11499	% Female tertiary graduates from all graduates in unspecified programmes
sK11500	% Female tertiary graduates in agriculture
sK11501	% Female tertiary graduates in education
sK11502	% Female tertiary graduates in engineering, manufacturing and construction
sK11503	% Female tertiary graduates in health and welfare
sK11504	% Female tertiary graduates in humanities and arts
sK11505	% Female tertiary graduates in science
sK11506	% Female tertiary graduates in services
sK11507	% Female tertiary graduates in social sciences, business and law
sK11508	% Female tertiary graduates in unspecified programmes
sK11509	% Female to male ratio in secondary enrolment
sK11511	% Female to male ratio in tertiary enrolment
sK11512	% Female to male ration in primary enrolment
sK11513	% Female trained teachers in primary education from female teachers
sK11514	% Female transition from primary (ISCED 1) to secondary (ISCED 2), in general programmes
sK11515	% Female transition rate from primary to secondary
sK11516	% Female under-age enrolment ratio in primary education
sK11521	% Female vocational pupils in secondary education
sK11619	% Girls to boys ratio in primary and secondary education
sK11626	% Gross attendance rate in post secondary education
sK11627	% Gross attendance rate in post secondary education, quintile 1
sK11628	% Gross attendance rate in post secondary education, quintile 2
sK11629	% Gross attendance rate in post secondary education, quintile 3

sKPI #	Key Performance Indicator name
sK11630	% Gross attendance rate in post secondary education, quintile 4
sK11631	% Gross attendance rate in post secondary education, quintile 5
sK11636	% Gross female attendance rate in post secondary education
sK11637	% Gross female school enrolment in pre-primary education
sK11638	% Gross female school enrolment in primary education
sK11639	% Gross female school enrolment in secondary education
sK11640	% Gross female school enrolment in tertiary education
sK11645	% Gross male attendance rate in post secondary education
sK11646	% Gross male school enrolment in pre-primary education
sK11647	% Gross male school enrolment in primary education
sK11648	% Gross male school enrolment in secondary education
sK11649	% Gross male school enrolment in tertiary education
sK11654	% Gross rural attendance rate in post secondary education
sK11660	% Gross school enrolment in pre-primary education
sK11661	% Gross school enrolment in primary education
sK11662	% Gross school enrolment in secondary education
sK11663	% Gross school enrolment in tertiary education
sK11664	% Gross urban attendance rate in post secondary education
sK11680	% Higher education gross enrolment ratio
sK11833	% Individuals who reported never taking a computer course
sK11834	% Individuals who reported no willingness to pay
sK11835	% Individuals who reported never taking a computer course because of lack of time
sK11836	% Individuals who reported never taking a computer course because of the course costs
sK11837	% Individuals who reported never taking a computer course because the courses are too difficult
sK11838	% Individuals who reported never taking a computer course because there is no suitable offer available
sK11839	% Individuals who reported never taking a computer course in the last 3 years, although they would need one
sK11840	% Individuals who reported never taking a computer course in the last 3 years, because of lack of time
sK11841	% Individuals who reported never taking a computer course in the last 3 years, because of the course costs
sK11842	% Individuals who reported never taking a computer course in the last 3 years, because of their engagement in self-study or assistance from others
sK11843	% individuals who reported never taking a computer course in the last 3 years, because there's no suitable offer on content available
sK11844	% Individuals who reported never taking a computer course in the last 3 years, because they don't need one

sKPI #	Key Performance Indicator name
sK11845	% Individuals who reported obtaining IT skills through formalized educational institution (school, college, university)
sK11846	% Individuals who reported obtaining IT skills through self-study (learning by doing)
sK11847	% Individuals who reported obtaining IT skills through self-study using books, CD-ROMs
sK11848	% Individuals who reported obtaining IT skills through training courses and adult education centers, on demand of employer
sK11849	% Individuals who reported obtaining IT skills through training courses and adult education centrs, on own initiative
sK11861	% Individuals who judge their computer skills to be insufficient if they were to look for a job or change jobs within a year
sK11862	% Individuals who judge their computer skills to be sufficient if they were to look for a job or change jobs within a year
sK11959	% Internet use for formalized educational activities
sK11961	% Internet use for job search or sending an application
sK11964	% Internet use for other educational courses related to employment opportunities
sK12021	% Literacy rate of youth female of ages 15-24
sK12022	% Literacy rate of youth male of ages 15-24
sK12025	% Long first degrees considered to be part of the Bologna structure1 (duration 5or more years)
sK12039	% Male 3rd grade students at the highest level of proficiency on the mathematics scale
sK12040	% Male 3rd grade students at the highest level of proficiency on the reading scale
sK12041	% Male 3rd grade students at the lowest level of proficiency on the mathematics scale
sK12042	% Male 3rd grade students at the lowest level of proficiency on the reading scale
sK12043	% Male 6th grade students at the highest level of proficiency on the mathematics scale
sK12044	% Male 6th grade students at the highest level of proficiency on the reading scale
sK12045	% Male 6th grade students at the highest level of proficiency on the science scale
sK12046	% Male 6th grade students at the lowest level of proficiency on the mathematics scale
sK12047	% Male 6th grade students at the lowest level of proficiency on the reading scale
sK12048	% Male 6th grade students at the lowest level of proficiency on the science scale
sK12072	% Male gross intake rate in grade 1 from relevant age group
sK12073	% Male gross primary graduation ratio
sK12084	% Male net enrolment rate in pre-primary education
sK12085	% Male net intake in grade 1 from official school-age population
sK12086	% Male net intake rate in grade 1 from official school-age population
sK12087	% Male over-age enrolment ratio in primary education

sKPI #	Key Performance Indicator name
sK12089	% Male persistence to grade 5 from cohort
sK12091	% Male persistence to last grade of primary from cohort
sK12098	% Male primary completion rate from relevant age group
sK12099	% Male progression to secondary school
sK12100	% Male repeaters in primary education from male enrolment
sK12101	% Male repeaters in secondary education from male enrolment
sK12104	% Male trained teachers in primary education from male teachers
sK12105	% Male transition from primary (ISCED 1) to secondary (ISCED 2), in general programmes
sK12106	% Male transition rate from primary to secondary
sK12107	% Male under-age enrolment ratio in primary education
sK12142	% Master's degrees 4-8 years of cumulative duration (second degree)
sK12204	% Net attendance rate in primary education
sK12205	% Net attendance rate in primary education, quintile 1
sK12206	% Net attendance rate in primary education, quintile 2
sK12207	% Net attendance rate in primary education, quintile 3
sK12208	% Net attendance rate in primary education, quintile 4
sK12209	% Net attendance rate in primary education, quintile 5
sK12210	% Net attendance rate in rural primary education
sK12211	% Net attendance rate in rural secondary education
sK12212	% Net attendance rate in secondary education
sK12214	% Net attendance rate in secondary education, quintile 1
sK12215	% Net attendance rate in secondary education, quintile 2
sK12216	% Net attendance rate in secondary education, quintile 3
sK12217	% Net attendance rate in secondary education, quintile 4
sK12218	% Net attendance rate in secondary education, quintile 5
sK12219	% Net attendance rate in urban primary education
sK12220	% Net attendance rate in urban secondary education
sK12227	% Net female attendance rate in primary education
sK12228	% Net female attendance rate in secondary education
sK12229	% Net female intake rate for the first grade of primary education
sK12230	% Net female school enrolment in primary education
sK12231	% Net female school enrolment in secondary education
sK12235	% Net intake in grade 1 from official school-age population
sK12236	% Net intake rate for the first grade of primary education
sK12237	% Net intake rate for the first grade of primary education, quintile 1
sK12238	% Net intake rate for the first grade of primary education, quintile 2
sK12239	% Net intake rate for the first grade of primary education, quintile 3
sK12240	% Net intake rate for the first grade of primary education, quintile 4
sK12241	% Net intake rate for the first grade of primary education, quintile 5
sK12242	% Net intake rate for the first grade of rural primary education
sK12243	% Net intake rate for the first grade of urban primary education
sK12244	% Net intake rate in grade 1 from official school-age population
sK12246	% Net male attendance rate in primary education
sK12247	% Net male attendance rate in secondary education
sK12248	% Net male intake rate for the first grade of primary education
sK12249	% Net male school enrolment in primary education
sK12250	% Net male school enrolment in secondary education
sK12279	% Net school enrolment in primary education
sK12280	% Net school enrolment in secondary education
sK12281	% Net total enrolment in primary education
sK12282	% Net total female enrolment in primary education
sK12283	% Net total male enrolment in primary education
sK12315	% Out-of-school children, primary, dropped out, quintile 1
sK12316	% Out-of-school children, primary, dropped out, quintile 2
sK12317	% Out-of-school children, primary, dropped out, quintile 3
sK12318	% Out-of-school children, primary, dropped out, quintile 4
sK12319	% Out-of-school children, primary, dropped out, quintile 5
sK12320	% Out-of-school children, primary, dropped out
sK12321	% Out-of-school children, primary, dropped out, female
sK12322	% Out-of-school children, primary, dropped out, male
sK12323	% Out-of-school children, primary, dropped out, rural
sK12324	% Out-of-school children, primary, dropped out, urban
sK12325	% Out-of-school children, primary, late entry
sK12326	% Out-of-school children, primary, late entry, female
sK12327	% Out-of-school children, primary, late entry, male
sK12328	% Out-of-school children, primary, late entry, quintile 1
sK12329	% Out-of-school children, primary, late entry, quintile 2
sK12330	% Out-of-school children, primary, late entry, quintile 3
sK12331	% Out-of-school children, primary, late entry, quintile 4
sK12332	% Out-of-school children, primary, late entry, quintile 5
sK12333	% Out-of-school children, primary, late entry, rural
sK12334	% Out-of-school children, primary, late entry, urban
sK12335	% Out-of-school children, primary, never in school
sK12336	% Out-of-school children, primary, never in school, female
sK12337	% Out-of-school children, primary, never in school, male
sK12338	% Out-of-school children, primary, never in school, quintile 1
sK12339	% Out-of-school children, primary, never in school, quintile 2
sK12340	% Out-of-school children, primary, never in school, quintile 3

sKPI #	Key Performance Indicator name
sK12341	% Out-of-school children, primary, never in school, quintile 4
sK12342	% Out-of-school children, primary, never in school, quintile 5
sK12343	% Out-of-school children, primary, never in school, rural
sK12344	% Out-of-school children, primary, never in school, urban
sK12346	% Out-of-school in primary education, female
sK12347	% Out-of-school in primary education, quintile 1
sK12348	% Out-of-school in primary education, quintile 2
sK12349	% Out-of-school in primary education, quintile 3
sK12350	% Out-of-school in primary education, quintile 4
sK12351	% Out-of-school in primary education, quintile 5
sK12352	% Out-of-school in rural primary education
sK12353	% Out-of-school in urban primary education
sK12418	% Perception of education facilities
sK12419	% Perception of education quality
sK12436	% Persistence to grade 5 from cohort
sK12437	% Persistence to last grade of primary from cohort
sK12442	% Ph.D. and doctorates
sK12445	% Population age 0-14 from total population
sK12461	% Population by educational attainment, age 15+, total, incomplete tertiary
sK12462	% Population by educational attainment, age 15+, female, completed primary
sK12463	% Population by educational attainment, age 15+, female, completed secondary
sK12464	% Population by educational attainment, age 15+, female, no education
sK12465	% Population by educational attainment, age 15+, total, completed primary
sK12466	% Population by educational attainment, age 15+, total, completed secondary
sK12467	% Population by educational attainment, age 15+, total, completed tertiary
sK12468	% Population by educational attainment, age 15+, total, incomplete primary
sK12469	% Population by educational attainment, age 15+, total, incomplete secondary
sK12470	% Population by educational attainment, age 15+, total, no education
sK12471	% Population by educational attainment, age 15-19, female, completed primary
sK12472	% Population by educational attainment, age 15-19, female, completed secondary
sK12473	% Population by educational attainment, age 15-19, female, completed tertiary
sK12474	% Population by educational attainment, age 15-19, female, incomplete primary
sK12475	% Population by educational attainment, age 15-19, female, incomplete secondary
sK12476	% Population by educational attainment, age 15-19, female, incomplete tertiary

sKPI #	Key Performance Indicator name
sK12477	% Population by educational attainment, age 15-19, female, no education
sK12478	% Population by educational attainment, age 15-19, total, completed primary
sK12479	% Population by educational attainment, age 15-19, total, completed secondary
sK12480	% Population by educational attainment, age 15-19, total, completed tertiary
sK12481	% Population by educational attainment, age 15-19, total, incomplete primary
sK12482	% Population by educational attainment, age 15-19, total, incomplete secondary
sK12483	% Population by educational attainment, age 15-19, total, incomplete tertiary
sK12484	% Population by educational attainment, age 15-19, total, no education
sK12485	% Population by educational attainment, age 20-24, female, completed primary
sK12486	% Population by educational attainment, age 20-24, female, completed secondary
sK12487	% Population by educational attainment, age 20-24, female, completed tertiary
sK12488	% Population by educational attainment, age 20-24, female, incomplete primary
sK12489	% Population by educational attainment, age 20-24, female, incomplete tertiary
sK12490	% Population by educational attainment, age 20-24, female, no education
sK12491	% Population by educational attainment, age 20-24, total, completed primary
sK12492	% Population by educational attainment, age 20-24, total, completed secondary
sK12493	% Population by educational attainment, age 20-24, total, completed tertiary
sK12494	% Population by educational attainment, age 20-24, total, incomplete primary
sK12495	% Population by educational attainment, age 20-24, total, incomplete secondary
sK12496	% Population by educational attainment, age 20-24, total, incomplete tertiary
sK12497	% Population by educational attainment, age 20-24, total, no education
sK12498	% Population by educational attainment, age 25+, female, completed primary
sK12499	% Population by educational attainment, age 25+, female, completed secondary
sK12500	% Population by educational attainment, age 25+, female, completed tertiary
sK12501	% Population by educational attainment, age 25+, female, incomplete primary
sK12502	% Population by educational attainment, age 25+, female, incomplete secondary
sK12503	% Population by educational attainment, age 25+, female, incomplete tertiary
sK12504	% Population by educational attainment, age 25+, female, no education

sKPI #	Key Performance Indicator name
sK12505	% Population by educational attainment, age 25+, total, completed primary
sK12506	% Population by educational attainment, age 25+, total, completed secondary
sK12507	% Population by educational attainment, age 25+, total, incomplete primary
sK12508	% Population by educational attainment, age 25+, total, incomplete secondary
sK12509	% Population by educational attainment, age 25+, total, incomplete tertiary
sK12510	% Population by educational attainment, age 25+, total, no education
sK12511	% Population by educational attainment, age 25-29, female, completed primary
sK12512	% Population by educational attainment, age 25-29, female, completed secondary
sK12513	% Population by educational attainment, age 25-29, female, completed tertiary
sK12514	% Population by educational attainment, age 25-29, female, incomplete primary
sK12515	% Population by educational attainment, age 25-29, female, incomplete secondary
sK12516	% Population by educational attainment, age 25-29, female, incomplete tertiary
sK12517	% Population by educational attainment, age 25-29, female, no education
sK12518	% Population by educational attainment, age 25-29, total, completed primary
sK12519	% Population by educational attainment, age 25-29, total, completed secondary
sK12520	% Population by educational attainment, age 25-29, total, completed tertiary
sK12521	% Population by educational attainment, age 25-29, total, incomplete primary
sK12522	% Population by educational attainment, age 25-29, total, incomplete secondary
sK12523	% Population by educational attainment, age 25-29, total, incomplete tertiary
sK12524	% Population by educational attainment, age 25-29, total, no education
sK12525	% Population by educational attainment, age 30-34, female, completed primary
sK12526	% Population by educational attainment, age 30-34, female, completed secondary
sK12527	% Population by educational attainment, age 30-34, female, completed tertiary
sK12528	% Population by educational attainment, age 30-34, female, incomplete primary
sK12529	% Population by educational attainment, age 30-34, female, incomplete secondary
sK12530	% Population by educational attainment, age 30-34, female, incomplete tertiary
sK12531	% Population by educational attainment, age 30-34, female, no education
sK12532	% Population by educational attainment, age 30-34, total, completed primary

sKPI #	Key Performance Indicator name
sK12533	% Population by educational attainment, age 30-34, total, completed secondary
sK12534	% Population by educational attainment, age 30-34, total, completed tertiary
sK12535	% Population by educational attainment, age 30-34, total, incomplete primary
sK12536	% Population by educational attainment, age 30-34, total, incomplete secondary
sK12537	% Population by educational attainment, age 30-34, total, incomplete tertiary
sK12538	% Population by educational attainment, age 30-34, total, no education
sK12539	% Population by educational attainment, age 35-39, female, completed primary
sK12540	% Population by educational attainment, age 35-39, female, completed secondary
sK12541	% Population by educational attainment, age 35-39, female, completed tertiary
sK12542	% Population by educational attainment, age 35-39, female, incomplete primary
sK12543	% Population by educational attainment, age 35-39, female, incomplete secondary
sK12544	% Population by educational attainment, age 35-39, female, incomplete tertiary
sK12545	% Population by educational attainment, age 35-39, female, no education
sK12546	% Population by educational attainment, age 35-39, total, completed primary
sK12547	% Population by educational attainment, age 35-39, total, completed secondary
sK12548	% Population by educational attainment, age 35-39, total, completed tertiary
sK12549	% Population by educational attainment, age 35-39, total, incomplete primary
sK12550	% Population by educational attainment, age 35-39, total, incomplete secondary
sK12551	% Population by educational attainment, age 35-39, total, incomplete tertiary
sK12552	% Population by educational attainment, age 35-39, total, no education
sK12553	% Population by educational attainment, age 40-44, female, completed primary
sK12554	% Population by educational attainment, age 40-44, female, completed secondary
sK12555	% Population by educational attainment, age 40-44, female, completed tertiary
sK12556	% Population by educational attainment, age 40-44, female, incomplete primary
sK12557	% Population by educational attainment, age 40-44, female, incomplete secondary
sK12558	% Population by educational attainment, age 40-44, female, incomplete tertiary
sK12559	% Population by educational attainment, age 40-44, female, no education
sK12560	% Population by educational attainment, age 40-44, total, completed primary

sKPI #	Key Performance Indicator name
sK12561	% Population by educational attainment, age 40-44, total, completed secondary
sK12562	% Population by educational attainment, age 40-44, total, completed tertiary
sK12563	% Population by educational attainment, age 40-44, total, incomplete primary
sK12564	% Population by educational attainment, age 40-44, total, incomplete secondary
sK12565	% Population by educational attainment, age 40-44, total, incomplete tertiary
sK12566	% Population by educational attainment, age 40-44, total, no education
sK12567	% Population by educational attainment, age 45-49, female, completed primary
sK12568	% Population by educational attainment, age 45-49, female, completed secondary
sK12569	% Population by educational attainment, age 45-49, female, completed tertiary
sK12570	% Population by educational attainment, age 45-49, female, incomplete primary
sK12571	% Population by educational attainment, age 45-49, female, incomplete secondary
sK12572	% Population by educational attainment, age 45-49, female, incomplete tertiary
sK12573	% Population by educational attainment, age 45-49, female, no education
sK12574	% Population by educational attainment, age 45-49, total, completed primary
sK12575	% Population by educational attainment, age 45-49, total, completed secondary
sK12576	% Population by educational attainment, age 45-49, total, completed tertiary
sK12577	% Population by educational attainment, age 45-49, total, incomplete primary
sK12578	% Population by educational attainment, age 45-49, total, incomplete secondary
sK12579	% Population by educational attainment, age 45-49, total, incomplete tertiary
sK12580	% Population by educational attainment, age 45-49, total, no education
sK12581	% Population by educational attainment, age 50-54, female, completed primary
sK12582	% Population by educational attainment, age 50-54, female, completed secondary
sK12583	% Population by educational attainment, age 50-54, female, completed tertiary
sK12584	% Population by educational attainment, age 50-54, female, incomplete primary
sK12585	% Population by educational attainment, age 50-54, female, incomplete secondary
sK12586	% Population by educational attainment, age 50-54, female, incomplete tertiary
sK12587	% Population by educational attainment, age 50-54, female, no education
sK12588	% Population by educational attainment, age 50-54, total, completed primary

sKPI #	Key Performance Indicator name
sK12589	% Population by educational attainment, age 50-54, total, completed secondary
sK12590	% Population by educational attainment, age 50-54, total, completed tertiary
sK12591	% Population by educational attainment, age 50-54, total, incomplete primary
sK12592	% Population by educational attainment, age 50-54, total, incomplete secondary
sK12593	% Population by educational attainment, age 50-54, total, incomplete tertiary
sK12594	% Population by educational attainment, age 50-54, total, no education
sK12595	% Population by educational attainment, age 55-59, female, completed primary
sK12596	% Population by educational attainment, age 55-59, female, completed secondary
sK12597	% Population by educational attainment, age 55-59, female, completed tertiary
sK12598	% Population by educational attainment, age 55-59, female, incomplete primary
sK12599	% Population by educational attainment, age 55-59, female, incomplete secondary
sK12600	% Population by educational attainment, age 55-59, female, incomplete tertiary
sK12601	% Population by educational attainment, age 55-59, female, no education
sK12602	% Population by educational attainment, age 55-59, total, completed primary
sK12603	% Population by educational attainment, age 55-59, total, completed secondary
sK12604	% Population by educational attainment, age 55-59, total, completed tertiary
sK12605	% Population by educational attainment, age 55-59, total, incomplete primary
sK12606	% Population by educational attainment, age 55-59, total, incomplete secondary
sK12607	% Population by educational attainment, age 55-59, total, incomplete tertiary
sK12608	% Population by educational attainment, age 55-59, total, no education
sK12609	% Population by educational attainment, age 60-64, female, completed primary
sK12610	% Population by educational attainment, age 60-64, female, completed secondary
sK12611	% Population by educational attainment, age 60-64, female, completed tertiary
sK12612	% Population by educational attainment, age 60-64, female, incomplete primary
sK12613	% Population by educational attainment, age 60-64, female, incomplete secondary
sK12614	% Population by educational attainment, age 60-64, female, incomplete tertiary
sK12615	% Population by educational attainment, age 60-64, female, no education
sK12616	% Population by educational attainment, age 60-64, total, completed primary

sKPI #	Key Performance Indicator name
sK12617	% Population by educational attainment, age 60-64, total, completed secondary
sK12618	% Population by educational attainment, age 60-64, total, completed tertiary
sK12619	% Population by educational attainment, age 60-64, total, incomplete primary
sK12620	% Population by educational attainment, age 60-64, total, incomplete secondary
sK12621	% Population by educational attainment, age 60-64, total, incomplete tertiary
sK12622	% Population by educational attainment, age 60-64, total, no education
sK12623	% Population by educational attainment, age 65-69, female, completed primary
sK12624	% Population by educational attainment, age 65-69, female, completed secondary
sK12625	% Population by educational attainment, age 65-69, female, completed tertiary
sK12626	% Population by educational attainment, age 65-69, female, incomplete primary
sK12627	% Population by educational attainment, age 65-69, female, incomplete secondary
sK12628	% Population by educational attainment, age 65-69, female, incomplete tertiary
sK12629	% Population by educational attainment, age 65-69, female, no education
sK12630	% Population by educational attainment, age 65-69, total, completed primary
sK12631	% Population by educational attainment, age 65-69, total, completed secondary
sK12632	% Population by educational attainment, age 65-69, total, completed tertiary
sK12633	% Population by educational attainment, age 65-69, total, incomplete primary
sK12634	% Population by educational attainment, age 65-69, total, incomplete secondary
sK12635	% Population by educational attainment, age 65-69, total, incomplete tertiary
sK12636	% Population by educational attainment, age 65-69, total, no education
sK12637	% Population by educational attainment, age 70-74, female, completed primary
sK12638	% Population by educational attainment, age 70-74, female, completed secondary
sK12639	% Population by educational attainment, age 70-74, female, completed tertiary
sK12640	% Population by educational attainment, age 70-74, female, incomplete primary
sK12641	% Population by educational attainment, age 70-74, female, incomplete secondary
sK12642	% Population by educational attainment, age 70-74, female, incomplete tertiary
sK12643	% Population by educational attainment, age 70-74, female, no education
sK12644	% Population by educational attainment, age 70-74, total, completed primary

sKPI #	Key Performance Indicator name
sK12645	% Population by educational attainment, age 70-74, total, completed secondary
sK12646	% Population by educational attainment, age 70-74, total, completed tertiary
sK12647	% Population by educational attainment, age 70-74, total, incomplete primary
sK12648	% Population by educational attainment, age 70-74, total, incomplete secondary
sK12649	% Population by educational attainment, age 70-74, total, incomplete tertiary
sK12650	% Population by educational attainment, age 70-74, total, no education
sK12651	% Population by educational attainment, age 75+, female, completed primary
sK12652	% Population by educational attainment, age 75+, female, completed secondary
sK12653	% Population by educational attainment, age 75+, female, completed tertiary
sK12654	% Population by educational attainment, age 75+, female, incomplete primary
sK12655	% Population by educational attainment, age 75+, female, incomplete secondary
sK12656	% Population by educational attainment, age 75+, female, incomplete tertiary
sK12657	% Population by educational attainment, age 75+, female, no education
sK12658	% Population by educational attainment, age 75+, total, completed primary
sK12659	% Population by educational attainment, age 75+, total, completed secondary
sK12660	% Population by educational attainment, age 75+, total, completed tertiary
sK12661	% Population by educational attainment, age 75+, total, incomplete primary
sK12662	% Population by educational attainment, age 75+, total, incomplete secondary
sK12663	% Population by educational attainment, age 75+, total, incomplete tertiary
sK12664	% Population by educational attainment, age 75+, total, no education
sK12728	% Primary completion rate, quintile 3
sK12729	% Primary completion rate
sK12730	% Primary completion rate from relevant age group
sK12731	% Primary completion rate, female
sK12732	% Primary completion rate, male
sK12733	% Primary completion rate, quintile 1
sK12734	% Primary completion rate, quintile 2
sK12735	% Primary completion rate, quintile 4
sK12736	% Primary completion rate, quintile 5
sK12742	% Primary school enrolment ratio
sK12743	% Primary school public education expenditure of current education expenditure
sK12747	% Private enrolment in lower secondary education, general programmes

sKPI #	Key Performance Indicator name
sK12748	% Private enrolment in lower secondary education, technical/vocational programmes
sK12749	% Private enrolment in pre-primary education
sK12750	% Private enrolment in tertiary education
sK12751	% Private enrolment in upper secondary education, general programmes
sK12752	% Private enrolment in upper secondary education, technical/vocational programmes
sK12758	% Private school enrolment in primary education from total primary enrolment
sK12759	% Private school enrolment in secondary education from total secondary enrolment
sK12766	% Progression to secondary school
sK12773	% Public current education expenditure of total education expenditure
sK12780	% Public spending on education from GDP
sK12781	% Public spending on education from government expenditure
sK12784	% Pupil-teacher ratio in primary education
sK12786	% Pupil-teacher ratio in secondary education
sK12875	% Rural primary completion rate
sK12876	% Rural secondary completion rate
sK12877	% Rural transition rate from primary to secondary
sK12890	% Secondary completion rate
sK12891	% Secondary completion rate, female
sK12892	% Secondary completion rate, male
sK12893	% Secondary completion rate, quintile 1
sK12894	% Secondary completion rate, quintile 2
sK12895	% Secondary completion rate, quintile 3
sK12896	% Secondary completion rate, quintile 4
sK12897	% Secondary completion rate, quintile 5
sK12898	% Secondary school enrolment ratio
sK12899	% Secondary school public education expenditure of current education expenditure
sK12931	% Students continuing education after compulsory education
sK12932	% Students in higher education per 1 000 resident population
sK12933	% Students not completing compulsory education
sK12934	% Students reaching the advanced international benchmark in reading achievement
sK12935	% Students reaching the low international benchmark in reading achievement
sK12977	% Tertiary graduates in agriculture
sK12978	% Tertiary graduates in education
sK12979	% Tertiary graduates in engineering, manufacturing and construction
sK12980	% Tertiary graduates in humanities and arts
sK12981	% Tertiary graduates in science
sK12982	% Tertiary graduates in social sciences, business and law
sK12983	% Tertiary graduates in unspecified programmes

sKPI #	Key Performance Indicator name
sK12984	% Tertiary school public education expenditure of current education expenditure
sK12993	% 3rd grade students at the highest level of proficiency on the mathematics scale
sK12994	% 3rd grade students at the highest level of proficiency on the reading scale
sK12995	% 3rd grade students at the lowest level of proficiency on the mathematics scale
sK12996	% 3rd grade students at the lowest level of proficiency on the reading scale
sK12997	% 6th grade students at the highest level of proficiency on the mathematics scale
sK12998	% 6th grade students at the highest level of proficiency on the reading scale
sK12999	% 6th grade students at the highest level of proficiency on the science scale
sK13000	% 6th grade students at the lowest level of proficiency on the mathematics scale
sK13001	% 6th grade students at the lowest level of proficiency on the reading scale
sK13002	% 6th grade students at the lowest level of proficiency on the science scale
sK13014	% Elderly (65+) literacy rate
sK13018	% Gross intake rate in grade 1 from relevant age group
sK13019	% Gross primary graduation ratio
sK13021	% Inbound mobility rate in tertiary education
sK13024	% Net enrollment rate in pre-primary education
sK13035	% Repeaters in primary education from total enrollment
sK13036	% Repeaters in secondary education from total enrollment
sK13040	% Transition from primary (ISCED 1) to secondary (ISCED 2), in general programs
sK13041	% Under-age enrollment ratio in primary education
sK13046	% Youth literacy rate from people ages 15-24
sK13054	% Trained teachers in primary education
sK13055	% Transition rate from primary to secondary
sK13056	% Transition rate from primary to Secondary, quintile 1
sK13057	% Transition rate from primary to Secondary, quintile 2
sK13058	% Transition rate from primary to Secondary, quintile 3
sK13059	% Transition rate from primary to Secondary, quintile 4
sK13060	% Transition rate from primary to Secondary, quintile 5
sK13097	% Urban primary completion rate
sK13098	% Urban secondary completion rate
sK13099	% Urban transition rate from primary to secondary
sK13113	% Vocational pupils in secondary education
sK13146	% Young literate females to males ratio of ages 15-24
sK13147	% Young literate females to males ratio, ages 15-24
sK13151	% Youth illiterate, female population
sK13153	% Youth male literacy rate from males ages 15-24
sK13159	% Out-of-school in primary education
sK13161	% Over-age enrollment ratio in primary education

Science

Science is the body of human knowledge based on facts and principles, gained through scientific research.

sKPI #	Key Performance Indicator name
sK7913	# High Tech patent applications to the EPO
sK7914	# High Tech patent applications to the EPO per million labor force
sK7915	# High Tech patent applications to the EPO in aviation
sK7916	# High Tech patent applications to the EPO in communication technology
sK7917	# High Tech patent applications to the EPO in laser
sK7918	# High Tech patent applications to the EPO in micro-organism and genetic engineering
sK7919	# High Tech patent applications to the EPO in semiconductors
sK7920	# High Tech Patent applications to the EPO per million of inhabitants
sK8000	# ICT patent applications to the EPO
sK8001	# ICT patent applications to the EPO in ICT computer and office machinery
sK8002	# ICT patent applications to the EPO in ICT consumer electronics
sK8003	# ICT patent applications to the EPO in ICT telecommunications
sK8004	# ICT patent applications to the EPO in other ICT
sK8005	# ICT patent applications to the EPO per million of inhabitants
sK8006	# ICT patent applications to the EPO per million labor force
sK8446	# Patent applications to the EPO
sK8447	# Patent applications to the EPO aircraft, aviation and cosmonautics
sK8448	# Patent applications to the EPO Bookbinding; albums, files and special printed matter
sK8449	# Patent applications to the EPO in agriculture, forestry, animal husbandry, hunting, trapping and fishing
sK8450	# Patent applications to the EPO in ammunition and blasting
sK8451	# Patent applications to the EPO in animal or vegetable oils, fats, fatty substances or waxes, fatty acids therefrom, detergents and candles
sK8452	# Patent applications to the EPO in baking and edible dough
sK8453	# Patent applications to the EPO in basic electric elements
sK8454	# Patent applications to the EPO in basic electronic circuitry
sK8455	# Patent applications to the EPO in biochemistry, beer, spirits, wine, vinegar, microbiology, enzymology, mutation or genetic engineering
sK8456	# Patent applications to the EPO in braiding, lace-making, knitting, trimmings and non-woven fabrics
sK8457	# Patent applications to the EPO in brushware
sK8458	# Patent applications to the EPO in building
sK8459	# Patent applications to the EPO in butchering, meat treatment, processing poultry or fish

sKPI #	Key Performance Indicator name
sK8460	# Patent applications to the EPO in casting and powder metallurgy
sK8461	# Patent applications to the EPO in cements, concrete, artificial stone, ceramics and refractories
sK8462	# Patent applications to the EPO in centrifugal apparatus or machines for carrying-out physical or chemical processes
sK8463	# Patent applications to the EPO in checking-devices
sK8464	# Patent applications to the EPO in cleaning
sK8465	# Patent applications to the EPO in chemical surface treatment
sK8466	# Patent applications to the EPO in combinatorial technology
sK8467	# Patent applications to the EPO in combustion apparatus and combustion processes
sK8468	# Patent applications to the EPO in combustion engines and hot-gas or combustion-product engine plants
sK8469	# Patent applications to the EPO in computing, calculating and counting
sK8470	# Patent applications to the EPO in construction of roads, railways, or bridges
sK8471	# Patent applications to the EPO in controlling and regulating
sK8472	# Patent applications to the EPO in conveying, packing, storing, handling thin or filamentary material
sK8473	# Patent applications to the EPO in crushing, pulverizing, or disintegrating and preparatory treatment of grain for milling
sK8474	# Patent applications to the EPO in decorative arts
sK8475	# Patent applications to the EPO in disposal of solid waste; reclamation of contaminated soil
sK8476	# Patent applications to the EPO in doors, windows, shutters, or roller blinds in general and ladders
sK8477	# Patent applications to the EPO in drying
sK8478	# Patent applications to the EPO in dyes, paints, polishes, natural resins, adhesives, miscellaneous compositions and miscellaneous applications of materials
sK8479	# Patent applications to the EPO in earth or rock drilling and mining
sK8480	# Patent applications to the EPO in educating, cryptography, display and advertising; seals
sK8481	# Patent applications to the EPO in electric communication technique
sK8482	# Patent applications to the EPO in electric techniques not otherwise provided for
sK8483	# Patent applications to the EPO in electrolytic or electrophoretic processes and apparatuses
sK8484	# Patent applications to the EPO in engineering elements or units
sK8485	# Patent applications to the EPO in explosives and matches
sK8486	# Patent applications to the EPO in fertilizers and manufacture thereof
sK8487	# Patent applications to the EPO in fluid-pressure actuators and hydraulics or pneumatics in general
sK8488	# Patent applications to the EPO in foods or foodstuffs, their treatment, not covered by other classes
sK8489	# Patent applications to the EPO in footwear

sKPI #	Key Performance Indicator name
sK8490	# Patent applications to the EPO in furnaces, kilns, ovens and retorts
sK8491	# Patent applications to the EPO in furniture, domestic articles or appliances, coffee mills, spice mills and suction cleaners in general
sK8492	# Patent applications to the EPO in generating or transmitting mechanical vibrations in general
sK8493	# Patent applications to the EPO in generation, conversion, or distribution of electric power
sK8494	# Patent applications to the EPO in glass, mineral or slag wool
sK8495	# Patent applications to the EPO in grinding and polishing
sK8496	# Patent applications to the EPO in haberdashery and jewelry
sK8497	# Patent applications to the EPO in hand cutting tools, cutting and severing
sK8498	# Patent applications to the EPO in hand or travelling articles
sK8499	# Patent applications to the EPO in hand tools, portable power-driven tools, handles for hand implements, workshop equipment and manipulators
sK8500	# Patent applications to the EPO in headwear
sK8501	# Patent applications to the EPO in heat exchange in general
sK8502	# Patent applications to the EPO in heating, ranges and ventilating
sK8503	# Patent applications to the EPO in hoisting, lifting and hauling
sK8504	# Patent applications to the EPO in horology
sK8505	# Patent applications to the EPO in hydraulic engineering, foundations and soil-shifting
sK8506	# Patent applications to the EPO in information storage
sK8507	# Patent applications to the EPO in inorganic chemistry
sK8508	# Patent applications to the EPO in instrument details
sK8509	# Patent applications to the EPO in layered product
sK8510	# Patent applications to the EPO in life-saving and fire-fighting
sK8511	# Patent applications to the EPO in lighting
sK8512	# Patent applications to the EPO in locks, keys, window or door fittings, safes
sK8513	# Patent applications to the EPO in machine tools and metal-working not otherwise provided for
sK8514	# Patent applications to the EPO in machines or engines for liquids, wind, spring, weight, or miscellaneous motors, producing mechanical power or a reactive propulsive thrust, not otherwise provided for
sK8515	# Patent applications to the EPO in machines or engines in general, engine plants in general and steam engines
sK8516	# Patent applications to the EPO in making paper articles and working paper
sK8517	# Patent applications to the EPO in measuring (counting G06M) and testing
sK8518	# Patent applications to the EPO in mechanical metal-working without essentially removing material and punching metal

sKPI #	Key Performance Indicator name
sK8519	# Patent applications to the EPO in medical or veterinary science and hygiene
sK8520	# Patent applications to the EPO in metallurgy of iron
sK8521	# Patent applications to the EPO in metallurgy of iron c21, ferrous or non-ferrous alloys and treatment of alloys or non-ferrous metals
sK8522	# Patent applications to the EPO in micro-structural technology
sK8523	# Patent applications to the EPO in musical instruments and acoustics
sK8524	# Patent applications to the EPO in nano-technology
sK8525	# Patent applications to the EPO in natural or artificial threads or fibers and spinning
sK8526	# Patent applications to the EPO in nuclear physics and nuclear engineering
sK8527	# Patent applications to the EPO in opening or closing bottles, jars or similar containers and liquid handling
sK8528	# Patent applications to the EPO in optics
sK8529	# Patent applications to the EPO in organic chemistry
sK8530	# Patent applications to the EPO in organic macromolecular compounds, their preparation or chemical working-up and compositions based thereon
sK8531	# Patent applications to the EPO in paper-making and production of cellulose
sK8532	# Patent applications to the EPO in petroleum, gas or coke industries, technical gases containing carbon monoxide, fuels, lubricants and peat
sK8533	# Patent applications to the EPO in photography, cinematography, analogous techniques using waves other than optical waves, electrography and holography
sK8534	# Patent applications to the EPO in physical or chemical processes or apparatus in general
sK8535	# Patent applications to the EPO in positive-displacement machines for liquids and pumps for liquids or elastic fluids
sK8536	# Patent applications to the EPO in presses
sK8537	# Patent applications to the EPO in printing, lining machines, typewriters and stamps
sK8538	# Patent applications to the EPO in refrigeration or cooling, combined heating and refrigeration systems, heat pump systems, manufacture or storage of ice and liquefaction or solidification of gases
sK8539	# Patent applications to the EPO in ropes and cables other than electric
sK8540	# Patent applications to the EPO in saddlery and upholstery
sK8541	# Patent applications to the EPO in separating solids from solids and sorting
sK8542	# Patent applications to the EPO in separation of solid materials using liquids or using pneumatic tables or jigs, magnetic or electrostatic solid materials from solid materials or fluids and separation by separation of high-voltage electric fields
sK8543	# Patent applications to the EPO in sewing, embroidering and tufting
sK8544	# Patent applications to the EPO in signaling
sK8545	# Patent applications to the EPO in skins, hides, pelts and leather

sKPI #	Key Performance Indicator name
sK8546	# Patent applications to the EPO in sports, games and amusements
sK8547	# Patent applications to the EPO in spraying or atomizing in general and applying liquids or other fluent materials to surfaces, in general
sK8548	# Patent applications to the EPO in steam generation
sK8549	# Patent applications to the EPO in storing or distributing gases or liquids
sK8550	# Patent applications to the EPO in sugar industry
sK8551	# Patent applications to the EPO in tobacco; cigars, cigarettes and smokers' requisites
sK8552	# Patent applications to the EPO in treatment of textiles or the like, laundering and flexible materials not otherwise provided for
sK8553	# Patent applications to the EPO in treatments of water, waste water, sewage, or sludge
sK8554	# Patent applications to the EPO in unknown areas
sK8555	# Patent applications to the EPO in water supply and sewerage
sK8556	# Patent applications to the EPO in weapons
sK8557	# Patent applications to the EPO in wearing apparel
sK8558	# Patent applications to the EPO in weaving
sK8559	# Patent applications to the EPO in working cement, clay, or stone

sKPI #	Key Performance Indicator name
sK8560	# Patent applications to the EPO in working of plastics, working of substances in a plastic state in general
sK8561	# Patent applications to the EPO in working or preserving wood or similar material and nailing or stapling machines in general
sK8562	# Patent applications to the EPO in writing or drawing implements and bureau accessories
sK8563	# Patent applications to the EPO in yarns, mechanical finishing of yarns or ropes, warping or beaming
sK8564	# Patent applications to the EPO land vehicles for travelling otherwise than on rails
sK8565	# Patent applications to the EPO per million labor force
sK8566	# Patent applications to the EPO per million of inhabitants
sK8567	# Patent applications to the EPO railways
sK8568	# Patent applications to the EPO ships or other waterborne vessels and related equipment
sK8569	# Patent applications to the EPO vehicles in general
sK12431	% Perception of the quality of the ICT infrastructure
sK12844	% Research methodologies and tools addressing gender issues applied in technical work
sK13164	# High Tech patent applications to the EPO in computer and automated business equipment

Labor & Social Protection

Labor and social protection's role is to ensure that all men and women have basic social and economic security, to provide working opportunities for citizens and protection for the unemployed. It has to facilitate structural changes, advancing social justice and promoting economic dynamism.

Economic Activity

Economic activity referes to economic exchanges across boundaries, between private, public and non-profit organizations.

sKPI #	Key Performance Indicator name
sK8103	# Labor input index
sK8364	# Net office space that is vacant
sK9094	# Youth labor force
sK9472	$ GDP per person employed based on PPP
sK10614	$ Expenditure on social protection from GDP
sK10712	$ Wages or earnings of young workers
sK10737	% 3 Years change in nominal unit labor cost
sK11004	% Child employment agriculture from economically active children ages 7-14
sK11006	% Child employment in manufacturing from economically active children ages 7-14
sK11008	% Child employment in services from economically active children ages 7-14
sK11068	% Contributing family workers
sK11109	% Decomposition of the projected increase in public pension expenditure from GDP
sK11146	% Economically active children from children ages 7-14
sK11195	% Employment to population ratio, ages 15+

sKPI #	Key Performance Indicator name
sK11196	% Employment to population ratio, ages 15-24
sK11457	% Female labor participation rate from female population ages 25-34
sK11526	% Female youth labor force from total labor force 15-24 years
sK11998	% Labor participation rate from total population ages 25-34
sK12081	% Male labor participation rate from male population ages 25-34
sK12275	% Net office space that is vacant
sK13009	% Current pension expenditure from GDP

Labor Force Structure

Labor force structure is the breakdown of the working age population in relation to engagement in paid economic activities.

sKPI #	Key Performance Indicator name
sK7438	# Community health workers per 1,000 people
sK7597	# Effective labor market exit age
sK7631	# Employment financial intermediation, business activities
sK7632	# Employment in agriculture, fishery
sK7633	# Employment in construction

sKPI #	Key Performance Indicator name
sK7634	# Employment in mining, manufacturing, energy
sK7635	# Employment in NACE
sK7636	# Employment in public administration, health, education
sK7637	# Employment in trade, hotels, restaurants
sK7638	# Employment in transport, communication
sK7639	# Employment, work-place based
sK7728	# Female labor force
sK7729	# Female labor force aged 15-24 years
sK8172	# Male labor force
sK8173	# Male labor force aged 15-24 years
sK8816	# Provisions for a gender-sensitive and family friendly workplace strengthened and enforced
sK8817	# Provisions for combating harassment at the workplace strengthened and enforced
sK8999	# Labor force
sK11085	% Coverage of all offices with gender focal point
sK11128	% Discouraged worker rate of youth
sK11130	% Distribution of youth employment by 1-digit ISIC sector
sK11131	% Distribution of youth labor force by level of educational attainment
sK11184	% Employers of total employment
sK11189	% Employment in agriculture from total employment
sK11191	% Employment in industry from total employment
sK11193	% Employment in services from total employment
sK11422	% Female child employment in agriculture from economically active children ages 7-14
sK11424	% Female child employment in manufacturing from economically active children ages 7-14
sK11426	% Female child employment in services from economically active children ages 7-14
sK11430	% Female contributing family workers from females employed
sK11432	% Female economically active children from female children ages 7-14
sK11434	% Female employees in agriculture from total female employment
sK11436	% Female employees in industry from total female employment
sK11438	% Female employees in services from total female employment
sK11439	% Female employment
sK11441	% Female employment to population ratio, ages 15+
sK11443	% Female employment to population ratio, ages 15-24
sK11451	% Female labor force from total labor force
sK11452	% Female labor force participation rate from female population ages 15-24
sK11453	% Female labor force with primary education from female labor force
sK11454	% Female labor force with secondary education from female labor force
sK11455	% Female labor force with tertiary education from female labor force

sKPI #	Key Performance Indicator name
sK11456	% Female labor participation rate from female population ages 15+
sK11523	% Female wage and salaried workers from total employed
sK11769	% General service staff opportunities for training
sK11770	% Parity in professional posts
sK11991	% Labor force participation rate from total population ages 15-24
sK11993	% Labor force with primary education
sK11995	% Labor force with secondary education
sK11997	% Labor force with tertiary education
sK12003	% Labor tax and contributions from commercial profits
sK12050	% Male child employment agriculture from male economically active children ages 7-14
sK12052	% Male child employment in manufacturing from male economically active children ages 7-14
sK12054	% Male child employment in services from male economically active children ages 7-14
sK12058	% Male contributing family workers from males employed
sK12060	% Male economically active children from male children ages 7-14
sK12062	% Male employees in agriculture from total male employment
sK12064	% Male employees in industry from total male employment
sK12066	% Male employees in services from total male employment
sK12067	% Male employment
sK12069	% Male employment to population ratio, ages 15+
sK12071	% Male employment to population ratio, ages 15-24
sK12074	% Male labor force aged 15+ from total labor force
sK12075	% Male labor force from total labor force 15-24 years
sK12076	% Male labor force participation rate from male population ages 15-24
sK12077	% Male labor force with primary education from male labor force
sK12078	% Male labor force with secondary education from male labor force
sK12079	% Male labor force with tertiary education from male labor force
sK12080	% Male labor participation rate from male population ages 15+
sK12114	% Male work only economically active children from male economically active children, ages 7-14
sK12122	% Males self-employed from males employed
sK12356	% Over qualification rate for foreign born male population ages 25-54
sK12357	% Over qualification rate for EU born female population ages 20-64
sK12358	% Over qualification rate for EU born female population ages 25-54
sK12359	% Over qualification rate for EU born female population ages 55-64
sK12360	% Over qualification rate for EU born male population ages 25-54
sK12361	% Over qualification rate for EU born male population ages 55-64

sKPI #	Key Performance Indicator name
sK12362	% Over qualification rate for EU born male population, ages 20-64
sK12363	% Over qualification rate for EU born population ages 25-54
sK12364	% Over qualification rate for EU born population ages 55-64
sK12365	% Over qualification rate for female population ages 20-64
sK12366	% Over qualification rate for female population ages 25-54
sK12367	% Over qualification rate for female population ages 55-64
sK12368	% Over qualification rate for foreign born female population ages 25-54
sK12369	% Over qualification rate for foreign born female population ages 2--64
sK12370	% Over qualification rate for foreign born female population ages 55-64
sK12371	% Over qualification rate for foreign born male population ages 20-64
sK12372	% Over qualification rate for foreign born male population ages 55-64
sK12373	% Over qualification rate for foreign born population ages 25-54
sK12374	% Over qualification rate for foreign born population ages 55-64
sK12375	% Over qualification rate for foreign born population, ages 20-64
sK12376	% Over qualification rate for male population ages 20-64
sK12377	% Over qualification rate for male population ages 25-54
sK12378	% Over qualification rate for male population, ages 55-64
sK12379	% Over qualification rate for non-EU born female population ages 20-64
sK12380	% Over qualification rate for non-EU born female population ages 25-54
sK12381	% Over qualification rate for non-EU born female population ages 55-64
sK12382	% Over qualification rate for non-EU born male population ages 20-64
sK12383	% Over qualification rate for non-EU born male population ages 25-54
sK12384	% Over qualification rate for non-EU born male population ages 55-64
sK12385	% Over qualification rate for non-EU born population ages 25-54
sK12386	% Over qualification rate for non-EU born population ages 55-64
sK12387	% Over qualification rate for non-EU born population, ages 20-64
sK12388	% Over qualification rate for population ages 20-64
sK12389	% Over qualification rate for population ages 25-54
sK12390	% Over qualification rate for population ages 55-64
sK12398	% Part-time female employment from total female employment
sK12399	% Part-time female employment from total part-time employment
sK12400	% Part-time male employment from total male employment
sK12830	% Re-employed

sKPI #	Key Performance Indicator name
sK12900	% Sector employment
sK12992	% Labor participation rate from total population ages 15+
sK13025	% Part time employment from total employment
sK13038	% Self-employed from total employed
sK13045	% Wage and salaried workers from total employed
sK13130	% Women among ambassadors
sK13131	% Women among clerks
sK13132	% Women among craft and related workers
sK13133	% Women among government ministers
sK13134	% Women among judges
sK13135	% Women among legislators
sK13136	% Women among members of parliament
sK13137	% Women among researchers
sK13138	% Women employed in the non-agricultural sector from total non-agricultural employment
sK13142	% Work only economically active children from economically active children, ages 7-14
sK13149	% Young workers engaged in excessive work hours
sK13167	% Over qualification rate for EU born population, ages 20-64

Social Benefits & Care

Social benefits and care refers to services available for all people, regardless of social or economic standing and is a support offered by the government.

sKPI #	Key Performance Indicator name
sK9216	$ Accommodation means-tested as disability benefits
sK9217	$ Accommodation non means-tested as disability benefits
sK9218	$ Assistance in carrying out daily tasks means-tested as disability benefits
sK9219	$ Assistance in carrying out daily tasks non means-tested as disability benefits
sK9220	$ Benefits in kind means-tested as disability benefits
sK9221	$ Benefits in kind non means-tested as disability benefits
sK9223	$ Care allowance means-tested as disability benefits
sK9225	$ Care allowance non means-tested as disability benefits
sK9226	$ Cash benefits means-tested as disability benefits
sK9227	$ Cash benefits non means-tested as disability benefits
sK9228	$ Disability pension non means-tested as disability benefits
sK9229	$ Early retirement benefit due to reduced capacity to work means-tested as disability benefits
sK9230	$ Early retirement benefit due to reduced capacity to work non means-tested as disability benefits
sK9232	$ Economic integration of the handicapped means-tested as disability benefits
sK9234	$ Economic integration of the handicapped non means-tested as disability benefits
sK9235	$ Lump sum cash benefits means-tested as disability benefits

sKPI #	Key Performance Indicator name
sK9236	$ Lump sum cash benefits non means-tested as disability benefits
sK9237	$ Other benefits in kind means-tested as disability benefits
sK9238	$ Other benefits in kind non means-tested as disability benefits
sK9240	$ Other cash periodic benefits means-tested as disability benefits
sK9242	$ Other cash periodic benefits non means-tested as disability benefits
sK9243	$ Periodic cash benefits means-tested as disability benefits
sK9244	$ Periodic cash benefits non means-tested as disability benefits
sK9245	$ Rehabilitation means-tested as disability benefits
sK9246	$ Rehabilitation non means-tested as disability benefits
sK9247	$ Social protection benefits as disability benefits
sK9248	$ Social protection benefits means-tested as disability benefits
sK9249	$ Social protection benefits non means-tested as disability benefits
sK9274	$ Expenditure on administration costs
sK9285	$ Expenditure on benefits in kind means-tested
sK9286	$ Expenditure on benefits in kind non means-tested
sK9288	$ Expenditure on cash benefits means-tested
sK9289	$ Expenditure on cash benefits non means-tested
sK9313	$ Expenditure on lump sum cash benefits means-tested
sK9314	$ Expenditure on lump sum cash benefits non means-tested
sK9323	$ Expenditure on other transfers to other resident schemes
sK9330	$ Expenditure on periodic cash benefits means-tested
sK9347	$ Expenditure on social contributions rerouted paid on disability benefits
sK9348	$ Expenditure on social contributions rerouted paid on family and children benefits
sK9349	$ Expenditure on social contributions rerouted paid on housing benefits
sK9350	$ Expenditure on social contributions rerouted paid on old age benefits
sK9351	$ Expenditure on social contributions rerouted paid on sickness or health care benefits
sK9352	$ Expenditure on social contributions rerouted paid on social exclusion n.e.c. benefits
sK9353	$ Expenditure on social contributions rerouted paid on survivors benefits
sK9354	$ Expenditure on social contributions rerouted paid on unemployment benefits
sK9355	$ Expenditure on social contributions rerouted to other schemes
sK9356	$ Expenditure on social protection benefits
sK9357	$ Expenditure on social protection benefits granted to non-resident households
sK9358	$ Expenditure on social protection benefits granted to resident households
sK9359	$ Expenditure on social protection benefits granted to residents of other countries
sK9360	$ Expenditure on social protection benefits granted to residents of the EU
sK9361	$ Expenditure on social protection benefits means-tested
sK9362	$ Expenditure on social protection benefits non means-tested
sK9366	$ Expenditure on transfers to other schemes
sK9389	$ Accommodation means-tested as family and children benefits
sK9390	$ Accommodation non means-tested as family and children benefits
sK9391	$ Benefits in kind means-tested as family and children benefits
sK9392	$ Benefits in kind non means-tested as family and children benefits
sK9393	$ Birth grant means-tested as family and children benefits
sK9394	$ Birth grant non means-tested as family and children benefits
sK9395	$ Cash benefits means-tested as family and children benefits
sK9396	$ Cash benefits non means-tested as family and children benefits
sK9397	$ Child day care means-tested as family and children benefits
sK9398	$ Child day care non means-tested as family and children benefits
sK9399	$ Family or child allowance means-tested as family and children benefits
sK9400	$ Family or child allowance non means-tested as family and children benefits
sK9401	$ Home help means-tested as family and children benefits
sK9402	$ Home help non means-tested as family and children benefits
sK9403	$ Income maintenance in the event of childbirth means-tested as family and children benefits
sK9404	$ Income maintenance in the event of childbirth non means-tested as family and children benefits
sK9405	$ Lump sum cash benefits means-tested as family and children benefits
sK9406	$ Lump sum cash benefits non means-tested as family and children benefits
sK9407	$ other benefits in kind means-tested as family and children benefits
sK9408	$ Other benefits in kind non means-tested as family and children benefits
sK9409	$ Other cash lump sum benefits means-tested as family and children benefits
sK9410	$ Other cash lump sum benefits non means-tested as family and children benefits
sK9411	$ Other cash periodic benefits means-tested as family and children benefits
sK9412	$ Other cash periodic benefits non means-tested as family and children benefits

sKPI #	Key Performance Indicator name
sK9414	$ Parental leave benefit means-tested as family and children benefits
sK9416	$ Parental leave benefit non means-tested as family and children benefits
sK9417	$ Periodic cash benefits means-tested as family and children benefits
sK9418	$ Periodic cash benefits non means-tested as family and children benefits
sK9419	$ Social protection benefits as family and children benefits
sK9420	$ Social protection benefits means-tested as family and children benefits
sK9421	$ Social protection benefits non means-tested as family and children benefits
sK10029	$ Benefit to owner-occupiers means-tested as housing benefits
sK10030	$ Benefits in kind means-tested as housing benefits
sK10031	$ Other rent benefits means-tested as housing benefits
sK10032	$ Rent benefits means-tested as housing benefits
sK10033	$ Social housing means-tested as housing benefits
sK10034	$ Social protection benefits as housing benefits
sK10035	$ Social protection benefits means-tested as housing benefits
sK10291	$ Accommodation means-tested as old age benefits
sK10292	$ Accommodation non means-tested as old age benefits
sK10293	$ Anticipated old age pension non means-tested as old age benefits
sK10294	$ Anticipated old-age pension means-tested as old age benefits
sK10295	$ Assistance in carrying out daily tasks means-tested as old age benefits
sK10296	$ Assistance in carrying out daily tasks non means-tested as old age benefits
sK10297	$ Benefits in kind means-tested as old age benefits
sK10298	$ Benefits in kind non means-tested as old age benefits
sK10299	$ Care allowance means-tested as old age benefits
sK10300	$ Care allowance non means-tested as old age benefits
sK10301	$ Cash benefits means-tested as old age benefits
sK10302	$ Cash benefits non means-tested as old age benefits
sK10303	$ Lump sum cash benefits means-tested as old age benefits
sK10304	$ Lump sum cash benefits non means-tested as old age benefits
sK10305	$ Old age pension non means-tested as old age benefits
sK10306	$ Old age pension means-tested as old age benefits
sK10307	$ Other benefits in kind means-tested as old age benefits
sK10308	$ Other benefits in kind non means-tested as old age benefits
sK10309	$ Other cash periodic benefits means-tested as old age benefits
sK10310	$ Other cash periodic benefits non means-tested as old age benefits
sK10312	$ Other lump sum cash benefits non means-tested as old age benefits

sKPI #	Key Performance Indicator name
sK10313	$ Partial pension means-tested as old age benefits
sK10315	$ Periodic cash benefits means-tested as old age benefits
sK10316	$ Periodic cash benefits non means-tested as old age benefits
sK10317	$ Social protection benefits as old age benefits
sK10318	$ Social protection benefits means-tested as old age benefits
sK10319	$ Social protection benefits non means-tested as old age benefits
sK10515	$ Cash benefits non means-tested as sickness and health care benefits
sK10516	$ Benefits in kind means-tested as sickness and health care benefits
sK10517	$ Benefits in kind non means-tested as sickness and health care benefits
sK10518	$ Cash benefits means-tested as sickness and health care benefits
sK10519	$ Direct provision means-tested as sickness and health care benefits
sK10520	$ Direct provision non means-tested as sickness and health care benefits
sK10521	$ Direct provision of pharmaceutical products means-tested as sickness and health care benefits
sK10522	$ Direct provision of pharmaceutical products non means-tested as sickness and health care benefits
sK10523	$ In-patient care means-tested as sickness and health care benefits
sK10524	$ In-patient care non means-tested as sickness and health care benefits
sK10525	$ Lump sum cash benefits means-tested as sickness and health care benefits
sK10526	$ Lump sum cash benefits non means-tested as sickness and health care benefits
sK10527	$ Other benefits in kind means-tested as sickness and health care benefits
sK10528	$ Other benefits in kind non means-tested as sickness and health care benefits
sK10529	$ Other cash lump sum benefits means-tested as sickness and health care benefits
sK10530	$ Other cash lump sum benefits non means-tested as sickness and health care benefits
sK10531	$ Other cash periodic benefits means-tested as sickness and health care benefits
sK10532	$ Other cash periodic benefits non means-tested as sickness and health care benefits
sK10533	$ Other direct provision means-tested as sickness and health care benefits
sK10534	$ Other direct provision non means-tested as sickness and health care benefits
sK10535	$ Other reimbursement means-tested as sickness and health care benefits
sK10536	$ Other reimbursement non means-tested as sickness and health care benefits
sK10537	$ Out-patient care means-tested as sickness and health care benefits

sKPI #	Key Performance Indicator name
sK10538	$ Out-patient care non means-tested as sickness and health care benefits
sK10539	$ Paid sick leave means-tested as sickness and health care benefits
sK10540	$ Paid sick leave non means-tested as sickness and health care benefits
sK10541	$ Periodic cash benefits means-tested as sickness and health care benefits
sK10542	$ Periodic cash benefits non means-tested as sickness and health care benefits
sK10543	$ Reimbursement means-tested as sickness and health care benefits
sK10544	$ Reimbursement non means-tested as sickness and health care benefits
sK10545	$ Reimbursement of pharmaceutical products means-tested as sickness and health care benefits
sK10546	$ Reimbursement of pharmaceutical products non means-tested as sickness and health care benefits
sK10547	$ Social protection benefits means-tested as sickness and health care benefits
sK10548	$ Social protection benefits non means-tested as sickness and health care benefits
sK10550	$ Accommodation means-tested as social exclusion benefits
sK10551	$ Accommodation non means-tested as social exclusion benefits
sK10552	$ Benefits in kind means-tested as social exclusion benefits
sK10553	$ Benefits in kind non means-tested as social exclusion benefits
sK10554	$ Cash benefits means-tested as social exclusion benefits
sK10555	$ Cash benefits non means-tested as social exclusion benefits
sK10556	$ Income support means-tested as social exclusion benefits
sK10557	$ Income support non means-tested as social exclusion benefits
sK10558	$ Lump sum cash benefits means-tested as social exclusion benefits
sK10559	$ Lump sum cash benefits non means-tested as social exclusion benefits
sK10560	$ Other benefits in kind means-tested as social exclusion benefits
sK10561	$ Other benefits in kind non means-tested as social exclusion benefits
sK10562	$ Other cash lump sum benefits means-tested as social exclusion benefits
sK10563	$ Other cash lump sum benefits non means-tested as social exclusion benefits
sK10564	$ Other cash periodic benefits means-tested as social exclusion benefits
sK10565	$ Other cash periodic benefits non means-tested as social exclusion benefits
sK10566	$ Periodic cash benefits means-tested as social exclusion benefits
sK10567	$ Periodic cash benefits non means-tested as social exclusion benefits

sKPI #	Key Performance Indicator name
sK10568	$ Rehabilitation of alcohol and drugs abusers means-tested as social exclusion benefits
sK10569	$ Rehabilitation of alcohol and drugs abusers non means-tested as social exclusion benefits
sK10570	$ Social protection benefits as social exclusion benefits
sK10571	$ Social protection benefits means-tested as social exclusion benefits
sK10572	$ Social protection benefits non means-tested as social exclusion benefits
sK10573	$ Social protection benefits
sK10580	$ Benefits in kind means-tested as survivors benefits
sK10581	$ Benefits in kind non means-tested as survivors benefits
sK10582	$ Cash benefits means-tested as survivors benefits
sK10583	$ Cash benefits non means-tested as survivors benefits
sK10584	$ Death grant means-tested as survivors benefits
sK10585	$ Death grant non means-tested as survivors benefits
sK10586	$ Funeral expenses means-tested as survivors benefits
sK10587	$ Lump sum cash benefits means-tested as survivors benefits
sK10588	$ Lump sum cash benefits non means-tested as survivors benefits
sK10589	$ Other benefits in kind means-tested as survivors benefits
sK10590	$ Other benefits in kind non means-tested as survivors benefits
sK10591	$ Other cash lump sum benefits means-tested as survivors benefits
sK10592	$ Other cash lump sum benefits non means-tested as survivors benefits
sK10593	$ Other cash periodic benefits means-tested as survivors benefits
sK10594	$ Other cash periodic benefits non means-tested as survivors benefits
sK10595	$ Periodic cash benefits means-tested as survivors benefits
sK10596	$ Periodic cash benefits non means-tested as survivors benefits
sK10597	$ Social protection benefits as survivors benefits
sK10598	$ Social protection benefits means-tested as survivors benefits
sK10599	$ Social protection benefits non means-tested as survivors benefits
sK10600	$ Survivors function - Funeral expenses non means-tested as survivors benefits
sK10601	$ Survivors' pension means-tested as survivors benefits
sK10602	$ Survivors' pension non means-tested as survivors benefits
sK10635	$ Benefits in kind means-tested as unemployment benefits
sK10636	$ Benefits in kind non means-tested as unemployment benefits
sK10637	$ Cash benefits means-tested as unemployment benefits
sK10638	$ Cash benefits non means-tested as unemployment benefits
sK10639	$ Early retirement benefit for labor market reasons means-tested as unemployment benefits

sKPI #	Key Performance Indicator name
sK10640	$ Early retirement benefit for labor market reasons non means-tested as unemployment benefits
sK10641	$ Full unemployment benefit means-tested as unemployment benefits
sK10642	$ Full unemployment benefit non means-tested as unemployment benefits
sK10643	$ Lump sum cash benefits means-tested as unemployment benefits
sK10644	$ Lump sum cash benefits non means-tested as unemployment benefits
sK10645	$ Mobility and resettlement means-tested as unemployment benefits
sK10646	$ Mobility and resettlement non means-tested as unemployment benefits
sK10647	$ Other benefits in kind means-tested as unemployment benefits
sK10648	$ Other benefits in kind non means-tested as unemployment benefits
sK10649	$ Other cash lump sum benefits means-tested as unemployment benefits
sK10650	$ Other cash lump sum benefits non means-tested as unemployment benefits
sK10651	$ Other cash periodic benefits means-tested as unemployment benefits
sK10652	$ Other cash periodic benefits non means-tested as unemployment benefits
sK10653	$ Partial unemployment benefit means-tested as unemployment benefits
sK10654	$ Partial unemployment benefit non means-tested as unemployment benefits
sK10655	$ Periodic cash benefits means-tested as unemployment benefits
sK10656	$ Periodic cash benefits non means-tested as unemployment benefits
sK10657	$ Placement services and job-search assistance means-tested as unemployment benefits
sK10658	$ Placement services and job-search assistance non means-tested as unemployment benefits
sK10659	$ Redundancy compensation means-tested as unemployment benefits
sK10660	$ Redundancy compensation non means-tested as unemployment benefits
sK10661	$ Social protection benefits as unemployment benefits
sK10662	$ Social protection benefits means-tested as unemployment benefits
sK10663	$ Social protection benefits non means-tested as unemployment benefits
sK10665	$ Vocational training allowance means-tested as unemployment benefits
sK10667	$ Vocational training allowance non means-tested as unemployment benefits
sK10668	$ Vocational training means-tested as unemployment benefits
sK10669	$ Vocational training non means-tested as unemployment benefits
sK11009	% Children 0-4 in other day care

sKPI #	Key Performance Indicator name
sK11010	% Children 0-4 in private day care
sK11011	% Children 0-4 in public day care
sK11713	% Households reliant upon social security
sK11785	% Individuals reliant on social security
sK13162	$ Disability benefits: disability pension means-tested
sK13169	$ Periodic cash benefits non means-tested
sK7087	# 3 year backward moving average of unemployment rate

Unemployment

Unemployment is the degree to which a population group of working age is without paid work and actively seeking employment.

sKPI #	Key Performance Indicator name
sK8848	# Re-employed layoffs
sK10773	% Aggregate replacement ratio, excluding other social benefits
sK10774	% Aggregate replacement ratio, including other social benefits
sK11187	% Employment gap of immigrants
sK11194	% Employment rate of older workers
sK11197	% Employment-to-population ratio
sK11461	% Female long-term unemployment from female unemployment
sK11517	% Female unemployment from female labor force
sK11518	% Female unemployment with primary education from female unemployment
sK11519	% Female unemployment with secondary education from female unemployment
sK11520	% Female unemployment with tertiary education from female unemployment
sK11522	% Female vulnerable unemployment, from female unemployment
sK11667	% Growth rate of GDP per person employed
sK12027	% Long-term unemployment from total unemployment
sK12083	% Male long-term unemployment from male unemployment
sK12108	% Male unemployment from male labor force
sK12109	% Male unemployment with primary education from male unemployment
sK12110	% Male unemployment with secondary education from male unemployment
sK12111	% Male unemployment with tertiary education from male unemployment
sK12112	% Male vulnerable unemployment, from male unemployment
sK12393	% Own-account and contributing family workers in total employment
sK12420	% Perception of employment opportunities
sK12802	% Ratio of youth-to-adult unemployment rate
sK12901	% Sector unemployment
sK13042	% Unemployment from total labor force
sK13044	% Vulnerable unemployment from total unemployment

sKPI #	Key Performance Indicator name
sK13047	% Youth male unemployment from total labor force ages 15-24
sK13082	% Unemployment assistance
sK13084	% Unemployment with primary education from total unemployment
sK13085	% Unemployment with secondary education from total unemployment

sKPI #	Key Performance Indicator name
sK13086	% Unemployment with tertiary education from total unemployment
sK13087	% Unmet need for contraception from married women ages 15-49
sK13116	% Vulnerable employment rate
sK13150	% Youth female unemployment from female labor force ages 15-24
sK13154	% Youth male unemployment from male labor force ages 15-24

Peace & Justice

Peace reflects a state of harmony between humans, based on mutual respect and guarantee of anyone's rights. It is characterized by the absence of conflict or war and a sense of security ensured by resolving problems through dialogue and negotiation instead of violence.

Domestic and International Conflict

Domestic and international conflicts reflect long-term historical experience of conflict within and outside national boundaries. Ongoing civil and trans-national wars are included in this subcategory.

sKPI #	Key Performance Indicator name
sK7540	# Deaths from organized conflict (external)
sK7541	# Deaths from organized conflict (internal)
sK7692	# External conflicts fought
sK7693	# External peace index
sK8069	# Internal conflicts fought
sK8070	# Internal peace index
sK8118	# Level of organized conflict
sK8835	# Rating of relations with neighboring countries
sK10575	# Misery index
sK10577	% Children involved in internal conflicts
sK10680	% Crime rate
sK10682	% Crimes involving a firearm
sK10684	# Civil disobedience acts
sK10686	# Riots and protests

Law and Justice

Law and justice is the system of binding rules of conduct meant to enforce justice through social institutions. It shapes politics, economics and society and serves as a social mediator of relationships between people.

sKPI #	Key Performance Indicator name
sK6043	% Documents exchanged non-electronically among criminal justice agencies in the jurisdiction
sK10688	% Recidivists
sK10692	% Sentenced population
sK10696	# Imprisonments
sK10698	# Types of crimes recorded by police
sK10700	# Community service orders

Militarization

Militarization represents the level of investment in developing military capabilities, access to weapons and is directly linked to how a country feels internationally in terms of safety.

sKPI #	Key Performance Indicator name
sK7167	# Armed forces personnel
sK7168	# Armed services personnel per 100,000 people
sK7586	# Ease of access to small arms and light weapons
sK7681	# Exports (transfers) volume of major conventional weapons per 100,000 people
sK7892	# Heavy weapons per 100,000 people
sK8017	# Imports (transfers) volume of major conventional weapons per 100,000 people
sK9117	$ Arms exports in constant 1990
sK9119	$ Arms imports in constant 1990
sK9190	$ Contribution to UN peacekeeping missions
sK10151	$ Military expenditure
sK10849	% Armed forces personnel from labor force
sK10850	% Armed forces personnel from total labor force
sK12174	% Military capability (sophistication)
sK12176	% Military expenditure from central government expenditure
sK12178	% Military expenditure from GDP
sK12179	% Military expenditure out of GDP
sK12355	% Outstanding payments versus annual assessment to the budget of the current peacekeeping missions
sK12710	% Presence of peace keepers - number of troops, police, and military observers in mandate

Safety and Security

Safety and security reflects the perception of criminality in society and the respect for human rights.

sKPI #	Key Performance Indicator name
sK7343	# Battle-related deaths
sK7431	# Combined Polity score
sK7984	# Homicides per 100,000 people
sK7997	# Human development

sKPI #	Key Performance Indicator name
sK8060	# Institutionalized autocracy score
sK8061	# Institutionalized democracy score
sK8062	# Intentional crimes reported by UN Crime Trends Survey (CTS) per 100,000 people
sK8063	# Intentional homicides reported by government police sources per 100,000 people
sK8064	# Intentional homicides reported by international police sources per 100,000 people
sK8065	# Intentional homicides reported by international public health sources per 100,000 people
sK8071	# Internal security officers per 100,000 people
sK8072	# Internally displaced persons
sK8088	# Jailed population per 100,000 people
sK8117	# Level of disrespect for human rights
sK8120	# Level of violent crime
sK8121	# Level of violent demonstrations
sK8430	# Overall Mo index

sKPI #	Key Performance Indicator name
sK8435	# Participation and human rights
sK8682	# Police per 100,000 people
sK8685	# Political instability rating
sK8688	# Political Terror Scale (PTS)
sK8732	# Potential for terrorist acts rating
sK8870	# Revised Combined Polity score
sK9116	$ Arms exports
sK9118	$ Arms imports
sK11943	% Internally displaced persons out of the entire population
sK12018	% Likelihood of violent crimes
sK12019	% Likelihood of violent demonstrations
sK12137	% Marine protected areas from territorial waters
sK12143	% Material deprivation rate
sK12432	% Perceptions of criminality in society
sK12831	% Refugees out of the entire population

Population

Population is represented by the number of individuals living in a geographical area.

Demographics

Demographics represents the structure of the population based on a certain set of characteristics.

sKPI #	Key Performance Indicator name
sK7104	# Female age at first marriage
sK7105	# Male age at first marriage
sK7381	# Cases brought to prosecution, originating from STRs, CTRs and independent law enforcement investigation
sK7382	# Cases initiated by law enforcement agencies on the basis of STRs sent by the FIU
sK7384	# Cash Transaction Reports (CTRs) filled
sK7398	# Children 0-4 age in public or private day-care per 1,000 children
sK7401	# Children who directly benefit from ILO action
sK7506	# Crimes recorded by the police
sK7570	# Domestic burglaries recorded by the police
sK7576	# Drug trafficking crimes recorded by the police
sK7667	# Engel coefficient
sK7731	# Female life expectancy at birth
sK7741	# Female population
sK7778	# Female population ages 0-14
sK7786	# Fire accidents
sK7844	# Gender ratio of population: women/men
sK7983	# Homicides crimes recorded by the police
sK8175	# Male life expectancy at birth
sK8183	# Male population
sK8218	# Male population ages 0-14
sK8590	# Periodicity of agricultural census

sKPI #	Key Performance Indicator name
sK8591	# Periodicity of child malnutrition indicator
sK8592	# Periodicity of child mortality indicator
sK8595	# Periodicity of health related surveys
sK8599	# Periodicity of population census
sK8600	# Periodicity of poverty related surveys
sK8681	# Police officers
sK8692	# Population ages 0-14
sK8694	# Population density
sK8887	# Robberies recorded by the police
sK8959	# Thefts of motor vehicles recorded by the police
sK9000	# Total life expectancy at birth
sK9005	# Total population
sK9067	# Urban population
sK9078	# Violent crimes recorded by the police
sK9083	# Weeks of maternity leave
sK10734	% 15-34 year-old males out of overall adult population
sK10754	% Adolescent fertility rate in births per 1,000 women ages 15-19
sK10758	% Adult female mortality rate per 1,000 female adults
sK10765	% Adult male mortality rate per 1,000 male adults
sK11032	% Community structure
sK11039	% Compensation of employees from expense
sK11041	% Completeness of birth registration
sK11042	% Completeness of infant death reporting from reported infant deaths to estimated infant deaths
sK11044	% Completeness of total death reporting from reported total deaths to estimated total deaths

sKPI #	Key Performance Indicator name
sK11045	% Completeness of vital registration system
sK11118	% Demography
sK11181	% Emigration rate of tertiary educated from total tertiary educated population
sK11446	% Female gross intake rate in grade 1 from relevant age group
sK11458	% Female legislators, senior officials and managers
sK11470	% Females ages 0-14 of total population
sK11471	% Females ages 0-4 of female population
sK11473	% Females from total population
sK11487	% Female study and work economically active children from female economically active children, ages 7-14
sK11525	% Female work only economically active children from female economically active children, ages 7-14
sK11534	% Females self-employed from females employed
sK11715	% Households with Internet access
sK11718	% Households without access to Internet at home, because access not needed (content is not useful, not interesting, etc.)
sK11719	% Households without access to Internet at home, because access not wanted (content is harmful, etc.)
sK11720	% Households without access to Internet at home, because of a physical disability
sK11721	% Households without access to Internet at home, because of access elsewhere
sK11722	% Households without access to Internet at home, because of lack of skills
sK11723	% Households without access to Internet at home, because of other reasons
sK11724	% Households without access to Internet at home, because of privacy or security concerns
sK11725	% Households without access to Internet at home, because the access costs are too high
sK11726	% Households without access to Internet at home, because the equipment costs are too high
sK11733	% Immigration rate
sK11944	% International migrant stock
sK11946	% International migrant stock from population
sK12092	% Males ages 0-14 of total population
sK12093	% Males ages 0-4 of male population
sK12094	% Males from total population
sK12103	% Male study and work economically active children from male economically active children, ages 7-14
sK12144	% Maternal leave benefits, from wages paid in covered period
sK12291	% Non-nationals among residents
sK12292	% Non-nationals in the labor force
sK12416	% People living in jobless households
sK12451	% Population ages 0-14 of total
sK12453	% Population ages 15-64 of total
sK12456	% Population ages 65 and above of total
sK12459	% Population below 5 million

sKPI #	Key Performance Indicator name
sK12460	% Population below minimum level of dietary energy consumption
sK12672	% Population in urban agglomerations of more than 1 million from total population
sK12673	% Population living in areas where elevation is below 5 meters from total population
sK12716	% Prevalence of female overweight, from children under 5
sK12717	% Prevalence of female wasting, from children under 5
sK12719	% Prevalence of male overweight, from children under 5
sK12720	% Prevalence of male wasting, from children under 5
sK12723	% Prevalence of overweight, from children under 5
sK12727	% Prevalence of wasting, from children under 5
sK12763	% Professionals, from employed people
sK12869	% Rural completeness of birth registration
sK12874	% Rural population
sK12916	% Sex ratio at birth (females per 1,000 males)
sK12926	% Smoking prevalence in females
sK12927	% Smoking prevalence in males
sK12937	% Study and work economically active children from economically active children, ages 7-14
sK12941	% Survival to age 65 in females from cohort
sK12942	% Survival to age 65 in males from cohort
sK12974	% Teenage mothers from women ages 15-19 who have had children or are currently pregnant
sK12990	% Those employed in the city who are in-commuters
sK12991	% Those living in the city who are out-commuters
sK13090	% Urban completeness of birth registration
sK13095	% Urban population
sK13100	% Use of insecticide-treated bed nets from under-5 population
sK13140	% Women who were first married by age 18, from women ages 20-24

Density & Urbanization

Density and urbanization are population characteristics based on geographical distribution.

sKPI #	Key Performance Indicator name
sK7195	# Living area in m2 per person
sK7584	# Dwellings
sK7640	# Empty conventional dwellings per total dwellings
sK8605	# Persons per room
sK8695	# Population density in people per sq. km
sK8697	# Population in largest city
sK8729	# Population in urban agglomerations of more than 1 million
sK8836	# Ratio of average price to average rent for a house
sK8837	# Ratio of average price to average rent for an apartment
sK9121	$ Annual rent for a house per m2
sK9122	$ Rent for an apartment per m2

Global » Human Development Areas

sKPI #	Key Performance Indicator name
sK9123	$ Annual social housing rents per m2
sK9124	$ Price per m2 for a house
sK9125	$ Price per m2 for an apartment
sK9126	$ Price per m2 for apartment, from median household income
sK9128	$ Social housing rents to median household income
sK10826	# Rural population
sK10862	% Occupancy per occupied dwelling
sK11144	% Dwellings lacking basic amenities
sK11707	% Households living in apartments
sK11708	% Households living in houses
sK11709	% Households living in owned dwellings
sK11710	% Households living in private rented housing
sK11711	% Households living in social housing
sK12289	% Non-conventional dwellings
sK12424	% Perception of housing market
sK12669	% Population in the largest city from urban population
sK12670	% Population in urban agglomerations over 1 million
sK12671	% Population in urban agglomerations of more than 1 million from population
sK12799	% Ratio of girls to boys in primary and secondary school

sKPI #	Key Performance Indicator name
sK8852	# Refugee population by country or territory of origin
sK10772	% Age dependency ratio from working-age population
sK10836	% Annual population growth
sK11090	% Crude birth rate per 1,000 people
sK11092	% Crude death rate per 1,000 people
sK11449	% Female headed households from households with a female head
sK12252	% Net migration
sK12286	% Nights spent by non-EU residents inside the EU per 1,000 population
sK12298	% Old age dependency ratio from working-age population
sK12422	% Perception of green space provision
sK12425	% Perception of integration of foreigners
sK12426	% Perception of safety in the city
sK12429	% Perception of the quality and quantity of sports facilities
sK12667	% Population having paid bribes
sK12674	% Population living in hazard prone areas
sK12677	% Population using solid fuels for cooking
sK13022	% Migrant stock
sK13048	% Tourism nights spent abroad by residents per 1,000 population
sK13096	% Urban population living in slums
sK13145	% Young age dependency ratio from working-age population

Dynamics

Dynamics studies short-term and long-term changes in the size and age composition of population.

sKPI #	Key Performance Indicator name
sK7175	# Associations
sK7197	# Occupants of motor cars
sK7982	# Homeless people from resident population
sK7996	# Human and economic loss due to natural disasters
sK8035	# Individuals who booked travel and holiday accommodation over the Internet
sK8581	# People in accommodation for the homeless per 1,000 population
sK8582	# People in women's shelter per 1,000 population
sK8594	# Periodicity of gender equality in education indicator
sK8838	# Ratio of day-time to night-time population
sK8850	# Refugee population by country or territory of asylum

Housing

Housing refers to the social problem of insuring that members of society have a home to live in.

sKPI #	Key Performance Indicator name
sK7995	# Houses per 100 apartments
sK12391	% Overcrowded households
sK23256	# Rural households benefiting directly from USG interventions
sK10702	% Repairs finished on time
sK10704	% Non-decent homes
sK10072	% Satisfaction with housing repairs
sK12954	% Homes with valid gas safety records
sK12957	$ Purchase cost per dwelling
sK12960	# Time to complete repairs

Quality of Life

Quality of life relates to the satisfaction of human needs, so that the population lives in safe and healthy conditions, thus creating a positive impact in the life of citizens.

Income Distribution

Income distribution represents the dispersion of wealth across population.

sKPI #	Key Performance Indicator name
sK11617	% GINI index
sK11755	% Income share held by fourth 20%

sKPI #	Key Performance Indicator name
sK11757	% Income share held by highest 10%
sK11759	% Income share held by highest 20%
sK11761	% Income share held by lowest 10%
sK11763	% Income share held by lowest 20%
sK11765	% Income share held by second 20%

sKPI #	Key Performance Indicator name
sK11767	% Income share held by third 20%
sK12147	% Relative income ratio of people aged over 60
sK12148	% Relative income ratio of people aged over 65
sK12839	% Relative median at-risk-of-poverty gap of elderly people (65+, 75+)
sK23244	% People living on less than $1.25 per day
sK23245	# Underweight children aged under 5
sK23246	$ Per Capita expenditures of rural households (proxy for income) of USG targeted beneficiaries
sK23248	# Stunted children aged under 5
sK23249	# Underweight women
sK23250	# Wasted children aged under 5

Poverty Rates

Poverty rates are the characteristics of income distribution to citizens with limited financial resources.

sKPI #	Key Performance Indicator name
sK8597	# Periodicity of income poverty indicator
sK10731	% Relative median at-risk-of-poverty gap
sK10852	% At-risk-of-poverty rate for pensioners
sK10853	% At-risk-of-poverty rate of elderly people by tenure status
sK10854	% At-risk-of-poverty rate of elderly people who are owners
sK10855	% At-risk-of-poverty rate of elderly people who are tenants
sK10856	% At-risk-of-poverty threshold, as 60% of median equalised income
sK10872	% Below poverty line
sK11532	% Females at-risk-of-poverty rate
sK11694	% Household with dependent children, at-risk-of poverty rate
sK11695	% Household with one adult older than 65 years, at-risk-of poverty rate
sK11696	% Household with one adult younger than 64 years, at-risk-of poverty rate
sK11698	% Household with three or more adults with dependent children, at-risk-of poverty rate
sK11699	% Household with three or more adults, at-risk-of poverty rate
sK11700	% Household with two adults with one dependent child, at-risk-of poverty rate
sK11701	% Household with two adults with three dependent children, at-risk-of poverty rate

sKPI #	Key Performance Indicator name
sK11702	% Household with two adults with three or more dependent children, at-risk-of poverty rate
sK11703	% Household with two adults with two dependent children, at-risk-of poverty rate
sK11704	% Household with two adults younger than 65 years, at-risk-of poverty rate
sK11705	% Household with two adults, at least one aged 65 years and over, at-risk-of poverty rate
sK11706	% Household without dependent children, at-risk-of poverty rate
sK12120	% Males at-risk-of-poverty rate
sK12438	% Persistent at-risk-of-poverty rate
sK12444	% Poorest quintile in national consumption
sK12446	% Population aged 18-24 at-risk-of-poverty rate
sK12447	% Population aged 25-49 at-risk-of-poverty rate
sK12448	% Population aged 50-64 at-risk-of-poverty rate
sK12449	% Population aged 65 or over at-risk-of-poverty rate
sK12458	% Population ages less than 18 at-risk-of-poverty rate
sK12685	% Poverty gap at $1.25 a day (PPP)
sK12687	% Poverty gap at $2 a day (PPP)
sK12689	% Poverty gap at national poverty line
sK12691	% Poverty gap at rural poverty line
sK12693	% Poverty gap at urban poverty line
sK12694	% Poverty gap ratio
sK12696	% Poverty headcount ratio at $1.25 a day (PPP) from population
sK12698	% Poverty headcount ratio at $2 a day (PPP) from population
sK12700	% Poverty headcount ratio at national poverty line from population
sK12702	% Poverty headcount ratio at rural poverty line from rural population
sK12704	% Poverty headcount ratio at urban poverty line from urban population
sK12921	% Single female household at-risk-of poverty rate
sK12922	% Single male household at-risk-of poverty rate
sK12923	% Single person household at-risk-of poverty rate
sK12924	% Single person household with dependent children, at-risk-of poverty rate
sK13028	% Population at-risk-of-poverty rate
sK13143	% Working poverty rate
sK23263	# Households with moderate or severe hunger

Transportation & Infrastructure

Transport and infrastructure refer to aspects of human activity that relate to the movement of people and merchandise as well as the human built structures that enable economic activity.

Infrastructure Operations

Infrastructure operations are the set of interconnected structured elements and activities that enable the production and distribution of goods and services.

sKPI #	Key Performance Indicator name
sK7137	# Air transport freight
sK7139	# Air transport of registered carrier departures worldwide
sK7141	# Air transport of passengers carried

Global » Human Development Areas

sKPI #	Key Performance Indicator name
sK7809	# Forecast value of road costs vs. actual costs
sK7868	# Goods transported on railways in million tons per km
sK7870	# Goods transported on roads in million tons per km
sK8092	# Kilometres of network of roads
sK8094	# Kilometres of total network of roads
sK8150	# Long-term programs
sK8440	# Passengers carried on roads in million passengers per km
sK8828	# Quality management/audit programmes
sK8878	# Road density in km of road per 100 sq. km of land area
sK8888	# Roughness
sK8997	# Km of rail lines
sK9074	# Vehicles per km of road
sK9084	# WEF quality of port infrastructure
sK9127	$ Average road user costs
sK10453	$ Pump price for diesel fuel
sK10455	$ Pump price for gasoline
sK10476	$ Resources allocated for road infrastructure
sK10942	% Certified international aerodromes
sK11205	% En-route PBN routes implemented in accordance with the regional PBN plan
sK11931	% Instrument Runway ends with RNP/RNAV approach procedure
sK12014	% Level of satisfaction regarding travel time and quality of road-user information
sK12392	% Overhead percentage
sK12768	% Protected road-user risk
sK12866	% Road sector energy consumption
sK12868	% Roads paved
sK12884	% Satisfaction with road system
sK12930	% State of road bridges
sK13062	% Transport services from commercial service exports
sK13063	% Transport services from commercial service imports
sK13064	% Transport services from service exports
sK13065	% Transport services from service imports
sK13088	% Unprotected road-user risk
sK13109	% Value of assets regarding road administration

Transportation

Transportation represents the process, activities and devices used to move items or people from one location to another. Common forms of transportation include planes, trains, automobiles, and other two-wheel devices.

sKPI #	Key Performance Indicator name
sK7088	# Accessibility by air
sK7089	# Accessibility by rail
sK7090	# Accessibility by road
sK7092	# Accidents per 1,000,000 departures
sK7094	# Acts of unlawful interference against civil aviation worldwide

sKPI #	Key Performance Indicator name
sK7140	# Air transport, registered carrier departures worldwide
sK7142	# Air transports, passengers carried
sK7183	# Age of the bus (only buses) fleet
sK7184	# Altitude
sK7187	# ATFM delay per flight in the main airports
sK7191	# En-route ATFM delay generated by airspace volume
sK7193	# Horizontal en route flight efficiency
sK7201	# Speed of inner-city car traffic during the rush hour
sK7204	# Time of journey to work (minutes)
sK7211	# Waiting time for a bus, in minutes, in the rush hour
sK7350	# Bird strikes
sK7352	# Boats
sK7383	# Cases of increased alert level
sK7385	# Casualties in road traffic accidents
sK7428	# CO2 emissions related to inefficiencies in route extension
sK7463	# Container port traffic in TEU
sK7564	# Distribution of aircraft in the in-service fleet by NOx characteristics
sK7574	# Drivers injured in road traffic accidents
sK7575	# Drivers killed in road traffic accidents
sK7577	# Duplicate 5LNC eliminated
sK7623	# Eliminated deficiency related to non-implementation of ATS Routes
sK7698	# Fatalities in road traffic accidents
sK7699	# Fatalities per 100,000 passenger cars
sK7700	# Fatalities per 1,000 road traffic injury accidents
sK7701	# Fatalities per million inhabitants
sK7792	# Fixed distance along-path
sK7793	# Fixed flight level
sK7794	# Fixed look-ahead time
sK7825	# Fuel burned (and CO2 generated) per 100 RTK/AT
sK7828	# Fully cleared runway in relation to movements or business hours
sK7869	# Goods transported on railways
sK7871	# Goods transported on roads
sK7885	# GT (decked vessels)
sK8009	# IFR flights and flight hours per ATCO hour on duty
sK8056	# Injured in road traffic accidents
sK8057	# Injured per 100,000 passenger cars
sK8058	# Injured per million inhabitants
sK8059	# Injury accidents in road traffic
sK8093	# Length of rail lines
sK8095	# Distance driven within each region by all trucks, intra-regional trips are not included
sK8096	# Distance made by journeys attracted by the region, intra-regional trips excluded
sK8097	# Distance made by journeys produced by the region, intra-regional trips are not included

sKPI #	Key Performance Indicator name
sK8098	# Distanced made by intra-regional trips
sK8099	# Distance driven in public transport per capita per day
sK8116	# Length of bicycle network (dedicated cycle paths and lanes) per 1000 population
sK8127	# Liner shipping connectivity index
sK8229	# Maximum distance a truck can drive to reach another region (km)
sK8230	# Mean distance between a region and all other regions of the European Union (km)
sK8339	# Minimum distance a truck must drive to reach another region (km)
sK8351	# Motor vehicles per 1,000 vehicles
sK8352	# Movements on friction levels below 0.30, 0.25 or at 9
sK8353	# Multimodal accessibility
sK8400	# Occasions when birds were scared away
sK8429	# Overall logistics performance index
sK8432	# Park and ride parking spaces per 1000 cars
sK8437	# Passenger cars per 1,000 people
sK8438	# Passengers carried on railways per distance covered
sK8441	# Passengers carried on roads per distance covered
sK8442	# Passengers disembarked in maritime transport of passengers
sK8443	# Passengers embarked and disembarked in maritime transport of passengers
sK8444	# Passengers embarked in maritime transport of passengers
sK8578	# Peak altitude
sK8579	# Pedestrians injured in road traffic accidents
sK8580	# Pedestrians killed in road traffic accidents
sK8865	# Residents in the vicinity of major airports exposed to noise at or above DNL 65 dB
sK8867	# Resources out of service more than 'X' hours at a time
sK8890	# Runway incursions and excursions per year
sK8910	# Signs out of service
sK8927	# States having implemented RNAV 5 area in the level band FL160-FL460
sK8929	# Stops of public transport per 1,000 population
sK8930	# Stops of public transport per km2
sK8931	# Stops per 1 km of public transport network
sK8956	# Temporarily cleared runway in relation to movements or business hours
sK9059	# Trips attracted by but not originated in the region
sK9060	# Trips produced by and leaving the region
sK9061	# Trips transited through the region, without origin or destination in that region (trucks/day)
sK9075	# Vessels
sK9087	# Worn markings
sK9191	$ Cost of a monthly ticket for public transport for 5-10 km
sK9192	$ Cost of a taxi ride of 5 km to the centre at day time
sK10135	$ Maintenance and repair of motor vehicles
sK10743	% Access to an all-season road, from rural population

sKPI #	Key Performance Indicator name
sK10790	% Air navigation deficiencies priority "U" eliminated
sK10791	% Air transport conducted under liberal arrangements
sK10792	% Airport and air navigation charges
sK10859	% Spectrum frequency availability for future aeronautical utilization
sK10883	% Buses running on alternative fuels
sK11097	% Current Aviation Frequency spectrum is protected to extent possible
sK11129	% Disruption of primary power supply
sK11150	% Effectiveness of safety management
sK11352	% Exercise frequency
sK11409	% Fatal accident rate
sK11579	% Fleet age composition
sK11734	% Implementation of PBN approaches
sK11746	% Incidents and accidents on the apron
sK11982	% Journeys to work by bicycle
sK11983	% Journeys to work by bus
sK11984	% Journeys to work by car
sK11985	% Journeys to work by foot
sK11986	% Journeys to work by motor cycle
sK11987	% Journeys to work by other modes
sK11988	% Journeys to work by rail or metro
sK11989	% Journeys to work by tram
sK12012	% Length of public transport network from total land area
sK12037	% Major international traffic flows wherein performance-based navigation operations are conducted
sK12427	% Perception of the public transport quality
sK12811	% Reduced category in relation to traffic
sK12812	% Reduced serviceability of one or more light systems
sK12854	% Response time more than 90 seconds
sK13053	% Traffic that is transit traffic
sK13078	% Unauthorized personnel on the airside
sK13089	% Unserviceability of one or more light systems
sK13101	% Use of not fully qualified personnel
sK13110	% Violation of local traffic rules (vehicles)
sK23219	# People receiving USG supported training in transportation technical fields
sK23220	$ Public and private dollars leveraged with USG support for transportation infrastructure projects
sK23221	# Government adopted improved transportation related polices or plans this year as a result of USG assistance
sK23222	# Transportation infrastructure constructed or repaired through USG assistance
sK23223	# People benefiting from USG sponsored transportation infrastructure projects
sK23224	# People receiving USG supported training in transportation related policy and regulatory practices

Environmental Sustainability

Biodiversity

Biodiversity is the variation of life forms, like plants or animal species in a given environment.

sKPI #	Key Performance Indicator name
sK7165	# Area of stands dominated by invasive tree species
sK7507	# Critically endangered threatened forest species
sK7836	# GEF benefits index for biodiversity
sK7988	# Hosted Clean Development Mechanism (CDM) projects
sK7989	# Hosted Joint Implementation (JI) projects
sK8110	# Latest UNFCCC national communication
sK8356	# NAMA submission
sK8357	# NAPA submission

sKPI #	Key Performance Indicator name
sK9082	# Vulnerable threatened forest species
sK10724	% Current biomass (spawning biomass) to virgin biomass (spawning biomass) ratio
sK10847	% Area of critical habitat
sK10873	% Biodiversity index
sK11099	% Current population biomass or spawning biomass to MSY ratio (Bt/BMSY)
sK12136	% Marine protected areas
sK13072	% Trophic structure

Environment and Pollution

Environment and pollution refers to characteristics of the planet and its pollution.

Air Quality

Air quality refers to the maintenance of an optimal balance of air quality for living conditions on Earth.

sKPI #	Key Performance Indicator name
sK7136	# Air pollutant emissions from energy systems
sK7144	# Ambient concentrations of air pollutants in urban areas
sK8834	# Radionuclides in atmospheric radioactive discharges
sK12417	% Perception of air quality
sK12962	# Air quality index (AQI)
sK12963	# Air quality monitoring stations
sK12028	% Urban areas with a dangerously high AQI
sK11331	% Compliance with ecological standards
sK11332	# Air quality agencies

Climate Change

Climate change is a significant change in the statistical distribution of weather patterns over time. This can be caused by factors such as oceanic processes, volcanic eruptions and even by human activities.

sKPI #	Key Performance Indicator name
sK7154	# Apparent consumption of CFCs and halons
sK7176	# Atmospheric concentrations of ODS
sK7188	# Daily min/max temperature
sK7198	# Precipitation in depth
sK7353	# BOD/DO in inland waters
sK7377	# Capacity of SOx and NOx abatement equipment of stationary sources
sK7379	# Car fleet equipped with catalytic converters
sK7396	# CFC recovery rate
sK7450	# Concentration of N & P in inland waters
sK7451	# Concentrations in acid precipitation

sKPI #	Key Performance Indicator name
sK7478	# Country precipitation
sK7479	# Country temperature
sK7625	# Emissions of heavy metals
sK7626	# Emissions of N and P in water and soil
sK7627	# Emissions of NOx and Sox
sK7628	# Emissions of organic compounds
sK7671	# Exceedance of critical loads of pH
sK7884	# Ground level UV-B radiation
sK8029	# Index of acidifying substances
sK8030	# Index of apparent consumption of ozone depleting substances (ODS)
sK8355	# N and P from fertiliser use & livestock
sK8693	# Population connected to secondary and/or tertiary sewage treatment plants
sK8810	# Projected annual temperature change
sK8811	# Projected change in annual cool days/cold nights
sK8812	# Projected change in annual hot days/warm nights
sK23273	# Laws, policies, agreements or regulations addressing climate change proposed, adopted, or implemented as a result of USG assistance
sK23274	# Individuals who have received USG supported short-term agricultural enabling environment training
sK23275	# Institutions with improved capacity to address climate change issues as a result of USG assistance

Emissions

Emissions are pollution discharges in the atmosphere by residential, commercial and industrial facilities.

sKPI #	Key Performance Indicator name
sK7071	# CO2 emissions in kt
sK7078	# Country level of PM10 in micrograms per cubic meter

sKPI #	Key Performance Indicator name
sK7413	# CO2 emission in kg per 2000 US$ of GDP
sK7416	# CO2 emissions from gaseous fuel consumption in kt
sK7417	# CO2 emissions from liquid fuel consumption in kt
sK7418	# CO2 emissions from manufacturing industries and construction in million metric tons
sK7419	# CO2 emissions from other sectors, excluding residential buildings and commercial and public services in million metric tons
sK7420	# CO2 emissions from residential buildings and commercial and public services in million metric tons
sK7421	# CO2 emissions from solid fuel consumption in kt
sK7423	# CO2 emissions from transport in million metric tons
sK7425	# CO2 emissions in metric tons per capita
sK7426	# CO2 emissions per employee
sK7427	# CO2 emissions per household
sK7429	# CO2 intensity in kg per kg of oil equivalent energy use
sK7433	# Combustible renewables and waste in metric tons of oil equivalent
sK7464	# Contaminant discharges in liquid effluents from energy systems including oil discharges
sK7629	# Emissions per ton of pulp exported and paper produced
sK7852	# GHG emissions from energy production and use per capita and per unit of GDP
sK7853	# GHG net emissions/removals by LUCF (MtCO2e)
sK7874	# Grams of CO2 emissions per km
sK7912	# HFC gas emissions in thousand metric tons of CO2
sK8050	# Industrial nitrous oxide emissions in thousand metric tons of CO2
sK8107	# Land area where acidification exceeds critical load
sK8125	# Life time of proven uranium reserves
sK8328	# Methane emissions in kt of CO2 equivalent
sK8374	# Nitrous oxide emissions in energy sector in thousand metric tons of CO2
sK8375	# Nitrous oxide emissions in metric tons of CO2
sK8376	# Nitrous oxide emissions in metric tons of CO2 equivalent
sK8410	# Organic water pollutant (BOD) emissions in kg per day
sK8411	# Organic water pollutant (BOD) emissions in kg per day per worker
sK8418	# Other GHG emissions
sK8419	# Other greenhouse gas emissions including HFC, PFC and SF6 in thousand metric tons of CO2 equivalent
sK8420	# Other greenhouse gas emissions, HFC, PFC and SF6 in thousand metric tons of CO2
sK8609	# PFC gas emissions in thousand metric tons of CO2
sK8815	# Proven uranium reserves
sK8907	# SF6 gas emissions
sK8914	# Soil area where acidification exceeds critical load
sK8960	# Thousands of Issued Certified Emission Reductions (CERs) from CDM
sK8961	# Thousands of Issued Emission Reduction Units (ERUs) from JI

sKPI #	Key Performance Indicator name
sK8979	# CO2 emissions from electricity and heat production in million metric tons
sK9003	# Methane (CH4) emissions
sK9004	# Nitrous oxide (N2O) emissions
sK9183	$ CO2 emission in kg per PPP $ of GDP
sK10781	% Agricultural methane emissions
sK10783	% Agricultural nitrous oxide emissions
sK10870	% Bathing water quality
sK10895	% Carbon dioxide damage from GNI
sK11019	% CO2 emissions from gaseous fuel consumption
sK11020	% CO2 emissions from liquid fuel consumption
sK11022	% CO2 emissions from solid fuel consumption
sK11023	% CO2 reduction of implemented new PBN approaches
sK11024	% CO2 reduction of implemented new routes
sK11025	% Coal rents from GDP
sK11030	% Combustible renewables and waste from total energy
sK11916	% Industrial methane emissions
sK11918	% Industrial nitrous oxide emissions
sK12287	% Nitrous oxide emissions in industrial and energy processes from total nitrous oxide emissions
sK12397	% Particulate emission damage from GNI
sK12676	% Population using solid fuels
sK12822	% Reduction of land-based pollution
sK13118	% Water pollution caused by chemical industry from total BOD emissions
sK13119	% Water pollution caused by clay and glass industry from total BOD emissions
sK13120	% Water pollution caused by food industry from total BOD emissions
sK13121	% Water pollution caused by metal industry from total BOD emissions
sK13122	% Water pollution caused by other industry from total BOD emissions
sK13123	% Water pollution caused by paper and pulp industry from total BOD emissions
sK13124	% Water pollution caused by textile industry from total BOD emissions
sK13125	% Water pollution caused by wood industry from total BOD emissions

Freshwater Quality

Freshwater quality covers the assessment of water quality, including biological and chemical part.

sKPI #	Key Performance Indicator name
sK7186	# Precipitation
sK8809	# Projected annual precipitation change
sK8858	# Renewable internal freshwater resources per capita
sK10798	% Agricultural freshwater withdrawals
sK10833	% Industrial freshwater withdrawals
sK10838	% Freshwater withdrawals from internal resources

sKPI #	Key Performance Indicator name
Sk11333	# Water quality index (WQI)
sK11334	# Water quality monitoring stations

Ozone Layer

Ozone layer is a layer in Earth's atmosphere containing relatively high concentrations of ozone and it protects life on Earth from the sun's ultraviolet (UV) rays.

sKPI #	Key Performance Indicator name
sK7554	# Water turbidity
sK7409	% Dissolved oxygen in water
sK7395	# Stream pollution index (SPI)
sK7393	# Water pH
sK8932	# Stratospheric ozone level
sK8674	# Ground level ozone indicator
sK8669	% Excedances of standard ozone levels
sK8668	# Periods of 1-hour exceedance of ground level ozone

sKPI #	Key Performance Indicator name
sK8667	# Ground-level Ozone Standards Designations
sK11050	# Ozone awareness programs
sK11049	% Adherence to national ozone regulations

Waste Generation

Waste generation is the quantity of materials or products that enter a waste stream before composting, incinerating, landfilling or recycling.

sKPI #	Key Performance Indicator name
sK7093	# Accumulated radioactive wastes awaiting disposal
sK8841	# Ratio of solid radioactive waste to units of energy produced
sK8842	# Ratio of solid waste generation to units of energy produced
sK12800	% Ratio of solid radioactive waste awaiting disposal to total generated solid radioactive waste
sK12810	% Recycling rates
sK13013	% Effluent discharge

Natural Resources

A material source of wealth that occurs in a natural state and has economic value.

Energy Resources

Energy resources are renewable (sun, sea, wind) or non-renewable (coal mine, gas well, oil well) resources used for obtaining an energy source.

sKPI #	Key Performance Indicator name
sK9057	# Transport energy intensities
sK10796	% Alternative and nuclear energy
sK10874	% Biofuels
sK10875	% Biomass
sK11152	% Efficiency of energy conversion and distribution
sK12288	% Non-carbon energy share in energy and electricity
sK12801	% Ratio of solid waste properly disposed of total generated solid waste
sK12841	% Renewable energy share in energy and electricity
sK13156	%+B2679 Stocks of critical fuels per corresponding fuel consumption

Fish Resources

Fish resources refer to aspects such as the distribution, species richness and relative abundance of fish species in the aquatic ecosystems.

sKPI #	Key Performance Indicator name
sK8964	# Threatened bird species
sK8965	# Threatened fish species
sK8966	# Threatened mammal species
sK8968	# Threatened plant species (higher)
sK10901	% Catch per sustainable yield
sK11060	% Conservation Status Index

sKPI #	Key Performance Indicator name
sK11119	% Depleted stocks rebuilding
sK11575	% Fisheries GDP to national GDP
sK12943	% TAC per sustainable yield

Forest Resources

Forest resources include the existing forest reserves and non timber resources.

sKPI #	Key Performance Indicator name
sK7536	# Deadwood
sK7641	# Endangered forest species
sK7694	# Extinct in the wild threatened forest species
sK7812	# Forest area in sq.km
sK8152	# Lying deadwood
sK8678	# Plantations area
sK8904	# Semi-natural area
sK8925	# Standing deadwood
sK8940	# Surface area
sK11593	% Forest trees damaged by defoliation
sK12790	% Rate of deforestation attributed to energy use
sK471	# Deadwood volume

Freshwater Resources

Freshwater resources assesses the total water storage.

sKPI #	Key Performance Indicator name
sK7151	# Billion cubic meters of total freshwater withdrawals
sK7340	# Basin precipitation
sK7341	# Basin temperature

sKPI #	Key Performance Indicator name
sK9044	# Renewable internal freshwater resources in billion cubic meters
sK10803	% Domestic freshwater withdrawals
sK12973	% Technically exploitable capability of hydropower currently not in use

Land use

Land use covers the exploitation of land for agricultural, industrial, residential, recreational or other purposes.

sKPI #	Key Performance Indicator name
sK7112	# Agricultural area irrigated
sK7130	# Agricultural land
sK7166	# Area undisturbed by man
sK7811	# Forest area

sKPI #	Key Performance Indicator name
sK7899	# Hectares of arable land
sK7900	# Hectares of land area equipped for irrigation
sK7909	# Hectares of permanent cropland
sK8104	# Land affected by desertification
sK8106	# Land area
sK8227	# Marine protected areas in sq. km
sK10777	% Agricultural irrigated land
sK10779	% Agricultural land from total land area
sK10846	% Arable land from total land area
sK10941	% Cereal cropland from total land area
sK11086	% Coverage of natural reserves
sK11591	% Forest area from total land area
sK12004	% Land area below 5 m from total land area
sK12434	% Permanent cropland from total land area

Personal Productivity Areas

Finances

Refers to the management of an individual's financial resources and assets. In order to achieve the best results, banking and credit actions, investments, expenses and savings should be tracked.

Assets

Includes economic goods owned by an individual.

sKPI #	Key Performance Indicator name
sK13241	# Cars owned
sK13432	# Personal computers owned
sK13450	# Radio sets owned
sK13507	# Antiques owned
sK11048	# Collections of art owned
sK11047	# Jewelry pieces owned
sK8041	# Properties owned

Debt

Outlines the obligations an individual has towards a creditor.

sKPI #	Key Performance Indicator name
sK13414	# Mortgages
sK13536	$ Debt
sK13914	% Credit card debt
sK13917	% Debt to annual income ratio
sK13921	% Home loan debt
sK13927	% Personal loan debt
sK8040	$ Payday loans
sK22985	$ Rent-to-owns
sK22986	$ Leases value

Expenditure

Illustrates the variety of expenses generated by the purchase of goods and services.

sKPI #	Key Performance Indicator name
sK13538	$ Expenditure
sK13539	$ Expenditure on health insurance
sK13540	$ Expenditure on holiday trips
sK13541	$ Expenditure on over-the-counter medicines
sK13542	$ Expenditure on prescribed medicines
sK13544	$ Household consumption expenditure on tobacco
sK13545	$ Household consumption expenditure on cleaning equipment
sK13546	$ Household consumption expenditure on cutlery, flatware and silverware
sK13547	$ Household consumption expenditure on glassware, crystalware and tableware
sK13548	$ Household consumption expenditure on major durables for outdoor recreation
sK13549	$ Household consumption expenditure on motor-cars

sKPI #	Key Performance Indicator name
sK13550	$ Household consumption expenditure on optical instruments
sK13551	$ Household consumption expenditure on postal services
sK13552	$ Household consumption expenditure in insurance connected with the dwelling
sK13553	$ Household consumption expenditure on narcotics
sK13555	$ Household consumption expenditure on accommodation services
sK13557	$ Household consumption expenditure on actual rentals for housing
sK13558	$ Household consumption expenditure on actual rentals paid by tenants
sK13560	$ Household consumption expenditure on alcohol beverages, tobacco and narcotics
sK13561	$ Household consumption expenditure on jam and marmalade
sK13562	$ Household consumption expenditure on animal-drawn vehicles
sK13564	$ Household consumption expenditure on apples (fresh, chilled or frozen)
sK13565	$ Household consumption expenditure on audio-visual, photographic and information processing equipment
sK13566	$ Household consumption expenditure on baby food, dietary preparations, baker's yeast and other food preparations
sK13567	$ Household consumption expenditure on bananas (fresh, chilled or frozen)
sK13568	$ Household consumption expenditure on beer
sK13570	$ Household consumption expenditure on berries (fresh, chilled or frozen)
sK13571	$ Household consumption expenditure on bicycles
sK13573	$ Household consumption expenditure on books
sK13575	$ Household consumption expenditure on bread
sK13576	$ Household consumption expenditure on bread and cereals
sK13577	$ Household consumption expenditure on butter
sK13578	$ Household consumption expenditure on cabbages (fresh, chilled or frozen)
sK13579	$ Household consumption expenditure on cafes, bars and the like
sK13580	$ Household consumption expenditure on canteens
sK13582	$ Household consumption expenditure on carpets and other floor coverings
sK13584	$ Household consumption expenditure on catering services
sK13585	$ Household consumption expenditure on chocolate

sKPI #	Key Performance Indicator name
sK13586	$ Household consumption expenditure on cigarettes
sK13587	$ Household consumption expenditure on cigars
sK13588	$ Household consumption expenditure on cinemas, theatres, concerts
sK13589	$ Household consumption expenditure on citrus fruits (fresh, chilled or frozen)
sK13590	$ Household consumption expenditure on cleaning and maintenance products
sK13591	$ Household consumption expenditure on cleaning, repair and hire of clothing
sK13593	$ Household consumption expenditure on clothes washing machines, clothes drying machines and dish washing machines
sK13594	$ Household consumption expenditure on clothing
sK13595	$ Household consumption expenditure on clothing and footwear
sK13596	$ Household consumption expenditure on clothing materials
sK13598	$ Household consumption expenditure on cocoa and powdered chocolate
sK13599	$ Household consumption expenditure on coffee
sK13600	$ Household consumption expenditure on coffee, tea and cocoa
sK13601	$ Household consumption expenditure on combined passenger transport
sK13603	$ Household consumption expenditure on communication
sK13604	$ Household consumption expenditure on confectionery products
sK13605	$ Household consumption expenditure on cookers
sK13606	$ Household consumption expenditure on crèches, nurseries
sK13607	$ Household consumption expenditure on dental services
sK13609	$ Household consumption expenditure on domestic services
sK13610	$ Household consumption expenditure on domestic services and household services
sK13611	$ Household consumption expenditure on dried fruit
sK13612	$ Household consumption expenditure on dried vegetables
sK13613	$ Household consumption expenditure on dried, salted or smoked meat and edible meat offal
sK13614	$ Household consumption expenditure on dried, smoked or salted fish and seafood
sK13615	$ Household consumption expenditure on edible ices and ice cream
sK13616	$ Household consumption expenditure on edible oil
sK13617	$ Household consumption expenditure on education
sK13619	$ Household consumption expenditure on education not definable by level
sK13621	$ Household consumption expenditure on eggs
sK13622	$ Household consumption expenditure on electrical appliances for personal care
sK13624	$ Household consumption expenditure on electricity

sKPI #	Key Performance Indicator name
sK13625	$ Household consumption expenditure on electricity, gas and other fuels
sK13626	$ Household consumption expenditure on equipment for sport, camping and open air recreation
sK13628	$ Household consumption expenditure on equipment for the reception, recording and reproduction of sound
sK13629	$ Household consumption expenditure on equipment for the reception, recording and reproduction of sound and pictures
sK13630	$ Household consumption expenditure on financial services n.e.c.
sK13632	$ Household consumption expenditure on fish
sK13633	$ Household consumption expenditure on food
sK13634	$ Household consumption expenditure on food products n.e.c.
sK13635	$ Household consumption expenditure on footwear
sK13636	$ Household consumption expenditure on footwear for children (3 to 13 years) and infants (0 to 2 years)
sK13637	$ Household consumption expenditure on footwear for men
sK13638	$ Household consumption expenditure on footwear for women
sK13639	$ Household consumption expenditure on fresh, chilled or frozen fish
sK13640	$ Household consumption expenditure on fresh, chilled or frozen meat of poultry
sK13641	$ Household consumption expenditure on fresh, chilled or frozen meat of sheep and goat
sK13642	$ Household consumption expenditure on fresh, chilled or frozen meat of swine
sK13643	$ Household consumption expenditure on fresh, chilled or frozen seafood
sK13644	$ Household consumption expenditure on fruit
sK13645	$ Household consumption expenditure on fruit juices
sK13646	$ Household consumption expenditure on fuels and lubricants
sK13648	$ Household consumption expenditure on furnishings, household equipment and routine maintenance of the house
sK13649	$ Household consumption expenditure on furniture and furnishings
sK13651	$ Household consumption expenditure on furniture and furnishings, carpets and other floor coverings
sK13652	$ Household consumption expenditure on games of chance
sK13654	$ Household consumption expenditure on games, toys and hobbies
sK13656	$ Household consumption expenditure on gardens, plants and flowers
sK13658	$ Household consumption expenditure on garments
sK13659	$ Household consumption expenditure on garments for children (3 to 13 years) and infants (0 to 2 years)
sK13660	$ Household consumption expenditure on garments for men
sK13661	$ Household consumption expenditure on garments for women

sKPI #	Key Performance Indicator name
sK13663	$ Household consumption expenditure on glassware, tableware and household utensils
sK13665	$ Household consumption expenditure on goods and services for routine household maintenance
sK13666	$ Household consumption expenditure on hairdressing salons and personal grooming establishments
sK13668	$ Household consumption expenditure on health
sK13669	$ Household consumption expenditure on heat energy (ND)
sK13670	$ Household consumption expenditure on heaters, air conditioners
sK13671	$ Household consumption expenditure on hospital services
sK13672	$ Household consumption expenditure on hot water, steam and ice
sK13673	$ Household consumption expenditure on household appliances
sK13674	$ Household consumption expenditure on household services
sK13676	$ Household consumption expenditure on household textiles
sK13678	$ Household consumption expenditure on housing, water, electricity, gas and other fuels
sK13679	$ Household consumption expenditure on imputed rentals for housing
sK13680	$ Household consumption expenditure on imputed rentals for secondary residences
sK13681	$ Household consumption expenditure on imputed rentals of households housed free
sK13682	$ Household consumption expenditure on imputed rentals of owner occupiers
sK13684	$ Household consumption expenditure on information processing equipment
sK13686	$ Household consumption expenditure on insurance
sK13687	$ Household consumption expenditure on insurance connected with health
sK13689	$ Household consumption expenditure on insurance connected with the dwelling
sK13690	$ Household consumption expenditure on insurance connected with transport
sK13692	$ Household consumption expenditure on jewelry, clocks and watches
sK13694	$ Household consumption expenditure on kitchen and domestic utensils
sK13695	$ Household consumption expenditure on leaf and stem vegetables (fresh, chilled or frozen)
sK13696	$ Household consumption expenditure on electricity
sK13697	$ Household consumption expenditure on liquefied hydrocarbons (butane, propane, etc.)
sK13698	$ Household consumption expenditure on liquid fuels
sK13700	$ Household consumption expenditure on low fat milk
sK13701	$ Household consumption expenditure on maintenance and repair
sK13702	$ Household consumption expenditure on maintenance and repair of other major durables for recreation and culture

sKPI #	Key Performance Indicator name
sK13704	$ Household consumption expenditure on maintenance and repair of personal transport equipment
sK13705	$ Household consumption expenditure on maintenance and repair of the dwelling
sK13706	$ Household consumption expenditure on major durables for indoor recreation
sK13708	$ Household consumption expenditure on major household appliances whether or not electrical
sK13709	$ Household consumption expenditure on major tools and equipment
sK13711	$ Household consumption expenditure on margarine and other vegetable fats
sK13712	$ Household consumption expenditure on materials for the maintenance and repair of the dwelling
sK13714	$ Household consumption expenditure on medical products, appliances and equipment
sK13715	$ Household consumption expenditure on medical Services
sK13717	$ Household consumption expenditure on milk, cheese and eggs
sK13718	$ Household consumption expenditure on mineral or spring waters
sK13719	$ Household consumption expenditure on mineral waters, soft drinks, fruit and vegetable juices
sK13720	$ Household consumption expenditure on miscellaneous goods and services
sK13721	$ Household consumption expenditure on miscellaneous printed matter
sK13723	$ Household consumption expenditure on motor-cycles
sK13725	$ Household consumption expenditure on museums, zoological gardens and the like
sK13726	$ Household consumption expenditure on musical instruments
sK13727	$ Household consumption expenditure on musical instruments and major durables for indoor recreation
sK13729	$ Household consumption expenditure on newspapers and periodicals
sK13731	$ Household consumption expenditure on newspapers, books and stationery
sK13732	$ Household consumption expenditure on non-alcoholic beverages
sK13733	$ Household consumption expenditure on non-durable household goods
sK13734	$ Household consumption expenditure on oils and fats
sK13735	$ Household consumption expenditure on olive oil
sK13736	$ Household consumption expenditure on operation of personal transport equipment
sK13737	$ Household consumption expenditure on other actual rentals
sK13739	$ Household consumption expenditure on other appliance, articles and products for personal care
sK13740	$ Household consumption expenditure on other articles of clothing and clothing accessories
sK13742	$ Household consumption expenditure on other edible animal fats

sKPI #	Key Performance Indicator name
sK13743	$ Household consumption expenditure on other fresh, chilled or frozen edible meat
sK13744	$ Household consumption expenditure on other fresh, chilled or frozen fruits
sK13745	$ Household consumption expenditure on other imputed rentals
sK13746	$ Household consumption expenditure on other insurance
sK13748	$ Household consumption expenditure on other major durables for recreation and culture
sK13749	$ Household consumption expenditure on other major household appliances
sK13750	$ Household consumption expenditure on other medical products
sK13752	$ Household consumption expenditure on other non durable household articles
sK13753	$ Household consumption expenditure on other non-hospital services
sK13754	$ Household consumption expenditure on other personal effects
sK13756	Household consumption expenditure for the preparation of other preserved or processed fish and seafood
sK13757	Household consumption expenditure for the preparation of other preserved or processed meat
sK13758	$ Household consumption expenditure on other preserved or processed vegetables
sK13759	$ Household consumption expenditure on other purchased transport services
sK13761	$ Household consumption expenditure on other recreational items and equipment, gardens and pets
sK13762	$ Household consumption expenditure on other services
sK13763	$ Household consumption expenditure on other services in respect of personal transport equipment
sK13765	$ Household consumption expenditure on other services n.e.c.
sK13767	$ Household consumption expenditure on other services relating to the dwelling n.e.c.
sK13769	$ Household consumption expenditure on other sugar products
sK13770	$ Household consumption expenditure on out-patient services
sK13771	$ Household consumption expenditure on package holidays
sK13772	$ Household consumption expenditure on paramedical services
sK13773	$ Household consumption expenditure on passenger transport by air
sK13775	$ Household consumption expenditure on passenger transport by railway
sK13778	$ Household consumption expenditure on passenger transport by sea and inland waterway
sK13780	$ Household consumption expenditure on pasta products
sK13781	$ Household consumption expenditure on pastry-cook products
sK13782	$ Household consumption expenditure on pears (fresh, chilled or frozen)

sKPI #	Key Performance Indicator name
sK13783	$ Household consumption expenditure on personal care
sK13784	$ Household consumption expenditure on personal effects
sK13785	$ Household consumption expenditure on pets and related products
sK13787	$ Household consumption expenditure on pharmaceutical products
sK13789	$ Household consumption expenditure on photographic and cinematographic equipment
sK13790	$ Household consumption expenditure on photographic and cinematographic equipment and optical instruments
sK13791	$ Household consumption expenditure on postal services
sK13796	$ Household consumption expenditure on potatoes
sK13800	$ Household consumption expenditure on preserved fruit and fruit based products
sK13801	$ Household consumption expenditure on preserved milk
sK13805	$ Household consumption expenditure on purchase of new motor-cars
sK13806	$ Household consumption expenditure on purchase of second-hand motor-cars
sK13807	$ Household consumption expenditure on purchase of vehicles
sK13808	$ Household consumption expenditure on recording media
sK13809	$ Household consumption expenditure on recording media for pictures and sound
sK13810	$ Household consumption expenditure on recreational and cultural services
sK13811	$ Household consumption expenditure on recreational and sporting services
sK13812	$ Household consumption expenditure on recreational and sporting services equipment
sK13813	$ Household consumption expenditure on refrigerators, freezers and fridge freezers
sK13814	$ Household consumption expenditure on refuse collection
sK13818	$ Household consumption expenditure on repair of audio-visual, photographic and information processing equipment
sK13820	$ Household consumption expenditure on repair of furniture, furnishings and floor coverings
sK13822	$ Household consumption expenditure on repair of glassware, tableware and household utensils
sK13823	$ Household consumption expenditure on repair of household appliances
sK13825	$ Household consumption expenditure on restaurants
sK13826	$ Household consumption expenditure on restaurants and hotels
sK13827	$ Household consumption expenditure on restaurants, cafes and the like
sK13828	$ Household consumption expenditure on rice
sK13829	$ Household consumption expenditure on root crops, non-starchy bulbs and mushrooms (fresh, chilled or frozen)

Personal » Personal Productivity Areas

sKPI #	Key Performance Indicator name
sK13830	$ Household consumption expenditure on salt, spices and culinary herbs
sK13831	$ Household consumption expenditure on sandwiches
sK13832	$ Household consumption expenditure on sauces, condiments
sK13834	$ Household consumption expenditure on secondary education
sK13836	$ Household consumption expenditure on services for the maintenance and repair of the dwelling
sK13838	$ Household consumption expenditure on services of medical analysis laboratories and X-ray centers
sK13839	$ Household consumption expenditure on services of medical auxiliaries
sK13840	$ Household consumption expenditure on sewerage collection
sK13842	$ Household consumption expenditure on sewing and knitting machines
sK13844	$ Household consumption expenditure on small electrical household appliances
sK13846	$ Household consumption expenditure on small tools and miscellaneous accessories
sK13848	$ Household consumption expenditure on social protection
sK13849	$ Household consumption expenditure on social protection services
sK13851	$ Household consumption expenditure on soft drinks
sK13852	$ Household consumption expenditure on solid fuels
sK13854	$ Household consumption expenditure on spare parts and accessories
sK13856	$ Household consumption expenditure on spirits
sK13857	$ Household consumption expenditure on spirits and liqueurs
sK13858	$ Household consumption expenditure on stationery and drawing materials
sK13860	$ Household consumption expenditure on stone fruits (fresh, chilled or frozen)
sK13861	$ Household consumption expenditure on sugar
sK13862	$ Household consumption expenditure on tea
sK13864	$ Household consumption expenditure on telephone and telefax equipment
sK13866	$ Household consumption expenditure on telephone and telefax services
sK13869	$ Household consumption expenditure on television and radio taxes and hire of equipment
sK13870	$ Household consumption expenditure on television sets, video cassette players and recorders
sK13872	$ Household consumption expenditure on tertiary education
sK13874	$ Household consumption expenditure on therapeutic appliances and equipment
sK13876	$ Household consumption expenditure on tobacco
sK13878	$ Household consumption expenditure on tools and equipment for house and garden
sK13879	$ Household consumption expenditure on town gas and natural gas

sKPI #	Key Performance Indicator name
sK13880	$ Household consumption expenditure on transport
sK13881	$ Household consumption expenditure on transport services
sK13882	$ Household consumption expenditure on travel goods and other carriers
sK13883	$ Household consumption expenditure on other appliances, articles and products for personal care
sK13884	$ Household consumption expenditure on vegetable juices
sK13885	$ Household consumption expenditure on vegetables
sK13886	$ Household consumption expenditure on vegetables cultivated for their fruit (fresh, chilled or frozen)
sK13887	$ Household consumption expenditure on veterinary and other services for pets
sK13889	$ Household consumption expenditure on water supply
sK13891	$ Household consumption expenditure on water supply and miscellaneous services relating to the dwelling
sK13892	$ Household consumption expenditure on whole milk
sK13893	$ Household consumption expenditure on wine
sK13894	$ Household consumption expenditure on wine from grapes or other fruit
sK13895	$ Household consumption expenditure on yoghurt
sK13896	$ Household consumption expenditure other tubers and products of tuber vegetables
sK13897	$ Household consumption expenditure on passenger transport by road
sK13898	$ Household consumption expenditure sugar, jam, honey, chocolate and confectionery
sK13899	$ Household consumption expenditure on alcoholic beverages
sK13900	$ Household consumption expenditure on cheese and curd
sK13901	$ Household consumption expenditure on fresh, chilled or frozen meat of bovine animals
sK13902	$ Household consumption expenditure on other milk products
sK13906	$ Tax payments
sK13907	$ Household consumption expenditure
sK13956	% Variance form planned expenditure

Income

Indicates the amount of money earned, as well as their source such as employment or investments.

sKPI #	Key Performance Indicator name
sK13532	$ Adjusted disposable income plus housework
sK13533	$ Adjusted disposable income plus housework and leisure
sK13534	$ Adjusted disposable income plus housework and leisure per consumption unit
sK13535	$ Adjusted disposable income plus housework per consumption unit
sK13904	$ Income
sK13908	% Growth rate of income
sK13957	% Variance from income target

Investments

Refers to the purchase of financial instruments or other assets that can generate future revenues.

sKPI #	Key Performance Indicator name
sK13445	# Properties registered
sK13918	% Deposit interest rate
sK13922	% Investment return
sK13923	% Investments to equity ratio
sK22987	# Stock certificates
sK22988	$ Owned shares value
sK22989	# Insurance bonds
sK22990	# Property investments

Savings

The amount of money left from the overall income after all necessary expenditures have been made.

sKPI #	Key Performance Indicator name
sK13537	$ Equity
sK13958	% Variance from target savings
sK22991	# Savings accounts
sK22992	% Personal Saving Rate (PSAVERT)
sK22993	% Household saving rate
sK13420	$ Pension plan
sK13824	$ Annuities

Home Economics

Refers to the general household management.

Cleaning

Indicates the actions taken to ensure a clean environment inside and around the house, as well as their efficiency.

sKPI #	Key Performance Indicator name
sK13932	% Recycling rate
sK13569	# Complaints with house cleanliness from household members
sK13572	% Satisfaction of household members with house cleanliness
sK13574	# Hours dedicated to house cleaning
sK13833	# Times house cleaning performed
sK13835	% Glass recycling rate

Cooking

Outlines the individual/ family's every day diet.

sKPI #	Key Performance Indicator name
sK13263	# Cooking using the microwave
sK13264	# Cooking using the oven
sK13318	# Gas ovens owned
sK13485	# Time spent cooking
sK13955	% Use of kitchen

Purchasing

Reflects the efficiency of the buying process for newly acquired good or services.

sKPI #	Key Performance Indicator name
sK13581	# Time spent shopping
sK13837	# Items bought per trip to shop

sKPI #	Key Performance Indicator name
sK13583	% Use of vochers and coupons
sK13841	# Shop visits per month
sK13845	# Shopping sessions
sK13847	# Items with a reserve supply available
sK13847	# Situations where an item was unavailable
sK13592	$ Savings achieved through smarter purchasing
sK13850	# Time spent with price comparisons
sK13597	# Items purchase based on price comparisons
sK13853	% Purchases made online

Utilities

Relates to household common services such as electricity, water, sewage, internet and TV cable.

sKPI #	Key Performance Indicator name
sK13231	# Business telephone subscriptions
sK13297	# Electric power consumption in kWh
sK13309	# Fixed broadband Internet subscriptions
sK13345	# Home satellite antennas
sK13348	# Household energy use
sK13366	# Internet bandwidth (Mbps)
sK13376	# KW consumed by existing appliances
sK13377	# KW consumed by new appliances
sK13407	# Mobile cellular subscriptions
sK13476	# Telephone lines
sK13477	# Television sets owned
sK13543	$ Fixed broadband Internet subscription

Personal Development

Outlines activities that improve awareness and identity, develop talents and potential, build human capital, facilitates employability, enhance quality of life and contribute to the realization of aspirations.

Education

Reflects all the aspects related to imparting and acquiring general knowledge, including schooling and results generated by instruction, training or studies.

sKPI #	Key Performance Indicator name
sK13199	# Bachelor's degrees 3-4 years of duration
sK13277	# Degrees obtained following the Bologna structures
sK13278	# Degrees outside the Bologna structures (ISCED levels 5A, 5B and 6)
sK13391	# Master's degrees 4-8 years of cumulative duration
sK13396	# Years of schooling
sK13436	# Ph.D. and doctorates
sK13528	# Years of primary education
sK13529	# Years of secondary education

Experience

Comprises aspects reflecting knowledge, skills, or practices gained from direct observation or / and active participation in events and activities of life.

sKPI #	Key Performance Indicator name
sK13189	# Visits to museums
sK13371	# Jobs changed
sK13390	# Major events attended
sK13409	# Full-time employment period
sK13410	# Part-time employment period

sKPI #	Key Performance Indicator name
sK13411	# Self-employment period
sK13413	# Unemployment period
sK13422	# New places visited
sK13440	# Points gained in the personal skills register
sK13497	# Training programs followed
sK13910	% Completion of learning targets
sK13911	% Condom use
sK13920	% Feeling of trust and belonging
sK13924	% Life satisfaction
sK13933	% Resilience and self-esteem
sK13935	% Social unrest
sK13954	% Trust in institutions

Reading & Thinking

Covers aspects relating to the action of reading written or printed matters and reflection activities.

sKPI #	Key Performance Indicator name
sK13217	# Books loaned from public libraries
sK13218	# Books read
sK13272	# Daily newspapers read
sK13346	# Time spent thinking about the self
sK13423	# Newspapers read

Planning

Illustrates the ability to carry out plans, implying the establishment of goals, policies, and procedures.

Plan Monitoring

Refers to the constant assessment of a plan or project progress.

sKPI #	Key Performance Indicator name
sK13928	% Planned tasks achieved
sK13930	% Projects progressing on time
sK13855	# Calendar conflicts solved
sK13602	# Plan reviews
sK13859	% Plans implemented on time
sK13863	# Time spent monitoring plans

Risk Assessment

Implies the identification, evaluation, and estimation of the levels of risks involved in a situation, their comparison and determination of an acceptable level of risk.

sKPI #	Key Performance Indicator name
sK13608	# Risks identified
sK13865	% Likelihood of risk
sK13867	# Risks documented
sK13868	# Risk control methods in use
sK13871	# Risks reviewed

Process Management

Reflects activities related to planning, tracking and monitoring the performance of a process.

Communication

Covers the systems, technologies and processes involved with the transmission of information.

sKPI #	Key Performance Indicator name
sK13257	# Computer use per week
sK13365	# International SMS sent
sK13406	# MMS sent
sK13467	# SMS sent
sK13520	# VoIP subscriptions
sK13873	# Minutes spent talking on phone per day
sK13618	# Emails sent per day

Reliability

Reflects the proven competency of being dependable and trustful.

sKPI #	Key Performance Indicator name
sK13919	% Emails responded within 3 days
sK13931	% Promises met
sK13953	% To do list tasks achieved as planned
sK13959	% Voice messages responded to within 1 day
sK13961	% Work deadlines on time
sK13875	% Accomplished tasks
sK13620	% Days arrived on time at work
sK13877	% Work calls answered on weekends

Time Management

Indicates the individual's ability to plan and execute activities in an efficient way that reduces time losses.

sKPI #	Key Performance Indicator name
sK13481	# Time per day of leisure
sK13482	# Time per day of paid work
sK13483	# Time per day of unpaid work
sK13486	# Time spent helping others
sK13493	# Time spent volunteering
sK13495	# Time spent watching TV
sK13909	% Bed time as scheduled
sK13926	% Meeting times on-time
sK13937	% Time spent commuting
sK13938	% Time spent doing housework
sK13939	% Time spent eating
sK13940	% Time spent grooming
sK13941	% Time spent making love
sK13942	% Time spent on the computer (non-work)
sK13943	% Time spent playing
sK13944	% Time spent praying
sK13945	% Time spent preparing food
sK13946	% Time spent reading (non-work)
sK13947	% Time spent relaxing
sK13948	% Time spent shopping
sK13949	% Time spent talking (non-work)
sK13950	% Time spent walking
sK13951	% Time spent on childcare
sK13952	% Time spent working
sK13960	% Wake-up as scheduled

Well-Being Domains

Fitness

Reveals the health status and physical condition, as the result of exercise and proper nutrition.

sKPI #	Key Performance Indicator name	sKPI #	Key Performance Indicator name
sK13197	# Assessment rating	sK13484	# Time spent bicycling
sK13274	# Days with at least 1 hour of vigorous physical activity	sK13489	# Time spent lying down
sK13275	# Time spent on moderate physical activity	sK13490	# Time spent sitting
sK13276	# Time spent on vigorous physical activity	sK13494	# Time spent walking

Health

Reflects a state of complete physical, social and mental well-being.

General Health

Relates to monitoring the general condition of the body and mind.

sKPI #	Key Performance Indicator name	sKPI #	Key Performance Indicator name
sK13177	# Albumin level	sK13253	# Cigarettes smoked
sK13179	# Allergies	sK13254	# Coagulation abnormalities
sK13181	# Allergy tests made	sK13255	# Cocaine use
sK13190	# Anterior cruciate ligament (ACL) injuries	sK13256	# Colds and flus
sK13192	# Antihistamine use	sK13259	# Consumption of energy drinks
sK13193	# Antioxidants supplements taken	sK13260	# Consumption of energy shots
sK13194	# Anxiety disorders	sK13261	# Consumption of sport bars
sK13196	# Ascorbic acid (Vitamin C) level	sK13262	# Consumption of sport drinks
sK13201	# Bacterial infections	sK13265	# Copper level
sK13202	# B-Alanine supplements taken	sK13268	# C-Reactive Protein (CRP) level
sK13203	# Beta2-microglobulin level	sK13270	# Creatinine level
sK13204	# Bilirubin level	sK13273	# Days of poor physical conditioning
sK13205	# Bilirubin, direct level	sK13280	# Dental injuries
sK13206	# Bilirubin, indirect level	sK13283	# Diastolic blood pressure
sK13207	# Bitot's spots	sK13293	# Ear infections
sK13208	# Bleeding time	sK13295	# Eating disorders
sK13209	# Blood chemistry abnormalities	sK13299	# Emergency department visits
sK13211	# Blood pressure	sK13301	# Episodes of heat exhaustion
sK13213	# Blood Urea Nitrogen (BUN) level	sK13302	# Eye infections
sK13214	# Body Mass Index (BMI)	sK13306	# Fears and phobias
sK13220	# Branched-Chain Amino Acids supplements taken	sK13308	# Fish oil/omega-3 fatty acids supplements taken
sK13229	# Broken bones	sK13311	# Folic acid level
sK13230	# Bromocriptine use	sK13312	# Food allergies
sK13233	# Caffeine intake	sK13315	# Frostbites
sK13234	# Caffeine supplements taken	sK13316	# Fungal infections
sK13235	# Calcitonin level	sK13320	# Glucose level
sK13236	# Calcium level	sK13326	# HDL cholesterol level
sK13239	# Carbon dioxide level	sK13328	# Heart rate
sK13240	# Cardiovascular abnormalities	sK13329	# Heat cramps
sK13242	# Central nervous system abnormalities	sK13330	# Heat strokes
sK13250	# Cholesterol	sK13332	# Hematocrit (HCT) level
		sK13333	# Hemoglobin level
		sK13343	# Home allergies

sKPI #	Key Performance Indicator name
sK13369	# Iron level
sK13374	# Knee injuries
sK13378	# LDH level
sK13379	# LDL cholesterol level
sK13380	# Lead level
sK13381	# Leukocyte count level
sK13386	# Lung and respiratory infections
sK13388	# Lymphocytes level
sK13389	# Magnesium level
sK13393	# Mean corpuscular Hemoglobin (MCH) level
sK13394	# Mean corpuscular volume (MCV)
sK13395	# Body temperature
sK13398	# Megavitamins and minerals supplements taken
sK13399	# Melatonin supplements taken
sK13408	# Monocytes level
sK13412	# Months of smoking
sK13416	# Multivitamins and minerals supplements taken
sK13428	# Parasitic infections
sK13429	# Parathyroid hormone level
sK13434	# Pet allergies
sK13435	# pH level
sK13438	# Platelet count
sK13442	# Potassium level
sK13443	# Probiotics taken
sK13444	# Progesterone level
sK13446	# Protein level
sK13447	# Pulse pressure
sK13451	# Red blood cell (RBC) count
sK13452	# Red cell distribution width (RDW)
sK13459	# Sexually transmitted diseases (STDs)
sK13463	# Skin infections and rashes
sK13464	# Sleep problems
sK13465	# Sleepwalking episodes
sK13468	# Sodium level
sK13469	# Stomach and intestinal infections
sK13470	# Suicide attempts
sK13471	# Sunburns
sK13473	# Sweat rate
sK13474	# Sweating abnormalities
sK13475	# Systolic blood pressure
sK13478	# Testosterone level
sK13480	# Thyroid stimulating hormone (TSH) level
sK13498	# Triglycerides level
sK13504	# Urine osmolality
sK13505	# Use of sport gels
sK13506	# Use of supplements/boosters

sKPI #	Key Performance Indicator name
sK13509	# Viral infections
sK13511	# Vitamin A level
sK13512	# Vitamin B complex supplements taken
sK13513	# Vitamin B1 level
sK13514	# Vitamin B12 level
sK13515	# Vitamin B2 level
sK13516	# Vitamin B6 level
sK13517	# Vitamin C level
sK13518	# Vitamin D level
sK13519	# Vitamin E level
sK13521	# Waist circumference
sK13522	# Water intake
sK13523	# Weight
sK13526	# Weight-loss supplements taken
sK13531	# Zinc level
sK13912	% Consumption of iodized salt
sK13915	% Days in good health
sK13934	% Self-perceived general health

Medical tests

Includes the medical procedures performed to detect, diagnose, or monitor diseases, disease processes and susceptibility, and to determine a course of treatment.

sKPI #	Key Performance Indicator name
sK13170	# Abdomen scans
sK13171	# Abdominal MRIs
sK13172	# Abdominal ultrasound
sK13173	# Abortion tests
sK13174	# ACTH tests
sK13175	# AIDS tests
sK13178	# Alcohol breath tests
sK13180	# Allergy tests
sK13182	# Amniocentesis for Rh sensitization during pregnancy
sK13183	# Amphetamines tests
sK13184	# Angiograms
sK13191	# Antibody tests
sK13195	# Ascetic fluid tests
sK13198	# Auditory brainstem response audiometries
sK13200	# Back X-rays
sK13210	# Blood cultures taken
sK13212	# Blood tests
sK13215	# Bone marrow biopsies
sK13216	# Bone scans
sK13221	# Breast biopsies
sK13222	# Breast cancer gene tests
sK13223	# Breast cancer screenings
sK13224	# Breast self-examinations

sKPI #	Key Performance Indicator name
sK13225	# Breast ultrasound
sK13226	# Breath tests
sK13227	# Breast enlargements
sK13228	# Breast reductions
sK13238	# Cancer tests
sK13243	# Cerebral angiograms
sK13244	# Cervical biopsies
sK13245	# Cervical cancer screenings
sK13246	# Chest X-rays
sK13249	# Cholescintigraphies
sK13251	# Cholesterol tests
sK13266	# Cortisol tests
sK13267	# Cranial sonograms
sK13269	# C-Reactive Protein tests
sK13271	# CT scans
sK13279	# Dental implants
sK13281	# Dental X-rays
sK13282	# Dermabrasions
sK13287	# Diseases
sK13288	# DNA fingerprinting
sK13289	# Doppler ultrasounds
sK13291	# Drug screening tests
sK13294	# Ear tests
sK13298	# Electrocardiograms
sK13303	# Face lifts
sK13304	# Face X-rays
sK13307	# Fertility tests
sK13313	# Foot X-rays
sK13317	# Gallbladder scans
sK13319	# Genetic tests
sK13323	# Gynecological exams
sK13325	# Hair transplantations surgeries
sK13327	# HDL cholesterol tests
sK13336	# Hepatitis B tests
sK13337	# Herpes tests
sK13344	# Home blood pressure tests
sK13372	# Kidney scans
sK13373	# Kidney stone analysis
sK13375	# Knee replacement surgeries
sK13415	# MRI scans
sK13426	# Ovulation tests
sK13431	# Pathology tests
sK13458	# Sentinel lymph node biopsy
sK13472	# Swab tests
sK13962	Endoscopies

Vaccinations

Indicates the inoculations with vaccines in order to prevent and protect against particular diseases.

sKPI #	Key Performance Indicator name
sK13176	# AIDS/HIV vaccinations
sK13185	# Animal vaccinations
sK13219	# Botulism vaccinations
sK13247	# Chicken pox (varicella) vaccinations
sK13248	# Cholera vaccinations
sK13286	# Diphtheria vaccinations
sK13290	# DPT/DTaP vaccinations
sK13296	# Ebola vaccinations
sK13300	# Encephalitis vaccinations
sK13310	# Flu vaccinations
sK13324	# Haemophilus influenzae B (HiB) vaccinations
sK13334	# Hepatitis A vaccinations
sK13335	# Hepatitis B (Hep B3) vaccinations
sK13349	# Human papillomavirus (HBV) vaccinations
sK13370	# Japanese encephalitis vaccinations
sK13387	# Lyme disease vaccinations
sK13397	# Measles (MCV) vaccinations
sK13400	# Meningitis vaccinations
sK13401	# Meningococcal vaccinations
sK13402	# Military vaccinations
sK13405	# MMR vaccinations
sK13417	# MUMPS vaccinations
sK13433	# Pertussis (whooping cough) vaccinations
sK13437	# Plague vaccinations
sK13441	# Polio vaccinations
sK13448	# Q fever vaccinations
sK13449	# Rabies vaccinations
sK13455	# Respiratory syncytial vaccinations
sK13456	# Rotavirus vaccinations
sK13457	# Rubella vaccinations
sK13460	# Shingles vaccinations
sK13466	# Small pox vaccinations
sK13479	# Tetanus vaccinations
sK13499	# Tuberculosis vaccinations
sK13500	# Tularemia vaccinations
sK13502	# Typhoid fever vaccinations
sK13503	# Typhus vaccinations
sK13508	# Viral hemorrhagic fever vaccinations
sK13530	# Yellow fever vaccinations

Nutrition

Reflects processes related to the administration of nutrients in the form of food in order to nourish the organism and support life.

sKPI #	Key Performance Indicator name
sK13237	# Calories intake
sK13252	# Chronic energy deficiency (CED)
sK13284	# Dietary energy supply (DES)
sK13285	# Dietary supplements
sK13292	# Drugs taken
sK13321	# Goiter (enlargement of thyroid gland)
sK13322	# Food intake
sK13331	# Height-for-age index
sK13351	# Intake calories from solid fats, alcoholic beverages and added sugars (SoFAAS)
sK13352	# Alcohol intake
sK13353	# Cereals intake
sK13354	# Intake of dark green and orange vegetables and legumes
sK13355	# Intake of fruit
sK13356	# Intake of fruit and vegetables per month
sK13357	# Intake of grains

sKPI #	Key Performance Indicator name
sK13358	# Intake of meat and beans
sK13359	# Intake of milk
sK13360	# Intake of oils
sK13361	# Intake of saturated fat
sK13362	# Intake of sodium
sK13363	# Intake of whole fruit (not juice)
sK13364	# Intake of whole grains
sK13367	# Iodine deficiency
sK13368	# Iron deficiency
sK13392	# Meals
sK13424	# Night blindness (inability to see in low light)
sK13427	# Pallor of palms or inside of eyelids or mouth
sK13510	# Vitamin A deficiency
sK13524	# Weight-for-age index
sK13525	# Weight-for-height index
sK13916	% Days with completed nutritional needs

Relationships

Indicate the mutual dealings, connections, or feelings that exist between people.

Family

Refers to long-term commitments between people who share similar values and goals.

sKPI #	Key Performance Indicator name
sK13258	# Conflicts between couples
sK13453	# Relatives who can be counted on
sK13487	# Time spent listening to family members
sK13488	# Time spent listening to spouse or partner
sK13491	# Time spent speaking to family members
sK13492	# Time spent speaking to spouse or partner
sK13496	# Time spent with family
sK13925	% Listening skills
sK13936	% Speaking skills

Friends and colleagues

Include people who share same interests and activities.

sKPI #	Key Performance Indicator name
sK13305	# Facebook friends
sK13314	# Friends who can be counted on
sK13382	# LinkedIn contacts
sK13501	# Twitter followers
sK13631	# Personal blog subscribers
sK13888	# Google Plus circles
sK13890	% Time spent with friends
sK13647	# Address book entries

Work-life balance

Outlines the equilibrium between an individual's professional activity and his personal time.

Achievements

Includes the actions accomplished successfully, especially by means of exertion, skill, practice, or perseverance.

sKPI #	Key Performance Indicator name
sK13232	# Businesses closed
sK13419	# New businesses registered

sKPI #	Key Performance Indicator name
sK13430	# Patent applications
sK13929	% Positive balance between good deeds and mistakes
sK13675	# Foreign languages proficiency certificates
sK13421	# Promotions
sK13677	# Awards received

Entertainment

Consists of the activities or acts meant to amuse the individual.

sKPI #	Key Performance Indicator name
sK13186	# Attendance at concerts
sK13187	# Attendance at theaters
sK13188	# Cinema attendance
sK13338	# Holiday nights spent on long domestic holiday trips
sK13339	# Holiday nights spent on long outbound holiday trips
sK13340	# Holiday nights spent on short domestic holiday trips
sK13341	# Holiday nights spent on short outbound holiday trips
sK13342	# Holiday trips taken
sK13383	# Local activities attended
sK13384	# Long domestic holiday trips
sK13385	# Long outbound holiday trips
sK13454	# Religious activities attended
sK13461	# Short domestic holiday trips
sK13462	# Short outbound holiday trips

Relaxation

Includes activities that have as purpose the refreshment of individual's body and mind.

sKPI #	Key Performance Indicator name
sK13650	# Time spent walking in nature each month
sK13653	# Meditation practices known
sK13655	# Massages received
sK13657	% Breaks from work
sK13662	# Time spent listening to relaxation music

Rest

Refers to the monitoring of sleep as it is an important element influencing the individual's health.

sKPI #	Key Performance Indicator name
sK13347	# Hours devoted to leisure and personal care
sK13418	# Naps
sK13425	% Dreams with nightmares
sK13527	# Work-rest minutes
sK13623	# Hours slept with the 10pm-2am interval
sK13627	% Nights with 6 hours of sleep or more

Made in the USA
Charleston, SC
02 November 2013